Lismore

My older brother Paddy Ballantyne, aged 4,
in the garden of our rented house in West Street,
Lismore, with Feeney's Garage repair shed
in the background. 1937.

Lismore
Autobiography of an Irish Town 1937–1954

JAMES BALLANTYNE

For the people of Lismore and West Waterford amongst whom I was born and grew up, and for my fifteen-year-old London-Irish son Joseph who should learn of, and come to appreciate in time, my formative and unforgettable Lismore years.

Published by The Heap, 9 Hollies Road, London W5 4UU

This commercially available edition first published in 2008
Reprinted with minor amendments in 2008

First edition (printed) published for private circulation in 1995
Second edition (microfiche) published for private circulation in 1997

Website: www.lismoreautobiography.co.uk

Copyright © James Ballantyne 2008

ISBN 978-0-9558221-0-0

All rights reserved. Apart from any fair dealing
for the purposes of research or private study, or criticism or review, as
permitted under the UK Copyright, Designs and Patents Act 1988,
this publication may not be reproduced, stored, or transmitted, in any
form or by any means, without the prior permission in writing of the author.

A CIP record of this book is available from the British Library

Designed by Nicky Barneby @ Barneby Ltd
Typeset in 11/13.75pt Monotype Sabon
Printed and bound in England on acid free paper by
Biddles Limited, King's Lynn, Norfolk PE30 4LS

Cover picture: Left to right: Peter 'Cox' Doherty, Dick Long
(Lismore Hotel) and the author watching the world go by at the
Monument, a favourite meeting place, in the early Fifties.
West Street leading up to Gallows Hill is in the background.
'Cox' was one of Waterford's best handballers of the period.
(Ballantyne family photo)

Contents

List of illustrations	vii
Acknowledgements	xiii
Maps	xvi
Introduction	xix
Letter accompanying first edition	xxiv
1. Earliest recollections	1
2. Home	24
3. The Rich	47
4. The Poor	57
5. The Middle Class	67
6. The Library	73
7. Religion	87
8. Gaelic Sports	119
9. Swimming	162
10. Other Sports	188
11. Horses, Dogs, Guns and Rods	208
12. The Land	231
13. Hunting	254
14. Gathering	276
15. Customs, Games and Gangs	295
16. Law and Order	335
17. Sickness and Health	349
18. Family Life	371

19. School	414
20. Sexuality and Sin	450
21. Politics	473
22. The World Outside	490
23. The Cinema	500
24. Show Business	534
25. Departure	550
Appendix	555
Index	566

List of illustrations

Frontispiece. My brother Paddy, aged 4, 1937

p. xxvi. An 1846 map of the County Waterford.

p. 2. My father Joseph Ballantyne with his father Patrick Ballantyne. *(Ballantyne family photo)*

p. 2. My grandmother Bridget Ballantyne (née MacDonagh). *(Ballantyne family photo)*

p. 4. My great-grandmother Mary Cullinane. *(Morrissey family photo)*

p. 4. My grandfather James Morrissey. *(Morrissey family photo)*

p. 6. My grandmother Anastasia Morrissey with her sons Jimmy and Mick, and Mam. *(Morrissey family photo)*

p. 6. My grandmother Anastasia Morrissey with her daughter Peg. *(Studio portrait by A. H. Poole of Waterford)*

p. 7. Mam and Dad in my grandfather James Morrissey's yard. *(Morrissey family photo)*

p. 7. My parents Joseph Ballantyne and Mary Morrissey on their wedding day in 1928. *(Ballantyne family photo)*

p. 11. Group of boys taken in our backyard c. 1943–44. *(Ballantyne family photo)*

p. 13. The LDF (later FCA) led by Jim Ormonde passing along the Main Street in Lismore in 1942. *(Photo and caption courtesy of Eugene Dennis)*

p. 15. Mam with Paddy and me in our back-garden in Lismore. *(Ballantyne family photo)*

p. 19. West Street pals. *(Ballantyne family photo)*

p. 23. Dad and 'Auntie Bab' Morrissey with Paddy c. spring 1934. *(Ballantyne family photo)*

p. 26. Easter Week 1916. The Scene at the GPO. *(Copyright: Thomas Kiersey of Dublin)*

p. 30. Mam, Dad, Paddy and me c. 1937–38. *(Ballantyne family photo)*

p. 30. My brother Paddy c. 1938–39. *(Ballantyne family photo)*

p. 31. Dad, Mam and Paddy. Mid-Thirties. *(Ballantyne family photo) p. 39.* My uncle Mick Morrissey with Paddy on the bar of Dad's bicycle. *(Ballantyne family photo)*

p. 41. Main Street Lismore in the late Forties or early Fifties. *(Period postcard produced by Photocraft Limited, Dublin.)*

p. 43. A 1778 print of Dromana House.

p. 48. Two prints offering contrasting early views of Lismore Castle.

p. 51. Mam with her first cousin 'Nurse Biddy' Morrissey and Paddy c. 1934. *(Ballantyne family photo)*

p. 74. The restored Lismore Library in September 1994. *(Photo by James Ballantyne)*

p. 76. An early roadside encounter with a written document. *(Ballantyne family photo)*

p. 100. Paddy Ballantyne wearing his altar-boy soutane and surplice, c. 1941–42. *(Ballantyne family photo)*

p. 102. A 1779 engraving of the mediaeval Old Bridge, Carrick-on-Suir.

p. 120. Lismore junior hurling team and supporters. Mid-1940s. *[Photo courtesy of Helen Landers (née O'Donnell)]*

p. 125. Sonny Bransfield and Dick Long. *(Photo by James Ballantyne)*

p. 148. The Lismore ball alley in summer 1990. *(Photo by James Ballantyne)*

p. 163. 'The Point' where the Blackwater and Owenashad rivers meet, 1994. *(Photo by James Ballantyne)*

p. 168. 'The Rock', our favourite swimming hole in the Blackwater. *(Photo by James Ballantyne)*

p. 172. A group taken at 'The Rock' in the early Fifties. *(Photo by James Ballantyne)*

p. 184. Denny Regan's preferred parking place at Clonea Strand. *(Photo taken by James Ballantyne in 2002)*

p. 197. Boxers. Jim Cully squaring up to Joe Baksi. *(Source unknown)*

p. 209. Penny ballad-sheets sold by tinker musicians at fairs, point-to-points and other public events. *(Source unknown)*

p. 216. Dad with his greyhounds outside Swanlinbar Garda barracks. *(Ballantyne family photo)*

p. 216. My brother Paddy with our uncle Jimmy Morrissey and two of Jimmy's greyhounds. *(Ballantyne family photo)*

p. 220. Period postcard of Lismore Castle, early 1930s? *(The photograph is from the Emerald series produced by the Irish Pictorial Card Co., Cork.)*

p. 233. My father Joseph Ballantyne by the River Blackwater in Lismore in the mid-Forties. *(Photo by James Ballantyne)*

p. 251. A *meitheal* poses at a threshing at the Denn family farm in Castlejohn, Co. Tipperary, in the late Forties. *(Ballantyne family photo) p. 255.* Philip Neville, Peter Neville and Mick O'Brien outside Feeney's Garage, Lismore in the early Fifties. *(Photo by James Ballantyne)*

p. 261. The Owenashad Bridge, Lismore in April 2006. *(Photo courtesy of Eugene Dennis)*

p. 285. 'The penitential drills.' A 1950s rural scene. *(Photo and caption courtesy of Eugene Dennis)*

p. 285. Thinning beet outside Waterford City in the 1950s. *(Photo and caption courtesy of Eugene Dennis)*

p. 321. Upper New Street (Botany) Lismore. Late 1940s. *[Photo courtesy of the late Ned Barry and his wife Siobhán Barry (née Neville)]*

p. 321. Boys skating on ice. Probably 1940s. *[Photo courtesy of Helen Landers (née O'Donnell)]*

pp. 324–5. Villa days. *(Ballantyne family photos)*

p. 338. Sergeant Joseph Ballantyne, front row centre, with colleagues in the late Twenties or early Thirties. *(Photo: Scholastic Real Photo Series)*

p. 345. Lismore gardaí in 1954, the year of my father's retirement. *(Photo courtesy of the Garda Archive/Museum, Dublin)*

p. 358. Studio portrait of my mother Mary Morrissey with her younger brother Jack, c. 1916. *(Morrissey family photo)*

p. 366. Nellie Morrissey, a younger sister of Mam's. *(Morrissey family photo)*

p. 367. My aunt Nellie Morrissey, her sister Nan Morrissey, younger brother Jimmy Morrissey and their cousin Jo Denn of Castlejohn. *(Morrissey family photo)*

p. 380. My mother holding my brother Paddy in her arms, 1934–35. *(Ballantyne family photo)*

p. 387. Paddy spinning on his tricycle, c. 1936–37. *(Ballantyne family photo)*

p. 387. Auntie Bab and Paddy on the 'Tallow' Bridge, Lismore c. 1938–39. *(Ballantyne family photo)*

p. 392. My aunt Nan Morrissey, Paddy and me in our back garden in West Street, c. 1938–39. *(Ballantyne family photo)*

p. 393. My aunt Biddy Morrissey with Dad, Mam and me in the back garden of the Morrissey family home in Greystone Street, Carrick-on-Suir, c. 1949–50. *(Ballantyne family photo)*

p. 394. Original colour postcard of Greystone Street and the West Gate, Carrick-on-Suir, 1910. *(Photo courtesy of the late Jimmy Power of Tullahought, Co. Kilkenny)*

p. 395. Morrissey family in front of Morrissey's Bakery, Greystone Street, Carrick-on-Suir, c. 1910. *(Postcard by Nuttall of Eltringham)*

p. 400. A 1778 engraving of Carrick-on-Suir.

LIST OF ILLUSTRATIONS

p. 401. Period postcard of the River Suir at full tide, looking in the direction of Clonmel, 1940s. *(The card was published by Cardall Ltd, Dublin. 1940s?)*

p. 402. Paddy Ballantyne up the bank by the Suir in Carrick-on-Suir, c. 1946/47. *(Ballantyne family photo)*

p. 402. My father Joseph Ballantyne relaxing in civvies, in Carrick-on-Suir, in the Thirties or early Forties. *(Ballantyne family photo)*

p. 404. My cousin 'Nurse Biddy' Morrissey and my uncle Mick Morrissey in Greystone Street, Carrick-on-Suir in the early 1930s. *(Ballantyne family photo)*

p. 406. 'Molly and me' in the early Forties. *(Ballantyne family photo)*

p. 406. My aunt Brighid Ballantyne (née Garvin) on the left, with my mother and Paddy at the Ballantyne family home in Carrowreagh, Co. Sligo. Late 1930s. *(Ballantyne family photo)*

p. 407. Aunt Brighid, Dad, Mam and Paddy at the Ballantyne family farmhouse in Carrowreagh, Co. Sligo, late 1930s. *(Ballantyne family photo)*

p. 416. School photograph of my classmates at the Christian Brothers' School, c. 1948–49. *(CBS school photo)*

p. 417. School photograph of my brother Paddy's classmates at the Christian Brothers' School, 1946. *(CBS school photo)*

p. 469. Jim [surname ?] and Dick Long outside the Devonshire Arms Hotel in the early Fifties. *(Photo by James Ballantyne)*

p. 479. My father Joseph Ballantyne in the uniform of an Irish Volunteer. Most probably taken in Keash, Co. Sligo c. 1917–1919. *(Ballantyne family photo)*

p. 481. Joseph Ballantyne in the centre with two unidentified men during the War of Independence. *(Ballantyne family photo)*

p. 481. Studio portrait of my father Joseph Ballantyne taken during the War of Independence. *(Ballantyne family photo)*

p. 482. Group shot. Joseph Ballantyne is seated front row on the right. Photograph taken most likely in Cammell Laird's shipyard, Birkenhead, Merseyside, c. 1920–21. *(Ballantyne family photo)*

p. 482. A receipt found among Dad's papers from the County Borough of Bootle Technical School, dated 18th November 1920. *(Joseph Ballantyne's papers)*

p. 491. Lismore Railway Station in 1964. The railway, sadly, was closed to all traffic three years later. *(Photo and caption courtesy of Eugene Dennis)*

p. 501. The Palladium Cinema, Lismore in summer 1990. *(Photo by James Ballantyne) p. 513.* Monthly programme of the Castle Cinema, Carrick-on-Suir for August 1955.

p. 536. The stage at Kilclooney Bridge, Coolnahorna in the townland of Clonea (known as Clonea Power) in the parish of Mothel. *(Photo permission of Maurice Quinn's niece, Mrs Maura Grace (née O'Dwyer) of Carrick-on-Suir)*

p. 551. The last photograph of my brother Paddy in Lismore. Summer of 1953. *(Ballantyne family photo)*

Acknowledgements

This book is published through the generosity of my late good friend John Turner, the British newsreel cameraman and war correspondent, who, I am sure, would have approved the use to which I am putting his most kind and wholly unexpected bequest.

John, a true English gentleman, died on 7 March 2007, three weeks and three days short of his 92nd birthday. I was privileged to be instrumental in persuading him to write his unique and greatly valued memoir which was published by my long-time employer, the British Universities Film & Video Council (BUFVC), in 2001 under the title: *Filming History: The Memoirs of John Turner, Newsreel Cameraman*. As we say in Irish, *beidh sé inár gcuimhne* (we shall keep his memory).

Certain names, dates, facts and events hovered tantalisingly beyond the limit of my recall. For a recollection of these, and other facts of which I was in ignorance, I am greatly indebted to Margaret (née Feeney) Madden and her husband, the late Michael Madden of Lismore, Eugene Dennis of Lismore and Cork, the late Edward 'Beaver' Doherty of Lismore and Nottingham, Frank Mason of Lismore and Cork, and to my late aunts Nan Morrissey and Bid Morrissey of Carrick-on-Suir, my late uncle Mick Morrissey of Carrick-on-Suir and Birmingham and my late brother Patrick Ballantyne of Carrick-on-Suir and Canada. Michael Madden, whose untimely death on the 11th of July 1996 left Lismore bereft, had an encyclopaedic knowledge of the town and its people and I shall always be particularly grateful to him for commenting on the 1989 typescript that preceded the first edition. He kindly corrected me on a number of points and supplied me with additional information that I incorporated in the 1995 text.

I am also further indebted to Eugene Dennis for going through the first (1995) edition and highlighting various misconceptions and errors, including many typos and misspellings. It is thanks to him also that I have now attributed the correct spelling of a number of surnames to the appropriate families, something that is always problematic and which I had hitherto striven unsuccessfully to get right. How many times have I asked myself, 'Is it Walsh or Walshe here, Scanlan or Scanlon, Sargeant or Sargent, McCarthy or MacCarthy, Crean or Creane?' Euge's incisive editing skills and independent judgement were much needed and, coupled with his insider knowledge of the town, have made a vital contribution to making this edition definitive. He also provided photographs.

Special thanks are due to my former BUFVC colleague Marilyn Sarmiento for bringing a completely fresh eye to the book. Marilyn, a native of the State of Michigan and an accomplished editor, knowing nothing of Lismore to begin with, has further edited the text with a neutral and eagle eye. She has lent the work a wholly professional finish and knows a lot more about Lismore and its citizens now.

Barrie MacDonald, former Head of Library and Archives of the UK Independent Television Commission, expertly indexed the volume. I thank him for his diligence, generosity and good humour.

The design of this book cover to cover is Nicky Barneby's. Kamila Naseova designed my website. Both have done a superb job. I am most grateful to them for their patience, expertise and professionalism.

My sincere thanks go to Michael Coady, Eugene Dennis and Donald Brady for generously providing the quotations shown on the back cover of the book.

I am grateful to Evelyn Coady of Lismore Public Library for her steadfast encouragement and for researching names and supplying photographs. Picture researcher Liz Heasman kindly advised me on copyright issues. Inspector Patrick McGee of the *Garda Síochána* Archive and Museum at Dublin Castle courteously clarified some matters relating to my father's service in the *Garda* and Commandant P B Brennan of the Military Archives at Cathal Brugha Barracks in Dublin kindly provided information relating to my father's active service during the War of Independence.

Others who have willingly helped with advice and encouragement have been Jim Lineen of Lismore and Dunboyne, Margaret Scanlon of Lismore, Séan Dennis of Lismore, Seamus McGrath of Carrick-on-Suir, Walter Dunphy of Carrick-on-Suir, Rob Sanders of the Trades Union Congress (TUC), and former BUFVC colleagues Nick Wray and Sergio Angelini.

It will be obvious to the reader that I am also beholden to my late parents Mary Frances (née Morrissey) Ballantyne of Carrick-on-Suir and Joseph Albert Ballantyne of Keash, Co. Sligo. I am grateful to my wife Anne Marie Reilly for finding the space in her own very busy schedule to scan the text and make further important suggestions, and to our son Joseph Ballantyne for solving my computer software problems and for willing assistance and support at the book launch, generously hosted by the Madden family at the *Summerhouse* in Lismore, on 10 August 2008.

My thanks to Weidenfeld & Nicolson, a division of the Orion Publishing Group, for their permission to reproduce the extract from *The Singapore Grip* by J G Farrell.

Every effort has been made to trace or contact the copyright holders of the photographs and prints reproduced in the book. I will be pleased to correct and acknowledge any omissions brought to my notice.

Raphael Samuel, the English historian, has noted that history is 'a social form of knowledge; the work, in any given instance, of a thousand different hands'. (*Theatres of Memory, Volume I: Past and Present in Contemporary Culture*. London: Verso, 1996, p. 8.) I thank the thousand contemporaries whose time capsule I shared in Lismore. This memoir of our small Irish town is a fruit of our lives together.

James Ballantyne
London, 30 January 2008

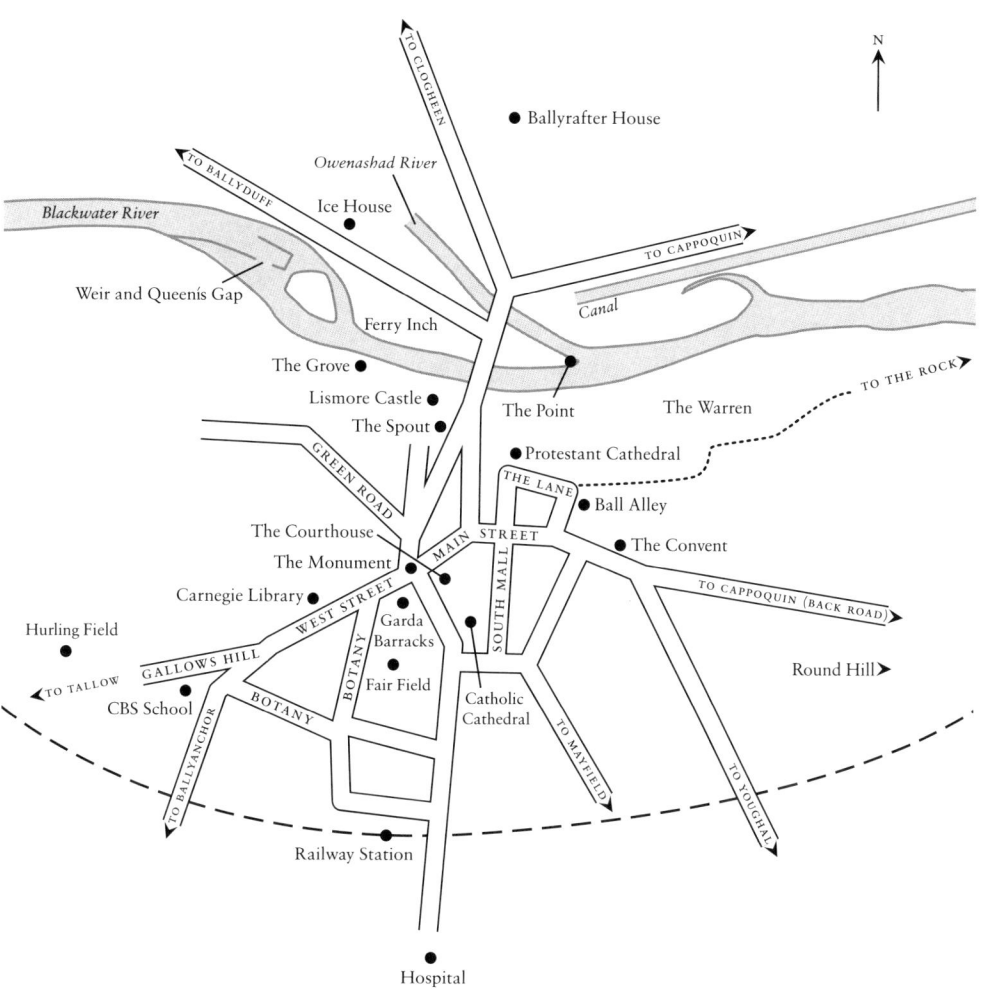

Lismore as I Knew It

Introduction

THE ADDITIONS, CORRECTIONS and amendments incorporated in this definitive edition of *Lismore: Autobiography of an Irish Town 1937–54* were prompted by a re-examination of the notes I had accumulated for the earlier editions of this book and by Eugene Dennis's rich compendium *The Lismoreian*, Volume I, 1998. (Volume II appeared in print in December 2007.) I use the term 'definitive' guardedly.

In the letter accompanying the first edition I wrote that I had tried to eschew nostalgia. Since then I have come to realise, particularly through Svetlana Boym's brilliant and groundbreaking analysis *The Future of Nostalgia* (Basic Books, New York, 2001), that nostalgia cannot be so easily dismissed. Somewhere I read a comment attributed to her by a reviewer, warning us that 'the past can't be recaptured and it never really was the way you remembered it.' It is not a comment that I have come across in her book (I may have missed it) but it is a necessary and cautionary, if possibly overstated corrective, with 'really' the critical word. I fully agree with her when she writes (page xvi) that 'nostalgia is about the relationship between individual biography and the biography of groups or nations, between personal and collective memory, and (page xvii) that it 'tantalizes us with its fundamental ambivalence; it is about the repetition of the unrepeatable, materialization of the immaterial.' Memory is fallible. It has played me false on a few specific occasions (1995 text) and I very much regret any hurt or embarrassment that may have been caused to individuals, friends indeed, as a result. I can say now that with the willing assistance of some fellow Lismoreians the work is as complete, and I hope, as honest as I can make it. Less obvious errors of one kind or another may still be lurking within the pages but I trust that these are at a minimum. The overall picture of life in the town during the years 1937 to 1954 is the important consideration.

It is often said nowadays that the early 1950s mark the divide between the 'old' Ireland and the 'new', whatever these convenient terms mean. I see only continuity. However, the accelerated pace of change of the new vibrant

Ireland has startled me. Few, if any of us, anticipated the huge benefits that membership of the EEC/EC would bring, the most important of which for me was the welcome confidence it engendered in us to seek opportunities beyond Britain and the English-speaking world on the continent of Europe. It is good to see our country playing an active and important role in the European Community today. Sadly, we also did not foresee the corrosive downside of our US-investment led capitulation to the rampant consumerism, 'propertyism' and greed of the anti-social, not to say cracked, Reagan-Thatcher belief set of the 1980s, dangerously and mendaciously barbed by George Bush and his neo-cons, that has seeded a virulent strain of racism and rightwing libertarianism (the antithesis of liberty), compromised our set of values and placed us in danger of losing our compassion, our imagination and our sense of beauty - our innate otherworldliness, if you like.

Not that our predicament is unique or even new, if fiction is to be believed. The following rhetorical passage in Chapter 22 of J G Farrell's great work *The Singapore Grip* (first published in 1978 and set in the period leading up to the Japanese invasion of Singapore in 1941-42) is uttered by the idealistic hero, Matthew Webb. *(The quotation is taken from page 177 of the 1992 paperback edition of the novel published by Phoenix.)* It may refer to a different society at a different time on the other side of the globe but, if not wholly analogous to our situation, is eerily prescient of it.

'Difficulties! Why, the rice merchants knocked Burma for six! The whole culture was destroyed. The old communal village life collapsed. Almost overnight it became every man for himself. People started fencing off grazing land which used to belong to the whole village and so forth. Profit took a grip on the country like some dreadful new virus against which nobody had any resistance. When the Burmese were reduced to becoming migrant seasonal workers in the paddy fields the old village life was finished off completely... and with it went everything that made life more than a pure money-grabbing exercise. At one time they used to hold elaborate cattle races, and water festivals, and village dances and theatricals and puppet shows. They all vanished. And what replaced them? A huge increase in the crime rate! To be happy people need to live in communities. If you don't believe me you can read it in the government reports!'

It is not too late to reassert and enrich these threatened Irish, indeed human, values and others that we used to cherish - openness, courtesy, kindness to strangers, for example - although, presently, the transient fads of tat economics and the baleful superficiality and glitz of much of the new-millennium Western lifestyle appear to hold us in thrall. Nor is it too late to call time on the endemic corruption, for example, in matters of tax evasion, rezoning of land for development purposes, bribery, and so on, in the political and moneyed echelons of our society. An abiding love of our unique Irish music, language and Gaelic games is evidence of an enduring core. Hurling and Gaelic football retain their amateur status (just about for senior intercounty players?) at a time of almost universal professionalism in the wider arena of sport. In Waterford we are as passionate as ever about our hurling and, although I was a poor exponent of the game, it is still the only sport that holds a visceral attraction for me (but I have to admit that Arsène Wenger's Arsenal in full flow stirs the blood as well). We take great pride in the superlative performances of our current county senior team, which counts among its squad superb representatives from Lismore and West Waterford, including Lismore's Dan Shanahan, the 2007 GAA, GPA, Munster Council *and* Texaco Hurler of the Year. It is gratifying to record also that in 2007 the Waterford senior hurling championship final was won in style by our neighbours Ballyduff and the county junior hurling final by neighbouring Ballysaggart.

There is, of course, an upside to this time of the Tiger too, although the benign effects may have arisen in spite of the booming economy rather than because of it, a combination of both, I suspect. Over the last twenty years or more Ireland has produced many new writers, poets, actors, theatre directors and designers, film-makers, musicians, singer-songwriters, comedians, artists, businessmen and businesswomen, young scientists of the year, and sportsmen and sportswomen of national and international renown. Citizens young and old have contributed admirably, both financially and through personal involvement, to countries stricken by disaster. The idealistic commitment of a large number of our young citizens, and indeed of a similar proportion of young citizens of the UK and the continent, is particularly praiseworthy. Our politicians, North and South, aided by a committed corps of civil servants, and their British counterparts, have finally brought peace and understanding to these islands. Sectarianism, regrettably, we shall have to live with for another generation or two, maybe longer.

So a debate is underway- a change in the positive sense, not the meaningless cliché of today's financial and technological jargon- as we begin to confront the gross inequalities in our society and establish our new multi-cultured identity, or identities. Present and future generations, I hope, will endorse a more honest and generous interpretation of our history and a more liberal and inclusive vision of what it means to be Irish, of what it means to be British, of what it means to be European, and of what it means to be a citizen of our troubled Earth.

If the Fifties signify a new departure I am pleased that I have been able to document life in our community in the early phase of this time of unwitting change. All the more reason not to apologise for what might be seen as an excess of detail in the book as one cannot know into which aspects of our lives social historians of the future will delve. The events, landscapes, thoughts and feelings I describe are coloured by my personality and are as I remember them (or, in the light of Boym's comments above, as I think I remember them?). Another person would perceive them in a different light, or might dispute my account. There is no one 'true' version of an event, an observation brought home to me in later years by Akira Kurosawa's innovative Japanese film *Rashômon*. I have tried to be as accurate as I can and apologise for any errors that may have crept into the work. Inevitably, my account constitutes only a chapter of the social history of Lismore during the period about which I have chosen to write. My canvas is of necessity incomplete as there were many people living in the town and surrounding area with whom I scarcely, if ever, came in contact. Other Lismoreians will recall other people, other stories and variants of mine.

I was a little over two months off my eighteenth birthday when I left the town of Lismore, in the west of the County of Waterford. Thus, the observations in this book are essentially those of a boy, then a youth, of the period 1937 to 1954, the infant years, of course, being the fruit of parental reflection. That I am recalling this period mainly with the eyes and ears, and indeed opinions, I had at that time implies that there are gaps, and potential pitfalls, in my account. In particular, what did the girls I grew up with really think about life then? How did they really spend their time? What did they really enjoy doing most? And the grown-ups, especially women, how did they feel about living in our small town? What were their worries about their children, and about their own and their children's futures? As to the world beyond our shores, we never took on trust the relentless myth making about American and British life and history peddled to us by the Hollywood and London film industries. On the other hand, caught up in our own myths, we were totally unaware of the pervasiveness of these cultures in our society and chose to ignore the stern admonitions of our Irish teacher Mícheál U. Ó Donnchadha (Vincent O'Donoghue) that our Gaelic way of life was being undermined by them.

In spite of the inevitable gaps in my own experience, I have tried to give a picture of the whole community and its activities, using my family as a study example. In doing so, I may inadvertently still give offence in some of the things I write but again there is no intention to wound. If I have raised the hem of the curtain on some of the weaknesses and foibles of others I have completely unveiled myself, and why not? Weaknesses and idiosyncrasies define us more than most traits. Not that I have dwelt upon these. I have shown our strengths too. My life in Lismore was happy and sad, uplifting and humiliating, hot and cold, but always rich. The value of those years to me is inestimable, though I have drawn away. Indeed, in a sense I have never left the place. Which is how it should be. Family circumstances compelled me to leave when I did. Others less fortunate than me might have quit the town more willingly.

For my 'narrative' I have chosen an impressionistic rather than a chronological framework. For particular pieces of information and for corroboration of dates I have relied frequently on the weekly *Dungarvan Observer*, the only West Waterford record for the period to which I had access at the British Library Newspaper Library in Colindale, north London. But I also checked a number of points in the *Dungarvan Leader*, the local weekly paper that my parents took, at the National Library in Dublin. Other aides-mémoire have been Ordnance Survey maps of Lismore and its surrounding area, and written works and articles about the town.

Three other books overlap the period with which I have concerned myself – Dervla Murphy's personal *Wheels Within Wheels* (1979), George O'Brien's poetic *The Village of Longing* (1987) and Paddy Vaughan's intimate *The Last Forge in Lismore* (1994). Dervla for me is still the vivid young woman of that time, Seóirse a little boy who holidayed first then later came to live at the top of Main Street during my teenage years, Paddy a member of a long-established Lismore family. To these I add *Images of Ireland: Lismore* by Eugene Dennis (Nonsuch Publishing, 2005), a superb and wittily captioned collection of photographs, many of which are contemporaneous with the time I lived there, documenting the people and places of the town.

The initial longhand manuscript of *Lismore - Autobiography of an Irish Town 1937–54* was completed in 1986, the typescript version in October 1989. This was followed in 1995 by the first printed edition, itself a corrected, amended and expanded redaction of the 1989 version. The 1997 microfiche text was a corrected and amended edition of the 1995 publication.

The positive reception accorded the 1995 edition by the townspeople of Lismore has encouraged me to expand, rewrite, amend and correct where necessary, that somewhat rough hewn work. I trust that this printed edition of 2008 has gained from further reflection and recall. It is my final word. Any misconceptions of mine that may remain I leave for others to address.

James Ballantyne
London, 30 January 2008

Letter that accompanied the first very limited printed edition of this book, outlining my reasons for writing it.

9 Hollies Road,
Ealing
London W5 4UU

Dear—

Lismore: Autobiography of an Irish Town 1937–54
Why This Book?

The spur to recalling what life was like in the town of Lismore during the period 1937–54 was a desire on my part to put back something of value into the community from which I came. Making a conscious effort to eschew nostalgia, I have worked on and off, at times intensively, on the project for over ten years. There's always a desire to improve on it, to get still closer to the 'reality' of the time, but one has to let go at some point and now is that point for me. That is not to say that I have exhausted my interest in West Waterford and its people, that I have got, or would want, Lismore out of my system. Far from it. I hope very much that the book will encourage others, especially students in the local schools, to delve deeper into the history – general, social and economic – of our town and region, using where accessible extant primary documents like minutes of meetings of official and voluntary bodies and political parties, old RIC and Garda Síochána reports, business records such as old shop ledgers, photographs, etc., etc. Here and there in my text I have loosely indicated some avenues that might be explored. Purely out of personal interest, I would love to see new archaeological research undertaken on the *Reilig Mhuire* and on the Round Hill and adjacent stretches of the *Rian Bó Phádraigh* and *Bóthar na Naomh*.

    I hope that the book may also find resonance throughout the County of Waterford and in the town of Carrick-on-Suir, the other community to which I owe a great debt. Carrick will always be special for me. The annual holidays of my childhood and youth were spent in the town and it was there that I began my working life among relatives and new-found friends and gained the confidence to go out into the wider world to earn my living and experience other cultures. My parents and only brother are buried in Carrick and the town and the beautiful surrounding countryside of the counties of Waterford, Tipperary and Kilkenny are as dear to me as my native place.

The dense and detailed nature of the book is such that I doubt whether it will ever find a commercial publisher, so its wider availability is problematical. These twenty copies I have had printed and bound for private circulation to family, friends, the Lismore Public Library, the Lismore Heritage Centre and the National Library of Ireland will at least put the period as I experienced it on record.*

James Ballantyne
London, 4 November 1995

---

*I also printed a further fifteen copies and had these comb bound.

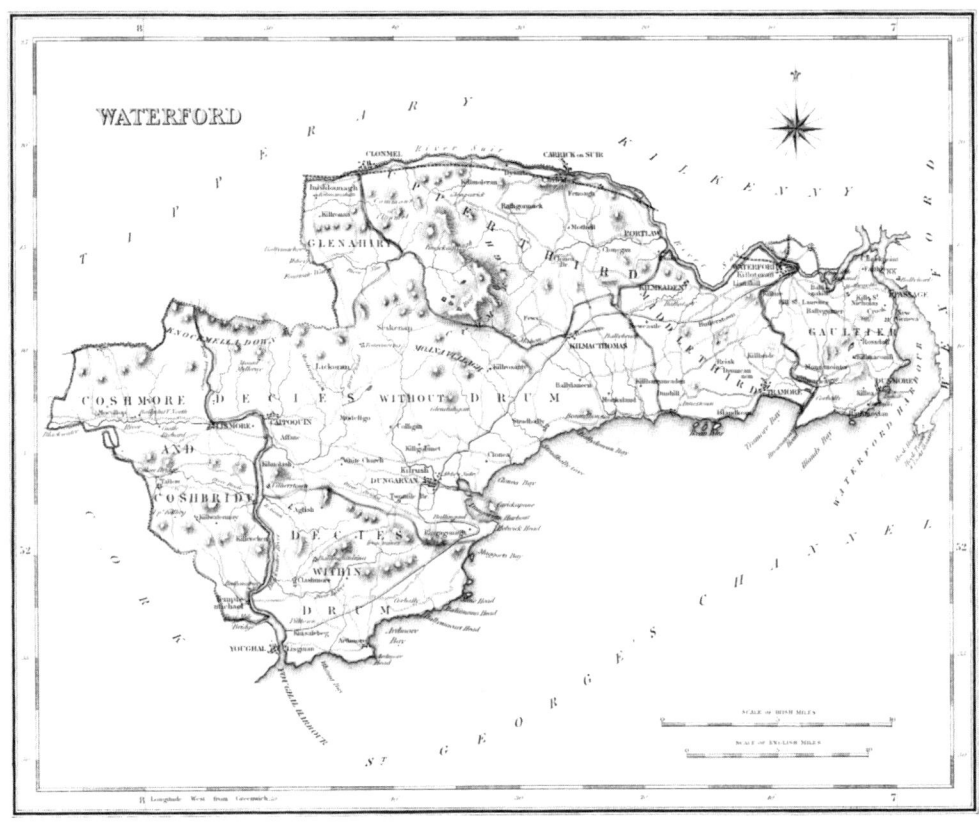

An 1846 map of the County Waterford showing the seven Baronies (divisions) of the Decies territory within the county, which are: Coshmore and Coshbride, Decies within Drum, Decies without Drum; Glenahiry, Upper Third, Middle Third, and Gaultier.

CHAPTER ONE

Earliest Recollections

FROM AN EARLY age I was captivated by the sea, although I visited it at most a mere three or four times a year, occasions when my father, a *garda* sergeant, shed his uniform for civvies and stood in for the Court Clerk of West Waterford when the latter was away on summer holidays. On completion of his work in the early afternoon Dad would have the family driven to Clonea Strand, a lovely stretch of beach, safe for swimming, that in midweek we had almost to ourselves. Occasionally, he would opt to take us farther along the Atlantic Coast to Ardmore, a shorter, more intimate beach that ran out from under a high cliff on the top of which stood the most perfectly preserved round tower in Ireland. And once or twice he took us in the opposite direction, to Stradbally, a narrow inlet in which the sea sparkled deliciously on the tidal rise of a sunny day. Aside from those and one or two fortuitous outings I only glimpsed the ocean through the window of the chugging steam train that carried us along the Dungarvan coastline to and from our annual holidays in Carrick-on-Suir.

The place from which Dad and Mam, my brother Paddy and I, and Molly McGrath, our maid, set out on these exciting trips was Lismore, a small market town of a thousand inhabitants (as many people as crowd into just one modern, eight-carriage, London tube train) situated in the west of one of the southernmost counties of Ireland, Waterford. (At the end of the nineteenth century *A Guide to Waterford and Wexford*, 1896, gave the then population as 1,600.) Here I was born, and grew up, in a terraced house in West Street, a short strip of road plugged in at one end to the Monument, a Victorian memorial to Ambrose, one of the Powers of Glencairn, and at the other to Gallows Hill, a place-name requiring no explanation. I was lifted from my mother's womb on the last day of February 1937, during what appears to have been a period of particularly harsh weather.

The 'Lismore Notes' in the *Dungarvan Observer* of June 12th of that year reported under the heading 'The Grim Reaper': 'The severity of the past spring on the health of the people has been exemplified in the case of the

Above: My father Joseph Ballantyne as a youth in County Sligo with his pipe-smoking father Patrick Ballantyne. c. 1912–13.

Right: Bridget Ballantyne (née McDonagh), one of two grandmothers I was never to know, on the threshold of the Ballantyne family home in Carrowreagh, Keash, Co. Sligo. Late 1930s.

number of burials that have taken place in Lismore, where 41 interments took place between the end of December and the end of May.' This frighteningly high figure, that may have been a factor in deciding my mother to adopt the somewhat overprotective attitude that she maintained toward my brother and me throughout our childhood, was, one hopes, to some extent offset by the births of my immediate contemporaries and me during the same period.

Lismore was not our traditional family home. My father, Joseph Albert Ballantyne, had arrived there in March 1934 to take up the position of sergeant in the Garda Síochána. (I hold receipt Number 158, dated 31 March 1934, from the Lismore Estates Company, acknowledging the sum of 17 shillings 2 pence received for the 'rent of tenement West Street Lismore from 19th to 31 Mar 1934'. It is signed by P W Henchcliffe.) Previously, he had served in Carrick-on-Suir, Fethard and Drangan, County Tipperary, and in Swanlinbar, County Cavan. He was a Sligoman, born in the townland of Carrowreagh and schooled and reared in the district of Gurteen at Keash, or Kesh, at the foot of the legendary *Céis Chorainn*. His father Patrick was a small farmer and cooper (a trade he learned in the USA and one in which he may have trained Dad as well). Dad's strong-minded mother, Bridget McDonagh, was also a small farmer. She came from Greyfield in the same parish. Patrick's family home was at Derrynane in Kilmactranny where the fine house still stands. He had returned from a spell working in America and was on the point of emigrating there for good when a matchmaker arranged a marriage between him and Bridget. They then went to live in Keash on McDonagh land given to Bridget by an uncle. Mary Frances Morrissey, my mother, was born on the northern bank of Carrick-on-Suir, which made her a Tipperary woman. Her mother, Anastasia Cullinane, was a Waterford woman from Ballyneale in the district of Rathgormack, at the foot of the picturesque Comeragh Mountains – the other end of the county from Lismore. Her family too worked the land. Her father, my great-grandfather, Michael Cullinane, known to my mother and her sisters and brothers as 'Daddy' Cullinane, was a dairyman when he married Mary Magrath. An old photograph owned by my aunts Nan and Biddy Morrissey of Greystone Street, Carrick-on-Suir, portrayed him as a large man with a black bushy beard. He was from the townland of Ross in the parish of Rathgormack where the Cullinanes still hold land today, including Crotty's Lake and the surrounding mountainside. As far as I know, Mary Magrath was from the Rathgormack area as well. 'Daddy' Cullinane's father's (my great-great-grandfather's) name was Philip Cullinane, also of Ross. Philip's brother Geoffrey emigrated to America 'about ninety year ago' i.e. in the Great Famine year of 1849, a family friend Philip Quinlan of Ballythomas, Rathgormack, wrote in a letter to my Aunt Nan in 1939. Michael Cullinane was living in Cregg, just north of Carrick by the time he died in 1908. My mother, only 7 at the time, remembered being taken to his burial in the graveyard of Mothel, across the Suir in County Waterford, in a horse-drawn, covered wagonette. It was a bumpy and dusty ride up over Grubb's Hill and along a dirt road and she got sick on the way. According to the noted Carrick antiquarian Hugh Ryan, Michael Cullinane is buried in one of two Cullinane graves in the churchyard – Number 30 that is marked by a rough stone. Mary Magrath survived her husband by seventeen years and when she died was interred in the New Cemetery in Carrickbeg. By that time the graveyard at Mothel was

Above: My great-grandmother Mary Cullinane (née Magrath) of Ross, Rathgormack Co. Waterford. Studio portrait by George D. Croker of Waterford. Date?

Right: My grandfather James Morrissey in the 1920s.

either closed to further burials or had become neglected and overgrown, and my grandparents, having already purchased a family plot in the Carrick cemetery when my uncle Jack died tragically at the age of 12 on the 18th of May 1921, decided unsentimentally to bury her locally rather than go through the bureaucratic process of seeking permission to lay her at her husband's side in Mothel.

Anastasia Cullinane's husband was a Kilkennyman, James Morrissey, a small farmer later turned stone mason and builder from Knockroe, Ahenny. His brother Jack farmed in Whitestown in the Parish of Mothel and it was probably through this connection that James met his future wife. His parents, John Morrissey and Margaret Phelan, who were married in Tullahought, County Kilkenny in 1866 are, according to family lore, buried in Windgap in the same county. Sadly, I was never to know any of my grandparents. James Morrissey died on the 10th of June, 1936 (obituary in *The Nationalist,* Clonmel, 13 June 1936, page 5? - funeral details in *The Nationalist,* 17 June 1936, page 5?; obituary also under 'Carrick Notes' in *The Munster Express,* 19 June 1936, page 5). Anastasia, or Statia, as known to her friends, followed him on the 2nd of May 1937 (obituary in *The Nationalist,* 8 May 1937, page 3). I was told that she held me in her arms once. My paternal grandfather, Patrick Ballantyne, died as early as 1918. Bridget McDonagh survived him half a lifetime and died on the 12th of July 1954. It had never been possible for me to visit County Sligo so I never met her either. My father was very upset when she died and I was saddened because it meant, at a time when I might have been able to travel to see her, that now I would be unable to say that I had known even a single grandparent. I envied pals in Lismore who had not only one, but two, or even all of their grandparents still alive. Some even had grand-uncles and grand-aunts. No one ever knew but in my own mind I sort of adopted my pal Billy Hogan's grandad Garrett as a surrogate grandfather. I liked his wife too. It seemed to me that he was an ideal role model, being a good-natured, good-humoured man, and something of a legend in that he was one of the last surviving members of the great Lismore senior Gaelic football team of the early years of the century, the Blackwater Ramblers. I would have been proud to have a grandparent like him.

My father's attachment to his mother impressed me. Once, toward, or at the end of, the Second World War, when he was told that she was seriously ill, he rode all the way from Lismore to Keash and back on his big 28-inch-framed heavy bicycle to be at her side. It was a return journey of some 300 miles or so over roughly surfaced roads and en route he slept in the cells of *garda* barracks. It wasn't the only time he cycled up. On another occasion he took a train to Athlone and biked it from there, possibly to attend her interment in the picturesque little graveyard of Knockbrack. She must have been much loved and I envied my brother who did get to visit her on the farm.

Paddy was four years older than I. He was born on May Day 1933 not in Lismore but in Carrick-on-Suir, in the back ground-floor bedroom of my mother's family home, and was to maintain more of an attachment to that town than to Lismore. A third child had preceded us, stillborn in 1928 or 1929 after three or more months of pregnancy (what family comment I could elicit on the precise term was indeterminate), I was to learn indirectly

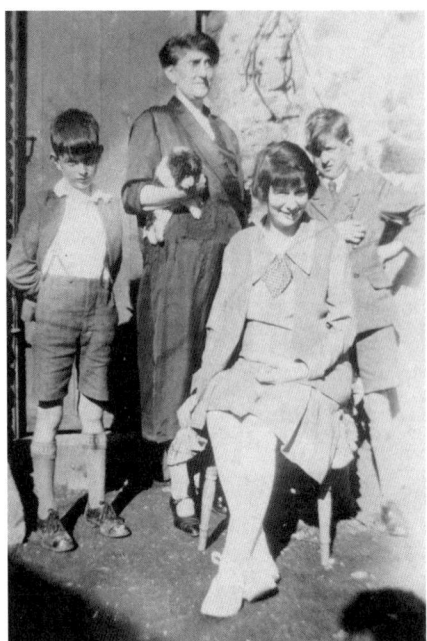

My maternal grandmother Anastasia Morrissey with her sons Jimmy and Mick, and Mam, Early Twenties.

Anastasia Morrissey here seated with her daughter Peg, later the wife of Liam O'Mara of Carrick-on-Suir.

very many years later. Parents did not talk to their children about such matters. According to my aunt Nan, who confided in me further in August 1994 as Paddy lay on his deathbed, my mother was told by a specialist in Dublin that she should not attempt to have another child for at least four years. Hence Paddy's birth in 1933. There was a further complication for the family following the birth. Dad was transferred to Swanlinbar in Cavan. At that time evidently, there was a rule, written or unwritten, in the Gardaí that a guard could not serve in a town or area into which he had married. It seemed that my maternal grandmother, a figure I always found forbidding from photographs, decided that she should take charge of my newly born brother until my parents 'got settled in' in Cavan. What my mother thought of this arrangement I do not know but she went along with it, as did my father who, like most men at that time, would have allowed the women to decide such matters. Perhaps she was to regret it later because the absence from her son was to last a whole year.

During this time Paddy was reared by my grandmother with the assistance of Nan, who was his godmother. What a wrench it must have

Mam and Dad in my grandfather James Morrissey's yard in Salt Yard Lane off Lower Greystone Street, Carrick-on-Suir during their courting days, late 1920s.

My parents Joseph Ballantyne and Mary Morrissey on their wedding day in 1928. Their marriage precipitated a move to Swanlinbar in County Cavan. Typical studio photo of the period by Stanley.

been for the little child when Mam came to collect him in 1934 I can only imagine, but the seeds of his lifelong inability to establish a permanent relationship, and perhaps the alcoholism of his later years, may be found here? On the outside charming with a caustic and cynical wit, he was throughout his life to remain a private and lonely individual inwardly. He was a man of high intelligence, widely read and a fluent player of the piano in his early manhood. The tragedy is, he never learned how to apply that intelligence to the business of life. My own relationship with him was always fraught and it is the greatest regret of my life that we never established a real understanding. It took my baby son Joseph, born on the 12th of October 1992, to finally bring about some kind of rapport between us. Paddy's immediate joy in his presence greatly surprised me and, improbably perhaps, at that moment I felt there was nothing my brother would have wished for more than to have had children of his own.

Once settled in the small West Waterford town my parents did not travel often out of it. The lack of a motorcar ensured that we were not a mobile family. The sea, though a mere fifteen miles distant at its closest point, was an outing away; Carrick, the best part of a day's travel by train and taxi because of the route the railway line followed in that era of leisurely locomotion. In a sense, I think that this was an advantage for me and for most of the pals with whom I grew up. As our sense of distance was so confined we did not need to travel very far to look for adventure. I had lots of time to spend on adventure but not all my boyhood pals and acquaintances were as lucky. Many had their youth cut short at the age of fourteen when they had to conclude an often desultory schooling and go looking for full-time work, most emigrating to London or Coventry, the main English magnets to which Lismoreians were attracted. There was a constant haemorrhage abroad but, at least, there was work to be found in other lands.

I was two years old when the Second World War broke out, eight when it ended. I scarcely knew it had taken place. The horrors of that appalling conflict fortunately passed us by in our quiet backwater, indeed in our young republic as a whole, though many thousands of our fellow-countrymen gave their lives in the struggle against fascism. I knew scraps about a few local people who served or died in the British Army, but nothing of other Waterford men who died or were seriously wounded, and in some cases decorated for valour, in the armies, navies and air forces of Britain and the United States of America, and in the merchant marine. But the signs of war were there for my infant's eyes to see.

I was 5 when first sent to infant school at the Presentation Convent that lay at the easternmost boundary of the town where the Deerpark Road forked off from the back road to Cappoquin. On the right leaving town, just before the corner, there was a large old mansion called simply the Hall and here, during the entire period of the War soldiers of the Irish Army were garrisoned. The Army did not use the main entrance to the building that was protected by sandbags. On the flat roof above the pilastered doorway there was a sandbagged machine-gun nest. Military access to the barracks was through a wide gate and up the driveway at the side of the building opposite Devonshire Cottages. Soldiers always stood on guard at the gate. Sometimes you caught a glimpse beyond the driveway of marching men in the Military Field at the back and now and again you saw a platoon marching in or out of the place, which greatly excited all of us children – the boys anyway. But away from these warlike preparations there were other people in which to delight, like Sister de Lourdes, the smiling young postulant robed all in white who used to take me by the hand and show me how to play games in the small, leafy, sombre convent schoolyard and who was, until then, the most beautiful creature I had ever laid eyes on. An angel certainly compared to the flinty black-garbed Sister Baptist, the nun in charge of the early years who was somewhat strict with us. There was only one other nun I could stand near me and that was Mother Brendan, the reverend mother, who was a Cullinane cousin of my mother's from the east of the county. She was a kindly, smiling woman and whenever my mother took me along to see her in her shiny parlour she would produce big red apples from the convent orchard from inside her voluminous black sleeves and give them to me. It used to puzzle me why she was called by a boy's name. I asked my mother about that once or twice but never got what I considered a satisfactory answer. Mother Brendan was okay in spite of that, but it was Sister de Lourdes I had the crush on.

There was an angel nearer home too who used to look after me: Auntie Bab, my mother's sister. She had a lovely, playful personality and when she visited us in Lismore, which was often, had lots of time for me. I think it was she who potty-trained me because I used to have fantasies about that later. In any case, I had a crush on her as well. But the women who took me in hand day by day, and night after night, were Mam and Molly McGrath from Carrick. Molly was known in Lismore as Molly Ballantyne and, indeed, I always took her to be one of the family although I found it strange that she used to sleep in one of the two attic rooms of our essentially two-storey house and only had a skylight instead of a window. She was low and dark-skinned and laughed easily through protruding front teeth. I was a handful for her at times but she did not stand any nonsense from me and, when I merited it, would smack me on the behind or on the back of the hand. I used to be confused when my pals asked me about her; I was unsure about her exact status in the household but assumed that she had as much right to be there as I had. She did a lot of the housework but then, so did Mam. So I never thought of her as a maid, nor was it ever intimated by my parents that I should think of her in this way. She was one of the family and that was that. It was on one of our holiday visits to Carrick, when I queried why she was not staying with us at my aunts', that I first realised she was neither a Ballantyne nor a Morrissey. It was then I was told that she was staying at her own mother's place. I can think of only two reasons why we had a maid: one, my mother's health may have been impaired in giving birth to me and she needed help to cope, and two, my grandmother, who seems to have been a bit of a martinet, and maybe even a bit of a snob, may have insisted upon it. In any case, Molly was good for us all. The only complaint, if you could call it that, I ever heard Mam voice about her was that she used to forget things when she went shopping. Molly would laugh when reminded and exclaim, 'My head!'

Wartime intruded in the home in the form of food rationing. Each member of the family, including Molly, was given a jam jar with his or her name stuck on it with one of those rectangular little white paper labels edged with red or blue borders that were used for labelling home-made jams and jellies. I received approximately one jar of sugar at the beginning of the month and that had to last me until the end – unless I managed to trade some butter or jam for a portion of someone else's. At mealtimes I became so adept at eyeing Dad's plate when I had finished my own piece of meat that he invariably slipped me an extra slice off his when Mam was not looking. Once she caught him doing this and angrily rushed me from the table. Thereafter, she saw to it that my chances were few and far between.

The house was kept warm enough with open fires. We burned home-produced turf and wood mostly. Wood was won the hard way by Dad and three of his colleagues, Guard Paddy Martin, Guard James Dennis, and Guard Michael Mason. Every year they used to purchase a full-grown beech tree between them from the Lismore Estates Company that administered the Duke of Devonshire's lands. This they would then fell, cut up and take home by hired horse and cart. Felling was a skilled, and potentially dangerous, art and when they ordered a particularly large tree they would pay a local lumberjack to fell it for them. Their tools for the job were the two-handed crosscut saw, sledgehammers, iron wedges, and self-made wooden wedges. The work was hard, even for those whose regular trade it was.

The fireplace in the living-room had two hobs and Mam did some cooking there, but volume cooking was done on the sawdust stove in the open air of the yard at the back of our house. The latter was an ingenious system, for a time open to the elements. Dad later built a lean-to shelter with open sides and a galvanised roof under which it stood. It consisted of a full-sized, round, metal oil drum with a hole of about two or two-and-a-half inches circumference, drilled through the centre of the base. The drum stood balanced on some six or so bricks that raised it above ground level. In the nearby slate-roofed shed we had a supply of sawdust purchased from the Lismore Estates sawmill. To prepare the fire you first placed a long metal pipe with a two-inch diameter through the hole in the bottom of the barrel. Then you filled the barrel with sawdust and packed it down tightly. This accomplished, you slowly extracted the pipe so that a hole remained in the sawdust. Then you lit a fire with paper and kindling under the barrel. The sawdust took time to ignite properly but, after it did, burned slowly, giving off a tremendous heat all day. To cook anything, all you had to do was place two flat iron bars on which large pots could rest across the top of the drum.

Group taken in our backyard c. 1943-44. Left to right; Paddy Ballantyne leaning out of picture, Michael Feeney, Jim Lineen. Jim Ballantyne, Tom Feeney. In the background a pot can be seen steaming on the sawdust-filled 'stove' that Dad used to prepare. Later on he was to construct a lean-to roof over this. Mam's castor-oil plant behind it was to take over the whole corner in time *(see picture of my brother Paddy in Chapter 25)*.

As well as cooking stews and the like, Mam also boiled her washing over the smouldering sawdust. And my uncle Jimmy Morrissey of Carrick, who was a greyhound trainer, used the same system in the yard at Greystone Street to boil sheep's heads for his dogs.

My young eyes detected signs of war around the town other than the military garrison. The bridge over the river Blackwater had a double scar across its back where the Irish Army intended to place explosives in the event of any enemy advance from a northerly or southerly direction. Wooden planks, finely fitted, were inset in the footpath. A nest of reinforced concrete pillboxes, sited below the Strand Bridge, promised resistance to any potential aggressor approaching from a variety of directions. One was placed beyond the wall of the gas works in the field by the canal, covering the approach road from Cappoquin. A second, across the road from the salmon hatchery by Bud Sargent's garage commanded access to the Strand Bridge. Most spectacularly sited, however, was the third that lay concealed under a grassy mound on the summit of the hill near Ballyrafter House and that gave an unimpeded view over the two bridges leading to the town.

These minor, slit-eyed defence works would have carried a nice little sting when their Bren-guns opened up, you felt, yet you had to ask yourself how the soldiers inside would have escaped if the enemy managed to get behind the tiny entrances. We used to play games around the Ballyrafter box when it fell into disuse after the War and had ample opportunity to put our theories to the test then.

Overt evidence was provided by the manoeuvres that were sometimes held in the Lismore area. The soldiers would bivouac amongst the trees at the town end of the Hurling Field and I used to see their tents when I was taken for walks around the Green Road. It was exciting to see a patrol of Bren-gun carriers whizzing by, but even more so, a line of soldiers on motorbikes, wearing their camouflaged oilskin capes, and with Lee Enfield rifles slung across their backs. The most thrilling moment of all, and I witnessed it open-mouthed from my bedroom window in the mid-afternoon, was a mock attack on a Bren-gun carrier that was passing down a strangely hushed and empty West Street. Two soldiers with a machine gun were lying in wait under the archway of Feeney's garage next door – earlier in the day I had seen them settling in – and when the ambush was sprung smoke bombs were thrown, the guns went ack-ack, and the carrier was immobilised directly across from our house. It seemed an odd place to stage an ambush, I thought, but probably the Army did it to provide a display of their skills and to reassure the townsfolk that their homes would be defended to the last. It was, however, only one of a number of battles fought in and around our town that afternoon and evening. I was in no position to speculate on military tactics at that time as I was only coming up to four years of age. It was November 1940. Later that night I was lifted from my bed and taken downstairs to be presented to Mick Higgins, a captain or a major, who was an old friend of my father's from the County of Roscommon, and who had unexpectedly dropped in for a quick cup of tea between assignments. His face was smeared with mud and there were ferns stuck in the wire meshing of his helmet. He smiled and dandled me on his knee. I was intrigued by his helmet so he placed it upon my head. So heavy it was! I had never had anything so weighty on my head before. He laughed and quickly took it off. Then he finished his tea and was gone.

The Local Defence Force, the LDF as we called them, were also involved in the manoeuvres and were much in evidence throughout the Emergency. For the most part, their parades and marches were fairly unexciting compared to the real thing but once, in 1943, one of our neighbours in West Street, Jim Ormonde, led a really big Easter parade of some 400 men all around the town, with the salute being taken from a platform placed at the

The LDF (later FCA) led by Jim Ormonde passing along the Main Street in Lismore in 1942, very likely on a Sunday as businesses seem shut. The triple-arched house between Heelan's and the Red House public house (with wooden balcony) was Billy Baldwin's greengrocery and wild game and fruit buying store.

Monument. Drilled by Jackie Callaghan of Church Lane, the LDF took themselves seriously but the young lads would always try and get a rise out of them, or make them laugh when they shouldn't. 'Lift them knees, Jack!' 'Belly in Billy!' 'You're a real sharpshooter, Mikey!' and the like would be hurled at various individuals who would either scowl or try to keep a straight face. Later that same day practical demonstrations given by the trained regular soldiers down by the Blackwater covered such skills as grenade throwing by hand and rifle, section and platoon attacking, tree-felling using explosives, and trench digging (*Dungarvan Observer*) but I was too little to be allowed to see those. The regulars stationed at the barracks involved themselves generally with the townsfolk by holding the odd sports day in the Fair Field and an Army hurling team called McDermotts used to play matches against the Lismore lads.

On VE Day, the day the Second World War officially ended, Jack Campion, a renowned salmon fisherman and later local Labour Party politician, hung out the Union Jack from the upstairs dormer window of his small bakery in Botany. It took a bit of guts, or contrariness, or both, to do that and it provoked some adverse and ironic comment. In Dublin, a bunch of students in Trinity College caused a riot in doing the same thing but no one took much heed of it in Lismore. Besides, it would have demanded as much courage to accost the short-tempered Jack and tell him he should take it down because it did not represent our nation. I went up the street to have a gander at the object that was causing the flutter. Where he got it from I could not even guess but it was very stripy and very gaudy, and altogether something of a mess, I thought. I don't think I approved of Jack's gesture, probably on nationalistic rather than aesthetic grounds. My father was amused by the incident but a lot of people did not like it. No one seemed to question Jack's motives, though. He was a man who did not mince his words and, in retrospect, I am sure that it was his way of showing that he welcomed the defeat of the Nazis.

In the immediate postwar years I would hear my parents remark on this or that man who had returned home after having been a prisoner of war of the Axis powers. One man in particular they knew personally: Joe Dooley, the son of Paddy Dooley the water bailiff. Paddy and his wife lived in a beautifully situated cottage at a place called the Glen, a mile or so out the Mountain Road. Joe had been captured at Singapore and had spent the rest of the War in Japanese prison camps and by all accounts had been very lucky to survive. His parents had given him up for dead. I was taken for a walk up the Mountain Road one sunny afternoon by Molly and Mam to see how Joe was convalescing. All I remember is that he was sitting in a chair outside on the gravel terrace amid the many-coloured wallflowers; he smiled wanly; and we got tea and cakes. What I totally, and not surprisingly, lacked was an understanding of the sheer horror and magnitude of the Second World War. There was some talk about something called an atomic bomb but nobody seemed to know exactly what this was other than that it would be the most powerful weapon ever engineered by man. In geographical terms, I was only beginning to come to grips with the scale of our planet. Sometime around then there was an air crash in New York and I remarked to Dad, on hearing him read out the details to Mam, 'Gosh, 'tisn't often things like that happen in Ireland.' He looked at me in puzzlement, as if I should have known that the city lay 3,000 miles across the Atlantic Ocean in another country. 'New York isn't in Ireland,' he said. 'It's in America.' 'Oh?' I sighed and shook my head.

I was learning other lessons for life in our own backyard, too. Dad had constructed a swing in the garden for Paddy and me. One day I was swinging on it while he was scything the long grass nearby. Intrigued by the delicacy and skill of this operation, I got off the swing and moved in for a

Mam with Paddy and me in our back-garden in West Street, Lismore, c. 1938.

closer look. In doing so I walked into the butt of the handle and received a hefty clout on the side of the head. I immediately started bawling and gave Dad a fright. He cuddled me in his arms and rubbed my head on which a sizable bump was already beginning to rise. Then he took me down to the kitchen and deposited me with Mam who, I thought, made light of the incident. But I stayed well clear of the scythe after that.

In early 1944 two people died locally in circumstances remarkable enough for me to note. The first was Lord Charles Cavendish, brother of the Duke of Devonshire and owner of Lismore Castle, who died of alcohol abuse in April at the early age of 39. He was well liked locally and people had an understanding of his affliction. I had my own inconsequential personal memoir of him. One day, when Mam and Molly were out walking with me on the Green Road near the tennis club pavilion he chanced by in his horse and trap, stopped, chatted a little, then, seeing the enthralled eye I was casting over his shiny vehicle, asked if I would like a ride. He would have had to appear very unpleasant for me to refuse such an offer – as it was, he had a slightly balding head, gold spectacles, and a kind of grave smile – so I immediately said 'Yes, please' and looked appealingly at Mam. She gave permission and away he and I went on down the Green Road to the Castle Farm where we turned and drove back to Mam and Molly. The man was affable company as far as a little boy could ascertain. I only ever saw him once or twice again, going next door to the Wine Vaults – the finest bar and grocery for miles around and much frequented by the local gentry – for a drink. When he died it was decided to bury him locally in the graveyard of the beautiful old Protestant cathedral. Indeed, it was probably his own wish. Once I heard people saying that he was going to be interred in a 'silver coffin' I just had to get a sight of it. In fact, it was made of silver oxide, i.e. chromium plating.

For the event the business of the town came to a standstill. The funeral was a huge one, peopled with all the nobs in the area, in addition to immediate family and, of course, the townsfolk. The order of the procession seemed to be family, nobs, town commissioners, shopkeepers, employees of the Castle and the Lismore Estates Company, then anyone else who wanted to march. A big although sad day for Dean Charles Stanley. It was beyond my understanding why the respectable band of Catholics at the front, on reaching the gates of the cathedral, stepped aside and did not go on to join the prayers at the graveside. Catholic Castle employees, with the liberal-minded sawyer Bishop Scanlon to the fore, showed no such scruples. I distinctly recall Michael McCarthy, our next-door neighbour who owned and ran the Wine Vaults, and his brother Danny remaining outside, their bald heads glistening piously through the green wrought-iron railings. It was a neat footnote that Michael also used to give me a spin in his horse and trap from time to time. The McCarthy brothers never missed *anybody's* funeral so I was particularly struck by their missing out on a chance to mouth a graveside prayer on this occasion. It was especially curious as the grave was located no more than forty or fifty yards from where they stood, tucked out of their line of vision in the corner at the left-hand side of the church. Somebody explained to me that while it was okay for Catholics to show their respects by walking in a Protestant funeral procession it was wrong for them to participate in a Protestant service because this would imply that the Protestant faith was on the same level as the Catholic faith that was, of course, the only true faith. It still only made a kind of sense to me, but not until after my pals and I had squeezed through many adult legs to get to the hole in the ground. And there it was, in close-up, the glittering conveyance to the other world, balanced on two thick planks. It was no ordinary grave either, as the muddy sides were lined with dark green moss. I had already seen ordinary graves - you could hardly miss the men digging them when you were out playing around chapel or cemetery - and I had tagged on to the odd funeral for the spectacle of it. So I knew this was something special. I watched fascinated as the silver box was lowered into the hole. Even though I knew who was in it, I could not grasp the meaning of it all. After a while the mourners began to drift away. Then we did. Later we wandered back to watch the gravediggers placing the last few sods on the grave and ornamenting it with no more than a simple bouquet of flowers, or maybe two.

The second man to die was Tommy Crotty, a grocer who lived in the Main Street. He had been a town commissioner for many years, chairman of the Commissioners often, and was a much loved local figure. I cannot remember him physically but I know we used to meet him on walks occasionally and my parents thought very highly of him. I happened to be within earshot when Dad told Mam that he had been killed in an accident. Tears came to her eyes and the two of them spoke in hushed tones. They remained subdued for days over it. It appeared that the man had slipped off the highest point of Lady Louisa's Walk in the Warren and had fallen down the jagged cliffside, smashing himself on a slab of rock by the edge of the river Blackwater. His neck was broken. It was Guard Boyle's son Jerry who found him. His was a huge funeral, too, but I did not manage to attend that for some reason – I was probably left at home with Molly. Soon after, however, I and a couple of pals sneaked down to the Warren to see the height off which he fell. Mam had always warned me to stay away from that dangerous pathway but morbid curiosity made me want to check it for myself. It was a high cliff all right, as high as the top of the roof of a three-storey house at least, and it was at the point where the path cornered that Tommy had stumbled. The flat rock below looked sacrificial. A few years later, whenever I used to pass that spot on my regular way to and from our swimming place beyond the Warren, I would sometimes feel a *frisson* as I pictured Tommy Crotty toppling over the edge of the precipice like Uncas in *The Last of the Mohicans*. It was a sobering vision, especially when you were galloping along the path.

There was another significant loss in early December of that same year – C. P. Hynes, the vet, who died after practising in the town for over forty-three years, but I have no memories of him. He was well-known for being the steward and starter at the Lismore Point-to-Point.

Being taken for walks by Molly and Mam was a regular feature of my brother's and my early years. In Lismore it was not difficult to find picturesque routes. All you had to do was take any road or byroad that led from the town. Our favourite places for short walks were the Grove, the Green Walk and the Green Road, all in the proximity of the castle. The Green Road was a working dirt road that meandered gently through tall deciduous trees, mainly beech, and from which at a certain point you had a fine view of the Knockmealdown Mountains in the distance. Around the wooded slopes of the Grove, that was situated outside the west wall of the castle, pathways, well-maintained by the billhook and broom of Paddy Cassidy of Ferry Lane, snaked among periwinkles, bluebells, wild onion, ferns and attractive shrubs above one of the darkest and deepest stretches of the Blackwater. (Eugene Dennis has pointed out to me that the workman's real surname was Connery though he was known in the town under the name Cassidy.) The main entrance to the Grove lay just beyond the castle sawmill. The Green Walk, in contrast to the other two, was a long straight path that shortcut the loop of the Green Road to emerge by the crossroads just up from the Castle Farm. It too was beautifully kept and on either side of it there was a variety of small trees and shrubs, bounded by holly and beech hedges, that provided perfect nesting cover for thrushes, blackbirds, robins, tits, wrens and finches in the spring. The Tallow Road and the Ballyanchor Road were other favoured routes. If you timed your walk right along either of those you could catch the steam trains shooting under the bridges. My favourite summer walk was down the New Way, across Lismore Bridge, left along the lower road to Ballyduff until you turned right just before the ice house in Ballyin, then left around the house through an iron kissing gate and up through a short stretch of wood and along by a stone wall to Johnny McGrath's place with its large garden. Johnny was a great gardener and sold fruit and vegetables. Mam and Molly would always stop and chat to him for a while and on the way back buy some of his produce. Mam was not above attempting a bit of matchmaking either and now and again would embarrass Molly by trying to pair her off with her bachelor namesake. Then we would resume our walk, the exciting stretch for me. We followed a path up by the side of the sand pit, in the steep slopes of which used to nest sand martins that you could watch flitting in and out of their holes. And there were lots of rabbits in the area. On top of the hill above the pit there was a grassy place, well-cropped by sheep, topped by a half-dozen Scots pines, and here we used to base ourselves for a picnic. Away to the south-west you could enjoy a view that took in the sylvan slopes above both banks of the Blackwater although you could not see the river itself. Because of its aspect the place caught the best of the afternoon and evening sun. We used to spend hours there, sneaking up on rabbits and watching them scurry away, playing hide-and-seek in the bracken, and putting together bunches of the abundant wild flowers. Dad was rarely with us on these occasions but sometimes he would join us for the early part of the evening. Generally, because of the nature of his work, it was more convenient for him to fit in shorter walks, along the picturesque Green Road or the Green Walk or out to the 'Tallow Road' railway bridge or a bit out the Glencairn Road.

All my memories of the Tallow Road route are not happy ones. Once, out

West Street pals. (From left) Mike Feeney, Cora Ormonde, Paddy Ballantyne, Teresa Ormonde and John Ormonde. Taken in our back garden c. 1938.

beyond Frank O'Donnell's farm where we used to pick field mushrooms, I was skipping along with my hands in the pockets of my tiny overcoat when I tripped and fell flat on my face. That hurt! Even the combined cuddling and coaxing of Mam and Molly could not kill the pain of it. My nose was all cut and my lips swelled up so much they had to pipe me liquid food through a kind of straw for a couple of days, after which I had to sup my food from a special cup with a spout on it for a further few. It was a lesson for life and I never walked with both hands tight in my pockets again.

Sometimes, when both Molly and Mam were busy, I would be entrusted to my brother, who was four years older than I. He did not relish looking after me and usually found a way to offload me onto girls of his age that he knew were keen to play mother. Often it was Teresa Ormonde up the street and maybe her cousin Cora from Dungarvan. When yet another Ormonde girl, Patty from Bottle Hill (Toortane) who was my age, was in town as well, the older ones would let her and me find something with which to occupy ourselves while they chatted to Paddy and his pals. It was Patty who showed me how to make mud pies in the Ormondes' small backyard, using empty shoe polish tins as baking trays, an activity I quickly tired of as it seemed pointless to make buns that you could not eat afterwards. On the other hand, Patty was more mature than I so maybe she saw some practical use for them.

When you are little you collect all sorts of bumps and bites and scratches and I had not received anything like my full share of them yet. Directly below Lismore Castle on the opposite side of the Blackwater there is a field called the Ferry Inch that is subject to flooding. In the middle of this there was a flat area, perhaps sixty or seventy yards square, that was marked off by raised banks about two to three feet high. Inside these banks clear mountain water, tunnelled off from the nearby Owenashad, could be retained through a system of locks and drains. Water could also be drained off from the enclosure. The system ensured that the depth of water within the banks could be maintained at a required level, perhaps a couple of feet or so, during exceptionally cold winter spells to allow the man-made pond to freeze over and form what was, in effect, an open-air skating rink. But the mere pursuit of pleasure, however enchanting figure-skating would have appeared in such a picturesque setting, was not the object of the earthwork. The ice house in Ballyin was situated on the Ballyduff Road at the farthest end of the Ferry Inch and the mass of water was trapped with the intention of freezing it solid so that blocks could be sawn from it and carted across to be stored in these shaded, deep-set, thick-walled, brick dungeons for domestic use. And for commercial gain - the salmon caught in the nets of the Lismore Estates Company were placed in wooden boxes, packed round with ice, and sent by night train and boat to England, mainly London, for consumption by the well-heeled on the following day. Any evening during the net fishing season one would see a number of boxes awaiting despatch at the railway station. The ice house served as a refrigerator. I never saw the ice-cutting enterprise in operation, probably it had been superseded by new techniques of refrigeration by my time, or perhaps the work was undertaken during my school hours, but I do recall seeing workmen going in and out of the chambers so the tomb-like construction was certainly still in use for storage purposes, at least.

What I did experience in the company of many other townspeople was skating, or rather sliding, on the ice rink. It hardly resembled a formal rink then, more a frozen-over pond. Possibly someone had real ice-skates but all I recall seeing was young men and women, and boys and girls, launching themselves out onto the frozen surface in ordinary shoes and trying to hold their balance for as far as they could. Once, when I happened to be standing nearby, looking eager to have a go myself but held back by an apprehensive Molly, two of Paddy's friends decided to do me a favour. John Crotty and Michael Feeney, who were enjoying themselves hugely, snatched me away and charged onto the ice, each holding me by an arm but not very effectively. Before I could decide whether I was liking it or whether I was terrified, the two of them fell flat on their arses and lost their grip of me so that I fell back and bumped my head hard on the glassy ice sheet that a few moments before had seemed so inviting. Molly froze John with a look and gave him the sharp end of her tongue as he sheepishly transferred me, bawling, back to her care. He was in the doghouse and I lost my enthusiasm for skating temporarily. In 2001-2002, during work on the town's splendid Millennium Garden in the Villa grounds across from the Monument another almost forgotten ice house was restored. This has now been elegantly incorporated as a feature of the new garden. As to the users of this particular construction, Tom Feeney has surmised that it might be connected with the Lismore Estates' Shipping Office that was situated in West Street in the building that was later to become Feeney's Garage. Fish was exported from this address. It may also have served the nearby Devonshire Arms Hotel during its glory days. Or it may have served the villa.

Another painful incident occurred when I was five or six. Nurse Knowles, the district nurse – known locally as the Jubilee Nurse – came round early one evening to work some of her medical magic on my tiny mickey that had become painfully swollen for some reason unknown to me. It was dark outside so it must have been winter. I was sat in a small tin bathtub of warm water that had been placed in the middle of the living room directly under the light bulb while Mam and the nurse chatted amiably. I was enjoying the sensation of being the centre of attention and I was expecting my pain to be eased fairly gently. Indeed, I was hoping that the mere act of soaking myself was going to clear up the ailment on its own. I was soon to be disabused of that idea. Nurse Knowles was a no-nonsense operator. She got down on her knees and, in her jolly way, complimented me in advance on being 'a brave little boy', which did nothing at all for my confidence because, I reasoned, she would not have said that unless something painful was on the way. Sure enough, she grabbed my prick and started squeezing the hell out of it. White stuff, like curd, leaked out into the water. I squealed but put up with it. There was no getting out of it anyway. 'Tis for your own good; has to be done,' Mam consoled me, although she was wincing too. After a while the nurse stopped, more hot water was added, and I was allowed to soak for another while. Then the whole horrible business began again. It went on like that for what seemed like an hour, and an hour to a child is a long time. The Jubilee Nurse, happily, never had to repeat the drastic treatment so whatever she did was effective. My malady had disappeared within days and I could freely pooley again. A couple of years later, in July 1945, Nurse

Knowles left town for good. Everyone was sorry to see her go. I was even sorry myself.

The end of the World War brought new things to our young lives, like bananas and oranges, fruit that we had hitherto only seen in the pictures. On the first few occasions when either arrived the word went around town like wildfire and within no time the entire stock was sold out, leaving many disgruntled customers. Molly rushed in excitedly one afternoon to tell Mam that some grocery up the Main Street had just got in a supply of bananas and should she go and get some. Mam, equally excited, said 'Yes!' and gave her the money but, by the time Molly got back up the town, the consignment had been snapped up. Next time she was quicker off the mark and I tasted my first banana, or part of a banana, as there was not enough to go around. I was favoured with a middle piece. It was enough to turn me on to bananas for life. There was a song we used to sing, 'Oh Ma, Will You Buy Me a – , Will You Buy Me a Banana', that possibly reflected the significance we lent to this fruit at that particular time of our lives.

Not long in the wake of the prisoners of war, another victim of the worldwide conflict came to live in our midst. Dr Michael O'Farrell, one of the local GPs who had been in charge of the local Red Cross throughout the Emergency, and who later became County Medical Officer of Health, and his wife took in a German war orphan by the name of Horst Selzner. The boy was the same age as their eldest son, Mickey, and they reared him as one of their own for a number of years until it was possible for him to return to his own country, then well on the way to reconstruction. The O'Farrell children were not ones with whom I often played, mainly for reasons of age but also, I suspect, on account of our different social standings, so I never really got to know Horst well although he attended our school (a class junior to me). He must have found us very strange to live amongst.

In the early postwar period a woman with a very odd name, Miss Pericho, closed down her shoe shop for the last time and retired to live in another town. Mam used to patronise her shop - I got a pair of sandals there at least - but I only remember her for her unusual name. Not long after, my pals and I suffered a more grievous loss when another woman with a strange name, Janey Canty, died. Janey had a sweet shop further up the Main Street at the top of Ferry Lane, opposite Eddie Nugent's, another shoe shop that Mam patronised. Her sweets were home-made and she stocked the biggest, tastiest and stripiest bulls-eyes that you ever saw in your life. At least that was what I thought, until Mam told me that Lucy Walsh's were even bigger and better. Lucy's shop had been situated in the Main Street also opposite Madden's public house but, unfortunately, as she ceased trading when I was very small, I never experienced the pleasure of tasting her delights. Lucy's sister, Mrs Mary Dunne of Botany, was also a confectioner who made classy sweets but she too operated before my time. In the absence of anything comparable, Janey's were more than good enough for me. When I first went to her place Molly would help me negotiate the step down from the street. Then I would stretch up my hand and place my penny on the counter to receive in exchange a little cone of newspaper full of bulls-eyes. Sadly, after the deaths of these three skilled confectioners, the art of sweet-making seemed to die out in Lismore.

The saddest event of my childhood was the death of my beloved Auntie Bab on the 15th of June 1947. Still a young woman, she had wasted away with tuberculosis, the killer disease of the time. I was taken in to see her on her deathbed for the last time in the upstairs double room of the Morrissey family home in Carrick-on-Suir. She was dressed in white and her face had a kind of peaceful smile on it I was assured. Her thin arms were outside the bedclothes. There was a rosary beads entwined round her white fingers. She was the first dead person I had ever seen, but I was more apprehensive than scared, and fearfully shy of all the women in black who were sitting around with tearful faces, muttering prayers. I held on tightly to Mam's hand. She had made it clear to me that after I whispered 'goodbye' I would never see Bab in this world again, but that one day we would all meet in heaven, a place of which I had, and always would have, a very imperfect understanding. But the explanation served its purpose. I was consoled.

Dad and Auntie Bab with Paddy c. spring 1934. Immediately behind is Feeney's garden which lay behind the big garage repair shed. In the background Lismore Roman Catholic Cathedral can be seen.

CHAPTER TWO

Home

THE HOUSE WE LIVED IN did not have a number on it, or if it did, we never used it. Letters were addressed simply to 'Ballantyne, West Street'. It was a grey-fronted, slate-roofed, two-storey house with an attic, and was roomier inside than the outside suggested. Our neighbour on the east side was Feeney's Garage, also a two-storey building with an attic and a kitchen added at the back, and on the west, the wide-fronted, three-storey select grocery bar, the Wine Vaults. Clearly at some time in the past our house too had been a bar or a shop, or maybe an office; a shop-front decorated half the exterior. (I have learned since via an early photograph in Eugene Dennis's superb 2005 compilation, *Images of Ireland: Lismore*, page 36, that it had been a bicycle shop in 1910.) On Feeney's side there was a wide window with four tall glass panels. Two metal bars ran horizontally across the lower half of the panels to protect them. On the inside of that shop window there was a two- to two-and-a-half-foot-wide ledge, of about the same height from the floor, that had served, no doubt, for display. It was possible to open back, like a half-door, the upper half of the panel nearest the garage and look out into the street. Standing on the ledge, I would do this often. Whenever anything was happening, like crowds streaming up Gallows Hill to the Hurling Field on a match day, or to the Fair Field in Botany on a Fair Day, you would be sure to find me leaning out of it, if for any reason, I had to remain indoors.

On the shop window there was a roller blind that was drawn at night, and farther in lace curtains hung from the ceiling to obscure the ledge. At night heavier opaque curtains were also drawn, especially in cold spells. This space was our living-room that in winter was the one room in the house in which a fire was always glowing from mid-morning, early morning on particularly cold days, till night. A big table stood next to the ledge and it was here that we ate. The five of us seldom ate together because of the unsocial working hours that Dad had to put in regularly and because Mam often used to feed Paddy and myself first so that Dad could have a bit of peace over his meal later. Often too Mam and Molly would eat together. Normally, I would sit facing the window. However, when we were all there at once, or when we had visitors, the table would be pulled back from the ledge to accommodate the extra bodies. I liked that because I was usually placed on the ledge instead of on a chair and I could see everything that went on in the room. Paddy would be alongside me, and on our left Mam, the place where she usually sat and kept the tea-pot warm with a cosy. Dad would be on the right, his usual place, and Molly opposite us. On the right, from the vantage point of the ledge, there was a wine-coloured dresser, the top half of which served as a bookcase – behind its glass panels stood such reference books as Charles Annandale's thick, grey-brown 1925 *New Gresham Dictionary of the English Language,* Cassell's six-volume, wine-coloured, *New Popular Educator,* and the eleven or twelve volume, light-green *New Gresham Encyclopaedia* (1923 edition, edited by Rappoport, Patterson and Dougall), all of which I would refer to increasingly as I grew older. In the lower half of this piece of furniture Mam kept her everyday china and kitchen utensils. On the left of the room there was a sizable open fireplace, with two hobs. Dad, at Mam's insistence, eventually prevailed upon the Castle, our landlord, to improve and extend this fireplace. On the right beyond the dresser was the doorway through which you entered from the hall. At the back of the room stood a mahogany dumb-waiter. To the right of this there was a small casement window that looked onto the kitchen – a built-on addition with a corrugated iron roof.

A sash window decorated the right-hand side of the house, facing it from the street. Generous in size but much smaller than the shop window, it had a wide low-slung ledge on which people used to sit often, which always annoyed Mam, firstly because she was afraid that someone might smash a pane of glass with an awkward movement of an elbow; secondly, because the presence of a body blocked the view from inside; and thirdly, because how dare anyone sit uninvited on our window-ledge anyway. The first reason was the most logical and, to give Mam her due, someone did smash a pane once. The second hardly counted as we so rarely sat in the room inside, that served as our sitting-room. Special guests and people my parents wanted to speak to privately, like nuns, priests, Christian Brothers, or the insurance man, were shepherded in there. It was always damp, even in summer. To counteract the dampness in winter Mam would keep a fire going in it all day, every two or three weeks. This was always a treat because you could sink into the soft sofa and armchairs in front of the blaze and read a book. Or play a game of ludo or snakes and ladders. Or just talk. Or, if you were feeling really lazy, let your thoughts wander in the brooding

Easter Week 1916. The Scene at the GPO, Dublin from the drawing by Wal Paget.
A large print of this hung in our sitting-room.

woodland of the oil painting that had seen better days that hung over the mantelpiece. Or, when we turned off the electric light, watch the long flame licking upwards in the mauve-coloured glass shade of the elegant bronze Victorian oil-lamp that stood on the sideboard, appropriately beneath the patriotic *Scene in the General Post Office, just before its evacuation – Easter Week 1916,* copyright Thomas Kiersey of Dublin. Nobody else in the town seemed to have this print and I used to proudly show it off to my pals and point out Patrick Pearse standing, gun in hand, in profile; Connolly wounded on a stretcher, Willie Pearse kneeling next to him taking notes, and so on through the seven signatories of the Proclamation of the Irish Republic. In the drawers of the sideboard were stored Mam's best tablecloths and, in the lower compartment, her best china, all that had survived of a fluted set, decorated with a flowing red floral design, that had been given to her and Dad as a wedding present.

I was not supposed to go into the sitting-room on my own but sometimes I did anyway, to listen to what the people sitting on the ledge outside on Fair Day were talking about – they could not see me behind the lace curtain – or just to have a different view of the street. When it was boredom that took me in there I was liable to get up to mischief. Once, when I was very little, I opened the drawer of the sideboard, lifted a carving knife out of its wedding presentation box and tested the sharpness of its edge on the lip of the piece of furniture. A sliver of polished wood some six inches long peeled over the blade and slipped to the floor. I gazed dumbfounded at the long knife held tightly in my two small fists, then at the tongue of wood at my feet. I sensed I had worked something irreparable. I put down the knife. I picked up the sliver and was despairingly attempting to re-attach it with spit to its former position when Mam entered. She let out a screech and pushed me away. I thought I was for it. What I had done certainly merited a flake, even if that was not Mam's style. What saved me, I think, was the fact that I had not done worse and cut myself with the knife. The fear of that was what really gave her the fright, although the sight of her lovely piece of furniture scarred for life could hardly have made her dance with relief. As it was, she merely slapped the back of my hand, muttered curtly, 'Your father will deal with you,' and ushered me out into the hallway. I remained in an agony of suspense until Dad came home an hour or so later. He inspected the damage that even he, with his carpentry skills, could not repair. 'Why did you do this?' he asked grimly. I stared at him dumbly, unable to muster either a reason or an excuse. 'Get up to your room,' he ordered. I scampered off upstairs, relieved that a hand had not been raised to me. Later on they relented and I was allowed down for supper, which I ate in silence, peering warily at them and my brother, who seemed amused by the whole affair, over the edge of my plate.

The concrete-floored kitchen was cool at best, except on hot summer days. In winter it was freezing. On the left through the window, also under the corrugated roof, was the flush toilet where you didn't tarry in winter. A white-washed, wooden partition separated this off from the kitchen. The kitchen had an outside window that overlooked a yard. By the window stood a wooden table that served as a surface on which to prepare food. Mam, not possessing a proper ironing board, also did her ironing on it, using as padding a couple of old blankets. She ironed with an old heated iron. This was a reddish-coloured iron contraption, in the hollow of which was inserted a red-hot, arrow-shaped slug of metal that had been pre-heated in the coal fire. The slug was held in place by a small trap-door that could be lifted up at the back. She would have a couple of these slugs in use alternately, as they cooled off fairly quickly. There was great activity in this area when the Christmas pudding was being prepared at the end of each November in advance of giving it its initial steaming in the big iron pot on the sawdust stove under the outside shed. On the right-hand wall of the kitchen hung 'the safe', a small pantry box with a mesh metal front to keep out the flies. Here was stored for daily use butter, milk, sugar, jam, marmalade, flour, etc. Below the casement window, kitchen-side, there was a deep, rectangular-shaped, porcelain wash-basin into which you could place a lot of pans and plates.

As you came through from the hall into the kitchen, on your right there was another doorway that we curtained off as no door hung there. This led to the slate-roofed outhouse that backed onto the bar of the Wine Vaults. We referred to it as 'the store'. Half of this space nearest the kitchen was paved with concrete and here were kept rags and polish for boots and shoes, brooms, Wellington boots, garden implements, and so on. The farthest end of the outhouse had a hard, earthen floor and against the end wall was piled up the coal and turf that had been delivered through an aperture that had once been a window – Dad had constructed a removable wooden board to close this off. In the middle, under a skylight, there was a cross-bench for sawing wood. When I was big enough I used to do my share of work on it with the bow-saw. Against the back wall Dad would place his bicycle. This was the one on which I learned to ride – leg under the bar, tortuously balanced. Whenever Dad had the time to indulge his carpentry skills it was here he worked. When I was little he made two wooden armchairs with upholstered seats that lasted us for years and years. He knew how to cut hair too and was my regular barber when I was little. I would be placed on a chair under the skylight regularly for a short-back-and-sides with a German-made Udahl hair clipper.

The lower half of the walls in the hall was wainscotted, the wooden panelling painted a dark brown. A heavy duty flowered wallpaper covered the upper surfaces. On the walls hung four of those romantic Victorian pictures in tall, dark-polished frames, two of the Scottish Highlands showing shaggy, long-horned cattle watering by the side of a misty lake, and two of pallid ladies in long, flowered frocks staring dreamily across flower-bedecked meadows. Beyond the door to the sitting-room you had the entrance to the living-room on the left, and beyond that immediately to the right a kind of walk-in cupboard that ran under the stairs. In the cupboard were stored odds and ends – superfluous wallpaper rolls, old coats and rags, bits of lead pipe, brushes, and the like. I used to hide in there for the fun of it sometimes and peer out through the crack between the door and the frame. Directly opposite this door on the facing wall hung a coat-rack.

Coming out of the cupboard, or utility room, if you like, you turned immediately right to go up the stairs to the second floor. As you ascended, the lower section of a tall window on the left looked out onto the slate lean-to roof at the back. At the first landing you turned right up a short flight of steps to the main level. To your right, through the banisters and window, was again the outside roof and, beyond that, the yard. The first room on the left was the bedroom shared by my brother and me. We each had a single bed and mine was in the furthest corner with the foot of it under the window that looked out onto West Street. The view was one I knew intimately. I was sickly as a child and whenever any disease was going around I was sure to get it – measles, mumps, chicken pox, whooping cough, colds, flu, even scarlatina when I was about fourteen, which kept me out of school for something like eight weeks because it was highly contagious. Standard enamel piss-pots stood under all beds.

The second room on the left was our parents', which contained, as well as a brass double bed, Mam's dressing table, a large mahogany wardrobe, and a marble-topped wash-stand on the top of which stood a porcelain jug and matching basin. On the bed was a thick O'Dearest mattress, 'the best there is', Mam used to say, and over the sheets and blankets a heavy, gold-coloured quilt. This room also had a fireplace, which our room did not have. Every year Mam liked to switch the furniture around in one room or another and once Paddy had done his Leaving Certificate and was spending most of his time in Carrick-on-Suir this room became mine and my parents moved into the smaller room. The move was dictated by one of my longer illnesses, probably when I had to be isolated for scarlet fever. Because of the fireplace my single bed was placed in the corner between the window and the hearth and it was a magical sensation to fall asleep on my horsehair mattress in the warm glow of the dying embers. In the absence of a fire the only form of heating anywhere upstairs was the ubiquitous earthenware or rubber hot-water bottle.

Immediately adjoining this room, straight ahead as you came onto the main landing, was the bathroom, a cold room with no running hot water. On the right as you entered was a wash-hand basin and in the corner opposite a large, free-standing white bath on four short legs. Next to the basin there was a window with a wide inside ledge that you could lean on, or sit on. From it you could look out over Feeney's yard, and ours, and right into Feeney's big, barrel-roofed, galvanised garage. Beyond this shed and to the left over the orchard garden of Bart Regan, Feeney's neighbour on the other side, you could see the bell tower of the Catholic church. Straight ahead, beyond our garden, your eye was drawn to Joe Kelly's field and the grey-stonewalled Fair Field and, away in the distance, Scarook Wood. I liked perching on that ledge. Sometimes I would climb out through the window and slip down onto the rusty galvanised roof of the kitchen and from there, along the slates of the lean-to roof. From this vantage point outside I could look in through the upper half of the staircase window at the wooden stairs that led up from the side of the bathroom door to the attic. At the top of this section of the stairs there was a brick wall that was badly in need of re-pointing and re-plastering. Both bricks and the mortar were in such a flaky

Mam with me on her knee, Paddy standing and Dad. Photo taken in the garden of our West Street home in Lismore c. 1937-38. The large repair shed of Feeney's Garage is in the background.

My brother Paddy Ballantyne, aged 5/6 on his tricycle coming out through the arch of the ruined outhouse that led into our garden in West Street, Lismore. c. 1938–39.

state that you could not stick wallpaper to the wall properly. Dad tried but gave up in the finish as the paper kept peeling away.

After one last turn to the right and a few more steps you reached the attic landing. The attic was divided into two and each room had a south-south-east facing skylight. The first room you came to was Molly's until she had to leave us when I was about twelve. It had a double bed with an iron bedstead and a very bumpy horsehair mattress. All the mattresses in the house, with the exception of my parents' O'Dearest one, were stuffed with horsehair, but Molly's seemed to me to be particularly bumpy. I used to ask her solicitously how she was able to sleep on it at all. She said it never worried her and used to show me the hollow in the middle where she could curl up. But I still was not convinced and would come back with the same question another time. The other room on this level was used as a storeroom. Dad's sizeable wooden tool chest was kept there and Mam would lay down apples, each one wrapped individually in a separate piece of newspaper, on the bare boards for the winter. Two rope lines, on which washing could be hung up to dry, were suspended from the rafters. Both this

Sergeant Joseph Ballantyne and Mary Ballantyne with their son Paddy in the backyard of our house in West Street in the mid-Thirties. Feeney's arch in background.

room and Molly's had alcoved ceilings, the boards of which were whitewashed. A wooden door and partition, stopping a couple of feet short of the skylight, separated the bedroom from the landing. From the top of the partition I was able to climb out onto the main roof and shin up to the ridge from whence I could look down into West Street and out over the Villa, an elegant house part-hidden by the tall beeches on the other side of the street. Looking in the opposite direction, I had an even better view across the fields to Scarook. Mam saw me up there once and got a fright. Thereafter I was forbidden ever to go up there again. But I did, of course, when I was older. By that time she had agreed to my sitting on the edge of the partition so that I could look out the back through the open skylight if I wanted to. It was a good point from which to look at the stars at night too, even if the edge, sometimes cushioned with an old pillow, was a bit hard on my bottom.

At the back of our house there was a long, narrow strip of land with distinct sections. Immediately at the back, off the kitchen, there was the yard bounded on the west side by the outhouse that backed onto the Wine Vaults and, around the corner from that, by the high stone side wall of the store's glass-roofed shed. On the east side, set in the five-foot-high stone wall that divided us off from Feeney's, hung a wide wooden gate that swung open in two halves. This gave us access to West Street through Feeney's arch and Dad used to bring in his supplies of firewood via this route. Our yard was about twenty feet long and at the end of it stood the walled remains of what had once been a large solidly built outhouse. A twelve- to fifteen-foot high wooden palisade, weathered black, still formed the front of this and we used to enjoy anchoring ourselves on the struts at the back and peering down over it into our own and Feeney's yards. A narrow pathway about seven to eight yards long ran between the side wall of the outhouse and Feeney's wall, culminating in a stone archway that led to the garden. Just on the right past this was an area where we dumped our rubbish and burnt what we could of it, there being no such thing as house-to-house refuse collection. Right next to the dump, overhanging McCarthy's stable, was a splendid lilac tree that kept us, and the neighbours, and the chapel altar, abundantly supplied with blossoms in the spring. A second, smaller tree was less fulsome with its blooms. On the grassy patch next to the tree stood the swing that Dad had constructed for us. After we had outlived this toy it was dismantled and the ground where it had stood re-cultivated. Even with the swing in existence there was still some forty feet of vegetable garden stretching up to Joe Kelly's field.

West Street itself, as it was so short, was an extension of home, and our neighbours knew each other well. A distinctive aspect of the street was that, with the exception of the Villa and the Carnegie Free Library, all the other buildings were on the one side, the south side. They began across from the Monument, the perceived centre point of the town, although not the geographical centre, with the imposing courthouse-cum- town hall. Next to that was the old Market House that in the early Fifties became Kathleen Hogan's ice cream parlour, a favourite place for the youth of the town to congregate. By the side of Hogan's there was an alleyway leading to a series of galvanised sheds with pens that, before my time, used to host a pig market and an annual potato market that was traditionally held on every St Patrick's Eve. The men's lavatory just on the left at the entrance to the market grounds remained in use and I would often frequent it myself even though I only lived up the street. Then came the *garda* barracks, a distinguished-looking, three-storey, granite building – office and gaol of the lawmen since the days of the old RIC. I got to know it well because Dad's office was on the top floor. The main block of the street commenced with the barracks and in succession came the Munster & Leinster Bank, Murphy's drapery, Bart Regan's newspaper shop, Feeney's garage,

Ballantynes, the Wine Vaults, Danny McCarthy's grocery and, finally, at the corner of New Street or Botany, Ormonde's dairy and grocery. The street then began to climb toward Gallows Hill. Round about this point the grounds of the Villa opposite came to an end and the library put in its appearance. On the more housed side of the street, directly across from the library, stood the National Bank, in my early years home to the Arthure family. Beyond that there was a small wooded area where we often used to play that stretched up as far as Hill Cottage, the Tudor-style home of Danny McCarthy before he sold it to a retired and returned major of the United States Army, one Walter Cullinane. Walter, or Wattie as he was known, always walked like he was on parade, swinging his arms across his ample belly like the Marines we saw in the pictures, and keeping in time with a kind of tune that he half-whistled through drawn lips and that you could never quite fathom – 'The Halls of Montezuma', maybe. Occasionally, presumably on some American national day or other, or possibly on St Patrick's Day, he would march out in his khaki US uniform. I used to take him off so successfully that Mam would parade me in front of visitors to do 'Wattie Cullinane's walk'. It amused her, at least, and I think Mrs Feeney got a laugh out of it too. Wattie and his missus were as amiable a couple as you would meet. I wonder if he ever noticed me taking the piss out of him. He probably did, because, as children do, I first learned the walk by following close behind and aping him. Hill Cottage was, in effect, the last house in West Street because the next dwelling along, Bushfield, was situated in beautiful wooded grounds on top of Gallows Hill itself, across from the Christian Brothers' School (CBS) where I spent most of my schooldays. Bushfield was home to Lady Godfrey and her two lanky daughters. Around the side, opening onto a little glade, was the large well-dressed kitchen from which Mam used to purchase eggs, fruit and vegetables. The daughters were considered a trifle eccentric by Lismore standards. A small legend was in circulation in confirmation of this. A local labourer encountered them in the middle of a meadow, apparently looking for something.

'Can I help ye find something?' he enquired helpfully.

'No thanks. We're looking for Fish,' one of them said and they went on their way without elaborating.

'Fish?'' the local scratched his head sorrowfully as he watched them disappear into the next field.

What he, and many others, did not know was that 'Fish' was the name of a horse they owned. Lady Godfrey had her moments too. When Adolf Hitler made some comment that annoyed her she is reputed to have remarked with quiet exasperation, 'Somebody should tell that bad man to shut up.'

The school, fronted by the handsome stone building in which the Brothers lived, was located on a triangle of land formed by the junction of the Tallow and Ballyanchor Roads, the former branching in from the right and the latter from the left, as you went up the hill. A quarter of a mile out the Ballyanchor Road, on the left, there was another fine house called Woodview, in which the Ellis family lived. I would call there to pick up country butter and cans of buttermilk for Dad, who loved the taste of both. I could take neither the milk – too sour, nor the butter – too tangy. Sometimes when I arrived Miss Ellis would be in the farmyard, still hand-churning the butter in the wooden churn, and I would have to wait until she had finished to watch her pour off the milk for me. Her brother Alec was noted for his forty-acre field and for breeding prizewinning cattle. Whenever my pals and I mentioned the Forty Acre it was understood it was Alec's to which we were referring. Jimmy Howard, who farmed extensively a few miles out the Tallow Road, also owned one but that was beyond the immediate environs of the town. As far as I recall, there were no other fields of this acreage in our area.

Lismore was a good place in which to grow up, magical for me, which is not to say that I experienced no pain, humiliation or sadness there. I had encounters of one kind or another with all of these sensations but was lucky enough to be cushioned from extremes. I came from a family that always had enough to eat in the house and I was adequately clothed and warmly housed in winter. People who grew up in Botany and Church Lane, the poorest quarters of the town, had it infinitely harder and yet it was in these two streets that I spent my happiest days.

Our locality was a region of rich and musical place-names – Shanavoola, Seemochuda, Glenaraha, Cooldrishogue, Monalour – though some, like the last-mentioned, disguised tragic associations. Monalour, *Móna na Lobhar* in Irish, has the English meaning, 'The Moor of the Lepers'. As against that, streaming, sometimes torrenting, down from the Knockmealdown Mountains came the Owenashad, in Irish *Abha na Séad*, in English the 'River of Pearls'. We learned early how the English distorted our place-names out of ignorance, but to give them their due, they quite often managed recognisable approximations to the sounds of our native tongue.

The area had a rich mix of surnames too. Alongside such well-known Munster names as McCarthy, Ormonde, O'Brien and Power there were those that made you wonder from where the people wearing them originally came: Pericho, Ussher, Bible, Veale, Heaphy, Paxman, Beecher, Kingston, Collender, Keniry, Looby, Mills, Brunnock, Searson, Uniacke, Cuffe, Neville, Fives, Behegan, Copithorne, Hornibrook, Pollock, etc., not to mention my own. And, of course, a vast weight of nicknames was apportioned – whether the wearers liked them or not. Jimmy Meade, a rather taciturn ex-British soldier, was known as 'the Gurkha'. Billy Neville was known for many years, and for reasons nobody ever knew, as 'Fisser' until he went to work in the Arcade, the biggest drapery store in the Main Street, whereupon he was quickly re-nicknamed 'Guiney' after the name of the big Dublin storeowner. Tommy O'Brien, a sharp-featured man who walked with a limp sustained in lumbering, went under 'Tommy the Hawk', or simply 'The Hawk', although they were not many who would call him either to his face. Then there was 'Moses' Kennedy. I don't think I ever worked out to my satisfaction whether Moses was a nickname or whether it was his real name, but either way his bearded presence impressively called to mind the old lawgiver. 'Storc' and 'Phopper' Stapleton, two stocky, powerfully built and fiercely industrious brothers, were lumberjacks, the former feted as one of the strongest men for miles around when it came to lifting anvils. They had a brother, Pa, who was awesomely as indolent as they were indefatigable and it was 'Doshin' (Donie) Keating and 'Sucky', also known as 'Blackie', (Philip) Neville who put the name on him – 'More Gravy Ma'. The two lads, who lived in Upper Botany, happened to be passing home by Stapletons in Lower Botany one evening when they overheard Pa – who was no chicken but fortyish at this time – say to his elderly mother, 'More gravy, Ma.' 'No more for Pa', she responded with an inspired flash of poetry, and this little rhyme became an instrument with which we youngsters used to torture her son, although we stood well back when we hurled it at him. At first it used to infuriate him but eventually he saw the funny side of the situation, or accepted the hopelessness of trying to frighten us into giving up the nickname, and used to join in the fun by making playful runs at us.

'The Gandóg' Scanlon was another who reacted a bit in this way. He was Mike the 'The Gander's son and both were tall, powerfully-built farmers with long necks, hence the nickname, who lived at Ballynelligan Cottage which we used to pass regularly in summer on our way down to the Rock for a swim. In the case of Jim 'Slog', the nickname, in effect, supplanted the surname. His real name was Jim Ahearne but nobody called him that. He received his soubriquet because he was the town crier who advertised events in our streets with his big brass bell. If you were given a nickname you were stuck with it for better or for worse. Some people, like 'Fisser', did not mind what they were called and could give as good as they got. Others, like Dan Colbert, the tall thin stationmaster, who was known as 'Gandhi', put up with it. Still others, like 'More Gravy Ma' and 'The Gandóg' did not relish their nicknames at all. One of my classmates, Tom Lineen, was not impressed with being named 'Tom the Bull', though his elder brother Jim had no objection whatsoever to being called 'Thumper' – both were big lads. What the handsome Paddy Barry thought of being called 'Snobby' I was never sure. Peter Kiernan, who played soundly in goal for many years for the Lismore junior hurling team, was none too keen on 'Jammy Jam', or 'Jammy', to give him the shortened version. Nor was Mick O'Brien, the town's best male ballrooom dancer, enamoured with 'Mick the Bird', abbreviated 'The Bird'. To my thinking, there was nothing objectionable in any of these – but then I was not wearing them. I was accorded a very nondescript one myself, a mere variation on my surname – 'Baler' or 'Bally'. At least, that is all I think I was called – in that line anyway.

Botany, or 'Botney' as we pronounced it, and Church Lane were not just the poorest sections of the market town of Lismore; they were also rightly or wrongly, considered the toughest. (For an explanation of the origin of the place-name 'Botany' as it applied to Lismore see Paddy Vaughan's book *The Last Forge in Lismore*, page 12.) To me these streets were centres of irreverence and wit, antidotes to the authoritarian attitudes I encountered elsewhere. I learned things about life in those two streets that were more important to me than most things that were drilled into me at school, arguably more important than anything I learned behind the desk. I would not wish to belittle the benefits of the formal education I received. I had little interest in being schooled so my teachers faced an uphill task from the start. On the other hand, few of my teachers filled me with any enthusiasm for the pursuit of knowledge. The library was far more persuasive in this respect. It was an irony that the schools I was educated at shared the same poles as the streets I was educated in, the Collegiate School of the Christian Brothers and Botany the westernmost, the Presentation Convent School and Church Lane the easternmost.

The north-south axis of the town ran from Ballyrafter and Ballyin (pronounced 'Ballin') in the North to Townparks in the South. Along the northernmost boundary ran the river Blackwater, overlooked by the impressive bulk of Lismore Castle. The view from the flag tower of the castle looking downstream, or from the drawing-room on a lower level, was breathtaking, I was assured by locals who either worked in or on the building and had been privileged to experience the sight for themselves. I only ever got as far as the Castle Gardens myself, and mostly there as an uninvited guest. But I felt I knew the view from on high because there used to be a popular black-and-white postcard of it that took your eye out over the elegantly arched Lismore Bridge down a gently wooded valley, past the confluence of the Owenashad and Blackwater, beyond Bullsod Island to the Bishop's Fishery, Monamon, Glenribben, the foothills of the Knockmealdown Mountains and probably even beyond Cappoquin. The view upstream and west I can only conjecture at. I am not aware that anyone ever marketed a postcard with this vista. Looking east again, immediately downstream of the bridge on the southern bank lay the Warren, a thickly-wooded cliff that climbed to the hill on which sat St Carthage's Cathedral, the fine Protestant church, the slender spire of which was a landmark for many miles around, that dated back in part to the twelfth century. Access to the Warren was through a heavy iron gate, painted green, that led to Lady Louisa's Walk, the cliffside right of way that rose first then fell away until it exited through a rusty stile onto the boggy mass of the inch across from Big Island. When you turned right immediately on going through the green gate, and climbed, you came to a shallow cave that bit in under a high, ivy-covered outcrop of rock. This recess, always bone dry, was known as Jackie White's Cave, after the man who chose to live there for a number of years not so long before my time. Jackie came originally from nearby Church Lane (and died there), and supplemented a meagre British Army pension with a bit of poaching. It was said that he possessed an exuberant wit. As evidence of this, Dad would tell me of the occasion when Jackie was surprised early one morning by the then Duke of Devonshire, out for a constitutional on his preserves.

'You're out early, Your Grace,' commented Jackie who was hiding a dead rabbit, or possibly a salmon, down the leg of his trousers.

'Yes. Looking for an appetite for my breakfast,' said the Lord, 'And what are you doing?'

'Looking for a breakfast for me appetite,' responded the poacher.

The story of the encounter is supposed to have been passed on by the highly amused Duke. A recognisable tale in other cultures?

One thing is certain. Whatever Jackie eventually died of, it could not have been thirst because directly across the road from his chosen place of residence was the Spout, a constant stream of delicious, fresh, spring water that has refreshed, and is still refreshing, generations of Lismore's citizens and passing travellers. It gushed out through a flue in the castle wall with the same intensity all the year round and spilled into a large smooth stone basin that was as high as a man's chest and as wide as the biggest cart pulled by a horse. The Spout was the centrepiece of a wide, semi-circular indentation in the castle walls and was set well back from the road. Large blue cobblestones, worn with time, led up to the limestone basin, and over these men would back their carts to fill their churns and barrels. The Castle itself had a water-cart, a big wooden cask placed on its side, mounted longitudinally on a chassis, and pulled by a single horse. The cask was filled from the Spout by way of a long chute to a lidded opening on the top, and drained by removing a wooden plug set low at the back. If memory serves me right, the Presentation Convent also had a water-cart. Sometimes you would see a queue of one or two carts waiting in line.

From the Protestant cathedral on the heights above Jackie White's Cave, a wide road called the Mall stretched south to Fernville. (The 1925 ordnance survey map of Lismore designates this short street as Chapel Place but we always knew it as Fernville.) The North Mall that ran from the cathedral to Upper Main Street was a short boulevard with wide grassy banks. It had only four houses on it, the Deanery and Castle View directly on the west side, and on the east side a house on the corner with Church Lane and, at the other end and indirectly, the Mall House, because the entrance to this was on Main Street. Church Lane was an L-shaped street and the other end of it met the very top of Main Street. On turning left into Lower Church Lane as you exited the cathedral gates you walked along by the cathedral wall until you came to a short row of cottages with pretty porticoes behind which the Warren Gardens, a reputed daffodil breeding enterprise, was located in the early years of the 20th century. On the eastern corner of the North Mall with Main Street there was an old, barred, iron seat, wide enough to accommodate four or five men on it – it was men who usually sat there – known to everyone as the Mall Seat ('Sate' as in 'fate' as we pronounced it). This was one of the main places where we used to congregate to watch the world go by and was a centre of experiential learning where different generations of males passed on their acquired wisdom of the ways of the world. On the Mall Seat end of South Mall there were one or two businesses, including a small hotel, and the tiny post office, where you tried to get served by the good-humoured Dorothy O'Brien rather than the lanky Miss Pender who peered at you severely through a brass grill, but it was the fine row of private residences, terraced houses on one side, villas on the other, that really gave this elegant street its air of well-being. At the top-west corner, behind tall walls, the Catholic St Carthage's Cathedral reared into the sky. A striking and imposing edifice in the Lombardo–Romanesque style, it was put up in the post-Famine times when you would have thought people had more pressing problems on their minds than building churches. On the other hand, it would have provided much-needed employment for the hard-pressed people of the area for a number of years. Probably it was conceived in the wave of triumphalism that followed Catholic emancipation to raise two fingers to the Protestants whom it was felt had expropriated the ancient church of Mochuda, the patron saint of the town.

The green gates of the Protestant cathedral were surmounted by a kind of papal mitre and crossed keys and there was a local fiction that this ornament of Catholic origin was once stolen in the dead of night and tossed into the deepest hole in the Blackwater below the castle by a malicious Protestant or renegade Catholic only to be found back in its rightful place next morning. What this proved, of course, was that the Catholics had a nifty diver in their midst. However, it was not customary to put this complexion on the anecdote. The hand of God had worked a miracle and that was that. In the face of such partiality on the part of the Deity who, after all, belonged to both sides, no effort was ever made to remove the insignia again, proving that the Protestants were just as cute as we had been led to believe they were.

South-west of the Catholic St Carthage's lay the Fair Field. Here the monthly fairs were held, on the second Wednesday of the month. Conveniently situated beyond the Fair Field was the railway station. Just across the railway line, on the site of an old sawmill, Jackie Scanlan the Main Street newsagent did himself and the young people of the town and surrounding area a favour by opening the Happydrome dancehall and general entertainment centre in April 1944. The place had been christened the Hippodrome initially but quickly and felicitously the rogue version was adopted.

From the station you could circle around by Botany, go down into West Street, and then down the New Way to the entrance of the fine avenue, lined with tall elms, that led to the main gate of the castle. If you turned left at this entrance through heavy wrought-iron gates you would eventually come to the Grove that, although formally on castle grounds, was accessible to the public all the year round. Close to the castle walls the ground was

My uncle Mick Morrissey with Paddy on the bar of Dad's bicycle on the New Way in Lismore. 1940? It looks like the occasion of Paddy's first communion. Note the rough state of the road surface.

high, but less craggy than the overgrown Warren, then it fell away progressively westwards over a distance of some four or five hundred yards to where an iron kissing-gate led onto the inch opposite Cottage Island and the Queen's Gap in the long salmon weir. (I am uncertain whether we used the name 'Cottage Island' or the alternative 'Betty's Banks' – 'from an old lady who once kept a school here', according to Canon Patrick Power in his *Places Names of Decies*, Cork University Press, 1952.) If you did not choose to exit at this point you could go further into the wood where the Teampuileen Caves were located. These scarcely merited the plural 'caves' any more than Jackie White's Cave merited the singular but they did go deeper than the latter and there was a tantalising glimpse through a fissure in the rocks of a darker hole to which even a small boy could not gain access. It was Molly who introduced me to them when we were out for a walk. In later years my pals and I continued to play around the area. The Grove was a favourite place with all age groups. The varied paths, the ferns and flowers, the trees that overhung the dangerously dark water below, the gracefulness of the swans around Cottage Island, the flashing blue and gold of kingfishers, the froth of the Queen's Gap, all these delights it could offer and more. Here and there there were long wooden seats on which you could relax and read or just rest for a while.

The texture of the town was grey and slaty, but there was a pleasing symmetry in the variety of domestic architectural styles, which ranged from the tiny, porticoed cottages of Church Lane and the larger porticoed ones of lower Botany through the small, plain cottages of upper Botany, to the three-storey shops, like the Co-Operative Stores (in earlier times the Blackwater Vale Hotel) and public houses along the Main Street, the imposing family residences with their walled gardens on the east side of South Mall and the smaller but still impressive houses (one the Commercial Hotel) on the west side and the walled and gardened houses like the Villa, the Deanery, and the Manse. The most eye-catching public buildings were the Courthouse/Town Hall and the Devonshire Arms Hotel, both of which faced the Monument. There was a third, equally well-known building at this junction, Con O'Neill's pub, appropriately named because of its red-brick appearance, the Red House. O'Neill's corner was another rendezvous much favoured by men and boys for monitoring the activities of the town, and on long summer evenings especially you invariably found a small platoon of males strung along its walls, the men on the Main Street side, the boys along the side wall in Chapel Street. Alternatively, we would arrange ourselves on the stone steps or wooden seats (many rotted away until restored for the Tóstal in 1953) that surrounded the Monument across the way.

Main Street Lismore in the late Forties or early Fifties. Photo taken from West Street. Devonshire Arms Hotel on the left behind the Monument, the Red House pub on the right. The railings of the Courthouse in the right foreground. Note scars on road, from laying new pipes for the town's water supply, most likely. More cars than usual in the street. Couple taking no chances crossing at the junction.

All roads led to and from the Monument, whether they were main thoroughfares or byroads filtering in through the southern and western approaches of the town, somewhere along which was sure to be situated a 'big house' or two. Lismore straddled one main road, the trunk route from Waterford City to Cork City. Five miles to the south-west lay Tallow with its glorious Sweep that offered the thrill of a long freewheel down on your bicycle – as long as your brakes held together for the hairpin bend halfway. Past the Sweep, it was a straight run across the bridge over the river Bride into the town itself. A couple of miles out from Lismore on this road on the left-hand side lay Toortane House.

To the east on the trunk route was the small town of Cappoquin. A more or less flat, winding four-mile stretch, bordered by woods on your left and the northern meadows of the Blackwater on your right, took you into it. You skirted the water's edge at the Kitchen Hole, reputedly the deepest spot on the river and part of the Bishop's Fishery, where the fishermen of the Lismore Estates Company fished for salmon with nets. Halfway along this road on the northern side lay Salterbridge House.

On your way out of town across Lismore Bridge a sharp left turn took you west along a shady road to Ballyduff, the fourth small town, including our own, that formed a nexus. [I should point out here for those unfamilar with this western region that there are two Ballyduffs in the County of Waterford, the one formerly in the Parish of Lismore and Mocollop in the Barony of Coshmore and Coshbride, sometimes designated as Lower (or now West) Ballyduff, and the other (Upper, now East, Ballyduff) in the Parish of Kilmeaden in the Barony of Middlethird (Waterford) in the east of the county.] Away to your left the Blackwater snaked out of sight to stay parallel until it rejoined you at the town six miles on. Along this road on the right-hand side were a number of interesting buildings, the disused mill at Ballyin; the thickly-walled ice house built into the shoulder of a hill so that it was half-covered with earth and shaded by broad-leaved trees; the folly called the Towers, built by the Kiely-Usshers and lying far into the still and ghostly Barranamanoge Wood in the Tower Glen at the base of a narrow waterfall. The adjoining wood to Barranamanoge is called Knocknagapall and on the fringes of this lay Ballysaggartmore House with the, for us children, scary Woodroofe and Kiely-Ussher family vaults. Imagine somebody not being buried in the ground but stored in a house alongside many other bodies! The trees around this great house were said to have been planted to represent the position of the armies and troops at the Battle of Waterloo – the kind of nutty exercise that a certain type of patriotic Anglo-Irish planter would have undertaken with relish. A little farther on from Ballysaggartmore House was Glenmore House, and in Glenmore Wood there was a bigger waterfall than the one at the Towers. On the left on the Ballyduff Road, past the ice house was Ballyin Gardens which, with the Castle Gardens, held the greatest variety of rhododendrons in the area. In the month of June on a few occasions my pals and I climbed in over the wall to savour its floral abundance. A beautiful residence attached to these gardens was usually leased to wealthy clients by the Castle.

Cross the Strand Bridge leaving town, turn left at the weigh house by the salmon hatchery and you were at the foot of the Mountain Road. Follow it and it took you north over the lower slopes of the Knockmealdown Mountains to the Gap. Eight miles of uphill slog on a bike, murder if the wind was against you. But what a joyride returning! Freewheel all the way in a quarter of the time it took you to climb. Five hundred yards along this road on the right an elegant driveway sloped up among tall chestnuts to Ballyrafter House on the hill. This fine house was the home of Arthur and Mrs Paxman. Across the side road at the back of it that ran up to Sruh and Glentaun West and beyond they possessed an extensive walled orchard garden from which they sold quality fruit and vegetables. In earlier years they had also run Paxman's Butter Factory, presumably on the same site.

A 1778 print showing Dromana House situated on the bluff to the left and the broad sweep of the River Blackwater along this tidal stretch.

The manager of this was Pat O'Sullivan of Fernville, who was first president of the Lismore Sinn Féin Club shortly after the 1916 Easter Rising. From the front lawn of the house you could look back and survey the dip below, called Glen View. Your eye panned easily across the road from the small, green-painted weigh house to Bud Sargent's garage on the left-hand side of the Cappoquin Road, then followed the row of granite-built stores on the right of that road, the disused mill and the old gas works of barrack stone, and some dwelling houses, behind which ran the disused canal that stretched out of sight on your left beyond the edge of Ballyrafter Wood. The gas works had remained operative until the end of the Thirties and had been managed by a close friend of my parents, Denis Drohan of Carrick-on-Suir, who died before his time in 1938. The short canal – it was only about two miles in length – ran on through Ballyrafter Flats to mouth on to the tidal waters of the Blackwater downstream of Ballygallane House.

There was a second road to Cappoquin, what we referred to as the 'back road', on the other side of the river but you would not have realised this along the main road until you were well on your way. This road ran in tandem with, although not quite parallel to, the railway line. At Ballyea, a mile out of town, this road branched off left to circle around the foot of the

Round Hill, an ancient Norman motte-and-bailey that we imbued with the magic of a fairy rath. This was stepped with Scots pines, the rich red bark of which glowed or glistened according to the prevailing mood of sun, wind and rain. Ride on further – we usually travelled along this narrow side-road on bikes – and you came to the Kennel Heights with its ruined mansion on the right, a bit of a climb on the way out, a great stretch to belt down on the way back. The Blackwater was wide at Cappoquin where it right-angled south toward the Atlantic Ocean. On the left and right of this southward flow there was a succession of fine houses, Dromana Castle, dramatically poised on a huge outcrop of rock with Dromana Wood behind it; Camphire House near Villierstown; and, beyond the confluence of Blackwater and Bride, Strancally Castle.

Immediately west of Lismore there was another back road, this time leading to Ballyduff, via Glencairn, and thus called the Glencairn Road. It veered right from the Tallow Road a half-mile or so beyond the town at the railway bridge we knew as 'Tallow Bridge'. At Glencairn itself on the banks of the Blackwater away to the right were located Fortwilliam House and Glencairn Abbey, the last-mentioned a convent run by the Cistercian order of nuns, an enclosed order bound by a vow of silence. Once a great house, the abbey stood on a promontory and faced directly across the river towards Glenmore House on the main Ballyduff Road. In its grounds was a place known as the Khyber Pass (there was even a Khyber Pass Wood), testimony to the foibles of earlier ownership. A secret escape tunnel was said to run from the house under the Blackwater and come up somewhere in Glenmore Wood. We had a similar fiction about Lismore Castle from which a tunnel under the same river was also supposed to lead to freedom at some long-lost exit on the Ferry Inch. So we were twice as well-endowed with hidden tunnels as most Irish towns.

I was taken along to Glencairn Abbey once by Mam who was visiting a young distant relative or friend of the family who was getting close to taking her final vow of silence after which she would never speak again. Sign language from an older nun led us eventually to Mam's communicating in a low voice through a lattice in a wooden panel with the teenage girl who seemed as happy as Larry with her lot. I must have been only about eight or nine years old myself at the time but already it was clear to me that this form of self-denial was something I viewed with a vague unease. After the abbey, Ballygally House, Glenbeg House and Ballyduff Castle dotted the landscape in quick succession, so, all in all between both banks, it was clear that this stretch of the Blackwater was much-favoured by the well-to-do.

The roads that undulated south from our town were all side-roads, macadamized rather than tarmacadamized, and all with level crossings, where the railway line traversed them not far out. The Deerpark Road ran south-east and provided a back road to Youghal in the County Cork, via Camphire House and Strancally Castle. It joined the Dungarvan–Youghal Road at Youghal Bridge, which crossed the Blackwater before the river widened out into a muddy, reed-lined estuary. In the late Forties and early Fifties this bridge was falling apart. Obstacles consisting of tar barrels filled with cement forced motorcars – the only vehicles with bikes and motorbikes allowed access – to zigzag gingerly over the shaky metal superstructure at the tightly-restricted speed of 5 miles an hour. Endless hassles in County Council meetings centred on constructing a new one a quarter of a mile upstream. Delaying a final decision was the strongly held view that the inevitable disruption of any building operations could be detrimental to fishing in the long term – a vital consideration for a famous salmon river. The site was eventually approved in October 1953 and the new bridge completed some years later. Whether the fishing was affected or not I do not know, but I suspect that the foreign fleets overfishing the Waterford coastline years later did more damage to stocks in a few short seasons than any spoliation caused by the destruction of the old bridge and the building of the new.

On the Deerpark Road, a couple of miles out from Lismore at the southernmost end of the townland of Tourin, there was a disused cornmill and the remains of an old mill race by the side of a stream known as the Owbeg. River and road ran on side by side through Killahala Wood, which extended itself along the west bank of the Blackwater opposite Dromana Forest. North Tourin was bounded by *Bóthar na Naomh*, an ancient extension of another ancient route, the *Rian-Bó-Phádraig*, and ran east from the Round Hill. Along this byway lay Drumroe House and the ruined Tourin Castle, the seat of the Roches until Cromwell dispossessed them. At Drumroe were remains of an early Christian settlement, according to tradition the birthplace of St Declan, patron saint of the Decies. Tourin achieved a later brief fame in the early 1950s as the home of the finest senior hurlers in West Waterford, and of some of the finest in the county.

The other south-radiating side-roads from east to west were the Mayfield Road, Townparks Road and Ballyanchor Road. Mayfield took you past Mayfield Lodge through Ballysaggartbeg Glebe, over the Owbeg Bridge in the dip at Ballinwillin, to Scarook (*Scarbhach* in Irish) Wood on Ballysaggartbeg Hill that I could see from the back of our house in West Street and where we would go to pick whorts every summer. Townparks led out by St Carthage's Hospital, a big, forbidding-looking block that had once been a Victorian workhouse, passing Ashbourne House at the end of an avenue of trees on the right, to Bishopstown Wood of which Scarook formed the easternmost part. An ancient ecclesiastical earthwork, An Lóistin, was located close to this road, in the waist of the Wood. The continuation of the road took you to a high point at Ballinaspick (in Irish *Baile an Easpuig*, which was how the locals pronounced it) that overlooked the River Bride on one side and gave you a charming aspect of Lismore on the other. Ballyanchor Road snaked through the townland of Burgess Anchor via Ballyanchor House to Curraheen North.

Many roads then led to and from our town and into these fed other minor byways that took us to places like Shrough (off the Mountain Road) via Rath House, or Monatarive, Glenshask and Ballysaggart (off the lower, or main, Ballyduff Road). By the time I left Lismore I still had not explored the nooks and crannies of many of these townlands nor, indeed, even once visited some of them. In this sense I was, perhaps, no different from a lot of my contemporaries. The one schoolmate who never failed to impress me with his knowledge of the geography of the area was Tom Lineen, who unfailingly seemed to know where places were and who lived in them. I used to excuse my ignorance in the face of such omniscience by telling myself, 'Ah sure, he has a lot of relatives dotted around the town', which he had not really – not over the whole geographical spread. But you had to make an excuse for yourself.

CHAPTER THREE

The Rich

IN DISCUSSING THE gentry around Lismore we knew what we were talking about. One of the premier dukes of England, the Duke of Devonshire, owned the town we walked in, as well as the castle and half of West Waterford, and when he was in residence up went the flag with his coat of arms on the highest turret. And, if that was not enough, at the end of the Forties another of the premier aristocrats, the Duke of Westminster, who was also of the Cavendish family, bought Fortwilliam House from the Hickmans and set up a holiday home there. However, fabulously rich as he was, we did not take him too seriously. In comparison to the Devonshire lord, who, according to what someone told my father, liked to boast that his family had lived in Lismore – on and off, of course – for going on three hundred years, the London magnate was a mere blow-in. And anyway, a man who lived in a stylish two-storey manor, however grand, could hardly be equated with a man who lived in a *castle,* and whose family seat, inexplicably at Chatsworth in Derbyshire rather than somewhere in Devon, was a *palace four or five times the size* of his Lismore residence. Which showed you how you could be mistaken in life. It was many years later I discovered that while one man could own all of Lismore, another could own half of the richest borough in London. So maybe the Duke of Westminster considered Fortwilliam to be no more than a simple fishing lodge from which to sally forth to practise a little encroaching on his cousin's waters. Whatever our ill-formed ideas about them, it was clear that these two men represented, in terms of rank, privilege and wealth, the First Division. We even reckoned we had picked up the customary form of address to use, 'Your Grace', should they, or their wives, happen to engage us in conversation.

In the countryside about us lived, in great, big, and smallish houses, the Third Division – scores of minor aristocrats and would-be aristocrats – some of whom seemed remarkably well-heeled, and some of whom were. We did not really have a Second Division unless, perhaps, one counted Isaac Bell, a reputedly immensely rich Englishman, who was probably just plain

Two prints offering contrasting early views of Lismore Castle. The undated Neale print (bottom) is probably the earlier of the two and may be 18th century. The 1839 Bartlett print (top) is a reprint of the 1831 engraving. I fished many a time for trout and coarse fish along the stretch of water where the two fishermen stand.

wealthy, and who rented Ballyin Gardens from the Castle for a few seasons. We encountered him being pushed around in a wheelchair, or driven around in a big limousine. The only other representative of the middle division of which we knew in the whole county was Lord Waterford who owned Curraghmore House and its vast spread at Portlaw in the east. Army, i.e. British Army, service was a prerequisite for the Third Division. All on the bottom rung had done their time, long or short, and grimly and bizarrely held onto their ranks, an attitude of mind not so much military as colonial perhaps. There would be Colonel This and Major That, and a lot of captains. Anything less was inadmissible. Strangely enough we never accommodated a general, although Earl Alexander of Tunis (a field marshal) had relatives in the Alexanders of Mayfield House. You only heard mention of the wives of these warriors when there was an annual hunt ball somewhere – the local papers, the *Dungarvan Leader* and the *Dungarvan Observer,* would studiously chronicle the top-ranking participants, e.g. Major and Mrs Maxwell, Captain and Mrs Alexander, Colonel and Mrs O'Brien, Captain and Mrs Jameson, and so on. There was an exception though, one Major Morgan's better half, who made a name for herself as Mrs Morgan in international show-jumping arenas where the Welshman Colonel Harry Llewellyn and his gelding Foxhunter (Irish-bred, I think) were all the rage.

The Devonshire mystique was what mattered. When the Duke and his Duchess were in town things began to hum. Even his fellow-duke would put in an appearance to coincide with his visits, driven around in his shiny black limousine by Lismoreman Jim Willoughby, furnished with a chauffeur's hat and renamed James. What else? It was through Jim we learned that the Duke, when in transit through Dublin, always stayed at the Shelbourne Hotel, the last word it was said, in Irish luxury. The Devonshires and their glamorous guests, among whom they could count no less than Fred Astaire the scintillating Hollywood star, would regularly be seen calling next door to the Wine Vaults for their midday tipple and sometimes, while I was buying a half pound of tea from Mikey McCarthy's son Florence, or 'Mokie' as he was nicknamed, I would hear their jolly voices hohoing through the mahogany swing doors leading to the bar. You could understand why they patronised the Wine Vaults. It was the classiest bar and grocery not only in the town but also in the whole of West Waterford. Before the advent of motor and rail transport it had been the coaching station for the town, and, when people in the area emigrated to North America during and after the Great Famine it was here they booked their passage. Mikey bought the business early in 1942 after it was put up for sale following the death of the previous owner James Ahern. In tone with its name the predominant colour of the establishment was wine red – mahogany shelves stretching right the way up to the dark ceilings, generous counters of the same hardwood, rust-coloured tiles on the floors. It had elegant arched windows, sculpted glass-panelled doors and always smelt of spices, tea and port. The main counter in the grocery, one end of which was opposite the door, was long and straight, the side one, on your right as you entered, sensuously curved. I loved to run my hands along their polished rims. On the side counter sat the biggest bacon slicer in town, a finely tuned instrument with a red casing. Whenever Mary Mac, the daughter, cut rashers for me I used to watch, with a mixture of fascination and apprehension, her fingers coming closer and closer to the razor-sharp wheel. The bar I only knew second-hand, when slipping through it to get to and from the high-roofed bottling-store at the back, where I occasionally used to volunteer to do a bit of work. Or when I purchased a soda siphon or returned an old one to reclaim the deposit. (The thick glass siphons with their black taps were refillable and the deposit on them was a worthwhile shilling or more.) It is one of the great disappointments of my life that I have never had, nor ever shall have now, the opportunity of perching on one of its high bar stools and sampling a port or sherry from the cask because the whole interior, bar and shop, was butchered irrevocably in the Sixties to create a Spar supermarket. 'A mistake,' Florence admitted to me when I was on a visit to Lismore in the Nineties, greatly regretting that he had ever allowed himself to be talked into the so-called modernisation.

The Devonshires were well thought of in the town for a number of reasons. In the smallest of ways had I not occasion to remember them well myself, having enjoyed the ride that Lord Charles gave me in his horse and trap? That sad heir, who had inherited all his father's Irish property, was remembered for a much greater kindness. In the time of the Second World War during a particularly harsh winter he arranged for the timber of 100 trees to be distributed free amongst the poor. The mean-spirited might say that that was no great shakes for a man who owned forest from Scarook to the Knockmealdown Mountains, mere public relations, but it was a generous gesture just the same. His ancestors were said never to have turfed people off their land during the cruel evictions that convulsed the country during the late nineteenth century – unlike other big landowners, some of them native squireens, who happily applied proto-Thatcherite thinking in downsizing their peasantry. The Lismore Estates Company, the registered name under which the Castle estate was run, was one of the biggest employers in West Waterford, and was known to treat its work-force fairly, although how much the workers' weekly wage of fifteen shillings or so represented in real terms in the 1940s I am not sure. In 1942 fifteen shillings formed the basic wage of a Castle worker. This was also the going rate paid by large landowners and big farmers. Smaller farmers paid as low as ten shillings. CIE workers were receiving £1-14-9 a week, which highlights the low wages of farm workers. (I am grateful to the late Dick Power of Botany for recalling these figures.) Public walks on castle land like the Grove and the Green Road were scrupulously maintained, enhancing the environment of the town for all who lived in it.

Given the excess of wealth on the Cavendish side and the depth of poverty among sections of our community, the townspeople's relationship to the Castle was inevitably somewhat feudal. A similar ethos prevailed in Glencairn around Fortwilliam. I became sensitive about this, I think, one spring when Dad came home with an eight- or nine- pound salmon, wrapped in a sheet of newspaper under his arm, a gift from the ebullient Lismore Estates Company manager, Billy King. It was not the first such salmon he had brought home. We usually got one every year. You never knew in advance when it would come, or if it would come. It depended on the quality of the fishing season. One year we received two so there must have been exceptional catches. Dad would unwrap the silver fish and lay it out on the kitchen table for Mam to admire, for the rest of us too if we happened to be around at the time. On this last occasion I started to worry about the gift. Why did Dad receive one and not, as far as I knew, the other guards? But I never dared ask Dad to his face. He was a scrupulously honest man and any expression of doubt on my part would have been sufficient, in itself, to hurt him. Eventually, I reasoned that as his job required him to arrange extra security around the castle grounds when the Duke and Duchess were in resi-

Mam on left with her first cousin 'Nurse Biddy' Morrissey and Paddy in pram outside the Green Road sawmill/garden entrance to Lismore Castle. Mrs King lived in the lodge out of shot to the left. Photo taken c. 1934.

dence, the salmon was a way of expressing thanks for the effort. On the other hand, the present could have been simply a personal one from the Billy King. He and his wife were friends of my parents and sometimes when we went walking as a family around the Green Road Mrs King would invite us into their lodge by the sawmill for tea. My doubts did not prevent me from enjoying the salmon. It was delicious.

In an unexpected way the castle brought some international glitter to the town. Lord Charles was married to Adèle Astaire, the dancing sister of the dancing Fred. The famous brother stayed at the castle on one or two occasions. From time to time too, it was rumoured that Bing Crosby was coming, probably because the crooner, like Fred, had also charmed the English aristocracy, but whether he actually made it I cannot say. A fairly regular visitor was Shane Leslie, the writer and cousin of Winston Churchill. You would see him strolling around town, wearing a soft hat and a long tweed overcoat and carrying a walking stick. After the War, Rose Kennedy and some of her clan appeared on the scene. A Kennedy daughter, Kathleen, had caused a bit of a scandal in both Catholic and Protestant circles by marrying the Marquess of Hartington, heir to the dukedom, in a registry office. Registry office? A strange new term was added to my vocabulary. Getting married in an office? With grey filing cabinets, bare boards, and a plain wooden table like in my Dad's? I knew little of weddings at this time – they seemed to me to be an expression of some secretive adult ritual – but I was fairly secure in the idea that they took place in chapels, because I had made enquiries about those little scraps of coloured paper that I saw blowing around the chapel yard from time to time. No, I was told, it was not the lads on a paper chase who had scattered them about but grown-ups at a wedding. The stuff was called *confetti* and was tossed over the *bride* and *groom* – three more new words. When the unlucky couple both lost their young lives not long afterwards, Lord William sniped in Belgium in the autumn of 1944, Lady Kathleen the victim of a plane crash in the South of France in the spring of 1948, there were dark mutterings in the town about the Hand of God striking them down for their effrontery in flouting established religion, i.e. you did not insult a Catholic like Jesus Christ and get away with it. The Devonshires received a further lesson in this when the Tenth Duke cashed in his chips before his time while felling an oak, a hobby of his apparently, in 1950. As for the Kennedys... A visitor the Duke might have preferred not to entertain, even in his absence, descended on the castle during the week in December 1954 in which I was preparing to leave Lismore for good – Sir Oswald Mosley, accompanied by his Mitford wife who was a sister of the Duchess. The would-be Führer's home in

Galway had mysteriously gone up in flames a couple of weeks earlier. At least God got it right sometimes.

The Duke and Duchess, whichever number in line they were, hit town regularly in the early spring, but used to drop in on other occasions too. In older times their fluttering coat of arms was run up the flagpole, most probably, as a signal to the locals, gentry included, or maybe gentry especially, to be on their best behaviour, but in my time it read more like an invitation to the Anglo-Irish landowners to 'come up and see us sometime'. If God-fearing Protestants failed to notice the flag they would certainly not have missed seeing the Duke and Duchess at church in St Carthage's Cathedral the following Sunday. A small wicket allowed the pair to slip discreetly out of the Castle Gardens into the New Way, from which they could cross over into Ferry Lane and from there stroll straight ahead up the Deanery Hill (old Church Avenue) to the cathedral, which must have made Dean Stanley's day. Church Avenue was grandly named but consisted of no more than a mere alleyway between tall limestone walls, the shady one profusely overhung with ivy, the sunny or Deanery garden one tufted with swathes of red valerian in summer.

In 1949, when he could not have been all that long in possession of Fortwilliam House, the Duke of Westminster tried a bit of one-upmanship on his cousin. He threw a big Christmas party for a hundred children in the Glencairn area. (The dukes seemed to like doing things in hundreds.) To make up the numbers, as there were not enough kids in Glencairn itself, a few youngsters from Lismore were invited as well. Janey Dunne from the Lodge by the Hurling Field was one of those lucky enough to be invited and she told me about it afterwards. They all got presents, she said, and there was a magic lantern show and funny films. And lots of sweet things to eat. I did get invited to a similar party though, also at Christmas, possibly even the same year. Early stirrings of charity chic? Genuine compassion even? Whatever the reason, Mrs Bell from Ballyin Gardens decided to throw a party for the children of the town at the Palladium cinema owned by Doc Healy. Santa Claus himself, the sainted pillar of giving, was there in person, the first time I set eyes on the real thing, and he gave each of us a colourfully wrapped gift and some sweets on the way in. When we were all seated, our hostess, a painfully thin woman, walked into a spotlight – the first time I really noted such an effect – and told us in a reedy, high-pitched English voice, and at length, that we should be kind to 'little donkeys'. 'After all,' she said, 'Jesus rode into Jerusalem on a little donkey,' a remark that implied to me that she thought God was a light little slip of a fella. But I knew better because Ned O'Brien, the Bird's younger brother, had told me that Jesus

Christ was the only six-footer that had ever lived, or ever would live. I had differed forcefully with Ned about this statement, saying that my own father stood six feet in his socks and that there were a fair number of other men of similar stature around, but I was stumped when he pontificated that Jesus was the only man who measured *exactly* six foot – all other men were a teenshie bit over or a weenshie bit under. I was confounded by the certainty with which my pal related this nugget of information and accepted his word as gospel, well almost. It was a *bit* hard to credit. But what evidence did I have to refute it? Fair play to Ned, it was many years later that I saw certified in Dad's *Certificate of Discharge* from the *Garda Síochána* that his height was six foot and one-eight of an inch! Anyway, the main point was, we both accepted that Jesus was a tall man. So the ride into Jerusalem could not have been all that fun for the donkey.

There was another interesting known fact about Jesus Christ – the robe, or toga, or whatever it was called, that he wore was seamless from top to bottom. Not a stitch or cut in it. How the man got in and out of it, or how he came to own it, nobody knew. But that did not sound too impossible if all he wore was a rudimentary sheet. Anyway, before the party that brought these unresolved theological questions to the surface again, none of us had known of Mrs Bell's concern for the donkeys of Ireland. Looking back, I have to admit that she had a point. Unlike the English, we Irish rarely became emotional about our animals and were not renowned for the way we treated them. Neglect rather than conscious brutality was our failing. Sometimes you saw donkeys with hide chafed red by ill-fitting harness, or with open cuts on their legs – wounds left untreated in the belief, innocent or convenient, that beasts healed themselves in their own way and did not require the intervention of Man. You did not need to be an adult to recognise that some animals were driven too hard, those you saw straining their guts out to pull overloaded carts of firewood along muddy and uneven winter tracks, and being lashed on the rump with a stout stick for their efforts. It did not make you happy to see this but, as a child, you felt powerless to protest about it, especially when you knew that the men doing the driving were pushing themselves hard too, earning a living for themselves and their families. The more understanding men would have their shoulders to the cart in support of the donkey. All you might inadequately do was approach the beast when it was given a breather and stroke its snout sympathetically.

There used to be a Donkey Protection Society in Ireland around this time so obviously Mrs Bell was not alone in expressing concern. The society, however, appeared to vent its greatest spleen upon those who organised donkey racing and donkey driving at shows and fairs, events I never recall seeing in Lismore. You wondered if it ever occurred to the people running the society to question whether horses liked having riders on their backs? Anyway, after our benefactress had had her say we all cheered and clapped, more in appreciation of Kevie Noonan's reaching for the cords to pull back the curtains than of the well-intentioned homily. Her kindness *was* appreciated but her sentiments were on another plane. No doubt she learned from the experience too. She never repeated the party. The film show was less memorable than her speech, a few shorts along biblical lines, with Jesus on his donkey.

The Lismore Estates Company's farming operations were administered by English, or possibly Anglo-Irish, stewards. I was never sure of their precise role although I knew they were fairly big at the castle. Two served their time in my memory, a Mr Prileaux and a Mr Cantillon, both somewhere in their mid to late twenties. I liked the former better. He was more of a performer, more fun to watch. There was the uncoordinated manner in which he would pull his solid yet strangely vulnerable-looking frame out of the Land-Rover; the way in which he threw his limbs about when he walked; the gleam of unrealised efficiency and innovation in his eye. 'Morning!' he would shout out to all and sundry, pronouncing it like 'mourning', on his way into the Wine Vaults every other day; 'Morning! Morning!', with added amiability when there was an extra spring in his step. I used to take him off to Mam too but she did not get half as big a laugh out of my impression of him as she did of my Wattie Cullinane walk. There was something of the square peg about Prileaux. His aim of bringing order to the affairs of the company seemed always to be contradicted by an innate inefficiency, personal or corporate, or by dreams that never got beyond the experimental stage.

His most spectacular innovation to the husbandry of the castle in my eyes was undoubtedly the pilot field of flax that he grew just beyond the ice house on the way to Johnny McGrath's, where barley was the usual crop. I had never seen flax growing before and the dense ocean of golden-yellow blooms was something to see. I shared his enthusiasm for it, thinking what fine cloth the linen-makers of Belfast would weave from the harvest. But the harvest was never gathered in; instead it was allowed to wither and was ploughed back into the ground to be succeeded by barley again the following year. Perhaps it was the 'wee blue blossom' variety of the plant that Prileaux should have grown? Or maybe the Duke and Duchess were just not interested in diversifying their activities?

The indefatigable steward also tried to revive charcoal burning in the area, I think. Molly, Paddy and myself, out for one of our walks beyond the Teampuileen caves, came across this strange process by accident. We had gone further than usual, almost to the end of the Grove near the Glen Farm, when we stumbled on a cordoned-off glade in the silent wood. In the middle of it a mysterious-looking mound was steaming like a giant Christmas pudding. Only what it was emitting was not steam but smoke, pungent puffs of it. Two workmen stood near it, eyeing it watchfully.

Cantillon – odd that they both had surnames of French-sounding origin – had a drier personality and was not as affable as his predecessor. But he could smile too through his gold-rimmed glasses and leave you with the impression he had his own peculiar wit. One of the incidental tasks the steward had to perform was organise the annual West Waterford Hunt Ball whenever this was held at the castle – a job you felt either man would have undertaken with relish. Whether Cantillon ever got up on a horse or not, I do not recall. I never saw him in riding boots. Prileaux, on the other hand, was seldom out of them and I used to see him occasionally astride a big brown animal. The Hunt Ball was a lavish all-through-the-night affair, with the Wine Vaults providing drink from 9.00 p.m. to 6.00 a.m. And you can be sure that Mikey McCarthy, a master of tact and accommodation, did a first-class job. No other publican in the town would have been capable of matching his stock of wines and liquors. With regard to the two stewards, the general impression you were left with from comment in the town was that Prileaux was a nice chap who on a good day might just have known his arse from his elbow and Cantillon an okay bloke who could organise one hell of a party. Picking up the pieces behind the two was the dour Major Silcox, who performed the role of major-domo. A surly burly man on lease loan from Lord Waterford of Curraghmore into whose family he had married. Would have been impressive Trooping the Colour, or leading the Charge of the Light Brigade. Nobody joked about him. Except maybe the sawyer and ultimate gas man 'Bishop' Scanlon from the castle sawmill to whom no one and nothing was sacred.

Spud Murphy from lower Botany was the one amongst us who got closest to the gentry. When he left school at the age of fourteen he got a job at the castle giving the new Duchess of Devonshire a leg-up on her horse. 'Lovely thigh she has,' he confided to me once or twice with a wink, moving me to picture the flat of his hand on her sleek jodhpurs.

CHAPTER FOUR

The Poor

NO ONE IN LISMORE ADMITTED to being poor. Even at the extremes of deprivation pride would provoke a denial of the label. Yet outward signs of poverty were only too apparent, both in the physique of the town and in the physique of its inhabitants. Often it was the seemingly insignificant detail that was the most telling. Boils, for example, were a common complaint among children. I used to ask myself why I was so fortunate in not being badly afflicted by them when so many others were. For a long time I got away with nothing more harmful than a periodic enlarged pimple at the back of my neck. Then I got a real boil and learned what it was all about.

Clothing was scarce, patches unexceptional, hand-me-downs indispensable, and barefoot children the norm in the streets of the poor. The last child to run barefoot was Patsy Hickey who had grown to like going without footwear so much he was well into his teens before his elders could persuade him to pull on a pair of boots. On the face of it, the poor grew to adulthood seemingly inured to the cold and damp – your body had to adapt or you would not survive. But when you saw deprived children shivering in their thin garments on icy wintry days you ceased to believe in this hypothesis, if you ever had. One man, who more than any other had the ability to withstand extremes of cold, was Michael Ryan of Botany. In fact, he took an almost perverse pride in it. On a day so cold 'you wouldn't put a sprong out in it,' as an old friend of mine Jimmy Power from Tullahought in the County Kilkenny used to say, you would spot Michael striding down the *middle* of West Street like an Irish Guard, wearing a light jacket and a shirt unbuttoned to the waist. Hard men used to flinch when they saw his broad hairy chest and wonder how he stuck it. In summer I used to envy the children who ran around barefoot and when I got clear of home would take off my sandals, hook them over my shoulder, and let my own feet run free. Of course Mam always found out later because I would return with tar on my feet, or minor grazes. Once, in Carrick-on-Suir, I ran down Greystone Street on a glorious sunny morning savouring the sensuous warmth of the concrete – the Tipperary town was distinguished for me in having *concrete* streets – against my bare flesh. Mam saw me, hauled me back inside the house, and told me to put on my shoes *immediately*. The innocence of my fleeting joy and her apparent mortification, in case my aunts would be embarrassed, I suppose, is an image that has always remained clear in my mind. When you went paddling on the stones in the Owenashad you learned who had the hardened soles.

The effects of malnutrition were only too apparent in the short term. In the long term they were insidious. The deaths in early manhood some years after I left the town of Donie 'Doshin' Keating of Botany and John 'Cal' O'Callaghan of Church Lane, two pals who unfailingly delighted us with their wit, could well be attributed to this. Doshin was exceedingly frail and suffered from bronchial problems. Sometimes he would look hunched and miserable but he never complained and always brightened up in company. Cal was much more robust but frail too. I was sickly myself but, coming from a lower-middle-class family, was insulated from the worst. I had a warm home (warm by the standards of the time), shoes on my feet, an adequate if not very varied diet, and when necessary, hand-me-downs from one person only, my elder brother. The staple food for poor families was the thick cut of grey-white bread, buttered and with white sugar sprinkled on it. Indeed, not only poor families ate their bread in this way. I used to get a lot of bread and butter too, but I never developed a taste for it with sugar. When Sucky Neville's mother, Kit, pressed a slice of bread on me from time to time I was loth to take it because the Nevilles were a large family and I knew that she had lots of mouths to feed. But I did not want to hurt her feelings either so I did take the cut now and again. Spuds, of course, were also basic, and milk. Rabbits, providentially, were a free source of protein and the lads used to go out hunting and trapping them with terrier dogs, snares, ferrets and, at a later stage – a deadly refinement – with portable car lights with which they dazzled the animals. Trout and eels from the local rivers were also free.

Rabbits, as well as being a source of protein for the poor – the middle classes for some odd reason turned up their noses at this succulent meat – were also a source of income. Agents would buy them and ship them off to England where people appeared to have no such hang-ups. This stock of wildlife remained available into the early Fifties. In 1953, however, the farmers, who were always, and with some justification, arguing that there were far too many rabbits in the country, introduced myxomatosis from over the water. One could generously say that by then wartime rationing had ended in Ireland and more food was being made available from other than Irish sources. But the poor were adversely affected just the same. Rationing was more severe in Britain during the immediate postwar years than during the wartime period itself so there was still a ready market for rabbits there. Pocket as well as belly, thus, was hit by the disease. If the yields from the farmers' crops improved in the succeeding years it was at a high cost to the poor and to the rabbit population.

It was a common outdoor sight on cold winter days to see men and boys, inadequately clothed in jackets and open-necked shirts, swinging their arms across their chests in an effort to pump warmth into their bodies. I was amongst them whenever I was rash enough to venture out without my brother's hand-me-down brown woollen overcoat. Girls in flimsy dresses you saw blowing into their hands and jigging up and down on their toes. Amongst large families living in the tight spaces of the small cottages of Botany competition for clothing was acute. Though I never asked I used to wonder how my friends the Nevilles managed to lay their hands on their own garments when they woke up in the morning. 'You didn't,' Kathleen clarified for me in later years, 'First up, best dressed. That's how it was. You grabbed what fitted and put it on.'

A reddish criss-cross pattern on the inside of the calves was the giveaway for the woman who was accustomed to sitting too close to her open fire. 'ABC', Mam used to call this condition and she always kept a thick pair of brown stockings handy so that she could pull them on when the cold at her back forced her to sit too near to the blaze. Keeping houses warm inside was, in many ways, more taxing than keeping bodies warm inside or outside. Central heating was unheard of, except maybe in Hollywood pictures, and even the bodies of the middle class were accustomed to absorbing the chill and damp of the climate. The middle class had enough wood, or even coal, to light fires, when a particularly miserable day made it desirable in summer as well.

In the cottages of the poor a fire was necessary all the year round because meals had to be cooked over it. Mam used to cook over the fire in the living-room also. As there were hobs on either side of it, pots could be kept warm on these in winter. More of our cooking – plum puddings, fowl and the like – was done on the sawdust fire in the yard. When we first got an electric cooking device I cannot remember but it was an event for Mam. Getting hold of wood was, thus, a major preoccupation for everybody but, for the poor, critical. In the cold of winter the problem was acute. As we lived in a well forested area, wood remained our principal fuel – a wonderful one but it had the disadvantage of burning too fast. Whichever source of energy you used, quality was dictated by price so the poor got the worst. Beech and oak were the most expensive of all and only selectively felled. There were occasions, however, when even these hardwoods became generally available. Severe storms hit the region from time to time and when they occurred in winter were a blessing for the poor. The prized, graceful beeches that grew in exposed places were often toppled over, sometimes a whole row decimated. The exposed stands by the Tallow Road on the west side of the town usually suffered the most, sometimes blocking for a day or two the stretch along by the Christian Brothers School that we knew as 'the Plantation'. Once a tree had fallen word spread quietly through Botany and Church Lane and whole families would descend on the stricken giant and strip it of its limbs with crosscut and axe, handsaw and hatchet. Often people chanced going out while the tempest was still raging in order to be first at the kill but this was foolhardy as other trees and limbs could come crashing down. Mostly people waited until the winds had abated, then went out with all available asses and carts, old prams, and home-made box-carts run on old pram-wheels, to haul the timber home. What could not be fitted on these was shouldered home.

Such storms were infrequent so in normal times other methods were needed to supplement what could afford to be bought. 'Going for a limb' was an expression that was common among the lads from Botany and the Lane. You took a length of stout rope with you into the woods, selected a tree displaying a branch that looked as if it could be snapped off with a vigorous heave, climbed the tree, attached one end of your rope to the branch, descended, and trusted in your strength to do the rest. It required considerably more muscle power than I could muster to tear off a good-sized limb. Frequently, two or three of us would tug together but even this concerted effort was not always equal to the strength of one, if our timing was out. Sometimes a limb was just too stubborn and defeated all attempts to remove it.

Beaver Doherty was a wizard at getting limbs. One late, sunny spring day he and Pete Neville from the top of Main Street and I found ourselves up by the Owenashad on the Ballyin side of the river in a grove of birches and ashes glistening with budding leaves. We were not seeking a limb expressly. Often, however, when we were out walking in the woods Beaver would take a rope along with him in case we came across a branch that was too tempting to leave behind. On a tall ash we spotted such a limb. Beaver clambered up and attached the rope. Then the three of us grabbed hold of the loose end and heaved; once, twice, three times to no avail. The branch just would not give. 'Ah fuck this!' said Beaver, 'Stand back.' Pete and I let go of the rope and watched as our pal twined it around his powerful forearms. He concentrated for a moment, then with one mighty tug, tore the fresh young limb from the tree. I gawked in admiration. Pete just shook his head. In the Warren once, Beaver told me another time, he and his first cousin Peter 'Cox' Doherty brought down a limb so large and leggy they could barely shoulder it home between them. They gave it the name 'Tarantula', cut it into blocks for firewood and sold it to earn a couple of bob for a Saturday night pint.

Strictly speaking, obtaining firewood in this manner was illegal. It was permissable to take a limb if you found one that had broken off naturally, for example, one that had been snapped off in a storm, but you were not supposed to help yourself to fresh wood from a tree. The reasons for this were more monetary than conservationist. Beaver and Seán Dennis, who was even stronger than Beaver, and I were tested on this point when Paddy Dooley, the bailiff, caught us red-handed with a limb at our feet. Seán it was who had climbed a big oak in the Warren just behind the Protestant churchyard and smashed off a large, partly-dead branch with a powerful kick. From above he had spotted the lanky bailiff approaching and hurriedly concealed Beaver's rope in an ivy-clad fork. Dooley immediately accused us of fecking the limb. Seán coolly informed him that he had just been climbing the tree for the challenge of it and when he placed his weight on the limb it had snapped off. He was lucky not to have fallen with it and broken his neck. Beaver and I supported his statement but the bailiff insisted he was going to have us summoned. We bluffed further, I even saying that he did not have a legal foot to stand on. Didn't I know all about these things 'cause I'd read them in my father's lawbooks? Paddy eyed me dubiously. Above in the tree Seán was grinning and Beaver said, 'That's right. He knows what he's talking about.' The upshot of it was that we rattled Paddy's confidence enough for him to let us go. But we had to leave the limb behind. An hour or so later, we were sitting across from the ball alley on the dome-shaped pile of rubble known to us as 'The Heap' when who should we see carrying the same limb into his house down the Lane but Tommy Parker.

'Hey, Parker, that's my limb!' shouted Beaver, half in earnest.

'Heh, heh. Tell me another wan,' Tommy laughed, going inside with his lucky acquisition.

'Well, fuck me! How do you like that?' said Beaver good-naturedly, and the three of us burst out laughing. Then we ignored for the moment the business of procuring wood. Later on, Beaver went back for his rope and maimed a tree elsewhere.

Girls and women as well as youths and men also went for a *brosna* – a bundle of sticks that could be used for kindling. For that you needed a length of strong cord or binder twine, a few old ties knotted together, or a long leather thong, the last-mentioned being the most prized and durable. You would lay the cord on the ground, arrange small branches of dry or dead wood across it until you had as much as you could carry, then secure the whole into a bundle that you could shoulder home. When the Warren was too closely watched by the bailiff Beaver and Cox used to go farther afield for a *brosna*, to a wooded area between the old golf course and the Blackwater that they knew among themselves as the 'Twig Bog'. Great wood was to be found there, evidently. I carried a *brosna* myself now and again but not to my own home as my parents were not keen on the idea. Mam might have been a little snobbish about it but Dad would more likely have felt that I was unwittingly taking what should have been left for the poor.

In other ways, I perceived their feelings to be reversed. A destitute family of six or seven, the Cooneys, lived in Church Lane and Mam used to help them out regularly with scraps of food and old clothing, and the odd bob now and again. It was Dad who used to get a bit embarrassed about this, mainly, I think, because the eldest daughter Mary was as tough as nails and her lifestyle used to offend against the stuffy morals of the town. There was always a chance that he might have to caution her. And maybe also he was a little worried lest Paddy and I might become fascinated by her adventurous nature. Which, in a sense, I did. I liked her free-wheeling style that often showed in little ways. Maybe I was 14, she 18, the day I was walking down the Lane toward her, near a few boarded-up houses that were due for repairs. As she passed them, humming to herself absent-mindedly, she belted in a half-dozen panes of glass in the small windows with the side of her fist. She grinned mischievously at me and I at her. I liked the touch of cool about her act.

Mrs Cooney was the one who used to embarrass me. In the high-pitched piercing voice that could lay waste anyone who crossed her, she insisted on calling Paddy and myself 'Master Pat' and 'Master James'. I hated this and said so to Mam and Dad but they only laughed at my embarrassment. I could never find the words myself to plead with Mrs Cooney to call me simply 'Jim' like everyone else did so I had to put up with it. She had a hard life and somehow if she felt she was doing the right thing in calling me 'Master James' why should I have disabused her?

Her husband Mikey (Burke his real surname), being a part-time if not full-time cattle drover, was nearly always away foot-slogging it around the country. It was said of him that he moved beasts from one location to another faster than any man in the business and that nobody could lower a pint of Guinness in less time than he. Not that Mikey would be trying to win any contests. He just consumed alcohol with the same tigerish energy that he did everything else. Tom Lineen was standing at the door of Madden's bar in Main Street one Fair Day and he saw Mikey accept a pint, down it and leave the bar before the farmer who was buying it for him had time to place his silver on the counter. You couldn't be much faster on the draw than that we figured. Mikey was as tough as his daughter Mary and, as a tool of his trade, always carried a fierce-looking ash plant in his fist. The only man ever to tangle with him and come out the right way up was Mick Coleman, a neighbour from across the Lane. As the tired old gunslinger in the pictures used to say, 'There's always somebody faster than you,' and Mick was Mikey's nemesis. By all accounts the drover took a hammering but he had a cute revenge when he won a subsequent court case after accusing Coleman of assaulting him in the ball alley. Mikey was okay. Even in his haste he'd always bid you the time of day. His eldest son, Michael, used to help him with the droving but never showed the same zest for it as his Dad. A much more laid back character, Michael could have been a fair handballer if he had applied himself seriously to it but he had little time for sport either. Mary the mother and the younger daughter Agnes were the ones who usually called to our house. They would have a sweet can with them for scraps of bread that had gone stale on us, or for the fresh cuts that Mam gave them occasionally too. When Mam was busy in the kitchen with Molly she would hand me the bread, wrapped in a piece of newspaper or placed in an enamel bowl, and ask me to give it to the callers. I used to be very confused doing this and struggled, I think, to understand the depths of their poverty. Knowingly or unknowingly, it was right of Mam to confront me with it.

Mrs Cooney was the only woman who daily wore a black shawl in Lismore. In contrast, in Carrick-on-Suir, scores of women wore this item of clothing. In the Wide Lane, next to my aunts' house, and in the Rookery by the West Gate – quarters equivalent to Botany and Church Lane that were slowly being demolished when I first saw them – it was a uniform. The Wide Lane was fairly open but the Rookery was still dark and mysterious and echoed with ghostly steps and disembodied voices. I would inch my way down it sometimes, then scamper back out again when my imagination sensed the sweet danger that my aunts had instilled in me about the place. As the houses were being pulled down the former inhabitants were being re-housed in a new council estate, furnished with baths and indoor toilets, on the Clonmel side of town called Treacy Park after the famous IRA man. To the middle class way of thinking, providing baths for the working class was an unnecessary luxury. My own mother unconsciously demonstrated this prejudice in telling me with amusement, and some scepticism it has to be said, that when the first tenants moved into these houses it was rumoured they used to keep the coal in the bath, a myth, I am sure, picked up from the English middle classes who have been attributed with the same remark about the English working class. Molly was from a lane farther down Greystone Street, Salt Yard Lane, and her mother Johanna, known as Annie, – squat, wide-faced, and with a fierce glint in her eye when her blood was up – was the toughest shawlie in Carrick.

The shawl was a unique piece of clothing and no woman better expressed its language than Annie – the imperious whip around the shoulder expressing contempt or anger, the comfortable sawing across the back after standing up, the wide-bodied arms akimbo stance with the garment stretched across the shoulders and elbows, throwing out a challenge or threat... . The movement I remember most, however, was the everyday toss of the shawl end around the shoulders as a woman set off for somewhere. All these were obvious signals. No doubt there were other ones beyond my comprehension, or that of any male, that only women could interpret. With the exception of the red, plaid garments frequently worn by tinker women, shawls, like Henry Ford's Model T motorcar, came in one colour only, black. It was a bizarre sight for my eyes to see a phalanx of women shawled in that sombre colour following a hearse at a funeral. Or to see the same women trading insults from the opposing sidelines at the local hurling derbies between the Swan and the Davins. Or just to see the shawls arranged around the shoulders of a group chatting amicably at the freshwater spring on the Well Road.

Growing older, I began to appreciate more the reasons why I was reasonably well-clothed. In calling at the homes of my less fortunate pals I would see the crowded conditions in which they lived and, bit by bit, came to an understanding of just how little money their families had to survive on. Then, in looking at myself, I began to realise that, although I was fortunate, I was not all that well-clothed either. In terms of underclothing I certainly had vests and woolly combinations for winter, 'coms' as Mam called them, but for most of my childhood I did not wear underpants. None of us boys did. I was already in long pants before I really became conscious of the desirability of wearing this civilized piece of apparel. But I was in short pants the first time I noticed a pair on anyone. I was doing a pooley alongside Mickey McConnell, a well-off pal who had come to live in the Villa, the big house across from us in West Street, and could see from the way he was struggling to get his prick out that he was wearing some sort of white undergarment. After the initial curiosity I felt that this was not an item of clothing that I would ever require. The memory of it only resurfaced when I was given my first long pants – a beige-coloured gabardine pair that had belonged to my brother. I had not worn it long when I noticed that it had become slightly yellowed around the crotch. At first I paid no attention to the stain but after a couple of weeks when it had become distinctly yellow the obvious reason dawned on me. Washing failed to remove it so I refused to wear the pants any longer. It must have been about then that Mam decided that it was high time she found the money to buy me some underpants.

Girls among the poor were no better off with knickers. The little ones, especially, had to do without. As a boy, you noticed things like that. Some girls, indeed, were almost into their teens before their parents could afford a pair of knickers for them. Mickey told me of how he and one of his pals had been hiding in the old barn in the grounds of the Villa where we regularly played when a girl we knew, who was already eleven or twelve years old, stopped with one of her pals to have a piss at the muddy entrance to the building. 'She lifted up her dress, opened her legs, and just pissed away. She had no knickers on! We saw *everything!*' my pal said in a hushed voice. We felt that for a girl she was a bit too big to go without. More interesting for us, however, was the confirmation of a point about the female anatomy. It never occurred to me that I was old enough to be wearing underpants myself at the time.

If the poor in the towns had it rough it was the tinkers who really suffered. They lived totally exposed to the elements. Their brightly coloured caravans were fine in summer, bearable in spring and autumn, but freezing in winter. And only a certain number had the security of such shelter. Many had to make do with a strip of canvas thrown over iron hoops, or other forms of makeshift tents. The wettings, the cold, the malnutrition, the lack of protective clothing, all took years off the tinker's life expectancy. It was often said that you rarely met one above the age of 45. Many I saw looked older than that, although as a youth I was not very expert at ascertaining the age of my elders.

Tinkers had extended families and particular ones seemed to predominate in particular localities, for example, around Lismore it was the Connors family, around Carrick-on-Suir, the Cartys. And Dad used to talk good-humouredly of a fiery MacDonagh clan who roamed up Sligo way. One of the Connors half-settled into a house in Church Lane, half-settled it was said because when travelling was in your blood it was almost impossible to reject it. In general, and not without reason, the travelling people were wary of the settled community. They had their own cryptic language, Shelta, and it was said that they would scribble secret signs, inconspicuous to the unknowing eye, on houses or farm gates that indicated to each other whether the occupier or owner of the premises was welcoming or not welcoming to them.

The core trade of the tinker, and the one from which their name derived, was the honourable one of tinsmithing which extended to sharpening knives, saws and other edged instruments. They manufactured tin cans, billy-cans and milk cans and regularly knocked on our doors to enquire whether we had any pots that needed mending. Sitting on the kerb outside, they would mend the holes with a kind of double-sided tin washer with a red rubber insert while you waited. On the artistic side, a number of them were fine fiddlers, capable of playing a wide range of jigs and reels, and good traditional singers. Selling ballad-sheets was an extension of this musical activity. The seller would sometimes pin samples of the sheets he was vending to the lapels of his jacket and when you paid him a penny would peel off a long coloured strip of paper from what looked like one of those rolls of banknotes you saw farmers and jobbers handling on a Fair Day. Green, yellow, orange or blue they usually came in, with the text in black. Colours in general you associated with the travelling people. Hear Gallows Hill shake on a clear day and you might look up and see a group of these resolute nomads hurtling down over the brow of it – some women in plaid shawls, the men in dark attire – fair or festival bound in their painted caravans and swaying flat-top carts. A flurry of green and red, and tossing foxy hair. Admirable the way the women and children balanced unconcernedly on the carts, floating over unexpected potholes with the same aplomb as over the flat, their menfolk fiercely intent, spurring on the piebald horses as if they could not get through our town fast enough. In no time they would flame past to sweep out of sight around the Monument corner, scattering question marks in their wake. Other places? Other jargons? Other gatherings? Enviable in summer the freedom tinkers enjoyed; in winter no one would have wanted to take their place.

CHAPTER FIVE

The Middle Class

SANDWICHED BETWEEN THE countryfied rich and the numerous poor was the middle class, to which, I suppose, my family belonged somewhere on the lower register. A *garda* sergeant cannot have earned very much when we could not afford a wireless until 1951 and then only on the never-never. But we had a maid, Molly, for some years. How we managed that I do not know. It is one of these things I should have clarified with my parents while they were still alive.

Class barriers in Ireland were strictly defined and no section of the community was more jealous of its place in the pecking order than the middle class, with its obsession with respectability. Regrettably, the educational system did more than its bit to keep us all in our places. It was transparent how occupations with a high social standing i.e. medicine, law, and the like, were passed on automatically from father to son and, occasionally, daughter. I cannot say I was ever impressed by this concern with respectability because I never really understood why people used to fuss about so artificial a concept. The Protestant minority had the edge over the Catholics in terms of temporal respectability – they held the financial cards for the most part – but the roles were thought by the latter to be reversed in terms of the after-life. But neither sect spat on the bit of money. The Protestants with their nuanced entrée to the great dukes of England, and to Trinity College Dublin, were the ones who set the social standards to which we were supposed to look up. The only person we had on the Catholic side who could look them straight in the face was Mrs Willy Redmond, the Fine Gael TD from the other end of the county. A *very* respectable woman with a *very* superior way of talking.

Each faith was depreciative of the other but, in the changed political circumstances since the establishment of the Free State, could not afford to be beastly to the other. Which put some strain on their Christian tolerances. The Catholics were inching their way out of the forelock-tugging stage and the Protestants were having to take account of the fact that the Republic was here to stay. Protestant and Catholic, for the most part, only mixed in the best places, i.e. the hunt ball, the tennis club, the badminton court, the cricket club, and at the point-to-point, hunt and gymkhana. Those at the top level of contact shopped at the Wine Vaults and drank at the Wine Vaults and the Devonshire Arms Hotel. Those on the lower brackets played a hell of a lot of whist. I only made it to the cricket club myself, having fallen out with the GAA Committee which looked after the juvenile and minor teams. The cricket club was the most democratic of the 'foreign' sports clubs. As it happened, I was no better at cricket than I was at hurling and Gaelic football so the move was of little significance to either allegiance.

Springing from this obsession with respectability was the Catholic middle-class penchant for *being seen* at prayer. It was not that this exterior show was confined only to the middle class – far from it, the poor could be spectacular in their devotion – it was just that they were the most consistent at it. We were all expected to put on our best clothes on Sundays and holy days. Mind you, the Protestants did this kind of thing too. But they seemed to make less of a fuss about it. Or maybe it was because there were fewer of them around to create a noticeable trek to their place of worship. Unlike the Catholics who streamed to St Carthage's Cathedral all morning long, some attending two Masses as well as a rosary in the evening. The stylish way to go to church was by horse and trap, like the Howards of Toortane. Countrymen came on their bicycles, their dark trousers carefully clipped at the ankle. In the chapel the best positions were hogged by the smartly dressed better-off, the women providing the main spectacle. One thing about the women that always struck me was how noisy they were. For them, none of that male business of shuffling up the aisle on tiptoes and edging into a seat. They made sure God knew they were coming. Clitter-clatter on high heels over the tiles and wrought-iron gratings, tap-tap along the wooden kneeling rail, click to open the handbag and *snap* to shut it. And if that was not enough, they prayed and sang louder than the men.

One May evening when I was about twelve I took a leaf out of their book, came in out of the sun through the open doors and strolled up the middle of the centre aisle to the front of the chapel when Father McGrath was in the middle of the rosary, a loose steel tip on one of my heels making a fierce clatter on the grating. I was perversely conscious that I was making an entrance, and I enjoyed it. The priest even lost his way in the Hail Mary momentarily. But what could he say in the face of such an outburst of faith? Wasn't I, after all, only flaunting my middle-class respectability? In doing the right thing in chapel you could be forgiven a lot, almost even the sin of adopting airs above your station. Being possessive of their niche in society the middle class liked the other classes to know theirs too, especially those on the rungs below them. Nell Foley, who created her own dresses, was the best-turned out woman in town – and one of the best-looking – but she came from Botany. So occasionally after she passed by you would see middle-class women snouting comments that were plainly on the nitpicking side among themselves. Not that any of it would have worried Nell. She was also the best female ballroom dancer around and used to win prizes to prove it when she stepped out with her husband Bill.

The middle classes appreciated that their kind in heaven got a better deal than their kind in hell, so paradise was where they insured themselves to spend eternity. And how best could you insure against your own failings than by raising a priest in the family? The farmers were very enamoured of this strategy too, and there was a sprinkling of priests of working class origin. Owning a priest was like staking your claim to a heavenly plot. A nun wasn't to be sniffed at but, saving the Reverend Mother, most nuns were regarded as a simple-minded lot – rather like vicars in the Church of England. A priest had his foot firmly on the rung of eternal preferment and, if he watched himself, might even make it on the temporal scene by rising to monsignor or bishop, or even cardinal – positions which could do his family no harm at all in the eyes of God, and only good in the earthly scheme of things.

The ultimate insurance was the 'deathbed confession', a most popular safety-valve in the religious experience of the middle classes. Only men seemed to succumb to this peculiar form of last-second ejaculation – hard-drinking, cruel, lascivious, ungodly men who retained that tiny spark of human decency that could not be denied at the very end. I never recall being given an example of a woman who pulled back from the brink. But, I suppose, the nuns had a few examples up their sleeves for the girls as well. The Irish middle classes, in general, liked a flutter, especially on the well-dressed racecourse, so why would they not have considered laying a standing bet on a no-hoper in the game of cosmic roulette? It was a canny little number. No matter how bad you were in life – cut-throat businessman, inveterate masturbator, patriot, the worst torturer in the SS – came the moment when you sensed yourself about to pop off, you said 'Father (meaning God), forgive me,' and the slate was wiped clean. In a flash. You did not even have to verbalise it. You could *think* it. And right up to your very last breath. 'Twas as close as that. Not even a stopover in Purgatory, well possibly, if you had been a real scoundrel like a corrupt soldier, cleric, politician or policeman, and there were not very many of those about. Of course, it *was* a high-risk strategy. There was no knowing if God in his infinite mercy wasn't going to do the dirty on you and pull the rug from under you before your time. In which case you were in for a nasty surprise, but probably, some very good company as well, hell being known for the wide range of licentiousness it offered.

Probably nobody expressed the middle-class ethic as clearly as the shopkeepers of the town. They knew the value of commodities and the pockets of their customers, so much so that some of them demonstrated the distressing habit of keeping poor customers waiting unduly while they served the better-off, or worse, allowed the latter to queue-jump. As a kid, you came last in line and sometimes I left a shop in annoyance when an adult was allowed to barge in before me. The shopkeeper's argument in such situations was twofold: one, the well-off customer's time was more valuable (to the customer, of course) and two, who the hell were you to be getting uppity anyway? Sometimes they gave you a bit of economic theory to let you know how tough times were for them. Peg Quinlan of Chapel Street, a small wiry woman, used to lay that moan on me now and again when I came into her grocery. I listened because she sold a brand of boloney to which I became addicted for a time – once I ate most of half a pound of it between the shop and home, a distance of no more than three or four hundred yards, and got a very stiff talking to from Mam who had sent me out to buy it. Peg would give out to me about Perks or MacDonalds Amusements staying on an extra week at Jackie Scanlan's Happydrome. 'They shouldn't be allowed to stay,' she said, 'They take money out of the town and it never comes back.' I stared at her pinched face as she elaborated on her theory, but failed utterly to understand what she was on about. Once I had spent my pennies they had left me. That was all I knew. Where they eventually wound up after that I had no idea, nor did I care. I certainly could not see Perks getting very far on my odd bob or tanner. For me it was a thrill they stayed on.

The shopkeepers might have expressed the ethic but it was the banks that considered themselves the true custodians of middle-class values. A job in a bank was a job for life, we were told in school, and it was a wise man who set his sights on counting other people's money. The banks – and we had two of them in Lismore, the Munster & Leinster and the National – did not pay very much in terms of hard cash, but in terms of respectability they were oceans of possibility. The youthful clerk was expected to socialise with the best while surviving on a pittance. Every bank manager connived in this charade that was considered to be an essential part of the bank clerk's training. Had they not been through it themselves? But bankers were not entirely oblivious to the needs of their staff. Financial assistance was at hand to ensure that employees joined the local tennis club or golf club or other desirable source of contact between them and their clients, real or prospective. How the official payed for a round of double brandies in this company was his problem. Women bank clerks were few and far between and tended to come from better-heeled families than their male counterparts. In bar and clubhouse they probably had the dubious advantage of having their drinks bought for them, although not all would have taken advantage of this, but they had to be careful to toe the line of sobriety, unlike their male colleagues. It seemed a grey and frustrating world to many of us and, certainly, the profession never attracted me in the slightest. Still, not all bank clerks were grey and a number of them managed to project refreshing personalities of their own. Jack Fogarty of the National used to have audiences in stitches at local concerts with his comic songs. Peter Kelly-Lynch of the Munster eschewed the world of polite games for the rough and tumble of junior hurling and football. And Jack Frawley of the National, father of my classmate Des, used to turn up now and again at the ball alley for a game of handball, at which he was dead handy. The town no longer had a golf club when I was growing up although there had been a small links on the rolling slopes just west of Ballyin Gardens. The tennis club was fortunate to have a picturesque, log-cabin clubhouse made of pine, across the threshold of which I only managed to sneak a foot once out of season, when an uninformed architectural curiosity led a couple of pals and me to explore the exterior of the building close up. In doing so we noticed that someone had forgotten to lock the door. Inside we crouched below the resin-perfumed windows and pictured ourselves fighting off a band of marauding Mohawks with our long muskets.

The major indoor recreation of the middle class was whist. Forty-five drives were a lesser obsession and table tennis and badminton made their appearance later. At least, that was the case in our town. In Cappoquin forty-five was the favourite card game. Card players would drive to Lismore from as far away as Youghal, Midleton and Dungarvan – a radius of some twenty miles – to sit in on Monster Whist Drives. Whichever game was played the same people seemed to be winning week after week. You could not help being aware of this because the most stubbornly boring section of the 'Lismore Notes' in the *Dungarvan Observer* and the *Dungarvan Leader* was a list of prizewinners' names. The prizes for whist carried baffling titles for someone like myself whose interest in cards stopped at a round of snap at home, or a round of poker, pontoon or twenty-five in the portico of Johnny Baldwin's little house in Church Lane on a rainy day. You won something if you were 'the longest seated' or had the 'lowest score' for God's sake, when in every other game it was the highest score that counted. Then there was 'the miniature' which sounded vaguely like the name of a dance I heard my mother mention. Whatever they called the prizes, come Christmas time they were not to be discounted. A turkey, a goose, or a sack of spuds, and that meant a *large* canvas sack of spuds, could be yours. For the regulars who attended the prize could just as well have been a square of Sharp's toffee. The point for them was to win at all costs and if you happened to be the unlucky dabbler who caused any of them to drop a game he, or she, would tear strips off you. You wouldn't want to be mentioning any names but it was surprising how the mask of middle-class decorum could slip under the pressure of such combative competition. On a couple of occasions in my early teens I talked my way into St Carthage's Hall where these drives used to take place and was a somewhat unwelcome guest loitering around players' backs as I battled to unravel the meaning of the phenomenon. I did not have long to wait for the fireworks and was enjoying them until Billy O'Brien, who used to act as MC, made it plain to me that this was no place for a sensitive young boy. One of the dicers took a different view and told me to fuck off because I was upsetting his concentration – probably the straight-talking Michael Lineen. Some of my schoolmates developed an interest in the game in their teens and did okay at it. 'Master' Jim Lineen, i.e. 'Thumper', and 'Master' Pierce Colbert both won prizes at one time or another. A handful of working class players dealt a hand as well, Jack Campion, the Labour Party councillor and salmon fisherman, and no man to cross when he held good cards, being one. But the game was dominated by the middle class. Regular winners would be people like Mrs John Scott-Allen, the petite salmon-fishing wife of the lanky, salmon-fishing, piano-tuner John, both of whom held licences to fish the best stretches of the Blackwater, an honour not accorded Jack who was equally, if not more, proficient with a rod. Father Denis McGrath, the zealous curate who organised his flock as successfully as his cards; Aggie Healy, the proprietress of the Arcade, the biggest drapery in town; Nora Willoughby, an up-and-coming shopkeeper; Guard Houlihan, the senior guard at the barracks; the schoolteacher Miss Mountayne of Strancally; Jimmy Glasse, the electrician; and the fiery Hannah Drohan who hailed from Shrough but lived in the town, were others who took home the bacon.

I suppose it was Mam's unspoken desire that I should make my way in this middle-class world also. She never came on heavy about it and must have been disillusioned to see her gentle nudging elbowed aside by an indifferent younger son. With Paddy she was more successful. He was a good scholar, widely-read, had a gift for music, and possessed polished manners.

CHAPTER SIX

The Library

LISMORE WAS FAVOURED with a handsome library building, a good book stock and, just as important, a fine librarian with a committed sense of what librarianship was all about. I was favoured in that the granite-ornamented, red-brick building was situated on the lower end of Gallows Hill, no more than a hundred yards from where I lived. It required either a black sense of humour or a sense of justice, or possibly both, to establish a store of learning at the feet of ghosts, hanged for whatever reason. When the hill first acquired its grim name I do not know but possibly it was in the seventeenth century when Lismore Castle was caught up in the indiscriminate cycle of retribution during the wars of Charles I and Cromwell. The library was a Carnegie Free Library and the people of our town were fortunate that the Town Commissioners of the period when Carnegie grants for libraries were on offer had the good sense to say 'yes' to that strange Scotsman who gifted 3,000 libraries across the globe and who wanted Home Rule for Ireland as well as for the country of his birth. Dungarvan, the largest town in the county after Waterford City itself, seemed to have spurned the offer and, as a consequence, had no publicly funded library at all. The seaside town did, for a time, have a subscription library – Hill's Lending Library and Reading Room – but that could not in any way be compared in scope to ours. Even Carrick-on-Suir, a town of about the same size as Dungarvan with circa 4,500 to 5,000 inhabitants, could not boast of a public library. Perhaps only smaller towns in Ireland were eligible to apply for Carnegie money? Maybe there were some clerical or political ramifications? A history of the establishment of the Carnegie Free Libraries in the island of Ireland would be an interesting subject for study. (Since I wrote these lines in 1995 just such a study has been published, and it is an excellent one I am delighted to say, *Irish Carnegie Libraries: A Catalogue and Architectural History* by Brendan Grimes; Irish Academic Press, Dublin, 1998. Details of the Lismore library, accompanied by a 1910 photograph and an architectural plan are given on pages 188–90.)

The restored Lismore Library in September 1994.

The Lismore building, through the informed decision of the Commissioners, had evolved into becoming the headquarters of the County Waterford Library Service, the tentacles of which stretched even to Carrickbeg, the County Waterford quarter of the essentially Tipperary town of Carrick-on-Suir. So for a small town of its size, scarcely more than a village, Lismore was bountifully supplied with literature. And the townspeople were well aware of this, not just from the cultural aspect but also from the point of view of the jobs it provided. These jobs were pitifully few but in a town that possessed no industry whatsoever every single post had to be defended. Our hold on the library was thus tenacious, too tenacious for the county librarian, Fergus Murphy, who clearly saw the anomaly of having the county headquarters stuck away in a little place on the Cork border when the obvious geographical and demographic centre, Dungarvan, totally lacked a public-funded service. The modest library accommodation at Lismore hardly constituted an ideal base for a regional service. In effect, a library that in normal circumstances might have functioned as a branch, had been elevated, for historical reasons, to the status of Central Library. There was another factor in Dungarvan's favour; the regional county council offices were already based there. Aside from the question of population, the fifteen-mile span that separated our two towns was more than just a perception in people's minds at a time when there were very few motorcars on the road. At a more practical level, Fergus was able to weigh in with the argument that the fabric of the library building in Lismore was fast deteriorating and the shelf space offered was inadequate for the library's purposes. The Librarian's case was logical and, no doubt, eloquent but after years of haggling in the County Council the lobby for keeping the Headquarters in Lismore, spearheaded by Jim Ormonde, the Fianna Fáil milkman-farmer who lived up the street from us, won. And I have to admit I was glad when it did. We had little enough in Lismore and if our library had been downgraded a fair share of our pride would have sunk with it. I think Dad was happy to see the library stay as it was also, although he was sorry on Fergus's account because he felt that logic was on the librarian's side. It *was* tough on Fergus, who, at a personal level, would probably have welcomed the opportunity of setting up a new service in a lively seaside town rather than stay on in a quiet backwater. But he did not lose the battle entirely. Once the final decision was taken work soon commenced on the repair and renovation of the library building, and a new garage was raised next to it – unfortunately on the shrubby site where some of us children used to pick up the basics of courting, so we lost out too – to house the splendid new bookmobile that was to replace the big old blue pantechnicon that had, literally, been run into the ground. I got a lift to Carrickbeg once in that old van from Fergus's deputy, Matt Gough, and nearly choked on the petrol fumes coming from the engine. The new dark green van was a purpose-built sparkler and Andy Drohan was the lucky man who got the job of driving it.

Being county librarian must have been a tedious and thankless job in some ways. The worst aspect would have been the interference of the library committee in the process of book choice. The choosing of books for his or her users is one of the most important tasks that a librarian has to perform and is one that the librarian, who is sensitive to his readers' needs, welcomes advice about, that is, sensible and/or specialist advice, *not* busybody interference. I suspect it was the last-mentioned that Fergus and his homologues up and down the country had to put up with in the censorious atmosphere that pervaded our lives. A crusty old parish priest, inured to airing his prejudices, was invariably the chairman of the library committee. And there was no end of petty bureaucrats and politicians, male and female, on it, anxious to label everything outside their narrow experience of life 'objectionable' or 'suggestive', or just plain 'dirty'. Voluntary advice was lent the committee by busybody members of the public who had nothing else to do but ferret out 'bad language' and 'unwholesome situations' on the open shelves. Walter Macken used to regularly find himself stripped from the bookshelves of his native country for his earthiness.

Dad was a voracious reader, especially of Irish writers, and Fergus would occasionally lend him new books, particularly those of writers like Macken that his antennae told him were likely to be banned, in advance of their being processed and displayed. Fergus knew that the books were safe with Dad, who was a fast reader and would turn them around quickly. Besides, our house was on his way to work should he need to reclaim any of them at short notice. There *was* such an occasion in 1952 or '53. Dad had just started Macken's *The Bogman* when Fergus called to the barracks on his way home from the office to inform him, with an apologetic grin, that he would need the book back first thing in the morning because someone somewhere in the county had complained about 'the bad language in it'. Consequently, he was having to withdraw it. And return it to the bookseller presumably? Dad was working late that night and, when he got in, stayed up to finish the story. I had peeked through the book with prurient curiosity and could not fathom what was supposed to be objectionable about it. 'The language is coarse,' Dad laughed. 'But sure that's no reason to ban it'. He seemed greatly amused by the affair and that was the reaction of a man who rarely swore himself. Fergus, I can only imagine, must have been bloody exasperated.

The county was fortunate to have a man of Fergus's quality in charge of its library services. Dad and Mam thought very highly of him and all of my school pals and I greatly respected him because there was something transparently honourable about him. Though he was a shy man he never passed you in the street without exchanging a word or two in Irish with you. He was a fluent Irish speaker and always signed himself 'F. MacMurchadha, Leabharlannaidhe Chonndae' in his official capacity. And he always cut a striking figure – slight frame, long stride, long silvery hair, bunch of books or other documents clutched against his ribcage. He was anxious to see the books on his shelves borrowed and read, and must, I think, have been a very good librarian indeed. The only reproach I could make of him was that you seldom saw him in the library in the evenings when you went to borrow books as he always worked a nine-to-five and was then occupied in

An early roadside encounter with a written document. I seem singularly unimpressed. Lismore, c. 1939.

the backroom on administrative tasks. On the evenings that new items went on the open shelves it was a rare pleasure to see him buzzing about the publicly accessible areas.

I started using the library early. We were encouraged by our teachers. But also, I had had enough of Old Mother Hubbard and the Old Woman Who Lived In A Shoe with Hey Diddle Diddle singing a Song of Sixpence. In order to become a member you had to have a pale green card (postcard size) signed by a 'Responsible Person', i.e. teacher, *garda*, doctor, solicitor, or some other figure of authority. Once you had got over that hurdle your tickets were written out for you. It was a thrill to be handed your own set with your own name on them, even if you were restricted to borrowing from the children's section only until you were fourteen.

The biggest thrill was when the new books arrived, usually in the spring and autumn months. You knew when to expect them because the library would always be closed for a week before they appeared on the shelves. High with anticipation, I would queue at the entrance early so that I would be sure of getting first crack at the new arrivals. Well, I would not always get first crack but I would be somewhere at the front, usually close enough to get to sit on the few steps leading to the churchy wooden door. Those of us gathered there would while away our time with chat and maybe a hand of pontoon or twenty-five until we heard Ann Vaughan, 'Miss Vaughan' to us, slipping the bolts on the inside of the door. Then we were in, barely suppressing our excitement, politely pressing past her, increasing our steps as we approached the low shelves at the end of the room. Once at the point of take-up it was a quick grab for a half-dozen likely titles from which you would then select the number, four at maximum, that your tickets entitled you to borrow. At normal times you could freely use tickets belonging to other members of your family as well as your own but when the new books became available you were, quite fairly, restricted to the use of your own to ensure that everyone got a fair crack of the whip. An early trick you learned was to return your previous books a week or two before the new ones arrived - by doing this you would turn up with tickets at the ready and not get delayed at the desk returning books on your way in. In my early years I was generally on the lookout for the new Biggles and William stories. By that time the comics that had helped to instil the reading habit in me were beginning to lose some, but not all, of their appeal.

The Beano had been my favourite; 'Lord Snooty and His Pals', Hairpin Higgins, Skinny Lizzie, Snitchy and Snatchy, etc.; 'The Shipwrecked Circus', 'Pansy Potter the Strongman's Daughter', 'Jimmy and His Magic Patch', and so on, and Big Eggo the ostrich on the cover. It struck a good balance between text and pictures and straight cartooning. As you grew older you began to get more pleasure from the items that carried the most text. 'Jimmy and His Magic Patch' – "I wish I lived in ..." was all he had to say and 'Whoosh!' he was transported to another time and place. In 'The Shipwrecked Circus' you could follow the adventures of Samson, Danny and Gloopy the Clown on Crusoe Island as they battled with the dangers of the deep and the badmen of the South Seas. I liked 'The King on the Flying Horse' too because the king's name was Dermod. In the companion comic *The Dandy* Desperate Dan was easily my favourite of the cartoon strips. Laughs all through and a big cowpie from Aunt Aggie at the end. This publication had characters with unforgettable names too – Korky the Cat, Keyhole Kate, Whiskery Dick, and Poor Old Nosey whose nose was so long he had to trundle it around in a wheelbarrow. The best thing in *The Dandy*, however, was Black Bob, a story in text with some illustrations, about a sheepdog which, in trying to return to his master in the south of England, encountered all sorts of adventures and performed all types of good deeds along the way. Come Christmas, you had bonus hardback annuals of both comics.

It was curious the way I went for Biggles and Ginger, and Algie and Bertie, because other stories about the Royal Air Force singularly failed to interest me. These others were to be found in the second generation of comics to which I had graduated – *The Wizard*, *The Hotspur* (a title I never understood) and *The Rover*, which carried jingoistic prangs like 'Squadron X', 'The Phantom Flier' and 'Rockfist Rogan'. Rockfist was the best of these in my eyes, partly because he had an Irish-sounding name, but even with him I became bored, annoyed and sceptical in turn as the 'Britishers' were *always* winning. I knew nothing of the reality of the Second World War (this was to hit me in my youth) and was forced to ask myself if the Germans could really be as bad as they were portrayed. Of this second generation, *The Rover* was easily my favourite read. It was *The Rover* that had 'It's Goals That Count', the sporting adventures of Nick Smith, the Captain of Redburn Rovers, international inside-left and master tactician. Beefy, square-jawed, short-back-and-sides, he could find the solutions to all the problems of his team. Then he, the most sporting of players, was sent off for the first time in his life. We couldn't believe the headline, nor the illustration – the dejected slope of the shoulders, the look of shame. But he bounced back, of course.

The Rover had J.A. Slade, 'the deadliest gunman in the West', ambiguous anti-hero, boss of the Rocky Ridge Division of the Pony Express, whose skill with a six-gun was only equalled by his deadly enemy, Wal Loader, the Pony Express rider who had sworn to kill him. The odd thing was, that Loader, for one reason or another, always seemed to find himself in the embarrassing position of having to save Slade from the 'Redskins'. *Loader had sworn to kill Slade. Now he fights to save him. Why?* read the banner headline at the top of one of the stories. After Slade had had a successful run *The Rover* introduced us to another hero of the Old West, Deliberate Daniel, the immaculately dressed lawman who wore black from head to toe, rode a black horse, and wore a white carnation. (We took it for granted that fresh supplies of this flower were readily available.) 'What a dude!' the locals would sneer, until they saw him standing his ground coolly in the middle of Main Street, the bullets from the badman's six-gun screeching past his head. 'He's got nerves of rawhide,' someone would be forced to admit admiringly. Then Daniel, strategically placed out of range of the short-barrelled enemy fire, would slowly and surely draw his unique long-barrelled Colt from his shoulder-holster, carefully level it and loose off just one shot. And that was the end of the baddie. In those days, as today, the American hero relied on superior weaponry to win his war for him. In *The Rover* you had Morgyn the Mighty, a British strongman admittedly, but no less exciting for that, duelling to the death on a jungle-clad island with Banzu the Jap and Emil Ironfist. For down-to-earth athletics and realistic social background the comic gave us Alf Tupper, 'The Tough of the Track', found as often at his local employment exchange looking for work as running exciting miles in the stadium. At one stage *The Rover* even had an Irish hero – or was it simply a name change for the benefit of the Irish consumer? Barney Brannigan, I think his name was, a hobo boxer, a kind of middleweight on the run, who took on a different opponent in each number. One of the three comics had a gripping series to which I was addicted, the title of which now escapes me, about English marauders who slipped across the English Channel at night to inflict casualties and humiliation upon the forces of Napoleon which were massing along the French coast. The object of it all was to dissuade the power-hungry dictator from attempting to land on British soil. Resonant, no doubt, for an English audience.

I bought all my comics from Jackie Scanlan, the Main Street newsagent and Happydrome impresario. He had the widest range and I was probably one of his best customers. Calling to his shop in the latter half of each week filled me with anticipation. I would arrive clutching my few coins, place them on the high counter, and wait breathlessly while Jackie picked out the issues with my name scribbled on them. I seldom took less than one and seldom more than two at any one time. I would have taken an issue of every comic on his shelf had I been able to afford it. Then it was straight home to get stuck into the next thrilling or funny adventures of my heroes. Now and again an issue would get delayed and I would be very disappointed. When this occurred I would harry Jackie and his missus two or three times a day until the overdue item arrived.

Along with *The Rover* the other comic I took regularly was *The Wizard*, and that was because it featured Wilson, the ageless athlete. No one knew how old he was; he could have been a century, or ten centuries. Bony, muscular, taciturn, patriotic, indifferent to cold and pain, he lived and trained on the Yorkshire moors. He always wore black running gear, stylewise ahead of his time in his T-shirt and long-john track bottoms. Nobody knew his thoughts, except the lone newspaper reporter who recounted his exploits in the comic, and he was none too sure either. Wilson was reeling off sub-four-minute miles before anyone had heard of them. Sometimes he would come up to the starting line well after his rivals had been gunned away and would still outrace them, which really annoyed the nasty ones among his competitors, especially the foreign ones. He ran times worthy of the 1980s in the marathon, smashed records in jumping, boxing, pole-vaulting, the javelin, you name it. World records left him cold. "Oh?" he would shrug on being told that he had smashed yet another.

All the comics had a football hero, Nick Smith of *The Rover* being the archetype, of course, and 'Limpalong Leslie' was *The Wizard's*, interestingly, as his name suggests, a player with a permanent limp but with great sleight of foot. *The Hotspur* featured the best footballer of the lot, 'Cannonball Kid', and that was my only reason for reading that particular publication which I used to get hold of by swopping my *Wizard*. Cannonball was the best centre-forward in the game and when he lashed out with his right foot the ball was a leathery streak that often tore the goal netting. It was in *The Wizard* I came across my first motorbike hero, Whizz Morgan, the ace of the speedway track. Schoolboy yarns never turned me on – the quaint customs of the public school, in which, for some arcane reason, they were invariably set, held little interest for me. *The Wizard's* yarn, 'Smith of the Lower Third' was, at least, readable. It was this comic too that featured a bizarre cover tableau, 'Spadger Isle'; if it wasn't racist it certainly peddled stereotypes – the white Captain Sam and Spadger, the funny, rubber-lipped blacks called Rastus and Sambo, and the like.

American comics rarely came my way until I had the bright idea of introducing myself to my first cousins in the United States whom I had never met and suggesting we do a swop. I did not really expect to hear from them and was thrilled when my uncle John Ballantyne's daughter Catherine wrote and agreed. When I opened the first parcel that arrived it contained a brown Kelloggs cornflakes carton out of which popped *Superman, Batman, The Joker, The Phantom, Mandrake the Magician,* etc. I gasped in delight and uttered my first 'Wow!' Then I thought of what I had sent them, and compared my dull-looking British publications with the spectacular and multi-coloured thrillers laid out before me. Clearly, I was getting the better of the deal. But what else had I to exchange? Soon another box arrived by post. This time, *Spider-man*, and an even bigger sensation, *The Life of Joe Louis*, my greatest boxing hero, told in comic-strip form, in two coloured parts.

For a long time I refused to let any of those comics out of the house. Pals were welcome to come in and read them. Then once when I was ill – it was after I had had a bad fall off a tree, I think – I relented and in one go lent all of them to someone who did not even come from Lismore, one of the Dungarvan Spratts who was holidaying at Ormondes, our neighbours. I had grown to like him and thought he was trustworthy. I never saw him or the comics again. Was I sore! I wrote him a couple of times and never even got a reply. There was one saving grace. I had not lent him absolutely everything. The Louis biography I kept back. But it was not the comics that worried me – by then I had read them so many times I knew them by heart. What irked and hurt was that I had misjudged the fucker. It was a lesson I took in.

The American comics stood out for their brilliant design, outlandish characters like the Joker, and little felicities like the passionate kiss between a flame-haired temptress and a naval lieutenant in a Phantom episode. The Phantom himself, with whom beautiful princesses seemed ever to be falling in love, was never the beneficiary of more than a chaste peck. You did not forget things like that. I chuckled at funny characters like Mutt and Jeff, Popeye, Olive Oyl, Wimpy and Swee'Pea. But I was not totally receptive to American humour any more than I was to British. Donald Duck and Goofy were rib-ticklers but Mickey Mouse was just Mickey Mouse. As for the Katzenjammer Kids, I saw no humour in them at all.

In 1950 a new departure in British comics was fanfared – *The Eagle*. It certainly looked and felt different. In size more like a tabloid newspaper, it was printed on art paper, and was vastly more colourful than any other British comic I had seen. But I was uncertain about how seriously I should take it. Its main attraction was 'Dan Dare, Pilot of the Future', a wholly conventional and recognisable RAF type with perhaps a dash of Dick Tracy, the American crime-buster whom I could put aside at any time. Very un-American, however, was Dare's roly-poly jolly batman Digby, who always called him 'Sir'. Rather than these two, it was the green inhabitants of the planet Mekonta, particularly the evil little Mekon, that made you go back for more. The strange animals encountered on other planets held a fascination too. By comparison, Dare and his pals appeared somewhat ridiculous – all 'Up chaps and at 'em', 'Come on the fleet', etc. The strip I liked most in *The Eagle* was 'Harris Tweed, Extra Special Agent', and this only appeared in black and white. Harris had a big jaw, furry black moustache, wavy black hair, and was really funny. Other than that there was only Lash Lonergan, an Australian cowboy who, as his name implied, was handy with a bull-whip and who, from his surname might have had Irish ancestry. An extra panel I always turned to was 'Learn Boxing with Freddie Mills' as it was about his time also that I began purchasing a periodical other than a comic, Nat Fleischer's *The Ring*. You could not buy *The Ring* in Lismore because there was no call for it the newsagents supposed, but in boxing-mad Dungarvan it was available. Whenever Dad had business in that town he would buy me the latest issue at the big newsagents in Grattan Square.

Comics were very much a form of literature for boys, and were so marketed. You looked twice if you saw a girl immersed in one. There *was* a girls' comic for a time, *The Schoolfriend,* and it was not bad. The main serial in it, set in a public or independent school, was much more interesting than the male equivalent in the pages of our comics, although the formula was the same – heroine and her friends in conflict with nasty head prefects and the like; secret panels and hidden tunnels in and around the old school building, and so on. Stirring stuff, but ultimately predictable.

The English comics were widely available and, though we Irish children liked them, we did not swallow all the British heroics uncritically. A similar, healthy scepticism tempered our enjoyment of the endless victories of the US cavalry over the 'Red Indians' in the pictures. I suspect the British publishers knew this too. Hence their giving us the odd Irish or Irish-sounding hero. Indeed, we sometimes used to wonder whether the jingoism we encountered wasn't a toned-down version for Irish consumption. In spite of such doubts, I myself remained an avid reader of the British product. Not all of my schoolmates, however, shared my enthusiasm. Most of us would have dearly liked to have Irish comics of the same quality as the English ones but the economics of the comic publishing industry would have been unfavourable to such a venture, I am sure. We did have our Irish monthly, the *Our Boys* published by the Irish Christian Brothers, which featured the scary, gripping, ghost stories of 'Kitty the Hare'. When Kitty drew her shawl around her shoulders and settled down to stoke the imagination of her enthralled readers with the latest of her supernatural tales we were riveted. I think I believed a lot of what she told. It was a lovely feeling to be curled up safe in your bed reading her on a dark winter's night with the wind howling outside and the rain lashing against the window-panes. You could almost see her sheltering under a tree, and hear her voice. There were stories of leprechauns and crocks of gold in *Our Boys*, too, but Kitty was the ace attraction.

It was she who inspired us to a macabre game of dare. The challenge was to cross the Old Graveyard of St Carthage's on one's own on a dark, preferably foggy or stormy winter's night. It was no joke I tell you because in addition to the images conjured up by the storyteller our minds harboured vivid graveyard scenes from the pictures of Boris Karloff and Bela Lugosi. The routine was that the one accepting the dare was given a leg up over the wall on the Fernville/Chapel Street side of the New Cemetery. Then he was on his own, just he and the ghosts of the dead who might pop up from behind any tombstone at any moment and freeze him with a cold stare. In the meantime the rest of us would dash around via Chapel Street and up the elegant avenue of yews that led into the cemetery to await his exit at the other side. I never did it by myself. It was one thing to be in the graveyard with a couple of your pals – I could hear my heart pumping even then – totally another to be in there on your own. Not many did the solo run, and run they did, with the possible exception of Tommy Hartnett who would have sauntered through a steam of vampires without turning a hair. Around Hallowe'en the lads from Townparks had another stunt. They would carve skulls out of large turnips, put lighted candles in the hollow of them, and thrust the spectral heads onto the top of the wall from inside the cemetery, at the same time uttering an unearthly wail, when some unsuspecting person, usually a woman or group of girls, was passing. That made a few people jump because the road was gloomy and quiet at the mouth of Hospital Lane, known to us simply as the Boreen.

Other than *Our Boys* the only other Irish comic I used to see was the annual Christmas cumulation of the bizarre antics of 'Count Curly Wee and Gussie Goose'. The *Irish Independent* featured this cartoon strip in its daily editions and I have to confess that I found it impenetrable. The reason may have been that I so seldom read this newspaper and when I did, it was at Feeney's. We took the *Irish Press* in our home. In annual form the strip made a kind of sense but it still left me cold. Just as our parents were divided into those who read the Fianna Fáil *Irish Press* or the Fine Gael *Irish Independent* we youngsters could probably have been segregated into those who understood Curly Wee and those of us who were clueless about it. Our elders might well have been cute enough to exploit this where they wished to sound out the political leanings of people they did not know very well. 'And what do you think of Curly Wee?' the seemingly harmless question might go. If you reacted blankly your parents would be put down as Fianna Fáil supporters or, just possibly, readers of the *Irish Times*. A positive reaction would classify them as Fine Gael.

As I grew out of the comics I got locked into the *Old-Time Stories of*

Erin, retold by Alice Dease, which I reread many times. *Swallows and Amazons* started me on a succession of the Arthur Ransome stories, from which I picked up useful hints on lighting camp fires, reading spoor, handling boats, and so on. After this transition period I graduated to the adult section of the library and gorged myself on a course of westerns. By the time I was 16 I had read every one on the shelves, except the Zane Greys that were tediously worthy and lacked sufficient gun-play. The others I could finish on the day I started them, often after lights-out under the bedclothes with the aid of a torch (you stayed downstairs until it was bedtime). I did finish one Zane Grey and, curiously, the only scene I can recall from all the westerns I devoured is from that. Of the countless other stories of the Wild West that I read, I remember only that a lot of them were written by Max Brand, a fair number had Texas Rangers in them, and they carried titles like *The Untamed, Six Shooter, Along the Rio Grande* or *The Wyoming Trail*. As well as what I got in the library there was a series of softcover adventures of the Texas Rangers that I used to buy in newspaper shops, mainly in Dungarvan. They all brought a new dimension to the B-westerns that I never missed at the Palladium. And their gunpowder fuelled the reading habit.

Thrillers were the logical next step so I launched myself into *The Saint, Bulldog Drummond* and *Blackshirt*. I must have read Sapper's hero very uncritically because the fascist in his makeup entirely escaped me. At this point in my life our own domestic politics were confusing enough. What happened elsewhere in the world only reached me through occasional headlines. Still, I recognised an underdog when I came across one and that was something. The Saint was, perhaps, less spine-tingling than Drummond but as a character was more satisfying and entertaining. Bruce Graeme's 'Blackshirt', alias the successful writer of thrillers Richard Verrell, was no fascist, in spite of his pseudonym. Rather a toff with a fetishistic taste for silk – black silk scarf, black silk socks. Did he wear black silk knickers as well? His expensive tastes did not stop at silk. Oh no. He wore shoes, black of course, 'that could only have come from a modelled last' and a Gibus opera hat, whatever that was. A sound chap with contacts in the right places, nonetheless. You easily got through one of his cases in a night.

By the time I was 15 or 16 I was edging toward 'serious fiction', but still eschewing the classics. The closest I got was a book I picked up not in the library but in our own bookcase at home, *The Sword of O'Malley* by Justin Mitchell (Talbot, Dublin, 1920). I read it while I was ill in bed. A Ruritanian romp, maybe, but O'Malley, the Wild Goose exile, was a dashing hero. A master swordsman, pictured in the frontispiece as tall and elegantly attired, a sardonic grin on his face, sitting back against the edge of a table, effortlessly parrying with a long poker the deadly rapier of his wild-eyed foe. And that scene where, seriously wounded after he has fearlessly rescued the beautiful Princess Irene from a blazing building, he utters in a fever his forbidden declaration of love, 'Irene, beloved, come, oh come!' You don't forget high romantic drama like that. I also attempted a long Russian novel, well fairly long, one volume only. The title of it escapes me but in its pages I was surprised and excited to encounter a vivid scene in which one of the male characters had it off with a farm maid on the flat of a discarded barn door in a muddy haggard. Very Russian but also a scene that an Irish country lad could envisage. Rattle the latch! On checking out the book at the library desk, I discovered that, although it wasn't a new item, I was the first borrower. Long Russian novels were evidently not to the taste of the readership of Lismore, or to that of the beady-eyed censorious busybodies who might have caused the book to be removed from the shelves for its frank description. Furtively, I congratulated myself and filed another image of humanity's sexual quest in my mind. The novel, sadly, was heavy going otherwise.

My tastes in literature were, on the whole, divergent from those of my parents and brother. Dad would read everything he could lay his hands on about Irish life and history and was widely read in Irish fiction. But his interests went beyond this. For example, he enjoyed T. E. Lawrence's *Seven Pillars of Wisdom* and it was clear that he greatly admired the man, both as writer and soldier. And he and Mam loved the short stories of O. Henry (as well as those of Frank O'Connor, of course). I never recall hearing him humming, let alone singing, a song but, from his Garda Síochána training days in 1923, he retained a leather-bound copy *of The Poetical Works of Thomas Moore* (Reprinted from the early editions, with explanatory notes, &c. London: Frederick Warne and Co. no date). We also had in the house gramophone records of John McCormack singing some of Moore's popular melodies, e.g. 'Tis the Last Rose of Summer', 'Oft in the Stilly Night', 'Believe me if all those Endearing Young Charms', 'She is Far from the Land', and 'The Harp that once through Tara's Halls'. I assume that Dad liked to read the poems. The book was fairly well thumbed.

When he got into a book that deeply interested him he could not put it down. Coming in late at night after a spell of duty he would pick one up and lose all sense of time. Mam would invariably wake up in the middle of the night and go down and call him. On one occasion she found him asleep in the armchair in the dining room at four o'clock in the morning with an open book resting on his hands. From all this reading he had amassed a store of anecdotes that he could draw on. One he liked to relate about George Bernard Shaw concerned the time Winston Churchill put one over on the Irish wit. It appeared the writer had sent the politician two complimentary tickets for the opening night of his latest play with the note, 'For you and a friend, if you have a friend.' To which Churchill replied, 'I'll go on the second night, if there is a second night.' Dad would laugh heartily at this and, though he had strong reservations about Churchill's attitude toward the Irish, was tickled that the Englishman had proved himself more than a match for the opinionated Shaw.

Mam's favourite writers were probably Daphne Du Maurier and A. J. Cronin, her favourite book possibly *Gone with the Wind*. She would occasionally be found reading biographies of the saints and out of piety she read the Irish Catholic paper *The Standard* and later on the English equivalent, *The Universe*. Piety too led her to take a little red devotional periodical called *The Messenger* but this, unlike the weekly newspapers, seemed to lie around unread. Dad wasn't much into the Catholic press, and neither were my brother and I. Papers that were full of pictures of nuns, priests and bishops, and had no sport to speak of, were hardly geared to attract my attention. What Mam enjoyed reading most, I think, was the daily paper. At the end of the day she would sit down and read it from first to last, commenting on various events as she went along. Paddy was passionately interested in European history and in the lives of the English monarchs, and he regularly took the English periodical *Everybody's*. Molly I would only see skimming through the newspapers. She claimed she found my *Beano* and *Dandy* silly but I caught her having a giggle over them once or twice all the same.

That I acquired the reading habit myself was undoubtedly due to the example of my parents and my brother. It was no harm for me either to be aware that not everyone in the family, let alone those outside it, shared my own tastes in reading matter. That I became a librarian in later life is in no small measure due to the use I made of the Lismore Carnegie Free Library and to the positive image of librarianship projected by Fergus Murphy and Matt Gough, who, in the midst of their duties, would occasionally allow Paddy or me into the workroom, a musty Aladdin's cave piled ceiling high with books of all descriptions and sizes, and let us ferret out a withdrawn item or two to keep.

CHAPTER SEVEN

Religion

RELIGION IN LISMORE, and probably in the whole of the island known as Ireland, was in turn funny, sad, elevating, mindless, consoling, cruel, bizarre, exotic, grim, grotesque and ridiculous, but, for all of that, you never took it less than seriously. It gave you a hard time and promised you nothing but a dream in the pre-Sputnik sky called paradise. Who wouldn't have wanted to live out eternity in a place that rolled off the tongue so sensuously and poetically? We only had Christianity in one form or another, and my direct experience was of Catholicism, the faith in which I was brought up. With the other limbs of Christian belief I had but tangential contact, regrettably. I was, I think, a pretty devout practitioner of my faith. Indeed, at times, I went through moments of such exaggerated holiness I scarcely knew myself. But my feet never really left the ground. I certainly never for one moment felt like succumbing to the blandishments of the missionary priests who used to come on extended visits to our school in the hope of recruiting some of us in our impressionable years for the task of civilizing the pagan. The obstacle for me was, that in spite of the indoctrination to which I was being subjected, I could see nothing wrong in being a pagan. On the contrary, paganism in many ways seemed a much more attractive proposition than Catholicism, or any other brand of Christianity within my experience. Not that all proselytizing stopped with the pagan. Protestants were encouraged to see the light as well. You heard of people being given 'instruction' in Catholic dogma. (Muriel Sutton of Mayfield underwent this in order to marry Jackie Walsh, the cobbler.) After successfully clearing this obstacle, they became converts, figures often so committed to the faith we took for granted they put you to shame. A pagan, it seemed to me, was onto a much better option. He could go through life without a guilt trip and still get to his own peculiar heaven.

The recruiters usually came around during the school retreats, which were sometimes slammed on us at fairly short notice if the brothers or priests perceived that our religious standards were slipping. There was usually an annual one in the autumn. During the three or four days of the retreat we were expected to display a heightened fervour. We would set up an altar in one of the classrooms where Mass could be said. You padded around in silence from one room to another, looking for a private niche in which to meditate but also, perhaps, a window to look forlornly out of when you realised just how bad you were. Silence was never total. There was always a whispered aside to a pal. 'What time is it?' 'Jasus, you're looking very holy.' An attempt to make you giggle, 'Did you hear the one about – ?' And non-verbal communication was maintained at all times – a nudge, a wink, a glance to exchange feelings about what was going on, or what might go on afterwards. Undeniably the best thing about the retreat for me was that I had time off from lessons. I think I performed as well as the next fellow, and a sight better than some. It never sank in that I was supposed to use this period to map out a pattern for my future life on earth as well. As far as I was concerned, I could see no end to the charming life I was leading in Lismore. The end result of the retreat was always a bit depressing, even if I did feel on a temporary high after confession. I knew I would never make it straight to heaven so I was forced to lower my sights to a stopover in purgatory.

Retreats were all very well – you *had* to think about something – but what really made you feel good and bad in turn was the annual mission. This was Catholicism in earnest. Up at the gates of St Carthage's Church every May or June went the tents and stalls of the mission hucksters, with their bewildering display of statues, crosses, rosary beads of mother of pearl, of wood, of silver and of bone; badges, scapulars, indulgences, prayer books, prayer sheets, missals, pictures, fancy bottles of holy water from all the holy wells of Europe, Pope's blessings, and any other devotional aid you would care to mention with one exception, flagellants' whips. We had many religious excesses in Ireland but flagellation was something that never appealed to us, although a similar practice, wrapping oneself in chains, was known. The Dubliner Matt Talbot, happily a minority of one, was the national exponent of this testing manner of contemplation.

Among the statues, the various guises of the Blessed Virgin and the Sacred Heart were the bestsellers. Saint Anthony, Mam's favourite saint for the practical reason that he helped her find things she had lost, was also popular, as was Blessed Martin de Porres (we pronounced the surname 'pores') who was heading for sainthood at this time. Of the saints, the two I had the most time for, St Francis of Assisi and St Francis Xavier were less prominent, the latter in particular. I admired the Italian because he could make animals come to him and speak to them, something I longed to be able to do and something I tried with various animals and birds to no success. The Spaniard won my applause for his courage and compassion in administering to the lepers of the Far East. Leprosy was the most harrowing disease I could imagine, dire beyond belief in its physical manifestations, cruel beyond words in the way in which those afflicted with it were ostracised.

Tents up, the parishioners readied, it only remained for the two Redemptorists, Fathers O'Carroll and McHugh, who were to stay in our midst at the invitation of the parish priest Canon Michael Walsh for two weeks, to arrive. A week for the women and girls, a similar stretch for the men and boys. They always came in pairs, these troubleshooters of the Lord, one easy-going, the other a flamethrower. I wonder if the police and secret services of today appreciate where the interrogation tactics they regularly apply were honed? Being excluded from the women's and girls' sessions, I can only comment on the boys' and men's event, which always followed the women's. Big expectation the first night. A time for taking up positions. Word had already gone around from the women and girls of the preacher who was the soft touch and of the one who was going to scorch us with the *Sermon On The Sixth Commandment* on the Thursday. As a result, males had already decided to whom they were going to go to confession at the end of the week. Church packed – the farmers and the hard lads from Botany and the Lane falling out the back door. And it was a very large church for a small town. As if the man who ordered it built had been banking on a local apparition to keep it full. But we were proud of it. It was far more arresting than anything our fellow-Catholics in Cappoquin, Tallow or Ballyduff could boast of, although the bizarre-looking *garda* barracks in the last-named ran it close in architectural terms. (Ballyduff police station, designed for the RIC, looked like something that had been been intended for the Orient. The story went that it *was*. But His Majesty's architects got their plans mixed up. So the West Waterford village got the Anglo-Indian building and somewhere in the vast continent of India – no one has yet pinpointed where – there is an Anglo-Irish police station, presumably serving the same purpose. From similar stories I have heard about other public buildings in these islands, e.g. Dungannon police barracks in County Tyrone, the Keeper of Plans of the then equivalent of today's British Property Services Agency must have been either monumentally inefficient, and I would not discount that, or had a fantastic sense of humour.)

Anyway, the chapel is full. Low-key start with a rosary. Slow. Slower than our own Father McGrath. Much, much slower than our Father Michael

Ahearne who used to go flat out. Then a stately bit of benediction with added candles and flowers. A few announcements. The first sermon. From the quiet man. General stuff, to ease us into things. Wouldn't want to scare us off the first night. Finally, the main benediction. We're over the first hurdle. Outside on the steps we mix with the adults – great excuse to stay out late – and pass judgement on the sermon. The next couple of nights are not very different, just more specific in content. Come Thursday, however, we boys are excluded from the spine-tingling *Sermon On The Sixth Commandment*. Our ears are too tender for such explicit matters. 'Aw shit!' we say disgustedly and hang around by the side door, picking up the occasional roar from the hard man in the pulpit, until our ashen-faced elders emerge looking very serious, or shattered, or both. 'What was it like? What did he say?' we demand of the older lads who were allowed in. They shake their heads and hurry on down town for a pint. 'Jasus, you have to be a man to go through something like that,' I think admiringly.

Eventually, my own turn comes – the month of May 1954, my seventeenth year. It's Thursday night. I'm sitting in the middle, right-hand aisle, a few rows down from the altar. Time for that *Sermon*. Father O'Carroll, a squat, fat man with a neck like a bull on him, is mounting the steps to the pulpit. The place is hushed. We all know what we're in for. Hell and damnation. The preacher gets to the top, draws breath, measures his audience with deliberation. Opens a book. Glances at it. Closes it. Takes a deep breath. I feel my Adam's apple up in my throat and worry that I'm sitting too close to the front. He begins with a relevant quotation, possibly the Sixth Commandment itself. It's not looking promising to a young man who has already learned to masturbate and has had his first feel of a girl, but there was one consolation. 'Whatever he says, I won't be seeing him again for another year.' Before long Father O'Carroll is in full flight. I begin to get the feeling I'm a very poor specimen of Christianity indeed. Better keep my hands to myself for the next month, if not quite for eternity. 'If Virginia Mayo offered herself to me right now, I think I might even have it in me to say no.' I banish the lovely image from my mind. Concentrate. I do.

But then something happens. The Redemptorist begins to get carried away by the voluptuous excesses of which he imagines we are capable. His face gets redder and redder. He pounds the red baize of the pulpit top with his fist. A mistake. It's been a long time since anybody shook out that item. Clouds of dust rise up and envelop him. Fascinated by this unexpected and theatrical development, I lose the thread of what he has been on about. He begins to cough and choke but carries on regardless, waving the dust cloud aside with his arms. It's too much. I can't stop a grin breaking across my face. I fight off a desire to laugh out loud. It is an odd feeling: one second faced with an avenging angel putting the fear of God into me, the next with just a comical human being. I glance around. Other faces are stifling grins too. Father O'Carroll has overcooked it. The cyclone subsides as abruptly as it began.

That was my one and only *Sermon On The Sixth Commandment*. I cannot recall ever having attended another although there must have been at least one other opportunity at a men's mission. It may be that Father O'Carroll's performance was so bizarre all previous efforts faded into insignificance alongside it. I was on the receiving end of one other talk on that subject, a small seminar that Brother P. D. Lee gave to our Leaving Class. A totally different and more intimate affair, it was not so much about the Sixth as about the birds and the bees. He wanted us to have the facts of life from him rather than the 'corner boys', he said. In that he was too late. The corner boys had long beaten him to it. I had the facts from them but P.D. synthesised the subject so much better, I had to admit. Our Brother Superior was a wholly devout man, much into Mariology, and we could see how difficult it was for him to approach the subject, yet he persisted, quietly and gently, knitting and unknitting his hairy alabaster hands. We had never seen him so nervous and, for us, out of character. It was strange to see this man who was built like a tank, and could probably have turned one over with his bare hands, approaching the subject so delicately. I certainly was very touched by, and greatly appreciated, his show of concern for our future wellbeing. From the subdued silence that followed his presentation, and from what we said among ourselves afterwards, it was clear that my classmates shared my opinion. Nobody else among our seniors, and that included our parents, had ever even tried to broach the subject of sex. And he only threw in one shocker. Urging restraint upon us he told us about 'a brute that insisted on having his way with his pregnant wife and so caused her to lose her baby'.

Father O'Carroll, it turned out, was not that bad either. The Saturday afternoon following the *Sermon* I went up to the chapel to go to confession. The pews were packed around Father McHugh's box. He was the slim, easygoing doe-eyed one. 'Jasus!' I muttered to myself, 'I'm not going to hang around all day waiting for him,' so I gritted my teeth and joined the only man waiting outside Father O'Carroll's box. In a way, I felt sorry for Father O'Carroll because it was so obvious that nobody wanted to have anything to do with him. He had given us all a roasting, sure, but maybe that was because he had been so instructed. Nevertheless, I expected a grilling. To my great surprise, the guy already in the confessional was out soon and the guy in front of me in and out in a jiffy. 'Well, maybe this isn't going to be so bad,' I thought and went in and said the piece that I had been composing in my mind. He *smiled* at me through the grill, then asked me softly whether I intended to keep my hands to myself in future. I said 'Yes, I will,' and meant it. He gave me a few Hail Marys, blessed me, and off I went, hardly able to believe that I had been in the lion's den and come out of it in one piece. Felt a bit let down too though. I was obviously not as great a sinner as I had thought. 'Easy as pie,' I congratulated myself, coming out into the sun, and laughed at the eejits who were queueing up for hours to be given a lengthy, and no doubt embarrassing, going-over by the nice, quiet fella. I felt I had learned something about humanity that day.

The missions used to literally end in a blaze of glory with what was called 'the renewal of baptismal vows'. Everyone was supposed to hold a lighted candle in his hand during this ceremony and in the big interior, which could at a pinch have accommodated the population of the town itself, this was quite a sight. And your nostrils got a lift from the pungent intermingling of smoke and incense. You had to hand it to us. We were dab hands at laying on the bit of pageantry. Looking back at it, the burning candles must have constituted something of a fire hazard. The biggest satisfaction of the mission came when the soft priest uttered a few final words congratulating the people of Lismore and surrounding district for the 'grand manner' in which they had attended throughout the two weeks. You went home with a glow in your heart, and some doubts about how long you could hold to your promises. But, on the whole, it had been great entertainment, brought the crowds to the town, business to the pubs, and livened up the place for a while. What more could you ask?

Retreats were another speciality of the churchmen with the *blas* but these totally lacked the razamatazz of the mission. These would be targeted on specific groups like the Children of Mary (women only), the Pioneers (teetotallers), and so on. In 1950 we were given a major injection of faith – the Proclamation of the Dogma of the Assumption. A new Article of Faith! Straight from the Bishop of Rome himself. You didn't experience many of those in a lifetime. For months before the formal proclamation our teachers slogged away, trying to pound into our unreceptive skulls some appreciation of the word 'dogma'. I can honestly say I could neither make head nor tail of it.

One bunch of missionaries used to hit town with a form of entertainment that should have been to our liking – the Mill Hill Fathers' picture show. Only their choice of films was dismal – travelogues of the Holy Land and Lourdes, and mission set-ups in the 'Dark Continent'. It wasn't much of a laugh going there and you had to pass over a few pence to help the priests in their great work of bringing the light of faith to the pagan multitudes, especially the 'black babies', for whom also there used to be regular collections in the schools. The collection box was novel. It was fun to place a halfpenny on the outstretched palm of an iron head-and-shoulders 'baby' and lever the coin into its mouth. I passed on willingly the few pennies my mother had given me for the purpose but ignored the priests' appeals for a chat on the side. You had no business in that line of operation unless you were sure you had it in you to sail past Purgatory. As it was, I was only going to be able to avoid limbo because my parents had had the good sense to have me splashed. Limbo. Now there was a place that lacked all attraction. Nowadays, I suppose, the closest thing to it would be the holdover halls of Her Britannic Majesty's Immigration Service at Heathrow Airport. You weren't going anywhere and you certainly weren't having a ball. I'd take what was coming in purgatory any time. Not that I could discount hell. One false step and I could be hopping up and down on hot coals for all eternity. Still, we were better off than the pagans in one sense. Look at the choices we had.

In spite of the glamour of the missions it was the home-bred religious spectacle that was best. Nothing could compare with the annual Corpus Christi procession that took place each June. There were days of preparation to delight in before the event itself. In Botany many of the families would paint the fronts of their one-storey terraced cottages with a mixture of whitewash and cow-pat, which gave an attractive, pastel-green patina to the walls. A big wooden altar had to be erected at the front gates of the Christian Brothers School at the top of Gallows Hill. Buntings and flags would go up all over town. We had two strings of bunting at home but no flags so Mother Brendan, the Reverend Mother of the Presentation Convent and Mam's second cousin, used to lend us a pair for the day, one a large white-and-yellow papal flag with the keys of St Peter on it. We used to hang the buntings from the bedroom windows across the street to a limb of one of the trees inside the Villa wall. The Feeneys and our other neighbours would hang theirs at the same time, Jim loaning out his long ladders to all and sundry while Tom and myself had great fun climbing the trees to give a hand. And there were flowers to be picked, or fecked.

In June of 1951 or 1952 I realised one of my greatest ambitions. Mikey Coleman of the Main Street, head altar boy, knacky corner forward in hurling, and, above all, prince of orchard robbers, quietly took me aside and suggested we go on an expedition to the Castle Gardens to feck flowers for the procession altar. Just me and the legend! I jumped at it. Everybody in town knew Mikey robbed orchards, especially everybody who had an orchard, but nobody had ever been able to lay a glove on him. We all stole fruit, though Foxy Flynn and Patsy Bray preferred raw carrots – they knew their Bugs Bunny. But Mikey was a pro. We rumoured it amongst us that he even had a fence for the produce he gathered in his neighbour Billy Baldwin, the jovial, big-bellied dealer in game and vegetables, regarded by us as a chancer who cruised skilfully on the edge of the Law. In our eyes Mikey's carefully-selected produce would have slipped onto Billy's shelves as naturally as the wild duck and pheasant, many victims of the dealer's own prowess with a double-barrelled shotgun, that ended up on the meat-hooks in or under the counter out of season. The Law never touched either of them, although a warning may have been muttered now and again. Mikey was a loner. His only Tonto was the occasional apprentice like me whom he chose to initiate, or maybe take along simply to highlight the gulf in practice between his professionalism and our amateurish grabbings, when the mood came upon him. Perhaps this was how he consciously or unconsciously fed his legend?

In the quiet of a late, cloudy evening I followed his small, wiry figure in over the castle wall opposite St Carthage's Well. We threaded our way through the stands of bamboo and along the majestic avenue of yews, the Monks' Walk, my confidence brimming because I knew I was in the hands of the Master. Summer had been late coming and Mikey was concerned that there might be a shortage of blooms even in the carefully tended gardens of the castle. But we needn't have worried. We soon came across exquisite roses in abundance, stocks with massive heads on them and other flowers of which we did not know the names. As we neared the walls of the castle itself, and came in full view of the wide windows above us, I began to get the wind up. But Mikey, for whom the exercise seemed to be a mere stroll, was in no hurry at all.

'We can get all we want here, hah?' I enthused nervously, 'No need to go any farther?'

'No,' Mikey agreed, surprising me, 'But before we take 'em I just want to check the strawberries.'

'Hah?' I blanched.

''Tis all right,' he said confidently, 'There's no one about.'

I gulped but knew I had no option but to follow him or I'd never be able to look him straight in the face again. He led me with assurance along a route I had never been before, through the riding house and out into the upper garden where the vegetables and fruit were grown. We came to the strawberry patch. Beds of them like nothing I'd seen! And all protected from the birds by heavy, green, string netting fixed at a height of three feet or so. I had a feeling, however, that these two birds were not going to be inhibited by it.

Sure enough Mikey commented, 'I want to have a look at these. 'Tis a bit early for them yet but you never know.'

We were now right under the windows near the Carlisle Tower. My heart was pumping. 'Mightn't somebody see us from the windows?' I said, trying to keep a stammer out of my voice.

'No, no, they're all away," the Master said casually and dropped to his knees and crawled in under the nets. 'Come on,' he held the netting up for me to join him.

There was nothing for it but to get down on my knees alongside him. 'Jasus!' I thought, 'If anybody comes along now we're fucked.' And I pictured a bailiff releasing a concealed cord to spring the net on us. But I was feeling elated too. In spite of my worries I had not chickened out. Mikey, cool as a Cagney, was already moving up a drill, examining the state of the berries with a practised eye. I followed up another and, following his example, fingered a few. Clearly, although there were a few reddish ones, they were not ripe yet. Mikey plucked one and chewed on it fastidiously. I tried another. It was a bit sour but okay. Mikey shook his head, however.

'No, they're not ripe yet.' He scuttled across the beds and examined some other plants. 'No,' he shook his head again, 'We'll leave 'em. I'll come back for 'em when they're ready.'

Greatly to my relief, we got out from under the potential trap and ambled back to the flowers – that is, Mikey ambled. I gritted my teeth, maintained a grin of a kind and aped his amble. By the time we got to the flowers I was willing to stretch out my arms and bundle up the first blossoms that fell into them. But not my partner. Under his direction we calmly selected the best on offer until we had a huge armful each. I'd never held such a noseful of scent. 'Even if we're caught now,' I reasoned to myself, 'what can anybody say? Aren't we only doing it for the greater glory of God?'

At the end of 1952 Mikey turned his back on his sinful life and went off to America to become a priest, an irreplaceable loss to the art of orchard robbing. But, I suppose, he'd have grown out of it eventually anyway. That single exploit suggested to me the possible reason for his success – timing. He knew *exactly* when to go in. The knowing gardeners for miles around must have breathed a sigh of relief when they thought of him winging his way to the Wild West; the innocent ones would have wondered why they had such bountiful crops the following years. God bless you, Mikey, you were an example to us all. In retrospect, there was a touch of swansong about his performance on that still evening. Maybe it took place in June 1952 and maybe he never did go back for a last haul of the Duke's strawberries?

The procession used to start at 3.30 p.m. *sharp*, which in itself was something, at St Carthage's Parish Church. There was an established order in which the marchers paraded and each section would sing its own hymns. A huge papal banner led the way. Then came the males; Boy Scouts and schoolboys at the front followed by the members of the Men's Confraternity sporting their red-ribboned, silvered medals of the Sacred Heart; and last, the 'ordinary' men of the parish. Females adopted a similar pattern; first the Girl Guides and schoolgirls; then the Children of Mary (amongst whom in a blue gown and under a white veil of lace would be Mam); and finally, the 'ordinary' women of the parish. It all seemed like a dress rehearsal for heaven in which everyone knew their place.

In the wake of the women came the centrepiece of the procession, the Blessed Sacrament, borne in the golden sacred monstrance by the parish priest under a gold-embroidered canopy supported by four Christian Brothers who each held a pole. In front of the Sacrament Petey Gillen, the sacristan, raised high a jewelled, golden cross and immediately behind him altar boys lofted the heady scent of incense into the air with their swinging thuribles. And just after them, the final touch, little girls dressed in white, strewing the way of the Host with rose petals from their wicker baskets. Somewhere among the throng also sang the choir. During the Emergency the Army and the LDF, who availed of every occasion to show off their steps, used to march as well.

The route was picturesque, never more so than at the beginning. Left up quiet Chapel Place (Fernville as we knew it), then left again around the back of the church grounds into posh South Mall, from the rise of which you had a lovely view along the North Mall, past the slender spire of the elegant Protestant cathedral, to the purple slopes of Knockmealdown in the distance. Then down Main Street. On the window sills of the private houses and in the windows of the shops altars of varying dimensions were mounted. By the time you got to the Monument the procession had begun to halt now and again to allow the ranks to close up. As the sound of shuffling feet faded your ears picked up the different hymns that the different sections of the march were singing – 'Hail, Queen of Heaven' seemed singularly processional – now echoing and now merging into one another to form a fleeting new composition. At times we were all supposed to be singing the same number and when the beat got out of synch the Confraternity men who were stewarding the march would scurry up and down the line, speeding up the tempo a bit here, slowing it down a bit there.

Amongst these marshalls of rectitude strode 'Parrot' Doherty, a strict disciplinarian whom Euge Dennis and his pals delighted in subverting by singing out of rhythm or out of tune or both. Along West Street I would gaze up proudly at the papal banner strung across from our house to the Villa grounds, but also a little guiltily knowing the item was only borrowed and not our own. But I could admire honestly the little altar that Molly and Mam and Paddy had put together on the outside sill of the sitting-room window. Then it was up Gallows Hill from which you could look right back up Main Street and watch the end of the procession still coming around by the Co-op. On the summit we halted at the altar erected outside the CBS gates and were arranged into ranks along the Ballyanchor and Tallow Road prongs of the fork to wait the tail. The women coming up behind would arrange themselves on the brow of the hill. When all was set for benediction off would come the men's caps or out would come their handkerchiefs to be placed upon the ground, some fastidiously, to protect the right knees of the Sunday-best trousers. After the brief service the procession resumed. Botany was the high spot of the route. It was striking how the poor of the street spared neither expense nor trouble to devise the most colourful and devotional altars and displays. After that it was an anti-climax to return via the Boreen and Upper Chapel Street to the church for the final benediction and dispersal.

What captivated me about the procession was not so much the religious fervour as the intoxicating scent of blossoms that made my nostrils tingle and my mind wander all along the way. But if the open-air spectacle of June was rich in such earthy sensations it was the Forty Hours adoration of May that really made your senses sit up and take notice. The church altar would be flooded with flowers and bathed in extra candlepower continuously from last Mass on Sunday to early Tuesday morning. During this round-the-clock event a vigil was kept by the men's and women's confraternities and we school children were sent along in guilds according to age groups. I used to pop in at times other than my appointed stints and would sit and gaze at the beautiful scene and breathe in the perfumed air. In silent contemplation you began to wonder if paradise wasn't a little like this.

Another event of the church calendar that I really liked was the simple celebration of St Carthage's Day. Nothing exotic here, little to assail your nostrils but the dampness of the shady undergrowth, a scent so familiar you hardly remarked upon it. A day so low-key we did not even get time off from school for it. St Carthage's Well, as we knew it, lay behind high walls in *Tobar na Ceárdchan* off the New Way and was a totally neglected place on any other day of the year. The Boy Scouts took it upon themselves to clear a path through the undergrowth the day before the Saint's day and I gave them a hand once or twice. On the day itself the wide, green wooden gates to the *Tobar*, which were normally kept shut, would be left open so that the townspeople could go in and pray at the well and fill bottles with its clear cool water which was reported to have effected cures in the past. Only a few adults used to wander in during the day's vigil. In the early evening the scouts, led by their scoutmaster Kieran Fenton, used to march down to the well and say the rosary. If it hadn't been for the scouts nobody except us children, who used to shin over the wall to play now and again, would have gone near the place. I was always a bit surprised, and even ashamed, that adults thought so little of our holy well, especially as the water tasted good enough for me to take a hearty slug of it any time I was playing there. Perhaps the well had some pagan connotations not to the Church's liking? Certainly the local priests did nothing to foster it as a centre of devotion. At a similar well out the Mountain Road in Carrignagour an annual pattern used to take place in honour of Saint Colman but I never got to attend this.

The last major event of the religious year was, of course, Christmas and we always had a fine crib in the chapel, peopled with sizable wooden figures painted in warm colours, including a set of the Three Wise Men for the appropriate time. The same one year in year out so that there was a welcome familiarity about it each time it reappeared. It was a time for candles too. Nothing like the Forty Hours Adoration though. Someone started a 'Bring Back Christ to Christmas' campaign in 1953 – almost certainly Father Denis McGrath, one of the local curates who was always coming up with bright ideas to occupy our idle minds. P. D. Lee, if he did not play a part in this, would doubtless have approved. The superior of the Christian Brothers used to plead with us always to write 'Christmas' rather than 'Xmas'. Of course, a cagey shopkeeper might also have been the spirit that moved the campaign. It was around this time also that loops of coloured bulbs appeared in the Main Street for the first time to add to the festivity of the window displays. Small cribs also appeared in some windows. Until this time it had been left to Teasy Meade and Nora Willoughby, the town's main stockists of toys, to provide us with a little festive glitter. Whether the campaign had anything to do with religious fervour was immaterial. The important effect was that it brightened our short winter days.

At one stage in my life I became an altarboy. It was not a career that lasted very long – I stuck it for less than a year – or shone very brightly. The problem was, I couldn't get up in the morning in time for eight o'clock Mass. Canon Michael Walsh, never exactly the soul of fun, told me off a few times for coming late. Once he was very scowly because not alone did I arrive late but the other server didn't appear at all. I had not been long at the game at this time and spent a trying sacrifice munching through the Latin on my own. It helped that the old priest was hard of hearing (or maybe he liked to give the impression that he was) so I could throw in a mumble here and there when the text failed me, which was more often than I would like to admit. When I came to ring the bell at the raising of the host I met with further embarrassment. I shook the bell too vigorously and the hammer just kept racing around the inside of the cloche instead of going ding-dong. 'Jasus, he can't even ring the fucking bell,' I could hear the Canon thinking as he glared down at me through his upraised arms. Still, between the two of us we finished the Mass.

On other occasions Mikey Coleman carried me. Mikey was great with the thurible. Effortlessly he would swing it high and send out reams of smoke. Others of us, experienced and inexperienced, trying to emulate him sometimes ended up tipping the thurible plate over at the highest point of an over-ambitious swing and spilling hot incense onto the red carpet that already bore evidence of previous mishap. The perpetrator then had to jump to his feet and frantically stamp out the resinous embers, earning himself severe scowls from the officiating cleric and sacristan and sarky grins from friends and enemies in the congregation. I was very envious of Mikey's skill and was only beginning to get the hang of the swing when I gave up my budding career in the church. In fact, I'm not sure whether I stopped voluntarily or whether it was suggested to me that I was not quite altarboy material. But I missed the thurible-swinging and the bell-ringing which I did eventually master.

Handling the cruets with the wine and water for the priest when he was saying Mass was another aspect of the business I enjoyed, more because it told me something about human nature than about anything to do with the preparation of the silver vessels. Some of the priests liked to polish off all the wine and others only took an ostentatious sip. You quickly got to know who liked his drop. If you were not pouring enough wine into the chalice the priest would lower it to encourage you to continue. If after that you were still too hesitant he would lower it further and if you failed to cop on at that stage he would help you to drain the cruet with a downward thrust of his thumb. What I missed most though was lighting the high candles for benediction with the six-foot wooden pole to the brass tip of which a wax taper was fixed, then snuffing them out after the service. It was quite a trick to light the candles. You had to bend the taper so that it could better reach the wicks. Sometimes a candle just would not light and your upstretched arms would be quivering under the weight of the pole as you tried again and

Paddy Ballantyne wearing his altar-boy soutane and surplice, c. 1941-42. He looks much more the part than I ever did.

again. It did not help that you knew the eyes of the whole chapel were upon you. Sometimes a more experienced server would have to come to your rescue and if he failed as well the uncooperative wick would be left unlit. Snuffing out the candles was a cinch but you had to do it gently. One reason why a wick would not light was because someone had snuffed it flat.

The bit of serving I had least trouble with was lying back on the steps looking idly down at the congregation when the priest was giving a sermon, but even that could have its hazards. A pal might make funny faces at you from the front pew. An excessive show of fervour by a member of the congregation might strike you as funny – if Boxer Dennis happened to be reclined next to you and noticed the same behaviour you could be sure he would crease you with some pointed and caustic aside – 'Will you look at that feckin eejit in the second row …!' If you could not contain a laugh you had to get up, hold your breath, genuflect and, as if you were going about a bit of the service, make for the sacristy, there to let it all out. There were other moments of fun in serving too. We used to carry our soutanes and surplices in black cotton bags that had long black cords to draw the necks tight and we could often be seen on the way home thumping one another with them. Some of the lads enjoyed chewing a host but I found them tasteless. I did not think much of the altar wine either but, as with the hosts, I enjoyed being dared to sample it. Altarboying was very much a middle-class occupation. It was rare for anyone from Botany or Church Lane to volunteer for it. There was certainly one good reason for this: even when at school, and that meant primary school, disadvantaged children had to use their free time to try to earn a few bob. On top of that, their parents who saw little enough practical use for the Irish language saw even less for Latin, which was left to the middle classes.

You could earn an odd bob for private serving and my little earner was none other than a bishop – the stationmaster's brother, home on holidays from South Africa where he was Bishop of Port Elizabeth. Shy, sincere, and retiring, he had the gentlest of eyes behind his large glasses. All he wanted was to be able to say Mass in private at the station every morning at a reasonable hour, but he was having trouble finding a regular server. Pierce Colbert, his nephew and my classmate, in desperation asked me if I wouldn't mind coming out of retirement – I had quit the practice by then – to do the job. Well, you had to do your best for a pal. I still had my gear so, having warned him that I was no great shakes at the business, I took it on. Mind you, I wouldn't say I wasn't influenced by the thought of a few bob either. Bishop Colbert was a different kettle of fish entirely to the cranky parish priest and we quickly established an efficient working relationship or, at least, so it seemed to me. The Masses in a small dim room at the station seemed to go okay and I operated with much more confidence than I did on the public altar. On two counts I reckoned he must have felt that I was doing a reasonable job: 1) he kept me on, and 2) he interrupted a holiday he was taking somewhere else to come and visit me when he heard that I had been taken off to hospital.

My hospitalisation was no big deal, just a standard appendectomy of the time, so it was extra nice of him to call by. A couple of days after the operation when I was lying in bed recuperating who should I see padding quietly into the ward with a big brown bag under his arm but the bishop. To my delight the bag was full of juicy Jaffa oranges. He stayed a little while and chatted amicably. I was very pleased that he had gone out of his way to come and see me as a friend. The ward sisters, who were nuns, only realised he was a bishop when he was on his way out because he had kept the collar of his overcoat up so that no one would see his purple. However, the gimlet eyes of one of them spotted the tell-tale flash and before you could spit they were dropping to their knees all over the place to kiss his ring, causing the poor man no end of embarrassment. I felt sorry for him. After he had managed to escape a nun came smiling up to me to tuck me in, even though I did not need tucking in at that moment, and said, 'Aren't you an important little fella, having a bishop call to see you?' I just shrugged and started peeling one of my gifts. They were the best oranges I had ever eaten and gave me a lifelong taste for Jaffas.

When priests, particularly missionaries, came home on holidays to their families they were treated like minor gods. No longer referred to as just 'Joe', for example, but as 'Father Joe'. By their own mothers and fathers! And by the brothers and sisters who had grown up with them. The mothers were the worst. 'Father Joe, would you like this? Father Joe, would you like that?' From morning to night the priest would be cossetted. In a large family a room for himself would be somehow engineered and he would be given the run of the main living space by day so that he could say his prayers. They

A 1779 engraving of the mediaeval Old Bridge, Carrick-on-Suir with the then ruined parish church in the background. On the bridge can be seen a house in which a nailer plied his trade well into the first half of the 20th Century (my mother remembered him). Note the terrier standing on the prow of the fishing cot. This was a familiar sight in my own childhood, and still is today.

seemed to have an awful lot of praying to get through, these visitors. Day in, day out, you would encounter them on walks, thick black breviary open, mumbling away. On the hottest summer's day. But then the heat we knew was nothing compared to what they experienced as missionaries in Africa, we were told. On what was a good day for us, you used to come across them huddled over an open fire. It was the damp of the Ould Sod that got them, we learned. They could not cope with it anymore. The Yanks were the same – shivering without their central heating. Moan, moan, moan, about the damp. (The Yanks even brought their own bog paper with them. Could you imagine that? As if the *Irish Press* was not soft enough.) Still, the missionaries came across with a bob, too, if you served Mass for them.

Nuns were less of a bother. They knew how to make their own beds and cook a meal, and they clearly had far fewer prayers to say. What impressed me most about them was the strange names they adopted. Sister Scholastica or Sister Borgia and the like. 'Where did they get them from?' you asked yourself. Bishop Colbert, I would say, was a refreshing exception to all this pampering. He would have none of it and besides, Dan Colbert and his family were much too level-headed and down-to-earth to fuss about the house all day after a brother who happened to be a bishop. Dan had enough on his hands to get the trains through on some approximation of time.

With regard to our own priests, we all had our favourites and mine was Father Michael Ahearne, a slim, nervous man who moved like quicksilver. He replaced Father T. Gorman who left after twenty-one years in April 1943. I think he was Mam's favourite too, although Father Hennebry, as a fellow-Tipperary native, ran him close. I had a good reason for liking him. He was the fastest rosary and Mass sayer in the business. Or so I thought, until a year or two after he had left Lismore. I came across Carrickbeg's answer to him – the legendary John McGrath of the Parish Church. The comparison was not quite straightforward. When it came down to prayers the Carrickbeg man edged it. But when you took sermons into account Father Aherne held a distinct advantage. McGrath had one fatal flaw; when the mood struck him, which was not infrequent, he could launch into a sermon of an hour's duration. Great homespun stuff, laced with biting wit, and ad-libbed all the way. His own unique style of putting the boot into wavering souls and, at the same time, making them laugh heartily at themselves. Aherne, in contrast, never believed in wasting time on sermons. Five to ten minutes was more than enough for him to say anything he wanted to say. On most occasions Father McGrath matched him in this but you could never set your watch by the Carrickbeg cleric. His Sunday slot was 11.00 a.m. and that was the only time of which you could be sure. A wise man, intent on getting away to a hurling match or the seaside never said to a friend, 'I'll meet you after eleven o'clock Mass,' because that could mean twenty past twelve as easily as twenty past eleven. The hard and hungover lads who regularly attended that last morning service of the day used to come prepared for the unexpected. They would always hang around at the door of the little chapel where they could make room to sit down on the steps leading up to the gallery and choir, or on the broad window sill by the stairs. And they would take along a pack of cards so that they could while away a lengthy sermon with a hand of poker. 'Pissin' agin the wind!' Father John was capable of snorting with a lift of his jaw if he had seen them, turning abruptly on his heel to bring his talk to a premature conclusion. His sermons always came to an abrupt ending anyway and usually left you hanging there awaiting a structured flourish.

Every quicksilver priest is matched by a sober-sided colleague and in Lismore we were saddled with the dour and sour Father Michael Murphy until, happily, he left us in 1945. The man who replaced him, Father Denis McGrath, was something of a mixed blessing. A fiercely energetic man to be landed on a sleepy town, he was always exhorting us 'to be up and doing' and had a mania for organising people and starting things. He had barely arrived when he announced the founding of a Lismore branch of the Pioneer Total Abstinence Association. I remember that because we schoolchildren were given an offer we couldn't refuse – a mass pledge. That exercise climaxed a couple of years later in November 1948 in a huge rally at Jackie Scanlan's *Happydrome* at which we were treated to a series of discourses on the evils of intoxicating drink. Father McGrath next sank his enthusiasm into the founding of the Legion of Mary, or so I thought at first. After a while I discovered that it wasn't he but one Frank Duff who had set that ball rolling. I did not join that body. There were limits to my piety. But I did give the legion a hand cleaning up the neglected Old Graveyard when 'Irons' O'Brien and Michael Nolan, two staunch legionnaires, asked me to help out. The best moment of that exercise came when we got back down to Con O'Neill's corner later on. It was a scented sunny evening and Dorothy Boam, the handsome daughter of the then English owner of the Devonshire Arms Hotel across the way came over and asked me where I had been. 'Clearing out the Old Graveyard,' I said innocently, at which Dorothy laughed, embraced me and fleetingly placed her warm, rouged cheek against mine. Which brought to mind a more celebrated and romantic legion.

But Father Denis had further ideas for us. By the early Fifties he was demanding a crusade of rosaries for world peace. This was at the height of the Cold War and was also the time when I first heard a reference to the dreaded Third Secret of Fatima, one so terrible, it was said, that the Pope himself had quailed before it and shut it away for all time. Another mystery for us to dwell on. I got caught up in the fervour of this crusade and demanded of my parents that the family should kneel down and say the rosary together every evening immediately before supper. Mam eyed me extremely dubiously. Dad left it up to her because he often had to be at the barracks at this time. It was not that they were not religious; they just did not feel the need to overdo things. Paddy just shrugged when it was put to him. Eventually Mam allowed herself to be coaxed, or coerced by her Red Guard of a son. 'Okay, we'll give it a try then,' she said wearily. I set up the schedule – joyful, sorrowful and glorious mysteries in turn. We all knelt, Mam leaning over the arm of one of the armchairs, and Dad, Paddy and myself on the seats of the kitchen chairs. We got through the first couple of evenings with a full house and no problems. Then my pal Tom Feeney wanted in when I told him what I had organised because his mother was not bothered about the business. 'Sure,' I agreed with missionary zeal and Tom turned up with his sister Margaret. Fortunately too as both Dad and Paddy chose to be absent on that same evening. It meant that I still had the same complement of souls. Down on our knees. We got through the first decade okay, then Margaret started to giggle. Then Tom. Then I saw the humour of the situation myself and joined them. Mam glowered at us. Were we saying the rosary or weren't we? Restart. Soon we were giggling again, and pinching each other's bottoms. Mam jumped to her feet and put away her beads. 'No point in going on with this,' she snorted. I hung my head sheepishly and Tom and Margaret looked embarrassed. And that was the end of the family rosary crusade in our house. I had to admire the way Mam had handled the situation. She had never wanted to take part in the charade in the first place but knew that my fervour would not last long. If Father McGrath happened to say to her later, 'Isn't it a wonder you wouldn't think of saying the family rosary in the home, Mrs Ballantyne?' she could honestly reply, 'Ah sure, didn't I try, Father; but Jim and his pals were too skittish so I had to give it up.' Wise woman. She had covered herself from all angles.

The rosary business had blown up mainly on account of a naïve Irish-American priest (born, in fact, in Attymass in the County Mayo), Father Patrick Peyton. In a land of crackpot redeemers his unique contribution was the unvarnished statement, 'The family that prays together stays together'. It worked and, as novelty tends to do in the United States, took that country by storm. You had to hand it to him. All he did was stand up before the people and say the rosary. At the time it was rumoured that he had Irish blood in him, probably on account of his first name, so there was a bit of a nationwide clamour to get him over here. You asked yourself, 'What can he teach us about saying the rosary?' Weren't we passed masters of the art? However he wanted it said – slow? very slow? lightning fast? mumbled? flowing? – we could accommodate him. He came. The 11th of July 1954 saw the climax of the whole campaign in West Waterford. An open-air gig on that Sunday evening at the GAA's Fraher Field in Dungarvan. An event not to be missed. There was a special excursion from Lismore for two shillings and sixpence and Dan Colbert got the train away on time. Sucky, Boxer, Foxy, Spud Murphy, Dodo Cahill, Mada Cahill, Nuala Tobin, Breda Behegan and I piled into a carriage like we were going to hear a concert by Nat King Cole. Our motives, one could honestly say, were mixed. Number one on the agenda was a night out in Dungarvan and number two a bit of harmless blackguarding. Number three, a visit to Fraher Field, hardly came into it. On the way down the wail of the rosary was heard from all the carriages but ours. From that only laughter and squeals came. A sour face looked in on us from time to time but failed to make any impression. Arriving at our seaside destination, we split up. Spud and Foxy and the women headed off in one direction, Boxer, Sucky and I in another. To our surprise the others said they were going to the field first. The three of us set off on a ramble in the opposite direction, expecting to find a bit of life in downtown Dungarvan. We should have been more realistic in our assessment of the impact of the Rosary Priest. The bloody place was like a ghost town. Not one pub open. Not even a stray mongrel in the street. Disconsolately we wandered down to the fine open-air swimming-pool. Surely somebody would be having a dip? Not a splash.

'Where the fuck is everybody?' Sucky bawled.

'Come on out!' shouted Boxer.

'Hallooooo!' I megaphoned through the palms of my hands.

'I reckon we done hit us a ghost town, pardners,' Boxer munched like an old sourdough.

'Water, I gotta have water,' Sucky held onto a wall and clawed his way along it like he was dying of thirst.

'Hang on pardner, we ain't gonna say the prayers over you yet,' Boxer puffed and lent him a shoulder.

'No sir,' I joined in. 'We'll have you round to the Rosary Man in no time an' he'll fix you up real good.'

Then we laughed loudly and ran up the street shouting other nonsense. Not a nose shimmered behind a lace curtain. We clowned our way along with similar sporadic outbursts, keeping to the waterfront as much as possible until boredom eventually drove us to the Fraher Field. At least the whole of Dungarvan would be there. The business was winding down when we reached the place. Thousands of heads between us and the podium prevented our seeing more than what might have been the back of the American's head. I only remember the man from his photo – big, placid and handsome, with a hangdog air and a pair of fists roped together with a string of beads. We met up with the others on the fringe of the multitude and dispersed in the direction of the railway station, wondering what all the fuss had been about. I think that must have been the general impression that this priest left in his wake. A couple of years later the man might never have existed for all you heard of him.

Father McGrath was given plenty of rope to develop his ideas because from 1951 the old Canon was throwing all the energies of his remaining years into the building of a new mortuary at the south transcept of the church, and a new wall running around the outside of the church graveyard. Great care was taken to choose sandstone and limestone in keeping with the fabric of the existing building and two local stonemasons, Johnny and Tom Keating from Botany, were contracted to do the job. Tom, Doshin's father, was a great button accordion player as well. The brothers had not practised their art for some years owing to a lack of this kind of work but such was their professional reputation that the parish priest had no hesitation in taking them on. For Johnny, in particular, the job was no more than what was due a pair of masters of their trade. Tom, who had a large family to support, would willingly have dropped his sights during the hard times and gone to work with cement blocks, but Johnny, the bachelor purist, refused to allow his younger brother to soil his hands with labour that was beneath their dignity. In such times their sister Minnie, with whom Johnny lived, did all she could to help feed Tom's children and, with what Tom brought in from hauling wood and playing at *céilidhes*, they somehow got by. It was only when the two men went to work on the site that most of the townspeople realised what fine craftsmen they were. It became a source of pride to us that we had local artisans capable of undertaking such highly skilled work and often my pals and I would stop to admire the deftness with which they dressed the stones with their hammers and chisels. By 1953 the new mortuary was completed, the old Canon's legacy to his parishioners. He died in November 1954 as we Ballantynes were setting in motion our final preparations for leaving the town for good. His successor was Canon Frank McGrath. Father Denis McGrath, the tireless senior curate who by now had us onto midnight Masses, eventually became Canon in his turn in 1973.

Other priests who came and went made little impression on me. One of them, Tom Murphy, a big solid man with a posh voice – definitely from somewhere up the social register – became more famous for the red setters and gundogs he bred than for any distinction at religion. A medium-paced Mass-sayer only. And no fun at reading out the names of the parishioners who paid their termly dues. But then we never had a priest who divined the entertainment possibilities of this somewhat notorious practice. In our town there would be subtle hints – a pause, a pursing of the lips – that a particular contribution might have been larger, but no more. Elsewhere in the country, straight talk would be employed. Dad used to tell of a PP from his part of County Sligo who commented on the inadequacy or otherwise of each individual contribution. 'Ah sure, John,' he admonished a rich farmer whom he reckoned should have been good for more than he gave, 'is that the best you can do?' In County Waterford he had a match in Father John McGrath of Carrickbeg who could deflate a contributor who was short with a mere glint or a tut-tut, or the whole parish if it fell down on its dues with a spiky clout over its collective ear: 'The collection is well down on this time last year. *What* are ye spending yere money on?' In this company the Lismore clergy were very dull. The best you could do was go to Father Ahearne's Mass on the Sunday when the list was to be read out. At least, he would whip through it the way he whipped through every other religious duty he performed. Dad always gave something between half-a-crown and five bob, which I thought was a lot and which maintained us somewhere in the middle of the scale. On hearing the names, arranged in order of size of donation, read out you came to a realisation of where your family fitted into the social order. And it would not have done you any good to contribute beyond your means. That was considered bad form. Dad considered this public accounting to be both unnecessary and distasteful.

Canon Walsh did his best to keep us on the straight and narrow but he did not have the legs for it anymore as we discovered when a few of us were forced into an impromptu game of hide-and-seek with him. Sucky, Doshin, Boxer, Bishop Scanlon and I were playing twenty-five on the steps of the side door of the church facing the Iron Room in Fernville while the rosary was being said inside. In age we ranged from 12 to 15 maybe, Doshin being the eldest, Patsy the Bishop the youngest. We were killing time until the rosary and benediction were over so that we could mingle with the crowd coming out and give the impression that we had been in attendance as well. The side door was not in use and it was a simple matter to dag around the corner and position yourself by the iron rail on the main steps as the worshippers emerged. The subterfuge was necessary as our parents had sent us out to evening devotions. Well, that was not quite true for some of us who had parental assent to either go out to the rosary or stay at home. What we were not allowed to do was go off somewhere else. Hence you went to, and did not go to, the rosary. Word always seemed to get back home if you weren't around after the service. As long as you were seen on the front steps it was naturally assumed that you had fulfilled your parents' hopes of you. The Bishop was the exception amongst us because his parents were easygoing about the outward show of religion. He just came along for the company.

'He's taking a long time tonight,' muttered Sucky, throwing down a jack.

'That's not worrying us, is it?' said I, hitting it with a king.

'Go in and see what mystery he's at, Bishop,' Foxy said to our pal who had an even more casual approach to religion than the rest of us.

The Bishop laughed. 'Sure 'tis all a mystery to me.'

Doshin took the trick with an ace.

'Where did that come from?' Foxy demanded suspiciously.

'From me hand. Where else?' grinned Doshin innocently.

'Wait a minute! How many aces... ?'

'My deal.' Sucky cut in and scooped up all the cards and started to shuffle them.

'Aw fuck it, Sucky! I wanted to check - ' Foxy began.

'Wanted to check what? This is a clean game.'

'Shh!' I cautioned, 'They'll hear us inside.'

'Let 'em,' Foxy snarled, 'I want to know where...'

'Foxy, never mind the cards. Go in and see what mystery the Canon's at,' Boxer chuckled.

Foxy regarded our grinning faces. 'What a fuckin' shower to be playing cards with,' he said wearily and got to this feet. 'I want 'em shuffled again when I get back.' He went off around the corner to check the mystery.

He was back in a flash. 'The Canon! He saw me,' he hissed.

'Take it aisy,' said Doshin who was leaning against the door lighting a butt. 'Sure he's not goin' to come down off the pulpit to chase you.'

'He's not in the pulpit, you feckin' eejit! He's standin' outside on the front steps.'

'Jasus!' we all exclaimed and scattered, leaving Doshin's butt and a few cards in our wake.

The Canon got to the corner just in time to see us bolting around the transcept. We halted, puffing and giggling, around the back.

'See if he's comin',' said Doshin.

Boxer had a peek. 'He is,' he chortled, 'No. Wait. He's gone back round the other way. Go over and watch that corner.'

Foxy and I made a dash toward the other side.

'Take it aisy,' said Doshin calmly, 'Sure 'twill take him a week to get round there.'

'Hey. Why don't we climb out over the wall there?' Foxy pointed.

'And be seen by the Miss Byrnes?" Boxer said. 'You know they're always at the window.' (The ultra-respectable Fernville was sometimes referred to as 'The Valley of Squinting Windows'.)

'Wouldn't you think they'd be in chapel sayin' their prayers instead o' spyin' on us?'

'I'll see if he's comin'.' I ran around to the other side. Sure enough he was, and raising more dust than was decent for a man of his age. I hared back to the others. 'Here he is!'

As we melted back the other way the organ began to play inside.

'I know what we'll do,' said Doshin. 'We'll slip in for benediction. He'll never think o' lookin' for us inside.'

We slid into the chapel and knelt just inside the door of the men's side, ignoring the reproachful glances of the old men in the short last pew, one of whom, Jim Hogan, hissed loudly, 'Close the door. There's a breeze.'

Bishop, making one of his rare appearances at a Christian service, complied.

'Hey!' Doshin hissed, and pushed his way in before the door was closed.

'What kept you?' Sucky whispered.

'I stopped to pick up me butt.'

'Did you get the cards? I dropped a couple.'

'No. He must have got 'em.'

'Shit! That's the end o' that deck.'

'Shhh!' a disapproving elder whispered loudly.

The congregation had begun to sing the 'Tantum Ergo' and Boxer joined in.

'Will you shut up out o' that, y'eejit!' said Sucky.

'Listen, lads,' Doshin said coolly, 'when 'tis over, don't go out first. The Canon will be out there. If he sees us comin' first he'll know we went in last. When everyone stands up hop into a seat and let most of them go out. And don't leave in a bunch. One by one.'

'Right,' we all nodded.

When we were regrouping on the steps outside the Canon was doing his usual bit of chatting to the respectable members of his flock.

'Didn't I tell ye he'd be there?' said Doshin out of the corner of his mouth and grinned. He knew very well that the PP was nearly always out there at this time.

We drifted into a group of boys of our own age range who had been to the devotions.

'He's starin' at us,' said Foxy nervously.

With a profound splashing of holy water, Boxer emerged from the chapel just then, dutifully saluted Canon Walsh with the index finger of his right hand, and came over to join us.

At the same moment John O'Riordan, Michael Crowley and Pat O'Connor, junior schoolmates, slipped into the group from around the corner. 'Who said the rosary, lads?' asked John. They had not been to the devotions either and wanted the same piece of information that we in their position would have wanted in case our own parents sprang the innocent-sounding question on us when we got home. It was a giveaway if you chanced your arm and came out with the wrong name.

We sparred good-humouredly with them over the name for a while then admitted it was Father McGrath.

Presently the Canon wandered over. 'And how did you enjoy the rosary,

Foxy?' he asked, sour glint and amusement fighting for supremacy in his eye.

'Very nice, Fa-, ah, Canon,' responded our pal coolly.

'Good night, boys.' The Canon shuffled off, his thigh-length black cape swinging gently from side to side. He could be pleased with himself. Didn't he succeed in getting us into the chapel after all?

'He didn't offer us the cards back,' observed Doshin.

When you thought about it, the men who ran the Catholic Church were never stuck for an idea to grab our attention. The lovely Latin that none of us really understood – *Dominus vobiscum, et cum spiritu tuo* – we only had to be told how to pronounce it for it to drip off our tongues like honey. Almost the way countless popes have mastered countless obscure languages in ten seconds flat. The endless occasions for pageantry – e.g. Holy Year, Marian Year. Didn't they even get the Government to issue stamps for these? As they did, I think, when President Seán T. O'Kelly came down to Mount Melleray, the renowned Cistercian abbey near Cappoquin, to open the new chapel there. President O'Kelly was the tiny little man with the big burly wife about whom Dad enjoyed retelling the crack made by a Dublin jackeen when the man walked out onto the greensward of Croke Park to throw in the ball at the start of an All-Ireland Final: 'For God's sake, why don't they cut the grass and let us have a look at him?'

The pageantry started early, at the age of seven, First Communion; at twelve, Confirmation. Both welcome events in a youngster's life because you made a few bob, and, if your parents could afford it, got a new set of clothes, and maybe even shoes. The parish priest welcomed you to Communion. For Confirmation you got the Bishop, a Corkman, Daniel Cohalan, with his funny little skullcap and his funny high hat, and his huge purple ring for us to kiss, up from his palace in Waterford City. When he came to town in the month of May he administered Confirmation not just to the boys and girls of our schools but to those of outlying districts like Ballysaggart and Ballinvella as well. The Bishop was cute too. In with the Confirmation he used to slip a pledge of abstinence from intoxicating drink that bound you until you were 21. Not that that worried me. I was not thinking of going on the drop at the age of 12. And a pledge wasn't to be taken all that seriously anyway. You couldn't be mortalled for breaking it.

In advance of your going on to First Communion and Confirmation a kind of Grand Inquisitor would come around to the school to check that you had acquired the necessary level of religious knowledge. 'Diocesan Inspector' they called him officially but he was just known as Father Lawn. No man was better titled. He was as soft as the cloth that bore his name or the grass you'd walk on. It could have had a sinister ring to it but there was nothing of that in the man at all as far as we could see. Sure he only came to test us in the catechism – 'Who made the world?' 'God made the world.' 'Who is God?' 'God is the Creator...' and so on. If you did not know the answers he would put words into your mouth. He was that anxious to see you pass. As indeed was Brother Murphy, the tetchy, thin-lipped Corkman who used to wig our ears and knuckle the sides of our heads, hovering menacingly in the background. Father Lawn, in fact, would keep an annual eye on us and invariably expressed himself 'well pleased' with the standard of religious knowledge we displayed.

Not that we could demolish the arguments of the first Protestant who might challenge us about our 'one true faith'. We were warned not to get into discussion about religion with strangers anyway, especially if we suggested we might one day be going to work in England. You could lose your faith that way because those fellows were specially trained for the purpose and could flummox you. Maybe. But in our own circles we could hold our own. 'Where is God?' The answer came like lightning, 'God is everywhere.' Snap. Next question. As we grew older we learned to cope with the concept of papal infallibility, a little tricky to get your head around, not to mention your tongue - 'infallibility' often came out with a couple of rogue stammered 'lls', like 'infall-ible-abil-lity' or the like. And I used to wonder why 'papal' and not 'popal'? We took the ex cathedra bit on trust although scepticism lingered – after all, we were all accomplished liars. More relevant epistemological conundrums demanded quick interpretation. For example, 'Why are certain hit songs banned on Radio Éireann?' Answer: 'Because they are suggestive.' 'What does "suggestive" mean?' It was a puzzle. In our youthful years three songs at least were banned: 'Only Five Minutes More', 'My Resistence is Low' (sung by Hoagy Carmichael), and 'Enjoy Yourself While You're Still In the Pink'. The last one really had me perplexed until Barney Walsh, my pal from lower Botany, gave me a critical reading with meaningful gestures of his fingers, of what the physical reality of 'being in the pink' could mean. Later, I felt confident enough to attempt interpretations of my own, wondering, for example, whether the words 'rub down with a velvet glove' from Guy Mitchell's 'Just in Love' were as innocent as they sounded. It was hard staying clear of the occasions of sin.

The Church was never above a bit of folklore and on Ash Wednesday it was graphically pointed out to you that you were only a speck of dust on the landscape. The priest's soft thumb came down on your forehead at morning Mass and you were left with a charcoal smear for the rest of the day. (If you were feeling lazy you could always smudge up from the fireplace at home.) Dust to dust so you had better watch it for the next 'forty' days. During Lent you were exhorted to give up things you really liked but I never felt I liked anything strongly enough to make giving it up a sufficiently meaningful sacrifice. I did start off sometimes by going to daily Mass in the mornings but that wasn't so much giving something up as taking something on. I think I may have given up taking two spoons of sugar in my tea one Lent to make do with just one. There was only one man in town that we all knew who annually made a supreme effort of willpower. Jim O'Donnell, the lanky postman, who was fond of a pint, used to come off the booze *entirely* for the whole of every Lent. Jim probably went on to become the longest-serving postman in the town after John O'Grady retired in October 1946 with forty-seven years' service. Come midday on Easter Saturday the binds were off and he would deservedly allow himself the liberty of staggering in late with the second post. I used to admire the man's fortitude although I had no way of gauging the thirst he must have endured.

May was the Virgin's month when you had rosaries in the lengthening evenings and went to the budding woods to pick bluebells for altar and home. Rosaries were said every evening during October too, and what you sought then in the woods was the edible chestnut. We consumed chestnuts by the score and one of our regular points for eating them was the choir, where we used to sing hymns between chewing them. Some evenings the wooden floorboards under us used to be ankle deep in shells by the end of the service.

The choir in the church was reached by climbing a wide, creaky stairway that was fixed to the bell-tower walls. On your right as you ascended was the wall, on your left a none too reassuring wooden banister. On the landing where you entered the choir though a doorway the bell-rope, dangling past you from a hole in the loft floor above, drew your eye vertiginously down to its furry red tail, hooked to the panelling at the side. On and off, you might look down from the landing at the red-tiled floor below and wonder what a body would look like if it splashed onto it.

The undisputed mistress of the choir was Kate O'Connell, or Kate Connell as we called her. Choirmistress and organist rolled into one substantial person, a solidly built matron who commanded respect when she settled her ample bottom on the organ seat and flicked out the stops. She had a heart-arresting glare through her heavily framed spectacles for the unfortunate chorister who drifted out of key, no time for frills, and she liked to keep the numbers going at a brisk pace. Sometimes when we'd be singing along lazily, which we were inclined to do, we would hear her voice soaring above ours, rallying us to a heightened tempo. In these moments Boxer used to delight in leading us on to give her more lung power and pace than she bargained for. Soon we'd feel Kate's glare on the backs of our necks as she belted out an extra decibel and strained to rein us in. 'Not so fast!' she'd hiss and send her brother Niall Darragh in from the adult section to re-establish order. Niall, a surly and moody troubleshooter, did not care much for youthful antics and we largely ignored him. But eventually we would throttle back, impishly overdoing it but not enough to give Kate an excuse for throwing us out of the choir. We knew her limits.

In the choir, as in the chapel generally, there was the men's side and the women's side but curiously the arrangement above was the opposite of that below, that is, the women and girls were on the right and the men and boys on the left. We juniors generally found ourselves in the choir-stalls while the adults liked to stand at either side of the organ. Compared to the girls the boys had more space because the choir was L-shaped and the arm of the 'L' was behind our stalls. This was very convenient for us because you could slip back into that niche out of Kate's angle of vision to peel your chestnuts, have a chat with a fellow choirboy, or just idle around till the service was over if you did not feel like singing. I liked the front row of the stalls as you had a terrific view of the whole church from above. Standing, you could look down over the parapet, with its wooden ledge angled steeply for music sheets; sitting, you could peer through the *oeils-de-boef* beneath it at worshippers scratching themselves, fidgeting impatiently, nodding off, whispering asides to one another. That I stayed in the choir for a number of years was due in no small way to the fact that I liked the view so much. That, and because it was fun eating chestnuts up there – we'd get through pocketfuls on a good night. But I liked the singing too. We could really make the 'Tantum Ergo' and the 'O Salutaris' move when we were in the mood.

None of us was really in a position to judge Kate's organ-grinding though we had the feeling that she came down a little heavy on the keys. We were better qualified to judge her singing – she should have stuck to the organ. Singing was better left to Mrs Kitty Endersen and Chrissy O'Brien of the Main Street who did solos for High Masses and weddings and the other public events. Mrs Endersen was a stalwart of the choir and it must have tried her patience, not to say her artistic appreciation, something fierce to have to put up with the rest of us bawling around her. On 22nd of December 1953 for the first time members of the choir went around town singing carols – and collecting for the parish fund.

What I remember the choir most for, however, is the bright May evening that I inadvertently lobbed a gob of spittle onto Annie Campion's nose, and the reason I'll never forget it is because I was scared shitless for days afterwards. Annie, who was probably in her late forties then, was a fierce Christian who gobbled up prayers like they were succulent marshmallows while at the same time shooting her eyes heavenward as if to ensure all was noted above. I would say that there was only one other person in the town who could devour a Hail Mary with the same vigour, Paddy Flynn of Botany, who eventually went off to join the monks in Melleray, where he became known as Brother Gregory. As they usually sat in separate parts of the chapel it was a rare treat to line the two of them up in your sights at the communion rail with their mouths going like the clappers. Peering along the pew at a row of lips moving in unison was one of the things I liked to do anyway when church services dragged on too long for my liking, and my eyes would brighten up whenever Annie or Paddy came into focus. You might also spot them when peeking through your fingers at the raised Host or when turning around to track a bird that had come in through the open doors to flutter from window to cornice and cornice to window. Not that I didn't pray seriously myself. There were times when I felt so holy I didn't know myself. I was just less exuberant about the business.

Christianity aside, Annie was no woman to cross. She could paralyse you with a glare at fifty yards and that bony, angular body of hers could shift at a lively pace. And she was a very determined woman. After a neighbour had hanged himself down the Grove she talked a female friend into accompanying her to inspect the limb from which the body was found dangling. Unfortunately for the pair, a couple of wags overheard them discussing the matter beforehand and, going on ahead, hid in the bushes nearby to await their arrival. No sooner did the women look up at the branch than the lads set up a ghostly wailing. The women screamed and took to their heels. Even for Annie the sombre Grove was no place to tangle with an unknown spirit.

On the evening I dropped the spit I was about 13, bored stiff above in the front choir-stall with the slow pace of the rosary. I was leaning over the shiny parapet, peering idly down at the congregation below when my eyes were drawn to Annie sitting directly under me in her usual place – aisle seat, last row of the middle aisle, women's side. I became fascinated by the mechanics of her routine – head rising and falling like it was on the business end of an Egyptian shadoof. The mischievous thought occurred to me that it would be fun to lob a spit onto the tip of her long nose when it was on the up and, though I had no intention of attempting this difficult feat, a ball of spittle began to form in my mouth. I withstood the temptation for a while but then lazily began to play a game of spittle roulette with the nose below, lifting my head up and down gently in time with it. Once, twice, three times, I dangled the spit from my lips, closed one eye, aimed with the other, then on the point of release skilfully drew the gob back into my mouth. The next time I slipped up. I had failed to appreciate how the spittle had grown in volume with each successive manoeuvre. I watched in horror as it spun down with precision accuracy, turning gently in a hazy ray of sunshine like a pearl falling to the bottom of a tropical sea. The nose rose. Plop! Timed to perfection. I sat back in my seat rigid with fright and prayed aloud like hell while I collected my thoughts. 'Jasus, I'm in for it now!'

I glanced nervously around. Unbelievably, no one appeared to have noticed what I had been up to – the rosary must have really sent everyone off to sleep that evening. The question was, had Annie seen me? If she had, there was no way out. If she hadn't, I had a chance. I doubted very much whether she would simply ignore the incident. That would not be Annie's style. I sang like a lark during benediction to give the impression I hadn't a care in the world but inwardly I was imagining the sublime forms of retribution that Annie might visit upon me if she found out. A Stations of the Cross maybe, with me as Christ? Having to face Annie's wrath was in itself the nearest thing to being thrown to the lions. There was nothing for it but to brazen it out. She would be waiting at the foot of the stairs like a vengeful Medea, if not right on the landing outside the choir door, to comb our faces with an icy eye. To my surprise and great relief there was neither sign of her on the landing nor in the stairwell below. But when I came out onto the front steps of the chapel with other members of the choir – we were usually the last out – there she was, clearly filling in the Canon on the incident, and fixing us each in turn with a scowl that could have stunned an elephant. I skipped past her with the innocence of the others and went off out the gate.

However, I knew the episode was not over yet – far from it. Annie wasn't one to let go a bone. She would complain to Kate too when the choirmistress emerged. Much as I wanted to confide in my pals I decided to keep the matter to myself. Aside from any fears that someone might inadvertently let it slip that I was the guilty party, I was ashamed of what I had done, even though it had not been intentional. The next day Annie appeared at the Christian Brothers School, still doggedly in pursuit of the miscreant. She had already been to the Convent and others of our classes. The net was closing in inexorably. P.D. Lee showed her into our room – I was in the Second Year then, I think – and she said her piece. There was an embarrassed silence. I knew I would have to own up if anyone else looked like being blamed for it. It was a question now of whether my nerve would hold. It did. Annie drew another blank. 'When I didn't shit in my pants then I never will,' I told myself as she left. Naturally, no one in the remaining classes could throw any light on the matter so I was off the hook. I was the cause of the Superior's giving us a brief lecture on behaviour in church just the same and Kate Connell kept a close eye on us during the ensuing week. Subsequently, I thought of going up to Annie privately and admitting to her that I was the culprit but there was a limit to my courage. She never got the apology that was her due.

In November 1946 parishioners, many for the first time, came to appreciate fully the eminence of Lismore's ecclesiastical past. Canon Patrick Power, the noted County Waterford antiquarian, published his *Historical Sketch of Lismore Parish*. It was announced at all Masses one Sunday that the booklet would be available at the door of the chapel from the following week, price sixpence. The cover came in two separate colours, green and orange-red, but the contents were exactly the same. It went like hot cakes. The writer drew together and expanded upon information that we previously only knew by hearsay, ranging from the founding of the town as a seat of learning by Mochuda, or Carthage, in the seventh century, through the time of Saint Malachy, our other local saint, through the history of Lismore Castle, to the early twentieth century. Along the way you picked up interesting nuggets. Mochuda was a Kerryman. The castle at one time had passed from the hands of the notorious Myler McGrath to Sir Walter Raleigh to Richard Boyle – the father of Robert Boyle, the famous scientist who was born in the town. The Presentation Convent was designed by Joseph Paxton, head gardener and architect to the sixth Duke of Devonshire at Chatsworth House He later went on to design and build the Crystal Palace in London. The Protestant cathedral had been built in its present form in the twelfth century. In 1814 the Lismore Crozier and the Book of Lismore, the contents of which do not relate to the town, were discovered in a cavity in a wall of the castle by workmen carrying out repairs. Tim Healy, first governor-general of the Irish Free State, went to school in Lismore.

The sad thing was, all this history on our doorstep was ignored by our teachers. Or, perhaps, not so much ignored as taken for granted. No teacher ever took us on a guided tour of the Round Hill, the castle, the two cathedrals, or the holy wells in and about our area. No one ever took us along the canal to explain its purpose and operation. No one discussed the history of milling in our area. The history and operation of ice houses was another subject that could have been explored easily; Castle employees could have explained this to us. But, at that time local history was not considered a worthy tool to fire the imagination. Canon Power later went on to complete the second, corrected and revised edition of his *Place Names of Decies,* a volume toward the publishing costs of which a number of Lismore residents, including Dad, contributed. Published in 1952, it is still the major work on the subject although scholars have since amended and corrected it on many points.

No discussion of religion in Ireland should end without a reference to funerals. They were always an event, from the tearful but sociable wake, to the processional walks to the chapel and the cemetery, to the climax when sturdy family members and close friends of the deceased would often pick up shovels to participate with the gravediggers in the final act of interring the coffin and shaping the displaced earth which was then bedecked with flowers and/or wreaths. Grief was tempered according to the circumstances of death and the age of the deceased.

Many people in town never missed a funeral, irrespective of how intimately they knew the departed. Foremost among these would be Michael and Danny McCarthy, who were ever-present in their severe dark suits and undertaker's mien. The pity was, they were not funeral directors themselves. Undertaking, you felt, was the profession for which they were made. No one could walk you to your grave with more gravitas and if you had been a customer of theirs they would put on a black armband for you as well. Somewhere in heaven someone must have been taking note of it all.

CHAPTER EIGHT

Gaelic Sports

WEST WATERFORD WAS an intensely physical environment in which to grow up. In any of our towns and villages you could not help but realise this. Take Lismore itself: the beauty of its mixed forest; the seasonal moods of the deep, meandering Blackwater and the clear Owenashad; the smoothly summiting Knockmealdown ever present in the distance; the earthy aromas of town and country; the striking architecture of so many buildings, from the modest little cottages in Church Lane to the grey stone castle perched on its promontory. All of these and more heightened, consciously or unconsciously, our awareness of the physical. Many years after I had left, a West of Ireland woman visiting a relative in Glencairn Abbey, and who as far as I could surmise knew something of the town, told me that she found the people of Lismore 'strange and gentle'. 'Unlike others in the area,' she added in some puzzlement. She did not enlarge upon the statement and I did not know her well enough – we chanced to be travelling by bus on a brief stretch of the road to Cork – to question her further. She could have been right on both counts. I think she definitely was on the second. For example, the hurlers and footballers of Lismore never acquired the ferocious reputation of those of our neighbours Ballyduff and Tallow. On the other hand, you would have made a great mistake had you assumed that the Lismore lads were there to be sat upon.

There were quiet men in our town, some of whom took little part in sport, or if they did, in sports of their own devising, and whom any man would have been advised to treat with respect. Tall heavyweights like Ned Coleman, Pad Lineen or Bill Landers and stocky men like Harry Vaughan or Storc or Phopper Stapleton were capable of doubling any trouble that might have been unwisely forced upon them. These were men who used to hold anvil-lifting competitions amongst themselves. Another Lismoreman, blacksmith Ned Brackett, could level a heavy wooden wheelbarrow at shoulder height, grasping it only by the ends of its handles, and was known as the only man who could perform this formidable feat. You would not

A fine portrait of some members of a Lismore junior hurling team and some of its supporters. Mid-1940s, probably. Players include Ronnie O'Donnell, a stalwart of the club for many years, seen kneeling on the left with his father J F O'Donnell standing behind him. Other players that I can positively identify are Michael Broderick, Billy Hogan (Main Street), Mossie Pollard, Georgie O'Brien, Bill Lineen and Johnny Vaughan. Among supporters I see Harry McGrath (who was very active in selection and training of the minors), Paddy Flynn, a young Richard Broderick, and a young Jim Lineen. The others I should know (many look so familiar) and will be reminded of them. Is that John 'Cal' O'Callaghan just being J F and Michael 'Lala' Crowley third from Cal's left? Time, unfortunately, did not allow for a proper and full checklist of those included. The occasion I also do not know.

have been advised to cross Nabsy Whelan or his brothers Mickey and Gordon Keyes – work that relationship out – on the hurling field. Nor anywhere Tommy the Hawk, a swarthy man who kept to himself, limped from a lumbering accident that, if anything, caused him to stride more purposefully, and who had a kind of an ever-present glint in his eye that cautioned 'keep off'. If Tommy came toward you fixing you with a look that suggested you might be more comfortable on the other side of the street you crossed over. Not that he would be looking for trouble, just maybe coming from it. There was no gentler middleweight around than his son Pedro, a man we youngsters greatly admired for his strength and fearlessness. The ashplant of Mikey Cooney, the cattle drover, was reputed to have seen men off the length and breath of Ireland. A couple of my schoolmates, Bernard 'Barney' Walsh, whom I was pals with for a long time, and Tommy Hartnett, with whom I was less friendly, could fist it out with the best of the bantamweights. And nobody got it soft from wiry hurlers like Pat

O'Donoghue, Ronnie O'Donnell, Mick Behegan, Michael Broderick, Kip Tobin or Tony Ahearne.

Pat O'Donoghue was one of our very best players. Trim but solid, skilful, fast and stylish, he could really belt a ball and was fiercely competitive. He played minor for Waterford and later went on to star for the University of Galway team when he went to study there. During his university years he would return to play for the Lismore juniors in the summer and was the main danger in our attack, popping up to ram in goals when the other forwards were getting nowhere. In 1951 he took part in a memorable game against Ballyduff. The Lismore lads, who usually came off second-best against our fearsome neighbour, had amazingly been running away with the game until the last five minutes when the opposition suddenly woke up and powered in four goals. It was a typical Ballyduff fight-back but it was not quite enough this time. Mick Madden and the rest of the backs regained their earlier dominance and Lismore held on to win.

Our sporting endeavours were mainly orchestrated by the Lismore Hurling & Football Club of the Gaelic Athletic Association but there was a surprising number of other options available: cricket, lawn tennis, table-tennis, badminton, swimming (in river and stream), for example. The main thrust of the town's ambitions was centred on the junior and minor hurling teams, the standard of play in my time not being up to senior level. At junior and minor, although we possessed some fine individual players, we weren't doing so well either, usually succumbing to stronger opposition during the opening rounds of the Western championships in early April. Certainly we were out of contention for any honours by the end of May. We held onto naïve hopes in Gaelic football, seeking inspiration in the legendary exploits of our famous Blackwater Ramblers who dominated the County scene during two periods, 1899–1902 and 1911–14, when they won a string of senior and junior championships. Since those early years, sadly, the centre of gravity of Waterford Gaelic football had shifted inexorably east until in the late Forties and early Fifties it was located along a five-mile strip of countryside that stretched from the foothills of the Monavullagh Mountains to the sea. From there came the gifted Stradbally and Kilrossanty senior teams of the period. It was left to Ballyduff and Knockanore to keep the west in contention at junior level. We called our junior football team the Lismore Ramblers, keeping alive the hope that one day the magic of our grandfathers would rub off on us.

The last members of the Blackwater Ramblers were still alive when I was growing up, none more hale and hearty than the brothers Garrett and Jim Hogan. A more charming man than Garrett you would be hard put to find.

He had the reputation of being tough as nails in his playing days and occasionally he would betray this aspect of himself to us when he was sitting on the sideline growing increasingly irritated by any player in the away team who was giving the Lismore lads a hard time. 'Stick in to him, damn it!' he'd roar, or 'Give that fella a belt!' Then he would turn around and chuckle good-naturedly at us youngsters who were sitting near him, hanging on his every word. The younger quiet-spoken Jim was held in memory to have been the better player, in fact, one of the greatest Ramblers of them all. Another Rambler was Joe Geary, who owned a pub in Ferry Lane and was also the local agent for international shipping lines. I was only 9 when he died. Dad told me laughingly how he and Joe had played a game of cat-and-mouse for a long time because of late-night drinking in the pub. Dad used to watch the place, knowing that Joe had some men inside, but whenever he raided it the drinkers had vanished. This line of police work was something for which Dad showed little enthusiasm. Quite how much it bored him I never knew until many years later Peadar Hickey of the Main Street told me an anecdote about him. The garage owner and his friends enjoying an after-hours drink used to be highly amused by a stunt Dad had devised for whiling away the time as he kept an eye on the pubs. He would hit the peak of his cap with the side of his fingers so that it spun around on his head a full 360 degrees and came to rest again in its original position. Evidently he became quite expert at this and would perform it many times during his surveillance stint. In retrospect I seem to recall Dad delighting me with this trick when I was very little but my recall may be faulty here.

The case of Joe Geary's vanishing clients, however, was out of the usual run of pub-busting. There was an obvious mystery to be solved. The matter achieved its resolution as Dad was preparing to leave the premises after yet another abortive raid. He noticed that a large framed poster, or portrait, on one of the walls was slightly askew, something he had not remarked upon on his previous visits. He went over and slid it aside and there behind it, crowded into a small chamber, were three or four grown men, grinning sheepishly. He found the episode so funny and was so pleased with the success of his sleuthing that he let Joe and the lads off with a warning. He knew the publican would have to toe the line in future – at least for a time – or build a new cubby-hole in which to stash his customers. Joe and he used often to laugh about the incident afterwards. After Geary died in 1946 the pub came into the hands of Joe O'Donnell. Appropriately, it was in the snug of this establishment that I gained my first experience of pub life.

Throughout the years of my childhood and my youth the old Ramblers were slipping away. A year before Joe Geary, Tommy O'Donoghue of

Chapel Street died; in 1952, Bill O'Neill of the same street. The Rambler whose death I remember most was Jacko Keyes of Botany who died in 1953. He was well-known to us all, not least because his daughter Kitty's house was a place of hospitality and fun for those of us who enjoyed Botany life.

My own career in the black-and-amber colours of Lismore was limited to one juvenile football match against Cappoquin, whom we considered our arch-rivals, and perhaps a juvenile or school hurling match at Lismore. And I played minor handball once at Stradbally – a singles game in which I got licked because I could not make head nor tail of the four-wall court, my first experience of such an alley. No more successful was the football match in Cappoquin. This was played on a Blackwater-soaked pitch – the southern half of the Cappoquin field was liable to flooding when the river broke its banks, as it had a few days earlier – on a sunny spring day. I only got on the team as a half-back because we were short of better players. And I had to endure a moment of supreme humiliation. Mickey Mason, a very tidy and fast Cappoquin forward, got round me and left me floundering in his wake. As he sped away from me up the right wing I could hear Harry McGrath, our coach, bawling after me despairingly to stop him. I didn't have to picture Harry's face, nor hear his language, when Mickey's shot flew over the bar. We lost the match, though it was not wholly my fault. Had it not been for Seán Moynihan's holding us together at full-back we would have taken a real hammering.

It was not so much the formal scene in the colours that I enjoyed as the informal puck and kick in mixed rig-out. Going up to the Hurling Field day after day on endless summer evenings to train with minors and juniors was great. We would arrive at the field between six and seven o'clock and change into our gear – togs and boots for those of us who had them or canvas slippers or old shoes and short trousers for those who had not. It would be the same for the men, except that some of them would be wearing long trousers. Nor did some of the men just wear ordinary pants in training. It was common enough to see junior players turning out for a competition match in such attire, especially the substitutes who came on. The trousers, indeed, might be the only item of his own that the sub would take onto the pitch with him, having borrowed boots, jersey and even hurley. In impoverished communities there was little cash for sartorial frills. When Ballysaggart put together a team in the early Fifties after a gap of some years half the side appeared in full-length trousers.

The Lismore Gaelic Field was pleasantly located and you took your time changing under the tall beeches at the town end in the lazy sunshine. The sun was still high when we started playing, long after sundown when we stopped. Juveniles, minors and juniors used to puck around together with three or four *sliothar*s during the warm-up period. Then the juniors, with those of the minors who were good enough to hurl with them would play a practice match in the town three-quarters of the field while we children were left to our own devices at the far end. When a championship game was in prospect the juniors would commandeer the whole pitch, in which case we youngsters had to make do with the space between the town goal and the beeches where we changed.

We were intensely proud of our fine Gaelic Field. It had undoubtedly the best playing surface in West Waterford, and probably in the county, but it had no sideline seats for a long time and was never furnished with changing rooms. The changing place on match days was under the tall hedge on the south side of the pitch beyond the sideline, one team near the entrance gate, the other further along at the back of Roseville, the ghostly manse on the Tallow Road where the elderly Millses lived. Occasionally, when a big match came to town, the teams would change at J. F. O'Donnell's pub in the Main Street. It was a constant complaint in Lismore that the town was not allotted its fair share of games even though it had the best pitch. In the late Forties a Gaelic Field Renovation Fund was set up with a view to providing better ancillary facilities. By 1947 the field possessed new railings and by 1948 sideline seats. The improvements, however, still failed to attract the important games for which the Lismore club was angling. Senior teams rarely came to town, and then to play exhibition matches mostly. At intercounty level we were only asked to host the odd junior football match. Our main problem was that Lismore, in spite of having some fine individual players, was not winning championships at that time so we lacked clout with the County Board. At the end of the Thirties and the beginning of the Forties the picture had been rosier. The classy hurlers we fielded during this period peaked in lifting the County Senior Championship in 1942, although this was subsequently taken from us by the Munster Council because of a dubious objection concerning the transfer of a player lodged by the opposing finalists, Erin's Own. At least, that was how Lismore viewed it. On their build-up to the senior victory the team had beaten the same Erin's Own side convincingly in the Junior County Final of 1940, following a victory in the Junior Final of 1938 over a team called St Stephen's.

Emigration was the main factor responsible for the decimation of sides throughout the Forties and Fifties. After Joe Duggan and a number of other players left for England in 1943 Lismore hurling went into a decline. Duggan went on to captain and play great games for the London Irish team Cuchulain's. I first saw him when he was home on summer holidays and came up to the Hurling Field to do a bit of training. Although he was probably past his best by then I could see for myself, if not from the faces of the regular juniors who clearly held him in awe, that he had form beyond the level of the usual players in our area. Another migrant who demonstrated class in training was Mick Regan who, like Duggan, had been a member of the 1942 team (he captained it) and was then also with a London club. In the 1950s one other of our best players was to enrich Cuchulain's, Sonny Bransfield, who was as delightfully stylish a hurler as the county ever produced. In October 1952 both Joe Duggan and Sonny played for London against Dublin in the All-Ireland Junior Hurling Final. Duggan at centrefield was voted man of the match and Sonny had a good game also. Lismore was only one of many teams that was bled of its talent by the exodus.

Sonny Bransfield, one of Lismore's and Waterford's most stylish hurlers (on left), and Dick Long sitting on Lismore Bridge in the early Fifties.

It would be an over-simplification to place all the blame for the depletion of teams on emigration, however. There was another factor at work, the GAA 'Ban' on participation in 'foreign games'. 'Foreign games' basically meant the classical English field sports of soccer, rugby, hockey and cricket. Tennis did not seem to count though it was frowned on too. Probably it was regarded more as mere recreation rather than sport. That was certainly my view. The Ban could only have been the product of Catholic minds. It was founded on true faith – the tenets of the Gaelic Athletic Association – and was wholly defensive in character. The most ridiculous aspect of it was that it demonstrated precisely the contrary, i.e. a lack of belief in the ability of two of the finest sports to be found anywhere – hurling and Gaelic football – to attract and hold players. The formal banning of a player usually came about when some stoolie or other whispered in the ear of the right person that he had seen so-and-so at a soccer match, not playing, mind, just *attending*. So embracing was this Ban that a player could even be fingered for being seen at a *dance* held in aid of a 'foreign game'. Naturally, some GAA committees saw in the Ban a useful instrument for weakening opposing teams where they could identify a top player who might have strayed from the green over the winter. Often this kind of information about a player was held in confidence for his transgression to be revealed at a critical moment in the championship. The 'rule' was hypocritical in the extreme and caused a great deal of acrimony. How could it have been otherwise, encouraging people as it did to inform upon others? Eventually nobody took it seriously and the GAA was forced to repeal it, but it took a long time dying. It was not until 1974 that it was formally written out. Players' reasons for non-compliance with the ukase varied: the natural tendency of an athlete to test his or her ability at different sports; dissatisfaction with the way a club was being run; social climbing (if you got to play interprovincial, or especially international, rugby you were on the ladder of success as an insurance salesman or something), the urge to spit in the eye of authority; plain distaste for hypocrisy.

The classical field game of hurling was above all such pettiness. We had all read how the legendary Setanta used to flake a *sliothar* the length and breath of Ireland for the fun of it, just as we knew how Christy Ring used to stop his Shell petrol tanker by the nearest level field every lunchtime to get out and practise again and again the lifting, catching, striking, lobbing, solo-running, swerving and free-taking that made him the greatest technical player of all time, a deadly and clinical finisher with a wholly professional approach to the game. Myself, I did not aspire to such heights of excellence, though that is not to say that I didn't harbour my own dreams of glory, like slashing my way through a thicket of hard men and flying *camán*s to escape up the wing, blood flowing from a gashed thigh, the whole town cheering me on, to evade a defender's last despairing tackle and lodge the *sliothar* in the corner of the net to steal the County Minor Championship for Lismore in the dying seconds of the game. Ah, what a joy that would have been had it happened in real life! A modest-enough ambition but one that few realised for their home town. On other occasions I dreamt right out of my class and pictured myself scoring that same golden goal to lift the All-Ireland Minor Championship for my county.

There was a real enough event to fuel that fantasy. In 1948 the Waterford senior and minor teams achieved a double that was rare even amongst the greatest hurling counties; they both won All-Ireland titles. It was the senior team that caught the imagination. Lismore had a man on the team, Ned Daly who was born and reared near the hospital and was then teaching in the capital, and was married to Tom Lineen's sister, Kitty. He treated us to a goal in the Final too. Ned it was who gave me my first glimpse of what senior hurling was all about. The year after the All-Ireland win he came up to the Hurling Field one evening to train and I happened to be standing near him on the sideline when he struck his first ball. He was all of thirty-five yards from the goal. There was a solid whack and the leather sizzled to the net, maintaining along its trajectory a height of no more than two or three feet from the ground. I had never seen anyone hit a *sliothar* so hard and so accurately, not even Willie Bob Lineen or Ronnie O'Donnell, two of Lismore's best forwards who could really rasp them home. There was another admirable distinction between him and those two players. When any of us youngsters got in his way during the puck-around he softened his swings and his tackles. Willie Bob and Ronnie never did and came flaking in at you in true junior style as if you were a grown man, which did nothing at all for your confidence.

After their All-Ireland victory the Waterford seniors took it in turn to tour the McCarthy Cup around the county's schools. The players who displayed it at the Lismore CBS were, appropriately, our own Ned Daly and the midfielder Eddie Carew. Tom Lineen, sitting in the desk next to me, flushed with pride when his brother-in-law held out the big silver trophy for us to touch. Then we all asked the two men excitedly to give us their own account of how they won it. We wanted to hear first-hand how John Keane, Waterford's greatest hurler, scored his three goals; how Johnny O'Connor, the other midfielder, linked up with Carew; how Christy Moylan, the all-rounder who was also on the county football side, fared; how Mick Hickey played – the powerfully built Portlaw man could give and take it with the best – in particular give, it used to be said. The win was doubly pleasing for Keane, Moylan, Hickey and the goalkeeper Jim Ware because exactly ten years earlier they had been on the county team that lost to the same rivals in the first and only other All-Ireland in which Waterford had appeared. Of all people it was a Carrick-on-Suir man, Mick Daniels from Greystone Street, the street in which I annually spent many enjoyable holidays, who captained the Dublin victors of 1938. I was chagrined when Mam passed me that nugget of information. Now in 1948 though, it did not matter. For the coming year the McCarthy Cup was the property of the boys in white with the blue cuffs and collars. Among the winning minors had been some of the men who a decade on were to figure in the classic All-Irelands of 1957 and 1959 against our neighbours, Kilkenny; the centrefielders Philly Grimes and Seamus Power of the famous Mount Sion club; Mickey O'Connor of Cappoquin, the fastest and arguably the most stylish player the county ever produced; John Kiely of Dungarvan who was to become as automatic a choice on the Munster Railway Cup sides as John Keane still was, and who was also a fine handballer.

In 1948 as well the Lismore camogie team brought a different dimension of excitement to the town. We had had a women's team, run by Monica Noonan and Sheila Daly, for a number of years, its success rate equalling that of the men's of the period, which was not saying too much. What intrigued me most about the women's game was the way they always seemed to go for goals even when a convenient point was there for the taking. In this instance, however, it was not the play of the Lismore Camogie Team that was causing the excitement but the fact that Miss Violet Nolan, Ireland's recently elected first beauty queen, had been invited to throw in the ball to start an inter-county challenge match between the Waterford and Tipperary camogie teams. And that was only half Miss Nolan's engagement. She was also to present prizes at a monster *céilidhe* in the Happydrome the same evening. Such a woman merited attention and I and my pals trooped up to the Gaelic Field to have a gander at her. In the blaze of publicity surrounding her the match had become incidental. She did not disappoint us. Her long red hair, more soft flaming mane than the foxy locks I knew in our area, wouldn't have disgraced Maureen O'Hara and she threw in the ball as well as any bishop or PP. The men on her side of the pitch outnumbered those on the far sideline and kept throwing admiring and hopeful glances in her direction. All to no avail, as far as I could see. I got as close to her as any of them and had as much chance of getting off with her as they had. I think Tipp won the medals.

We had to make the best of 1948. The next year began a long decline for Waterford hurling with one exception. Mount Sion, the perennial county champions from Waterford City, remained one of the most phenomenally successful club sides in Ireland, regularly winning challenge games against the best senior teams of Cork, Tipperary and Kilkenny. 1949 saw another of the weaker hurling counties, Laoighis, fight its way to the All-Ireland Senior Hurling Final. There were three unforgettable things about that Laoighis side: it trained on raw eggs, it was captained by a man with the unlikely name of Paddy Rustchitzko; and it was trounced by Tipperary. Tipp's easy win also turned out to be the first of three All-Irelands in a row for that county. I was sorry for the Leinstermen but happy for my mother's county. In supporting Tipperary, after Waterford had gone out of the competition, I was at odds with most of my pals in Lismore. I was even more at odds in supporting Kilkenny whenever they came up against Cork. That was my grandfather's county. Kilkenny had the added attraction for me of wearing the black and amber, although they wore their colours in narrow, vertical stripes while we wore ours in wide horizontal bands. Kilkenny was something of a bogey team for Cork at that time and could always rely on their elegant forwards Jimmy Langton and Terry Leahy to slot over winning points in the closing stages of a close and hard-fought game. As happened in 1947 when Leahy scored with virtually the last puck. My pals seemed to look at things from a different angle. Lismore being near the Cork border, they felt they owed their allegiance to that county when Waterford was out of the running for the championship. It was simply a matter of geography. For the same reason the more mobile citizens of Lismore looked toward Cork City rather than toward our own city of Waterford. I, on the contrary, resented the Corkmen because they were the ones who usually knocked us out, often in the first round, and often, more unluckily for us, by the slimmest of margins. So many times Waterford almost beat them! 'The Corkmen!' Mam would laugh with just a hint of malice, 'They're so cocky.' As for Christy Ring, much as I admired him, I knew he could be dirty when things weren't going his way. Supreme in all the skills of hurling, he had also mastered the art of the professional foul, sometimes getting away with murder, it was said. Aside from clipping opponents with the heel of his stick and digging them in the ribs with the end of the grip he had a fund of other niggling tricks for putting men off their game, and he used to browbeat referees.

But every man eventually meets his match and when John Doyle of Tipperary came on the scene Ring learnt to be very careful about how he conducted himself. We in Lismore took pride in the fact that the first referee to send him off was our own Johnny Vaughan, no mean senior hurler himself in his playing days. The Christy I used to see delivering petrol next door to Feeney's garage was a totally different individual, shy and withdrawn, in no way seeking adulation – he never sought that anyway as far as I could see; displaying his skills on the playing field seemed to be reward enough in itself. No hurler before or since approached the game with such dedication and even those who viewed him with a jaundiced eye had to admit that he was the greatest player the game had seen. Other Corkmen aroused no conflicting feelings in me. I had unqualified admiration for men like Liam Dowling, Allan Lotty, Jim Young and Paddy Barry. But I still did not want to see them win! Waterford being out of the way, I reserved my cheers for Tipp's John Doyle, Tommy Doyle (who kept Ring scoreless in two matches), Paddy Kenny, Tony Reddan and the big full-forward Sonny Maher who always hurled with his cap on.

One of my greatest regrets on leaving Lismore was that I never got to attend any of the classic series of Cork–Tipperary encounters in the Munster Finals of the early Fifties. Mam did not allow me to travel to county matches, even though I could have been accompanied by parents and uncles of friends. So I had to settle for the wireless and for the first-hand accounts that I got on the Monday after the match from Tom Lineen or Sucky Neville, who never missed these games. And it was not just the match and the crowds you missed. There was the whole adventure of getting to Thurles and back. Like what happened to Sucky and Doshin when they shared expenses with Jimmy 'The Hawk' O'Brien. Jimmy had a temperamental little Ford – up to the early Fifties you could guarantee that any Ford on the roads of West Waterford was temperamental – and it broke down on the way home on the Clogheen side of the Gap, the famous beauty spot high in the Knockmealdowns. Sucky and Doshin had pushed it more than halfway up when Jimmy, sitting cushily behind the wheel, came up with a bright idea. 'Leave 'er go, lads,' says he to my shagged-out pals who could push no more, 'If I run her back now she should start.' The lads looked at him dubiously and against their better judgement let the Hawk have his way. They knew they had made the wrong decision when the car disappeared around the first bend without a kick. They set off after it and eventually found it on the flat of the Vee, the hairpin bend in the foothills. 'Sorry lads,' said Jimmy. And they started pushing all over again, vowing that this time they would take the motor right up to the Gap from where they could freewheel down the other side to Lismore.

Dad would not have minded my going to the county games, I think, but having no interest in sport he was content to acquiesce in Mam's wishes. It may have been that money was tight; probably it was more because Mam thought I might get lost, or be beaten up in a fight. In the world of the GAA pitch encroachments were commonplace and occasionally reached the stage where there were running battles between rival supporters. Punch-ups on the field of play by rival players were frequent and hurleys were raised and used. Some men were even vicious enough to club an opponent from behind when the ref was not looking. What Mam failed to comprehend was that such incidents were far more likely to occur at a junior match in Lismore than at a senior championship game in Thurles, the temenos of the mainly Catholic game of hurling where bishops flocked to throw in balls and lead the singing of the 'Faith of Our Fathers '– 'We will be true to thee till death' – before the contest. Two of our neighbouring villages, Tallow and Ballyduff, had fearsome reputations and the Lismore lads always approached matches with either team with some trepidation. There were always scores to settle from previous years. But though the Lismore lads were not warlike, they had their breaking point in the face of excessive provocation. I saw Pad Lineen, the broad-shouldered Lismore Estates Company fisherman, normally the calmest of men, kayo with a single punch a Ballyduff man who made the mistake of getting to him. There was one local match I was not even allowed to attend – I was very young at the time. It was a county championship game at Lismore between Tallow and Ballyduff that fully lived up to its hype. Games between the blue and gold of the former and the red of the latter really packed in the crowds, however ambiguous the crowd's reasons for attending. This time things got so out of hand the *gardaí* had to draw their batons and make some arrests. Men were carried from the field, gashed from belts of hurleys, and maybe from batons too. From the front window of our house I saw a couple of Ballyduff players being helped along toward the changing room at J. F. O'Donnell's in the Main Street, coats thrown casually over their shoulders, the blood on their heads indistinguishable from the red of their jerseys. Then I was hooshed away from my perch by Mam. That night it was later than usual when Dad came home. He looked tired and grim.

Mick Hickey of Portlaw, a sound half-back on the county senior team for many years, was reputed to be the toughest and most ferocious hurler in the east, a reputation matched in the west by a couple of Ballyduff men, Mick Beecher and the excitable Mikey Quirke who in Dungarvan, according to the late Beaver Doherty, flattened a referee whose decision he disputed. Beecher was a big, handsome rogue of a man with a Ronald Reagan quiff and a wide smile. Whether he played at half-forward or half-back the well-brilliantined quiff seldom turned a hair during the course of a match. 1953 was his greatest year when Ballyduff achieved the rare double of winning both the Junior Hurling and Junior Football county championships. He captained the hurling team and, I must admit, that we in Lismore were not unhappy to see a side from the west administer a beating to Mount Sion, even if it was only the eastern club's junior team. Coincidentally, the Mount Sion seniors were also completing a double, stopping Kilrossanty from making it five in a row in the football. Disagreements within clubs often led to players turning out for different sides in different years. Some players were particularly free with their talents and Beecher was one of them, even going so far as to declare for Ballyduff's arch-rival Tallow. There was another explanation for a player's moving from club to club – an understandable desire to play at a level commensurate with his talents. A hurler or footballer of senior quality would not have wished to spend his peak years shoring up a junior team that showed no hope of winning the county championship and advancing to senior grade. Nonetheless, it was strongly felt that allegiance was owed to the place of one's birth. Beecher wore the black and amber on one or two occasions as well, albeit in football. You could store up a lot of ill-will for yourself with that kind of chopping and changing but Mick was able to give as good as he got. Off the field, typically, he was the most amiable of men they used to say. Like Christy Ring, another Jekyll and Hyde. How he came to play for us I'll never know. We had no reason to like him – on their way to the 1953 double Ballyduff had given Lismore a fierce hiding. In spite of that the Lismore lads did not begrudge our neighbours their championship win. Considering that Ballyduff had also roughed up the clean-playing Lismore side in 1951 this attitude was even more astounding.

When Ballyduff met Tallow there was good hurling to be seen as well as blood and guts, however. Charlie Daly and the white-haired young defender Pat Rafferty of the reds were fine hurlers and experienced intercounty men. Tallow could count on the Curley family – Mick, who had played a blinder in goal for the Waterford senior team in the 1938 All-Ireland Final; Con, who had been on that same Waterford side when they beat Cork in the Munster Final; the evergreen Sonny without whom Tallow would not have been Tallow; Billy, Joe, and Paul, the youngest and most promising. There was probably only one other hurler in the county who had a longer playing record than Sonny, the fanatically fit Cappoquin veteran Paddy English. English already had grey hair when I was following the fortunes of the Cappoquin seniors and he played on long after I had left the region, finally hanging up his stick at the age of 46. One of my classmates, Peadar Henley, a cousin of the Curleys, played on the Tallow junior team while still a minor. A small, chunky, surly lad with an insolent slouch, he was as tough as teak. We were not exactly close friends but I had to admire the courageous way he could hold his own with grown men. He used to ride point-to-point too and I once saw him in Lismore jumping a ditch, neck-and-neck with another jockey, each flaking out at the other with his whip, and bumping and boring as they galloped off to the next obstacle. Any man who was in that league knew how to handle himself. But West Waterford junior hurling was not all rough-house. As I intimated above, Tallow and Ballyduff often belied their reputations as hard physical sides with skilful displays of team hurling.

Cappoquin consistently and successfully fielded elegant, fit and clean-playing teams in all grades. The Geraldines of Aglish were a new strong hurling side of the early Fifties, with a particularly attractive player in 'Stylo' Riordan, as his nickname suggests. And the great Tourin senior hurling team of the same period that came from an area between Aglish and Cappoquin fired the imagination of every hurling follower. Tall, rangy men, height accentuated by their strip of red-and-white vertical stripes, they carried themselves like Texas rangers and swept the county in 1950. They got to the Final again in 1953 but, sadly, this time they were trounced by the almost automatic holders of the championship, Mount Sion, and the meteoric ascendancy of the glamorous West Waterford side was over. As with Tallow, a couple of talented families formed the backbone of the team. Of four Fives brothers, two of them, Mossie and Jimmy, went on to play for the county. The Duceys supplied a brace in Dick (who also liked to referee) and Tom. The character of the team was George 'Haudles' McGrath, the left back, who looked like Dan Duryea, the fast-talking Hollywood actor who specialised in laconic anti-hero and not-so-baddie roles in the Forties and Fifties. With his lank hair combed straight back 'Haudles' cut the same kind of rakish figure as the American and, like the American in his screen persona, could mix it when the heat was on. Against all this neighbourly success the Lismore juniors could only muster the occasional unexpected, but well-deserved, win in the early stages of the championship. Cappoquin, their regular victims in the Thirties and, to a lesser degree in the Forties, were now the more imaginative hurlers with players of particular quality in Mickey O'Connor, Billy Conway and Mick Lacey. In the centre of the county two new sides were emerging with some success, the oddly named Fourmilewater and the metropolitan-sounding Brickey Rangers, snappily abbreviated 'The Brickeys', who took their title from the River Brickey, a stream that flowed into Dungarvan Harbour.

What Lismore did produce in the early Fifties was good refereeing, although we regarded this skill as a somewhat dubious compensation for the lack of a winning championship side. John F. O'Donnell, 'John F.' as he was known, another of the Blackwater Ramblers, was probably the man who established this tradition in the town. He was very much the elder statesman of Lismore GAA when I was a boy and still very active in the affairs of the club. Another of the older referees, Seán O'Hugain, was only a name to me. One of Dad's colleagues, Jim Byrne, refereed hurling and camogie. We had two intercounty refs, Johnny Vaughan, who was in the process of winding down a successful hurling career at senior, junior and intercounty level, and the long and lean ex-junior Mossie Pollard, aptly nicknamed 'Legs Eleven' by Sucky Neville. It tickled us to see 'Legs' – we abbreviated him after a while – loping out onto the pitch like a giraffe, uttering brisk brrr-brrr-brrrs on his whistle. Like Johnny Vaughan, Mossie felt it was his duty to stamp out rowdyism. Unlike Johnny, he never achieved the distinction, or had the opportunity, of sending off the most famous player in the game of hurling. Christy Ring didn't go to the sideline meekly and used all the weight of his reputation to pressure Johnny into changing his mind but the Lismoreman stood by his decision. The only other ref in the county to make an impression on me was Jim Pinkert of Dungarvan, and that was only because of his unusual surname. I vaguely wondered whether he was distantly related to the ace Pinkerton detective agency that we used to come across in the American pictures.

We had two boys' teams in our town, the minors St Malachy's and the Christian Brothers School's St Carthage's. The school team used to acquit itself fairly well in the Dean Ryan and Dr Hackett knockout cup competitions, the major trophies for schools' hurling in our region. One of our neighbours in West Street, Franco McCarthy, starred in a side that beat Mount Sion to win the Dr Hackett Cup in 1940. After that, however, no trophies came the school's way. At the end of the Forties and the beginning of the Fifties the most successful schools' team in Munster was North Monastery, 'North Mon' of Cork City, who practically monopolised the winning of the big competitions.

I might have stood some chance of getting onto a Lismore team but I did not have a hope in hell of securing a place on the school one. To be picked for St Carthage's you had to fight for your place not just against the lads of the town but against the lads from a radius of ten miles or so who attended the school. So on the school team we had at various times strong hurlers like John Osborne of Aglish who later played for the Geraldines, John Herr and Frank O'Donoghue of Cappoquin who went on to play minor for the county, Charlie Bolger of the same town who if he didn't play for the county afterwards certainly got trialled for it, Peadar Henley of Tallow, and others. The problem with the school team was that the lads never had enough time to establish any real teamwork. My role in it all was merely as a kind of sparring partner. Wednesday was sports day at the CBS and in the afternoon the Hurling Field would host two games simultaneously, the senior boys occupying the town end of the pitch, the juniors the other. Both football and hurling were played, the choice of sport being dictated sometimes, but not always, by forthcoming competition. I never enjoyed these occasions as much as the summer evening training sessions amongst the Lismore minors and juniors. They always seemed so frenzied and competitive. Perhaps it was just the atmosphere of the curriculum. Still, it was preferable to being stuck behind a desk.

The hurling and football I liked most of all was when we youngsters organised matches and competitions amongst ourselves. I really did train extra hard for these – as much as I did in spring to get myself fit for the start of the season. Keen as I was, Tom Lineen, a strong hurler who could lob over seventies even as a boy, was keener. One spring we started particularly early. No sooner had daylight reached beyond the threshold of evening than we were regularly hurling in the field behind the library, taking frees, practising solo runs and tackling one another on the matted winter grass. In a way, I suppose, I was little more than a ball retriever for Tom but I got a lot of enjoyment out of it just the same and was pleased that he considered me a good enough partner with whom to practise.

Curiously, the one moment of glory in my short hurling career occurred against Tom. We were on opposing sides in a competition we were holding in the Fair Field in Botany and happened to find ourselves competing for the *sliothar* in the outfield. By a sheer stroke of luck I managed to get ball, hurl and hip in line and beat my pal to the stroke. A satisfying sting ran up the handle of my stick to the palm of my hands as the boss met the ball full on. At the same time my hip caught my opponent off balance and sent him sprawling. As he fell I heard Sucky, who was on my team, yell, 'Atta boy, Baler!' I felt very proud of myself but also a little overawed by the unaccustomed skill I had demonstrated. Tom was the best player on either team so I knew the measure of my achievement. Needless to say, he was none too pleased at my momentary success but he was not a person to bear a grudge over it. If he was, I would have had cause to worry.

These competitions in the Fair Field were played in a carnival atmosphere. We would set up a kind of knock-out league between the different streets of the town, the ostensible prize being the mere satisfaction of winning, the real one just taking part. I used to be on the Main Street team or one of the Botany ones, from which sides the winners usually came. But Townparks always had a good team too, with the likes of Willie Ryan, Pat 'Bags' Murphy, Bishop Scanlon and Michael 'Murph' Murphy on it. Our non-official contests received official recognition during the first Tóstal in 1953. One of the brothers in our school, Brother Beare, I think, organised a seven-a-side Gaelic football competition for which a set of medals were to go to the victors. There were sixteen teams in all, each captained by a strong player. Aside from the medals there was another difference between this contest and those of our own devising. Because it was open to all juveniles attending the CBS lads from outside the town also took part. Pierce Colbert, who was very good at picking off points from a distance, was my captain. I would have preferred to have been on Seán Moynihan's side – he was the best footballer amongst us – but that was the luck of the draw. Tom Lineen captained another team and it was his turn to put me down when his side defeated ours and went on to appear in the final. And not so surprisingly, it was a Cappoquin man, Frank O'Donoghue, who captained the winning squad. Frank, a nephew of our Irish teacher Vin O'Donoghue, went on to play minor football, as well as hurling, for the county. I was glad to see his side win because my pal Boxer Dennis was in it. But I had another best pal on the losing side, my neighbour Tom Feeney, and I was sorry that he and Tom Lineen, who did not like to lose, had to fall at the finish. They were especially disappointed because they had already beaten O'Donoghue's team earlier in the competition. One way or another most of us were disappointed. But the whole thing had been great fun and had attracted a lot of people to the Fair Field.

Aside from competitions we were always arranging impromptu one-off games among ourselves, the kind where numbers did not matter. We just split up whatever players were available into two sides. The selection of the teams for these games was always a tense affair as far as I was concerned. We all knew who the captains were likely to be and we all knew roughly where we came in terms of ability. I was very conscious of this. Some of the lads could not have cared less who wanted them or didn't want them in their team. Murph, i.e. Michael Murphy, was like that. Cool, easy-going, he would just toss his lank, fair hair and amble across, grinning with indifference, to whoever picked him. But he could hurl when he wanted to. I was not captain material any more than he was but, unlike him, I used to wait tensely in the hope that I would be chosen by one of the captains whose selections I liked to be on – Seán Moynihan, Tom Lineen or Jim Crowley. It was always a great disappointment to me if the player I favoured failed to pick me. Even worse was the blow to my self-esteem when I found myself relegated to a spot further down the list than I had anticipated – the weakest players were the last ones to be chosen. Occasionally I would find myself picked earlier than expected and that pleased me no end, although attendant upon this was the trust that I would lift my game accordingly. Maybe I earned it. There was a time when I used to practise hurling for hours – lifting, striking, taking cuts and frees, solo running with the sliothar balanced on my boss... . I must dearly have wanted to be a good hurler.

Our self-organised games would take us outside the limits of the town now and again. One spring Saturday a dozen or so of us juveniles – some of the Dennises, Tom Lineen and Sucky Neville amongst us – set up a match against a group of lads from Rath. Rath was a townland that lay north of Lismore on the way to Sruh and the shortest way for us to approach it on foot was through Ballyrafter Wood. We entered the wood just beyond Paxman's, hurleys with boots laced to the the boss slung over our shoulders, and followed the right of way uphill until we came out near Rath House, the residence of Miss Jacob, a courteous, grey-haired woman whom I often saw shopping at Macs in West Street. She was distinguished in belonging to the Quakers – an odd sort of Protestant sect, very peaceful, and not a lot of them about, as far as I could gather from what I had been told. Beyond the house we came out onto a small plateau of green fields. A bitter wind was blowing from the Knockmealdowns but the day was clear and sunny, or at least it was until we changed into our gear and trotted out shivering onto the frozen ground that was to be our pitch. We had only just started playing when the wind carried a flurry of snowflakes across our field of vision. During the ensuing minutes we chased the ball from end to end in packs in order to stay warm. Barely ten minutes had elapsed when I looked up the field from my position at left back to witness a curtain of white descending over the halfway line. The tail end of it swirled down towards me. It rippled clear of the green and I saw play continuing at the other end. But soon it was down again. We hurled on for another few minutes before we were forced to give up. Not long after we had changed back into our ordinary clothes the weather perversely cleared up again. On our way back through the wood the sun was shafting light along the tips of the trees. We came across a badger's sett and examined the large mouth of it warily. We all knew how fearsome an enemy that shy and peaceful creature could be if you attracted its hostility. Then we continued on our way again. In sporting terms the day might have been a failure but in terms of a day out it had been interesting and educative, not least the experience of organising an away game in our own right.

Although Gaelic football took second place to hurling in Lismore the club made determined efforts to ensure that it always fielded teams at minor and junior levels. But in the Forties and early Fifties, while we had some chance of winning through to the Western Final in hurling, we had no hope at all in football. Our best footballers were outsiders from footballing counties – Walter Creane, the eldest son of the *garda* superintendent, who was a Dubliner; Seán Moynihan, a *garda*'s son, and a Kerryman; and, at junior level for a time, Tommy Keane, our English teacher who was also from Kerry. My classmate Pierce Colbert was our best locally produced juvenile. Although lightly built for the game he was a nippy forward with an accurate boot. Unlike the rest of the GAA players in the town the three lads, aside from Tommy Keane whom I never saw with a hurley, were footballers first and hurlers second. Unfortunately, we did not hold on to Walter for long. No sooner had he completed his Leaving Certificate than he left the country to take up a position in the British Colonial Service in Salisbury, Southern Rhodesia. There was one all-rounder in the club, Ronnie O'Donnell, who was equally proficient in both codes. At school we were urged to try our hand at the two. I liked football myself but not half as much as hurling. For one thing, football was miserable on a wet surface because the leather ball that we inflated with a bicycle pump absorbed so much water it really took it out of you to kick it any distance. High fielding was one of the paramount skills of this game and you needed height and brawn, allied to a keen sense of timing, to become expert at that. I quickly realised how difficult it was when I misjudged the drop of a high ball and took it right on the top of my outstretched fingers. I still have a bent third finger from that miscalculation. I was lucky I did not break it.

My first glimpse of what senior football was all about did not come until 1953. In April of that year, again as part of the Tóstal celebrations, Kilrossanty, the Waterford County Champions, played Fermoy who were, I think, the Cork Champions in an exhibition game at Lismore. There was a huge crowd at the game and the minute the players stepped out onto the pitch there was a buzz that told you this was going to be something special. These were big powerful men and the way they swatted the leather around in the warm-up suggested they knew how to play football as it should be played. All eyes searched out in particular two Kilrossanty men, Billy Kirwan and Cheasty Lonergan, top-class footballers who had represented Munster as well as Waterford. 'Which one's Cheasty?' 'Which is Kirwan?' we asked our elders eagerly. Recognising well-known players from the scratchy photographs in the Dungarvan newspapers was not always easy. Cheasty, who had been playing for years, was said to be past his best and certainly the grizzled look of his massive, chiselled head suggested venerability. 'Past his best?!' I asked myself incredulously as he picked off some lovely points from difficult angles, one a sideline free from all of fifty yards, taken right in front of where I was sitting, that he booted over unceremoniously with a thunderous drive. The fielding skills on display by all thirty seniors on that day were a revelation to me and from then on I took a heightened interest in the game of Gaelic football. That great Kilrossanty team had inspired a resurgence in the county game too, so much so that the year before Kerry had only managed to scrape through by a point against Waterford in the Munster Championship – an unheard of feat by our predominantly hurling county. That performance had fuelled our anticipation of the Kilrossanty–Fermoy challenge. Kerry was always *the* team to beat in football and when I was growing up the likes of Paddy Kennedy and the Brosnans were among the finest players to have appeared in the green and gold. Not that Kerry had it all its own way. Dad, who came from the footballing county of Sligo, was pleased to see the teams from the West of Ireland doing well, even though he expressed little interest in sport. He was particularly disappointed when Roscommon, his neighbouring county, failed to beat Kerry, after first taking them to a draw, in the 1946 All-Ireland Final. Paddy Kennedy was matched in those games by a Roscommon star with the unusual name of Bill Carlos.

The year 1947 brought an even more eventful All-Ireland Senior Football Final because it was played not in Ireland but in the famous Polo Grounds of New York City. It was to be the first and only time that a Senior Final was exported, an imaginative attempt by the GAA, nonetheless, to show Irish-America, and in particular the Mayo-born Mayor of New York, William O'Dwyer, the real thing. There was also a low-key commemorative link as 1947 was the 100th anniversary of the height of the Great Famine, that catastrophe of Empire still on the fringe of living memory which many Irish-Americans, in particular, found hard to acknowledge had befallen their impoverished forebears. But to me, and many others, the export of what was one of our national occasions made little sense. How could you have an All-Ireland Final in some other country? Not that it made any odds to me really, Dublin or New York being equally inaccessible, and either way I would be relying upon Mícheál O'Hehir to bring me the game on the wireless.

My pals and I were very proud of our national Gaelic sports commentator and relished his many clichés. His greatest assets were his ability to keep up with the game and his sense of humour. He was also skilled at setting the scene and giving you a sense of the atmosphere. Once you got locked into his commentaries you almost felt you were at the match yourself. As we did not have a wireless at home until 1951 I listened to most of the games at Feeney's or, if they were away for the day, in the *garda* barracks day room that looked across to the Monument. I was lucky to have a choice of places. At the barracks a couple of guards and some other men would be ranged around the walls, lounging on wooden chairs, one or two others by the large oak table, when I would poke my head around the door and ask whether I could join them. Guard Dennis or Guard Moynihan would nod me inside and I would find a vacant space on which to perch. Waiting expectantly for the game to begin, I would take in the knowledgeable opinions of my elders on the state of the teams and of the world. Guard Murphy, in particular, with his placid smile suffusing his full, round face, impressed me with his comments. Outside the sun would be blazing down on West Street, melting the tar into dark glistening pools here and there. Only the odd mongrel would be moving, and he lazily. Then suddenly we found ourselves in Thurles, or Cork, or Limerick, or Dublin. At half-time I used to go out into the street and stretch, and when the mongrel was there, pat it on the head if it came across to me. It was usually one I knew from Botany. From the day-room would echo the voice of O'Hehir, above the pipes of the interval band, discussing the action that had transpired so far and what was likely to come.

Listening at Feeney's was a different experience. The large wireless occupied the full space of a wide window-sill, all but shutting out whatever light the curtains let through to the living-room at the back of the shop. Indirect light filtered in through the doors that led from the kitchen and the shop. A number of us sat on the dark shiny sofa and in the deep matching armchairs, and stayed in the cool shade from start to finish of the match. When Tom or Michael or their Dad wanted to listen my presence would always be tolerated, but if Mrs Feeney was on her own she was understandably not very happy when I knocked on her door and roused her from a nap on the one afternoon of the week that she had off. When lending an ear to the odd game with us she would also get very annoyed when a customer looking for petrol would ring insistently on the doorbell. The way she reasonably looked at it, everyone around knew the garage closed on Sunday afternoons so drivers should have taken account of that fact when estimating their fuel requirements for the day of rest. Her husband Jim was more laid-back about it and did not mind topping up a wayward traveller.

Whichever of the two venues I patronised I used to find it a very lonely experience coming out into the street after a game in which the Waterford hurlers were involved because not one of my pals would be about. They would all have gone off to the match by car or excursion train and it would seem to me that I was the only youngster left in town. It was a cinch, however, that nobody from Lismore was away at the Polo Grounds final. An extra thrill on that occasion was being allowed to stay up late as the match did not commence until 8.30 p.m. Irish time. Feeney's was full. O'Hehir's voice was clear but it had an unaccustomed faraway crackle to it. Kerry, the favourites, seemed unhappy on the foreign turf and Cavan, with its clutch of O'Reillys, Mick Higgins, and especially Peter Donohue, upset them. Dad was happy to see a team from what he saw as his region of the country – he had served in Swanlinbar for a time – make up for Roscommon's loss of the previous year. The next day brought another novelty. Wire photos that had been sent directly to Dublin for the first time appeared in the daily newspapers. The strange immediacy of the lined and fuzzy images was reminiscent of the pictures of the Joe Louis–Billy Conn heavyweight championship fights. The Polo Grounds experiment was a one-off. Afterwards, the All-Ireland rightfully came home to stay and, over the next few years, Cavan and Mayo gave Dad more to cheer about.

Though I never managed to be the hurler of my dreams I did succeed in kitting myself decently. I only ever owned one set of hurling/football boots and I used to savour the gladiatorial click of their studs on the tarred road. They gave me a sense of growing up. They lasted well because I took care to keep them smeared with dubbin. Hurleys did not last long. I broke a number of these. Obtaining replacements was only a problem when you did not have the money to purchase a new stick. We were fortunate to have a fine hurley-maker in Lismore, Bertie Fitzgerald, a tubby man who had a small sawmill on the corner of Fernville and the Mayfield Road, opposite the tree-lined entrance to Ardagh, Dr O'Farrell's fine house and grounds. Bertie had a trained eye for a good piece of ash and used to supply *camáns* to many hurlers in the area. Choosing the plank of ash from which your hurley was to be cut was exciting. You would go through the open galvanised gate and find Bertie in his workshop at the far end of the premises, around you the delicious aroma of freshly cut wood and under your feet the springiness of the carpet of sawdust. Bertie would amble over to you with a canny smile, size you up for price and height, show you a half-dozen planks within your range, then leave you to make your choice. You cast your eye over the timber, noting the disposition of the knots and, above all, the grain. A good grain, i.e. one that curved naturally where the boss of the hurley was to be, was vital, otherwise you would find yourself with only half a stick in your grip at the first clash of the ash. At my age you never got the best, of course. You would gaze enviously at some perfect planks that Bertie had put aside for adult hurlers who needed sound equipment. What point was there in wasting a fine piece of timber on a young lad like me? But hurleys could be unpredictable. The finest-looking *camán* could unaccountably split in two at the first wallop. It was common at matches to see new hurleys getting smashed, some cleanly, some jaggedly. This was an occurrence welcomed by youngsters on the sideline, who would pounce on a discarded stick and carry it off home to give it a new lease of life with a strip of metal band from a packing case and black insulating tape. Your only guarantee from Bertie was that you would leave his shop with as well-crafted a piece of workmanship as could be had.

After you had chosen your plank you gained the immediate satisfaction of seeing him block out the rough shape of the hurley with the circular saw. Your initials were pencilled on the handle of the rough, which then took its place alongside others in various states of completion. A week or so later when you called back Bertie would hand you the almost-finished product and ask you to test it for length and grip. You took a few swings with it, leant on the middle of it to test its spring, ran your hand up and down the handle. You and he would exchange a few comments. Then he would double-check the height of the hurley against your hip. After that he would fix the object in a vice, plane off some shavings here and there, grunt with satisfaction, and ask you to return for the finished product in a day or two. At the final try-out he might take off a few more shavings, sandpaper smooth the alteration, then the hurley was yours. Twelve and sixpence was the last price I paid Bertie. The fine hurley I got for it lasted me quite a while. If I had been a better hurler it would not have lasted me half that long, I'm sure. No reflection on the maker. Merely that a better player would have tested its capabilities more intensively. I was a well-satisfied customer, even though I missed the weight of my hard-earned 12/6 out of my pocket.

To ensure a longer life for my stick the first thing I did as soon as I got home was put a metal band around the boss. This I always did at Feeney's garage. Strips from packing cases were always lying around the workshop and Kieran Fenton or John 'Panzer' Behegan would give me a copper rivet and allow me to use the vices. First I sized and bent the piece of metal around the centre of the boss, cutting it so that the join I was about to make was on the heel. Then I hammered a hole through the overlapping ends with a nail, pushed the rivet through from the inside of what was now the narrow base of a triangular band and beat it flat. All I had to do then was slip the band up over the boss from the toe and tap it into place as tightly as it would go. For added insurance I hammered a couple of light nails through the sides of the band to make certain that it would not fly off during play. Such reinforcement was very effective although it offered no guarantee that the hurley would not give elsewhere. A hurler's favourite stick might end up with three or four bands on it, with added strips of insulating tape, from repeated repairs. The black tape was often wound round the grip as well, to prevent slipping when hands became sweaty. I tried not to use it there because my hands used to get black and sticky. However, after a hurley slipped away from me once or twice I resorted to the tape as well. The extra weight on the boss lent by the metal bands was favoured by some players as it helped to lengthen their puck. Badly riveted joins were murderous and at times players received nasty gashes from opponents' defectively repaired sticks.

A small town like Lismore was lucky if it could produce a team at minor and junior grade. A large one like Dungarvan could support a number of clubs, any one of which might produce teams at all grades. I had no real knowledge of GAA activities in the seaside town but did of Carrick-on-Suir, a place of comparable size. Carrick had three clubs, two of which, the Swans and the Davins, were based on the northern bank of the River Suir and consequently played in the County Tipperary championships. The third, the Mollerans, was based on the County Waterford bank of the town where the players trained on a tight saddleback pitch below Grubbs Hill. They participated in the Waterford championships and only ever met the Carrick Mór teams in challenge games. The real confrontation, thus, lay on the Tipp side of the river. And confrontation it was. The Swans and the

Davins were deadly rivals and whenever they, or their minors the Cygnets and the Stars, met you could cut the air in the town with a knife during the run-up to the game – irrespective of whether this was a championship encounter, or a mere challenge. The Davins' headquarters was located across the street from my aunts' house, either at the Temperance Hall that was, or, a few doors further down, at the horse-collar adorned premises of Paddy Harraher, the saddler, who single-mindedly trained them.

As with Lismore, this club was going through a lean period during the late Forties and early Fifties, and it was due to family involvement and geographical proximity that I supported them. Uncles and cousins at one time or another played for, or were involved with the club. My uncle Jimmy Morrissey was talented enough a hurler to be nicknamed 'Doyle' after Eddie Doyle, the great Kilkenny defender of the early twentieth century, whose style of play on the left wing Jimmy was said to emulate. The Davins or, to give them their official name, Seán Treacys, which nobody but the local newspapers seemed to call them, were essentially a hurling team. That they ever produced a junior football side, which they managed to annually, and which caused consternation if they got beyond the first round of the championship, was due solely to the club's anxiety to hold onto an extra vote on the county board. Again, like Lismore, they possessed an excellent Gaelic field, the only one in the town, which because of the club's lack of success was not getting the class of match it deserved. It was, after all, called the Davin Park after the famous south Tipperary athletic family of the early part of the century. Carrick was renowned for its all-round athletes in those years, another, Tom Kiely of nearby Ballyneale, being world champion in 1904 and 1906. In Clonmel lived the jovial Corkman Dr Pat O'Callaghan from Kanturk, Olympic hammer-throwing champion of 1928 and 1932. Mam seemed to know him and I met him once or twice when he called to Greystone Street to see the Morrissey family. The Davin Park, located at the beginning of the Clonmel Road, may have been the Davins' pitch but they did not train there. Their training ground was a mean triangle of public land on the corner of Greystone Street and Mill Street, known as the Wad. The Swan – they were always referred to in the singular locally – were having as much success as the Davins were experiencing failure, even going so far as to break the stranglehold of the great North Tipp teams on the Tipperary Senior Championship. They may have had no Gaelic field but they did have a relatively better training ground than their rivals, i.e. the Fair Green, or simply the Green as it was known, also public land. Another advantage they had was a proper clubhouse, situated across from the Level, which was anything but level.

Encounters between the two sides filled the Davin Park, no matter what grade was playing. The rivalry was so intense supporters had to choose carefully where they stood; Swans ranged on the Treacy Park side, Davins on the West Gate side, neutrals, such as there were, at either end. Among the supporters none were more vocal than the women in black shawls. Insults were freely traded across the width of the pitch and it was an unfortunate son who let his mother down by playing badly. He would not hear the end of it until he redeemed himself at the next derby. If he was a Davin the chances were that he had little hope of redemption. If, on the other hand, he was a Star he had every hope of revenge. The Cygnets, unlike their seniors, did not have it all their own way. The two minor sides were involved in a number of exciting clashes, one of which I was delighted to witness because my favourite cousin Brendan O'Mara, who played not only for the Stars but for Tipperary as well, had a cracking game in a Stars win. A couple of years later in 1947 Brendan turned up unexpectedly at the Lismore Gaelic field as a sub on the Tipperary junior *football* team which, not unexpectedly, lost to Kerry in the Munster Semi-Final.

My own single hurling exploit in Carrick occurred not on the Wad but on the nearby Well Road. I was about 8 or 9 at the time and Dad was taking me up the river bank for a walk. He was deep in thought. I was messing along after him, hitting out at loose stones on the road with the hurley I was carrying. Coming on a small heap of loose chippings that council workmen had left in their wake after repairing potholes, it occurred to me that it might be fun to have a wallop at it. Coincidentally, a green CIE bus from Clonmel came past Bóithrín na gCapall, the side road that led down to the Suir a hundred yards farther on. I was standing on top of the pile at this time and, though I suspected that what I was about to do was bold, I was unable to hold myself back. As the bus drew level I lashed out and sent a volley of pebbles against the side of it. Perhaps some of them flew in through the windows? Whatever, the bus shuddered to an abrupt halt and out jumped the conductor and stomped over to me with a thunderous face.

'Don't you know that's a dangerous thing to do!' he yelled angrily, catching me by the shoulder and shaking me. 'You might have hurt someone.'

I was helplessly silent in my guilt.

Dad came to the rescue. 'That's all right. He's my son. I'll take care of him,' he rapped.

The conductor was not satisfied and wanted to question me further.

'I'll take care of him,' Dad repeated grimly and silenced the man with an authoritative stare from under the brim of his brown hat.

The bus conductor seemed cowed by this and returned to his vehicle. All the passengers were looking at me. I felt shamed and humiliated.

'That was a very silly thing to do. You could have hurt someone,' said Dad quietly, echoing the words of the conductor. Then he told me to run on ahead and left me to stew in my own juice. It showed on my face that I realised I had done wrong and that was enough for him.

It was a huge disappointment to me that I never made the grade at hurling. I did try and I did train but I lacked two basic attributes, confidence and real guts. I had not much of the latter, which was drawback enough, but I was totally short on self-confidence. Of the two, confidence was the more important. My frequent bouts of illness and Mam's constant warnings that I was frail and needed to look after myself had sapped all my sporting belief in myself. I grew ashamed of my skinniness and felt reluctant to strip off in the company of my more muscular companions. It used to be a source of wonder to me when I saw skinny players handling themselves with confidence on the hurling pitch against physically stronger opposition. Charlie Bolger of Cappoquin was just as skinny as I was but he could mix it in any hurling company. As noted earlier, he got trialled for the Waterford minor team and while still a minor turned out at junior level for his town. Such confidence was beyond me. Then there was the Lismore bank clerk, Peter O'Kelly-Lynch, who was very insistent that you put the 'O' in his name though we all knew him as plain 'Kelly-Lynch'. Peter, if that were possible, seemed even skinnier than I, and used to take the field like a lost Egyptian mummy with his legs swathed in bandages. He was neither a great hurler nor a great footballer but he loved both games and played regularly for the junior team, at times way above himself, turning in performances that surpassed those of his more muscular team-mates. What impressed me most of all about him was his ability to ignore the cruel jibes and ironic cheers that we launched at him when he ran on as a substitute. My muscular pals, like Seán Dennis and Seán Moynihan used always to have a go at him and I joined in, half-heartedly, because I knew that in doing so I was having a dig at my own skinny frame.

But Kelly-Lynch was a target for us on more legitimate grounds too. He was always on the committee of the club, as treasurer usually – he was, after all, a bank clerk – and went on to become treasurer of the Western Board. In this capacity he did little for us juveniles and minors, we felt, so we gave him a ribbing on this account as well.

Discontent among the minors about the way the Junior Committee as a whole viewed minor affairs rumbled on over a number of years until the minors took matters into their own hands in 1954 and decided to run the

Malachys themselves. My own eventual break with the club came about partly as a result of this air of neglect. Later, better players than I were to give it as the main reason for their decision to give up hurling – a loss of talent the club could definitely not afford. But you had to hand it to Peter the way he took the field, calmly adjusting the soft cap he always wore, allowing our jeers to run off him like water off a duck's back. To shrug off that sort of thing you had to have confidence. At senior intercounty level it used to please and baffle me to hear of the phenomenal point-scoring of Jimmy Kennedy of Tipperary, the frailest-looking player ever to play for a major county. All his teammates had to do was create space for him around the midfield, pass him the *sliothar*, and watch it sail over the bar.

If skinny Jimmy Kennedy was frail, not quite so skinny Jimmy Brohan of Cork, who was just emerging on that county's minor team, was indestructible. No better full-back was to go out on a field. He claimed every inch of his own corner and frequently whole areas inadequately covered by his fellow backs. It was a stirring sight to see his lean frame breaking through a half-dozen burly forwards, beating off their despairing thrusts with his stick before sending down a long clearance to his own front men. As he was to do in senior ranks in the late Fifties with a regularity that defeated the best forwards put up against him. With *that* confidence I could have hurled a quarter as well as he and been happy!

Dissatisfaction with the GAA committee was not only something that concerned the minors. The juniors had their troubles too. Problems came about usually over selection or training, or over access to the club funds. The situation got so fraught one year in the early Fifties that the Botany lads, feeling they were getting a raw deal in selection terms, opted out en masse and made serious efforts to set up a rival team of their own, called the Nemo Rangers after the Cork team of the same name, I suppose. It was a refreshing idea to try to put together a team that was not named after some obscure saint or other, and they did not immediately seek a priest as patron. Pedro O'Brien and Mick Behegan, two sound hurlers, were involved in the venture and may have instigated it. A number of trial games were played against scratch teams from the surrounding countryside but, owing to a shortage of players, the Nemos never really got going and the hopes of Botany foundered.

One summer's evening they played a Glencairn selection in a friendly at Glencairn and I walked there to support them. I had given up hurling myself by that time but during the game someone on the Lismore side got injured so I was dragooned into minding goal in my ordinary gear. Luckily, I did not have much to do as I did not possess sharp enough reflexes for that position.

It was dusk by the time I was really tested. An opposing forward got round the Nemo backs and charged in on me after the incoming ball. I had the *sliothar* clearly in my sights and confidently reached out my left hand to grab it at the same time swerving to the right and drawing back my hurley arm for the expected clearance I was about to make. Unfortunately, my hand closed on air as the ball chose to hop away to the left on the uneven ground. It was in the net before the forward reached me. Soon afterwards the whistle blew for full time. I was on the winning side, which did not say much for the opposition. Walking home the two-and-a-half miles later, Tommy 'Gawkser' Cahill got up my nose by accusing me of being windy, saying I had leapt aside when I saw the forward bearing down on me. The accusation was ironic as Gawkser himself was no more a hero than I on the field of play and got his nickname because his eyesight was weak. But I could forgive him. I was fond of his sister Dodo. Other new teams that did hold together for a time were Glen Rovers (the 'Glens') from Araglin way and Shamrocks from the Tallow direction.

Years later, Mikey Coleman, by then a Catholic priest home on holidays from Japan, was to tell me of a similar moment of embarrassment when he was playing for the CBS school's team, St Carthage's, in Fermoy. Normally a cute corner forward, where his tally invariably amounted to a goal a match, he found himself on this occasion unaccountably guarding the net, a position for which he felt he possessed no talents. As all the action at that period of the game was taking place at the other end of the pitch, he stood alone and bored in his own half. On the end line near him, Vin O'Donoghue, our Irish teacher, and Brother O'Connor, the CBS superior, who were responsible for selecting him in goal, were observing the action. Suddenly, one of the half backs on the opposing side unleashed a freakishly long clearance from his end of the field. Mikey, so far untested, but under no pressure whatsoever from the opposing forwards, none of whom was within thirty yards of him, advanced calmly from his goal to deal with the unthreatening situation. The ground was somewhat bumpy and the ball hopped once, then twice. Mikey, heedful of Vin's dictum that whenever your square was threatened you did not mess around trying to lift the ball but pulled first time and cleared it out of the danger area, decided unwisely on this course of action and, instead of covering the *sliothar* with his body and attempting to catch it in his hand, he elected to pull on it. As with my Glencairn experience, the ball danced away from him at the critical moment and, slipping past his flailing *camán*, went straight into the net for a giveaway goal. *'Amadán! Gligín!'* he heard Vin hiss furiously. It was, he said, the nadir of his hurling career. But he experienced a perverse glow of

The Lismore ball alley on the elbow of Church Lane in summer 1990, showing the former home of Jack Dunne and family immediately on the right. 'The Heap' was located directly opposite the mouth of the alley, nearside of the low wall that didn't exist in my time.

satisfaction in having graphically illustrated to his teachers why he should never have been put in goal in the first place.

The Gaelic game that captured my imagination when I was 13 or 14 was handball. The town had a number of concrete ball courts. The least impressive was that of the Christian Brothers' school, a mere single wall. A large and well-preserved four-wall racquet alley existed in the grounds of the Presentation Convent. One summer a few of us persuaded the nuns to let us try out a game of handball there. We reached the informal conclusion that it would be an ideal court for us to gain experience of the four-wall game but, for some reason known only to themselves, the sisters refused to let us use the place on a regular basis. It was an irritating and incomprehensible attitude because, as far as we knew, the girls attending the school seldom if ever used the court. Perhaps they made more use of it than I remember? The town's public ball alley was the one in Church Lane, erected by the Duke of Devonshire at the end of the nineteenth century. It was a well-constructed three-wall court, although not as spacious as the convent one. The first time I saw it I was overawed by its huge, dark-grey, lichen-flecked walls. There had been an element of danger for a young fellow with Botany affiliations in venturing down the Lane in the first place, but I was in no way prepared for the discovery of this deep canyon behind the row of small houses.

Handball came naturally to the lads who were born and reared in the Lane. They grew up hitting a ball around the alley. Before the Lismore Handball Club was revived in 1949 after a gap of many years the Landers, O'Callaghans, Colemans, Dohertys and Dunnes were accomplished handball families who played the game among themselves for the love of it. But it was not until the beginning of the Fifties, when the lads started thinking about competing as a club, that the town really came to appreciate the talent that had existed all the time. The Dunnes' home adjoined one wall of the court and we were forever plaguing Jack and his wife Molly, seeking access to their well-stocked vegetable garden to recover the standard (the special ball for handball) that one of us had mishit or deflected over the side. Jack had been a good handballer himself and his son Pa, who was a year or so younger than I, was keeping up the family tradition. The family's good humour only gave out after we had knocked on their door for the sixth time in an hour.

A couple of doors up from Dunnes lived Jackie O'Callaghan and he too had passed the game onto his sons. And Pakes Lynch of that generation, a gillie by trade and a good one, was still playing. Mick Landers and Mick Coleman, who were in their late twenties or early thirties, and others of their age group, were the inspiration for the Lane's many handballing successes of the early Fifties. Mick Landers was regarded as the best player ever to have come out of Lismore and was the driving force behind the formation of the new club. His brother Bill was also a powerful hitter of the ball. Another Landers, Dick, (from Glengarra and no relation to the Church Lane family) was Chairman of the Club throughout the early Fifties. We nicknamed him 'Fellow Gaels' because he always initiated his brief, painfully shy speeches with this fraternal greeting.

It was the softball game, using the standard, that we played. But you first had to pick up the fundamentals with either an ordinary rubber ball or a tennis ball. The specialised standard was for a long time unobtainable from any shop in the town so it had to be purchased in Dungarvan or elsewhere. It was also not cheap. I was very proud when the day came that I was considered good enough to be able to cope with the electric bounce of this ball. One day outside Madden's Bar and Bakery John 'Cal' O'Callaghan showed me a standard for the first time, and not just one but two, a new example and one that had 'cracked' from constant usage. The new one was firm and had a translucent look about it. You could sink your fingers in the pith of the older 'muddy' example where the insides had cracked, but even this one, with the best hammered out of it, jumped away from me when I hopped it on the flagstones. Both were yellow-brown in colour and very smooth, with a circumference appreciably smaller than that of a tennis ball. During play in the alley someone would often loft the ball not only over Dunne's side wall but over the other side wall or the high front wall as well, to land in Guard Boyle's field. When this happened we were adept at dodging around to the side to catch the hop of the rogue shot or at visualising from the trajectory at which the standard flew over the front wall the approximate patch in which we expected to find it. When the grass was allowed to grow too long we would curse 'The Rancher', as we had nicknamed the guard, because it cost us extra time to locate the ball – sometimes it might take five or six of us as many minutes to unearth it. The front wall had an attraction for us other than handball as well. The back of it, unlike the playing surface which was cemented flat, was coarse and it was possible to climb up it, finding grips in the decaying masonry, and peer down into the alley. Sometimes during a game a face, often that of Michael Cooney who took a particular joy in it, would appear and grin down at you. If a serious match was in progress the face would be quickly warned to fuck off.

Three really good handballers brought success to the newly re-established Lismore Handball Club: Cal, Ned 'Beaver' Doherty and his first cousin, Peter 'Cox' Doherty. But the best player in town, as those three were the first to point out, was a non-competitor, Peter Neville, who lived at the top of Main Street in a distinctive grey-stone house at the mouth of Church Lane. Pete was only coaxed into playing once for Lismore, I think, partnered by Beaver in a minor softball doubles match against Tooraneena, which the pair won without sweating. He was a natural. A big, soft, playful youth with a ready grin and a penny-sized patch of grey hair on one side of his otherwise black head, he had style, strength and intelligence to throw away. Whether he struck the ball fiercely, or stroked it gently, his timing was perfect and he could place his shots with clinical accuracy. No one could butt like him and he could point out the exact spot on the front wall where he was going to place his shot. Sometimes for a laugh he would tell you he intended putting the ball in a particular corner and, when you went haring in that direction to play the return, would send it to the other corner or whip it back tantalisingly over your head, leaving you floundering like an eejit. I never minded him making a fool of me in this manner. He did it so agreeably and with such an infectious chuckle that you could not take offence and, of course, his skill was so admirable I was glad to learn from him. Though naturally right-handed, if he had really wanted to he could have beaten me with his left. And I was a reasonable player. It was a pleasure to play with him, or to watch him play. Always, but ineffectively, I was trying to model my style on his. The problem with him, from the club's point of view, was that he was also naturally slothful and devil-may-care. The idea of training was foreign to him and he had no time for club competition. He played the game for his own enjoyment and was happy to leave it at that. I respected his view but, like the other players, felt it was a shame that he did not want to develop the excess of natural talent with which he had been endowed. We all pleaded with him to play for the club, none more than Cox who was constantly at him, but to no avail. Commitment would have made him invincible. As it was he could be beaten.

Beaver Doherty also had loads of natural talent. Raw power compensated him for not being as gifted and as quick-witted as Pete. He was stocky, hard-muscled, with broad shoulders and strong arms – the perfect build for a handballer. Pete could strike a standard as hard as he, exquisite timing giving him the velocity to match Beaver's strength. The latter had another physical advantage: his hands were harder than the former's, hard enough for the hardball game which he had a go at when Billy and Jack Walsh of Midleton, two well-known senior hardball players, came to Lismore to play an exhibition game.

The hardball deserved its name. It had a hardwood core, moulded round with leather and rubber. A hand as hard as a cricket bat was required to play it consistently. And you needed to be very quick on your feet to keep out of its range when an opponent sent it flying around the alley. If it caught you on the head it could lay you out. I tried striking it a few times after the exhibition but did not fancy it at all. Apart from the discomfort caused to the palm of the hand, it was woefully short on bounce compared to the standard. (Eugene Dennis remembers it differently, 'skiddy with a fierce erratic bounce'. He's probably right.) Beaver did not take to the game after the experiment.

Another game, very much a minority sport of brawny men, in which he tested his ability along the back road to Cappoquin, was road bowling. It was Jessie Gallagher of Cappoquin, a noted West Waterford player, who taught him the skills of this. In Munster it was very much a Cork game and was dominated by a man called Mick Barry who could loft and spin the 'bullet', as the iron bowl was called, with a skill and strength that no one then could match. Beaver showed me the bowl with which he played. In size it came somewhere between a *sliothar* and a golf ball, nearer the first-mentioned than the second. Weighing its twenty-eight ounces in my hand I could easily imagine the power that was needed to send it hurtling along a country lane.

That Beaver had that power I had no doubt. He would amply demonstrate this from time to time, one of his accomplishments being to launch, with an underarm throw, a sizable stone from the height at the end of Ballynelligan

Cottage boreen, which overlooked both the inch below and the full width of the Blackwater, onto the opposite riverbank. It seemed an awesome distance and although he was only 16 he was the only man we knew who was capable of this feat. One day, in our company, from the same eminence he deliberately landed a stone in the water near to where a man was fishing from the bank opposite. The man peered about him perplexed. He must have known it was not the kind of splash that a fish would make but he could detect no one within range of a stone's throw. We saw him look up at us but clearly he dismissed the possibility that anyone might have tossed one from there. Eventually he settled down to his fishing again. A few minutes later Beaver lobbed another missile just short of the bank. Before it had had time to splash our pal had dropped onto the grass alongside us to enjoy his victim's outraged and totally mystified reaction to the second interruption.

If Pete Neville's game was physically surpassed by Beaver's, it was surpassed in quickwittedness by Cal's. Cal was the cutest player in the county. Playing him was like playing a ghost. You never knew which side of you he would appear at next, or in which direction he was going to send the ball. He was a master at switching play and sending out conflicting signals – when you came dashing forward expecting him to go for a butt he would loft the ball back over your head and when you held back expecting a long lob he would cut short the swing of his arm and gently butt the ball so that it peeled back from the base of the wall leaving you stranded. His skill at reading a game allowed him to conserve energy to such a degree that he often played with a lighted fag in his mouth. A singles match between him and Pete was fascinating to watch – cat-and-mouse and full of entertainment as both were noted for their quips. Cal was another of those physically frail sportsmen whom I admired. He was tall and quite thin, with a right shoulder that was pronouncedly higher than the left. His reflexes were razor-sharp, which made him a fine goalkeeper at hurling as well. As long as he had a sound set of backs in front of him, and the bespeckled carpenter Georgie O'Brien usually gave him solid cover at full, nothing, or very little, would pass him. What he did not have if the backs gave way was the strength to fend off burly forwards. He played many good games and some brilliant ones for the junior hurling team, plucking seemingly unstoppable shots out of the air with hand and hurley. Beaver was also a talented hurler and could have won himself a regular place at half-forward on the county minor team if he had applied himself to that game. As it was, he played some fine games for the Malachys. However, with the sudden growth of interest in handball promoted by the Landers family both men decided to devote their skills to that sport.

Cox Doherty was the linchpin of the handball club. Unlike his cousin Beaver who lived at Devonshire Cottages, a neat row of artisans' dwellings across from the Hall near the Presentation Convent, Cox lived in the Lane – at the extension beyond the ball alley, and one could almost say, *in* the ball alley. He was as possessive of the alley as he was competitive as a player. Slight of build, he was stronger than Cal but not at all as sturdy as his cousin. Quick-witted as a player, he was almost a match for Cal. A perfect doubles player he was strong in singles play also. Being the most competitive of the Lismore handballers, it used to annoy him intensely to see Pete Neville and, to a lesser extent, Beaver, not exploiting their natural talents to the full. He could be fun, Cox, but he could also be peevish. Playing with him, you were expected to take the game seriously. At times though, when Cal and Pete Neville were in a caffling mood, he fell around laughing like the rest of us. It was murder for opponents to encounter Cal and Cox at the top of their form in a doubles. The two frequently dominated to an extent that was embarrassing.

The handball club's good years really began in the summer of 1951 with the holding of a town tournament to choose the best players for the first championship match against Tooraneena. There was never any doubt about the top players. It was the second rung that had to be filled. As well as those mentioned earlier there were other contenders from the Lane itself. Andy Ahearn, trim, with muscular arms, and wearing well-sweated leather straps on both wrists, which gave him the swashbuckling appearance of a trapeze artist, could swat a ball as hard as anyone. Tommy Parker, a lazy, shambling kind of lad, not to be taken seriously you might think, could play a cagey game when the mood was on him. By now, interest in the game had burgeoned beyond the immediate environs of the alley to the whole town, in part, perhaps, due to our inability to achieve any success in hurling and football during this time. Handballers like Brooky Lynch from Townparks, Seán Dennis from South Mall and Ritchie 'Bawgie' Broderick from Main Street were strong prospects for doubles roles. But I did not discount myself. I had developed a passion for the game and used to be up at the alley training at ten o'clock on summer mornings, whatever the weather. At times I would even use only my left hand in order to strengthen that side of my game. Being accepted as a doubles partner by Cal, Beaver, Pete and Cox had done wonders for my confidence and I reckoned I had as good a chance as any of the younger players of getting picked for the minor squad. In the evenings of that July the area around the alley was crowded with lads waiting for a game. Church Lane was a narrow L-shaped street, its right-angle positioned directly across from the alley. At the angle there was an empty space where a few houses had been cleared and on that space was that hump of rubble that we called 'The Heap'. There we would lounge around waiting our turn for a game, sizing up the strengths and weaknesses of potential opponents. I knew I was developing into a useful, if limited, player and my confidence was boosted by a couple of wins in the initial stages of the boys' tournament. It began not to seem too far-fetched that I might even have it in me to beat strong-hitting lads like Bawgie or Seán. My opinion of my abilities suffered a rude shock when I met Pa Dunne toward the culmination of the minor knockout competition. That Pa was a worthy competitor I did not doubt, but as he did not take the game as seriously as I did I cockily convinced myself that I could defeat him. I had reckoned without the pedigree of the Lane boys. Pa had observed a fatal flaw in my game and he exploited it ruthlessly. My long game was lacking in strength so he used his fist to belt the ball out to the back of the alley, and even onto the road, pinning me in the outfield when I needed to be closer in. I was given little opportunity to butt, at which I was reasonably adept, and Pa sailed through convincingly to the next round. It was a crushing blow to my self-esteem and I went home dejectedly that night. I had failed in another game that meant so much to me.

Seán Goulding of the Main Street, Seán Uí Guilídhe as he was officially known in his capacity as a Fianna Fáil senator, opened the softball championship proceedings against Tooraneena. His interest in the sport had come as a surprise to us youths. The small, mild-mannered politician with the glistening spectacles had not shown himself around the alley until then. His participation brought luck to the club. Beaver annihilated his opponent in the minor singles (21-2, 21-0) and Pete Neville and himself easily won the minor doubles (21-6, 21-2, 21-12). Cal and Brooky Lynch eased through the junior doubles (21-10, 21-10, 21-13) and Cal had no trouble in winning a singles challenge match (21-10, 21-10). We only had one disappointment. In the junior championship singles Mick Landers was below his best and lost 21-9, 21-11. It had been a successful debut by the club.

In April 1952 another event in which Seán Goulding took a hand fired the ambitions of the club. The Senator, in generously presenting a cup and a set of medals for the winners of a senior tournament involving some of the County Cork's and Ireland's best players, gave the lads the opportunity of appreciating the intercounty game at first hand. Until then the Lismore team had had no genuine idea of where they stood in terms of quality vis-à-vis other teams – with the sole exception of the Touraneena challenge match which seemed to indicate that we had players as good as any in Waterford at least. (Touraneena was an established club.) The players who had agreed to appear were Billy and Jack Walsh, who were also to demonstrate the hardball game, and John Fox and Jimmy Hanlon of Fermoy, the latter Munster Junior Softball Champion at the time. Dick Landers was expecting a huge crowd to attend, even though handball had nothing like the following of hurling or football. He had laid on the Éire Instrumentalists Céilidhe Band to march the imported gladiators to the arena. He instructed us to extend the Heap with pick and shovel, which we duly did, so that it would accommodate more spectators And on the Sunday, to avoid an anticipated last-minute crush at both ends of the Lane, he sent us out after the last Mass to sell advance tickets. We had expressed some doubts about the necessity for this but, Dick in his role as chairman insisted upon it, so a few of us youngsters were sent out, furnished with rolls of green tickets and green canvas bags in which to carry the loot. Boxer and Michael Dennis and I were strung across the road in Chapel Street between Quinlan's shop and St Carthage's Hall. It was a grey bitterly cold day, unseasonal for the month of April, and we exchanged jokey asides with one another as we shouted out, 'Get your tickets now for the big handball tournament! Avoid the crush! Get your tickets here!' The mass of punters weaved past the pitiful barrier we represented as if we were a leaky sieve, not *one* of them buying a ticket. We were looking very sheepish when Mr O'Connell, the debonair manager of the National Bank came across to us, snug in his expensive crombie overcoat, and with his handsome wife dangling on his arm. He was the one who was to be handing out the medals to the winners later on. 'Look lads,' he said, 'I won't be able to get to the alley until late so here's a sixpence for my ticket.' We protested that he did not have to pay as he was doing the club a favour by supporting our endeavour but he pressed the tanner on us anyway so we took it. And that was all we had to take back to Dick. To put it mildly it was a meagre profit for our morning's work and suggested ominously that the icy sullenness of the weather was going to have a dire effect upon the gate. Dick, however, shining with optimism, maintained against all the evidence that we would be fighting off the crowds come three o'clock. Sadly, his confidence was again misplaced and the expected hundreds never materialised. Indeed scores would have been an exaggeration. But, although the club may have lost money on the venture, to those of us playing the game the exhibition was a revelation. The two Walshes were grown-up versions of Beaver Doherty and they struck both standard and hardball with clinical ferocity. Cal was the only Lismoreman involved, playing a softball singles game against Dick Slattery of Fermoy. We watched this with intense interest as we knew that Cal's performance would be a measure of the standard of our game. In spite of playing well, our representative was comfortably beaten by his more experienced opponent. Clearly, we still had a lot to learn.

That year the club took off. With Peter Neville declining to take part, Bawgie had won the right to partner Beaver in minor doubles. In early May Beaver won his minor singles match against Touraneena opposition 21-0, 21-0 and he and Bawgie won their doubles against the same club 21-19, 21-0, 21-10. Cal was the junior singles choice and Cox and Mick Landers the junior doubles pair. Pa Dunne and Seán Dennis were standing by as substitutes. Beaver's reputation had spread so fast he was already picked to play minor doubles for the county with a player from Dungarvan. The County Board's faith in him was not misplaced. As well as winning the County minor singles title (21-12, 21-1) at Stradbally he later got to the final of the senior softball singles where he was only beaten with difficulty (21-17, 21-12, 21-12) by Guard Seán O'Connell of Tramore, a much more experienced opponent. The *Dungarvan Observer* of 20 September 1952 commented, 'Experience showed but Doherty with a few more years in which to gain strength and experience could become a powerful force in the handball world.' And, as if that was not enough, he and Ritchie took the minor doubles title. With Cal's winning the junior singles, our club celebrated its first full season in the county championships with a *céilidhe* in the Town Hall at the end of August.

In championship games the Lismore lads encountered one great disadvantage – our alley was a three-wall one. Championship matches were played in four-wall courts. I only ever had the opportunity of competing once in a four-wall alley, in the one in Stradbally that was the best in the county. It was a scorching hot day and the team had driven down to the seaside village in a hired Ford V8. Beaver, Cal and Cox were playing championship games and they had kindly set up a challenge singles for me against a local player so that I could gain some experience of the back wall. The sun had been blazing down all day and when I entered the court through the small wooden door at the back heat came at me from all sides. Given a bit of sand it could have been a Roman arena. If I felt nervous to begin with, I was quickly disillusioned further. My opponent, engaged in his warm-up, was hooking balls effortlessly off the back wall. I scrambled to do likewise. Above me, Cox leant over the wall to say a few words of encouragement. My challenge did not last long. I could make no fist of the four-wall game and was swiftly dispatched two sets to none. My despondency at my poor showing was compounded when I saw how successfully my teammates had adapted to the four-wall alley. It hardly seemed to trouble them at all. Cox, indeed, played better there than he did at home. I realised then, if I hadn't before, that they were in a totally different league to me.

The year 1952 was also the year in which Beaver, Boxer, Seán Dennis and I cycled down to Kilgobnet with Cal and Cox to see the latter pair compete in a medals tournament arranged by the local handball club. The Lismore GAA committee, who showed little interest in handball, had refused to pay for a car for our two players. Again it was a sultry day and fourteen miles or so on the old bikes we possessed was no joke, especially for Cal and Cox who were the ones who had to play a game at the end of the journey. We experienced the worst bit of the trek along the side roads that led from the main Carrick road to the small village that lay at the foot of the Monavullagh Mountains. We were getting tired and thirsty by this stage and only vaguely knew where Kilgobnet was. 'Only a mile up the road,' we were assured at different points by a number of locals. When the one mile began to seem like four we figured we must have taken a wrong turning somewhere. Eventually we arrived, shagged out after the final pull, and somewhat later than expected. The Kilgobnet lads crowded round us, relieved to see Cal and Cox in our midst. In appreciation of the effort we had made in journeying there by bike they treated us with great hospitality, bringing us refreshments before the game and feeding us afterwards. They had a fine three-wall alley like our own and in the intervals before and after the Lismore challenge the rest of us had a chance to fire a few shots, and Beaver, naturally, raising gasps of admiration among the onlookers. We had the added pleasure of seeing the Lismore pair win through to the final of the tournament, which was to be played on the following Sunday. In the face of such determination and winning ways the GAA committee was shamed into paying for a car to take the two players to the final in which they beat Dungarvan. The hurling element on the committee, in particular, was envious and depreciative of the success of the handball club at a time when the hurlers were going through very lean times. Disparaging remarks about the sport made by a couple of Main Street hurlers in the presence of Beaver and his Lane pals in Madden's Bar one night led to a few punches being thrown.

The year of the club was 1953. It began in April with a home tournament linked to the town's first Tóstal celebrations. Players from Lismore, Fermoy and Dungarvan took part. The big name was John Kiely of Dungarvan, the great senior hurler whose prematurely grey head was to become instantly recognisable at senior county and interprovincial level during the rest of the decade. He was not as proficient at handball as he was at hurling but he and his partner were good enough to beat Cox and Mick Landers in junior doubles just the same. Beaver and Cal won their singles games. The Lane lads went on to qualify for no less than five of the six County Finals in the autumn, with the evergreen Mick Landers bowing out of championship handball by winning the junior singles title. Beaver, representing Waterford, defeated a Kerry player in the Munster Softball Singles Minor Final at the Horse and Jockey court near Thurles. Later in the All-Ireland series the new Munster champion lost to a Roscommon player. Cal and Cox had represented the county in junior doubles but went out early against stiff opposition. The lack of regular training in a four-wall court undoubtedly told against the Lismore players in spite of their adaptability. There had been some talk amongst ourselves of constructing a back wall in the Lismore alley but nothing ever came of this. For a start, there was no money for the volume of building materials that would have been required, and there may have been a problem regarding planning permission. What the club did manage to do, and Mick Coleman and the lads from the Lane did the job themselves, was extend the playing area beyond the side walls of the alley right up to the road, by concreting over what had previously been a pitted patch of earth that was quite dangerous for players, particularly on the left-hand side. The GAA went some way toward addressing the training problem by paying Beaver's bed, board and travel for a two-week stay in Stradbally to allow him to train intensively in the four-wall court there before the Munster Championship Final. Beaver himself used to say that, as the weather was so sunny while he was there, he spent more time relaxing in a pub (O'Brien's or Whelan's?) down the road from the alley than honing his skills in the four-wall game. 1952 and '53 were the peak years for the club. After that the lads seemed to lose interest. Beaver had never been a great one for training and Cox got fed up with prodding him. All argument became irrelevant when the star of the club emigrated to England in 1954. Sadly, soon the club was in decline, never having realised its full potential. In general, the lack of proper facilities, and of any kind of structured coaching scheme, proved a severe drawback to the development of young GAA talent. The only way a player could refine his skills was by observing better players than himself and seeking tips from them, then practising, practising and practising. When it came to administration, however, the Lismore GAA held one trump card. Its chairman of many years, our Irish teacher Vin O'Donoghue, formally Mícheál U. O'Donnchada, had risen through the ranks to become first, chairman of the Munster Council, and then in April 1952, president of the GAA.

Field athletics was another sport controlled by the GAA in our area through its affiliated organisation, the National Athletic and Cycling

Association (NACA). There was another national athletics body in the country, the Amateur Athletics Union (AAU), which was more internationalist in spirit – GAA supporters would say pro-British. The existence of the two, entirely separately run, national authorities served only to harm the progress of athletics in Ireland. For example, AAU and NACA athletes did not compete against one another. The division also seemed to mean that any athlete of class who wanted to compete internationally had to join the AAU, because this was the only Irish organisation that was recognised by the international athletics authorities. My own interest in athletics was marginal, though I knew of, and admired, the exploits of world-famous sportsmen. And sportswomen. The first big female name to come to my attention was that of Fanny Blankers-Koen, who greatly increased women's awareness of the contribution that they could make in the sporting arena. Mam certainly was intrigued by the huge success of the Dutch 'Flying Housewife' in the sprints at the London Olympics of 1948 though, from the self-conscious way she laughed in discussing it, she seemed to imply that there was something unfeminine about women taking part in so male-dominated an endeavour.

Blankers-Koen did not steal all the headlines at the Olympics, however. Emil Zatopek made a name for himself in running the 10,000 metres in record time and, for the following four years, was to remain supreme in distance running. It was no surprise that he won the 10,000 again at the Helsinki Games of 1952, even after first having won the 5,000. What made people really sit up and appreciate his exceptional talent was his winning of the marathon gold medal as well. Our only Irish athlete of note during this period was the miler John Joe Barry who left Ireland to attend an obscure American university called Villanova, which no one had ever heard of before. Apparently, it was one of those institutions that had pots of money and lots of glasscases that it wanted to fill with sports trophies. Not having enough quality athletes of its own, it offered special coaching facilities to foreigners who could produce the inter-varsity goods. It worked for Barry anyway. He ran many fine races although he never quite made it to the top. That was left to Britain's Gordon Pirie, with whose skinny-framed successes I identified. The English tradition of phenomenal miling culminated, appropriately, with Roger Bannister's sub-four-minute run in May 1954, about which I amassed a file of newspaper cuttings and photos. A month later, the psychological barrier having been breached, the Australian John Landy broke the new record.

A novice sports day used to be held periodically in the Hurling Field. One summer, in particular, there was a flurry of athletic activity in the weeks preceding it. I tried my hand at a number of events - the 400 yards, 100 yards hurdles, high jump and pole vault. Nobody achieved much height in the high jump because we employed the scissors kick method. For the pole vault we used a long, stout bamboo that might have been somedody's curtain pole. Willie Ryan was the best of us at that and climbed to a fair height. I don't recall whether I took part in the sports on the day, but if I did, I certainly did not win any medals. I can say that with authority because I've never won a medal, or trophy of any kind, for anything. Occasionally, there used to be county championship sports meetings at the field, too, and one year cycle races were run around the perimeter of the pitch. Tommy 'Bomber' Whelan and and Paddy Whelan were the two most successful runners in the town. Bomber, who was the older of the two brothers, ran in the County Cross-Country Championships at Aglish in the winter of 1953-54, I think, and Pat won many races after I left Lismore. The last athletics field day I attended was a Tóstal event held in April 1954.

Cycling was a popular sport up and down the country but, strangely enough, because in Jimmy Foley we possessed a cyclist of national reputation, it never seemed to arouse much interest among Lismore sportsmen. Most townspeople had never seen Jimmy race – the events he competed in were always held elsewhere – but they were proud of his distinction. When I was growing up he no longer lived in the town, but in Cappoquin, where he owned the Railway Bar just up from the Gaelic Field. It was in this pub that the Lismore lads always changed when they played hurling or football in our neighbouring village. Half of Lismore seemed to want to crowd into the small room at the back to shout words of encouragement before the contest, or words of commiseration in the sweaty and subdued aftermath. Now and again though, there would be whoops of joy after an unexpected victory and the narrow entrance would be plugged tight with bodies. The minors, and juveniles, were rarely accorded the honour of using Jimmy's as a changing room and had to make do with the lean-to shelter on the town side of the pitch. The cyclist did his best riding in the early Forties when he won races all over Munster. One-, three-, and five-mile sprints were his speciality and he was picked to ride for Ireland. Probably, as he rode under NACA rules, he never came up against Reg Harris, the famous Englishman who was world professional sprint champion for years. You did not need to be interested in cycling to come across Harris's name. It often cropped up in snippets in the comics or in the daily newspapers. Nor, if you were interested in sport generally, could you have failed to note the exploits of a wiry Italian called Fausto Coppi who, in the late Forties and early Fifties, seemed to be dominating most of those strange and gruelling road races that went on for weeks on the Continent. That was when I heard of the Tour de France for the first time.

Cycling brought a whiff of excitement to Lismore in August 1954 when the NACA-organised Rás Tailteann – the amateur Tour of Ireland – passed through, or rather by, the town. It was the first time that this annual event had been routed our way and hundreds of spectators lined the canal straight and the bridges to watch the cavalcade of cars and riders approach from the direction of Cappoquin and turn right at the bottom of the Blackwater Bridge to head off toward Ballyduff and, ultimately, the stage ending in Cork City.

CHAPTER NINE

Swimming

SWIMMING WAS THE only sport that permanently held my attention. I took to it from an early age. I don't know that I ever regarded it as a sport. It was just a highly pleasurable physical activity. In Lismore it seemed natural to want to learn to swim. There was a variety of rocky pools along the Owenashad, grassy bathing places along the Blackwater, and we even had a swimming pool in the town itself, albeit a private one in the Castle Gardens.

A high dive off Lismore Bridge was probably the greatest aquatic thrill the town could offer but this was frowned upon on two counts. It could be lethal to the amateur and the diver would be impinging on the Duke of Devonshire's prime fishing preserves when he hit the water. Any daring young man who managed it, as John Noonan of the Main Street was said to have done, did so in the early hours of the morning before the Law was out and about. A few were said to have jumped rather than dived. Michael Madden remembered an uncle telling him about an ex-British soldier who came to live in the town after the First World War and who would plunge from the bridge regularly for a few pence. Presumably the Duke of Devonshire and the Law had no objection to a man who had been through the hell of the Western Front, and was clearly an accomplished diver, earning a crust in this manner. The man's stunts ended the day he went in for added drama. He had built a wooden gantry on the wall of the bridge with the object of increasing the height of his dive. On his launching himself from the platform on the top of this structure the whole thing collapsed backwards under the weight of his kick, causing him to strike the parapet on the way down. He was lucky to escape with a badly damaged shoulder and, understandably, never tried to dive off the bridge again. Somebody wrote a poem about his feats but I have never come across this. It may well survive in a local newspaper of the period.

The waters of the Owenashad were ideal, but cold. They streamed all the way down from the rounded, heathery humps of the Knockmealdowns through beautiful wooded glens, and it was a delicious sensation to immerse

The Point, where the Blackwater and Owenashad rivers meet below Lismore Bridge, in September 1994. The Owenashad flows in from the right. The flag tower of Lismore Castle can be glimpsed in the centre backgound. The poplars weren't there when I was growing up.

yourself in the slow-swirling eddies trapped by the rocks. Sunlight stabbed your back, wildflower and hazel tingled your nostrils, stones glistened where you splashed them. You scarcely remarked on any of these effects. They were simply there. In contrast, the Blackwater was a major river, so deep in places you could not see the bottom on the brightest day. This you joined from the open fields that gave off a healthy tang of cowshit, dandelion and cropped grass. Its waters were slow and temperate. The accepted thing was to acquire your basic skills in the Owenashad and graduate to the Blackwater from there. There were five places where the boys and girls of the town bathed in the mountain stream – at the Point, i.e. the confluence with the Blackwater, where the flow slowed between grassy banks; in a pool by the salmon hatchery; in the quietly trickling stretch above the weir at Ballyin House where you could jump in off sandy banks; in the deep, swirling pools immediately below the weir where you could dive in off the slippery, moss-covered cement; and in the shady stretch by a small field that could be found a mile or so up the Mountain Road before you cornered to Lady Louisa's Bridge. At the nearby Bark Yard, (so-called 'from its use as a site for skimming bark off trees which had been cut for scaffolding' – Paddy Vaughan, *The Last Forge in Lismore*, page 57), there had formerly stood another weir that sluiced water off to a mill race at Ballyin Mill. Pit-props were also fashioned in the yard and shipped to Britain from Killahaly.

You learned your first strokes at the Point. Molly used to take me there and keep a close eye on me from the riverbank. She did not swim herself. On a sunny day there might be a couple of dozen of us little ones, boys and girls, playing in the water – paddling, looking for elvers under the flat stones, picking up the elements of the dog- paddle, or dog's paddle as we called it, where the water deepened by the opposite, Ferry Inch, bank. Occasionally, we would give ourselves a scare by standing at the tip of the Point where the two waters merged and imagining ourselves slipping down the acutely shelving side of the big river into the blackness beyond the clear water. Sometimes too, there would be shouts of excitement when a large fish suddenly slid up out of the depths then sped off again with a powerful flick of its tail at the sound of our voices, or the shadows we cast.

Catching elvers, or eels as we called them, was a favourite pastime. We would gently raise the stones to flush them out, scoop them up when the moment was right in one-pound corned-beef tins or jam jars, or simply with cupped hands, then take them home and keep them in larger containers, the bottoms of which we would cover with sand and gravel. Fry, or *bricíns*, we also caught in this manner until Teasy Meade, the toy shop owner in the Main Street, got in a stock of children's fishing nets. The unfortunate creatures we trapped seldom survived the well-meaning attention we lavished on them so we were constantly restocking. When we found we had caught too many we always put the ones we did not need back into the water. Elvers were plentiful in Lismore but I never saw numbers in the Blackwater to equal those I saw in the River Suir in Carrick. On hot summer evenings up the river bank in Carrick when the tide was in you would see millions of these tiny animals swimming upstream in one seemingly never-ending and unbroken shoal. It was a sight that never failed to fill me with a sense of awe. Could they really have made it to Carrick all the way from the dense seaweed of the forbidding Sargasso Sea which, according to the comics, mariners feared, and in which, according to what I had picked up at school, all the eels of the northern hemisphere bred? And where were they heading for so purposefully now?

Our parents put up with our keeping fish in two-pound jam jars and the like and, sometimes, temporarily in the bath. What they did not approve of was our using glass vessels to catch the elvers. Now and again a jar slipped from somebody's hand and broke and one had to be most careful to retrieve all the sharp and jagged pieces. This was not always done and cut soles were the result. Mostly the cuts were minor but sometimes there would be bad gashes. Once I saw a mother carrying her screaming little girl up the Blackwater Bridge, a bloodied handkerchief gripped tightly around the child's foot to staunch the flow from the wound. I got minor cuts myself from time to time, as we all did, not always from broken glass. You could gash yourself on sharp stones as well. It taught you to be careful in the shallows and wear an old pair of sandals, if you had one.

We received no formal swimming instruction, nor did any of our own teachers ever try to coach us. We learned by observing one another and by exchanging experiences. All of us began with paddling, and immersing our bodies in knee-deep water. From there you taught yourself to balance on outstretched arms and hold your body horizontal by waving your feet. After a time you acquired the confidence and courage to lift your hands off the bottom and try to propel yourself forward. It cost you many mouthfuls of water. To begin with, you stayed afloat for no more than a stroke, or possibly two, then with practice you found that you could dog-paddle a couple of yards. I loved going to the Point because it was a complete summer playground. In the field by the river there were clumps of shrubs and briars round which we used to chase one another and sometimes in the afternoon Mam and Molly would take Paddy and me further downstream for a picnic by the fast-flowing current. It must have been trying for our elders keeping an eye on us but they seemed to enjoy it too.

Tom Feeney embarrassed Molly once when she had him and his sister Margaret, as well as myself, in her charge. When we were changing into our togs Tom looked down at his naked sister and exclaimed, 'Oh Jasus, Margaret has no mickey!' And he laughed uncertainly. Molly blushed, hurriedly covered Margaret's nether parts with a garment and hooshed us away. 'Get off out o' that with ye!' she said, not quite concealing a grin and sent us round the back of the clump to change into our togs. Tom changed quickly and headed for the water. I was slower until suddenly my naked arse began to sting like hell. I jumped to my feet with a yelp and looked down. I had been sitting on a small, sandy anthill. I frantically brushed the ants, real or imaginary, off my backside, dragged on my togs and tore past the astonished Tom into the water. The cold bath took away the stinging and, I supposed, washed away the few pismires that remained. Tom and the others stood on the bank laughing their heads off.

The essentials of the dog-paddle having been mastered, it was time to trust myself to the Owenashad above the Strand Bridge. There was an intermediate place behind the salmon hatchery where we used to turn over stones for elvers, paddle and dunk ourselves in the deepish water but the next real step in swimming terms was the weir. First I tried the stretch upstream of the weir where the water was at its clearest. Here too there was the added fascination of the pond-skaters that moved in fits and starts along its surface. They had a grace that was singularly lacking in the other water bugs that scuttled from stone to stone along the river-bed. And there was the mystery of why they could walk and run *on* the surface of the water while all other creatures sank or swam. It was here I opened my eyes underwater for the first time and, having learned how to keep them open, went under time and time again to watch the shafts of sunlight reflecting off the pebbles on the bottom and off the waves I generated. Here too I became aware of that spicy, tingling sensation you get when cold water runs up your nose. By this time I had a pal who took more eagerly to the water than I. Billy Hogan, 'Hoagy' as we called him, was the grandson of the old Rambler Garrett and he could not have been more at home in the water if he had had fins. Small and round, he used to frolic in the stream like a young seal and, once in, never wanted to come out of it.

For fun, as much as for safety, we were now using discarded rubber tubes from the wheels of motor cars as water-wings; black in colour with the occasional red one. We got them from Jim Feeney, or the lads in the garage, patched them up and inflated them with the air pump. A rarer plaything, when later we gravitated to the Rock (our natural Blackwater swimming pool), was the back-wheel tractor tube. Three or four, or even six or seven, of us could raft along on this and it was fun to capsize it or pitch one another off it. Sometimes we would all pile onto it and try to submerge it, with a car tube a simple feat for one person, but not so easy with the massive tractor one. The car tube was, on the whole, the more useful of the two, and easier to transport – you simply wore it around your body like a bandolier. It was easy to bounce it off the water, or off the back of a pal's neck. And, unlike the tractor tube, it functioned as a serious swimming aid. Lying back on it, paddling with your arms, you were unconsciously picking up the technique of swimming on your back – and floating, a skill we perfected above the weir with much trial and error, assisting each other by supporting the back of the swimmer's head with the palm of a hand. It was with the tube around our waist that we gained the confidence to master the breast-stroke, the basic stroke that we developed out of the dog-paddle. The backstroke we acquired was more a reverse breast-stroke than a reverse crawl.

But there was more to the weir than just swimming. The surrounding trees and shrubs made it an ideal place to play hide-and-seek and in the narrow sluice that led to the hatchery we used to race twigs or simple wooden boats that we nailed together at home. As soon as I had acquired enough experience to handle myself above the weir I began jumping and diving into the deep and frothy pool immediately below it. Although a good six or seven feet in depth, the pool did not really represent any danger to us as we were never more than a few strokes out of reach of the shallows. Once you got that far you could not wait to test your ability in the Blackwater.

I only swam in the pool up the Mountain Road a couple of times. It was not that it was that far out of town. It was just that it was the preferred spot of a set of young people who liked to keep themselves apart – *habitués* of the tennis court with whom I had little in common. To some extent the pool was a Protestant reserve. Dean Stanley's sons and daughters and Peter Dowd and some of their friends favoured it. But then, so did the Catholic sons and daughters of Mr O'Riordan, the head cashier of the Munster & Leinster Bank. Atypically, the sons and daughters of Superintendent Creane used to go there too, atypically because aside from the eldest son Walter, who liked to give himself intellectual airs, that numerous and endearing family was most down-to-earth.

I am, no doubt, misjudging the Protestants since, sadly, I had no close contact with them. It was more a social than a religious divide as far as I was concerned. I was curious about their religion, of course, and now and then sought to inform myself a bit more about it. However, it was all I could do to cope with one arm of Christianity so I never got very far with my researches. Those of us who swam in the different reaches of the Owenashad may have had misconceptions about each other but that did not prevent us from maintaining amicable, if distant, relations.

The Rock was not really a rock but the end of a wall that marked the boundary between Ballynelligan Glebe and Ballyea. Through land erosion the extremity had collapsed and it was this that jutted out some ten feet to twelve feet from the sandy riverbank into the Blackwater. There were two parts to it: the very end had broken off irregularly and jutted out of the water to form the Rock proper from which we dived; the extension that still clung to the land was known as the Wall and you walked along this to get to the diving point, although you could take a running dive off the end of the Wall as well – most easily acomplished when the river level was high as you had to clear some underwater debris before you hit the water. The older boys used to tell me how good the swimming was there. It was located downstream from the town on an inch that extended east from the Warren and was situated directly opposite Bullsod Island, the largest of the three sandbanks found in the middle of this broad stretch of water. A kind of stony weir on the town side of the first island ensured that the main flow of

'The Rock', our favourite swimming hole in the Blackwater.
The Rock is seen bottom left with the Congoola flowing from left to right
by the far bank. The downstream tip of the middle-sized island is on
the left, Ballyrafter Wood in the background.

the Blackwater ran along the far side of the islands. The water was deep and fast-flowing there – the deepest hole behind Bullsod was known to us as the Congoola (phonetic). On the Rock side the stream maintained a surge for some fifty or sixty yards before broadening out into the wide pool in which we swam, then it ran on to rejoin the main flow at the easternmost tip of Bullsod Island, the point to which the river was tidal. The town's sewage was piped into the river just below Lismore Bridge, some three-quarters of a mile or so upstream, but the water seldom showed any overt signs of pollution. Exceptionally a fragment of turd might be spotted bobbing by. It was not enough to worry us, although it did stir passing visions of involuntarily ingesting the wandering item.

Before I graduated to the Rock I set myself one small exploit – a swim in the castle pool. Hoagy had first shown me this and I had made up my mind that I would swim in it one day. Hoagy, who lived at the Lodge a few hundred yards away, had never swum in it either. The Lodge lay just down from the Monument at the top of the New Way alongside a big, wrought-iron gate, hung between granite pillars, that guarded the entrance to the Green Road, from which one gained access to the Castle Gardens and the sawmill. Every evening before darkness fell Hoagy's grandmother used to shut this gate. First thing in the morning it would be opened again to allow vehicles through. A wrought-iron wicket at the side was accorded the same routine. Beyond the gates on the right was the Reilig, an ancient graveyard, now a tiny field in which a couple of cows were occasionally kept. At the end of this, just over the high wall by the Broghill Tower, lay our target.

It was a humid, cloudy evening when we made our play – Hoagy, Tom Feeney, who was sometimes nicknamed 'Twiddles', and I, togs already on under our short pants, towels shoved surreptitiously up our shirts. We strolled up the Green Road as if we were going for a walk but, once we were out of sight of the Lodge a hundred yards on, climbed in over a break in the wall of the Reilig opposite an iron gate on the other side. Inside a minute we found ourselves at the foot of a ten-foot-high stone wall, a more formidable obstacle than the wall we had just scaled. But its height was deceptive. A tree on the Reilig side, branching in over the top, promised easy access. Having climbed it stealthily, there below us lay the pool, mounted like a jewel in a manicured lawn, the length, perhaps, of two goalmouths, the width of one, designed and installed by Adèle Astaire herself in her role as Lady Charles Cavendish, so in conception at least, all the way from Hollywood. I pictured the stars lounging around its grey, stone verges, sipping cocktails. The water was still and clear, inviting us to furrow it. The area was totally enclosed by walls and set in the one opposite us was a wooden wicket that led to the gardens. We perched on top for a few minutes, ears pricked up for the sound of an approaching voice or footsteps from beyond the gate. Not a murmur. Even the birds seemed to have been overcome by the lethargy of the evening. One by one we slipped down off the wall, noting in doing so the holds that we would employ again on the way out. Quickly we stripped off and planked our clothes and towels behind a bush. I ran across to the gate and had a screw through a crack in it. Not a soul to be seen. Three discreet splashes and we were luxuriating in the private waters of the Duke and Duchess of Devonshire. The water was cold, a relief from the steamy air, and we tumbled in it like a trio of porpoises. At first it was all whisper, whisper, and scarcely a splash, but then, as our pleasure increased so did our squeals of delight. Soon we threw caution to the winds and began diving and jumping in. Hoagy, particularly, was in his element. After maybe a quarter of an hour or so Tom and I felt that we had pushed our luck far enough and got out and started to shake the water off our bodies, running around on the grass. We had towelled ourselves down and pulled on our clothes before Hoagy was finally persuaded to come out. And then he didn't stay out for long. After he had shaken the water off himself like a wet pup he suddenly decided on one more length and dived in again. After that he did stay out, but with regret. Because of his tubby build cold water never seemed to bother him. He could happily have stayed in all night. The water had almost resumed its stillness when I threw a last glance at it from the top of the wall. The wetted stone surrounds would show evidence of intrusion for a while yet. From time to time the three of us talked of repeating the exercise but, for some reason, we never got our act together again. I certainly never got round to swimming in the castle pool a second time. It could have been that I never dared. More likely the pleasures of the Rock, and the company I delighted in there, made a replay seem superfluous. No doubt Hoagy made it back.

Another balmy summer's evening a further exercise in forbidden pleasure occurred, this one wholly impromptu. Willie Ryan and I, and a couple of the Dennises happened to be strolling down at the Point when, on the spur of the moment, we decided to cool our sweaty bodies in the Owenashad. By the Ferry Inch the water reached a depth of three or four feet over a stretch of some ten or twelve yards so it was just possible for us older lads to swim in it. Bathing naked was a lovely sensation. Your whole body seemed to let go. We were enjoying ourselves enormously when a bunch of girls we knew, led by Kathleen Scanlon of Botany, appeared out of nowhere and sat down next to our clothes.

'Enjoyin' yereselves, lads?' Kathleen grinned knowingly.

'Go away now,' we urged, embarrassed.

'What kind o' togs are ye wearin' at all?' another girl wanted to know.

'Never mind what kind o' togs we're wearin',' we said, circling warily. 'Buzz off now and leave us alone.'

'Do ye know, I think they're not wearin' anythin' at all,' said Kathleen.

'You mean they're naked!' one of her pals gasped in mock horror.

By this time we were slinking up to our necks in the deepest water under the opposite bank.

'Go away with ye now,' we shouted, more from embarrassment than anger.

'Don't talk to us in that tone of voice,' said Kathleen confidently. She knew that she and the others had us in a spot.

We decided it was best to ignore them and started swimming again, although keeping our nudity as far removed from our tormentors as we could.

The girls just squatted and grinned.

'Ah go 'way now, girls, go on,' we said, irritation beginning to creep into the voice that spoke for us.

'Ah sure, we have nothin' else to be doin'. We'll wait for ye to come out.'

'We're comin' out now,' I bluffed and arched my neck unconvincingly out of the water.

'What did you say, Jim? I didn't hear you?' Kathleen got to her feet and came right up to the edge of the bank from where our nudity would have been clearly evident.

By now her pals were on their toes as well. We slunk back to the deep.

'Go away. We're comin' out,' Willie said with deliberation, his tone indicating that he was no longer in a mood to put up with the hassle.

'Come on. Sure we don't mind,' they invited.

We look at one another, baffled. How the hell were we going to get rid of them?

Then they upped the stakes. 'Would ye like us to look after yere clothes, lads?' one of them said and picked up an armful of our garments.

The matter was now definitely getting serious. If they ran off with our clothes we would have to wait until darkness before we could sneak up the bridge to our various homes. And what if we ran into a guard, or a woman, or a priest on the way?

There was only one thing for it. As one we rushed forward as if we really meant to get out, but taking care to keep our privates below the waves we were creating. The girls squealed, dropped our clothes and scampered off. We looked around cautiously. Had they really gone or were they hiding behind the nearest clump of briars waiting to embarrass us further the minute we appeared on the bank in the nude? We decided to keep going and made a dash for our trousers. They had run off towards the mill and we were able to drip-dry in peace.

The Rock was an institution – a centre of male entertainment and street learning. It had evolved as such although the area was not totally a male preserve. A hundred yards or so downstream of it where the water was shallower women and girls used to congregate on the grassy bank. They bathed rather than swam and did not spend at all as much time in the water as we did. Not that our type of water sport was so special. Real swimming was done in Dungarvan where the nearest public pool was located. I never had the opportunity of swimming in that although I often gazed wistfully down on it from the pathway above. But swimming there would have meant as qualitative a leap for me as playing handball in a four-wall alley. After all, didn't Paddy Arrigan, the son of my parents' old Carrick friends Mick Arrigan and his wife, who now lived in Abbeyside, learn his swimming in it? And he was winning medals all over the place, eventually becoming Irish backstroke champion. I was very proud the day I met him. The favourite swimmer amongst us youngsters, of course, was Tarzan, Tarzán as we

A group taken at 'The Rock' in the early Fifties. Back row, standing left to right: Pa Dunne, Pat Murphy, Willie Madden, Seamus O'Donnell, Seamus Furey. Middle row, kneeling left to right: Michael Dennis, Tom Feeney, Peter Dennis, Willie Bob Lineen. Front row, sitting left to right: (unidentified but tantalizingly familiar), John O'Riordan, Paddy Whelan, John Ryan, Billy O'Riordan.

accentuated it, in the person of Johnny Weissmuller, whose surname we also somehow managed to get our tongues around. All our efforts to do the crawl were attempts to emulate him.

On a good day you would find anything from a dozen to twenty of us gathered at the Rock. A good day might be sunny, cloudy sunny or sunny showery. A poor day would be cloudy and grey, attracting depleted numbers. In addition to swimming we used to amuse ourselves with informal contests to see which of us could scud the farthest underwater from a dive off the Rock, or off the Wall. Lounging on the grass, we would amuse ourselves telling yarns, talking about the pictures and, of course, the girls. Everyone waited on Cal's next wisecrack. And he did funny turns too, like jumping in off the Rock and surfacing feet first, or swimming around with a lighted fag in his mouth, which he did anyway because he liked Woodbines. Other times he would leap up, go purposefully along the Wall and continue walking out over the Rock onto the water, going under with a loud splash, perhaps accompanying the stunt with his own madcap version of 'Ma, He's Making Eyes At Me'. Once with Beaver, he drew the ire of John Lynch, the testy castle bailiff and licensed salmon fisherman, by swimming down the fast flow, known to us as the Current, from the Big Island to the far side of Bullsod, which was off-limits to swimmers as it was a fairly good stretch for salmon. In the event, the lads were more buffeted by the rocks underwater than by anything Lynch said to them and picked up a number of abrasions and cuts on their limbs and torsos. But Cal had his reflective side too and at times would just sit quietly and stare into the distance.

Once in my experience, we did a bit of nude sun-bathing. Brooky Lynch, back from England for a while, was the one who introduced this note of sophistication amongst us. The fashion did not last long as the rest of us felt too shy about parading our nudity. You could never be sure that you were entirely out of sight of prying female eyes. Once when we were in the process of changing into our clothes after a swim Fisser Neville erupted on us from the other side of the Wall, brandishing a fistful of long nettles, and tried to drive us toward a few girls who were at the women's bathing place. We scattered, all but one of us, Foxy Flynn, with some stitch of clothes on. Fisser singled him out and the hapless victim had no option but to make for the trees on the high ground away from the river. We who were lucky laughed, of course, at the sight of our pal's pale arse bobbing over the long grass like a rabbit's, but we did not laugh for long. As soon as he had driven Foxy into the wood Fisser returned and set upon us again. By this time we were fully clothed but even clothed you were wary of stinging nettles. Then a couple of girls happened along on their way downstream.

'Hey Foxy!' Fisser shouted, 'What are you doin' up there in the bushes? Come on down out o' that.'

Foxy did not reply.

The girls, aware that something was going on, giggled and passed. Soon we saw them in a huddle with those already at the women's bathing place who had seen our pal haring nakedly across the field and their merriment was evident.

By this time our pal, not unnaturally, was anxious to get back into his trousers. 'Aw come on, Fisser, let me down,' he pleaded.

'Come down any time you want. Sure I'm not stoppin' you?' Fisser called back, then laughed and sought participation in the faces of the rest of us. He must have sensed that we were becoming more apprehensive on Foxy's behalf. Fisser was older than us by about five years and, though I liked him, there was a certain one-sidedness about his sense of humour that I could not always take.

'Aw bring us up me trousers,' Foxy called our plaintively and showed himself from the waist up at the perimeter of the wood.

'They're here, waitin' for you. Come on down,' said Fisser, chuckling, and rearranged his bunch of greens.

Foxy knew Fisser well enough and withdrew back into the trees. His tormentor, sitting over his clothes, eyed us as if daring us to go to his assistance. We sat around uneasily and made small talk. Suddenly Fisser sprang to his feet and jumped over the Wall, waving the nettles. He had spotted Foxy sneaking down the other side of the ditch. Again our pal had to seek the protection of the wood. Again he resumed his pleas and again Fisser made fun of him. Eventually we could not stand by any longer and see Foxy humiliated. One of us, I do not recall who, braved Fisser's nettles, grabbed Foxy's trousers and ran off to the wood with it. When the two reappeared it was a very irate Foxy who confronted an unrepentent Fisser. And rightly, he did not spare the rest of us the tongue-lashing that we merited. After a time though, his sullen mood left him and he became his old self again. Fisser's stunt, typical of him, had been genuinely funny to begin with but he had made too much of a meal of it and soured things.

When I first started swimming in the Blackwater I did not go straight in off the Rock itself. The water was very deep in its immediate vicinity and you had to swim out more than a few yards before you could find your depth. Seven or eight yards downstream you were able to walk in off the bank and find enough depth to swim in comfortably. Little by little you learned to handle yourself in water that came up to your neck and, finally, the day came when you felt you were ready to go in off the Rock. It was easiest to jump, or dive, in off the tip and there I sat for what seemed a long time, trying not to let my eyes follow the sunrays down to the point at which they exhausted themselves in the dark water. Cal was floating on his back further out, gently coaxing me on. I knew he would fish me out if I panicked but I still wondered what was awaiting me in the depths. We had all heard stories of people drowning in seemingly innocuous situations. What if I went so far under Cal could not locate me? My other pals were uttering words of encouragement too and I was conscious of their eyes on my back. It was time to go. I stood up, paused a second and jumped in feet first. I surfaced quickly and swam, spluttering, out towards Cal. I felt exhilarated but knew I was not out of danger yet. I reached Cal. We swam out another couple of yards together. Then I was able to find my depth. Once on my feet I was greatly pleased with myself. I turned and waved to my pals on the bank.

'It's great! Come on in,' I shouted.

But most of them already knew. They had been through the same initiation themselves. Later on, I in my turn, would encourage boys younger than I to make the same leap. That was how we taught one another, and learned from one another, and we experienced a great deal of satisfaction in acquiring and passing on skills.

Once you had mastered the art of going in off the Rock, first by jumping then by diving, or vice versa, and swimming out across the flow you had gained direct access to Bullsod Island. The alternative was to ford across to the little group of islands at the top and bottom of the light current and make your way to Bullsod via these. It was fun to explore the aits. You could imagine yourself a castaway like Robinson Crusoe, climb the alder trees for the best vantage point, seek out the empty nests of the water birds that used the islands as a sanctuary, marvel at the bold and threatening swirl of the Congoola on the other side, and rummage among the flotsam and jetsam of the long-gone winter floods. Once with more than mere pleasure in mind Beaver Doherty, Seán Dennis, Richard Broderick, Willie Ryan and I built a sizable raft from driftwood and a few fresh limbs torn from the alders. The real object of the exercise was to collect firewood for Beaver, and after the vessel was completed we all got on it and floated it down the Congoola and on to the mouth of Tom Coleman's boreen under the Round Hill. From there Beaver took the wood home on a borrowed ass and cart. On the opposite bank once, on Big Island, I found amongst the reeds part of a large deer antler. Hoagy and I examined the slimy green hardness of it with wonder but then, deciding that it was incomplete, threw it back into the water again. A day or two later I met Billy O'Riordan shouldering it up the Bridge, like a prize trophy. He seemed a bit put out when I told him that I had found it first and slung it back in the river. He went off home with it nonetheless, after suggesting that it might have come from an ancient Irish elk. Perhaps he showed more sense than I did in hanging on to it?

Now and again in summer our swimming would be interrupted by an unexpected flood. Once the rain-clouds had moved on we were always eager to resume but were forced to wait until the floodwaters had abated. Usually our impatience got the better of us and we did not wait for the river to subside to its normal level. By then it was hued a pale Guinness and was so cold it stung at the first touch. The sting quickly suffused your body and you swam to a new sensation.

Next I adapted to the side-stroke. This was the one we saw the Indians use in pictures like *The Last of the Mohicans* when they wanted to glide silently past an enemy. Being merely a variant of the breast-stroke, it was not a difficult one to learn. More than any, it was the Weissmuller crawl that we wanted to master. Not an easy stroke to pick up without expert tuition. The best any of us could do was the overarm. There was an exception, and he an unlikely one. Crony O'Gorman, the skinny, hollow-chested publican from the Main Street who walked with a stoop, was the only man I ever saw doing the crawl in Lismore. We were amazed even to see him in swimming togs. It was a particularly warm day that had brought him out. Sitting on the high, sandy bank some thirty yards upstream from the Rock, he looked white as a snowball and, from the way he was hugging himself, seemed to feel just as cold. 'Chain-breaker', Seán Dennis instantly and cruelly nicknamed him and the name was to stick. A little later Seán and I came back up to that spot to go in and swim down past the Rock when who should we see cruising by us below but Crony, doing the most perfect crawl either of us had seen outside the silver screen!

'Jasus, isn't he a quare fella!' gasped Seán admiringly, 'Where did he learn to do that?'

There was something quite nice about having our earlier perception of the publican contradicted. I would have liked to ask him how he did it, and whether he would teach us the stroke, but for us boys he had never appeared the most approachable of men, so we let it go. Which was our loss for, who knows, he might have been delighted to have been asked and equally happy to tutor us. I certainly would have benefited from his tuition because by the time I left Lismore I was able to do no more than a crude overarm.

Muscles were things that preoccupied us too and the Rock was a place where general physical attributes were on display. Seán was the nearest to Charles Atlas perfection among the *habitués* though Beaver ran him a close second. I saw myself cast in the role of the skinny guy who got sand kicked in his face in the American muscleman ads. Whenever I sat behind Seán's desk at school I used to wonder at the width of his shoulders and, when he was stripped to the waist, at his slabs of pectorals. These were the muscles that gave him the edge on Beaver. When it came to doing push-ups on the grass I did not even try to compete in that company. 'It must be great having a body like that,' I used to think ruefully, unconsciously reflecting the thoughts of the skinny guy in the ad 'You'd be able to take care of yourself in any situation. And the girls would fancy you more.' In spite of our mild obsession with physique we paid little overt attention to the comparative sizes of our genitalia. A throwaway remark here, a furtive glance there, was the norm. Rarely a group appraisal. Knowing more about sin than sex, our attitude was, perhaps, not surprising.

It was typical of the Catholicism of our upbringing too that while boys and girls would swim together when very young, in adolescence they gravitated through some unstated mechanism to separate bathing places. I only ever swam among girls at the Point and above the weir in the Owenashad. In boys this separation led to some feelings of depreciation for the swimming abilities of the girls, wholly unfounded because, not swimming among the girls, how could we be in a position to assess their skills? A shameful episode from my own life was typical enough to suggest that maybe the girls were better off without us anyway. Berry O'Riordan, who was a little younger than I, said something to which I, rightly or wrongly, took exception while we were bathing above the weir. My angry response was to dunk her head repeatedly under the water. Though she came up spluttering I saw no danger in what I was doing until Molly came running up and angrily ordered me to release her. I did so immediately and it was only when the girl's head emerged gasping for air that I realised I had overreacted and done something nasty. Once clear of the Strand, however, I shook off that uncertain feeling of guilt. It was only when I went to the Munster & Leinster Bank a few days later to change a five-pound note for Mam that the full extent of my nastiness was brought home to me. I was the only customer in the place and Mr O'Riordan, comfortable and stout behind his brass grill, challenged me about my recent conduct.

'What was that you did to Berry the other day down the Strand?' he asked quietly but sharply.

I was taken aback. Even though it was commonly held among us boys that girls were tell-tales it had not occurred to me that Berry would tell her father of her experience. I defended myself with some show of indignation but was forced to listen to him as he counted out the change.

He spoke calmly and gravely and concluded, 'Aside from the fact that it's no way to treat a young girl, do you realise how dangerous it was? You could have drowned her.'

'Drowned her?' I caught my breath.

He must have noticed the fright I got for he went easier on me after that. Before I left I apologised for my bad conduct and promised I would never do such a thing again. Then I slunk out with my tail between my legs, deeply ashamed. I do not remember whether I ever apologised to Berry herself. The chances are, I did not. Boys didn't do things like that.

In an area criss-crossed by rivers and streams we were constantly warned of the danger of drowning. *Never go swimming alone. Never get too far out of your depth. Never go swimming in places that aren't recognised as being safe for bathing. Beware of currents and whirlpools.* One thing I did not need to be cautioned about was whirlpools. I had seen in the movies and read in the comics how enormous examples of these could even drag ships under. The thought of being sucked into a bottomless, black vortex, there to be devoured perhaps by a giant, lurking octopus, gave me no joy at all. When we read in the papers of drowning incidents these seemed to happen mostly at sea, which did not seem unusual. It was more frightening to hear of fatalities in rivers and streams. After all, rivers and streams had banks and islands, and overhanging branches of trees, which gave them limits. You could only venture so far from land. The sea was without end. As for lakes, they were something else. *Never go swimming in lakes,* we were told. *They have treacherous, hidden currents even though on the surface they may appear calm.* On the whole, people seemed to believe this but once or twice I saw swimmers in the shallows of Baylough, the picturesque lake nestling under rhododendron groves in the slope above the Vee. There was an added hazard in this particular lake, one Petticoat Loose, the mention of whose name always drew a naughty chuckle from Mam. In my imagination this wild female assumed the proportions of a quasi-mythological ogress. The historical Petticoat Loose was a big, tough, free-living, farmer's daughter called Mary Hannigan who lived in the early 19th century. She led a Dionysiac life and after a scandalous death returned to haunt the borderlands of Waterford and Tipperary, it was said, until her ghost was banished by a priest to the bottom of 'bottomless' Baylough.

But you heard more about people nearly drowning than actually drowning, which invariably brought up the hoary old trick question, 'Would you rather be nearly drowned or nearly saved?' One such incident occurred when a classmate of my brother's, Seán O'Connell of Chapel Street, got into difficulties in the deep water at the Rock. Apparently he had been in the water on his own and the others on the bank, amid the usual hubbub of conversation, had not noticed his predicament until almost too late. When they did there was a mad scramble led by Cal. Seán was towed back to safety. I was told about it in whispers later on and the close call was held up as a warning to others thereafter. *Never get out of your depth when you're alone in the water.* Understandably, Seán got such a fright he never went near the water again, or if he did, not for a very long time.

The wide, slow-flowing stretch of the Blackwater a few hundred yards up from the Queen's Gap was the deepest water in which I swam around Lismore. One approached this bathing place, if it could be called that, from the Grove, emerging through an iron kissing-gate onto a narrow strip of rough meadow, lined on the riverside with sallies, opposite the Queen's Gap. From there, one followed the river upstream, crossing over a wooden stile into a larger, grazed meadow until one reached a place beyond the osiers where it was possible to slip into the water off the bank. Only strong swimmers like Dervla Murphy, the daughter of our librarian, or John Noonan, or Hobson the vet of the South Mall, were reputed to go swimming in this isolated place. That Dervla liked it was no surprise. She was a sturdy, solitary woman of the hiking, biking, tennis-playing type, well able to take care of herself. And if, as was said, she liked to swim naked she could accomplish that here with complete privacy. I was not the first member of my family to go there. Paddy and some of his pals had been too. It was Willie Ryan who took me along, one evening about seven o'clock. He had been once or twice before so he knew where to go. Not a breeze raised a rustle in the dense wood behind us and the river moved with scarcely a whisper. In the distance downstream one could just about hear the hiss of water jetting through the Gap. Birds called lazily. Fish rose and fell with a plash, occasionally with the hard smack that signalled a large salmon. Or possibly a pike? There were pike in the Blackwater and I felt a sense of apprehension that one of those voracious creatures might sink its array of sharp teeth into a part of my flesh that mattered. But they were not noted for biting chunks out of humans, I told myself, and in I went. The black surface peeled away, still and dark as a primeval lake, from my chin. I could have been the first living thing to cleave its waters. The fanciful notion was quickly dispelled by the silver belly of a white trout that plopped by the far bank. It was dangerously thrilling to know that beneath you was a depth of anything from ten to twenty feet. I swam breast-stroke and side-stroke, Willie backstroke. We crossed toward the other side, Willie pulling away strongly upstream. I cruised lazily around where I was while he went on a hundred yards or so. I was not yet confident enough of my abilities to swim that far against the flow. The water was surprisingly temperate and we stayed on in it another while after Willie had floated back. It was my last summer in Lismore and one of the last swims I had in my home town. I enjoyed the swim but not the place so much. Certainly it was a hole for serious swimmers, but a lonely spot. I would not have exchanged it for the camaraderie of the Rock.

 Floating on your back and backstroke swimming was most fun in the sea and I was privileged to be able to get to Clonea Strand beyond Dungarvan, or Ardmore further west, a few times every year. These occasions arose when the court clerk for West Waterford, Mr O'Keeffe, who lived in the Main Street, took his family away on annual holidays. Dad was *au fait* with the court procedures and used to deputise for the clerk during this month or so, earning himself some extra money. At the same time, he managed to treat his family to a day at the seaside, a trip he could otherwise not have afforded; the extra taxi miles beyond the return journey to Dungarvan were at his own expense. We used to set off around 8.30 a.m., which suited me fine; I could not wait to get away. Denny Regan, the local taxi-driver, would call for us in his Ford V8 and Dad, Mam, Molly, Paddy and I would pile in, Mam mostly in the front passenger seat because she used to get carsick in the back (she travelled badly by bus also). Paddy and I were always fighting over the other space in the front and were placated by being given turns. Dad and Molly were indifferent about where they sat. It was only fifteen miles to Dungarvan and the court did not start until 11.00 a.m. But Dad had to arrive for work an hour or so earlier than this. Denny wasn't our only driver I have discovered although he was the usual one. Paddy Vaughan, the author of *The Last Forge in Lismore*, in a letter to me of 18 February 2003 writes, 'I recall being in Ardmore with your father and family. I had a car for hire at the time, c.1948, and felt I had to drive extra careful with the Sergeant beside me!'

With Denny at the wheel you needed to start early. Anyone else would cover thirty miles in the time it took him to cover fifteen. He was a slim, quiet, dark-suited, conservative man who considered that any speed in excess of thirty miles an hour was fast driving. Anything above forty-five was reckless. In all the years we travelled with him he never overtook anything faster than an ass-and-cart or a man on a bicycle travelling on the flat. Small wonder that I, in my impatient little way, found it difficult to understand why every other vehicle on the road used to pass us out. On the other hand, what would we have gained by hurrying? Dad made sure he would arrive in plenty of time, and anyway, we had to hang around Dungarvan until his work was done. There were two things I always looked forward to on the way down, the level crossing at Cappagh because we always seemed to arrive there when a train was due, and the Master McGrath Monument at the cross where the Dungarvan and Carrick-on-Suir roads converged, because seeing it meant that the seaside town was now no more than a couple of miles away. The chances were that when you reached Cappagh the gates would be closed for anything up to fifteen minutes. The train was never on time. People in cars and lorries would curse to be let through, knowing full well that the train was miles away yet, but the gatekeeper would not budge. The signal had come through. The train was on its way. The gates had to remain closed. Pedestrians and cyclists were luckier. They could slip across by the side gate. On occasion, as many as a dozen vehicles, including ourselves, were held up, causing me to wonder how many motor cars might be delayed in similar circumstances across the length and breadth of Ireland at any one time. Dad would let us get out and lean through the white gates to catch the first sight of the train as it came whistling into view. Then, as it approached, the gatekeeper ordered us back. Soon it powered across the highway, spitting smoke and steam. Most of all, I liked seeing the passenger trains because the people aboard waved back to you as they passed, but I got a kick out of the goods trains as well.

The first time Dad told me that we would soon be passing the memorial to Master McGrath I expected to see an imposing statue of some great Irish hero. Imagine my disappointment when all that came into view was a small spike of a thing on which, on the side of the plinth facing toward Dungarvan, a white marble dog was chiselled in relief! Even at the pace Denny was going you could not catch more than a glimpse of it. Then Dad, who took a great interest in coursing, told me all about the champion greyhound and his winning of the Waterloo Cup, the most prestigious prize in that sport. I failed totally to share his enthusiasm for this exploit and thereafter when he would say, 'We'll soon be coming up to Master McGrath,' it conveyed little more than a milestone to me. Later on, when I was to learn the words of the song, I gained a better appreciation of the greyhound's prowess.

A landmark I awaited with more anticipation, particularly on the return journey in the evening when the sinking sun was scattering its rays through the dancing leaves, was a funnel of trees beyond Cappagh where the foothills of the Monavullagh mountain range tailed into fields on the right. In such light it seemed an enchanted place where fairies might gather and play. It never failed to send a tingle down my spine when we passed through it. In these moments I was grateful for Denny's leisurely driving.

In Dungarvan Denny would always manage to find a parking space right outside the courthouse in Thomas Francis Meagher Street, if not at once then the instant a spot became available. When, initially, we were forced to park elsewhere he pulled up round the corner in Grattan Square, the wide and elegant market-place, where he would pace fretfully up and down until he spotted somebody vacating the desired space in front of the courthouse. It was a professional thing with him to gain parking there. Unacceptable even was a slot across the road in front of the Devonshire Arms Hotel. Yes, Dungarvan had one too, *and* it had a Lismore connection. The manager and joint owner was the charming and elegantly dressed Nicholas O'Kelly who was married to Babe Lineen – sister to Pad and Michael – of our town. Mam had a lot of time for the pair and occasionally, Nicholas, who was also involved in local politics, would invite us in for refreshments. Eugene Dennis recalls a political rhyme that I never remember hearing. It is worth recording as a measure of O'Kelly.

> When Fianna Fáil were on their back
> and crawling on their belly,
> the man who put them on their feet
> was Nicholas G. O'Kelly.

In any event, Dad had to get out and go to work the minute we arrived. The rest of us had time to kill until the court was over. Sometimes we would wait in the car with Denny, always when it was raining, but mostly we would go off for a stroll and leave him to his own devices. We got used to leaving the car in one place and finding it parked somewhere else later, always inched that little bit nearer to, if not already in position in, the ideal spot seaward side of the main entrance, which was where Denny prided himself in setting down and picking us up. On a warm sunny day killing time before getting away to the beach was a drudge. The problem was, that Dad could never say in advance with any certainty just how long the court proceedings were going to take. He could guess but always there was the possibility that some solicitor or other would bring up some matter that required unexpectedly prolonged discussion. We counted ourselves lucky when he finished at noon, unlucky when he did not manage to get away until three o'clock. As a consequence, we could never stray too far from the car. In general, Dad would get clear between 1.00 p.m. and 2.00 p.m. Denny was good at popping in and out of the courtroom to check how things were going. It was not always simply a matter of the court being over. After the district justice had left, Dad had to stay on and write up the proceedings in massive wine-coloured and green ledgers, the sets so official and grand they looked as if they might have been intended as registers for Saint Peter at the Gate. When Dad seemed to be taking too long over the task Mam would allow me to go into the dark-panelled courtroom to hurry him up. It was a claustrophobic place, furnished with dark wooden benches, the arrangement of which made no sense to me. I could not imagine what went on there. Dad would smile and say that he would be along shortly. I might go straight out to report to Mam or I might stay around and wander along the benches, trying them out for size. Mam did not mind hanging around the town as much as I did. Dungarvan with its population of just over 5,000 inhabitants was marginally bigger than Carrick-on-Suir, the population of which numbered just under 5,000. In a town that was five times the size of Lismore she could shop for things that she could not get at home. She might take Paddy with her, leaving Molly to walk me down to the nearby bridge and along the quay to watch the small boats bobbing up and down in the harbour. There we could also savour the tang of the sea and the reflection of the clouds in the water – clearest at full tide. On days that were warm and moist the cloudbanks seemed whiter and fluffy and when the tide was low the mudflats whiffy. When we got back to the car Mam would have bought buns with icing on them, and lemonade maybe, and we would snack on these. If, before he went into the court, Dad signalled that his working day was definitely going to be a long one (because of the unusual number of cases on his list) we used to take a longer walk up by the open-air swimming pool where I would gaze enviously down at the boys and girls splashing in the blue-lined basin, and at the blue-green waves that lapped against the rocks into which it was set.

The moment we had all been waiting for arrived when Dad, dressed in a light-grey suit and wearing on his head the soft, brown hat that so suited him – he always dressed in civvies for these court jobs – came striding out of the granite building with a carefree smile on his face and got straight into the taxi. Denny immediately took us away over the bridge and out via Abbeyside. When time permitted my parents always stopped off at that suburb to visit their close friends, the Arrigans. Mick had played senior football with the fine Grangemockler side (the Mocklers) of the post-World War One period, some members of which were on the Tipperary team that played Dublin in the Bloody Sunday All-Ireland Gaelic Football Final of 1920. Time not permitting, we would head straight out to Clonea Bay, skirting the causeway that carried the train in which we travelled to Carrick on our holidays. We always took the narrow road that branched off to the quieter, middle section of the beach rather than following the main road to the busier castle end. Busier? In the middle of the week? In Ireland at the end of the Forties, beginning of the Fifties? Well, relatively. Court Day in Dungarvan was always on a midweek day, often, I think, on the town's half-day, so on a really hot afternoon a surprising number of cars would gather at the strand. On such days Denny would make negative remarks about the way everyone else drove or parked. At the seaside he would seek out a parking place near the front, if arriving early enough on the right between the grassy ditches where the narrow road dipped towards the beach. Now and again, for whatever reason, the car would not be in the same place at the end of the afternoon as it had been at the beginning. You were in another world the minute you stepped out of the car onto the sand-strewn ground. A light breeze filled your nose with seaweed and your ears with singing larks. You hurried along to the brow of the beach and the vastness of the Atlantic Ocean ran away with your eyes.

Denny would already have ascertained how the tide was running but I was always anxious to get Dad's on-the-spot opinion because it was the tide that would dictate the pattern of the afternoon. The wide beach at Clonea had no lifeguards and when the sea was a little on the rough side Dad would only allow us to bathe if the tide was coming in. When it was going out, he said, there was a danger that you might get carried out to sea. But there were another reasons too; the warm sand took the chill out of the incoming

Denny Regan's preferred parking place at Clonea Strand. He would park on the right roughly across from the 'No Road' sign.

Atlantic waters, making them more pleasant to bathe in, and it was easier to judge your depth because you knew the slope of the beach. On still days he had no objection to our swimming in the outgoing tide as long as it was not too far out. I had no awareness of the dangers of the shore when I was small and had to be held back by the hand while the picnic baskets and swimming things and my bucket and spade were taken out of the boot of the car. The adults seemed to take ages over this but eventually they were ready to go and I was allowed to run free – almost. Molly was never far from my heels as I picked my way over the pebbles and scampered onto the sand. We walked halfway along the beach in the direction of Ballynacourty Point until we came to our favourite picnic site on a long strip of grass above the shingle.

If the tide was coming in, and was in far enough over the warm sand, Dad, Paddy and I would immediately change into our togs and go for a swim. Mam and Molly, who never went swimming, were content to stretch out on the grass and enjoy the sun and scenery. Mostly we were lucky with the weather though sometimes it was cool and sunny-cloudy. There were times too when a morning rain did not let up and there was nothing one could do but drive straight back to Lismore in total disappointment as soon as Dad had finished his duties. Even worse, on one or two occasions the weather was so bad in the morning, and the forecast for later in the day so devoid of hope, that Dad did not even take us to Dungarvan. As against that, there were cloudless days when the blue of the sky and the sea were so in hue, you could hardly tell in looking at the horizon where the one began and the other left off.

Dad's swimming costume was a strangely old-fashioned garment, an orange-red loincloth with black stripes and a black section where he pulled the single strap over his left shoulder in the fashion of a circus strongman. He dressed and undressed very decorously, removing himself to a hollow apart. Molly pointedly looked in the opposite direction to which he had gone but Mam seemed easier about where she glanced. I never saw Dad in any other togs and he never went for a swim with Paddy or me in any place other than Clonea, Ardmore or Stradbally. He was not a great swimmer, being accomplished only in the breast-stroke, but this, it appeared to me, he did competently. When he was ready he would take Paddy and me by the hand and run down to the waves with us, as eager as we were to plunge into the water. When I was little I would be left to potter at the edge of the sea with my bucket and spade while Molly watched over me but as I grew older I was allowed to join my brother and Dad for a splash. Dad would play happily with us for a while after which it was his custom to swim out on his own, having warned us to stay well back in the shallows.

It was not easy to coax me out of the water but in the end the prospect of the tasty picnic that I knew Mam and Molly would have laid out on a white tablecloth on the grass proved sufficient enticement. Indeed, I was usually ravenous by the time I got back to be rubbed dry by either when I was little, by myself when I grew older, which was not as pleasurable in one sense but more to my liking in another because I hated having my ears poked by them. On the plates were laid out ham or corned beef sandwiches with lettuce, hard-boiled eggs and tomatoes. There would be flasks of hot tea for the grown-ups and fizzy lemonade for my brother and me. Denny could have joined us – it was not for lack of invitation – but, in his professional way, he preferred to remain aloof. He always brought his own sandwiches and a flask of tea and, even on roasting-hot days, it was his custom to eat in the car and afterwards pull the hat down over his face and take a nap, rather than enjoy the bracing sea air. You would see him emerge from the car in the late afternoon to sit on a rock or on the shingle at the top of the beach, still in his dark suit and with his hat low over his eyes. Not a beach person, Denny, although I did actually spot him once or twice with his white shirtsleeves rolled up to the elbow and his jacket draped over one arm. My parents were always wary of the sun because they knew from experience how easy it was to get burnt at the seaside. In spite of their attention and warnings I managed to get redder shoulders than were good for me. By the time I left Lismore at the age of seventeen I still had not learned to avoid getting sunburn every year. Once in my mid-teens I overdid it to such an extent I could not sleep and for a couple of nights stretched out on my back on the cold linoleum of my bedroom floor in an attempt to cool my itchy skin.

After we had eaten Dad liked to take out his racing binoculars and scan the ocean for coasters and ships. When he fixed on something he would lift me up on his lap and hold the binoculars to my eyes so that I could pick up the object too. At that early age my eyes were not wide enough apart for the narrowest setting of the eyepieces so he would turn the glasses on their side so that I could peer through one. It was difficult to get small boats in my sights but eventually I would focus in on them with a squeal of wonder. Steamships were easiest to locate because they trailed a long plume of dark smoke. The binoculars were not very powerful and often I found it more fun to focus on near objects and view them through the wrong end of the lens. I specially liked to distort faces in this way.

Having eaten, Paddy and I were impatient to get back into the sea again but we were not allowed another swim until our meal had been digested for at least an hour. To fill the interim, and give Dad and Mam a few moments to themselves and maybe have a snooze, Molly would take the two of us farther up the beach where it was rocky. There we could look for conch shells to put our ears to and hear the sea in, or make half-hearted attempts to prise tortoiseshell limpets from the smooth rock-faces, or examine the activities of the small crabs and other seashore animals marooned in the pools among the cracks and sandy hollows by the ebbing tide. Later on we would see Mam and Dad strolling up the beach, arm in arm, deep in conversation, or lightheartedly running around one another, to join us. You could sense their closeness and playfulness. She would be calling him 'Bal' perhaps, the pet name that the Morrissey sisters had for him. In our presence she was more accustomed to calling him 'Dad' or 'Joe'. I saw nothing exceptional in their mutual warmth. That was how they were together. Of the two, she was the more protective and, maybe, the more realistic. He was shyly romantic and, in spite of the strict exterior he could assume, soft. When they reached us we would all walk on a bit more, then turn and go back for another swim if the conditions were right. After that there would be time for a last snack before, come seven or eight o'clock, we would return to Denny for the ride home.

If the tide was out when we arrived at the beach we used to reverse the day's activities – paddling and picnicking first, followed by the stroll up the beach, then swimming when the tide had turned and was far enough in over the warm sand. The pattern was the same at Ardmore, a shorter, cosier strand with a grassy bank higher than that of Clonea. The added attraction of the seaside village was its small fishing harbour and picturesque cliff walk. At the Cliff Hotel Mam and Dad could have a quiet afternoon tea, unencumbered by Paddy and me who were exploring the rock pools around the harbour with Molly. I loved the traffic of the dinghies, particularly when they came in with their catches of mackerel and herring. In August, when the shoals were in, you could see the mackerel voraciously driving the frantic sprats right up to the base of the rocks below the cliffs. Which meant we went home with a dozen fresh fish bought for a song.

On one occasion when Paddy was in Carrick-on-Suir on holidays, and after Molly had returned to live in the same town, Dad asked Denny to take us a little further afield to the beautiful cove at Stradbally. Aside from its idyllic setting, this hamlet was renowned for three things: its Gaelic footballers, the number of orders of nuns who had summer residences there, and its 'missing postman' who disappeared on Christmas Day 1929 and was never seen or heard of again and about whom no one, not even the Law, dared anymore ask questions of the clammed-up locals. On that splendid sunny day I could not miss the black-robed sisters strolling along the cliffside paths above us and felt sorry for them that they had to go so covered up. The mirror-bright tide was funnelling steadily up the strand through the narrow inlet between the cliffs, dislodging knots of sunbathers from the rocky niches on the western side. Along the eastward side the ripple of a small stream grew fainter as the swelling sea pressed it back up its channel. On the slopes figures other than nuns picnicked and took the sun. I was delighting in the contrast of being now under the water, now under the sun. My sea-level eyes were drawn to the wider sea that beckoned beyond the cove and I wished I were a strong enough swimmer to stroke out and greet it. But I was too young to be allowed beyond my depth and had to be content with splashing within my inches. After the beach we visited Mam's cousins, Mary and Mattie Kiely and their family, who then farmed in nearby Monakerka. Another cousin, Mary Glendon from Cork, was holidaying with them and I was much drawn to her sparkling personality. A bountiful farmer's meal detained us too long at table. Then my cousins and I were let loose on the land to play hide-and-seek among the cocks of hay. If that day had an end I never saw it. When the time came for us to depart the sunlight was still clinging to the horizon.

CHAPTER TEN

Other Sports

CRICKET, WHICH TOOK MY FANCY for a season in my early teens, was a game I came to by default. It featured in the summer comics I read and, though the cricket stories held no interest for me, names like W. G. Grace (lavishly-bearded), the Compton brothers (all-rounders), Len Hutton and Don Bradman (big hitters) were known to me. The Cricket Ground adjoined the Hurling Field so it was not unusual for us in the course of our Gaelic games to allow our gaze to stray across from time to time to what was happening over the fence, especially when Pad Feeney of the Castle Farm was swiping sixes and fours all over the place. The game was one I classified with tennis and badminton as just another sissy English pastime, not to be taken seriously. They broke off in the middle of the game for a cup of tea, for God's sake! What I knew about the rules when I started could be summed up in a few words – one man threw the ball, one stumped, two batted, and nine hung around as catchers. With increasing interest and a closer perusal of the comics, I began to acquire a more sophisticated vocabulary, but one that was largely meaningless to me, e.g. 'silly mid-on', silly mid-off'. Happily the Lismore lads did not confuse one another with this inane terminology, not even Dean Stanley, who doubtless, with his theological turn of mind understood it perfectly. The bowler (the thrower of the ball), whoever it was, directed you to stand 'over here', 'over there', 'more to the left', 'more to the right', 'farther forward', 'farther back', or just flagged you into position with the motions of a hand, the way one might guide a car through a gate.

I was first put to work as a fielder (a catcher) and for a time suspected that I was merely being used as a ballboy. My suspicions grew when I found that I never seemed to be sited where the catches were taken. There were other aspects of my apprenticeship that I was not overexcited about either, like giving the women a hand with the tea in the small shed at the north-west corner of the playing field that served as a pavilion, learning to score a game, or helping to roll the pitch. But all these things had to be endured, I supposed, before I could be given my chance at the crease, and little by little I began to realise that there was more to cricket than its cool, white exterior suggested. For a start, the shiny wine-coloured ball with its heavily stitched seams was as hard as a rock – harder by far, and bigger and heavier, than the *sliothar* with which I hurled. Then there was the bat, a solid block of wood, no easy cudgel to handle. Just learning to catch the ball was more than I expected; if you did not let your cupped hands fall a foot or so with the trajectory of it you got a phop as hard as anything laid on you by the Christian Brothers. The biggest eye-opener was seeing the fast bowlers in action close up. There were two in particular, Pad Feeney, as ferocious in his pitching as in his batting, and Jim Casey, a publican from the Main Street who also owned land out Glencairn way and in other parts around the town. Pad was able to mitigate his bowling when faced with budding, would-be master batsmen like myself but Jim was only let loose on the men. The publican-farmer, whose nickname was 'Bladder', or maybe 'Blather', didn't seem to know his own strength and the sight of his blocky figure lumbering up to the crease like an angry rhino must have put the heart across many a tail-ender. Pad enjoyed putting the frighteners on me sometimes when I was batting by going back a long way from the crease and charging in, but then at the last second he would draw back and lob me a ball I would have some chance of striking. Once or twice he did not slow his arm and I felt the wind of the bullet just before it whipped my stumps out. In heart-stopping moments like that I prepared to jump out of my skin. The game merited practice and in the backyard at home Tom Feeney and I would alternately bowl and bat using a hurley and a tennis ball, or we did until Tom put through the kitchen window and gave Mam an awful fright. To our relief she only laughed, surveyed the broken pane, and told us to take out cricket elsewhere.

    Lismore had a very useful team at the end of the Forties, beginning of the Fifties. It chalked up a string of successes against sides from the counties of Waterford, Cork and Tipperary. Regular rivals were Kanturk, Midleton, Mallow, Cahir, Tramore, Cork City (a Church of Ireland selection), and Newtown School, a posh Quaker boarding establishment in Waterford City. Dean Stanley captained the side and, though he was pushing on a bit, was a fair batsman and bowler. He was, in fact, a sportsman of some renown, having in his heyday excelled as a triple Munster interprovincial – at cricket, hockey and rugby – but I did not know this at the time. Evenings he would appear for practice in his grey suit, throw off his dog-collar and jacket, slot into a vacant fielding position and peer purposefully at the batsman through his spectacles. For matches he would be in his whites like everybody else. The slow bowlers were Pad Feeney's brother Jack, and Matt Gough. Both had deceptively easygoing ways about them and their little jigs up to the crease gave you the impression that even you could flog either of them to the tennis pavilion for six but, nine times out of ten you would hit air and seven times out of ten you would hear a sharp click behind you as your stump took a wallop. Jack was the man who most troubled opposing sides – figures like 6 for 9, or 6 for 19 were not unusual for him. But Matt, unlike his roly-poly counterpart, had another string to his bow. He was a handy batsman as well and his calm application often saved a game when the openers went cheaply. The biggest hitter was undoubtedly Pad. With his powerful physique he rated as the village slogger and could as easily be out for a duck as score 60, which was as high as anyone scored in the league in which Lismore played. Sixes onto the roof of the tennis pavilion, which was situated beyond the grass courts from the cricket pitch, were his specialities. Almost as big a hitter as Pad, and probably more consistent, was Frankie Tierney, the wicket-keeper. Frankie was tall and rangy and there was a sinewy elegance about his play both in front of, and behind, the stumps. An innings of 55 that included three sixes and five fours, was a fair measure of what he was capable. When Pad and Frankie threw their wickets away with rash strokes the carefree Gus Kingston, or Willie Clements, could be relied upon to steady up the middle order of the batting.

As to my own accomplishments, I was a fairly useful fielder and bowled with a reasonable aim, if not with any great pace. The pinnacle of my achievement was the time I skittled Pad out at practice, which tickled Jack because he was the one who taught me most about the art of bowling. My coup was a pure fluke but the lads gave Pad a great ribbing on his way back to the line nonetheless. The batsman had his revenge on me a few evenings later when I dared field too close to him. I had only stood where I was put. Well, maybe I had crept a little nearer for the gas of it. If I did, I was taught a rude lesson. I was crouched about fifteen yards away, at a right angle to the pitch, level with Pad (the suicide position when fielding against a slogger, I was later to learn; no doubt there is a whimsical technical term for it) when he swifted around, unexpectedly light-footed, and thumped the ball in my direction. A blur whizzed toward me and before I could take any kind of action, evasive or constructive, it caught me full on the kneecap. I dropped like a stone, yelping.

'That'll teach you to field too close to me,' Pad grinned.

I could barely walk home afterwards and limped the whole of the following week.

In line with the other sports I tried my hand at, I only once had the chance of striking a ball for Lismore against outside competition, and that was by way of a concession, a double concession as it turned out. Matt Gough had kindly arranged for me to travel to Waterford with the team to watch them play posh Newtown School. He could not have anticipated that he was letting me in for one of the greatest humiliations of my sporting career. The match was over. Lismore had played poorly and lost and the Newtown team of young bloods was still out on the pitch, having scarcely had a canter. Matt asked them to let me have a knock as a kind of supernumerary twelfth man and the boys, who were of the upper-sixth type I used to read about in the comics, graciously agreed. With a sense of foreboding I said there was no need for me to be put in pads; I would hardly be at the crease for long. But the boys insisted that I should be properly protected so I had to endure the laborious routine of strapping on both pads. I had rightly gauged my skills as a batsman. After a long walk from the pavilion, and it was a proper pavilion, I was bowled clean first ball. Great embarrassment all round, not least my own.

'Aw sure, he's only learnin', give him another shot,' Matt pleaded and the captain again graciously agreed.

I did not know whether to thank Matt or curse him as I took centre, surveyed the full complement of fielders around me, and faced the incoming slow bowler, a youngster not much bigger than myself, one more time. The ball floated down tantalisingly. I hit out and held my breath, hoping against hope that I would hear the sweet smack of the leather against the willow of the bat and feel the tingle of a well-struck ball running up to my palms. There was a sharp click all right but it was only my stump going over for the second time. Stupefaction across the pitch, most of it mine. I rushed from the crease before Matt could suggest that I be given another attempt to redeem myself. The lad cast in the role of my tormentor gave me an embarrassed and apologetic look. I smiled weakly as I passed. 'Will I ever get back to the pavilion?' I thought. Later over tea, the lad and Matt expressed understanding words again.

'He's only starting,' Matt said.

I was already thinking of retiring.

Better lads than I defected to the world of cricket from the GAA, sometimes returning to hurling later, or surreptitiously trying to play both games to avoid the GAA Ban. Kip Tobin was undoubtedly the best of my age group and put the striking skills he had learned on the long Gaelic pitch to good effect on the twenty-two-yard strip. Vin O'Donoghue, though he hated the smell of anything *seoinín* was surprisingly undemonstrative when he learned of my activities on the cricket scene. Aside from a passing a *searbhasach* remark, made more in sorrow than in anger, he did not try to make a meal of it. His attitude might have been different had I been a useful cog of the hurling team.

The only other sport I had a go at in Lismore was table tennis, which was played in the courthouse during the winter months. I did not rate it as a sport though, more as a pastime. On the other hand, I had heard of a Hungarian called Victor Barna who was raising it to the level of a fully competitive sport in England. What started my interest in it was a table tennis set I got from Mam and Dad one Christmas – one of those wide cardboard boxes that contained two sandpaper-lined bats, a couple of hollow white balls and a green net fitted with two clips that you could string across the middle of any table big enough to play on. Mam was my usual opponent in the family and was often too cute for me. A game that was also known as ping-pong would not, under normal circumstances, have held my interest for long but when I was given a chance to handle and use the rubber-studded bats of the Lismore Table Tennis Club I was forced to upgrade my estimation of it. Matt Gough was to be one of my tutors in this game as well. He was probably the town's number one player, more adept at spinning the light ball than the heavy cricket ball. Frankie Tierney, surprisingly for a long bat slogger I thought, also had time for the game. I did not get very far with this sport, either, but, at least in this case, I could plead lack of commitment. Two of my school pals, Willie Ryan and Jimmy Colbert, were good enough to hold down places on the club team. Other male regulars were Ca O'Donnell and Paddy Tyers.

Table tennis had been going for a number of years when it was somewhat elbowed aside by another pastime, badminton, that seemed to bring with it the social affectations of lawn tennis. Indeed, the practitioners of the new racket game were mainly, though not totally, winter migrants from the summer sport. The courthouse was again the venue. When eventually a team was formed it had problems finding opponents within a reasonable radius. The only town I remember them playing against was Midleton, where every game under the sun seemed to find a home. I would not be surprised to learn that it was the Cork players that encouraged the formation of a team in Lismore so that *they* would have someone to oppose. Among our best players were Monica Noonan, Dorothy Daly, Claude Colbert, John Crotty and the McCarthys, Mary and Mokie. My brother Paddy also played, but less seriously.

As for lawn tennis, sometimes I used to laze around on the grass outside the high wire netting that surrounded the courts and watch the swishing around. Florence 'Mokie' McCarthy was clearly the best player, even to my untutored eye. I enjoyed watching him play. The lanky John Crotty was handy, too. But there was another aspect of the game that drew our young eyes, the 'bit o' leg' you glimpsed, especially the unfamiliar show from the ladies of visiting teams. On the whole, I concluded, even though Paddy was involved in this club too, that it was not really a sport to be taken seriously. My brother, like me, was an ineffectual sportsman, and I used to feel that his interest was really in the social side of both badminton and tennis. It was the opinion of most of us boys that a game that attracted the active participation of a lot of girls hardly merited the name of sport. Not that the women of the town did not know how to compete in their own right. Ann Madden, Dervla Murphy, Monica Noonan and Mary MacCarthy always looked spirited in their play, as far as I could judge.

Other games we knew of second-hand. Our interest in sport was catholic in spite of the GAA Ban and we never knew which activity would engage our attention next. Cappoquin had a rowing club, which was okay by the GAA, and a fine shingle Boathouse with a wine-red galvanised roof, large enough to accommodate six or seven hundred patrons for a dance. Some of our Cappoquin classmates used to row for the club. The most successful was Paddy McGrath of Modeligo who was one class under mine. Paddy went on to become one of the club's best oarsmen and rowed for many years. His younger brother Liam was also a fine rower. On an August Bank Holiday or two I cycled to Cappoquin for the annual regatta. The weather was usually good for this, and when it was, the event attracted a large crowd. The races were held on the broad southern arm of the river bend when the tide was full and we used to congregate under the trees along the Killahala Road to watch the fours and eights sweeping by. Although a different kind of spectacle, it failed to rivet me and I attended every other year rather than annually. What I liked most about it was the swish of the slim boats and the rhythmic splash of the oars on the still, black water; what I liked least, the lengthy periods of inactivity between the races. I was attracted by the crowds too. In our rural area crowds were always interesting, whether they flocked to a sporting event, a political meeting, a circus or a funeral; they brought with them new faces and sometimes new models of cars or lorries or bicycles. The sight of so many human beings coming together in one place was something to be enjoyed – perhaps a chance to spot a well-known personality, perhaps an occasion of sin, certainly an opportunity for a bit of entertainment, no matter how serious the occasion. Willie Sargent, who was stroke on the Cappoquin Rowing Club's senior team, was something of a matinee idol. A fine tenor who sang at concerts throughout Munster, he was also a daredevil motorcyclist. With his brother Michael, he was a regular participant in scrambling and road racing events. No road races were held in our area but scrambles took place in the vicinity of Cappoquin. Willie was tragically killed while taking part in the Leinster 100 Road Race in 1953, deeply saddening our two towns. His uncle Bud owned the garage below the Strand Bridge in Lismore so the family, though living in Cappoquin, were always up our way and were felt to be one of our own.

I never had much interest in cars, other than a short period jotting down licence numbers, or in motorcyles, other than the wartime excitement of seeing soldiers racing by in formation. But, in the glittering heyday of Fangio and Ascari, our next-door neighbour Michael Feeney was mad on racers, especially motorcycles. Unfortunately for him, his mother, having heard of too many accidents on bikes, forbade him to own one of these. It was only when she was away, and when a bike had been left in for repair, that he could indulge his passion, taking the repaired machine, a BSA, AJS or Norton usually, for a burst up Gallows Hill and out the Tallow Road for a mile or two. He was always promising me a ride on the pillion but never actually got round to taking me with him. I did not blame him really, although I was disappointed. So infrequent were his chances of a ride himself – eventually it reached the stage where the garage foreman Kieran Fenton was instructed never to let him have access to any motor-bike on the premises – that he had to grab every opening that came his way. It was really tough on him when a gleaming new machine went on display in the shop. All he could do was sit on it and finger the controls longingly.

Defeated in his hopes of glory on a bike he then upgraded his interest in car racing. He announced that he was going to construct his own racing model and enlisted his brother Tom and me in the project. On the promise of getting regular test spins in this future bullet of the highway and track, and a share in the glory it would certainly win for itself, Tom and I became his eager assistants. The scheme was to strip an old Ford down to its chassis, insert a recharged engine in the place of the clapped-out one, and solder together a new body. For weeks Tom and I toiled over the rusty framework, chipping bits off here, sandpapering there, preparing for the day when the rebuilding could begin. The hulk was straddled across wooden blocks by the wall that divided our two houses, near the entrance to the high, galvanised work-shed. Every now and again Mike would come up to us and say, 'Ye're doin' a fine job, lads,' then direct us toward a new aspect of the operation. Panzer Behegan, the garage mechanic, was more mischievous with his comments. 'She's shapin' up like a real flier, lads,' was one, delivered with a sceptical grin. We took him at his word and were not infected with the slightest doubt. No sooner had we completed the stripping, however, than we had cause to remember his nudges and winks. Mike's interest in the project suddenly waned to zero. We harried him to no avail with requests for further tasks until, finally, our own dreams of glory bit the dust too. We had laboured for nothing but our imaginations, at least, had glimpsed the silver of a finished roadster.

Rugby stormed into the headlines with the Irish team's International Championship and Triple Crown doubles of 1948 and 1949. Tom Lineen took a keen interest in these notable victories, though he remained a GAA man through and through, and was the only one of us who could make sense of the rules of that game. The thing that used to intrigue me about the rugby players was how beefy and tough they looked. I used to wonder how they could be, or appear to be, physically stronger than the lads who used to labour on the roads or in the fields. The advantages that the doctors, solicitors and insurance men held, of course, were in diet and the time they could devote to training. Another aspect that intrigued me was their curious penchant for parading initials. The Catholics on the squad were usually one up on their Protestant team-mates in this respect, possessing sets of three rather than two.

The extra Catholic one came at Confirmation when we were allowed, indeed encouraged, to add a third forename of our choice. In my own case, I was given James Joseph at birth and, out of religious fervour and patriotism, chose Patrick for my third – I had always felt cheated that my brother had been given full title to this forename. Mam had chivied me toward Oliver, after Blessed Oliver Plunkett, the martyr who was hanged at Tyburn, but I was determined to get the 'P' in there. So, if I had played alongside Jackie Kyle I would have out-initialled him J.J.P. to J.W. Funnily enough Dad never had a third forename or, if he did, I never heard of it. His second was quaint enough, Albert. An enquiry as to how that one sneaked into the family never drew a satisfactory answer.

If rugby made any impression on me it was in the newsreels I saw of Kyle jinking through massed defences. Names like Mick Lane, George Norton, Karl Mullen, Ernie Strathdee and Harry McKibben also became familiar. And, as much as any of them, Tom Clifford, the burly Limerickman whom we had a lot of time for because one, he was a Munsterman in a sport dominated by Ulstermen and Leinstermen and two, he was not averse to telling the hidebound ruling body of the game, which had cold-shouldered him for years, to go and jump in a lake.

From the comics I read it was far easier for me to relate to soccer rather than rugby, though this sport too was scarcely less remote. It was not played anywhere in West Waterford, but interest in it was growing locally. Mick

Madden, Mokie McCarthy and some of the other men from the town began to motor to the Mardyke ground in Cork City and Kilcohan Park in Waterford City to see Cork Athletic and Waterford United in action. I had some understanding of the rules of the game though the concept of offside, unknown in Gaelic football, was something my mind reacted against. The biggest puzzle to me was how a man could head that heavy leather ball on a wet day and not knock himself out. And yet the players were doing it all the time! Irish soccer produced few household names but in Johnny Carey of Manchester United we undoubtedly possessed a world-class performer. His bald head became instantly recognisable after he had captained the first successful United side to victory in the 1948 Cup Final and then led Ireland to a win over England in 1949. There wasn't much more you could have asked of a man. Whether it was rugby or soccer, we used to revel in England's defeats, even if we were not doing the defeating. Their loss to the USA in the 1950 World Cup and the routs by the classic Hungarians in 1953 and 1954 were music to our ears. Well, to a point. In spite of this partiality the exploits of the famous English League clubs impressed me. The Wizard of the Dribble's medal in the 1953 Cup Final was like something out of the comics. And when Cork Athletic imaginatively signed Raich Carter, the illustrious English inside-forward, for a season in 1952–53, this hitherto unknown name to me instantly became the Christy Ring of football. The ex-Hull player, already at the end of his career, won the FAI Cup for Cork on his own.

A sport that never failed to engage our interest, though it was not formally practised in Lismore, was boxing. Any lad who was handy with his dukes merited respect, even if you did not like him as a person. Peter 'Pedro' O'Brien was reckoned to be a good and stylish boxer, maybe the best in town. I only had that on hearsay from my Botany pals but never had reason to doubt the stories about one or two who had made the mistake of taking him on. Pedro was a clean fighter who, if he got involved in a flare-up on the hurling field, would throw down his hurley and trade fists rather than sticks – in the eyes of us youngsters the mark of a real man. Mick Coleman of Church Lane was another with whom no one was anxious to exchange blows. Mick, unlike Pedro, was capable of starting a scrap as well as finishing it. The two never had the occasion to test their skills on one another as far as I know, but if they did I cannot help thinking that Mick would have had the edge. He was heavier than Pedro and the extra poundage would almost inevitably have favoured him. Pound for pound though, and when it came to pure boxing skills, my feeling is that the Botany man was the better.

The only real boxing action the town of Lismore experienced came at the end of the Second World War. Jackie Scanlan staged a tournament or two at the Happydrome at which the soldiers garrisoned in the Hall demonstrated their skills. At that time I was too little to attend and, anyway, my interest in boxing was to develop later. To see amateur fights you did not have to go any farther than Dungarvan, which had a thriving boxing club, and an amateur of international reputation in Peter Crotty, also a soldier, who represented Ireland at welterweight and who was especially unlucky to be beaten at the Helsinki Olympics of 1952. His career I followed with interest. The high point of Irish professional boxing was provided by the frail-looking Northern Irish flyweight champion Rinty Monaghan who won the world title from the durable Scottish Champion Jackie Patterson in 1948 – a great year in general for Irish and Waterford sport – and defended it successfully for a couple of years. It was less easy to keep up with the appearances of Martin Thornton, the Irish professional heavyweight champion who never seemed to fight in Ireland and seldom seemed to win. Jack Doyle was a hard act to follow! A professional boxer who did come to Lismore was a big Tipperary man, Jim Cully, who appeared not in the guise of a pugilist but as an ordinary hand with Perks or MacDonalds Amusements. He was some six-foot-six-to-eight inches tall with a broad slab of back and his feats of strength were colossal. He could crouch under the chassis of a long fairground truck and raise the back of it off the ground by straightening his legs, which he did sometimes to amuse, other times out of necessity when a vehicle got bogged down in the muddy field. He was an amiable man and we boys loved to be around him and peer up the full length of his giant body. Many years after he had put in his last appearance in the town and gone off to earn his bread in the ring I came across a photo of him in some boxing journal or other squaring up to Joe Baksi. He towered over the tough Polish-American heavyweight contender but looked curiously frail in comparison with the latter. I suspect he operated more in the role of sparring partner rather than full professional because I never saw his name on a card. Nonetheless, he was

This photo of Jim Cully squaring up to Joe Baksi has somehow survived with me. I have failed to trace which boxing magazine or newspaper I cut it from. Late 1940s.

a man to remember. And perhaps he did fight Baksi? [I have since discovered via the Web, from which 'facts' should be sifted with care, that he was 7ft. 2in. tall and did indeed have a couple of fights as a professional in 1948 – one kayo win and either one or two kayo losses after which he vanished from the boxing scene.]

My favourite boxers were all black: Joe Louis, Sugar Ray Robinson and Archie Moore – at the top of their form and at the right weight invincible. But I greatly respected Jersey Joe Walcott and Ezzard Charles as well. The first big fight to snare my attention was the Louis–Conn rematch of 1946. Billy Conn being Irish-American, and very much the underdog as he was really only a light-heavy, meant that my loyalty to Louis was in question. Joe won by a knockout in the eighth – nobody ever got a second shot at him and lasted to the end – but Conn again displayed the fine skills that had almost defeated Louis in their first battle. That was the fight that encouraged me to start a scrapbook of newspaper cuttings about boxing. I cut out the fight report with its grainy wire photo from the *Irish Press* and carefully pasted it into an old *Wizard* annual. Eventually I was to fill two annuals, and after that a cardboard box in which I stored the overflow. I also extended my collection to include such events as the Bannister four-minute mile, the All-Ireland hurling and Gaelic football finals, the Munster finals, Sherpa Tenzing's and Edmund Hillary's ascent of Mount Everest, and so on. *The unluckiest loser against Louis was Jersey Joe. Even the great champion felt the result should have gone the challenger's way at the end of fifteen rounds in December 1947. The result of the rematch in June 1948 was inevitable. The Brown Bomber, though again outboxed, dropped his valiant opponent in the eleventh.

We had not long had a wireless at home when Sugar Ray, on the last leg of a European tour, put up his crown against England's Randolph Turpin at Earl's Court in London on the 10th of July 1951. That evening Tom Lineen, Hoagy and I were bunched around the set that stood on the dumb-waiter in the living-room, riveted to Raymond Glendenning's commentary, less than enthralled by Barrington-Dalby's plummy inter-round drawl. Turpin started well to our surprise. We knew that he was not a bad fighter but, as he had never come up against anyone of Robinson's calibre before, there was no reason to suspect that he would not go the way of all the other European challengers the champ had recently iced. Mam sat behind us sewing – something she hated doing – but her ear was tuned to the set as well. She liked listening to boxing on the radio although, understandably, she became apprehensive when a fighter was being cut up. Halfway into the fight Turpin was still steaming into Sugar Ray with confidence enough to suggest to Glendenning and Dalby that he might just stage an upset. We were having none of that. We knew our man. He was just biding his time. Any minute of his choosing he would unleash a salvo and that would be the end of the Englishman. The thought of an Englishman beating the great American world champion appalled us, even if this particular Englishman was black and consequently evoked more sympathy in us than if he had been white. Turpin continued to do well. So well Barrington-Dalby was salivating.

'Jakus, he's leavin' it late?' Tom looked at Hoagy and me in disbelief.

Was it possible that – ? Oh yes, it was. Turpin had the legs of the Champion who had spent more time than he should have hoofing it round the floor shows of the Continent. Bang went the final bell and off went Ray's crown. We waited without hope for the referee's verdict. It wasn't long in coming.

'Turpin's won! Turpin's won!' Glendenning exulted and our hearts took a dive into our boots.

Immediately we turned off the set. There was a hush. We didn't know what to say to one another, such was our state of shock. It could only have been worse if Barrington-Dalby had been doing the punching.

Mam looked at the three of us and laughed. 'Sure 'tis only a fight,' she said.

'Only a fight!' we thought collectively, 'Didn't the woman realise the gravity of the matter at all?'

I saw Tom and Hoagy down the hall to the door. They went off shaking their heads. Took us days to get over it. It was another couple of weeks before the newsreel of the fight reached the Palladium. At least then I saw for myself that the Englishman had won fairly. A fitter Sugar Ray duly won back his title the following September, but not before taking another pasting from Turpin. The second time, surprisingly, I felt sorry for Turpin because he suffered the kind of technical knockout that made you feel the American boxing promoters had pulled a fast one on him. Robinson's eye had been cut so badly by the end of the previous round the fight should have been stopped in the Leamington man's favour. But it had been allowed to go on and Robinson, who knew the score, produced the goods. The ageing champion had been desperately lucky. Third time round he would not have been able to withstand the powerful Turpin. But the third fight never materialised and, with great regret, I witnessed the rapid and inexplicable decline of the great English fighter, through the hammering he took from the American Carl 'Bobo' Olsen and his ignominious KO at the hands of the Italian, Tiberio Mitri. Both of these were rugged boxers but at his best

Turpin, who had it in him to be an all-time great, would easily have beaten them.

Other fighters I liked to follow were the welterweight Kid Gavilan, the Cuban with the bolo punch – a version of the shifty Kid McCoy's corkscrew – and Willie Pep and Sandy Saddler whose four featherweight battles at the end of the Forties and beginning of the Fifties were fearsome roughhouse encounters. Close to home there was plenty to enthuse about in the Irish amateur scene, especially the many wins of Mick McKeon, Johnny Caldwell and the heavyweight Gerry Ó Colmáin. But it was not just the current boxers, amateur and professional, in which I was interested. Reading *The Ring* I was captivated by the blood and guts of the Manassa Mauler, the Michigan Assassin, Jack Johnson, Joe Jeannette and, above all, Sam Langford. Langford, a middleweight, possessed a reach and punch that allowed him to take on heavyweights, all of whom feared him and only the greatest of whom were capable of beating him. I also took the British weekly *Boxing News* regularly but for action, glamour and presentation this fell far short of Nat Fleischer's publication. Its plus was that it covered all-important amateur bouts as well as the professional arena, which meant that the Irish international matches were always reported in detail.

In my fantasies I now began to see myself as following in the footsteps of the greatest battlers. There was no reason why I should not put together a wallop as lethal as that of the slim Kid Gavilan, or the spidery Sandy Saddler, or even Sugar Ray – if I were not to discover to my joy that I already packed one. But first, I had to put some slabs of muscle in the right places. And that was not going to be easy in a town like Lismore where people would not take you seriously if you announced that your ambition was to be champion of the world, at featherweight for a start, maybe. A regular place on the Irish amateur team was my fall-back position. I filled a rough canvas bag with sawdust and trundled it up to the attic room that Molly had vacated by then to serve as my punch bag.

'What are you doing with that old bag hanging up there?' asked Mam with some annoyance in her voice. Perhaps she had visions of its retaining rope snapping and the whole thing crashing down through the ceiling and landing on top of Dad and her as they slept?

'I'm going to be a boxer,' I announced.

'A boxer!' she laughed, 'What do you want to be a boxer for? You'll get a flat nose.'

'I don't care,' I snapped and walked off.

She might not have realised it but her comment gave me something to think about. Until then I had never noticed that indeed, all boxers, give or take the odd one, had flat noses. Now, on checking through my issues of the boxing periodicals, I found they had, sure enough. But, once I had corroborated that fact, the prospect of having my schnozzle bashed flat failed to deter me from my stated ambition. I dug out an old pair of ordinary leather gloves that used to belong to Dad and, though they were too big for me, pulled them on and set to work punching the bag regularly. I knew I had to toughen up the skin over my knuckles because one day when Barney Walsh and I compared fists I discovered that my pal, having to do much more physical work, like sawing and chopping wood, at home than I, had thicker folds of skin over his knuckles, and calloused palms. I read in *The Ring* that some old-time fighter used to toughen the skin of his hands by soaking them in salt water, so I tried that out. Not for long though. Judging by the meagre results in the short term, it was a process that required a far higher degree of patience than a boy in a hurry could muster. Then I read about Georges Carpentier's legs. It appeared that for a light heavyweight they were unusually strong and muscular. Poses of the fighter confirmed this. He was quoted as saying that he had practised *savate* as a young man in French Indo-China and used to kick a punch-bag in order to enhance his kicking power. Unlike the business of soaking one's mitts in brine this was a routine that seemed to me wholly logical so I went in with the boot for a few weeks. Again, however, the results were disappointing. The slabs of muscle were just failing to materialise. I was at my wit's end.

Then I remembered Charles Atlas and his Dynamic Tension. Something I had previously dismissed as highly unlikely to produce the kind of miraculous physique it claimed to build. In my comic collection I quickly dug out his persuasive ad with its classic storyline of the hapless weakling having sand kicked in his face by the beach bully in front of a bevy of bathing beauties who seem to have nothing better to do than admire the passing beefcake. The weakling, of course, returns a short few weeks later, pumped-up to a he-man, and Cagneys his tormentor in the face with the flat of his hand, earning the full attention of the fickle cheesecake. 'Dynamic Tension? Hmm,' I thought. I felt I knew what the words meant individually, but conjoined I was not certain. The dictionary did not help. Left to my own devices I figured out that the phrase had to mean lying on the floor on one's back, stretching one's limbs to the utmost, and willing power into one's musclature. It was a touching belief on my part in the power of auto-suggestion but, unfortunately, as a body-building technique it was wholly ineffective. I perused the photos of Atlas again. You had to hand it to him. He looked like a god. Or what my uninformed mind conceived to be the Grecian ideal of a god. Not a ripple out of place, not a mark on his face, ageless. The World's Most Perfectly Developed Man. What wouldn't I have given to have looked half the man he was? Yet, my appreciation was not completely uncritical. I was forced to ask myself what he did with all those beautiful muscles. After all, not all world boxing champions had legs like Carpentier – Sugar Ray's were skinny as rakes. Why, for example, wasn't Atlas like that other Adonis, Jim Londos, a real Greek, the champion wrestler of the world? Or like our own Steve Casey or Danno Mahony? Or, as he liked to pose in the act of throwing a discus, the world's best discus thrower? Or as good a swimmer as Johnny Weissmuller, not renowned for the shape of his legs? No matter, I thought, if he can teach me to put muscles on, I'll do the rest in my own way. I wrote off for details of his course and duly received the same with an application form giving his fee.

The only problem now was how, at the age of 14, was I going to raise the money? I felt sure that my parents would not wear the idea so I did not even bother to ask them. Anyway, they did not carry the kind of spare cash that I needed to fund my hopes. I was at a loss until I saw a Dungarvan scrap-merchant's advertisement in the *Dungarvan Leader,* asking for scrap metal, in particular, lead. I remembered there were a few lengths of lead piping lying in the cupboard under the stairs and decided to go into business. To those first pieces I added others that I scavenged here and there, caching all under old rags and blocks of wood under the stairs. After a few weeks I had amassed a reasonable amount but nothing like the shipment I required. I decided I had to have a partner and talked Paddy Creane into helping me, not mentioning, however, the specific purpose for which I needed the money. The understanding I gave was that once we had enough for a consignment we would split the proceeds. Paddy scoured the Manse and came up with some more odds and ends. Another couple of weeks went by. Then I managed to unearth a few further scraps. I needed something like a fiver to pay for the Atlas course of exercises so that meant that we had to put together lead to the value of a tenner for an even split. So far we were nowhere near that amount. I was on the point of giving up when I was over in the Villa playing one day and noticed lead flashing protruding from under loose bricks in a long strip along an outside wall where a lean-to outhouse had formerly stood. My eyes lit up. The Villa at that time was unoccupied so there could be no harm in removing the apparently unwanted metal, I reasoned. It would have been taken down by the owners when they removed the outhouse had they had any use for it. Next day, in the quiet of the early evening, Paddy and I went across with a hammer and chisel and a canvas sack. It was a simple matter to climb the wall and the sixteen- or eighteen-foot strip of lead came away in our hands. We didn't even have to use the tools we brought. Following the success of this mission I surveyed a number of other likely walls in the town but to no further avail. It was clear that we had collected all we were likely to get.

Time thus to write to the Dungarvan address saying that I had a shipment of scrap lead for sale and could someone please come and collect it. The man wrote back in an uncertain hand with instructions to put it in a sack and send it on by goods train. On receipt of the consignment the appropriate amount of money would be forwarded. Aware of the somewhat iffy reputation of scrap-merchants, I was dubious about this response but felt that I had no option but to comply with the request. 'It might be better this way,' I thought, 'because Mam and Dad won't get wind of the deal then.' I did not really mind them finding out about the metal. What I wanted to keep to myself was how I was going to spend the proceeds of my small venture. Paddy Creane and I borrowed a wooden trolley from Feeney's garage, wheeled the consignment up to the goods store at the railway station, labelled it, and sent it off. But after it was weighed I was dismayed. In monetary value we only had just over seven quids' worth. Split down the middle that meant that my share of £3-10s would not be enough to pay for my Charles Atlas course. From where would I get the other couple of quid? To further postpone the course after all the time I had already invested in it would severely dent my hopes. I was thoughtful as we returned from the station, but shamefully so. 'How can I go back on my commitment to my friend?' I was asking myself, 'The truth of the matter is that I collected most of the lead. I was the one who discovered the long strip at the Villa that really gave us our breakthrough. I must have collected at least two-thirds of the stuff. With two-thirds of the dough I can pay Atlas.'

A few days' later a brown envelope containing a cheque arrived for me in the post. The merchant was as good as his word. But a cheque? 'Jakus!' I thought, 'what am I goin' to do with that?' I had expected the green stuff or at least a postal order. I went to the post office, hoping that I could exchange it for cash there. Miss Pender eyed me suspiciously and turned it over in her hands. 'What's a young brat like him doing with a cheque?' I read in her gaze. Then she told me that I would have to take it to a bank. As I was used to going to the Munster & Leinster to change notes for Mam, that seemed the obvious one to try so I took a deep breath, walked up to the counter and presented my cheque for encashment. Mr O'Riordan looked at me in some surprise.

'I can't cash this for you,' he said.

'Why?' I wanted to know.

'You're underage. Your father will have to countersign it first.'

'What!?" I said, getting all apprehensive.
'Your father'll have to sign his name on the back of it.'
'But it has nothin' to do with him.' I protested.
'I'm sorry. But that's how it is,' he leant forward confidentially. 'Tell me, how did you get this?'
'I sold the man some scrap lead.'
'That was very enterprising of you,' he said, almost admiringly, and he began to view me like I was a prospective client, 'Now don't worry. You'll get your money once I have your father's signature.' He waved the cheque. 'On the back of it.'
'All right,' I said, pocketing my troublesome piece of paper and thinking, as I went off in some trepidation to find Dad, 'Why didn't that bloody man send me cash?'

What was worrying me was that strip from the Villa. I rehearsed my earlier self-justifications. It wasn't as if I had stolen it. It was on an outside wall. No one but me had noticed it up there. After all those years. And anyway, no one was living in the place. But I knew Dad. He would ask questions. Hadn't he caught some men who had stripped lead off the Kiely-Ussher vaults in Ballsaggartmore and arrested them?

Sure enough, a worried look crossed his face when I showed him the cheque and asked him to sign the back of it. 'Who's that from?' he asked curtly.

'A scrap-merchant in Dungarvan,' I replied, mustering all my innocence before the six foot of blue uniform.

'What would a scrap-merchant be paying you money like this for?' He held out the cheque and touched it with the long finger of the arm that carried the silver stripes.

'Ah, I, ah, sent him a sackful of lead,' I said, not quite as smartly.

'Lead?' His eyes narrowed uneasily, 'Where did you get lead to the value of this amount?'

'I collected bits and pieces over a long time. With Paddy Creane. We did it together.'

I looked up at him hopefully.

'Hmm.' He toyed with the piece of paper that was causing me all the bother. 'How much lead did you send for this?'

'Couple o' hundertweight.'

'Hmm.' His shoulders rose and fell with a sigh.

''Tis all okay,' I hastened to reassure him, 'I found bits around the house and Paddy scoured the Manse. Other bits we got here and there. I used to store them under the stairs.'

'You have to be *very* careful with lead, you know.' He gave me a warning look. 'Lads get into trouble over that.'

'We didn't *steal* any of it,' I put on an aggrieved air, hoping desperately that he would not demand more precise sources of me for he was a man to whom I could not lie easily. What if he forced me to disclose the lode I had discovered at the Villa? What I saw as honest scavenging he might conceive as not so innocent thieving?'

'Oh, I'm not suggestin' ye stole any,' he said guiltily.

I felt a sense of relief and was probably not totally oblivious to the guile I had unconsciously employed to embarrass him.

He changed tack. 'And ye're satisfied with the price ye got for it?'

'Satisfied!' I thought. I had never seen so much money in my life. Well, in theory. I still had to get my hands on the real stuff.

'Oh yeh,' I assured him, as if it couldn't be otherwise. I knew what he was getting at. The guy in Dungarvan was probably selling it on for twice the price he had given me. But I wasn't complaining.

'Aw well, I suppose 'tis okay then.' He reached into the breast pocket of his uniform and took out his fountain pen. Then, at last, he signed the back of the cheque.

'Thanks, Dad,' I held out my hand before the ink was rightly dry.

But he wasn't letting go of it yet. 'That's okay. But I don't want you doing anything like this again without first asking my permission. Is that clear?'

'Yes,' I said contritely, 'I'm sorry I had to bother you.'

'That's all right,' he patted me on the shoulder and handed me the slip of paper.

On the short walk to the bank to finally claim my hard-earned notes I could now visualise those slabs of pure meat beginning to form across my shoulders.

Mr O'Riordan beamed when I went up to him. I watched him verify the signature then focussed on his soft, pudgy hands counting out first the notes, then the change. He handed me the lot to check. It was all there. I turned to go. He beckoned me back and waved a savings book at me.

'Wouldn't you like to put some of that in here for safe keeping?'

I regarded him with incomprehension. Put the money back in? After all the trouble I had to get my hands on it? I shook my head. 'No. I need it for something.'

He sighed and put away the booklet. 'Another time. Good luck.'

I left quickly in case Mr Hudson, the manager, might appear behind me and pressure me further.

Outside in the street I breathed triumphantly and balled my fist tightly around the small fortune in my pocket. That part of the operation had been successful. It was the next move that was worrying me. Guilt settled on me as I went off to find Paddy Creane. There were no two ways about it. I had faithfully promised to split the proceeds down the middle and I was about to go back on my word.

Paddy was a cool and unflappable character. Generous to a fault, he had even less sense than I about money, and that was what I was counting on. I showed him the whole amount and suggested that as I had scavanged over two-thirds of the lead I should really be entitled to two-thirds of the money. I agreed I had said that we would split two ways but, on reflection, as he had come into the operation late and had gathered less, it was only fair that I should be entitled to the higher cut. Besides, I was the one who had found the buyer. Paddy was a little taken aback, and must have felt hard done by, but he quickly shook off any disillusionment and happily accepted the share I was offering.

'That's fair enough,' he said, couldn't care less.

After we parted I turned around and watched him going off up the street, his slim frame ambling along unconcernedly. I was elated that I now had the money for the Charles Atlas course, apprehensive lest I had sacrificed a friend. Most of all, I was disgusted with myself for going back on my word. Fortunately, Paddy was never to hold it against me and we remained good friends.

The following day I went to the post office, bought a postal order and sent it off with the completed application form to the Great Physique himself. Then I was broke again. As against that, nobody would be kicking sand in my face for much longer. A few months' time? Well, realistically a year maybe. A fortnight later, a fat, discreet, white envelope with just my name and address on it arrived from England. It was waiting for me when I came home from school at lunchtime. I grabbed it, went upstairs to my room and tore it open. It contained an acceptance form for me to sign and the first set of exercises. The accompanying letter, predictably, was along the lines of, 'Congratulations, you have now committed yourself to being the possessor of a superb physique...', but less predictably, the exercises seemed little different from those which our gym teacher Sidney Fraser taught us every Wednesday afternoon. 'Aw well,' I consoled myself, 'this is only the loosener-upper; the real dynamic tension will come later. And then the beach bullies, wherever and whenever they surface, better take care not to get on the wrong side of me.' I curled a mean lip and hid the letter away under my comics and things.

Every Tuesday thereafter for many months a similar envelope with the next batch of exercises would be waiting for me at lunchtime. Mam, who probably knew by now exactly what I was up to, always placed it in the wire mesh safe in the kitchen for me. She only once asked me what was in the envelopes and, when I muttered something noncommital about comics, left me to my juvenile secrets. That the promised muscles never materialised can hardly be blamed wholly on Charles Atlas. I did commence the regime in a mood of high application but after a few weeks when the tape measure showed no accretions where these should have appeared I began to lose interest. Nothing happened to enlighten me about the expression 'dynamic tension' either, unless the bathing of one's balls to aching point under ice-cold water had something to do with it. Atlas seemed to believe that that part of a man's anatomy was an inexhaustible storehouse of power and energy. No less curious a belief, it had to be admitted, than others that came my way. The exercises, I suppose, did me no harm in the long run.

A new American magazine, *Boxing & Wrestling,* brought wrestling into focus for me. It was a revelation that an Irishman, Steve Casey from Sneem, County Kerry, had won the world heavyweight wrestling championship from Lou Thez, the massive Hungarian–American, in February 1937, the month and the year in which I was born, and went on to remain champion throughout, and beyond, the Second World War. Why had I never heard of him before? Why did he not wrestle in Ireland from time to time? In the late Forties and early Fifties the big pro names were Gorgeous George and Killer Kowalski. The former was fun, the latter mean. Neither, I felt from what I read, would have troubled Casey.

CHAPTER ELEVEN

Horses, Dogs, Guns and Rods

THE BIGGEST ANNUAL EVENT IN Lismore was undoubtedly the Point-to-Point, usually run in the month of February but sometimes, due to severely inclement weather, in March or even April. It was organised by the West Waterford Hunt and took place at the Castle Farm course beyond the Hurling Field and the cricket ground. The number of runners for each race, or the 'fields' as they were called, varied very much from year to year. Thirteen horses would be considered a huge field and we did not see many of them. Five represented a small field though sometimes you got as few as three or four. The finishing straight was staked out at the bottom of a slight dip below the cricket ground, a flat-topped trailer serving as the judges' stand.

Of paramount importance to us children, aside from the excitement generated by the crowds, was the day off we got from school. The holiday really started the late afternoon before the races. We were allowed home a bit earlier than usual and, after a quick call home to toss in the schoolbag and grab a slice of bread and butter, we dashed off to the railway station to watch those of the racehorses that were arriving by train being unloaded at the siding beyond the goods yard or at the short ancillary one on the near side of the tracks by the water tower. The evenings would just be starting to stretch in anticipation of spring, the rare mild and sunny ones treasurable. A special train would pull up and, one by one, a half-dozen animals with colourful monogrammed blankets thrown over their backs would be led out of the cars, whinnying and snorting, their tightly bandaged hooves beating a nervous tattoo on the wooden ramps, their immaculately braided tails dancing in the glow of the sky. We sat well back on the railings, fascinated by the haughty behaviour of the thoroughbreds and by the way their handlers soothed them with whispers and caresses, or curses when the soft approach failed to produce the desired behaviour. I knew they were special and, though I loved to watch them, I never had any inclination to ride one. Magical in themselves, it seemed an affront to sit a human being on their backs.

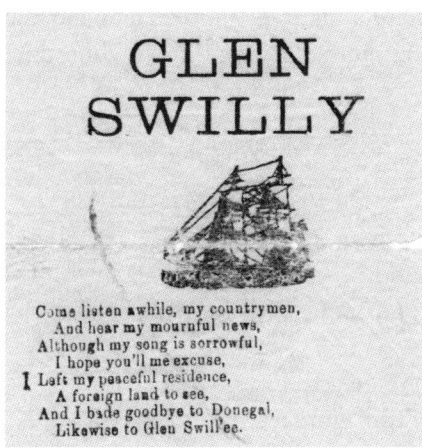

Typical penny ballad-sheets sold by tinker musicians at fairs, point-to-points and other public meeting places.

The tinkers would also have arrived en masse during the preceding days and would have set up their encampments on the wide verges by the railway bridges out the Tallow and Glencairn roads. Their hooped caravans and high flat carts, painted in striking combinations of red and green, were eloquent testimony of the skills and mettle of their owners who, early in the morning of race day would be out on the streets offering fiddle music, and songs on penny ballad-sheets. There would be a woman to tell your fortune too, if you were so inclined. Earlier still, the race field would fill up with caterers' vans and small amusement stalls which, ranged behind the bookies' stands, would offer sweets, soft drinks and chips, and roulette later in the day. A canvas marquee would house a bar. Mam and Dad always gave me a few bob for the day, more to buy sweets and snacks than to gamble, but I usually managed to place a small bet or two. I was warned, above all, to stay clear of the three-card-trick man. One afternoon I learned why. It was one of the least welcoming race days, having rained throughout all the night before and long into the morning. The area around the bookies' stands was a quagmire. But the sun eventually came out to mitigate the cold wind that was icing across the exposed field. In place of the three-card-trick man, his counterpart the thimblerigger was already doing business, deftly manoeuvring three silvery thimbles and a single green pea to and fro across the surface of a light foldaway table, when Boxer Dennis and I happened by. He was a small, wiry man with a sharp face and wore a shabby brown gabardine coat. His hands moved now meanderingly, now with blinding speed.

'Come on lads, try yere luck,' we were invited by the man with him.

Boxer and I shook our heads.

'Go on, lads, ye can beat him,' someone else behind us teased.

Just then a young lad won half a crown. Not much older than us, his sun-scalded face told us he worked on the land. The belt of his brown woollen overcoat dangled freely from one of its loops, one end almost trailing in the mud.

'That's the stuff! You see,' another man next to us urged.

'Good lad!' yet another congratulated the winner.

'Hit 'im with a ten-bob note,' the first man crowded him.

'Don't!' Boxer said.

But the lad would not listen. Down went the orange-coloured banknote.

The thimblerigger's hands whirled over the playing pieces, then came to a stop. We watched apprehensively as the lad made his choice amid conflicting counsel. He lost.

'Didn't I tell you it wasn't that one?' one of the men turned over the correct thimble to reveal the pea. 'Go on. Have another go. He won't beat you a second time.'

But the manipulator did and relieved him of a second note for the same amount.

The victim was now fingering his last ten bob.

'Don't!' we cautioned. We could see that he was thinking of recouping his losses.

A minute later the third note disappeared into the swindler's pocket and the lad withdrew, dazed, to the fringe of the small group, or maybe it was the thimblerigger who imperceptibly shuffled his coterie aside to establish a new orbit into which to tempt prey. Our attempts at consoling the lad were roughly shrugged off. When you realise you have been suckered like that you just want to go away and kick yourself. He was not the only creature to have it hard that year. In the soft going several horses fell.

Though the whole town had a stake in the Point-to-Point it was predominantly a day for the nobs and the gentlemen farmers and their wives who came out from under their elegant eaves in flocks, all rubber macs and shooting-sticks and radiating bonhomie and hard cash. The cream would congregate round the judges' stand and suck on their hip-flasks. Those that had no business on the trailer would balance solidly on their sticks. That year there was one exception to this, an old boy who toppled sideways off one into the mud. The soft going had got to him too. A lot of the men had red, well-fed faces and hung around the beer tent, or whiskey tent perhaps, between the races, twanging away animatedly in their loud, high-pitched voices, in which they were matched note for note by their women. It was their day all right, but the rest of us had fun too.

Willie Connors, the Castle Farm manager, and a great friend, he and his wife, of my parents, used to be the Hon. Sec. of the meeting. He mostly got the races off on time every half-hour. The big race of the day was the Lismore Town Plate. Other events would be a lightweight race, a heavyweight race, a maiden, a hunt and a farmers'. Most were open to all-comers. Top winner's money would be of the order of £25. Only two of the jockeys were personally known to me: George Heskin, a local farmer and acquaintance of Dad's, and Peadar Henley, one of my classmates. Heskin won a number of races down the years and Peadar, who started racing young, was not afraid to tussle with the most experienced riders. When it came to horses there was only one animal in it for me, Springfield Boy, a pacey jumper owned by the Curleys of Tallow, which eventually notched up over fifty point-to-point victories. Other horses passed through Lismore as unknowns and went on to tackle the most fearsome steeplechase of all, the Grand National at Aintree. Lovely Cottage, the 1946 National winner was reputed to have had an outing at Lismore. Paddy Vaughan gives details of other well-known horses on page 53 of his book *The Last Forge in Lismore*. One year my cousins the Kielys, who by then had moved from Monakerka to Lisfennel near Dungarvan, ran a filly named Sgéal Shee, which later came home a winner a number of times at real race courses up and down the country, in the process enabling John Kiely to make a name for himself as a steeplechase jockey. His brother Paddy Kiely rode too and went on to complete the course in the Aintree Grand National. In horse-racing generally I scarcely showed an interest and the little I showed was for steeplechasing, and then only for the big races. Flat races like the Derby, heard on the wireless or seen on the newsreels, were over so quickly they did not seem worth bothering about. However, I could not but be aware that Gordon Richards was the greatest jockey on the flat, especially in 1953 when he followed Stanley Matthews' success in gaining a first F.A. Cup Winner's medal by scoring his first Derby win on Pinza. For both sportsmen they were to be their only such successes. Dad had little interest in horse-racing and was not a betting man. Mam, however, would usually place a bob or two on her choice for the Grand National at Aintree or the Epsom Derby and, in addition, would buy tickets for the Sweep run by the Irish Hospitals Trust.

My favourite vantage point at the Lismore Races was the jump nearest the finishing straight. From there, standing well back on the ditch, you could see the horses coming over the previous jump, then racing across 300 yards or so of open field before soaring onto and over the high, wide obstacle beside you. They would then branch round to the left, first or second time round, and go on to tackle the next few jumps which lay out of sight at the back of the course before coming into view again. The most dramatic moments came last time round. The horses came over the penultimate ditch with added fire and charged toward you, their jockeys lashing out with the whip at the unfortunate animals, and sometimes, cursing at one another. The thud of the hooves grew louder and, with a fierce onrush of sweat and steam, beasts and riders swept over the final obstacle and sprinted down the dip toward the straight, straining for victory. It was not always that dramatic, of course. A field of three, four or five sometimes came in so strung out it looked more like a time trial than a race. At times I preferred to locate myself by the straight to get a close-up of the finish. There the tension would rise just before the horses jumped the last ditch. A steward on a large stallion, the whipper-in, would appear out of nowhere and come pounding up ahead of the competing riders, forcing punters back from the railings with the crack of his whip and the broad belly of the animal under him. Seconds later the leading horses would come belting in in his wake. By the time the last horse came into view spectators would have strayed onto the course again so that the jockey invariably had to shout to clear his way to the line.

Another fascination of pointing was the bookmaker. Bookies, on the whole, were a fairly seedy-looking bunch, with the odd snazzy dresser thrown in, and were accompanied by even seedier-looking clerks. The bookie stood on wooden steps alongside a black slate with his nameplate on it; the name was often in red and in various fonts and sizes. Below at his side, standing or perched loosely on a high stool, the clerk scribbled furiously in a dog-eared ledger, or erased or chalked up new odds on the slate. The bookie might also be writing on the slate the nearer it came to the off. The fascination with the bookie lay in the way he never stopped talking or gesticulating while transacting business. The clerk, in contrast, hardly uttered a word. Both men's eyes barely landed, or barely seemed to land, on the punter as they took his money. In return the punter received a small brightly coloured card, often in red, with the bookie's name and number on it in large lettering. When you won something, which in my case was never – hardly surprising as I placed so few bets – as if by magic the clerk knew exactly how much you were owed, even though no odds were pencilled in on your card. He must have got it right because you rarely saw anyone argue over the payout. Most bookies had permanent offices in town as well – the Lismore one was owned by the R. Power chain – although some operated only on the racecourse. The Lismore premises boasted a discreet, black-windowed frontage in the Main Street with the words 'Turf Accountant' emblazoned in gold letters across it. For years I passed it by, wondering why I never saw anybody coming out of the place with a bagful of turf under his oxter. Eventually, and I must have been all of 15 at the time, Tom Lineen patiently explained to me what the word 'turf' in 'Turf Accountant' signified. It was to take me a further fifteen years to discover what an accountant was. When you came to think of it, the term 'bookmaker' did not exactly suggest a man with a leather bag handing out calling cards in exchange for cash either.

The trek away from the course got underway the minute the last race was over. We youngsters hung around watching the stalls wind up, scouring the ground casually with our eyes in case anyone had dropped a coin or a note. The sun would have set and the night would be inching in. You felt a sense of loss in your heart seeing the horse vans depart. You knew that you would not experience a day like that again for a whole long year of your young life. Down the town later the bars of the Devonshire Arms Hotel and the Wine Vaults would be handing out the shorts as quickly as the well-heeled and lucky racegoers could put them away. All the other bars in town, too, would ring with tills and glasses amid a litany of winners and losers. That night there would be a point-to-point dance at the Town Hall to look forward to – for those old enough to take part. For those of us too young, a chance to stay up a bit late and watch those old enough going to the festivities, and look forward to the day when our own turn would come.

Horsey events did not stop with the Point. In nearby Tallow a huge horse fair (established in 1904 by Canon [William] Meagher, according to a notice in the Clonmel *Nationalist* of 6 September 1919) was held every first week of September. Horses of all kinds would be brought to this annual event from the neighbouring counties of Munster and used to start arriving from early morning. We would see the animals passing through our town to and from the fair, many being walked and some being driven in horse vans. Very large sums of money would change hands during the day. In Lismore in the month of April or May an annual gymkhana was held in the Fair Field. Compared to the Point the Gymkhana was deadly boring so we were forced to generate our own thrills, the sweetest of which was getting into the ground for nothing. The formal entry was through either of two galvanised gates, one in lower Botany opposite Stapletons, the other diagonally across the field opposite the old graveyard in Upper Chapel Street. High walls surrounded the enclosure but there were gaps here and there where the stonework had partly collapsed. Stewards were posted at these vulnerable points to prevent people getting in for nothing. The biggest breach was the one in the wall that backed onto Joe Kelly's field behind our garden and that was always too closely guarded. Naturally, none of us youngsters wanted to pay to get in so our strategy was to climb onto the walls away from the gaps at the Botany side and perch there like amiable vultures until a steward's attention wandered. At that moment we would pounce off the wall and dash across the open space into the crowd as fast as our wings would carry us. Sometimes you got picked up and were frogmarched back out again, looking sheepish but determined to have another go. Your getting hunted down opened up a window of opportunity for your other pals because one man chasing you meant one fewer on the lookout and that gave them a chance to slip through. The earlier you got in the more respect you won from your peers. To make it in the first half-hour when the stewards were fresh and at their most vigilant was noteworthy; to make it halfway into the afternoon won you no plaudits at all.

Once inside there was little to do except wander about. One horse at a time, however tastefully adorned, jumping over a few walls, a few poles and a pool of water wasn't our idea of excitement at all but, given a sunny day, it was pleasant to lounge on the grass and observe people passing to and fro. It wasn't all horses, though. There were also sheepdog demonstrations in which a trained dog would shepherd a few sheep or a few geese into a white pen. It was the fringe which offered something approaching real entertainment, country contests like tug of war, sheep-shearing, and later on, tractor-reversing with a trailer attached. The West Waterford Hunt, without whom neither the Gymkhana nor the Point-to-Point would have taken place, availed of the occasion to send its red-coated master, probably Colonel Chavasse, on a gallop around the jumping enclosure, tally-hoing on his little brass horn with the funny toot, and trailed by his slavering hounds. A harmless canter, as inexplicable as it was dull.

The same outfit appeared in West Street one autumn and presented an entirely different aspect. The master, in civvies, was then finding it difficult to keep control of the spotted, yelping dogs and freely laid into them with his whip when they threatened to get out of hand. Each dog on its own might have posed no danger but in a pack and under the lash they seemed capable of ripping any living creature apart. As indelible as the visual image was the sharp tang of the identical piles of hazel-coloured shit that pimpled the roadway after they had gone. It stank to high heaven, someone explained to me, because of the exclusively raw meat diet of those specially trained hunters. It was easy to feel sympathy for the foxes they would soon be tracking down, even though I was aware of the terrible depredations of these wild and beautiful predators when they broke into a chicken run. The Hunt seldom met in the immediate environs of Lismore. Bishopstown, I think, was its nearest hunting ground. Otherwise it assembled in places such as Clashmore, Modeligo, Ballysaggartmore, Tallow, Beary's Cross or Curraglass. Traditionally, the opening meet was held on St Stephen's Day, an opportunity too for the Wren Boys to put in an appearance at the pub where the stirrup cup was being passed around. The nobs would be in a jolly mood and could be counted upon to come across with a festive bob or two. Subsequently the meets were held on Sundays, the last at the end of March, after which the fauna and flora could coexist less dangerously for another nine months.

An incident occurred in Feeney's yard that illustrated indelibly for me the manner in which hunting dogs were often brutalised. Sam McBrearty, a Donegalman and friend of my parents, who worked for Dr Michael O'Farrell of Fernville, was noted for training gun dogs. On this particular day he had two young pointers with him on stout leather leashes. For some reason one of the two was being a little refractory, nothing excessive as far as I, with my seven- or eight-year-old eyes, could make out. Suddenly Sam lost his temper with the animal and started to thrash it unmercifully with its leash. It was as if he had become incensed that the dog had dared disobey him in front of the man to whom he had been showing off the pair. The unfortunate pointer howled in pain but still Sam lashed it, his face bright red with a fury I had never seen on a man until then. I was frightened and appalled by the uncontrolled ferocity of the attack on a creature that a few seconds earlier I had been about to stroke.

'Stop it! Stop it!' I shouted.

But Sam ignored me. By now Mrs Feeney, Panzer Behegan and Kieran Fenton had been drawn to the ugly scene. They too looked shocked but did not intervene, probably on the mistaken principle that one did not interfere between a man and his dog. I ran next door to call Dad but he was not in.

'Sam McBrearty is beating a dog to death. For no reason,' I shouted tearfully to Mam and went back out again.

By then the flogger's fury had subsided through sheer physical effort and the dog lay whimpering at his feet. I went to pat it on the head but was pulled away by Mam who had followed me there. I looked at Sam with hate in my eyes. How could he, a man I had so often seen laughing and smiling good-naturedly in Dad's company, a man who had always been friendly toward me, have acted with such cruelty?

Dad and his greyhounds outside Swanlinbar garda barracks, County Cavan, c. 1929.

My brother Paddy, on the left, with our trainer uncle Jimmy Morrissey and two of Jimmy's greyhounds in the garden of the Morrissey family home in Greystone Street, Carrick-on-Suir, c. 1947.

When I remonstrated with Dad about it later he tried to excuse his northern friend's behaviour, saying that the Donegalman was an expert with gun dogs and that the animal he had beaten must have done something very wrong earlier to have merited such treatment; I probably did not have the full story. But he did not seem very convinced by his own explanation, having concocted it probably more to assuage my horror than to excuse Sam. I took my own decision on the matter and neither spoke to Sam McBrearty, nor looked him in the face other than with undisguised antipathy, ever again.

In coursing the hunt had its doggie equivalent, with the hare rather than the fox being the unfortunate victim. Dad always showed an interest in this, indeed, when he served in Drangan, Carrick-on-Suir and Swanlinbar he used to keep greyhounds of his own. And my uncle Jimmy Morrissey, whose company I dearly loved, made his living from coursing and the track. The Lismore Coursing Club had a fairly low profile. Outings seemed to be held sporadically at the Castle Farm, on the lands of which hares were preserved, if that is the right word, for coursing. Keen members were Mrs Willie Connors, who owned a champion dog, and Jack O'Gorman, the boisterous and voluble solicitor. The most active coursing club in the west of the county was the Dungarvan one of which Johnny O'Connor, the great county hurler, was a member. Only once did I ever attend a meeting myself, and that one was neither at Lismore nor Dungarvan, but at the Cappoquin & District Club's venue out the Dungarvan Road. Jimmy Morrissey coursed a dog there one post-Christmas day and I went out with Dad to see how he fared. The dog did not do so well and altogether it was a day for the hares. I only saw one being caught. All the others made it safely through the traps, safely that is, to course another day. (At the time I assumed they were free forever.) Even though he no longer kept a dog, Dad maintained an interest by taking the coursing paper regularly. He would tell me how difficult it was to slip the two dogs in a heat and that there was only one man in Ireland who did it to perfection, Mick Horan, the regular slipper at all national events. End of September the season began.

Fishing and shooting were blood pastimes in which I personally took a hand. My shooting experience in the fullest sense, that is, using a double-barrelled shotgun, was limited to one well-into-the-season September outing on which Mike Feeney took me to show me how to handle and discharge this dangerous weapon. Up until then I had held mastery only of a pellet gun, although I had loosed off a couple of rounds with a .22 also. It was a dank, misty evening when the two of us got out of the car out Bridane way. We were hopeful of a shot at the wild duck as they flew over toward the River Bride. I was feeling very adult for my 17 years in the knowledge that I was about to be entrusted with a shotgun. It was an important step in my initiation into manhood, I thought. As we made our way over ditch and field to a vantage point on the summit of a low ridge Mike carried our one weapon broken open and quietly lectured me on its handling, at one point illustrating graphically how Nabbsy Whelan had blown off a finger a couple of years earlier when he was climbing though a hedge to collect a rabbit he had bagged. We lowered our voices to a whisper and settled into the far side of a ditch from the direction in which we expected the birds to appear. The mist let up, allowing us to focus more clearly on the pale ribbon of water in the distance. We had come inadequately clad for the drenched conditions but, as we intended to be out for no more than a couple of hours, this did not worry us. In the eerie stillness we heard only the periodic rustle of a small animal in the undergrowth, or the faraway call of a bird about to settle down for the night. Mike touched my arm and locked the gun barrel into position. What had he detected? He pointed and motioned that I should keep my head down. Approaching from the north-east was a vee of ducks. Mike did not move as they flew overhead. I gave him a quizzical look.

'Too high,' he whispered. 'No point.'

I nodded. I knew the range of a shotgun was limited.

'They may circle back,' he said.

But they didn't. A second, then a third necklet of birds flew over, still at too high an altitude. And that was that. It was now getting dark. By this time I was feeling miserable as well as disappointed.

'We'll see if we can bag a rabbit,' Mike said.

We sneaked along by the hedge and peered through a gap into the next field. Sure enough, a couple were grazing within range.

Mike handed me the loaded weapon. 'Have a go,' he invited. 'Now remember, hold the stock very tightly against your shoulder.'

I raised the gun as instructed, having been doubly warned that if I did not cushion it in this manner it would recoil and might smash my chin or collarbone. I took aim. Just then the rabbits detected us and scampered off.

'Shoot!' Mike urged.

I pressed the trigger. The gun went off but I missed my target. I cursed.

'Never mind,' said Mike. 'You held it right.'

We managed to loose off another barrel each before rejoining the car but still our quarry eluded us. Driving home in what was now a persistent drizzle we came across a rabbit sitting in the middle of the road. I thought we had dazzled it the way it huddled there ignoring us. We got out of the car and walked up to it. Even though we came between it and the headlights still it did not move. Then we noticed its horribly swollen eyes.

'Myxo!' Mike said through tight lips.

He went back to the car, got the gun, inserted a cartridge and put the unfortunate creature out of its misery.

'They go deaf and blind,' he explained, tossing away the empty shell. 'You can go right up to 'em in broad daylight. I'd like to shoot the bastards who brought that into the country.'

It was my first glimpse of the deadly disease that, within a year, was to almost wipe out the rabbit population.

From the age of 10 or 12 through until I was about 16 fishing occupied my attention. In a town favoured with a famous salmon and white trout river in the Blackwater, and a brown trout tributary in the Owenashad, it was always likely that, for a period at least, every youngster would become hooked on angling. I certainly did, thanks to the patience and skill of Andrew Drohan, one of the best trout fishermen in the area. Andrew, who worked for the library, introduced many of us to fly-fishing. Our very first taste of hunting underwater life had been acquired, of course, scrabbling around under the smooth flat stones of the mountain stream by the Strand Bridge and the Point, catching elvers and fry with jam jars and corned beef tins. Later on some of us might have purchased a length of bamboo with a white muslin net at the end of it, to reach out into deeper waters. Still later, you graduated to your first semblance of a rod – a length of ash or hazel to one end of which was attached a piece of strong twine, a piece of cast, and a black hook on which your wriggling worm-bait was impaled. At first, Andy observed your crude efforts with amused detachment. He would come upon you on his way to the downstream fishing below Bullsod Island, his greenheart rod pointing behind him, his black waders flapping round his thighs. Each time he would impart some nugget of advice or other until, eventually, when he saw that you were serious about learning how to fish, he took you in hand.

'Get a good length of bamboo,' he said to me, knowing full well that I would have to shin over the castle wall at the New Way to feck the required item from among the prolific stands in the Castle Garden, "and we'll make a decent rod for you. You'll need a reel as well but I'll take care of that."

I duly arrived at his house in Chapel Street with my seven-foot length. It was not as springy as I had hoped but it tapered nicely and was straight as a die.

'Fine,' said Andy, appraising it. 'Now the next thing we have to do is make the rings for the line.' And he proceeded to show me how to bend a short strip of netting-wire into an eye with two half-inch tails that pointed in opposite directions. 'Now you make another four of the same and then we'll make the top ring together because that's slightly different.'

When we had made all the rings Andy produced some fine, strong twine, the kind they used in the better shops, and carefully bound to the shaft the tails of the ring that was to be located nearest the reel. 'Now you tie the others on in the same way. As tight as you can. Remember you must be able to look straight through all the rings, otherwise the line won't run through freely. Leave approximately the same gap between them.'

I did my best, eliciting his help only when I needed his index finger pressed on the twine when I came to knot it. On completion of that part of the job I passed the bamboo, which was already taking on the appearance of a real rod, to my instructor for inspection. He peered down the length of it from the top to check that the eyes were aligned, then he tested the ring bindings to make sure that these were tight enough. He nodded approvingly and I, with growing excitement, watched him bind on the top ring which he had fashioned into a double eyelet with two tails pointing the same way. Finally, he explained that I should seal the bindings with some of my mother's nail varnish to make them waterproof. Then he produced a small reel.

'This is an old one I had myself.' He spun the wheel to demonstrate that it rasped freely. 'You're welcome to it. It'll do for the time being.'

In this period postcard of Lismore Castle, shot from the inch downstream of the Blackwater Bridge, the common alder trees on the left are those surrounding the Pond where we fished for perch and roach.

We identified the spot on the butt of the rod where I could most comfortably manage the reel, then we bound the reel on too.

'You'll need a proper line now,' said Andy. 'What you want is a medium weight one. About thirty foot. You'll get it at Feeney's.'

Now that I had a proper rod I could start coarse fishing in earnest. For dace I used to fish off the cement table of the second sewage outlet below the Blackwater Bridge, for roach at the Pond, a small sheet of deep water surrounded by tall alder trees just downstream of the bridge on the Ferry Inch opposite. I tended to set my rod on the grassy bank just upstream or downstream of the Pond when I wanted eel. When we wanted to be really specific we referred to the Pond as the Roach Pond, a not entirely accurate designation as perch were more in abundance than roach there. The perch population always seemed to remain in it, even though the Blackwater regularly flooded the inch in winter, and irregularly throughout the year. We used to wonder why the fish neither swam off in, nor were swept away by, the rapidly flowing current that used to swirl past the prowed base of the main pillar of the bridge. On hot sunny days you could lean over the parapet of the bridge and watch the red fins and lazily turning silver flanks of dozens of them basking just below the surface of the muddy water. You might toss a stone in to frighten them under, then wait to see them float back into view again. Below the surface the water was always impenetrable to the eye, muddy in normal conditions, Coca-Cola after a flood. None of us knew how deep it was.

We suspected that the Pond was not a natural pool but some kind of artificial hole cut into the inch by the Castle at some time in the past, possibly connected with the ice-house, or conceived simply as an ornamental lake stocked with colourful roach. With the dense vegetation around it, it was obviously unsuited to fly-fishing but ideal for us tyro fishermen with our home-made rods, lead-shot weights, penny hooks and the corks of bottles that we used as floats. Worms were our bait. There were a couple of natural gaps in the undergrowth and we trod down one or two others so that we could cast over the whole expanse of water. When the 'roach' were biting you usually took two or three without any difficulty. Other days they seemed to sink right down into the mud at the bottom and show no interest in feeding. In the Blackwater itself roach and perch were relatively uncommon, dace plentiful. At the sewage pipe it was child's play to catch dace, which we then employed as bait for eel.

Our juvenile angling did not require a licence so, naturally, when we graduated to fly-fishing it never occurred to us to apply for a trout-fishing permit. This cost five bob a year, a lot of money in our eyes. Besides, we only fished for brown trout, and it wasn't as if we over-fished. For my own part, I was rarely to catch a good-sized fish. The water bailiffs really only came down on you if they suspected you were fishing for white trout (the local name for sea trout) or salmon. Anyone caught out of line there received a smart fine. The gripe of the licensed salmon men was that the best waters were reserved for the Duke of Devonshire and his guests. Dad, not an angler himself, did not see it quite that way. He argued that as the Duke was stocking the river the man was entitled to limit access to his fisheries. If the State were running the hatchery it would be a different matter. It was not an argument that carried much weight with me. I could not see why one man, particularly an English aristocrat, should have the right to stop us fishing in our own river. But the issue was academic in that I was still a long, long way from taking the big ones.

Aside from bailiffs, fishing was not without other kinds of hazards. One early evening, not long into my fishing career, Mickey McConnell lent me his father's solid, burgundy-coloured six-foot sea-fishing rod to go angling for big eel in the Blackwater by the Pond. Barney Walsh and I were manning this rod and his one, using as bait chunks from a couple of dace that we had first caught across at the sewage pipe. These sizable pieces were fastened on large hooks. Downstream of us sat Hoagy, eyes fixed intently at his own line, and behind us on the inch, Willie Ryan and Boxer were lazily pucking a tennis ball around with hurleys. We often carried a hurley or two with us when we went for a stroll, sometimes to have a flake around when we got bored with everything else, sometimes to beat the undergrowth and flush out rabbits when we went hunting with terriers.

Willie and Boxer had put down the hurleys and were messing about on the upstream side of the Pond somewhere when I felt a pull on my line fiercer than anything I had ever experienced before.

'Jasus!' I exclaimed, 'What's that?'

Barney came running over, as always full of directions. 'Play him. Give 'im a bit o' line.'

'Do you think 'tis a salmon?' I gasped hopefully, trying to unlock the catch on the fat, complicated reel, 'Feck it, I can't free the thing.'

'Pull on it then. 'Tis a strong line.'

I pulled and a monstrous set of sharp teeth broke the surface of the water.

'Jasus Christ, what's that!' I repeated, the heart put across me.

'A pike, I think,' said my pal. 'Pull 'im out. There's nothing else you can do.'

The fish dived again, threatening to take me and the rod with him. I looked at Barney in disbelief, then took a tight grip on the butt of the rod and heaved with all my strength. A long black thing rose out of the water and went flying back over my head into a tuft of long grass. I dropped the rod and ran back a few yards.

'Did you see that!' I cried, my heart pumping with dread and elation. I had never seen anything remotely as big and savage looking on the end of a line.

'I did,' said Barney, back on his heels too.

'What is it?'

'Conger eel, maybe.'

By now even Hoagy, who until then in his phlegmatic way had been ignoring our cries, taking them for needless exaggeration, had abandoned his own rod and run up. The three of us crept gingerly nearer our catch which was writhing helplessly in its strange environment.

'Look at the size o' that!' I gasped.

'Look at them teeth!' said Barney. ''Tis an eel all right. But I don't think 'tis a conger. You only get them in the sea really.'

'How are we going to kill it?' Fearsome as the poor landed creature appeared, I did not like to see it thrashing about in such distress.

'You have to whack it on the tail,' said Barney.

'On the tail?'

'Yeh, that's right,' put in Hoagy. 'No point in hittin' 'im on the head. You can't kill an eel that way.'

I looked around in vain for a stick then I had a bright idea. 'I know. I'll get a hurl from the lads.' I ran around to Boxer and Willie and brought them hastily back with me. I grabbed Willie's stick and started flaking the tail of the unfortunate eel with it. Boxer joined in and gave it a few cracks over the head for good measure. Still it writhed.

'You can't kill an eel,' muttered Hoagy lugubriously. 'I've seen 'em hoppin' up an' down on the fryin' pan and they cut into pieces.'

Eventually, in spite of Hoagy's observation, we managed to bludgeon the animal senseless. I did not attempt to recover my hook that was lodged deep in its gullet. I was taking no chances with those teeth. When we laid its carcass out straight it measured about a yard in length. At its thickest it was almost as fat as a jam jar. Sizewise, this was to be the peak of my angling career; I was never to catch anything remotely as big again. Not that anybody took much notice of my success. We gave the eel to Hoagy's grandmother on the way home and she had it on the pan the next day.

'It didn't jump,' Hoagy told me later, man enough to admit that his theory about panhopping eels did not always hold good.

I never got to taste it. I would have brought it home myself, only Mam refused to cook eels. To be honest, I did not feel deprived on this occasion. That particular specimen had done its scavenging a bit too close to the town sewage outlet for my liking.

Soon afterwards Barney, Willie and I tried out the same rod in the same place with a wholly different outcome. Earlier we had been under the bridge at the other side of the Pond having the piss taken out of us by an average-sized eel that skilfully, or otherwise, refused to impale itself on my hook. The two-footer used to hold itself vertically and allow my bait to slide down six or seven inches into its gullet so that I was sure I had it hooked but each time I pulled on the line, gently or with a jerk, the barb would come sailing out again, with the piece of dace still dangling on it untouched. It seemed to be more interested in playing Russian roulette than in feeding. Eventually it tired of the game and meandered back under a stone. There had to be something wrong with it, we told ourselves.

Back at our usual spot we encountered a problem. The grass and dock weed had grown so high we could not cast properly anymore. Because the rod was so short and the reel cumbersome the method we had worked out was for one of us to go ten yards behind the person who was casting, tread flat a small window of meadow, place the bait in the middle of it and then give the all-clear for the launch. The snag with this was that the hook took a tuft of fresh green grass with it. No eel was dumb enough to approach a chunk of cut-up dace laid out like a salad. After a number of trials, we were on the point of giving up when Barney, who was then casting, got a bright idea. Barney often came up with bright ideas, not all of which were very practical but this one seemed straightforward enough. One of us, i.e. Willie or myself, because Barney, having the rod in his hands wasn't putting himself forward, would stand behind with the baited hook laid on the flat of his outstretched hand. That way there would be no chance of the hook getting entangled in the grass. As I was the one who had set up the evening's entertainment I reluctantly volunteered to go first. Barney stood with the rod poised high.

'Are you ready?' he asked.

I flattened my palm like I had never flattened it before and tried to avoid eyeing the barbed hook. 'Right!' I shouted.

Barney threw the rod forward with a slashing movement and dragged me part of the way with him.

'Christ!' I yelped as the barb harpooned into the soft base of my thumb.

'You didn't hold you hand flat enough,' said my pal accusingly, paying scant heed to the blood that was beginning to seep along the side of the hook.

'Like hell, I didn't,' said I, trying to dig out the hook with my blunt penknife.

'You won't get it out with that.'

He was right. 'I'll cut it out with a blade when I get home,' I was forced to concede.

'Let me have a go,' said Willie.

'No, I'll have to cut off the hook.'

'I mean at holding the bait.'

Barney's eyes lit up.

I looked at Willie dubiously. 'Are you sure?'

'Yeh.'

We tied and baited another hook.

'Are ye right?' Barney called, rod held aloft.

'Okay,' said Willie coolly.

The line swished. I watched it coil back toward the outstretched bait. Then Willie yelped, only louder than I had. Barney had thrown an extra bit of muscle into the cast and had succeeded in lodging the barb much deeper in the pad of Willie's thumb than he had in mine. So deep it was not something you could scratch out with a razor blade. An immediate and unanimous decision was taken to call a halt to the evening's fishing. It was about eight o'clock on a Sunday evening and the problem now was to find someone medical to cut the hooks out. There seemed to be only one solution, to traipse across town to the Hospital and get one of the nurses to do the job.

'Aren't ye a pair of quare fellas!' Nurse Foley, I think it was, grinned when we told her how we had come to lodge the hooks. She snicked mine out first then dashed some clear disinfectant that stung onto the cut. By the time she had tied a white bandage around the hand I had a nice sense of being battle-scarred, though really I knew that all I had suffered was a scratch. She was scooping into Willie's flesh for ages until, finally, she got a sort of pliers, clipped off the eye of the hook and threaded the rest in one side and out the other. Willie winced but took it like a man.

The day came when I said to myself, 'Isn't it time you stopped catching things you can't eat and try catching something you can?' By this time Andy was letting me accompany him evenings when he fished the Bishop's Fishery below Bullsod. Usually we went down the Ballyrafter Flats side of the river to where the *Rian Bó Phádraig* forded it. Opposite us the copse of Scots pine on the Round Hill would sparkle in the setting sun. Occasionally we fished the Ballyea West side of the water as well. When we first went Andy fished and I watched and learned. We would leave home about 7.00 p.m. and set off downstream at a leisurely pace. Along the way we would meet other good trout fishermen – Nabbsy Whelan, or Gordon and Mickey Keyes.

The immediate topic of conversation was the state of the fishing at that moment. I was always eager to see the size of fish the others had caught and, invariably, was left wondering whether I would ever be capable of landing the glistening one-and-a-half- or two-pound white trout they showed me. The brown trout they had would be smaller – a one pound fish was considered a fairly unusual catch in the Blackwater. Andy was wise to the ways of the river and could always tell from the way a fish splashed what kind it was and how heavy it was. He knew the sounds of other water creatures too – otters, water-rats, and the different waterbirds. Laying out his gear, he would show me how to tie casts with either two or three flies. I learned names like the Spinner (black and red varieties), the Butcher, the Black Gnat, the Black Spider, Invicta, Wickham's Fancy, and Greenwell's Glory. The Red Spinner was the basic evening lure and Invicta was used when all others failed. Andy sometimes switched flies two or three times in the course of an evening. I learned too about the different kinds of rods there were, and the different woods of which they were made. Greenheart was the most-highly prized wood, but it was highly priced too. I was left behind when he tried to explain to me that what he was doing was called wet-fly fishing, logical enough, but that there was also a skill called dry-fly fishing. Dry? How could you keep a fly dry when you were dancing it on the surface of the water? Eventually I accepted that the dryness was relative but, as I still could not visualise the techniques of dry-fly fishing, Andy kindly gave me a demonstration along by the canal beyond Ballygallane Bridge where briar and bush impeded normal casting and where brown trout were to be found. He used a tiny furry black fly and managed to land a couple of small fish. The technique looked very fiddly and my instructor made no effort to hide his dislike of it. As for me, I quickly decided it was too esoteric and let my attention wander with the green, blue and red-brown dragon and damsel flies that floated from leaf to leaf like wind-blown satin.

Serious wet-fly fishing did not start before nine o'clock, by which time the trout were rising to feed on flies. Andy would hitch high his black waders, caution me to remain still, and wade out into the water from the sally-lined bank. He was fairly tall and slim and stood very straight, snaking the line out across the surface of the water with regular, elegant sweeps of his right arm, and drawing it back into a long loop with the fingers of the left. I would be downstream of him where he could keep me under observation, so that he would not have to worry about sticking a hook in me. No doubt also, he wanted to be sure that I was not fooling around where there were deep holes in the river-bed. As well as being instructive, these evenings were hauntingly beautiful. While Andy fished I was able to sprawl on the bank and give drift to my senses. In the slow fade of day the overriding stillness chuckled with life – the eddy, rush and deep flow of the river, the flutter of wings, the scamper of small animals in the undergrowth, the fitful cries of birds settling down for the night. But it also screeched with death – the anguish of a rabbit caught by a stoat, or of other prey plucked by a sparrowhawk. With the peppery scent of the vegetation in my nostrils and the texture of reed, sedge and shrub under my thumb I had the feeling of being a wild thing myself.

The thrills came when Andy hooked a sizable white trout. Such trout were renowned as fighters and it took a good fisherman to land one. Andy would play it patiently, giving it time enough to tire itself out before finally reeling it in. When the fish arched out of the water in a desperate last attempt to free itself Andy would pronounce on its weight. The trickiest bit was getting it into the net and it was at this stage that Andy, for all his experience, lost the odd one. When that happened he would mutter admiringly, laugh ruefully at the fish's cunning, examine his cast, and start all over again. The fish he did catch he would kill immediately by pressing back the head until the neck broke.

'You should always kill your catch at once,' he told me. 'It's cruel to leave it gasping there until it suffocates.'

A few times the fishing was so good we stayed on into the night. On the way back to the bridge there seemed to be only the two of us in the world, swishing along the familiar paths, Andy patiently answering my many questions or entertaining me with fishing stories, pulling us up now and again to marvel at the stillness, or the vestigial daylight stratified in the sky. He would see me home on these late occasions, give Mam a couple of trout and apologise to her for keeping me out so late. She never worried when I was out with him because she recognised that, even though he could not swim, he knew the river.

In due course under my friend's tutelage I acquired a nine-foot fly-fishing rod made of greenheart from Sam Hick of Cappoquin, the quality dealer in rods and guns in West Waterford. The quantity of tackle in his shop window was remarkable enough. Inside, my eyes widened further. Racked on the walls was a variety of rods the like of which I had never seen before, ranging from light, elegantly crafted fly ones to thick, bullish sea ones; behind glasscases, shotguns and .22 rifles; under the glass counter, flies, lines and other tackle. A fishing bag I didn't need – we youngsters always carried our catch home with the aid of a twig, hooked at one end, threaded through the gills of the fish. And waders I couldn't afford. Completing the inventory were clocks and watches, for Sam was a jeweller too. Andy made plain the extent of my means and, while I gazed longingly at the superb, burnished rods with the creamy, bone rings, Sam sought out and sold me the workaday item I could afford. Then there were flies to choose, tied by the shopkeeper himself, a fisherman of repute, from feathers of pheasant and wild duck. If I couldn't catch a fish now I had no business being in the game.

I began to fish seriously with Andy. A pair of ordinary black Wellingtons dictated less positional choice than Andy's thigh-length waders but I could still find footholds enough from which to cast. Usually we would stand about twenty or thirty paces apart, he downstream of me to avail of the better chances. The first few times I got stuck in a white trout Andy came up and, standing on the bank, directed me how to play the fish. I was unsuccessful in these attempts but Andy told me not to worry. That was part of the learning process. When I hooked a three-quarter-pound one I was so amazed at the strength of its pull I thought I was wrestling with a two- or three-pounder.

'It's the current,' Andy explained. 'Makes them appear much heavier than they are.'

I was so fearful of losing that one I begged Andy to land it for me, which he did. Though in time I managed to catch a few half-pound brown trout on my own, the biggest fish I landed on our expeditions was a three-quarter-pound roach, a big fish of its kind, which I struck in the Bishop's Fishery at Ballyea West. It gave me a ferocious tug to begin with but then, unlike a white trout of similar poundage, showed no fight at all. I was delighted to land it just the same.

Andy spoke very disparagingly of sea-fishing. 'No skill to it at all,' he would say. 'Once you've hooked the fish you just reel him straight in. You've seen it yourself with the mackerel. They give you one fierce pull and that's it.'

While I admitted he was right, I liked fishing for mackerel too. It was crude, but you caught a hell of a lot of fish when the shoals were in along the Waterford coast. Which made you wonder what you were doing spending hours by the Blackwater to reel in a few sprats and the odd decent fish. Not that I went mackerel fishing often. For one thing, the shoals only came inshore for a couple of weeks in August, right up to the rocks in exceptionally warm weather. For another, I was dependent on friends for a lift down to the sea. Ardmore, where Dad sometimes took the family during his court clerk stints in Dungarvan, was a favourite place to go fishing for mackerel. Unfortunately, the rare occasions on which we went there rarely coincided with the onrush of the big shoals. Dad did hire a dinghy for us once or twice and a local fisherman rowed us out to try our hand with a spinner – the kind that was red on one side and bronze on the other. We caught enough fish for a meal or two.

Appropriately, Ardmore was the setting for my greatest haul of mackerel. I was 12 or 13 at the time. It was an exceptionally hot day in Lismore. When Jim Feeney heard that the fish were shoaling in such numbers they were biting the rocks he decided, on the spur of the moment, that he wanted a bit of the action too. Tom called for me excitedly at six o'clock in the early evening and asked me if I would like to go with them. Margaret and his mother were going as well. Mam said okay and I was off like a shot. Jim fashioned a couple of crude 'rods' for Tom and me, each consisting of a five-foot length of hazel to the end of which was knotted a yard of binder twine which trailed a couple of feet of strong cast. Our bait was a silver-and-green lure that looked like a small fish. We then piled into a black Ford V8 and drove off. Tom and I were beside ourselves with excitement and for me there was the added thrill of being in a car with someone who knew how to drive twice as fast as Denny Regan. Margaret, our junior, observed us with the kind of amused detachment that young girls reserve for the antics of young boys. When we arrived crowds of holiday-makers and day-trippers were bubbling around the harbour with excitement. As Jim led us down across the slaty rocks we could already see silvery flashes like cloudbursts rippling across the surface of the sea.

'Jasus, look at that!' Tom pointed when we reached the water's edge.

Three feet below us mackerel were steaming in after the millions of sprats racing to escape their gaping jaws. Again and again they came round, insatiable in their appetite. All we had to do, and we did it, was scoop our lures through the water and we had a fish. In no time a small rock pool behind us was filling up with thrashing fish. It was so easy it became boring. I remembered what Andy Drohan had said about sea fishing.

But then something pleasant and unexpected happened that was to make my day one above all to remember. A girl of my own age approached with her parents to watch us. The parents were dressed in formal, expensive clothes that made them look strict and out-of-place in the seaside setting. The girl wore pigtails tied up over her head. I threw yet another catch into the pool, lightly splashing the end of the brown overcoat she wore. When I apologised she smiled at me with big eyes and laughed sweetly. The coat struck me as odd on such a warm evening. It implied that she was delicate and that her parents wished to protect her from potentially harmful sea breezes. Confused, I turned aside and launched into my fishing with renewed vigour. The more fish I caught the more often I could turn around and catch her eye. No girl had ever smiled at me so sweetly. I fell in love with her straight away. After a while I summoned up my courage and asked her if she would like some fish. We had many more than we needed. She looked up at her parents who gravely nodded approval – the mother even smiled. Mrs Feeney had brought a couple of brown paper bags with her to carry home the few fish she had sceptically expected Jim to catch and she kindly gave me one of them. I carefully selected six of the best fish, wrapped them up and handed them to the girl who had set my heart beating faster. She thanked me with a winning smile. Her parents thanked me too, then they led her slowly away. She looked back, wistfully it seemed to me, and I, equally wistfully, looked up at her. Then she was gone beyond the wall of the cliff walk. I imagined her staying in the Cliff Hotel, or in some other big house above the town. My enthusiasm for fishing departed with her.

Fortunately, Jim was bored by now and said it was time to call a halt. We had so many fish we would scarcely be able to give away the ones we could not use ourselves. One hundred and fifty we counted. Jim asked other nearby spectators if they would like some and a few did. The remainder we somehow managed to string together and carry back to the car. On the way out of the small town I scanned the streets for a last glimpse of the girl, but without much hope as it was already getting dark. I felt sad because I knew I would be unable to return to Ardmore in the ensuing days. Travelling home my thoughts were full of her. What had started out to be an unforgettable evening's fishing had ended up the most romantic night of my young life. I would never be the same again.

We did have trouble getting rid of our overload of mackerel. Lismore was awash with them and, nobody having fridges, there were not many places cool enough to store them for long. We had mackerel for breakfast, dinner and tea over the next two days. I persuaded myself that the girl, if she were on holidays as seemed reasonable to suppose, would turn up in our town to see the sights during the succeeding days, but she never did, or if she did our paths did not cross. For months, maybe years, afterwards I used to think of her and dream that she would reappear.

Worm-fishing for brown trout when the rivers were flooded was another kind of fishing that I used to enjoy. Sometimes this was marginally out of season but the practice seemed to be tolerated by the fishing authorities. The salmon season that opened on the 1st of February, for net fishing at least, usually ended in the last week of July or the first week of August. The trout season began later and went on until the end of September. The big floods came in November, especially to the Owenashad, but it was more the October ones that we fished. Small trout, firm and succulent to eat and rarely weighing more than eight ounces, used to flock to the mouth of the mountain stream to feed on the bounty brought down by the muddy waters. At the Point, where the youngest of us swam and played in the summer months, the stream that usually flowed placidly five or six feet below the bank would now be level with the inch, backed up by the powerful and irresistible flow of the Blackwater. Along this grassy verge you would encounter maybe twenty of us, ranged two or three yards apart, dipping our worm-baited hooks into the water with a fixed length of cast. The trick was to flick the point of your rod upwards the second you felt a nibble, so sinking the hook into the jaws of the fish. To be really good at this you needed very quick reflexes because the fish fed exceedingly delicately. It was easy to mistake a ripple of the current for a bite. Each time you struck and missed you lost a worm because the whiplash sent it flying off the hook; so you had to put on a new one. This cost time and worms and I lost a lot of both. A classmate of mine, Chris 'Scanner' Scanlon, was a dinger at this kind of fishing. The slightest brush at the bait and he had a fish wriggling on the end of his line. His reactions were so fast that sometimes he hooked trout on the outside of the mouth or in the flank. It was nothing for him to catch six while I laboured for one. Boxer and Euge Dennis also pulled in a good few. Nor was it just us youngsters who reaped these unexpected harvests. Nabbsy Whelan and Mickey Keyes and other accomplished adults did so as well. But not Andy Drohan. Andy never dirtied his hands with a worm. For him, fly-fishing was all. Worms were for the birds.

CHAPTER TWELVE

The Land

THE LAND AROUND Lismore was drained by abundant waters and streams of which the most imposing was the majestic Abha Mhór or Blackwater, a direct source of wealth as well as pleasure for the area. Many livelihoods other than those of the professional rod-fishing people like John Scott-Allen and his wife, and Jack Campion, and the net fishermen of the Lismore Estates Company depended upon it. The town commissioners were always anxious about the state of the fishing, in particular the salmon fishing, which varied in natural cycles from year to year. Lismore's reputation for good fishing brought much-needed tourism to the town. The Lismore Board of Fishery Conservators, which in effect meant the Lismore Estates Company, was the statutory regulatory body for the area. It met once a month and regularly issued statistics on net catches, the use and state of the weirs around the Queen's Gap, illegal netting, spawning beds (in the Blackwater and its tributaries some 2,000 to 2,500 visible beds might be counted in any one close season), migration of salmon smolts (a smolt is a young river salmon when it is bluish along the upper half of the body and silvery along the sides) and so on. The inspector for the area was Dr A. E. J. Went, the historian of Irish fisheries, a stout man who wore black-rimmed spectacles and whom you saw fairly regularly in town. The monitoring of effluent disposal was one of his prime concerns. Combatting illegal fishing, i.e. poaching, was the immediate task of the water bailiffs, Paddy Dooley and John Lynch, and they came down hard on any lads they caught. Among items they confiscated would be illegal nets and trimmed stakes for use in constructing illegal weirs. In general, the type of net in use on the Blackwater, especially with regard to mesh size, was strictly watched; the *Dungarvan Observer* reported in May 1940 that there had been a controversy over trammel nets at a recent meeting of the Lismore Fishery Conservators.

The salmon net-fishing season commenced on the 1st of February and the best net fishing on the Blackwater was the Bishop's Fishery which extended from Bullsod Island, the tidal limit, to the Avonmore Bridge in Cappoquin. The prime stretch of this fishery began at the river bend by the Kennel Heights on the back road to Cappoquin and ended a mile downstream near the main road on the other bank. Exactly halfway between these two points where the river skirted the main road, and often flooded it, was the deepest water, known as the Kitchen Hole. Sometimes when we passed this on our bicycles we used to stare at it in awe through the trees, thinking that we had never seen such a dark and forbidding sheet of water. It was here that the crews of the Lismore Estates Company laboured. Powerful men like Pad Lineen hauled in the heavy nets, heavy enough when empty, back-breaking when laden. The mesh of their nets was fine enough to take white trout as well as salmon. A dearth of fish in a season would hit the company and its men hard, the independently licensed crews even harder – nets and the wide, flat-bottomed boats did not come cheap and there was the price of the net-fishing licence to consider as well. A maximum number of salmon netted in any one day in the height of an average season by the crews of the Lismore Estates Company might be forty or fifty, with catches of up to seventy or eighty exceptional. In 1945, when the company resumed salmon fishing after the Second World War, eighty salmon were netted in one July day, 'the greatest number taken for very many years' according to a contemporaneous issue of the *Dungarvan Observer*. Overall, in any one month in the Lismore area an average of 2,500–3,000 salmon would be killed in the nets by the company and the independent crews, and rod fishermen would take from 300–400. Over 2,000 grilse (a grilse is a young salmon on its first return from salt water) and some 300–400 fully grown white trout (i.e. sea trout) would also be netted. The *Observer* of 3 May 1952 reported the precise figures for the previous March, given at the recent meeting of the Lismore Fishery Conservators – 2,830 salmon killed in the nets, 332 with the rod. At the same meeting it was reported that large migrations of salmon smolts had been observed in the second and third weeks of April. In June 1954, according to figures given in the *Observer*, 2,688 salmon and 2,316 grilse were taken by the nets, rods and illegal weirs; and also 326 sea trout weighing 484 lbs.

Not all salmon appeared in the Blackwater by natural design. The Lismore Estates Company operated the hatchery by the Strand Bridge and as youngsters we used to delight in staring down through the wire-netted fences at the big fish cruising in the channel by the side of the building. Sometimes there would be hundreds of them, meandering up and down with lazy sweeps of their powerful tails. Then one day they would all have disappeared, or maybe only a few would remain. We knew it had something to do with spawning but no one ever organised a formal school visit to the place so that we could learn about the skills required for this small industry that was so important to our region. It may have been that the company had to take extreme precautions to avoid the possibility of disease, which could wipe out whole fish populations. Whatever the reason, my pals and I were only ever shown around the place by the foreman Mr Copley, or one of the workmen, when there were hardly any fry in the sluices. Just the same, it was fascinating to see the system of channels through which the clear water of the Owenashad flowed.

Winter brought a regular hazard to the hatchery – flooding. No fish would be there at that time but severe torrents sometimes tore away the timber supports and the wire netting around the outside channel where the spawning salmon were kept in summer. The hatchery sheds themselves survived all floods although they too took a battering on occasion. Flood waters played havoc with the system of weirs on the Blackwater as well. Upriver at Ballyin an ambitious development at the Queen's Gap was destroyed in one night, that of the 31st (or 18th? – I am not clear about the date) of January 1945. The hatches on the big weir that was used to control the running of the salmon up to Careysville near Fermoy (renowned as the best stretch of salmon water on the Blackwater, if not in the whole of Ireland, and owned by the Duke of Devonshire) and the gate or gap through which fish descended from upstream, had been in need of renewal for a long while. At the time the works on the construction of a new gap were well underway. But the huge wall of floodwater that swept down on that night ripped away the new reinforced-concrete foundations. Dad happened to be on duty down by the ice house at the time and heard the great

I think this photograph of my father Joseph Ballantyne was taken by the River Blackwater in Lismore in the mid-Forties. The stones on which he is standing are possibly part of the remains of the concrete foundations for the new weir at the Queen's Gap that were destroyed by a huge wall of floodwater in January 1945.

crack as they collapsed. The company suffered a severe blow and the costly project was never resumed. Flooding was a common hazard of our winters and annually caused blockages of one degree of severity or another on the main Lismore–Cappoquin Road at Glenview and the Kitchen Hole, and on the back road, at the foot of the Round Hill and on the level stretch on the Lismore side of the Kennel Heights.

Most fearsome for farmers were the unexpected floods of late summer. When they occurred they were liable to wash away hay, crops and livestock. August 1946 saw the worst surge 'in living memory' (according to the 'Lismore Notes' of the *Dungarvan Observer* of 17 August), worse than the huge Owenashad floods of November 1944 which had overflowed Lady Louisa's Bridge (*Observer*, 25 November 1944), and even worse than the massive flow that had wrecked the Blackwater weir the year before. It had stormed and rained nonstop in Munster for almost the whole of two days. The Owenashad, as was customary for its short run, had risen quickly. Huge boulders and full-grown trees were driven along by the torrent, undermining parts of the wall along the Mountain Road. In Ballyin the homes of the Ansons, Farrells and Lineens were flooded to a height of up to four feet. The gas works, the McCarthy's and Co-op stores, and Bud Sargent's garage were inundated.

All this happened at night and it was only the beginning. As the Owenashad began to subside the Blackwater, flowing down from its source in County Kerry, began to rise inexorably. By the time Molly was allowed to take me down to the bridge to see the spectacle the rain had stopped and an awesome, fast-flowing current was spread out over all the inches as far as the eye could see. The bridge was lined with townspeople who uttered 'Ohs!' and 'Ah!' whenever a tree trunk, or a piece of household furniture, or the bloated carcass of a cow or bullock, was carried beneath the arches. And somehow from our safe vantage point there was the fear that the next thing we might see floating by would be the corpse of a human being. Looking east, it seemed as if the whole valley was filled with water, right up to the woods on the high ground at either side. And it was. The Lismore–Cappoquin and Lismore–Ballyduff roads for a good stretch either side of the Strand Bridge were flooded to wall-top level. Molly held my hand tightly and my body even tighter when she let me sit on the parapet for a better view, for I was quivering with excitement and dread. Over the next few days I returned with increasing freedom of movement to the spectacle until, finally, with great disappointment, I saw the waters subside. But that only opened the way to a new show. Now we could walk up by the Strand, and up the Mountain Road, to see the destruction wrought by the Owenashad, and gape at the massive boulders that were standing where none had stood before. On page 21 of Seán Sexton's excellent *Ireland: Photographs 1840–1930* (Laurence King Publishing, 1994), a graphic early photograph of the power of the winter floods shows a wide breach in Lismore Bridge where a couple of the dry arches were carried away by the flood of 2 November 1853. The photograph, taken the day after what may have been the severest flood of all, also interestingly shows the Owenashad, and Glen View with its fine mill and the canal in the background. It was shot by Francis Edmund Currey, the Duke of Devonshire's land agent who took a number of priceless early photographs of Lismore and its people, including a fine study of the Spout, taken around 1855 and also shown in Sexton's book. Miss Frances Wilmot Currey, the daughter of the agent, as well as being an artist and writer, was a prize-winning professional bulb grower and plant breeder in the first decade or so of the 20th Century. She was the proprietor of the walled Warren Gardens that were situated behind part of the Protestant Cathedral wall and the adjacent cottages in Lower Church Lane. Copies of her excellent bulb catalogues are held in the Lindley Library of the Royal Horticultural Society in London. Frank Mason, an old schoolmate, drew this enterprise to my attention in 2006. His maternal grandfather, Thomas O'Connor, was the head gardener there and Frank (in 2007/08) is researching the exact extent of the gardens, the possible current availability of the daffodils and anemones that Miss Currey bred and sold widely and how the whole business was run. In the meantime, *The Newsletter of the Irish Garden Plant Society* has published a most informative preliminary article by him on the gardens in issue 104, April 2007, p.16-22. The piece reproduces from Eugene F Dennis's *Images of Ireland: Lismore* a fine accompanying photograph, taken on site, of the redoubtable lady and her staff.

In the main though, floods were predictable in their volume and in the time of year they struck. When I was big enough to go out on my own I used to go down to the Owenashad in daylight hours, after it had rained incessantly for a time, in the hope of catching the first surge of the flash flood that was certain to come roaring down from the mountains. (This small river was itself fed by the Glendeish, Glenaveha, and other burns.) Some of my pals had had the luck to witness this wall of water shooting down the narrow ravine by the Mountain Road, or charging at the Strand Bridge. It was a rare stroke of luck to catch the initial onrush because this mostly occcured in darkness or very early in the morning after rain had persisted into the night. One late and dull wintry afternoon my efforts paid off. What I saw, standing alone on the Strand Bridge, was not the full fury I had hoped for but a respectable swell some three or four feet in height that stretched across from the Ballyduff Road to the hatchery. It bore down not with a great roar, but with a hiss and a crackle, as it thrust aside the rhododendron branches in its path before slapping against the columns at my feet. I ran to the other parapet and watched it peel away toward the Point. It was all over in seconds but was still something to tell my pals about.

Storms and westerly gales were as destructive as the floods. Many trees, most sadly the tall straight beeches, were blown over, to lie like stricken Gullivers, their rootstock soles sentinelling the jagged craters they had created. Electricity poles were felled, causing sudden blackouts. Slates were blown off roofs. I liked it when the lights failed. It was magical sitting in the glow of candles and oil-lamps. The tall, bronze lamp from the sitting-room with its upturned, mauve-coloured glass shade threw out specially soft reflections. But this mood was always followed by a deep sense of disappointment when the lights suddenly sprang on again. Not that they always came on and stayed on. Often they would go off again a few minutes later. Or flicker and splutter for a couple of hours before the Electricity Supply Board would succeed in restoring normal service. Such work was slow and difficult and often the linesmen were brought out dangerously at the height of a storm. Mam did not share my disappointment. She was always pleased to see the electricity back, or mostly. She had to be in the mood for candles or lamps.

Since rural electrification had got underway after the War there were always teams of trained electricians in the area. Here and there by the roadside you would come across piles of wooden poles, treated with creosote, waiting to be set in place. Those that were already erected bore the spike holes of the spurred, iron climbers that the linesmen used. I always wanted to climb a pole with a pair of these but no ESB man I asked was willing to let me have a go. Probably on grounds of safety. Even so, it was an event to observe them ascending, then leaning back into their leather safety-straps while they disentangled broken lines and connections after a storm.

Blizzards seldom hit the area, although they occurred commonly enough in winter on the exposed slopes of the Knockmealdown Mountains and used to sweep across the coastline around Dungarvan with some fury from time to time. Naturally, we boys were on the lookout for snow every winter. From the top of Gallows Hill, on the way to and from school, we could see in the distance the top of Knockmealdown itself, the highest peak in the range to which it lent its name. When that smooth summit turned white there was hope. As late as May exceptionally we might see a mantle of snow on it, but that was unlikely to herald a white Lismore. When I was 9 or 10 years old a couple of icy winters brought lots of snow, as much as six inches outside our front door; fine and dry, it stayed for days. It stayed white too, there being so little traffic. A time when the redwing – 'Norwegian thrushes' we called them for some reason of our own – were over from Scandinavia. The unexpected harshness caught them unprepared in a land in which they normally wintered with ease. You saw them hopping along on the ground exhausted by their efforts to find food in the sealed-off landscape.

My brother Paddy and I came across one being worried by a cat and rescued her just in time. Fatigued though she was, it still was not easy to catch her. Eventually, we managed to corner her in a drift. Paddy held her inside his jacket and warmed her against his breast. Getting home, we made a bed for her in a shoebox and left her alone in front of the fire in the living-room with some bread and water so that she could thaw out and eat, and, hopefully, lose her fear of us. Mam was busy in the kitchen, so she did not mind. Later in the afternoon we transferred the bird to our room. That night we fell asleep to the sound of her claws lightly scratching the top of the wardrobe where she had perched. Next morning, in spite of the cold, she flew off through an open window.

Over the ensuing days we rescued others – thrushes, a robin, a wood pidgeon. This time we kept them indoors, which did not please Mam because they left their droppings all over the place, but she agreed to let us harbour them until the thaw set in. I had become attached to them by then and, when the time came to release them, watched apprehensively as they nervously edged toward the open window that beckoned them to freedom again. I was hoping that one of them, at least, might stay to become a pet but all flew off without hesitation once they got to the window. Later, in the mild weather of spring, I caught a jackdaw that had not yet learned to fly. It stayed around for about ten days, long enough to make me think it had grown accustomed to me, but once it had found its wings it too followed its instincts. It did seem to display *some* hesitation though, transferring its weight undecidedly from claw to claw before taking off. At least, that was the interpretation I put upon its movements. For weeks afterwards I kept a lookout for him, hoping that we would recognise each other, that he would suddenly land upon a fence beside me, or better, on my shoulder like Long John Silver's parrot. But it was not to be.

Never wanting the snow to disappear, I never welcomed the thaw. There was an added bonus to take into consideration. On particularly cold spells I might be fortunate to be allowed a fire in my bedroom, lit to counteract the ice that formed on the inside of the window panes. The fireplace was near the head of my bed and I loved falling asleep in the glow of the dying embers. By morning, however, the windows would have frosted up again and the linoleum on the floor would feel just as icy under my naked feet. During such weather also we would run out of blankets and all available overcoats, the most desirable of which were Dad's thick *garda* greatcoats, would be thrown on top of the eiderdowns for added warmth. The eventual thaw was inevitable and, while I never wished for it, there was much that was pleasurable in the thawing process itself – the icicles dripping pearls from the roofs and branches, the vegetation reviving after its spell in cold storage; the return of birdsong. I might slope up Chapel Street from the Monument, narrowing my eyes against an iridescent townscape melting in the sun. I'd lash out with my turned-down wellingtons at the loosening lumps of snow at the side of the pathway and delight in the arrows of ice that shot into the air. The last pastime of winter.

You learned to have great respect for the elements, above all, thunder and lightning. Thunder, I accepted in time with some scepticism, was caused by the collision of clouds. I was sceptical because I could not visualise such soft and fleecy things colliding with a wallop. Then someone told me to listen out for the thunderclap the second after I saw a flash of lightning. I liked the crack of thunder and flashes in the night sky, the latter preferably from behind the safety of a window-pane, for I knew that lightning could be unpredictable. Sometimes you heard of farm animals, particularly cows, being killed by a bolt and, now and again, you came across a tree that had been split. You were warned never to stand under a tree in an electric storm because the tree could act as a conductor to your warm body. I do not think I ever quite believed this though I heard it said often enough. I figured I would be a much easier target if I stood in the middle of a field. On top of that, I'd get drenched by the accompanying rain.

The night sky could offer other spectacles too, one more rare and more impressive even than lightning. Paddy and I used to borrow Dad's racing binoculars, sit on the low wall that divided our garden from Joe Kelly's field and comb the heavens. Sometimes the sky was so crisp you felt that if you threw a stone at it you'd hear the tinkle of broken glass. Paddy could identify a number of constellations. I was only sure of the Plough. One night a new and different kind of brilliance appeared – vertical, purple-green streaks like the brushstrokes of a cosmic artist. They hung like curtains way beyond Botany, shifting a little from side to side. Excitedly, we called Mike Feeney. He was as puzzled as we were. Then Dad came up and said that it was the aurora borealis, the northern lights! He had seen them in Donegal. They were still there when I was sent off to bed. The next night they had vanished. I never witnessed the phenomenon again.

If you had been asked to suggest a daytime metaphor for the night sky you might well have thought of the country's road system as the potholes in the highways and byways seemed as innumerable as the stars. And County Waterford was reputed to have the best roads in Ireland! Lismore streets were tarmacadamised, with two exceptions, the Station Road that swung around from Botany to Townparks and the Boreen (Hospital Lane) that ran straight across from Botany to the Old Cemetery. The Station Road, the responsibility of the CIE rather than the council, was stony and gritted and, because of the heavy usage it got, was always torn and rutted. The Boreen carried lighter traffic and was okay. Metalled or not, all roads were pockmarked with potholes which the county council workers were forever filling. A band would descend on a street or stretch of road without warning, provisioned with tar barrels, a brazier for melting the tar, thick tar-brushes with wooden handles at ninety degrees, shovels, brooms, and a cartful of loose chippings. While the tar was being heated the potholes would be swept free of mud and debris. Later one man would go around with bucket and brush, tarring the holes, followed by another shovelling in the chippings. It was a leisurely activity, relieved by long moments of straightening up to let the world go by. This kind of patching extended the life of a road until, inevitably, the only remedy was a complete new surface. Which called for a larger scale of operation. A small tanker with tar-spraying equipment was followed by a gang of men distributing chippings evenly with wide sweeps of their shovels. After them came the steamroller, always exciting to watch, its tall chimney spurting smoke, its heavy iron drive-wheel spinning rapidly, its massive front roller and rear wheels crushing everything in its path. Goal-sized recesses in ditches – that often also displayed ridged, triangular-headed iron milestone markers painted white with black lettering and digits – were used to store the chippings and, sometimes, the equipment needed for the job. There was one behind the weigh-house by the hatchery and whenever that filled up with the familiar red sandstone you knew that a repair of some significance would soon be underway in or around the town.

Major repairs, as far as motorists were concerned, were laudatory but they did nothing for us children. You could neither spin your tops nor roller-skate because the chippings were so coarse. It was not even any fun rolling your hoop on them. Biking could be hazardous too; if you fell off you came away with a limbful of tarry scratches. There was a positive side to it though; on hot days it amused us to poke around in the pools of tar with sticks. Great for us, not so great for our mothers when we returned home with the familiar black stains on our sandals and white slippers, on our clothes, hands, face, and even hair. You were given a pat of butter, the only household remedy that removed tar, and were told to clean yourself up. When the stains proved resistent to butter Mam would send me over to Feeney's for a drop of petrol, the last-hope detergent.

The country came to town on the second Wednesday of every month, Fair Day. Before the Second World War there had also been a pig market that was held in the Market Yard, up the alleyway by the side of the *garda* barracks. By the beginning of the War the market took place every fortnight; by the end of it, it seemed to have petered out. I only have vague memories of hanging around one and that may not have been a pig market but the Annual Seed Potato Market that used to be held every St Patrick's Eve, and which ceased too by War's end. Up a lane by John F. O'Donnell's in the Main Street there was another market yard where visiting dealers traded in household goods and clothes every Friday. This market held little interest for me. In contrast, the monthly fair was always a welcome event, bringing farmers, jobbers, drovers, animals, carts, cars and trucks, and the tinker musicians and ballad-sellers to Lismore for the day. The streets steamed up with the earthy tang of the farmyard and the grunts and squeals of livestock protesting the slash of sticks and the rough manhandling – *bainbh* being lifted by the ears and tails; calves being 'bagged' in canvas bags to stop them moving around when being transported in carts. But a big crowd was not always guaranteed. Some fairs could be very quiet and trade, from the cattlemen's and jobbers' point of view, dull. Sometimes fat sheep and cattle would be scarce to the point of unavailability. Cattle formed the main trade of the fair – bullocks, heifers, and 'springers', i.e. cows very close to calving. The last-mentioned were so-called, Eugene Dennis informed me, because the cow's dug 'literally springs to accommodate milk for the new-born; springing is a classic sign that a cow's time is nearing.' The breeds sold were mainly Hereford, Dairy Shorthorns, Red Poll or Friesian. Curiously enough for a Munster county, Kerry cows were rarely, if ever, seen. I first laid eyes on a herd of these over Carrick-on-Suir way and puzzled over the half-grown look of them until Dad explained to me that the Kerry did not grow any bigger.

Farmers, jobbers and drovers might spit on their hands in West Street and the Main Street but the bulk of their business was conducted in the five-acre Fair Field. The field was owned by the Duke of Devonshire through the Lismore Estates Company and was first made available to the people of Lismore in 1879 for the purpose of holding fairs, sports meetings, shows, gymkhanas, and similar events. It was a walled, purpose-built, enclosure. The sheep-pens and cattle-pens ranged along the northern boundary of the field were serviced by drove, lorry, and train. By the goods yards at the railway station there was a further series of cattle-pens to and from which animals were railroaded in wagons. Two stands in the middle of the field had been torn down before my time because they had fallen into a state of disrepair and become dangerous. Most of the year, because we had to be in school, we youngsters did not see much of the fair. If you were feeling energetic you could get up early and catch the beginning of it before going to school, which was what I did on occasion, calling up to the Walshes in Botany on the way to collect Barney. There, across the road, you could observe the livestock being unloaded from lorries at the main gate. You missed all this if you did not get up early. By the time we were let out for dinner the focus of activity would have shifted from the field to the Main Street and West Street where the farmers who had sold their animals drank and gossiped while their wives shopped. Only when a fair was exceptionally large would there still be life in the town when school was over – three o'clock for primary, four for secondary.

P.D. Lee, the Superior of the Christian Brothers School, had little time for Irish farmers. To him they were a lazy and inefficient bunch who preferred leaning over their five-bar gates and moaning about the weather, no matter what the state of it, than getting up off their backsides and extracting the most out of the land. 'Look at the Dutch!' he would say impatiently, riding off at a tangent on his hobby-horse, 'Look at the way they cultivate every inch of the land. They even win back land from the sea and farm that. And we with so much acreage we don't know what to do with it. And what about the Far East where they've been constructing rice terraces up the sides of mountains for hundreds of years? The Dutch don't have five-yard headlands like us. They slim down their ditches and plough right up to them so they can reclaim some more. Irish farmers! All they're good for is putting the cows out to grass...'

There was more than a grain of truth in his criticisms and the farmers' sons amongst us pricked up their ears and reddened when he lashed out. Some of them, like Dan Howard or Tom O'Connor, would have been members of the recently formed Macra na Feirme, looking outward for new ideas and techniques. With the advent of rural electrification the farming community no longer felt as isolated as formerly. Its sons and daughters were beginning to hold formal debates among themselves in the Devonshire Arms and the town hall about ways and means of increasing the productivity of the land. The compulsory tillage of the Emergency (introduced in February 1940), when inspectors were sent around by the Department of Agriculture to ensure that farmers maintained their quotas, may also have been instrumental in improving farming methods. In town allotments for the unemployed began in 1941. The farmers were already into chemicals VAP for putting cows right, i.e. curing sterility; BIP for eradicating fleas; CAW for poisoning crows and pigeons – a few of the graphically named proprietary brands you saw advertised in the local papers. But the farm labourers were still working six- and seven-day weeks, more seven than six.

Milk production was being given priority at this time. We still got our milk from Jim Ormonde, who lived up the street from us. Jim had a small farm just past the railway bridge on the Ballyanchor Road and used to milk his cows himself twice a day, every day of the year. He delivered to your door, using half-pint and pint measures to ladle out the milk from the three-gallon pails he carried, one in each hand. But creamery-filled bottles were on the horizon. Lorries carrying large tanks, from the Ballinamult and Dungarvan Co-operative creameries, were becoming an increasingly common sight on our roads. As these always ran to a schedule dictated by the times cows were milked they served another purpose also. People knew when to expect them and would wait by the roadside to thumb a lift. The drivers, for their part, quickly got to know the people living along their routes and became noted for their kindness in picking up travellers. There was talk of starting a creamery in Lismore at one stage but nothing ever came of it.

I did manage to see the interior of a couple of creameries. My curiosity had been aroused by the cylindrical, steel churns I saw on railway stations awaiting transport or on crude, wooden platforms by the roadsides awaiting collection by the lorries. Mill Vale Creamery on the County Waterford side of Carrick-on-Suir was a place I regularly passed, going on walks over Grubb's Hill with Dad, and once, at my insistence, he asked one of the workmen if we might come in and look around. It was in the afternoon, the day's work was done, so the visit was fairly uninformative. Much more satisfying was my trip to Grangemockler Creamery nine miles north of Carrick because we had an inside contact there, Mam's first cousin Peg Grant (née Denn), who worked as a butter-maker. Peg was finishing her day when we arrived. The corrugated-iron building was much bigger and more interesting-looking than its Mill Vale counterpart. Peg showed me how the capacious revolving drums worked and how she made butter and shaped it into one-pound blocks. Everywhere was spilling water as the place was being hosed down. White curd-like residues from the butter-making process flowed along cement channels and out under the sides of the giant shed into a small stream where brown trout, unconcerned at the presence of humans, fed eagerly on them. A local lad of about my age, 11, told me that you could tickle the fish easily. I tried but could not manage it. And neither could he. I then told him about Andy Coleman from the Main Street of Lismore who had the reputation of being able to catch trout in this way in the pools of the Owenashad. Not that I ever saw him do it. But he had confirmed to me that he could. After the visit, Peg took Mam and me back to Johnny Sweeney's house nearby, where she then lived, for tea. Soon afterwards her daughter Phyllis arrived home late from school. She had been bucking an orchard with her pals, she explained, and produced the goods to prove it. I laughed, recognising a kindred spirit, and willingly accepted the apple she offered me. Her mother pursed her lips severely.

Milking machines were also coming in. I first saw one at the Castle Farm buildings on the Green Road. While Pad Feeney was attaching the red rubber milkers to the cows' udders he let me have a go at milking by hand. I gripped the cow's teats gingerly and pulled gently. Nothing came.

Pad laughed and roared, 'Squeeze it, man!'

I did, but still no milk came.

'Harder,' Pad grinned.

I looked at the cow's hind legs anxiously. Jim Canning, a schoolmate of mine, had been kicked by an animal he was milking, so I wasn't taking any chances. I had heard of grown-ups getting kicked as well. I pulled a little harder and out flew a squirt. But Pad had lost patience with me by then. He grabbed one of the other teats and squeezed, and immediately a stream of milk shot from it, turned the flow onto my face like he was holding a water-pistol. He roared with laughter again. I ruefully rubbed the warm liquid from my face and tried once more. This time I was only marginally more successful. Clearly, there was more to milking a cow than pressing a teat.

A kick from a cow could be painful, and embarrassing, but it was one of the lesser accidents that could happen with farm animals. Farm labourers also got kicked by more powerful animals – jennets and bolting stallions and mares. Sometimes horses bolted in towns and raced through the streets until someone had the courage and the know-how to stop them. John Troy of Church Lane stopped two runaways in one week after they had been startled by swarms of wasps. The lethal animal was the bull. Fiercely territorial, he was capable of attacking people instinctively, at times goring an unfortunate victim to death. When recalcitrant at a fair he might require four or five strong men to restrain him but when paraded at a Show would allow himself to be lead by the nose by a single handler. Alec Ellis of Woodview on the Ballyanchor Road kept a massive bull, which often had the run of his forty-acre, and whenever we were on his land hunting rabbits, or picking blackberries, or just walking through the fields, we kept a sharp eye out for him. The Castle Farm used to move a red one around from field to field in the patchwork of land between Gallows Hill and the Green Road so you had to be extra careful when you cut through there. Sucky and I were chased by him once in the field behind the library. We never expected him to be there and, fortunately, happened to be close enough to the ditch when he made a drive for us out of a group of grazing cows. We had a suspicion that the Castle used him more to keep us off its land than to service the cows because we never saw him mounting a female, something for which we used to be casually on the lookout. Only once did I manage to see a cow being bulled, and that was only a glimpse in the lane that led from the ball alley to Ballynelligan Cottage, where 'the Gander' Scanlon farmed. A few of us were playing handball when we heard a bull roaring nearby. We immediately raised our heads as no such animal grazed in the fields around there. Looking across we could see the animal rearing up above the top of the wall. Obviously, the Gander had had the bull brought in to service a cow, so it merited closer attention. When we came nearer, however, his son the Gandóg threatened us with his stick and ran us off. He was grinning like he was enjoying himself.

Accidents with farm machinery were the most numerous. The sharp knives of mowing machines cruelly wounded the unwary child who happened to stray into them unnoticed, and cut to pieces many a sleeping or unwary wild animal. Adults met their deaths when tractors they were driving overturned. Misfortune occurred most frequently at threshings, possibly due to the fact that it was usual for workers to slake their thirst with pints of stout over a hearty dinner. A man might injure or kill himself in a fall from the top of a rick, which could be as high as fifteen to twenty feet, when it narrowed as the threshing neared its conclusion. A labourer might blunder into the belt that drove the thresher. Beyond any man's control, the beaters of the threshing set might suddenly break up and cause havoc.

It was odd how being a townie in a small Irish town, a village by the standards of the densely populated nations of Europe, could cut you off from the way of life of those who lived out the country. I was curious about country people, how they existed, often miles from the next house, on the fringes of dark and threatening woods, halfway up mountainsides where the icy blizzards of winter might seal them off for days on end. I asked myself whether I could ever live on the land. Putting my doubts and fears to a classmate, John Fitzgerald, who lived at Carrignagour in the shadow of the Knockmealdowns, I quickly saw that he regarded my question with incomprehension. For him, living in the country was neither lonely nor threatening. On the contrary, he liked the sense of space around his home. In a town the size of Lismore even, he would have felt fenced in. And he was right. We townies just made assumptions about country people. I could also, I suppose, have queried the inconvenience of not having shops near you, but that never occurred to me, nor to him, no doubt.

But we were not entirely ignorant of the ways of the land. Far from it. From observing farmers at the fair, listening to things our parents said, scanning the local papers and, most of all, taking note of images – deliberate and unintentional – provided by our schoolmates from the country, we built up a fairly coherent picture of farming life. When later on, as teenagers, we took summer jobs on the land – thinning sugar beet or picking fruit, etc., – we augmented our knowledge, acquiring, for example, a greater understanding of the changing seasons and of the hazards that could destroy crops. Hazard number one, for historical reasons, was potato blight. We learned early of the calamitous Famine that had devastated our land and people in the nineteenth century. Once I myself had absorbed the horrific scale of this, I never again came across the word 'blight' without a shiver of apprehension. And blight was still around. Now and again you heard a report of an outbreak in some part of the country which galvanised spraying of potato crops in June and July was urged on farmers by the Department of immediate preventive spraying on the part of those who had been lax. Repeated Agriculture. *Spray early, Spray thoroughly, Spray often during the season* the posters stuck on telegraph poles and other convenient places exhorted, posters which we often defaced for fun to read *pray early, pray thoroughly, pray often during the season*. It was strange that the farmers needed persuading. One would have thought that the financial consequences of a failed crop would have been a strong enough deterrent, aside from the potent folk memory of the Great Famine. But the small farmer, in particular, had to weigh the cost of prevention against the probability of an attack.

Nor was blight the only enemy of the potato. In early summer dry spells crows might damage crops by locating the seed potatoes via the young stalks and eating them. Less of a threat was the black-and-yellow-striped Colorado beetle although one year, when a couple of the creatures were discovered in grain sacks from the USA at one of the ports, we were lectured in the schools on the dangers of an infestation of this. Other crops were prone to other diseases. 'Root eelworm' was a dread of beet growers and 'wheat midge' could destroy a whole crop of wheat. In August 1951 the *Dungarvan Observer* reported that over 2,000 acres of wheat along the Blackwater in the Ballyduff region had been eaten away by the midge. But weather could be the greatest hazard of all. Heavy rain hitting the ripened corn could negate a season's hard work. Beautiful sunshine for us townies could spell trouble for the farmer if it persisted at the wrong time. When the weather was really out of joint the bishops would hustle to the rescue, directing that 'prayers for fine weather', 'prayers for rain', or whatever, should be said at all Masses. The clerics were onto a pretty sure thing. For a start, the weather had to be *bad,* i.e. bad from the farmer's point of view, for a considerable period before divine intervention was invoked. Then it was the convention that the decree would apply for a period of four to five weeks. Given such latitude, the bishops could hardly fail. Still, the prayers probably gave the farmer psychological rope to hang onto.

Of animal pests, the rabbit was the one that did most damage to green crops. That meant cabbage, of course, a staple Irish vegetable, and the young corn – oats, wheat and barley. Literally thousands of acres could be eaten up in a short time, we were told, a scale of devastation difficult for us townies to appreciate, let alone accept. I certainly found it hard to credit. How could those fluffy, cuddly creatures, whose white powder-puff tails we saw popping in and out of ditches everywhere, chew away so much? Surely the farmers were seeking advantage in exaggeration as usual? In time, I came round toward the farmer's point of view, but only toward. There remained the fundamental conflict between the townie's and the farmer's impression of what constituted a pest. In this case, the farmer's pest was, for the poor people of the town in particular, a basic source of food and income. Rabbit stew was a regular dish on Botany tables. On my own family table, sadly, it never appeared. Mam turned up her nose at rabbit as she did at eel and everything else I caught except trout. A couple of times I brought home rabbits and begged her to cook them for me but she wouldn't. I had heard that farmers did not eat rabbits either, which made me wonder if, coming of farming stock herself, she did not regard wild things as proper food.

It never occurred to me to try and cook the rabbits myself. I could just about boil an egg. Otherwise, cooking was an art known only to women. Mam herself would point out that there was no reason why men could not cook. All the great chefs she had ever read about were men, after all. Their pre-eminence she put down to the hard physical grind of being on one's feet in a hot kitchen all day long. A man could stick that better. To me it seemed a curious profession for a man to adopt, another of the quare things that went on in big cities. Sucky's mother, Kit, was the one who gave me my first bite of rabbit and, while I did not go overboard for it, I felt it was certainly something for which I could develop a taste.

You did not have to go far beyond the town to experience the real *métier* of the farmer – working the land. Less than a mile out the Mayfield Road you could observe Michael Whelan's pair of magnificent shire-horses engaged in the seasonal activities of ploughing, harrowing with gate or disc, pulling the sowing machines, mowing machines and reaper-and-binders. They were occasionally used for moving trunks of trees that had been blown down in storms, or felled deliberately, work mainly performed by the Irish draught horse. A shy person, Michael was renowned as a great ploughman, able, it was said, to turn a straighter and deeper furrow with his horses than any man could with a tractor. When Macra na Feirme started up ploughing competitions, however, he never showed any interest in participating. But he loved to show off his shires. The only such animals in the area, they were the envy of many farmers when they appeared, groomed in their leather and brasses at shows and parades. Some farmers would shake their heads and mutter about the cost of keeping the beasts, conveniently forgetting the multitude of operations they could perform.

By the end of March on most farms the cereal crops would have been sown, potato planting would be in full swing, and the ground prepared for the sowing of beet, mangolds, turnips and cabbage. Wheat and oats were the main cereals, but barley was also grown. The farmer had no sooner finished all this work than he began to worry about the hay. It would have been hard for him not to, given the uncertainty of the climate and the necessity of that crop for winter feed. A good June would see hay-saving up and away by the end of that month or the beginning of July; on any road out of town the whirring of mowing machines or the silky swish of a scythe would lead the assault on your senses. Haycocks would nose up soon afterwards.

In these warm months too the bees would swarm and you might see a cloud of them on the wing, undulating like a wayward puff of smoke. You were told to respect these insects, out of fear on the one hand, for their honey-making capabilities on the other. Never disturb a cluster you were warned, and stay well clear of them in wet weather. Lads, at their peril, did disturb them sometimes though, throwing stones at the football-sized agglomerations just to see what would happen. A couple of times I saw clusters form in West Street, one in a tree in the grounds of the Villa, directly across from Feeney's, and the other in one of the small beeches that formed part of the hedge between our garden and Feeney's. Jim Feeney used to dabble in bee-keeping when a swarm came his way and he smoked these two down off the branches from which they were dangling into large square biscuit tins. Vin O'Donoghue, who happened to be passing, acted as technical adviser on the first operation. Our science teacher was well-informed on bee behaviour and people would call on him for advice whenever they found an unwelcome swarm in their backyard, but only after they had tried to get hold of Brother Murphy first. Murphy was a skilled bee-keeper, possibly the best in the immediate area, and would never pass up an opportunity to acquire a new hive. In a good year he might have six or eight ranged inside the Tallow Road wall of the brothers' small orchard, all producing honey. A bad year might see him down to one or two. He was fearless and confident in his handling of the bees and, even though he would protect only his head with a black net worn over a wide-brimmed black hat, never seemed to get stung. Possibly the bees found him as acerbic as many of us boys did. The Ellises of Woodview also kept bees. Mam used to buy honeycombs from them. I was not always able to distinguish a bee from a wasp but I could distinguish their nests, on the general theory that bees nested in trees and wasps in holes in the ground or in rotting logs of wood. In Scarook Wood when picking whorts you moved carefully when there seemed to be more bees or wasps around than usual. Sometimes we had to leave choice berries unpicked because wasps had nested in the immediate vicinity. On occasion you got stung. This was always sore and affected some of us more than others. The wasp had a big advantage over the bee in this respect; it could sting you many times. A bee could only sting you once, after which it died. Which meant, we were told, that a bee had to get awful mad before he would sting you. Wasps were the ones that worried livestock. The bee minded its own business. Of stinging insects the most fearsome was the hornet, often called the horsefly because it could panic a horse. When you spotted one of these in the neighbourhood you kept your head well down.

Having saved the hay, the farmer could not just sit back and wait for the corn to ripen. Among other tasks there were potatoes to be sprayed and thistles and other 'noxious weeds' to be cleared from the pastures. If a farmer did not cut down such weeds he could be fined by Law. New potatoes came on the market in June–July, the earliest always from the Dungarvan area. Come August, the low-slung hay-floats drawn by single horses would be on the byroads, bringing in the dried yield to the haylofts. In a dry year the farmer was fortunate. In a wet one he salvaged what hay he could from the sodden fields and worried about the cost of providing extra feed over the coming winter. He might have to countenance selling off livestock he could not afford to feed in a consequently depressed market. But a dry year was not without its dangers either. One heard of hay-barns and their valuable contents catching fire and being burned to the ground, a loss not always covered by insurance.

Autumn brought the farming year to a climax. In the cornfields the ears on top of the stalks swelled with grain and turned from green to gold. Our nearest laboratory for observing this process was to be found along the Green Road where the Castle Farm grew wheat in adjoining fields. Near the headland Molly would break off a few spikes and show Paddy and me how to rub them in our hands to winnow away the chaff. The seeds were hard but tasty. Paddy saved some in a little box at home to chew at leisure, which led to a furious argument between us. As older brothers often do with younger ones, he talked me into exchanging an old piece of a rolled gold bracelet that Mam had given me as a plaything for his mini-hoard of corn. I agreed with some misgivings and we completed the swap. Very soon afterwards, with the prerogative of younger brothers, I decided I did not like the bargain and asked for my gold back. He refused point-blank.

'Gimme me gold!' I shouted in a temper.

'No!' he shouted back.

Mam heard the screaming match that developed and rushed into the living-room.

'Gimme me gold,' I wailed again.

'Give him back the bit o' bracelet, Paddy,' she said to my brother, 'What good is it to you?'

'It was a fair exchange. I won't give it back,' he shouted.

'Gimme me gold,' I muttered mournfully.

'Gimme me wheat,' he teased.

At which point Mam blew up, snatched the objects of contention from our hands, exchanged them, pushed Paddy out of the room and followed him muttering, 'You're big enough to have more sense.'

My show of temper abruptly subsided and I began to tinker with my plaything like a magpie.

'Gimme me gold,' Mam used to toss at me for a long time afterwards whenever I sulked. It never failed to bring me out of my mood and even raise a smile on my lips.

Harvesting operations generally began in mid-August and went on until about the second week of September. In an unusually sunny year they might begin a week earlier; in a wet one, they might be delayed until well into October. In the wet year the farmer faced two kinds of loss: lodging of the ripe corn by heavy rain, or a slump in income if the moisture content of the threshed wheat was above the specifications laid down by the Department of Agriculture. The reaper-and-binder, particularly when it was pulled by a brace of horses, was an exhilarating machine to observe in action but, as with the mowing machine, too attractive for children who were kept well away from its lethal blades, fatal to game that hesitated in its path. Before the reaper-and-binder could begin its operations a certain amount of corn had to be scythed around the headlands so that the horses, or Fordson tractor, could turn the machine first time round without trampling on or rolling over the corn growing there. Some farmers left unsown a headland wide enough to take the machine but this was considered wasteful.

Threshing began as soon as the corn had been gathered into the haggard and built up into a high rick. The threshing machines travelled around from farm to farm, farmer helping farmer on the threshing day, for which extra men were always needed. At least a dozen pairs of hands were required at the machine to toss the sheaves onto the drum, clear away the chaff, fill and tie the sacks of grain – which weighed over two hundredweight when full – and load them onto a lorry. On big farms a steam machine was occasionally still employed to drive the thresher. Generally though, an ordinary tractor engine was used. In both cases a long, wide belt made of some kind of rubberised hessian and running between engine and thresher kept the drums in motion. There was always an early start to the threshing day and when a steam engine was used the man operating this had to rise first because he had to have the traction engine up and running so that the work could begin by eight o'clock. Around Lismore I often saw threshing sets passing by and threshings going on at a distance. Only on one occasion, however, did I observe, and in my small way participate in, a threshing close-up for a whole day and that was at a farm belonging to my Morrissey/Denn cousins in Knockroe, County Kilkenny. I was about 10 at the time and came away with two abiding memories of a hot, sunny day, but with vivid recollections also of motoring through the lunar landscape of the disused slate quarries in the region and the general hum of an important event in which Dad exercised his long-dormant farming skills as well. The first was the fabulous dinner we got: lashings of home-cured bacon, plenty more of which hung from hooks in the ceiling; dishes of flowery potatoes; jugs of thick cream. I had never seen so much food in any one place before. Outside in the yard, on either side of the front door of the small, white-washed farmhouse, sat wooden casks of porter on trestles which the hard-working men gathered round eagerly. Everyone was in a good mood, keen to complete the threshing. My second memory was a less pleasant one. In the late afternoon when the work was nearing its end, Eddie Denn, in an excess of good humour, swung me into the air and threw me into the soft pile of chaff. I came out scratching all over, spitting chaff and blue murder, and threw my whole vocabulary of curses, modest as it then was, at him which, to my chagrin, only made him and the other men laugh all the more. I had to strip off and have all the chaff and fine powder beaten out of my clothes. Mam was not too pleased with Eddie but I think she contained a grin nonetheless.

In September silage had to be made from the young after-grass grown after the cropping of the hay in early summer. A new technique of making this, the 'trench' method, was being urged on farmers in the early Fifties. Whatever method was used your nostrils could not fail to detect the overpowering stench of the stuff. It was important to finish all these operations in good time as the sugar beet crop had to be lifted in October.

The first combine harvester arrived in Lismore about the time I was leaving it. Probably it was bought by Jimmy Howard of Curraghreigh, the most progressive, as well as the most hardworking and unassuming farmer in the locality. Claas of Holland was the manufacturer of this gigantic red machine which necessitated gates to be removed and ditches to be torn down to accommodate its width. There was much debate as to whether it was right for Irish conditions, the feeling being that in our climate corn needed a couple of weeks in which to dry out before it should be threshed, something for which the combine, reaping and threshing in one combined operation, did not allow.

A *meitheal* poses at a threshing at the Denn family farm in Castlejohn, Co. Tipperary, in the late Forties. A mound of chaff is seen in the foreground. This may well be the chaff that Eddie Denn threw me into. Eddie, wearing cap, is standing second to the right of my other cousin Phyllis Grant who is sitting down.

The summer shearing of sheep was an activity I only witnessed once, when it appeared as an event at the Lismore Agricultural Show. Sheep dipping, however, I could see any year, but not without some effort as the season for this was October. By then I was back at school, which meant that, with the dipping forming part of the normal working day, I could only be around for any length of time if I mitched. The alternative, my usual choice, was to join the end of the day's proceedings after school. It was possible to catch a quick glimpse of things over lunch hour, but no more than that, as the dipping took place at the other end of town in the lane that led from Glen View to the sawmill by the Strand Bridge. The fresh water sluiced from the weir on the Owenashad for the salmon hatchery was channelled under the road at the junction of the Cappoquin and Mountain roads to emerge as a stream on the right of the lane by the high stone wall of the mill. From there, a little further along, it was funnelled left through another underground passage to discharge itself into the still waters of the canal. Across this little stream, no more than six or seven feet wide, was placed a large and somewhat rusty-looking metal trough, deep at one end, tapering to shallow at the other. The water that poured into this unit assumed the colour of thinned-down porter when infused with the strong-smelling chemical dip. And it was into this, from a wooden ramp at the deep end, that the sheep, still wearing the marks of their summer visit to the shearer, were bundled. One by one they were dunked unceremoniously a few times by men who prodded them under with long poles before allowing them to scramble up the slipway at the shallow end and out into a dry pen. The procedure, accomplished with much energy and commotion, was intended to protect the animals from disease and ticks, I was given to understand.

In spite of his tendency to *ochón*, the farmer could enjoy himself – at the point-to-point and gymkhana, of course, and playing cards into the small hours, but also at the Lismore Agricultural Show, a well-attended event held at the Fair Field in July. There was an occasional autumn show in September as well, more suited, perhaps, to the gentleman farmer than the farming community in general but also well-attended. My pals and I looked forward to this show much more than the gymkhana. Among the prize displays of fruit and buns there was always something tasty to be fecked – after you had managed to slip past the stewards. And there was a greater variety of activities. The strong men of the area would gather in informal competition to see which of them could throw a 56-lb weight the farthest or, in the September event, toss a sheaf the highest. I particularly liked the last-mentioned. There was something elemental in seeing a powerful man sprong a heavy bundle of corn stalks into the air over a high crossbar. Ancestral nuances, perhaps? Prize competitions of all sorts abounded with horse-jumping, happily, kept to a minimum. Some of the alternatives, however – best bull, best shorthorn cow, best bullock, best poultry – did not exactly rivet us either. More promising were best craft work, jams, veg and flowers, and wholly up our street the best cakes and fruit, over which we used to hover like crows.

We took an active part in the judging of buns and fruit, sometimes pre-, sometimes post-competition. Doshin Keating was the one amongst us with the most say – for prize apples especially he possessed the fastest hands at the show. The post-competition period was the most fruitful for us as the stewards watched us like hawks before the judging. So much so that I once had to suffer the indignity of being thrown, well, firmly ushered, out of the marquee by Tom Fives, the secretary of the show, and a man I greatly admired as a hurler. He had caught me salivating a little too longingly over Mrs Chavasse's apples. A lady farmer from Cappagh, Mrs Chavasse was always winning prizes for her big juicy reds. Turfed me out Tom did, saying, 'Come on now. Off with you. We don't want anything fecked around here.' I fronted a mild show of outrage but left quietly. I knew that Doshin already had one of the reds in his pocket and would share it with us. Other consistent prizewinners at the show were Alec Ellis for his heifers; his sister for her cakes; John McGrath, the Main Street butcher, for his shorthorns; Lismore Estates for its cows; Major Maxwell of Moorehill for his flowers, and suchlike. After the judging it was a fairly simple matter to fill your pockets. The public would be filing through the marquee to see whose fruit and cakes were adorned with rosettes. In the crush you could hardly miss picking up something. And, if you did, you just went back in and did the round again. Boxer took the most risks. Once or twice I was lining up a beauty when he stretched out a paw and fecked it from under my nose. Another time Sucky and myself were going around for the third time, determined that one of us would lift a particularly mouth-watering apple in a well-guarded position, when Doshin calmly lent over in front of us and walked off with it. We looked at him open-mouthed then lowered our sights on the less appetising alternatives. We enjoyed doing one another down like that but afterwards shared our loot. It was all part of the show that the Lismore Agricultural Society would round off with an all-night dance at the Happydrome or Town Hall.

CHAPTER THIRTEEN

Hunting

BOTANY WAS WHERE the best rabbit hunters of the town came from and the best of the best were the 'Hawks', Jimmy and Pippa. Experts with snares, ferrets and dogs, they really came into their own when the new technology of 'dazzling' came into fashion. The technology itself was basic, a car battery and a car lamp that functioned as a spot. It was the application that was new. When you turned the light on a rabbit at night he would stare into it, mesmerised. All you had to do was walk up to it, grab it and despatch it with a chop of your hand, the so-called rabbit punch. You got top price for an animal killed in this way as it was unmarked. I did not approve of the casual practice of dazzling. It seemed unsportsmanlike, too much like shooting sitting ducks. I never tried it, although Pippa showed me his equipment and demonstrated how he used it. The practice of dazzling by the O'Briens and other hunters, I did not object to; it was a livelihood for them. Pippa might bring home as many as a hundred or a hundred and fifty kills on a good night, a week's work with snares. Farmers were quite happy to allow dazzling on their land as long as the hunters knew what they were doing and did not startle livestock. For them it was a cheap way of getting rid of pests that they could otherwise only have controlled by the expensive, in terms of time and money, and not very efficient method of shooting. They had neither the patience for snares nor the inclination for ferrets. In 1954 they hailed the advent of what seemed like the perfect solution to their problem, infectious myxomatosis, introduced, it was suspected, by some members of their own community somewhere in Ireland, from whence it spread like wildfire. The rumour may, or may not, have been true. Conceivably, the disease might have been introduced accidentally. But would it then have spread countrywide so rapidly? Whatever the truth, what pleased the farmers did little for the poor of the towns, who suffered a grievous loss of income and protein, both of which, at a time of much poverty and emigration, they needed. In time, everybody, farmers included, became revolted by a plague which condemned hundreds of thousands, perhaps millions, of unfortunate animals to an unspeakable death – pathetically rotting alive, blind and swollen, in huddled fear.

Before dazzling came on the scene snaring and ferreting were the professional methods used for trapping rabbits. They were less efficient than dazzling and also crueller. An animal might be caught in a snare for hours, desperately trying to free itself. The ferocious little ferret would terrify a rabbit but, at least, when the prey bolted into the hunter's net it would be quickly dispatched with a rabbit punch, a clean kill. The least efficient and least skilled method of hunting, and the one that I enjoyed, was going out the fields with a half-dozen terriers and greyhounds, or whippets, and flushing the rabbits out of the undergrowth.

I took up snaring seriously for a short time, practising it amongst the bracken above the sandpit. Mick 'The Bird' O'Brien was the pal who taught me how to read the rabbit runs and showed me where best to lay snares. The snare itself, bought cheaply from the Co-op or other hardware store, consisted of a coiled lasso of brass wire to the end of which was attached a length of strong wine-coloured cord. To set the snare you tied the cord securely to a wooden peg that you drove deep into the ground by the side of the run, using a convenient stone. It was important to do this properly as a noosed rabbit would run off with your trap if you did not hammer the peg

Left to right: Philip 'Sucky' (also 'Blackie') Neville,
Peter Neville and Mick O'Brien outside Feeney's Garage window display,
Lismore in the early Fifties.

sufficiently deep into the ground. Then, causing as little disturbance as possible to the immediate vegetation, you formed a noose of about four or five inches in diameter and angled this not quite vertically, rather slightly away from the direction in which you expected the rabbit to come, across the run. If you angled it toward the rabbit his head would meet the wire and knock it aside. The diameter of the noose was important too; if you set it too wide the rabbit would just pass through it. Finally, you disguised the trap with whatever vegetation dominated around the spot. You would lay a number of snares at a time, usually late in the day, and come back early next morning to check them. It was not always easy to remember exactly where you laid them, and sometimes you failed to recover one. Failure to locate a snare could also be due to your having camouflaged it too well, or to someone's having fecked it. If you found the vegetation flattened around the spot where you laid one, and there was no sign of the snare, you knew you had noosed some creature that had struggled desperately to break free. More difficult it was to conclude whether that creature had escaped with your snare attached to it or whether both had been stolen.

Mick and I got a hell of a fright once when we found the vegetation flattened around a wider area than usual at one of our snares. We could see that we had trapped something larger than a rabbit and when we bent down to examine it a large, brindled wild cat lunged spitting at us from the bracken, only to be pulled back by the wire that was coiled tightly around a blood-stained hind leg. We were at a loss to know what to do as the cornered animal would not let us approach to free it. After we had discussed the matter for a while I suggested going down to Johnny McGrath's to borrow one of his garden nets but Mick had another idea and was determined to carry it out himself. He took off his jacket, tossed it over the cat with a sudden movement, dived, held the animal fast and somehow freed its leg. Then he sprang to his feet and turned it loose with a flourish. I was lost in admiration. It was one of the bravest acts I had ever seen and so skilfully executed. I was struck too by his kindness in setting it free. At first we had thought that killing it was the only solution to the problem. But Mick had a very moral attitude to hunting. Another time we found a rusty spring-trap on the hill, obviously lost by another hunter. He squeezed the spring and showed me the savage-looking teeth, deprecating the use of so cruel an instrument. Such leghold traps were laid for larger animals like foxes, which sometimes escaped them, but only at the cost of a limb. Fortunately, they were vastly dearer than snares so you saw few of them about.

Ferreting was something that never attracted me. I was often shown the animals that were kept in small wire-windowed, wooden boxes and was fascinated by the confident way my pals handled them, holding them around the belly as if they were kittens or, if that were thinkable, pet rats. Only once, when a few of us were out with the dogs, did I see first-hand the technique of this method of hunting. We came across Mick Coleman of Church Lane and another man out Mayfield way just taking the nets down off a ditch, having had some trouble enticing their ferret back out of a small warren of rabbits' burrows. Ferrets were liable to do this. One could go wild on you which, given the price of a trained hunter and the difficulty in obtaining one, was a considerable loss to its owner. The two men were debating whether to have one more go. They only had a couple of kills to show for their afternoon's work. Deciding on one last attempt, they moved along the grassy ditch to another set of burrows. I watched as they pegged the nets over the mouth of every exit they could find. Then came the anticlimax. When it was time to insert the ferret they had to ask us to move on. They could not have our dogs diving at any rabbits that might get entangled in the nets, or worse, mistaking the ferret for a rabbit and killing it. I looked back as we climbed over a gate into the next field. The men were crouched expectantly, one either side of the ditch.

Hunting with the dogs, which we did all the year round, was what I enjoyed above all. It was not that we ever caught much. To the real hunters of Botany such expeditions were serious in intent but for me and my pals it was not so much a kill we were after as the excitement of flushing out a rabbit and giving the dogs a run. It was good to be out in the country, walking miles through the fields. The core of our group consisted of Sucky, Doshin, Boxer, Foxy, Barney, the young Bishop Scanlon, Bing and Val Foley and me. We were not always out together. Sometimes a few of us teamed up with others, or others teamed up with us. Pedro or Pippa accompanied us now and again and then, understandably, it became more serious. It was a simple matter to assemble a posse of terriers. Anywhere you whistled in Botany, out of nowhere would appear a scattering of happy-looking terriers and mongrels, half of them called Patch or Spot, wagging their tails and barking excitedly. Some terriers were dynamos at flushing out game and if you could rope in one or two of those you knew you were in for a good day's sport. But you had to be very careful in your selection. The best dogs were owned by men who supplemented their income by catching and selling rabbits and, understandably, they would not take kindly to your tiring out the terriers they might be intending to take out later themselves. Another problem was that a bunch of other lads might have set off not long before you, taking the best available animals with them, in which case you wound up with a couple of yappy pups and, perhaps, an easygoing mongrel that just wanted to tag along for the company.

Greyhounds were few and whippets rare. The whippet, small in stature and faster over a short run than the larger hound, was the ideal complement to the foraging terrier in this kind of hunting. The terrier would drive the rabbit out into the open where the whippet could pursue him around briars and shrubs and through gaps that the greyhound, because of its larger size, could not negotiate. The finest-looking whippets I saw around Lismore were not hunting animals at all, but mere toys owned by the rich Isaac and Mrs Bell of Ballyin Gardens. Sleek, light-brown purebreds, they always looked bored. You would have liked to take them out with the Botany pack to see if you could arouse their innate hunting nature.

Having gathered the dogs we would set off from the station along the railway line in the direction of the Round Hill, wellies, if we had them and I usually had, turned down pirate-fashion so that we wore collars of white around our calves and shins. Trains were not a problem. We knew when the regular ones were due and learned to keep our ears skinned for the unexpected, unscheduled goods train. From the Plains Indians of the cowboy pictures we learned that if we put our ears to the track we could detect the vibration of the oncoming locomotive long before we could hear the familiar sound of its whistle, or so we liked to imagine. In reality, I think, it was the ear pointing to the sky that did the detecting as the rails were not fused into a continuous line. We knew from school that the track-layers had to leave gaps between rails for expansion; if they did not the rails would buckle in hot weather and cause derailments. We noted for ourselves that this gap was indeed narrower in hot than in cold weather. It amused us also to place the odd penny or small stone on the rail for the passing train to flatten and crush. We tried flattening halfpennies into facsimiles of pennies too, but as forgeries these were not very convincing. In summer there was an added attraction on the slopes of the cutting approaching the Round Hill – wild strawberries. It was around this point that we would begin our leisurely hunt, branching away from the line to follow a series of ditches where we might hope to startle some rabbits. What we kept our eyes on particularly were the patches of thick briar and bracken. Into these the terriers would plunge willingly, or at least the keen hunters would. Some, especially the young dogs, needed encouragement. When we had a greyhound with us, which was not often, one of us would be holding it well out from the ditch so that if a rabbit were frightened out into the open the hound could be loosed after it. In the open the rabbit could nearly always outrun the short-legged terrier but it had little chance against the pacy stride of the hound. The rabbit could outfox the hound by beating it to a low or narrow gap that the dog could not get through. This was where the whippet showed its advantage. But you did not rely on the hounds only to catch the prey. The terriers cornered them in thickets too. However the unfortunate rabbit was caught, you had to act swiftly to snatch it from the jaws of the dogs and despatch it with a chop. If the dogs tore it in any way you could not sell it to anybody. No matter what you did there would be some track of a dog's teeth on it. Such kills were known as 'dog rabbits' and fetched less in the market-place. Billy Baldwin, the Main Street game dealer, would always make you an offer. A man to bargain with, he would dock you for every visible blemish, and some invisible, the lads used to say.

From Ballyea we would circle around in a wide arc through Deerpark and Mayfield until we arrived back at the station again. Occasionally we would reverse the route. By the time we got back we would have been out for three to five hours, always on the go, but never taking our hunting too seriously. There was always time to indulge in a bit if catapult practice, a bit of gossip, a bit of horseplay, and you could rely on Doshin to crease you with his quick wit. But we had our hunting moments too, flushing out the rabbits and pursuing them through the briars and scrub, whooping and waving the ashplants or hurleys that most of us carried. Doshin never carried a stick and Foxy seldom brought one. All in all, whether you came back with a few rabbits or whether you came back empty-handed you had an exciting, entertaining and healthy – though this never occurred to us – day in the open air. And there were pleasant surprises too. Once we were strolling aimlessly across the middle of a field in Deerpark when Foxy put a finger to his lips and motioned us to halt. We knew he had spotted something and stood still. He sneaked on ahead until he came to a clump of long grass. Then he pounced like a cat and rose with a beautiful, black baby rabbit cupped in his hands. We had caught young rabbits before but never a black one, an exceptional catch in the wild. It was a lovely creature and we all admired and stroked it. Foxy took it home and kept it as a pet for a long time. Unfortunately, the day came when it suffered the fate of all pet rabbits in Botany – the dogs got to it while Foxy was out. Sometimes when pet rabbits had outgrown their small homemade hutches their Botany owners would take them out to the fields and release them into the wild with a pang, hoping that if anyone trapped them later it would not be them. Other times the rabbits made their own escape.

Being out in the country brought other benefits. You became keenly aware of the moods and colours of the seasons. You saw or heard animals and birds you would not see in town, foxes at a distance, the cry of corncrakes. Sightings of foxes would vary with the fluctuations in population of this shy and cunning creature. When figures for sightings and population peaked the predator became a real menace to poultry-owners in the district, which paid a bounty for each fox killed. But it was not necessarily the number of foxes that led to more raids on chicken coops. In a bad winter, when the animal's normal supply of wild game became scarce, it naturally sought food elsewhere. The devastation of the rabbit population by myxomatosis had a similar knock-on effect. The fox crept closer to the farm and, when it struck, killed not just the birds it could eat but every one it could reach.

Badgers snuffled and played in the woods. Mysterious creatures. I never saw one. But I knew a number of their sets, or what we took to be their sets – burrows much wider and deeper than those of rabbits. We would peer down into the dark mouths, hoping for a glimpse of a stripy head, prepared at the same time to run like the devil if we saw one surfacing. We had no desire to attack the badger, but it might have interpreted our curiosity as a threat. Badger-baiting went on in the district and I had heard of terriers that had been killed or maimed by the powerful jaws of the intended victim. The only dog that was equipped to take on the badger was the English bull terrier and you did not see many of those around. In Lismore I only ever knew of one, a pure-bred owned by Mick Ward of Botany who kept it as a pet. Mick was a solid, pious, and somewhat humourless man, foreman with the county council and local fire chief. When I first encountered him coming down West Street with that sinewy animal I nearly leapt out of my skin. I had never seen such an ugly-looking creature – ugly to me at any rate – at close quarters. Its skin-tight bullet of a head protruded through a thick, studded, leather collar that I hoped was strong enough to restrain it. In time, I learned to accept him as harmless – as long as he was under Mick's firm hand. Baiters were not the badger's only enemy. Farmers also paid a bounty on them sometimes, on the tenuous evidence that they were carriers of diseases like TB that could be passed on to cattle.

The otter was another shy creature that came under attack, when it was perceived that its numbers had increased to the point where too many fish were being taken from the rivers. After a lot of trying I did manage to see one of these. I happened to be standing alone on the Owenashad Bridge looking upstream of an average autumn flood when I heard a strange whistling from downstream. I listened for a while before concluding, from descriptions I had been given, that it had to be an otter's call. I crossed the bridge cautiously and peered over the parapet at the undergrowth on my immediate left from where the sound seemed to be coming. It was getting dark but I could still see clearly. Suddenly I saw a movement in the water swirling by the bank. A sleek head with bright eyes popped up and whistled again. It *was* an otter. With growing excitement I watched its head turn from side to side as if it was looking for something. It whistled once more and

The Owenashad Bridge, Lismore from upstream, April 2006.
I first glimpsed the otter in flood conditions just beyond the arch on the left.

only then did I notice that it seemed distressed. Had it lost its mate, I wondered? Or was I just misinterpreting its actions? Its call pierced the stillness yet again, lonely and searching. Perhaps it was the one that was lost? It lurked by the bank for a while, then swam across the fast-flowing current toward the other side. En route it spotted me. It glanced again to double-check, then blended into an eddy and was gone.

Ballyin Wood was where we went to see red squirrels. You spotted them in other places too but in Ballyin you were sure to come across one in the beeches if you moved quietly. Gorgeous, dashing animals, their bushy tails lent them an illusory bulk. You ran beneath them, eyes trained high, trying to keep them in vision as they skipped ahead of you. At times, in your pursuit you fell over the roots of trees that stretched unnoticed across your path. Once in my hand I held a dead squirrel that someone had wantonly shot with a .22. Slayer of small birds and animals that I was myself, it was inconceivable to me that anyone would want to shoot so exquisite a living thing.

In spring you looked for frog-spawn under the tallest beeches in Lismore beyond the Canal Bridge, or in the marshes of Ballyrafter Flats. Easily found there in muddy pools and ditches, it quivered like jelly when you touched it and stared at you with a thousand eyes, each an embryo that potentially could develop into a full-grown frog. Could. A sudden dry spell might dehydrate it.

A flood might wash it away. The frog had to lay many eggs to ensure its survival as a species. Later on you would check the same sites for tadpoles. And later on again you might catch a young frog in your hand and stroke it before letting it go. Slugs you did not stroke, especially not the large black ones that inched their way across beds of dead leaves in damp woods. They filled me with apprehension when I was little, even though I accepted they could not do me any harm. Snails, on the other hand, I liked to touch and play with. In the interstices of our stone garden walls there were lots of them, too many for Dad as they used to devour his young cabbage. We used to hold them in our small hands and chant, *Shell-a kee, shell-a-kee, boo-kal-ee, stick out your horns,* elongating the last word to two syllables that sang 'haw-rons'. As much as the slug, the tiny earwig that used to fall out of the cabbages and the big castor-oil plant that grew in our yard by the kitchen window made me apprehensive because it was commonly said that it liked to get into your ear. Of insects, butterflies attracted me as much as, or possibly more than, the dazzling dragonflies that I liked to observe along the canal, with the exception of the large white, so common it was boring and which also, in its caterpillar state, devoured our cabbage. Multicoloured emperors, red admirals, painted ladies; fawn-coloured fritillaries and common blues flitted in profusion wherever there were blooms. Most mysterious were the moths that came out at night – flimsy greys, furry whites and marbled duns – startling you in doorways or bellying up to illuminated windows. Slow-moving insects, unlike the pond-skaters that legged it over the still pools of the Owenashad.

As well as giving shelter to red squirrels Ballyin Wood was home to more unusual birdlife. You would see treecreepers shinning up the trees and occasionally hear the drumming of a woodpecker or, at least, that was what we took the sound to be. For a time I assumed that treecreepers *were* woodpeckers. Jays too liked the place. A few of us were strolling in the wood when I first encountered one there, its cry a harsh echo in the hush and not recognisable as any bird we knew. Sucky unfurled the rubber thong of the small catapult he always carried in his inside pocket, picked up a suitable pebble and placed it in the leather pouch. We indianed toward the call. The bird took off through the high branches, leaving us with a tantalising glimpse of the rich plumage of its underbelly. Sucky saved his ammunition. We puzzled over what kind of bird it was. Boxer suggested it might be a jay and later we were able to confirm this. Subsequently we got close to one or two, but never too close. The jay was too wary of man. And with good reason. About that time, probably when I was 13 or 14, I had picked up the most environmentally destructive hobbies of my life – shooting birds with catapults and pellet guns, and collecting birds' eggs.

The first was totally home-inspired, the second a Victorian idea I had picked up from the English comics. In our world there seemed to be a limitless supply of wildlife, so what harm could there be in hunting a few birds? Or in carefully lifting one speckled egg from the five in a blackbird's nest, or one tiny fragile pearl from the sixteen or so in the wren's mossy hive? You were told that you should approach the nest early in the breeding season so that the embryos would not have formed in the eggs; if they did, you could not blow the contents out through the pinhead-sized hole that you made in the egg end – you made one in the other end as well through which to blow. It was also stressed that you should never take more than one egg and, that when you did take the one, you should on no account allow your fingers to touch the other eggs, or the internal parts of the nest. Not an easy operation where the wren was concerned. It was said that if the mother bird sensed a whiff of human presence in the nest it would abandon it and leave the eggs to rot. This code I strictly followed with songbirds. With crows – regarded as pests by farmers – I was less scrupulous. And with hawks, which preyed on songbirds and baby rabbits, I was unscrupulous – on the one occasion I contrived access to one of these predators' cunningly sited eyries. Under the term 'hawk' we grouped for want of the exact terminology the kestrel, the falcon and the sparrowhawk. The nest I robbed was, I think, a kestrel's.

Every year a pair of birds used to nest in a hole in the stonework of the first supporting column facing west above the main abutment of Lismore Bridge. Leaning over the parapet and looking down, you would see the 'hawks' winging in and out of this in the spring. I grew determined to add one of their eggs to my growing collection. But how to go about it? The wall was sheer and there were very few grips or holds to be seen, at least as far as an inexperienced teenager could make out. The easiest solution would have been to lower oneself down the ten feet or so from the parapet and reach into the nest, but without mountaineering know-how this was clearly an impossibility. I then reconnoitered from below. That approach appeared no less daunting. It was easy enough to clamber up the ten feet onto the grass-covered salient that supported the column. The problem was to climb the masonry that led up to the nest from there, a height of some sixteen or seventeen feet. I sought holds in the stonework but could get no further than a few feet without slipping back again. It quickly became apparent that only a ladder could get me up there. Not that that was a perfect solution either; there was little enough space on the rough surface of the salient to lean a ladder safely against the wall. So now I had to borrow a ladder? But from where? Paddy Creane had also taken up egg-collecting so I put my plan to him. He was enthusiastic and knew from whom he could procure a ladder, old Georgie O'Brien, the carpenter and joiner who lived across the street from the Manse. Against his better judgement Georgie kindly let us have his longest, a ten- or twelve-foot job. In the quiet of the early evening we shouldered it down the North Mall, down the Deanery Hill, down Ferry Lane, across the bridge and in over the high wall and onto the Ferry Inch at the corner of the Ballyduff Road. Getting onto the salient was no problem; pulling the heavy wooden ladder up behind us was more difficult; righting the ladder against the stonework of the column, tricky. But we managed it all. I knew the ladder would not be long enough to get me right up to the nest. At best I would have to balance on the second or third rung from the top, a somewhat precarious position. So I had brought with me a few six-inch nails to use as crude pitons and a hammer to drive them home, the means with which I hoped to steady my final approach to the nest.

To my dismay when I mounted the ladder, I found that I was still a couple of feet short of my requirements. Adding to my discomfort was the 'hawk', which had taken fright and was circling menacingly above me. I gazed down the length of the ladder at Paddy who was holding it steady at the bottom. If I slipped off it I was a goner because I would be thrown back over the point of the salient onto the cement below. I was scared but I wanted that egg so badly I overcame my fright. I climbed down. We moved the base of the ladder as close as we dared to the wall in order to gain a precious few extra inches at the top. Paddy looked dubiously at the almost vertical stand of it. But he could see that I was determined to have another go. He handed me the hammer and nails and gripped the rungs tightly. I took a deep breath and ascended. At the top I reached up and after some false starts managed to drive two nails into cracks in the masonry above me. Then I threw down the hammer and inched myself up onto the top rung of the ladder, using the nails as holds. I could go no higher, but the top of my head was now just below the hole with the nest. Holding onto one of the nails with my right hand, and with my cheek flat against the wall, I reached up toward the lip of the hole with my left. I managed to get my fingers in a few inches. But all I felt was stone. No twigs and definitely no eggs. I sensed the hole was much deeper but I could not reach in any farther. Sweating, I descended. The hawk was still circling above the bridge, shrieking angrily. We now had to worry that its behaviour might attract some elders of the town, or the guards. If anyone looked over the parapet and saw what we were doing they would order us off the salient at once, not so much because we were worrying the hawk but because we might break our necks. We had to work fast if we were to finish what we started.

'The hole goes in farther than I thought,' I said to Paddy.

'You're on the top rung already. You can't go any higher,' Paddy said with resignation.

'Can we move the base just a little bit closer to the wall?'

Paddy gestured. 'We can't come any closer than that. The ladder would topple over.'

'I'm almost there!' I said, frustrated.

'Let me have a go.'

'Okay, but I'm taller than you.'

Paddy shinned up to see for himself.

'You haven't much to hang onto,' he said calmly when he came down. 'We can't go any higher, that's for sure.'

I looked around. 'If I had something I could reach in with, I might be able to hook out the nest.'

There was a sycamore growing on the riverside of the salient. I reached up and broke off a branch from which I fashioned a foot-long baton with a crook at one end. Then I climbed up the ladder again. This time I reached my target. I hooked out two eggs to begin with but, in doing so, punched a hole in one. I descended with those then went up again. The second time I got two more but damaged one beyond redemption. When I put my feet on the ground for the last time my hands were shaking. I had never done anything so scary in my life before. But I felt elated. Paddy sat next to me and we examined our booty. The eggs were about the size of a pigeon's, creamy-white and speckled reddish-brown. And we had a good one each. No one else had a hawk's egg for sure.

When I got home there was a further moment of tension. Might this egg contain an embryo? I made a hole in each end of my good egg with a pin and succeeded in carefully blowing out the contents. I then discarded the damaged one that I had held onto as a fall-back. My collection I kept in a long wooden box that I had painted brown and half filled with sawdust. It had a flap lid that I could raise when I wanted to admire the eggs. Twenty eggs would settle comfortably on the sawdust. I had perhaps a dozen. The two eggs I most coveted, a crane's and a swan's, would not be able to fit into that box. They would require a special container. I was determined to secure these too, even if it seemed odd to want to have as a trophy an egg of those beautiful, elegant birds whose behaviour I so much admired. Pedro O'Brien had promised to come with me to the cranes' nests by the canal at Ballygallane Bridge and help me to get a specimen there. The nests were constructed on the very tops of the tallest beeches, the trunks of which were so long and slender I could not get a start up them on my own. As well as that, the nests were of such a density and width I did not know whether I had the skills to clamber onto one, particularly if a bird with a razor-sharp beak was in the vicinity. Pedro, I knew, had already climbed these trees just for the challenge they presented as climbable objects. Consequently, that egg was as good as got. I never did get it though because, fortunately, I was shocked into giving up my disgusting habit before I got round to it. My disillusionment started with the realisation that my actions had driven the hawks from the nesting place they had used for years. Standing on the bridge, I missed the flap of their wings as they flew in and out of the nest. I missed their soaring lifts, and sudden swoops onto the inch – even the shrill death cries of their small prey which reached my ear.

But it was the acquisition, or non-acquisition as it turned out, of the swan's egg that really brought me to my senses. There were always swans on the Blackwater. In Lismore you saw them mostly around the Queen's Gap and Bullsod Island, but also upstream of the bridge and downstream along the Bishop's Fishery. They nested on the middle island of the Bullsod complex and on Cottage Island at the Queen's Gap, and, shielded by the sallies or osiers, along the sluice wall of the weir beyond the Grove. Getting a swan's egg off an island was a kamikaze mission I had no intention of attempting. A swan could break your arm or your neck with a beat of its wing if it caught you in the water. And that excluded what it might do to you with its powerful neck. Only one nest was vulnerable, the one on the sluice wall. I decided to set up a raid and this time asked Barney Walsh to assist me. We reconnoitered the site and came up with our plan. One of us would frighten the hen off the nest with stones, without trying to hit her, then keep her and the cock, which was never far away, away from the nest with a further barrage of missiles, giving the other the opportunity of sneaking through the willows, grabbing an egg and hotfooting it back out of the place. Working it out, it became apparent to us that one person would not be enough to keep the two swans at bay. We needed an accomplice. Tommy Hartnett, a fearless and pugnacious pal of ours from Townparks, seemed to fit the bill. We were not particularly close friends with him but he agreed to come with us. In fact, he even volunteered to be the one to snatch the egg, the most dangerous part of the operation and the task I had assumed for myself. I was the egg collector after all. There was probably a law against taking swans' eggs but, if there was, we were unaware of it. In terms of life, a swan's egg to us was essentially no different to the chicken's that sat in our egg-cup. Yet had you asked us to compare the two birds in terms of beauty we would have derided the idea of any such comparison.

We chose the moment for our raid when the cock swan was downstream near the tip of Cottage Island. Barney loosed a hail of stones around the hen to frighten her off the nest. She fled, calling distressedly. Tommy dashed into the sallies and threaded his way through to his goal. He grabbed the solitary egg, brandished it above his head, and did a jig of triumph on the nest. The cock, out of vision of the nest, realised something was happening, and shrieking and beating its wings, lifted itself high in the water and sped toward the obvious source of the trouble, Barney and me standing on the bank. We tossed some stones in front of it and it shied away. On the other side of the weir the hen was churning back toward her nest but Tommy was safely clear, protected by the dense growth of willows. Barney and I threw a few more stones at the cock, then legged it across the open field after Tommy, who had emerged ahead of us. We ran through a ditch onto the next inch and, keeping close to it, made for the wood below the Teampuileen caves. In spite of the cover the sparse hedging gave us, I was half expecting the big swan to come lashing down on us with its fearsome wings. Instead, it pursued us with relentless shrieks and cries. The anguish in them shocked me but I did not immediately realise that I had instigated a very shameful act. Safe in the shelter of the trees I would still be happy to accept the egg which my pal was about to hand over to me. But when we halted, breathless, Tommy was in an exhilarated state and in no mood to part with the prize. He was the one who had performed the most dangerous part of the operation so why wasn't he entitled to keep it?

'But you don't collect eggs!' I protested.

'Yeh, but, I'd like to hang onto it, I mean, for a little while,' he said inexplicably, and stroked it covetously with his hand.

'That's not fair, Tommy,' said Barney, 'You promised to give it to Jim. After all, he was going to go in for it himself. So hand it over.'

'I won't!'

And with that, before Barney and I realised his intention, he hared off through the woods clutching the egg to his chest like a rugby ball. We recovered our wits and took up the chase but, with the jump he had on us, he eluded us. I was downcast. After organising the successful raid I did not even get to touch the egg. And the feeling that I had wronged two of Creation's most beautiful creatures was beginning to incubate in me. But I was angry too. Tommy had taken me for a ride.

'We'll get 'im.' Barney assured me, 'The double-crosser!'

That evening around seven o'clock the two of us met up with Foxy Flynn, who had a score of his own to settle with our runaway pal, at Con O'Neill's corner and from there we set off around town to find Tommy, with or without the egg, and give him a hiding. We were to do it fairly, not jumping him as a trio but letting him take us on one by one. Tommy was as tough as teak and could probably have handled the three of us together but our code demanded that we give him an even break, even if we were making it tough on ourselves. Not that we expected him to win. On the contrary, our plan was for Foxy and me to get our lashes in first, so softening him up for Barney, the best of us with his mitts, who would then administer the real hiding. The town seemed unusually quiet as we traversed it and there was an air of menace about. A feeling that Tommy, in anticipation of our move, might erupt on us out of a dark corner in a counter-attack, perhaps even with a scratch gang of his own. We kept our eyes skinned and spoke little, and when in mutters. An hour went by during which we scoured Townparks, Chapel Street, Botany, Main Street and Church Lane unsuccessfully. Half an hour later after a second pass around Townparks that included a taunt and a prolonged pause outside his house we still had not flushed him out. By then I had something else to worry about. I was staying out later than I was supposed to. Unlike the Botany lads whose parents took a more liberal line about kids staying out late, I was subjected to the respectable curfew of the Main Street, a disadvantage that always made me envious of my pals from around the corner. If I did not get home soon Mam or Dad, or both, would give me a sound scolding. Clearly, if we were to find Tommy now I would definitely have to be the first to tackle him. Another half-hour brought us no nearer our quarry. We split up in Chapel Street where our search had begun, the lads saying that they intended to carry on the hunt.

'Well give 'im a couple from me if ye find him,' I said shamefacedly, hoping that they would not think I was chickening out.

'We will,' they swore and headed off in the direction of Townparks yet again.

But Tommy had gone to ground. They never found him that night and by the following one our tempers had cooled. I often wondered if the fugitive even realised we were on his trail. He was not one to shirk a fight.

'Fuck 'im!' we decided and abandoned all thoughts of revenge.

I was sour about the swan's egg for another while but then lost interest in my hobby. Eventually, before I left Lismore, I passed the small collection that I had retained to the young Bishop Scanlon.

I never looked at the Queen's Gap swans, nor any other swans, again without a deep sense of shame. Tommy and I, accidentally or otherwise, seemed to avoid each other thereafter, robbing me of the chance to enquire what he had done with the egg. Soon he emigrated to England. Who knows, maybe he felt ashamed of the episode too and returned the egg to the nest? He would have had the courage to do such a thing.

Egg collecting had developed out of bird-nesting, an altogether more benign and more educational interest. Observation taught you where the different kinds of birds liked to nest, for example, blackbirds and thrushes in hawthorns, elders and holly; wrens and robins in dense beech and holly hedges, which grew in profusion along the Green Road; finches in field hedges; pigeons in beeches. Amid the rushes and tangled grass of Ballyrafter Flats a snipe's nest might be pinpointed, a find that excited you as snipes never flew straight off the nest when you startled them but ran along the ground for a distance before taking wing. Aloft they traced a zig-zag pattern which left you further confused. Waterhens nested on branches that overhung the canal or the Blackwater around Bullsod. Water-rats and unexpected flooding were their enemies. Sandmartins returned year after year to the sandpit above Johnny McGrath's. You learned to recognise the different kinds of nests – the mud and spittle-lined bowls of the blackbird and thrush; the smaller, looser bowl of the finch; the moss-ball of the wren; the pigeon's plate of twigs; the impenetrable, thorny football of the magpie. When you found a nest you kept it to yourself, or only told your closest pal or pals. Too many boys disturbing the area about the nest could cause the bird to desert it. Having found a nest, it was customary to return to it from time to time to observe the progress of the life inside it. A discreet glance to check that the hen was still sitting on the eggs; an ear to the cries of chicks; the fascination of the tiny gaping beaks, ravenous for food.

Bird-nesting could have been totally harmless but for the activities of some amongst us. It was not uncommon to come across a nest, new or known, and discover that all the nestlings in it had had their throats cut with a razor-blade. Most of us deplored this sadistic practice which offended against an unwritten and unstated code of honour that prevailed amongst us and, if we ever caught anyone in the act of doing it, told him in no uncertain terms what we thought of him. I myself never came upon anyone in the act but I did come close enough to have strong suspicions. When someone was caught strong arguments or even fist-fights ensued. Possession of a razor-blade was no evidence in itself. Most of us carried these as we carried penknives – for topping pencils, cutting paper, slicing and trimming the peashooters that we made from the stalks of hogweed, and so on. One edge of the twin-edged blade was usually slotted into a metal clip for protection. We carried them in card pouches, sometimes carelessly. It was not unusual for one of us to put a hand in a pocket and withdraw it abruptly, a finger dripping blood. For school we carried them more securely in our wooden pencil-cases. We asked ourselves why some boys were so cruel to innocent nestlings but never came up with an answer. It was hardly credible that they found pleasure in it. Possibly they found justification for it in the constant demands of farmers for the control of pests? That was certainly my excuse for slaughtering crows. Catapulting full-grown, or even young, crows counted as hunting. I did not see the cruelty in that. We went for a quick kill, as we did when fishing. The pleasure was in an efficient strike.

In late spring when the young birds were taking wing it was easy to bring them down. Our favourite killing ground was out the Convent Road. In a field across from Sullivan's farmhouse where a line of Scots pines fringed the road, there was a rookery where the young birds learning to fly made easy targets. We called them crows though they might have been rooks, choughs, or even jackdaws, for all we knew. (They were, in fact, rooks.) We were vague on species. It was easy to recognise the distinctive scald-crow, but we would have been amazed had we been informed that the colourful jay too belonged to the crow family. Sucky, Doshin, Boxer and I did the farmers a further service on the Castle Farm across from the Christian Brothers School where the crows nested in the thick, parasitic growth of the elms that stood in the middle of a field. It was here that I obtained a crow's egg for my collection, far less scrupulously than when I was collecting those of other birds. With our catapults we were merciless. Yet I never disliked crows. On the contrary, I loved the dry echo of their calls.

Starlings were the birds I really did not like. In my eyes they were peevish, crotchety scavengers. In winter, Barney and I used to lie in wait for them with a pellet gun at the Castle Farm chicken run across from Feeney's on the Green Road. The birds used to descend on the muddy ground in clouds to share as best they could in the feed scattered for the poultry. Barney and I would be squashed inside one of the small hen-houses, or sometimes we would occupy a hut each. It was not easy to pick off the starlings when they were on the ground on account of the low velocity of the pellet. You also had to contend with their busy motion. They seemed not to notice the report of the gun, only the phut of the pellet zinging into the mud near them that caused a mass exodus temporarily. Unaware of us, they were soon back. They returned more warily but, ironically, this presented us with our best chance of a hit because they alighted first on the wooden fences and rusty iron railings around the run where they made better targets. The gun being his, Barney did most of the shooting. I had a go from time to time. Later I acquired my own shooting piece, a Webley .22 pellet pistol, a useful target gun but of little efficacy for starlings. With smaller birds there was always a chance that a lucky shot would bring one down. The first starling we bagged was a revelation. The dark, scraggy-looking bird we knew at a distance displayed in our hands a subtly coloured, iridescent plumage.

Bird lime, a sticky, yellowish substance, was used by the lads who wanted to trap songbirds, particularly goldfinches, alive. I noticed it on branches sometimes but never wanted anything to do with it myself, picturing it gluing the wings of its unfortunate victims. A twig cage, an idea we had from the comics, was a kinder alternative. You criss-crossed a number of twigs into a hive-like frame, narrow at the top, wide – perhaps twelve to fifteen inches – at the bottom, and tied them firmly together. To set the trap you propped up one edge on a forked stick to which you had attached a long length of brown cord, scattered bread crumbs on the ground beneath the cage, and lay doggo behind a convenient bush to await a bird which was sucker enough to go for the food. A tug on the cord and you had your prey. Fine in theory but you needed a lot more patience than I had to catch something. Some of the Botany lads trapped goldfinches in this way and kept them in home-made twig cages as singing pets. I never liked to see birds in cages and tried to restrain myself from shooting goldfinches and bullfinches – I loved the singing of the one and the plumage of the other. It was not a difficult decision – they did not make easy targets. Even more difficult, well-nigh impossible, was it to bring down a swallow, swift or martin, birds for which I reserved a special affection. You had to admire their effortless elegance. I loosed the odd stone at them in the forlorn hope of winging one and examining it at close quarters. By chance I did get to touch a swift one day. Mike Feeney next door called his brother Tom and me over and showed us a sleek young bird clutched in the palm of his hand that had grounded in Kelly's Field and was unable to take off again because of the width of its wingspan. Having let us inspect its plumage, Mike tossed it up into the air and away it flew. Beauty *was* a deterrent. We did not shoot at the elegant little goldcrest, the tiniest of all our birds. We did not shoot at the kingfisher whose vivid blue and gold we glimpsed where the cliffs of the Warren and Grove met the Blackwater. They skimmed in pairs, unlike the lone cormorant you would see bobbing up and down in the current below the Queen's Gap. (An incidental point, this place on the river was known officially as the King's Gap but local usage, probably due to our Victorian past or possibly to a survival from the time of Elizabeth I, preferred the feminine form.) I seldom shot at the treecreeper either. The fascination there lay not in its beauty – its plumage is rather drab – but in the manner in which it used to dart jerkily around tree-trunks. It wasn't an easy target. The first cuckoo of the year was pleasing to hear but much more pleasing to me was another elusive bird that tantalised our ears, the corncrake. Though I strained to catch a glimpse of the creature itself, I was content to hear its crake which was as consistent and reassuring as the song of the lark at Clonea Strand. Rarely flushed from the middle of a grain field, the bird momentarily unveiled a dash of red and brown before quickly diving for cover again. Like the snipe, it was adept at throwing intruders off its track. I never located a nest although I sought one often enough in Mayfield and Deerpark, areas I particularly associated with it. This was too well concealed in the high corn which you wouldn't have wanted a farmer to catch you treading underfoot. But the advent of summer was announced not with a crake but with a squeak, that of the swallow, which every year took you by surprise. One minute it was not there; the next, there it was scything the skies. A day or two later a pair would return to nest under the eaves at the back of either McCarthy's or our house. Summer had really come. Down by the Owenashad the willy wagtail – our name for the pied wagtail – would confirm it, dancing from rock to craggy rock, stone to polished stone. Along this tributary too, in the middle reaches up the Mountain Road, you caught sight of the stubby dipper flashing its white breast as it hopped non-stop and dunked itself in the fast-flowing waters. This was the only place around Lismore where I remember seeing this busy little bird. When I first laid eyes on it I thought it was a semi-albino blackbird – you saw the odd one of this species flecked or banded with white.

In the eaves of our house a different flying creature, the bat, would have emerged from hibernation. When I was little I was nervous of bats but I liked them more than I feared them. There was something mysterious about the light flutter of their wings, their piping squeak, and the way they came out at dusk. Mam and Molly actively disliked and, perhaps, feared them because they had heard that bats could get entangled in a woman's long hair. On the other hand, Mam had no fear of its earthbound cousin, the mouse, while Molly was just as jumpy when this mammal was out and about too. Bats were common around Lismore. Coming home late from a picnic on the slopes about the sandpit we would encounter them all along the way back to the bridge. Amid the trees above the ice house they seemed to swoop so close you imagined you saw the flash of an eye. But they never touched you.

We had a curious attitude to wildlife. We could love and delight in the profusion of creatures around us and we could kill them without compunction. Possibly it was the very profusion that encouraged us in our double standards. Ultimately, a natural respect for living things put limits of its own on our attitude. In my own case, a slowly evolving concern culminated in a single incident that made me hang up my catapult. It happened in late autumn on the Green Road, past Greenmount, the red-tiled house opposite the Broghill Tower of the castle. Among the laurels and rhododendrons that lined a gravel footpath that led to the Grove there were two fine common yews on the soft red berries of which the big mistle thrushes, or stone thrushes as we called them, annually came to feed. Looming above these were tall, slender beeches. I was accompanied by Hoagy and Tom Feeney. For arms we carried a pellet gun and a couple of catapults. I was packing a particularly lethal form of ammunition for my slingshot, marble-sized balls of lead that I had hammered into shape out of a length of old piping. Our first shots missed and the birds took flight. One of them settled on a topmost branch of a beech. She was exposed but it looked an impossible shot. I fitted a piece of lead into the leather thong and aimed speculatively. The projectile sped on its way. A burst of feathers indicated that I had scored a hit against the odds. The bird spun off its perch but instead of falling away from me, as one might have expected, it opened its wings and swooped elegantly down towards me with ever-increasing speed until it hit the ground almost at my feet. The exhilaration of having aimed successfully gave way to apprehension when I saw the beautiful bird spreadeagled on its breast. The way it had flown suggested that I had merely nicked it and that it should still be alive. I knelt and touched the warm body. The neck flopped loosely. I turned the bird over. It was dead. I was horrified. It seemed as if the creature had deliberately thrown itself before me in accusation of what I had done. Tom and Hoagy noticed my dismay and muted their enthusiasm for my brilliant feat of markmanship. I dug a hole in the soft earth beneath the shrubbery with the heel of my boot and, after admiring the downy, spotted breast for the last time, buried the victim without ceremony. The incident, which should have been a triumph, threw a damper on the hunt. Half-heartedly we loosed off another couple of shots then gave up and went home. I never shot at birds again.

It was not so easy to hang up my catapult entirely. For targets I then turned to inanimate objects, specifically the white, porcelain insulators – 'cups' as we called them – on the crosspieces of electricity poles. These had always been fair game to us anyway but now I was able to give them my full attention. In this endeavour I was a fair shot but I could never match Sucky. Nor could anyone else. He was the acknowledged ace amongst us. The trick was to hit the lower half of the cup. Then you were rewarded with a satisfying, bell-like crack and saw a good-sized chip, or couple of chips, split off. If you hit the cup on the solid, rounded top your stone would only bounce off it. A hit, yet not a hit. Boxer got a kick out of the cups too and would laugh and do a little dance when he really knocked the stuffing out of one. Between the three of us we cracked a fair number of them in the area. Smashing them beyond the town and its environs, especially in Cappoquin where we often went to the pictures or to GAA matches, brought an added satisfaction. According to Boxer, and we had no reason to doubt the authority with which he expressed it, the cost of the broken cups was passed on in the rates of the affected street or townland by the

Electricity Supply Board. As a consequence, though we had little or no understanding of rates, we avoided shooting in our own streets.

'Cappoquin can pay for that one!' Boxer would chortle after an appropriate hit.

'Deerpark can pay for that one,' Sucky would grin.

'Chapel Street can pay for that one,' Doshin, who didn't carry a catapult himself but came along for the fun, might wink.

The CIE also unwittingly contributed toward our sharpshooting activities. Through uncles, fathers, brothers or cousins who worked for the railway some of the lads were able to get their hands on detonators, a supply of which was kept by signalmen for emergencies. If there was a power failure or heavy fog, for example, and the signalman wanted to halt a train he would place a detonator, or two or three, on the track before the oncoming locomotive so that when the driver heard them go off he would immediately pull up. The detonator was about two inches in diameter, half an inch thick, and had a strip of lead attached for affixing it to the track. In the centre of the usually black-painted object there was a pin of perhaps a quarter of an inch in diameter and it was this that sparked the detonation. We used to wedge the detonator in a cleft of rock and shoot at it in an effort to explode it. You had to stand fairly well back as detonators, though not inherently dangerous, could fly off in unexpected directions when set off in this manner. They were solid objects and we rarely managed to explode them with our catapults. The effective methods were to throw heavy stones at them or, drop rocks on them from a height which quickly produced the desired effect of creating a loud bang. Yes, it was always a cause of excitement when one of the Botany lads reached into his pocket and produced this mini-bomb.

We were now experts at making catapults and favoured the small stripped ash fork that nestled lightly in the breast pocket of our jackets. Sucky pioneered this model and he always took out and put away his with great fastidiousness. It was simply made and consisted of the usual components: the fork itself, the two strips of red or black rubber cut from an old car tube, and the tongue of an old shoe or boot, all held together by four pieces of, preferably, waxed cord. There were other models about. One of the lads had been given a shop-bought model from England, a curious wire-handled effort with black rubber strips a quarter-inch square in the cross-section. We all had a go at it and decided it was useless for our purposes. The rubber was too stretchy, which meant you lost both distance and velocity, and you could not aim properly with the thing. I myself had carved a heavy-duty model out of a piece of plank. Instead of a 'V', it had a 'U' shape in the well of which

I had centred a small tack to act as a sight. Slits cut in the arms of the 'U' formed grips for the rubber. It must have been a fairly successful model because I had fifteen notches in the butt of it, each signifying a kill – a habit I picked up from the gunfighters of the Old West – when I stopped shooting birds. The last bird I killed with it, the mistle thrush, went unnotched.

We did not fully realise how dangerous a catapult could be to humans as well. My own lesson came one day when a few of us were walking down the New Way on our way to the Rock. We encountered some of the O'Riordans and Trevor Endersen playing amid the laurel bushes and horse chestnut trees on the raised vee between Ferry Lane and the Way. Our two groups started slagging one another off for no particular reason the way boys do and, again for no particular reason, we suddenly got ratty with one another. I catapulted a couple of stones into, I thought, the tallest branches of the chestnuts to make our rivals duck for cover. Then our group laughed and went off for its swim unconcernedly. We did not like Trevor much because in our eyes his mother used to spoil him and keep him away from the likes of us, one of those unjust judgements that boys inflict on those they perceive as different to themselves. Later in the afternoon I was no sooner back home than Mrs Endersen appeared at our front door with Trevor in tow. She pointed to an angry red weal on his neck and accused me of deliberately aiming at her son with my catapult. Mam was appalled and asked me sternly whether this was true. I put it surlily, and with some insolence, that I had only fired high into the trees. A stone must have ricochetted. Both mothers now lectured me on the dangers of catapults, something I could have done without, and which only served to increase my growing sense of grievance against Trevor. At least, I did not have to be told that I could knock someone's eye out with a stone. I had never aimed head-high at any person, even amid the passions of gang warfare in the town; it was not customary amongst us to aim a shot above the legs or lower body. My truculent attitude was brought on not because I was indignant about being accused of deliberately aiming straight at Trevor but because I felt that his mother was doing all his talking for him. But I apologised. After all, it was not his fault that his mother had dragged him along, though I suspected he had run straight home and told her. On the other hand, she could hardly have failed to notice the ugly mark on his neck even if he had not pointed it out. In similar circumstances my own mother would probably have reacted in the same way. Eventually I was to outgrow my catapult. Impossible to say *when*. As one does in youth, I just moved on imperceptibly to other things.

CHAPTER FOURTEEN

Gathering

SLINGSHOTTING WAS NEVER pursued to the exclusion of other activities. Hunting small birds and animals went hand in hand with gathering in the fruits of the shrubs and trees. Gathering had a wild side – robbing orchards – and a respectable side– picking wild fruit and picking market garden produce. I became involved in all three operations. Stolen fruit was always the sweetest and robbing the most fun. As I was the son of the local *garda* sergeant, I had to be exceptionally careful not to get found out. It would have greatly embarrassed Dad were I caught in the act. And I would have felt very bad about putting him in such a spot. Not that he, or the other guards, did not know I went robbing. Or if they were not exactly sure of it they knew me well enough to have assumed it. And that went for my other pals too. Most of us went for the apples, pears, strawberries, raspberries, red- and black-currants, and gooseberries – 'goozegogs' as we called them – but tomatoes were appreciated as well. Two of our number, Foxy Flynn and Patsy Bray, had a curious appetite for raw carrots. While the rest of us were filling our pockets from the trees and shrubs they were down on the beds grubbing up the Bugs Bunny staple. I cannot say we were the most daring of robbers as, on the whole, we went for the soft options – the Presentation Convent, Dean Stanley's, Roseville, Doc Healy's, O'Riordan the bank clerk's, the Villa before the McConnells moved in. We patronised a few orchards and gardens out the country as well. The toughest nuts to crack were Arthur Paxman's at Ballyrafter and the Castle Gardens, both of which were professional and well-staffed operations. You had to be a ghost like Mikey Coleman to flit in and out of these with impunity. Lady Godfrey's and Alec Ellis's were no soft touch either. In season, these places had an almost constant watch on them. As did Roseville, the mysterious-looking ivy-shrouded grey building out the Tallow Road on the edge of town, owned by the Millses – Albert, Herbert, Frankie and their composer sister Laura.

Though well-watched, this fruit garden counted as a soft, well, fairly soft, option because the Quaker family was on in years. Albert was a fine horticulturalist and grew delicious apples, raspberries, strawberries and goozegogs, not to mention vegetables, and flowers that he grew for the English market. It was the Millses' misfortune that their garden backed onto the Hurling Field and presented a porous hawthorn hedge and leaky, barbed and net wire fencing as defence. Evenings after a game it was difficult to resist the lure of succulent fruit. Getting into the garden was easy but, the minute you were inside, nine times out of ten you would hear Laura cry out in her high, posh Anglo-Irish accent, 'Albert, the boys are in the garden!' Once you heard that you knew her brother was on his way with a stick. But you still had time because he could only move slowly. In that ten to twenty seconds you stuffed what you could into your pockets, then made for the gap you had created in the fence. In theory that was how it worked. In practice, Albert might give you the fright of your life by appearing suddenly from behind a bush where he had been lurking. It was then hide and seek in and around the fruit bushes before you got out. I was never happy about raiding the Mills family because Mam used to buy produce from them and, any time I was with her, I would be presented with an apple for nothing. So I only had a go on a couple of occasions and left it at that. It did not seem right to steal from such a nice, elderly and hardworking family, especially when, for all I knew, they depended wholly on the income they made from the garden.

Seán Dennis had first-hand experience of their generosity. Albert in one of his surprise forays had nabbed him in the act. Diving for the breach in the fence, Seán got himself entangled in the barbed wire. Instead of whacking his helpless victim with his stick the old gentleman freed him and marched him up to the house where the sister solicitously dabbed Lysol on his scratches. Then, on Seán's shamefacedly promising never to raid them again, Albert handed him a sixpence and let him out through the front door with a pocketful of apples. Needless to say, Seán never troubled them again. And when the rest of us heard the story we made similar silent promises to ourselves. Albert might have been slow on his feet but, when it came to human psychology, he was streets ahead of us. Even so, there was to be no let-up for him. The next generation of robbers would have to experience things in their own way and Laura would continue to shout, 'Albert, the boys are in the garden!'

Doc Healy's was always a pleasure to rob because there was a nice irony about fecking his best Coxes and going on to eat them in his picture-house, not to mention tossing the hearts back into the one-and-threes when the screen went momentarily black. The Deanery had a fine big garden, enclosed within high stone walls, easy enough to scale but you had to be watchful. The Stanley brothers and sisters might see you and the Dean himself was a nifty mover for his age. Once he plucked Michael Dennis off the top of the wall when Michael was all but up and away with his pockets full of goozegogs. Like the Millses, the Dean was understanding of such youthful escapades and, after giving our pal a lecture, let him go. Good gooseberries were available in most gardens but Paxman's grew the best. On one occasion Hoagy and I raided it of fat, fresh green ones and went on down the Strand and stuffed ourselves with them. Better it would have been to have waited until they were golden-yellow but the fact that they were a little sourish did not lessen our enjoyment of them one whit. We hung around the Strand most of the afternoon – I think we may have been mitching from school – during which, unknown to us, the fruit was working as a laxative. The point came when we both needed a shit. Each grabbing a handful of broad dock-leaves, the standard bog-tissue of the wild (also useful with a drop of spittle for easing the sting of nettles), we dagged behind separate bushes. My business done, I stood to pull up my pants. Idly glancing behind me to inspect my pile, I nearly jumped with fright.

'Jasus, me shit's all green!' I shouted.

'So's mine,' said Hoagy calmly, ''Tis only the goozegogs.'

I sighed with relief and peered inquisitively at my dark-green pile again, then went over to have a look at Hoagy's. Sure enough, his was the same. What had started out as a simple call of nature had ended up as a lesson in human physiology.

The convent was not as easy as might have seemed. On the plus side, the nuns could not chase you effectively in their long robes; on the minus, it was considered a rather ungallant act to rob their secluded orchard, and what we lacked in gallantry the guards made up for in keeping an eye on the place. And that could mean trouble. Compared to the nuns, the Christian Brothers' few apple trees scarcely constituted an orchard. The focus of their garden was Brother Murphy's beehives. Naturally, we were ultra-careful in this location but there were some possibilities. It was always possible to snick a few apples out over the wall at the Tallow Road side with your hurley. Mostly though, we just pocketed an odd one during school hours when we were being given a botany lesson. My skills in orchard-robbing were also exercised around Carrick-on-Suir. 'Bucking' orchards they called it in those parts and my cousin Brendan O'Mara took me with him on a couple of successful forays out by Dovehill Castle and Ballydine.

Picking whorts – our name for bilberries – and blackberries was legitimate business. Come mid-July we were out on the slopes of Scarook or Deerpark Woods harvesting the whorts that earned us one-and-three or one-and-six a pound. In late September–early October you would find us along the hedgerows, in any direction you wished to take, picking blackberries for four to sixpence a pound. The difference in price reflected the fact that much less time was required to pick a pound of blackberries than to pick the same amount of whorts, the whort, on average, being three times smaller than the bigger berry, and less juicy. The main agent for the berries in the west of the county was J. J. Budd for whom sub-agents like Billy Baldwin or Jim Ormonde or Coghlan's pub in Lismore would collect. Jim had given up his sub-agency by the time I started picking so Billy was the man with whom I dealt. There were no flies on Billy and when you brought in your berries for weighing he inspected them closely for signs of excess juice. Berries picked immediately after rain would naturally show some excess but some of us might have added a little water, occasionally of dubious provenance, to our cans to top up the poundage on the scales. But if Billy had to watch us, we also had to keep our eyes on him. His agile fingers could have your berries weighed to his advantage in a blink while he distracted you with his jovial blather. Once he had tossed your pickings into the large, purple-stained wooden tun there was no chance of a reassessment. We learned to slow him down and often argued the toss with him over the weight and quality of our produce before taking our money. In spite of, or maybe because of, the element of mutual distrust between us, I liked him and never offered my berries to anyone else. Besides, I went regularly to his vegetable shop next to Con O'Neill's pub for spuds and cabbage and, in the shooting season used to stare in wonder at the pheasants, wild duck, wild geese, wood pigeons, and the odd hare, that he had tied by the legs and hooked over high iron bars. The fruit we picked was shipped off to England daily by Budds. There was a further use for the tough little whortleberry shrub too. Stripped of its leaves and fastened to a broom handle with wire, it made an excellent besom for sweeping outhouses and yards.

Before you could pick any whorts you had the best part of a two-mile hike ahead of you out the Hospital Road to Scarook, the nearest wood where they could be found in quantity. You carried with you two, or maybe three, half-gallon sweet tins and a jam jar sized corned beef can that you had wired up with a crude handle. In one of the tins there were a couple of rounds of bread and butter, and possibly a hard-boiled egg, to see you through the day. Over your shoulder you draped an old coat to keep you dry should it rain. A few of us would head off about eight o'clock in the morning, sleepy-headed but full of chatter. Ahead of us, or behind us, on the road there would be other knots of boys and girls, all heading in the same general direction. Nearer the wood, however, we would fan out over a wide area, each group proceeding to its preferred patch, or second-choice patch if someone else was already picking at the first. The whort bushes were thick on the ground and in most years carried a good crop of fruit. To begin with, you hooked one of the sweet tins to your belt and picked straight into that, taking what seemed like an eternity to cover the bottom. When it got to about a third full it no longer felt comfortable on your belt so you exchanged it for the small corned beef can and used that as a filler for the larger tin. The obvious advantage of working in this way was that both hands remained free for picking. Speed and dexterity varied from person to person with the highest performance, of necessity, coming from the families of Botany and Church Lane. Kathleen Neville was the fastest picker I ever saw, her hands moving so fast she appeared to vacuum the berries off the bush.

For the poor, wild fruit provided a necessary seasonal income. Earnings were shared around the family, which was often a large one. For middle-class youngsters, and lower-middle-class ones like myself, it meant pocket money. It helped my parents, of course, that I earned a few bob for myself; they were able to conserve some resources they would otherwise have spent on me. I offered Mam cash from time to time but she seldom took it, and when she did, always paid me back later. The poor could not afford to snack on the fruit they were picking or, if they did, it counted as a necessary meal. Better off kids did not miss the weight of a fistful of berries. All of us, though, had the sense to know that the more we ate the less income we would receive so we disciplined ourselves. Well, almost. It was easy to be seduced into inactivity by the endless buzzing of the bees, wasps and flies, and by the sunlight that speckled the floor of the wood. And inactivity made you gaze longingly at the moist fruit glistening in your tin. Once, I confess, I was totally undisciplined. But so also were Boxer, Michael and Euge Dennis, with whom I had cycled up to the Vee to pick whorts for the first time on the slopes above the shimmering water of Baylough, beyond which the Golden Vale of Tipperary arrayed itself in an immense patchwork of fields. And, if that was not enough to distract us from our business, the sun beat down from a hazy blue sky and a delicious light breeze massaged our faces. We did start with the most serious intent and had filled about a third of a tin each when our surroundings got to us. It was a poor year for whorts generally, which was what had taken us farther afield than usual, and we had to rove over a sizable area to find berries. Remember too that we had had to cycle the best part of eight miles uphill to get to our destination. The warmth of the sun began to slow us down. Glancing across at Michael, I saw him shove a handful of berries into his mouth and suck contentedly on their sweetness. He grinned with pleasure. I ignored him at first and continued searching. When I straightened up and looked again he was taking another handful. I sat down and waited for him to take a third and, when he did, I followed suit. Euge, off to the left, was the next to succumb. We looked at Boxer who was scouring the fruitless bushes farther up the slope.

'Only a feckin' eejit,' said the wise Michael, lying back in the low shrubbery, 'would be pickin' whorts in a place like this on a day like this.'

A string of curses floated down over us before Boxer too gave up the hopeless hunt. We shared the rest of the day with the coloured butterflies that skipped over the heather, with a shepherd and his flock on the opposite slope, and with a handful of tourists that dotted the far shore of Baylough, pearling in its dark-green rhododendron setting.

One thing about picking whorts, you did not tear your hands with thorns the way you did with blackberries. The size of the blackberry was its plus. You covered the bottom of a tin in no time and with a quarter of the effort expended on bilberries filled the whole vessel. Blackberries could be picked along almost every hedgerow but my favourite site, one that Hoagy discovered, was at the bottom of a small sloping field that backed onto the Grove below Jack and Pad Feeney's place. Here briars grew in great profusion. As no one else seemed to know of the place, the fruit had time to mature into big, black, juicy berries, sweet enough to tempt me into eating them. Until then an earlier experience had put me off blackberries. I had been about to pop a handful into my mouth when I noticed a couple of white maggots on them. That handful went to England to make blackberry jam instead. Strangely enough, local housewives did not seem to make either blackberry or whortleberry jam. At least as far as I knew, women of my mother's generation eschewed this free harvest. No doubt, some of the local English or Anglo-Irish had the good sense to make proper use of it. Mam did, however, encourage us to eat whorts and blackberries with milk or cream.

The most galling thing that could happen to you when berry-picking was to fall over your tired feet on the way home and tip the contents of your tins onto the ground. When this happened in the wood you had a good chance of retrieving nearly all the fruit. On a dirt track like the Hospital Road you could lose half your crop because it was impossible to clean the grit off the berries on the bottom of the pile. A loss of one pound weight of whorts represented, for me at any rate, not less than half an hour's, and maybe an hour's, endeavour. So you learned to tread very gingerly when your tins were full. The two crops of berries were important to the economy of the town, especially in a good year. A potentially good year could be vitiated if the woods caught fire in a dry spell. On the happily infrequent occasions when this occurred large areas of the whortleberry crop were destroyed, not to mention full-grown trees and young plantation. Bad weather meant a reduced crop of both berries or, at least, a delay in ripening.

The firm of Budds also offered cash for sloes but I never saw anyone harvesting these. The blackthorn was common enough but fruit-bearing trees less so. Long and very sharp thorns were a deterrent to sloe-picking. On the plus side was the size of the fruit, twice or thrice that of the largest whort, and its habit of growing in bunches. What Budds paid for it per pound I cannot even guess but, given the comparative rarity of the crop and the consequent distances you had to cover to fill a sackful, it must have attracted a higher price than the whort. Dad loved to suck on sloes and whenever we went on autumn walks out the Tallow Road he would always pluck a few off the blackthorn that grew by the side of the railway bridge. I tried them a couple of times but they left me gasping, their dry bitterness draining my mouth of moisture. Dad generally liked edibles on the bitter or sour side – sloes, crab apples, the fresh green leaves of beeches, buttermilk. The elderberry was another fruit that no one seemed to gather, even though it was available in profusion.

Bob Nolan, who was married to Dodo O'Donnell of the Main Street, started an imaginative venture in the town in 1950, a fruit farm located on the left just beyond the railway bridge on the Ballyanchor Road. His idea was to supply fresh fruit daily to the Dublin market, 135 miles from Lismore, not an entirely risk-free enterprise in an era of poor road transport facilities. The emphasis was on strawberries and raspberries but red- and black-currants were grown as well. One of my schoolmates, Kip Tobin of Botany, became a summer foreman on the farm. I picked fruit there over two summers, after which I tried my hand at thinning beet, a much tougher proposition but one that was also better paid. At the height of the picking season Bob, a tall handsome man with curly black hair and a ready grin, might have up to a hundred of us youngsters, boys and girls, working on different rows of fruit. He did not mind if he caught you popping a berry or two into your mouth, seeing, with good sense, that he could not hope to keep an eye on a hundred kids all day and that we would soon get sick of the taste of the fruit. On our part we saw, as with the wild fruit we gathered, that the more we ate the less went into our baskets and the less we earned. We were paid per basket picked.

The alternative to eating fruit during work was to slip some of it out with you at the end of the day. We wore any kind of loose headgear we could confect, or lay our hands on, to keep the sun off the back of our necks while we worked. I wore an old brown hat of Dad's with a handkerchief stuck under the back, French Foreign Legion style. And, when the mood was on me, a half-pound of choice strawberries walked off under the crown. I looked on it as a sort of bonus for the hours I put in. In our eyes the pay we received was not over-generous, but then we had no conception of how tight Bob's profit-margins must have been on the ten-acre site. What the job offered, beyond any consideration of money, was the opportunity for us boys to enjoy working alongside the girls, and for the girls, maybe, the chance to enjoy working alongside us. Our thoughts were more on the opposite sex than on fruit picking and a fair share of snatched and experimental hugging and kissing went on amidst the greenery over the lunchtime break, and rendezvous were set up for the evening.

To inhibit such activities a certain amount of segregation was practised in the rows, although this may have had as much to do with comparative picking skills as with Bob's concern to keep the clergy happy by removing us from occasions of sin. Not that Bob himself would have given a damn about how we behaved as long as we brought in the harvest. When he chanced upon any of us in what to our innocent eyes was a compromising situation he would just laugh and roar in one breath, 'Back to work, ye lazy sods. Jasus, what am I payin' ye for?' Then he would stride off, grinning, up the row. Basically, the boys worked on the raspberries while the girls were given the strawberries and currants, but if any particular fruit was in danger of over-ripening a task force of both sexes would be put on that. Lunchtime was unpoliced. What we got up to then was our affair. My own preferred way of spending it was to lie on the straw between the strawberry beds, eating my sandwiches, popping the odd juicy berry into my mouth, blackguarding with my pals, male and female, and soaking up the sun when it was shining. When the hour ended at 2.00 p.m. we still had four hours' work ahead of us. Starting at 8.00 a.m., that made for a long day and we were pretty tired at the end of it. Heavy rain followed the next day by hot sun meant extra effort, sometimes Sunday work for which we were paid overtime. Those must have been tense days for Bob, wondering whether he would get the over-ripening fruit picked before it dropped off the plants. What could not be saved for the market would be tipped into wooden tuns and sent for jam-making.

Orchard robbers were his other worry. In a town with a long tradition of robbing he could not leave the farm unguarded outside working hours. A caravan was placed on the site and in it another O'Donnell spouse, Brendan

Hehir, a tight-lipped and humourless civil servant from Dublin, the antithesis of Bob in personality and manner, spent his summer holiday nights riding shotgun. But Bob kept an eye on the place too, as did Kip on his behalf. My schoolmate was a more than faithful foreman and gave me a smart lesson in economics one pay day. The system was that we formed a queue outside the caravan. Bob sat inside with the money and the book that recorded our week's work. Kip stood at the door and called us up one by one and handed us our wages, in cash of course. This time I was near the end of the queue and was looking at the silver coins in my hand with a stupefaction that was immediately apparent to Kip. I knew that I had worked long and hard that week but did not realise I had earned so much.

'Is it okay, Jim?' he asked solicitously and flicked a lock of lank, fair hair off his wide forehead with a sideward toss of his head.

'Yeh,' I said, pleased and innocent, 'I didn't think I'd earned all that.'

'Hang on.' Quick as a flash he took the money out of my hand. 'I'll check it with Bob again.' He went inside the caravan and, with as little time as it took to do an about turn, came back out again and returned to me the cash, minus five bob. 'There *was* a mistake. Sorry,' he apologised.

'Oh? Sure,' I said, bemused by the speed at which my unexpected income had been reduced.

'You can check it with Bob if you like.'

'No, no. 'Tis okay.'

No sooner was I out of the gate than it dawned on me that I had been suckered, either by Kip or Bob, or both. Rightly or wrongly, it was my pal I suspected, on the evidence of the speed with which he had been in and out of the caravan. When I told Sucky and Boxer about the incident later in the evening they laughed and said I was a feckin' eejit. Which was true. I should have taken my money and run. The chances were, I had earned the original amount, and maybe more. On the other hand, I had to admire the quick-wittedness with which Kip had reacted. If I was stupid enough to undervalue my labour why should he worry? It was a lesson for the future.

Sadly for Bob, the fruit farm failed not long after I left Lismore in 1954. Probably he was just too far from his market and when market-gardening developed in the County Dublin region the economics of the business must have been against him – a bitter blow after pouring so much effort into a project that he had made a success of for a time. Indeed, things were looking so rosy at one stage that he was talking of establishing a jam-making factory, which the area could well have done with, in the town. Tourism – we were on the scenic route for CIE bus tours – and fishing were the only industries in Lismore, aside from the Castle, of course. We envied our

'The penitential drills.' A 1950s rural scene.

Thinning the bittersweet beet outside Waterford City in the 1950s. The girl is steering the pony that is pulling a drill cleaner guided by the man behind.

neighbours in Cappoquin who had a thriving bacon factory in which, happily, a few Lismore people found employment. The Lismore town commissioners were tireless in their efforts to attract industry, any industry, to the town but, for one reason or another, these always came to nothing. An Industrial Development Authority they set up was, at various times, promised economic shots in the arm as diverse as a grass-meal factory – there had been particularly high hopes of this – a creamery, a braid-making factory and a bicycle factory. But all the projects foundered, I suspect, on our geographical location. We were just tucked away in too quiet a corner in the quiet west of the county. Waterford City and Dungarvan held all the infrastructural cards. Eventually, a consolation prize came the town's way, the Knockmeal Co-operative Society that ran a fine store in the Main Street from which you could buy anything from a pound of sugar to a tractor. In terms of employment, however, this was wholly inadequate for the needs of the town.

From fruit-picking I moved to thinning sugar beet, back-breaking work if ever there was back-breaking work - the kind of forced labour that might have been foisted on our unfortunate forefathers who were deported to the real Botany. And here I was doing it willingly. Michael and Euge Dennis, both younger than I, were my initiators into the skills of this toil.

'Now leave the haggling to us,' I was told as we approached the late Eugene O'Donnell's farm at the foot of Deerpark Wood before eight o'clock on a dull June morning. I did not feel at all insulted at being ordered to keep my mouth shut by my juniors as I knew they had experience of thinning and would strike the best possible deal. The farm was owned now by Eugene's widow whose three sons worked it for her. The sons were tall powerful men but Mrs O'Donnell, a stout, earthy woman with a round face, was undoubtedly the boss. The eldest son took us over a rise to the field of beet that sloped away in the direction of Lismore. He stopped at the headland.

'Well?' he said, keeping to himself his own idea of what he might be willing to pay per drill thinned.

'How long are they?' asked Michael.

''Bout a hundred yards,' the son supposed.

'Aren't you sure?' Euge laughed and Michael with him.

The son laughed too.

I was so fascinated by the exchange that was developing I only mustered a grin.

The son threw me a glance that suggested he was sizing me up for my capability of undertaking such graft, or maybe it was only for a sense of humour.

'We'd better see then, hadn't we?' said Michael and off he paced down the dip along a row of fresh green shoots.

O'Donnell followed after him along the next row doing his own count. Euge and I rambled along in their wake. I was still remembering the farmyard we had just come through, with its rusty machinery scattered about and the couple of sheepdogs that had loped lazily towards us as we approached up the lane pushing our bikes. I was also a little apprehensive that I might not measure up to the demands of the new line of work. Dad, a farmer's son himself, had warned me to be prepared for a hard week.

'Yeah, about a hundred,' Michael said when he reached the end of the drill, 'give or take a yard or two.'

'That's right,' agreed the son. 'But some of 'em are shorter than others.' He pointed to his left.

'An' some of 'em are longer than others,' Euge put in, pointing in the other direction.

'Good lad, Euge,' I thought, 'you're not lettin' him get away with anything.'

'Well, I'd say about one-an'-six a drill,' Michael offered.

'One-an'-six!' exclaimed O'Donnell.

'We'll do a top-class job for you,' said Michael. 'We're all experienced thinners.'

I put on a deadpan expression and stuck my hands deep into my pockets in case the farmer would notice how soft and white they were. It did not occur to my townie mind that he might have read the signs already.

'I don't doubt that, lads, But I can get *men* who'll do 'em for a bob.'

'A bob!' Michael and Euge snorted derisively.

'We'll throw in a bit o' dinner as well.'

'A bob is still too low.'

And so it went until they settled on one-and-threepence, which O'Donnell knew was the going rate that he would have to pay for drills of that length and which Michael and Euge knew was the top rate that boys could expect.

Michael, the youngest of us, signalled the end of the matter by saying grudgingly, 'Well, I suppose we may as well take the one-an'-three, seein' as we've spent half the mornin' comin' out here.'

'Fine, lads. I'll leave ye to it,' said the son and went off up the field about his other business.

I breathed a sigh of relief. I had had visions of him standing over us before the lads would have had a chance to show me the ropes.

'Is the price all right?' I asked.

''Tis okay,' Euge nodded, 'with the bit o' dinner thrown in.'

'We wouldn't have got more out of him,' Michael agreed, 'but we had to ask for more, you see? If we had asked straight out for one-an'-three he'd have stuck at a bob.'

'Ah!' I soaked up a further lesson about market forces.

We threw our old canvas sacks, essential equipment for thinning, on the ground and knelt on them. Then the lads gave me a few pointers. It was a good day for such work, cloudy and cool, but not too cool, I was told; thinning was murder under a hot sun. I was shown how to lean on the hand I would not be using as a tool, in my right-handed case, the left. Then I got a demonstration of how I should proceed to thin. You worked with the heel of your bare hand, scooping out from the slight ridge of six-inch seedlings the plants that were superfluous, leaving behind every seven inches or so a single beet to grow to fullness. The earth was hard and stony and I was warned that my working hand would become torn and sore for the first few days while it was toughening up. The wrist of the other arm would swell and the shoulder muscles grow stiff over the same period from supporting the weight of my upper body. After that it was time to go to work. I spat on my hands and looked up the long drill. From my vantage point on my knees it curved out of sight over the incline. A hundred yards? It seemed more like a half-mile, the way a hundred yards of water did when you were swimming.

By lunchtime I had thinned about two-and-a-half drills, not too bad the lads, who had started their fourth, reckoned. The son had returned after an hour to check that our work was satisfactory. I was glad when he okayed the standard of mine. The fact that I was slower did not seem to worry him. Mrs O'Donnell fed us spuds and tossed slices of fat from home-cured bacon onto our plates like she was feeding a clowder of cats.

'Did ye hear the bibe last night?' she asked quietly as she was snicking off another sliver with a long knife.

'The bibe?' queried Michael and we all looked at her in puzzlement. (In our ignorance we did not know that the word came from the Irish *badhbh chaointe* = banshee.)

'Don't ye know what the bibe is?' she asked, surprised.

We shook our innocent heads.

'That's what we call the banshee in these parts.'

'The banshee!' Michael, with a typically uninhibited lack of diplomacy, laughed in derision.

'Oh yes,' she said in all seriousness and not at all put out by my pal's reaction. 'It was very clear last night.'

We looked at one another and stifled grins. Was she trying to have us on? But she was not. Clearly she really seemed to believe in the existence of the bibe. A year or two earlier, when I was an avid reader of Kitty the Hare, I would probably have shared her belief but by now the banshee, like Santa Claus before her, roved only in the world of fairy tales. We might have pursued the matter with her except that another question was uppermost in our minds – when *was* she going to toss us a slice of succulent flesh instead of the fat? It was only when two of the sons came in and sat down that the knife cut into the pink. But the meat was not to be for us. Instead, she shamelessly cut off big thick slices and deposited them on the plates that she handed to the men. Then she mentioned the bibe again.

'Oh yeh, 'twas very clear last night,' the older of the two said, sticking a wedge of the delicious-looking meat for which our tongues were slavering into his gob.

'The bibe!' Michael laughed outright when we got out of range of the house after our indifferent meal, 'Jasus, I never heard that one before.'

At the end of the first day my hands could barely steer the bicycle home. Hardly surprising then that my thinning career lasted at most a couple of weeks. There had to be an easier way of making a few bob. And anyway, a fine spell of weather made it much more desirable to be down at the Rock and broke. A man whose hands and arms were inured to the work could earn a lot in the thinning season, though. Jimmy the Hawk had the reputation of being the king thinner in the area, so fast he could clear a hundred yards while the likes of me might be coping with twenty. The speed of his work was matched by quality so he was always in great demand. When I muttered to Dad how back-breaking I found the work he just laughed and said, 'You should try cutting turf sometime!' I did not need his graphic description of that toil. I had seen men at it myself out the

Mountain Road. But he was not prepared to let me off that lightly. 'That's only light turf,' he said, 'The stuff I was cutting was solid, wet, black peat. That *was* back-breaking work; the hardest I've ever done in my life.'

Ingathering the free bounty of the countryside was at its most pleasurable in going for mushrooms. Nothing could quite match the satisfaction, even the thrill, of finding a succulent white cup in a clump of mid-green grass. Except maybe finding a group of fresh ones. At times we might have a paper bag or two with us in which to place the mushrooms we intended to collect. On other occasions we just came across the fungi unprepared. In this instance, the common means of carrying them home was to pluck a strong stalk of grass (rye or couch grass or the like) with the root stock attached, then spear the mushrooms on to it from the top. Failing a root a knot might be fashioned at the base. Depending on size up to a dozen cups could be threaded on each stem.

It was not easy to predict a good year for field mushrooms. Even when the August weather appeared propitious the crop might be sparse. Frank O'Donnell's ten-acre grazing field, situated a mile out the Tallow Road on the left, was the best place I knew for them. Frank, who lived in the Main Street, never bothered collecting them himself. In this he was no different from most other farmers who shared his disdain for the edible fungus. Mam and Molly loved picking mushrooms, too, and the whole family enjoyed eating them, fried or boiled in milk. But, in setting out toward the late evening we never got the best of the crop. That was harvested at the crack of dawn by the Botany boys and girls to whom it was a welcome source of income.

It was Mam who taught me to appreciate wild flowers, which grew in abundance around Lismore. In spring she would point out the yellow-petalled primroses that dotted many ditches and railway banks, and encourage me to enjoy their scent. Violets too were common at this time of year and could be found amongst the primroses along the ditches, or on their own down the Grove. In May bluebells filled many glades along the Mountain Road. Summer hedgerows gave off the spicy-sweet scent of wild privet and meadowsweet. When I was very little Molly showed me how to make daisy-chains and we played at knocking heads off ribwort. She showed me how to suck sweet juice from the bells of fuchsia blossoms. Dad's esoteric taste for the spring leaves of the beech turned in autumn to the tiny nuts of that tree. The nuts tasted good but the prising open of the tricorn shells required more patience than I had to make them a consumable proposition. Wherever we walked in summer we would return home with at least a sprig of wildflower. From the flower-rich meadows we put together mixed bunches of poppies, marguerites, knapweed, and other flowers and purple-tinted grasses, the names of which we did not even know. There was wild woodbine from the hedges, heather from the hill above the sandpit. Thistles were not flowers I picked as they were so prickly to the touch but I loved their vivid purple blossoms, especially the large tufted head of the spear thistle, which attracted a continuous bustle of insects. I did not realise that knapweed too was of the thistle family, as well as the lesser burdock, the prickly autumn seed-cases of which we called 'sticky-backs', and which we delighted to toss at the backs of unsuspecting passers-by when not plastering them on one another.

The loveliest flower of all, in my eyes, was the mysterious and stately foxglove, a common flower in our area, mysterious because it was linked to the fairies, and deadly too, we were told, because it was poisonous. In spite of its dark reputation Molly showed me how to fit the bells on the tops of my fingers, the way she would slip on a thimble when sewing. This trick and the fairy connotation I later found wedded in the Irish name of the flower, *méiríní púca*. It is also known in Irish as the *méaracán dearg*. The one other wild flower we were warned never to touch was cuckoo pint or lords and ladies (Irish: *cluas chaoin*), particularly its attractive and succulent-looking, bright-red berries which were said to be even more poisonous than the juices of the foxglove. Again, because of this reputation, it seemed mysterious and we did not always refrain from touching the purplish spadix, which looked like a tiny baseball bat. We were more chary of the berries. That wild flowers had medicinal qualities we also learned. Our own common remedy for warts, which most of us got on our hands at one time or another, was the milky juice of the spurge. We used the juice of the dandelion too, but this was considered less effective. Part of the mystery of the foxglove was that it was said to possess healing powers but these were unknown to us children. Better known were the celebratory aspects of plants, trees, and flowers, bluebells and lilac for the May altar, shamrock on St Patrick's Day, berried holly at Christmas time. You learned how to tell shamrock from clover. I picked it in our garden in small quantities but for a large spray sought it in the grass between the Hurling Field and the tennis courts. Berried holly for Christmas was easy to find in some years, impossible in others. Well, never quite impossible. In scarce years I always managed to find some, perhaps just from a single tree, in Glenribben Wood out the Cappoquin Road.

The return to school brought an end to the high activity of the summer months but the edible chestnut season was still to come. In the meantime, the weeks in the run-up to late September were melancholy, concerned mainly with readjusting to school discipline. In those weeks we would avail of the light of the ever-shortening evenings to drop-kick a football around the field between Hogan's Lodge and Greenmount while, at the same time, keeping an eye on the condition of the spiky husks of the three great chestnut trees that grew in the middle of it. It was a rugby ball we played with and we had a choice of two. I had one that my uncle Mick Morrissey, home on holidays from England, had given me, and Mickey and Gerald McConnell had another. Hoagy and I thought we were not doing too badly at taking frees until Michael Langford, an ungainly barefoot youngster, happened by and lashed the ball twice as far as we did with his bare toes! After that we gave up. Besides the nuts were ripening fast.

Always impatient for the moment when we could start eating them, we sometimes jumped the gun and picked a few ahead of time. Once we knew they were really ripe we swarmed around the trees. There were various stages of approach, the easiest of which was to pick up the fallen husks and nuts off the ground; a windy hour or two would have sent many crashing down. When the nuts were fully ripe the husks would split open on impact with the earth. Next you climbed the lower boughs and either shook off, or broke off, the accessible husks on these. Then you descended and threw short sticks at the higher branches in an effort to dislodge the husks on those. Finally, you climbed into the highest branches to reach the most inaccessible fruit. There you could pick some husks by hand, shake off others, and hit off others with a long stick. The various processes at work in stripping the three trees of their fruit took about a month. Some husks would hang on tenaciously beyond the season but, in the end, they would succumb to the autumn gales. The best climber amongst us, indeed in the whole town, was Pippa O'Brien. Where the rest of us would crawl along a horizontal or sloping limb, Pippa would walk, or even run, along it, balancing himself with or without outstretched arms. I could walk along some limbs but never came near to equalling his head for heights. When, at other times, we climbed trees for the fun of it, Pippa would leave us gasping at his fearlessness and sense of balance. Even Boxer, another fearless climber, was in awe of him. In the woods by the Owenashad near Paddy Dooley's house, in Ballyrafter Wood and in Ballyin Wood near Kate Pender's cottage there were other good chestnut trees. J. J. Budd, the fruit merchant, was also willing to purchase nuts but we liked our chestnuts too much to want to sell them to anyone. Hazel trees were common in the Grove and along the Mountain Road but nuts were scarce on these, or appeared to be. It may have been that someone ahead of us was harvesting them for gain. In the near corner of the ten-acre beyond the chestnut field at Greenmount there was a massive and beautiful walnut tree but the few nuts we farmed off it from season to season never fulfilled the promise of the luxuriant foliage.

We took our woods for granted around Lismore. Living there, it never occurred to us that we inhabited one of the least-afforested countries in Europe. Until it was pointed out in a geography lesson at school. And later I learned from Dad that the rich variety of deciduous trees that surrounded us in the town did not come about entirely by an accident of nature. The enlightened planting policies of successive Dukes of Devonshire had played a large part in shaping the landscape. In the early 1950s re-afforestation became a policy of central government and spruce and pine plantations began to spring up on the lower slopes of the Knockmealdowns. From the bathroom window of our house in West Street I could see all the way to Scarook and Deerpark Woods and would note gaps appearing in the skyline where old trees were cut down and new ones planted.

Lumbering was a traditional trade in the town, with at least a couple of sawmills in operation at any one time. During my youth three were working, the major commercial mill at the castle, the mill by the Strand Bridge, and Bertie Fitzgerald's small-scale yard at the corner of the Mayfield Road. The one by the Strand Bridge was as much a warehouse as a sawmill, I think. There was talk from time to time of establishing another one to replace the old mill by the railway station that had closed down and been subsequently turned into the *Happydrome* by Jacky Scanlan, but this project, in common with other industrial hopes, never came to fruit. Sawmilling could be dangerous. A moment's lack of concentration on the circular saw could cost a workman a finger or two. The cool and slow-moving Bishop Scanlon had lost a couple, and a year or two after I left town Sucky Neville saw part of one of his fly off. Nor was it only the possibility of gashing his hand for which the sawyer had to watch out. Sometimes he was struck by a length of wood spat up by a fault in the timber, suffering a knockout or other injury.

Felling fully grown trees was also a dangerous occupation. The number-one lumberjacks were 'Storc' and 'Phopper' Stapleton from Botany, so skilled they could drop a trunk precisely where they wanted it. This most skilful task of a skilful trade was important because a tree dropped in the right spot minimised damage to young trees that were growing up to replace it. It took a lot of experience, years probably, to calculate how a tree would fall, and to gauge its length on the floor from its standing height. The only measuring instrument used was the lumberjack's eye. Tom Lineen and I watched some castle men felling a big beech at *Tobar na Ceárdchan*. The tree was to fall towards us and we had been told to stand beyond a certain point, which we did. As the giant keeled over in our direction it seemed to me that we were going to be struck by the topmost branches.

'Tom, watch it!' I exclaimed and hurriedly withdrew a few steps.

However, my pal, having seen trees felled before, knew he could trust the lumberjacks' mark and did not budge. The branches whipped the ground safely short of him. Tom gave me an amused look. I grinned sheepishly and felt a fool.

Other timbermen concentrated on smaller trees and supplied blocks of firewood to the town. A neighbour around the corner in Botany, John O'Donnell, known to all for whatever reason as John Jocklin, was one of those. Jocklin was a tall, rangy man with a pronounced stoop and was blessed with such prodigious energy he was in danger of meeting himself coming back. In keeping with the way he moved, he spoke flat out, sometimes so fast he seemed to be telling you three things at once. The timbermen usually operated with an ass and cart. Limbs and stout branches were loaded lengthwise on the cart between four-foot staves that tapered at the ends to fit into sockets at each side of the cart. Usually four staves were enough to contain the load but ropes had to be used as well to make sure the topmost wood would not slip. Jocklin was an expert at loading a cart. He always carried the maximum load possible, and maybe a bit more, which was unfortunate for his animal. Even more unluckily for it, the ass was expected to measure up to its owner's frenetic idea of pace. Jocklin made up for his practical lack of compassion for the over-stretched animal by feeding it well. As Molly our maid was a great friend of the Heaphy's, who lived next door to his yard, and as I was often up at Barney Walsh's house opposite as well, I saw a lot of him. When we judged his mood to be irritable Barney and I liked to take a rise out of him by shouting, 'Don't rush now, Jocklin,' or 'Isn't it time you got a jennet, like Storc and Phopper?' We did not always catch what he muttered by way of response but watching his mouth move was awesome.

Tommy Keating, the stonemason and musician, also brought in some income with an ass and cart. Unlike Jocklin, he never loaded his cart to the limit and he was as unflappable as the former was excitable. Tommy used to hire out his rig, or loan it to friends. Another who did this was Jack Connors. The Dennises would borrow Jack's to bring in timber they had cut. They usually got their wood up the Mountain Road, and there was one thing you had to be aware of when you took that particular ass in that direction. Jack was accustomed to leaving the animal to graze on a small patch of grassland at the Bark Yard by the Owenashad, downstream of Lady Louisa's Bridge, while he was engaged in lumbering in the dense woodland nearby. A five-bar iron gate that opened directly onto the yard was permanently open. Knowing where his feed was greenest, the ass had developed the habit of turning automatically into the gateway upon arriving there. Boxer and Euge gave me a demonstration of this that almost worked too well when I went along to give them a hand. As we approached the site, Boxer spurred the ass and the unloaded cart up the road as fast as it would go. When we reached the gate, still going full tilt, the ass suddenly veered sharply left and galloped into the yard, smacking a shaft of the cart against one of the posts and nearly spilling us onto the road. It was just as well that Jack did not see the experiment. The lads would never have got the cart again.

Mam did not like to see Dad handling timber, although he was adept at splitting the big limbs he brought home with wooden and iron wedges. Above all, she feared the iron wedges. They were not cheap so he would try to use them for as long as he could. When the heads grew jagged with use there was always a danger of metal flying off when the wedge was struck with the sledgehammer. More than once Dad gashed his hands as a result of this. Mam used to get very distressed when this happened as the tears in the skin bled a lot. Deeper and more persistent was another worry that nagged at her, that the dragging and strain demanded by his lumbering would harm him in the long run.

CHAPTER FIFTEEN

Customs, Games and Gangs

GAMES JUST HAPPENED. One day children would start playing hopscotch. Another week marbles would start. The next, whipping tops would be the rage. The one after that might see us rolling hoops. There was no logic to what started when. At least that was how it seemed. None of us ever figured out why all the children in the town took up particular games at particular times. Who started the ball rolling each time? The shopkeepers, maybe, by stocking up on particular goods at suitable intervals? But we did not need anything from the shops to play hopscotch, and hoops we made ourselves. Was there amongst us a games fanatic who was secretly imposing his or her wishes upon us by subtly starting off the game that he or she wanted to play at any one time? It was all very puzzling, as if some mysterious force were at the back of it. Not that we thought about it that much. On the contrary, we were happy to go along with the game of the moment no matter how it came about. The time for some games could be predicted, of course, i.e. those dependent on the four seasons. The ground elder and hogweed from which we fashioned our peashooters only reached the required maturity in autumn. More to the point, the ammunition we used in these, the abundant haws of the hawthorn, only acquired the hardness necessary for propulsion in late September. We could have used dried peas earlier, indeed at any time of the year, but never did, as we would have had to purchase those. The sticky-back was also autumnal as you had to wait for the burdock burr to dry out before it acquired its limpet-like 'stickiness'. Snow brought winter games – sliding on ice, tobogganing on crudely made sleds, snowballing. Most predictable of all were games linked to calendar customs, e.g. 'hunting' the wren on St Stephen's Day, ducking for apples at Hallowe'en (you had to duck your head in the water to achieve any success).

Boys and girls, when they were little, shared games. Thereafter, the tastes of both sexes altered in line with public perception of the games girls should be playing and those boys should be seen to play. But there were no hard-and-fast rules. Always amongst us there were exceptions who chose to play across the gender gap or who had no interest whatsoever in conventional games. Girls might join with us boys in a game of Cowboys and Indians, hide-and-seek, or arrow hunt. We, in our turn, might have a swing at ring-a-ring o' roses, or try skipping with a rope at which they were expert in all sorts of fancy steps. All of us joined in hopscotch. (Didn't we call it 'beds' as in other parts of Ireland?). See-saw with an old plank or long bough placed across a barrel or tree-trunk was another pastime we shared with girls. Board games like ludo, draughts, or snakes and ladders, were always unisex as were games of cards for adults, especially twenty-five, forty-five and whist, which were played a lot in the area. I have only a vague recall of the games that girls practised on their own. There was a ball game that was played against any convenient wall. It consisted of the non-stop lobbing and catching of the ball without dropping it and was accompanied by rhymes or chants. Sometimes the ball was tossed from under a leg; other times the player twirled 360 degrees before catching it. 'Queenie' was the name given to another ball game the girls played. The balls used were made of solid rubber with marbled colouring or were the conventional white tennis ones.

Tig (or tag) was the basic game of the school-yard, learnt when you were very little. You played it with your immediate classmates. During breaks, you saw boys and girls dashing about trying to tag others of the same age group. Giant steps, also popular, was more of a street game and boys grew out of this more quickly than girls. Margaret Feeney and Rena Murphy and their pals used to rope in Tom and me for a game in West Street regularly. To begin this game one of us stood against the Villa wall, facing it. The other five or six participants lined up on the opposite side of the road. The object for each of them was to try to be the first to touch the person facing the wall. The one to do so won the game. Conversely, the object of the child facing the wall was to frustrate all attempts to touch her, in which case, if she were successful, she would be declared the winner. She would call out instructions like, 'two giant steps', 'a baby step', 'three baby steps and a giant step', and other variations, and, while the others were attempting to carry these out, would whirl around suddenly to try to catch them in motion. If you were halfway through a step you froze in that position. If she caught you off balance you were out of the game. You did not have to respond to her every instruction and so could choose the moment when you wanted to advance. It was not easy to get to the person at the wall. The last few steps especially were a cat-and-mouse exercise in sudden movement.

Parlour games played from an early age were blind man's buff and follow-my-leader in which family and friends joined. Musical chairs was another but I was not so keen on this as the adults used to take it over. Slap hands

Paddy and I played with Molly and Mam. Dad amused us with riddles and rhymes. While tricking me with his thumb into half-believing that he was stealing my nose, then sticking it back on again, he would sometimes ask, *'Will I tell you a story?'*

'Yes,' I would say eagerly, knowing what was coming.

'About Johnny McGory?'

'Yes.'

'Will I begin it?'

'Yes.'

'That's all that's in it.'

He would play with my toes. *This little piggy went to the market,* (squeezing my big toe lightly), *This little piggy stayed at home* (squeezing the next toe a little harder), *This little piggy got bread and butter* (squeezing the third still harder), *And this little piggy got none* (squeezing the fourth fairly hard so that I tingled in anticipation), *And this little piggy –* (he would pause) *– went kweek, kweek, kweek, kweek, kweek!* (he would squeeze and pull my little toe vigorously while I squealed in delight).

Among ourselves, we children passed on riddles like:

> What goes up when the rain comes down? An umbrella.
> What gets bigger the more you take away from it? A hole.

Usually we found these silly but passed them along the line just the same. When we sensed that someone we did not like was funking something we might chant, *Cowardy, cowardy, custard...* The aggrieved one might respond, *Sticks and stones may break my bones but names will never hurt me.* Girls might taunt us with, *Georgie Porgie pudding and pie, kissed the girls and made them cry,* or just yell, *Goosie goosie gander* at us, intimating that we were being stupid. When selecting teams for games we often used the device:

> Eeny, meeny, miney, mo
> Catch a nigger by the toe
> If he screeches let him go
> Eeny, meeny, miney, mo.

The final 'mo' was stressed to indicate the individual selected. We, and our elders, who also used the verse in the company of children, were totally oblivious to its ugly racism. The word 'nigger' was also commonly used in specifying a particular dark shade of brown polish or leather, which further implied it was acceptable.

A tale without end that Dad was fond of telling us when he was putting us to bed was:

> It was a dark and stormy night
> And the captain said to the mate,
> 'Tell us a story,'
> And the mate began,
> 'It was a dark and stormy night…'

The first time he told me that I felt cheated but ever after, even though I knew what was coming, I listened with feigned bated breath and asked him to repeat it.

There were other rhymes beyond the first few lines of which we never seemed to get or, if we did, made up our own words:

> Dan, Dan, the dirty man
> Stole my shoes and away he ran…

> The boy stood on the burning deck,
> His feet were full of blisters…

> The bear went up the mountain,
> The bear went up the mountain,
> The bear went up the mountain,
> To see what he could see…

> Christmas is coming and the goose is getting fat…

> Fly away Peter, fly away Paul,
> Come back Peter, come back Paul…

With the exception of the second, for which boys contrived many lewd and corny endings, girls were more inclined to chant these.

Tongue-twisters we picked up mostly from the comics. One we especially liked was, *I saw three white rabbits down by the riverside.* Pete Neville, who had difficulty in pronouncing his 'r's, always came up with, 'I saw twee white wabbits down by the wibberside,' much to our amusement. 'Aw, go on Pete, say it,' we would urge and, when he was in the mood, he would oblige and make us, and himself, giggle. We did not intend any unkindness toward our pal and he did not seem to take offence. As against that, we should have realised that if he needed to be in the mood to attempt it he must have been at least somewhat sensitive about his 'r's. It illustrates again the unintentionally cruel manner in which children pick on differences from what they perceive to be the norm, even among best pals.

Toys were scarce in the wake of the Second World War and much of the time we relied on hand-me-downs and swops for new ones with which to play. Lead soldiers were favourites with boys, easy to swop and easy to repair with a matchstick when a head came off; you merely stuck one end of the match into the hollow head and the other into the hollow body. Broken arms and legs, which were solid, stayed broken. Forts and castles for your maimed armies were easily constructed out of cardboard shoeboxes after you begged them empty off Bobby Allison or Aggie Healy, the Main Street drapers. Eddie Murphy, the draper in West Street, did not sell shoes but you could try him for an old hat box to make a tower. Comics gave you ideas for constructing simple toys on your own. There was a sort of buzz-saw affair that we made out of the cut-off end of a corned beef can and a length of string. A couple of tin cans and a length of wire would make a kind of telephone with which you could signal from one room to another. Sword-fighting gave us the opportunity to play Errol Flynn (nobody wanted to play Basil Rathbone) or Louis Hayward. Hazel was the material of which our rapiers were made and we bored holes in the covers of old polish tins to provide guards for our hilts. But not all our heroes were drawn from the silver screen. We fashioned Celtic broadswords and short Roman blades and daggers out of the long strap-like leaves of a thick stand of New Zealand flax that grew on the edge of the lawn in front of the Villa. Then we metamorphosed into the demigods of the Fianna, Oisín or Goll or Caoilte, or Fionn himself. Then there was Brian Boru. But never a Roman, except maybe Horatius at the bridge. Bows and arrows were made of hazel, ash or holly. I once shaved and sandpapered a piece of yew in the hope of making an English longbow but, in the absence of a proper design, failed to get it to function. Girls had to make their own toys too. Most dolls and teddy bears were sewn together by mothers and daughters and stuffed with old socks.

The new toy that made the most impact with boys, and unwelcomingly with adults, was the water-pistol. It was made of tin and shot off a reasonable stream of liquid, but it was not very durable. Often it choked and often it broke down completely. Which led us to improvise a lethal variation, the bicycle pump, that never failed and that possessed a far higher deluge capability than the pocket pistol. Guns went down well with us, needless to say. For many years we had had to put up with the single-cap-shooter but then, a major advance in our parent-irritant potential, the cap-strip appeared. The old single cap had been a small circle of red paper, about a quarter of an inch in diameter. In the middle of it bulged whatever it was that made the bang when the hammer of your silvery piece struck it. Hell of a weapon to load when the bad guys were coming at you in force. The new strip, dark-red on the top, pink on the underside, carried about twenty shots, which gave it nearly as much firepower as the six-shooters employed in the B-westerns.

My first multi-shooter was not quite the shiny, silvered Colt in the fancy leather holster that I had weighed in the palm of my hand admiringly in Teasy Meade's bijou toy shop in the Main Street and for which I had penned an urgent request to Santa Claus. Instead, all I found in my Christmas stocking, one of Mam's much-mended cast-offs, was a tinny affair in a rubberised half-holster that looked like a mongrel version of a First World War German Mauser. I did not know what to make of this and complained bitterly to Mam that it was the other gun I had wanted. As it was very early in the morning and Dad, having worked late into the night before, was still asleep, she hushed me and took me down to the living-room and there, told me in plain but sympathetic language that she and Dad had been unable to afford the fancy pistol. I would have to make do with what I had got. For the first time, probably at the age of eight or nine, I realised that there were cash limits to my parents' generosity. But I could not help wondering who in the town was the lucky one wearing the gun of my dreams. As it happened, I was never to see it strapped to anyone's thigh so it must have been a stranger who rode into town and bought it. Mam then sent me back upstairs to get dressed and said she would have a better surprise for me when I came down again. I was back in a flash, pulling my braces over my shoulders.

'What's the surprise?' I asked breathlessly.

'Open the front door and look out into the street,' she said quietly.

I threw open the door and gasped with delight. It was snowing! Two inches already covered the ground and large, dry flakes were whispering down through the still air. I ran out along the shaft of light that pierced the dark and found I was the only person in the street. I was sliding in the snow when Mam called me back in. She put a coat and cap on me and told me I could play until she was ready to go to seven o'clock Mass with me. A few minutes later she took me by the hand and we went off to see the crib. By lunchtime I had accepted my tin mongrel of a pistol. At least it was a fast loader. From now on the baddies had to look out.

In my Christmas stocking I might find such things as sparklers, a cracker, a ball-bearing puzzle, a Dinky car, a few pennies, a few sweets, etc., accompanying my main present. This varied from year to year. Years when I did not get a gun might bring me any one of the following: a box of paints and brushes, which always delighted me as I liked painting and drawing, a game of ludo or lotto, a book, a stamp album, a small set of plain wooden building blocks, a game of rings, or a jigsaw puzzle. Once, I was particularly lucky and got a small train set. I liked rings and Mam and Molly could always be coaxed into having a game with me. Jigsaws never seemed to have enough parts in them to present a real challenge. By the time four- and five-hundred-piece puzzles appeared in the shops I had lost interest in them. A favourite game that did not cost a penny was noughts and crosses. We played it on the blackboard at school, in our copybooks, scratched it on walls and pavements with chalky stones and in the earth and sand with twigs, wherever. It was good that so many of our pleasures came cheaply. Without them what would poor children have done? By comparison, I had little to complain about. I was comparatively well-provided with formal games.

For many years Teasy Meade's was the Aladdin's cave of manufactured toys, the glow in an otherwise unadorned Christmas Main Street. We would stand in front of the crammed shop-window that glittered with coloured lights and tinsel and reflected the sparkle of our wondering eyes. Among the things we would have liked to take home: six-guns, lorries, cars, Indian warbonnets, cardboard aeroplanes for self-assembly... For the girls there would be dolls, even perhaps ones whose eyes opened and shut, and more dolls. Inside, Teasy would let you touch, and maybe handle, a toy that you were interested in having your parents buy for you. You could always find an excuse to be in the shop anyway, as sweets and chocolate were her normal trade as far as we were concerned.

On the 2nd of October 1949 a rival entered the field. Nora Willoughby, who for five years had managed Jim Feeney's general shop for newspapers, ice-cream, sweets, etc., a little up the street on the opposite side, bought out Jim and started up on her own. Come Christmas she bowled us over with the biggest display of toys the town had ever seen. And, unlike Teasy, she had the space in which to show them off. By then also, toys were beginning to be manufactured in quantity again in Britain. It was great for the smaller children but by that time I had outgrown my old wooden scooter and the old wooden rocking-horse that I used to ride in the attic of my aunts' house in Carrick.

What I had not outgrown, however, were roller-skates and both Nora and Teasy were now stocking those. They were the models with ordinary wheels. The classy, ball-bearing variety I had only vaguely heard about. These were unknown in our locality. With one exception, when a schoolboy of about my own age, Cyril Dunne, came home from England to live in Ballygallane. Cyril was a real skater and could move faster and do turns that the rest of us could not even attempt. Somebody said that he had been seen skating along the parapet wall above the dry arches of Lismore Bridge that extended over the Ferry Inch, a scarcely believable feat as the surface of this was pitted by erosion. It was okay for walking along as we often did, or trotting along as we sometimes did, or even running along on the odd occasion that we were accompanied by Pippa O'Brien, but skating along it! Who was to say that someone as good on skates as he was could not do it? He used to fly down Gallows Hill and the New Way on his way home from school, and could stop dead whenever he chose. The skates we others had never ran so freely, no matter how much we oiled them. Nor were they as robust.

The most unusual board game I played you could neither get at Nora's nor Teasy's. It was called Monopoly and was brought to the town by Paul Rice, an English boy of the same age as me whose parents had shortly before purchased the Devonshire Arms Hotel. Originally owned by the Duke of Devonshire, the hotel had been sold to a local man Tommy O'Donnell, in the thirties I think, for the price of £3,000, lock, stock and barrel. After O'Donnell died his widow sold it to a new English owner, a Mr Hunt, in October 1947. Hunt had it for about three years before selling it to Mr and Mrs Rice. The Rices, in their turn, were only to remain about two years before selling out to Mr and Mrs Boam. Paul introduced the McConnells, the Creanes, Tom Feeney, Hoagy and me to the game and once we had mastered its property-owning concepts, quite foreign to me at any rate, we were always keen to play it. The only trouble was, Paul's attitude to the game was intense and if he thought you were not being equally serious he would suddenly scoop up the board and pieces and flounce off in a temper. He did this once in our living room when Tom, Hoagy and I were ribbing him a bit. Mam was very angry with us and said later that we should not upset Paul like that. He was highly strung, which was true, and possibly shell-shocked in the War, which was debatable. She was right to have a go at us. Paul must have felt very much an outsider in Lismore. A Protestant, he did not seem to mix with fellow-Protestants like the Stanleys or Peter Dowd, and he went to the Christian Brothers' School. His father had bought him an ass on which to ride for pleasure. Sadly, he looked rather comical on it because he was tall for his age and it was fat. He finally tired of us and afterwards we would sometimes try to excite the animal with whoops and cries of 'Ride 'im cowboy!' whenever he rode down West Street. Once or twice we whacked the ass on the rump with a hand to start it running. Because of what Mam had said I never felt comfortable ragging him but I joined in. Maybe I felt offended that he had dismissed us so lightly. Whatever it was, something about him irked me. I do not think he can have looked back on his brief stay in our town with much relish. The whole fault was not on our side. We did try to make friends. Probably our backgrounds were just too different.

As in most homes, there was always a deck of playing cards in ours. Mam and Molly enjoyed playing snap and beggar-my-neighbour with Paddy and me. Dad was disdainful of cards. My own attention span for card games was very limited, so much so that snap and pontoon, games requiring little steady concentration, were the ones I liked best. I quite enjoyed a round of twenty-five and poker, too, but only as a fill-in when the lads were short a player. Johnny Baldwin's portico in Church Lane was my preferred venue. Johnny was a quiet, slim, middle-aged little man with a laconic sense of humour, and he was happy to let us use the picturesque portico of his house for card games when the rain came down and we had to interrupt our games of handball across in the alley. We used to play for small change if we had it, matchsticks if we hadn't.

When the weather was dry and we wanted to gamble we were more likely to opt for pitch-and-toss on the strip of bare earth outside Redmond 'Rem' Daly's black galvanized storage shed around the corner from Johnny's. (Frank Mason via Paddy Vaughan has informed me that this is the same shed in which the Warren Gardens staff used to pack daffodils for mailing at the beginning of the 20th Century.) This game I did like. It demanded a skill that was more to my liking. Maybe it was just that I preferred playing something on my feet than on my arse. You lobbed a stone on the ground, perhaps five to seven yards from where you stood. This was the bob. Then, in turn, we pitched pennies at the bob. The person whose coin landed nearest got first crack at the second phase of the game, the toss. You put two coins on a short strip of wood, or simply used your index and second fingers, and tossed the coins as high as you liked in the air. Every head that came up you could pocket. There was a knack in pitching – Pete Neville and Beaver were very skilled at it – and in tossing – Peter Doherty was a crack at this. It was really satisfying to see your coin slide in under the bob to take first place. Tossing styles varied. Some of us liked to give the coins a lot of air, others of us a quick and shifty twirl. Real gambling commenced with the toss. The tosser or any participant could bet on the disposition of the coins before they came to rest on the ground. 'A bob to head 'em,' the tosser might challenge and, if he succeeded in turning up two heads, he would pocket a shilling from the lad who took him on, as well as winning the two pennies. 'Half a dollar you won't head 'em,' an onlooker might say and if the tosser failed he had to pay that person half-a-crown. But an onlooker could place a bet with another onlooker as well, e.g. 'A dollar he won't head 'em.' Onlooker or tosser or other player could take on multiple bets and the stakes could go very high. For this reason the game was illegal. In our case, however, the stakes were never high. There simply wasn't that kind of money around in the Lane. The guards in Lismore never bothered when they saw lads playing pitch-and-toss, well almost never. There was an occasion when the 'The Rancher' Boyle gave a few of us, and in particular Beaver as he looked the eldest and thus the most responsible, a short lecture on the illegality of our endeavour. He was in belt and braces and shirt sleeves on his way to feed his cows at the time, which really got up Beaver's nose.

'He wasn't even in bloody uniform,' he snorted.

When there were not games to be played around the ball alley there were always the foibles of this person or that person to entertain us, Guard Boyle with his brace of heifers kept round the back of the ball court, or Rem Daly, for example. Sometimes we might be engaged in a game of handball when someone would say quietly, 'Hey lads, Rem is lockin' the shed.' A string of heads would then peer expectantly around the corner and over the side wall where it was low, as Rem put the key in the padlock and turned it. It was at this moment that our faces lit up. The key would be withdrawn but then to reassure himself that he had really turned the lock Rem would first tug the padlock to the left, then to the right, then left again, then right again, up to maybe half a dozen times, until he had really assured himself that the lock was engaged. Before he glanced around furtively to check whether anyone had observed his series of covert actions we would have ducked out of sight, emerging again a moment later to see him hop on his bike and pedal off via the North Mall to his grocery store in the Main Street.

At the Mall Seat we used to congregate for chat and a bit of blackguarding, and of course, a crude joke or two like:

Tommy developed diarrhoea at Mass and was making his way home with the scutter running down his legs when a woman stopped him.

'*Can you tell me the way to the chapel, please?*' *she asked.*

'*Follow the trail, Ma'am,*' *Tommy pointed.*

One of Beaver's favourite stunts while we whiled away the hours there was to whistle a tune in time and in keeping with the gait of a passer-by. Someone lightly skipping along would find himself accompanied by the Laurel and Hardy signature tune. A brisk stride might get 'Kelly the Boy from Killane'. A slow shuffle would elicit the 'Death March'. A woman going by purposefully on high heels would be accorded the air of a popular quickstep. When all of us at the Seat joined in it could be most disconcerting for the passer-by. Most people took it well, smiled, or even burst out laughing, but a few scowled angrily which, of course, gave us the most satisfaction. As the angered person swept off Beaver might add for our benefit, mimicking the style and acccent of the verbose American travelogue commentator James A. Fitzpatrick, 'And so, as the setting sun sinks below the horizon we say farewell to (the person's name), man (it usually was a man) of monumental glory and scenic grandeur.'

Quiet moments of tedium demanded other forms of entertainment. We might start pulling our fingers to see who could make them crackle the loudest. A spitting contest might evolve, the object of which was to see who could spit the farthest. Beaver was no slouch at this either but the one amongst us uniquely accomplished at lobbing a gob was Jim 'Plug' Lineen from the Main Street. When Plug was around it was simply no contest. A sharp hiss from his lips and the ball of spit went flying a yard or two beyond Beaver's best. Plug himself attributed his peculiar talent to the gap between his lower front teeth. It somehow aided propulsion he maintained. We took him at his word. On other occasions we would just hold our breaths and puff up our faces to see who could make the reddest face. In moments of dire boredom farting might erupt. As with Plug in spitting, we had amongst us an unassailable champion in this event also, 'Fisser', later 'Guiney' Neville, whose appearances at the Mall Seat were all too rare an occurrence. Fisser did not just toss out the odd number like the most of us. He could serenade us with a series of pieces – staccato, fortissimo, con brio, piano. We would have urged him to blow out lighted candles had we known of the outrageous theatrical accomplishments of *Le Pétomane* (Joseph Pujol). The champ without a doubt, Fisser. But you made sure you stayed upwind of him. His brother Sucky had a different line – pulling faces, doing funny walks and giving you the 'fox's bite', the last-mentioned an excruciating experience for the individual caught in the 'bite'. You might bring that upon yourself if, thinkingly or unthinkingly, you told Sucky to shag off, or put one across him in some way. When he next got near to you he would grab the inside of one of your thighs with a hand and squeeze his nails into your flesh until you said you were sorry. As you were hopping up and down with the pain of it, he did not have to wait long for his apology. His favourite funny walk was a little routine he did going up and down steps, or stepping on and off kerbs.

Fecking things was also a kind of game for us and, aside from robbing orchards and raiding the agricultural ahow, we always had an eye to opportunity. The things we fecked were minor, and mostly we stole for fun. Our victims, of course, did not necessarily see it that way. Some items that looked interesting at the fecking stage turned out subsequently to be useless, like the chrome cigarette roller I lifted at a Castle Garden charity fete. It looked shiny and attractive to my magpie eye so I took it. Later, when I could not get it to work, I gave it away. At that time I had just begun smoking and thought I could learn to roll my own.

Fags had to be experienced and Woodbines, being the cheapest, were the obvious choice. Not easy to feck though because they were always kept well out of reach of shop customers. Woodbines were ideal for the beginner. Not alone did they come in a small, green, paper wallet of five but you could also buy them one at a time from a collusive shopkeeper who turned a blind eye to your under-age puffing. I was fortunate to be able to wangle a few pence to fund my experiments. The bob Mam gave me to go to the shilling seats at the cinema matinee I apportioned in my own way. I went to the fourpennies and bought fags, or maybe sweets, with the rest. When Colonel McConnell came to live at the Villa in 1948 he brought with him from the Middle East an exotic new dimension in smoking, Passing Cloud. He used to order these by the hundreds – his elder son Mickey showed me a wooden carton once that must have contained at least a couple of hundred. Mickey stuffed a handful in his pocket and we went off for a smoke. His father would not miss them, he assured me, he smoked so much he never really knew how many were left in a box. Passing Cloud certainly looked the last word in luxury, thick and oval and with an aroma definitely a step up from the humble Woodbine.

When we fecked things we did not always appreciate where to draw the line. One incident left me feeling very ashamed. Next door to the cattle pound in Ferry Lane there was a small shop that used to be owned, I think, by a Mrs Bridget Moore. She sold it at the end of the Forties to a quiet, elderly couple, Mr and Mrs Sinnott, who reopened the shop, selling among other things Power's fizzy lemonade, chocolate, and plain buns, for which we developed a taste. The couple were very gentle and loving with one another and were most pleasant to their customers. The shelves were never very well-stocked and the light bulbs always glimmered with a low wattage so it was clear, even to us, that the place was run on a shoestring. It was about seven in the evening when we were in there. We had asked for something that seemed to be out of stock so the old man had gone to the back room to check with his wife if this was so. In the meantime I happened to notice that there was a cardboard box containing the kind of buns we liked on a high shelf behind me. I touched Doshin's arm and pointed. He nodded and moved closer to the door to the back room to keep an eye on the couple's movements. Quickly I stood on a settle below the shelf, reached up, raised the lid of the box, and slipped two or three buns into my pocket.

I just had time to place my feet back on the floor before the man returned. He confirmed that the item we wanted was out of stock so we left. Did I imagine that he gave me a strange look as if he guessed I had been up to something? When we got far enough down the road I took out the buns and we shared them. We laughed about my mean little feat as we ate them. But there remained with me for a while the aftertaste of reprehension. I never made proper restitution for my act and was too ashamed ever to admit to the nice old couple that I had stolen from them. I made a conscious effort to patronise the shop more frequently afterwards and whenever I was going down the bridge for a stroll would call in to purchase a bar of something, whether I wanted it at that particular moment or not.

Through my contact with Gerald McConnell I started taking stamp-collecting seriously. Before that I had acquired stamps in the desultory manner in which I picked up picture cards of football players, cars, planes, animals, etc. Gerald had an exotic collection that put faces on parts of the world that had hitherto been unknown to me. Also, he knew much more about the ins and outs of philately than I did; I could tell from the way he handled his stamps. Inspired, I began to write off to dealers for cheap packets of mixed stamps and started sticking them into a proper album, an inexpensive one I bought in Dungarvan, using minuscule gummed labels. I suppose I collected stamps for the best part of three or four years, for a brief part of that very acquisitively. During my serious phase Gerald happened to mention to me, when he was showing me his large collection in the front room of the Villa, that he was thinking of getting rid of the stamps of some countries and concentrating on others, a concept new to me. I immediately sat up on hearing this and began to sort out some of the biggest and most colourful ones of the possible rejects.

'Well if you *do* decide to give away some of your collection I wouldn't mind taking those ones off your hands,' I offered generously.

Gerald smiled but was non-committal. He had the good sense not to offer me the stamps and subsequently, on realising how greedy I had been in putting in such a direct request for them, I was too ashamed to raise the matter with him again. He probably saw that for me the fascination with stamps lay in what they taught me about distant places and not in what they might be worth as collector's items.

Other crazes were short-lived. With Gerald too I tried conkers for a season but that pastime failed to inspire me. Car-spotting, a hobby I picked up from the comics, lasted at most half a year. The same cars kept coming round, even on a Fair Day. My favourite was that which Bill Moore of Monatarive referred to as his 'golden chariot', an aged Ford 10, if I remember correctly, held together by Heath Robinson technology. The only thing I learned from this rather aimless form of endeavour was that KI was the registration indicator of County Waterford, WI that of Waterford City, HI that of County Tipperary and ZB that of Cork – city or county I cannot recall. Train-spotting, which might have been marginally more interesting, was a non-starter as only a handful of engines went through Lismore station.

When it came to calendar customs the one I preferred aside from Christmas was Shrove Tuesday. On Pancake Day I knew I could look forward to a plateful of pancakes, with warmed-up strawberry jam and castor sugar to spread over them. April Fool's Day gave us a licence to put one over on our classmates. That might have meant telling a tall story or sending a fellow-pupil to another pupil to say that so and so wanted to see him. Silly things. Adults used to try and catch one another out too. Molly used to be furious when she was fooled.

Christmas, of course, was the biggest event in a child's calendar. It meant presents, a few bob in your pocket, and more food than you got at any other time of the year. It seemed to go on for so long, too. The first week of December my parents would put up decorations in the house. Before that even, I would be scouring the newspapers and comics for the first picture, usually a line drawing in an advertisement, of Santa Claus. I would have gone out and picked the berried holly, branches of which would be placed on top of the pictures on the walls and on the mirrors over the living-room and sitting-room fireplaces. I used to help with putting up the decorations also. One square, blue-and-green chain was long enough to go diagonally across the living-room and had to be supported with drawing pins along the ceiling. Shorter ones were linked into this. We used the same decorations year after year, with Mam introducing a new one when a very old one finally fell apart. A pair of big white cardboard bells flecked with silver and a Santa on his sleigh, also flecked with silver, hung flat on a wall. The same cardboard crib went up annually on the window ledge that looked onto the kitchen. If putting up the decorations filled you with anticipation, taking them down left you flat. Paddy and I did not participate in removing them. Mam usually left them up until out first days back at school. She had no set routine about taking them down. Some day after the 6th of January we would come home at lunchtime to a cheerless room, that very quickly reverted to its habitual role.

Letters and cards were numerous at Christmas time, particularly during the run-up to the festive day itself when extra, temporary postmen were recruited to help Jim O'Donnell. The mail would be delivered at irregular intervals, three, four, or even five times a day. Every time you came in after being out playing there was a chance that another letter, or even a parcel, might have arrived. Above all, I was awaiting two letters; one carrying an English postal order for two-and-sixpence or five bob from Uncle Mick in Birmingham and the other a ten-bob or pound note, English or Irish, from Aunt Nan and Aunt Bid in Carrick-on-Suir. By parcel would come a goose, plucked and ready for the oven and shoehorned into a large shoebox, from my aunt Bridget Maggie (known to us as Aunt Brighid) and Uncle Larry, Dad's youngest brother, who ran the Ballantyne family farm in Keash, County Sligo. A home-made fruit cake would arrive from my Carrick aunts as well.

Mam and Molly would have made the plum puddings already. They made three round ones in November, one for Christmas Day, one for New Year's Day, and the third to be held over for an appropriate occasion, sometimes Easter. It was such a slog mixing the ingredients by hand Mam figured she could just as easily make three as one. Paddy and I would be drafted in to help her and Molly stir the heavy dough. I did not eat plum pudding myself but I was intrigued, and possibly put off by, the items that went into it – suet (a fatty substance that looked like dried soap); shrivelled-looking sultanas (hardly out of the Arabian Nights) and raisins, which I could not distinguish from them; and sickly-bitter things called collectively peel that looked like pieces of orange and lemon skin coated with sticky sugar. The fiddliest part of the whole operation was stoning the sultanas and raisins. Happily, I did not do this very well – apparently I threw away too much of the fruit – so Molly took me off it after scolding me for my fumbling efforts. I was only too delighted. I did not see why I had to be involved in preparing something I was not going to eat. The Christmas cake was also made in November. As far as I could judge the same mixture went into this as went into the pudding so I did not eat the cake either.

After the November flurry of activity, the first sign of the coming festive season, things proceeded as normal on the food front until nearer the time, when the cake reappeared for icing. First an unappetising layer of yellow almond paste would be smeared all over it. Then, after an interval of a week or so, the sweet white icing would go on it. I liked to be around for this phase of the operation because I would be offered the spoons and bowl to lick when the job was done. The same decorations went on the cake each year: a small red china Santa lying on his belly, and a rubbery green sprig of holly with a glossy red berry on it. And around the side would go the same red, green and white paper ruff. All in all, making a Christmas cake seemed to be much more demanding than making a pudding. Not least in terms of worry was the cooling off period after the cake had been taken out of the oven. Mam would be on tenterhooks worrying whether it was going to sink in the middle. There was one thing I did like about the pudding – the blue whisky flame that licked up the sides of the ball when it was set alight on the table.

St Stephen's Day was the day for colour. Mam always saved pennies for it because she knew that from morning until lunchtime a lot of youngsters, and some grown men, would be calling to chant a few verses that began with:

> The wran, the wran, the king of all birds,
> St Stephen's Day was caught in the furze...

or

> The wran, the wran, that do be seen,
> All along the holly green...

and ended with:

> Up with the kettle and down with the pan,
> Give us a penny to bury the wran.

The wren boys and girls would be carrying a thick branch of holly decorated with coloured ribbons and pieces of paper, and their faces would be blackened with burnt cork. Some of them would accompany their singing with papered combs. Youths and grown men might offer a more sophisticated musical overture, playing a jig or two on musical instruments before singing 'The Wren' and asking for money. They would expect a tanner at least for their effort. Willie 'Teller' Walsh and his pals always believed in putting on a good performance. The first rat-a-tat on the door would shake you out of bed at the first sight of day. Mam, after her exertions of the previous day, would not always be disposed to getting up so early and would ignore the first callers, or might hand me a few pennies to give them if I was excitedly looking out the window. As well as blackening their faces, the wren boys and girls cross-dressed and disguised themselves in outlandish garments. A major part of the fun for me was in trying to recognise their identities. The voice was the giveaway when a disguise was otherwise impenetrable. I would have loved to go off with the wren myself, both for the fun and for the money, but my parents rightly forbad it.

'The custom is for the poorer people of the town. It wouldn't be right for you to take money out of their pockets,' Dad pointed out in his quiet way. It wasn't really so with the custom. Anyone could go with the wren. But I knew what he meant.

The holly branch was supposed to carry a dead wren in it but I never saw one and would have been distressed if I had, because it seemed to me that the rationale for hunting down and killing the tiny bird was wholly unjust. It was guilty, the story went, of betraying Jesus to the Roman soldiers. The holy man was hiding in a bush when he startled it. Naturally enough, it promptly flew out, giving him away. How else should it have reacted?

Hallowe'en with its barmbrack and tanner was something we made a stab at rather than celebrated. On a number of occasions Mam filled the tin bathtub with water and floated apples on it for us to try to capture with our teeth. Duck apple we called this. Kneeling by the tub with your hands behind your back it was well-nigh impossible to sink your teeth into the bobbing fruit. Snap apple was another form of the game. To play this we hung an apple from a length of string at an appropriate height in the doorway between the living-room and the hall and sent it swinging in a circle. Again you had to hold your hands behind your back while trying to grab the passing apple with your teeth and bite off a mouthful. The apples always appeared to be too big for our juvenile mouths although Mam would say that she had tried to pick out small ones so that we would have a better chance of getting our teeth into them. When we tired of our conspicuous lack of success she would let us roast chestnuts on the open fire with the extendable fork that we normally used for toasting slices of bread. Once or twice she managed to buy some hazel nuts for us to crack.

If you wanted a dull night out in Lismore you picked New Year's Eve. With the heavy accent on Christmas it just got left out. You heard people moaning about this and saying that there ought to be a hop in the town hall, like they evidently had in some other towns in the region. New Year 1950 was notable for the determination of one man to welcome it in. Ned Barry of Botany had been one of the most persistent voices advocating change and had sworn that if nobody else started something that year he would have a think about it. On the 31st of December 1949 I had gone to bed around 9.30 to 10.00 p.m. but stayed awake, reading with a torch. Paddy was on holidays in Carrick-on-Suir. It was a dry night, pitch black. Coming up to midnight I opened my window and looked up and down the street. The town was dead. Not even a flicker of light from the Red House or the hotel. After a while I shut the window and went back under the clothes, disappointed that there was no sign of a hum around the Monument, the natural focal point if anything was to cut loose. Shortly afterwards, the newly installed electric town clock, of which we were very proud, started striking twelve. I lay there, counting off the hours. Immediately the last bell struck there was a wild roar from up the street near Ormonde's corner, followed by a great clatter. I sprang out of bed and stuck my head out of the window just in time to see a dark figure racing by on a bicycle, towing behind him a long tail of assorted empty cans, loosely strung together and hopping and sparking along the road like a party of mad march hares. I laughed as he headed on up Main Street and the lights in the houses came on one after another. By now my parents were standing at the front door and heard my delighted squeals.

Mam looked up. 'Who was that?' she asked, laughing.

'I don't know,' I lied, not wishing to give away Ned's name in case some spoilsport might complain to the guards about the stunt. Though I had barely made out the person's outline I was certain it was Ned and, sure enough, next day it was confirmed to me at Kitty Keyes's.

Birthdays were not much feted in Lismore. Your own was always a welcome event, usually just a small family affair. Some years the Feeneys might be invited round to us in the afternoon for cake and lemonade. And Paddy and I might be invited round to Feeneys for Mike's or Tom's or Margaret's birthday. There was no real pattern to it. The biggest party I went to was at the McConnells and it was rather formal. It was given for their daughter Popsie and all of us who used to play in the Villa at that time were invited. Mam gave me some money to buy a box of chocolate sweets as a present and I had to put on my best clothes. There were about twenty or thirty of us there, boys and girls, some of whom I did not know, like Colonel O'Brien's children from Salterbridge House. Everything was beautifully arranged and Mrs McConnell, a kind and charming hostess, had baked delicious cakes. And there was more orange juice and lemonade than we could guzzle. I felt very shy and awkward at first but got by without incident once the party was underway.

Self-organised games, often on the spur of the moment, we enjoyed a lot. These included arrow-hunt down the Grove, tree-climbing, jumping off high walls, rolling boulders down steep slopes, and playing hide-and-seek. No formal equipment was required to play any of them. Pieces of chalk for the arrow-hunt we picked up off the dirt roads. Any chalky stone good enough to scratch an arrow sufficed. The Boy Scouts used to organise paper-chases among themselves but, not being a member of the troop, I could not take part in these. On occasion the 'hares' rushed by me in the Grove, scattering Guinness bottle labels or scraps of newsprint from bags hung around their shoulders. Other times I came across their trails after the event. Always I wished that I could have joined in. But we non-Scouts organised the odd one of our own too. The Grove, above the Blackwater deep we knew as the 'X-Hole' (as Eugene Dennis has reminded me) was also one of our places, the favourite one, for rolling boulders. (Edward 'Beaver' Doherty has informed me that another deep, located downriver from the Bridge and across from the Point, was known as 'Miss Lattin's Hole', presumably from some unfortunate incident in the past.) The other escarpment we used overlooked Ballyin Mill. Both had their attractions. The object of the 'game' was to prize loose the biggest rocks we could manhandle and send them crashing down the slopes through the woodland. The louder their helter-skelter career the better we liked it. At the Grove there was the added *frisson* of seeing the rocks end their run with a great splash in the Blackwater. Those at Ballyin travelled down a more precipitous slope and ended their run on the flat scrubland at the bottom. The advantage there was that they had a clearer passage and consequently whizzed down. We had the good sense to make sure before launching the boulders that the way beneath was clear of living things. This was essential in the Grove as the boulders traversed at least two of the snaking pathways that were cut into its side. Not being able to see all the way to the bottom, one or two of us had to station ourselves along the chosen trajectory to ensure that no harm came to any person or animal when we released the rock.

Heights from which to jump could be found anywhere but the biggest challenges were the cliff above the sawdust pit in the Warren, the high brick wall near the turntable at the railway station, and the sandpit. Of these three the most dangerous was undoubtedly the cliff in the Warren, in reality the leftover wall of a disused quarry, where the lads from Church Lane liked to risk legs and pelvis. The surplus sawdust of many years from the castle sawmill had been dumped, and was still being dumped, here to form, unwittingly, the springy bed that formed a landing pad. The cliff was vertical and there were three distinct ledges from which you could jump: the lowest at fifteen or sixteen feet; the middle one, perhaps twenty-five to thirty feet; and, the most awesome, the top of the cliff, which was all of fifty or sixty feet high, or as high as the roof of a three-storey house. I only ever dared go off the lowest level. I myself saw Beaver jump off the middle, or second, one. Among others known to have braved the intermediate stage were Papa Hickey and Pete Neville. I never saw anyone go off the top. It was rumoured that it had been done but I never came across an eyewitness account. If anybody had risked smashing his legs on so foolhardy a leap, it would have been someone like Mick Coleman or Brooky Lynch. It is possible that some lads jumped from the top on to the middle level, which would have been a hair-raising stunt in itself as it meant a touchdown not on sawdust but on rock overlayed with a tangle of ivy and moss, and would have demanded a keen sense of balance on landing to avoid toppling over onto the lower ledge, or all the way to the bottom. The lads from the Lane were happy enough to regard the second level drop as a sort of initiation to manhood for the bravest. Looking down from that height, I was well able to believe it.

In comparison, the Botany test was tame. Not that the Botany lads tried to equate the two. But the ledge by the turntable was still a test. It might have been only ten to twelve feet high but you landed on grass and not on springy sawdust. The real test was to take a standing jump off it. I used to only trust myself from a sitting position and, even then, hit the ground with a wallop. A running launch from the grassy overhang boosted your takeoff at the sandpit. This jump depended more on style and athletic ability but, needless to say, nerve came into it too. The sand, sloping away from you, made a great break-fall. There was a possible danger of sandslide. Our parents never liked to hear that we had been playing at the pit and, because of previous accidents, even a fatality or two I think, constantly warned us against going there. In spite of their worries, we went. But I think we became reasonably sensitised to the danger and kept a close eye on the condition of the sand.

For me, sand-jumping was higher up the pleasure scale than the other two but for real uninhibited pleasure we turned to another variant, jumping off hayricks in barns. Farmers did not approve of this so you had to pick a quiet moment in the farmyard. The most accessible venue was the high, galvanised shed on the Castle Farm at Feeney's. Hoagy, Willie Ryan, the McConnell brothers, and Tom Feeney and I, used to have great fun jumping off the top of it, or sliding down its sides, onto the hay piled up at the base. Until one day Pad Feeney, in an unusually sour mood for him, caught us at it.

'Fuck off out o' that!' he ordered.

'Sure we're doin' no harm, Pad,' we protested sheepishly.

'How would ye like it if someone trampled all over yere breakfast?' he asked and sent us on our way.

His logic was irrefutable and I never jumped on hay with an easy mind again.

Pranks were always on the cards. Sucky taught us a new one with unexpected swiftness. Spud Murphy and Foxy and I happened to be chatting with him under the rookery in the Villa beeches. We though nothing of it when he withdrew a few steps from us and leant back nonchalantly against one of the trunks. Suddenly he roared and clapped his hands as loudly as he could. The three of us looked at him, wondering what he was up to. Too quickly we learned when a shower of crow shit rained down on us from the startled birds above that had taken flight. Close to the tree, he was out of the line of fire. How he laughed as we rubbed the shit out of our hair and off our jackets! The lesson was not lost on us. I had occasion to pull the stunt on a few innocents myself afterwards. With Sucky we went on to create a game out of it. All of us would stand on the fringe of the canopy of the trees then suddenly shout and clap our hands. After that it was a dash for the shelter of the trunks before the shit hit the ground.

Playing anything with Sucky could he hazardous, even hide-and-seek. Boxer and I were hiding under the laurels on the corner of the bridge and the Ballyduff Road when we heard our pursuers Sucky and Foxy jump on to the wall above us.

'Got ye!' shouted Sucky in triumph.

We stayed stumm, knowing that he could not see us through the dense foliage. There was more than a fifty-fifty chance that he was bluffing.

'Aw, come on, lads,' we next heard Foxy say in his plaintive voice. 'We know ye're in there. Let's go off somewhere else.'

We remained silent.

'Come on, lads,' he called again impatiently.

Still we lay doggo.

There was some muttering above us and the next thing it seemed to be raining.

'Fuck! He's pissing down on us!' Boxer twigged instantly and we dashed clear.

'Oh!?' said Sucky in mock surprise, packing his prick away. 'Were ye in there after all. Sorry lads.' And he and Foxy laughed uproariously, leaving us to eff and blind at them.

Effing and blinding came naturally to us, as to most Irish youngsters. To the odd Englishman or Englishwoman who chanced to hear us it must have appeared excessive, judging by some reactions I encountered, but to us it was often no more forceful than saying affectionately to a pal, 'You fuckin' bollocks!'

The Fair Field in late autumn was one of my favourite places for playing hide-and- seek. Its surface seemed flat when you glanced at it in daylight but at night when you were in there the dull glow of the street lights from Botany and Chapel Street revealed a multiplicity of hollows in which you could lie flat as a sniper. Often we carried torches or bicycle lamps so that we could rake an area where we sensed movement or thought someone was concealing himself; you had to be fairly certain in your judgement of this because, in showing a light, you gave away your own position. If you guessed wrongly you had to move out of the immediate area smartly. The torches I sought for myself were those with a good spot. I liked watching the strong beam disperse in the infinity of the black, starlit sky, or trace a pattern on the underbelly of a low-hung cloud. Less ambitiously, I employed it to puzzle the crows in the Villa rookery.

From our game in the Fair Field it was only a short progression to another enduring pastime – knocking on front doors and running away. Sometimes we would knock and not run away but duck behind a nearby wall or shrub so that we could giggle silently at the puzzlement or chagrin on the face of the man or woman who had opened the door. When we were really out to annoy someone we would return a minute or two later and repeat the process. We tried to vary our knocks, sometimes rapping like the postman, sometimes tapping politely, other times, bang, bang, bang. And sometimes we rapped the length of a street, bringing everyone to their doors. Now and again we got chased but, as we always had a head start on our pursuer, we never got caught, well nearly never. The chasers were usually those to whom we accorded special treatment – a salvo of haws from our peashooters in the back of the neck after they had checked the street and turned to go back inside. That brought out the worst in even the calmest of people and you had to scoot like a bat out of hell. If you really wanted to be daring you stole even closer and sprayed the householder using a water pistol or bicycle pump converted to a super-water pistol. That cut your head start to a minimum. And, of course, passers-by and cyclists became innocent accomplices in our game by obligingly walking into, or cycling into, dark thread that we had stretched across a pathway from knocker to electricity pole or across the road from knocker to knocker. We did not go in for this very much because it involved waiting around for someone to come by. In a quiet town like Lismore that was more of a wait than we had the patience for. But we gave it a whirl.

As plaything and public irritant the peashooter stayed with Sucky, Boxer and me for longer than was decently acceptable. Like the catapult, it was an instrument with which we had grown up, of which we acquired mastery, and which we took great pride in using. You did not throw all that out of the window lightly. Harmless compared to the catapult in terms of weaponry, the peashooter, nonetheless, had to be aimed with care. You never shot at a person's face where injury to the eye might occur. Down the years we tried out various models from the long and the short ground elder and hogweed ones to those fashioned from the best castle bamboo. The last-mentioned was the Parker pen of peashooters, some twelve to fourteen inches long, cauterised inside with the red-hot spoke of a bicycle wheel, and offering range and accuracy. Elegant and durable but not necessarily any more accurate than a ground elder or hogweed job of equal length. Ammunition for our shooters was inexhaustible, and free. The hedgerows of the surrounding countryside were red with haws in autumn. Targets, mainly town-based, were to be found in abundance as well. The haw was expelled singly or in a burst of up to ten. You usually put a handful in your mouth to give you either option.

One of my earliest, and most irresistible targets was, I think, the shiny bald head of a jovial uncle of Michael O'Farrell's who used to drink at the Wine Vaults. I was recovering from an illness at the time and was leaning out of my bedroom window chatting to Hoagy and Tom Feeney, who were below in the street, when I spotted it coming up by the barracks. I got out my shooter and signalled to the lads that they should just appear to be talking to each another. When the head was passing I peppered it with a mouthful of haws. They bounced off it like rain off a tin can. I pulled back and stayed still as a Sioux behind the curtain.

A good-humoured voice floated up, 'You have a good shot up there whoever you are.'

I peeked out as the head turned into Macs, a hand patting it ostentatiously.

But we did not pick on unarmed innocents only. Mainly we were bouncing haws off one another. The most forbidden places to spit a haw were at chapel, naturally, and at the cinema. Letting one go in church was probably high on the scale of sin. We certainly did not attempt it often. The Palladium did not carry the same weight of sacredness, but we were mindful of the danger of hitting someone in the eye and contented ourselves to lofting loose scatters from the fourpennies into the one-and-threes when the screen darkened. Of course, when we went to the shillings, which we did expressly on occasion, we had no compunction about spraying someone or other we knew in the fourpennies on the back of the head.

Three activities for juniors that were governed by indefinable seasons were playing marbles, rolling bicycle hoops and wheels, and whipping tops. Marbles we played in spring, I think, but sometimes in autumn too. Perhaps the British Marbles Championship held at Tinsley Green in Surrey at Eastertime influenced the beginning or end of our marbles season but, if this was so, it was wholly unbeknownst to us. Three different types of sphere were employed in playing marbles: the 'taw', made of white ceramic, with a diameter of about one inch; the 'glassie', made of multicoloured, translucent glass and five-eighths of an inch in diameter; and the 'marble', a dun-coloured clay piece, having a diameter of just under half an inch. Glassies were the prize items. They could not be bought in the town for a number of years so the same ones were recycled from season to season and were usually pretty chipped from use. From time to time a glistening new one would appear, brought home perhaps from England or the United States by a visiting relative. Glass taws also existed but these were rare. The ordinary clay marbles – what we called marbles in Lismore and they called 'mebs' in Carrick-on-Suir – we could purchase from Teasy Meade. White taws she also sold. Up to six of us might be involved in a game. The play area was generally a flat piece of pathway, earthen or tarred. Similar areas in the school playground were used as well. 'Flat' was relative; some of the pitches on which we played were pretty bumpy. The marbles and glassies were placed in a line about three inches from the base of the wall and about the same distance apart. The player rolled from the kerb, when there was one, a distance of four to five feet. The object was to dislodge as many items as you could with your taw. Every marble or glassie you hit, whether directly or on the rebound from the wall, you could pocket. It was usual, if you had first go, to throw from an angle as this gave you an increased chance of taking two or three items. If you ran low on marbles you could do a swop. The exchange rate was three marbles to a glassie. The rate for taws was negotiable. In Carrick they did not roll the taw but rested it on the index finger and released it with a flick of the thumb. Barney Walsh and I played a lot of marbles and could usually hold our own.

A posse of us rolling hoops could create quite a din. The hoop was simply the rim of an old bicycle wheel. The knack was in keeping it under control with a foot-long stick or baton that you cut from the branch of an ash or hazel tree. There were various ways of doing this. To start the hoop off, you held it vertically on the ground on your right side with the left hand stretched across your body and hit it on the back with the baton you held in your right, vice versa if you were a *ciotóg*. You then kept it rolling by belting it at regular intervals as you ran alongside it. To deflect it or turn it you could either touch the near edge or far edge with the stick or otherwise steer it by holding the stick vertically against the concave hollow of the back. Braking was achieved by pressing the stick down horizontally on the concave hollow of the top. Sometimes when you were really bowling along you might hit the hoop too vigorously and see it run away from you. Other times it might take a deflection on an uneven road surface and career into somebody's legs, or in through a shop door, in which case you would run up breathlessly, grab your hoop, say you were sorry, and take off again with the sharp edge of a tongue in you ear. If you sensed the hoop was in danger of running out of control, or if you had to stop it in an emergency, you hooked it off the ground with the baton, there not being time to brake it in the conventional manner. Pile-ups were common during street races. One hoop straying off its line would bring the others down. It easily happened as the wheels, scavenged as they were from old bicycles, were not always as round as they might have been. With Feeney's garage next door selling and repairing bikes, and having Tom as a pal, I was assured of a good source of hoops. You needed a new one every so often because they went out of shape from crashing into walls and other obstacles. The constant lash of the stick took its toll as well. Under the guidance of Kieran Fenton and Panzer Behegan, Tom and I developed more streamlined models using whole wheels with tubes and tyres. These were less controllable than the hoops when you bowled them in the conventional way. An added refinement gave you complete control. One end of a five-foot length of strong fencing wire was hooked through the hub of the wheel, the other bent back on itself to form a crude handle. This device allowed you to run as fast as you liked, pushing the wheel before you. Interesting, but it could not compare with the free-wheeling clatter of the hoop.

The spinning tops we whipped were of three types and all were made of wood. The ace was the one we knew as the Tommy top. This mushroom-shaped object had a head with a diameter of an inch and three eighths and a thickness of five eighths, a stem with a diameter of six eighths at its widest coming to a point at an inch and a half. Total height, two-and-a-quarter inches. The stem was usually decorated with a red and a blue strip. A metal stud was hammered into the point. The Spitfire of tops, it could be whipped comfortably through the air thirty, forty or fifty yards and still be spinning when you caught up with it. Ordinary tops were much less elegant and aerodynamic. More conical or pear-shaped than mushroom-shaped, they came in two varieties. One had a diameter of an inch and a half at its head and tapered to a point into which a metal stud was also hammered. Its height was two-and-a-half inches. The other had a head diameter of an inch and seven eighths and tapered two-and-a- quarter inches to a metal-studded point. The bodies of both tops were ribbed, the first narrowly, the second broadly. These tops, especially the fatter one of the two, required less skill to keep them spinning than the Tommy and could be whipped no more than a quarter or a third of the distance that you could whip the ace. They were the models with which you started off. Only when you had mastered these could you take on the Tommy. It took some skill to get a top started. You wound the end of your lash around the body of it and with a quick flick of your wrist released it onto the surface of the road. If it stayed spinning you were on you way. If not, you had to begin again. On the flat heads of all the tops we gummed pieces of coloured paper torn from chocolate or sweet wrappers so that when the tops were spinning we got an attractive rainbow effect. The whip, or lash, which you could employ with all models, was a one-and-a-half- to-two-foot branch of ash or sycamore to the end of which you tied a length of binder twine, perhaps two or two-and-a-half feet long. After it had been run-in the twine had a frayed tail. Tom and Margaret Feeney and I used to whip our tops up and down West Street, Main Street and Gallows Hill mainly.

Mike Feeney, who by then had outgrown the pastime, liked to give us an occasional demonstration on the Tommy at which he was a wizard. He could send it further than anyone else we knew, from the garage to the guards' barracks and beyond, the best part of a hundred yards. And it would still be spinning on its point when he caught up with it. Adults were wary of our Tommies because there was a fine line between hitting them straight and accidentally curling them. Frequently a shop window or a car or a person took a rap. Not a popular top to be seen with. When we appeared in the Main Street shopkeepers would peer out at us anxiously. In time we learned to restrict the length of our shots there and saved the daring drives for West Street and Gallows Hill where there were fewer windows. Traffic was hardly a problem. Whether we were whipping tops or rolling hoops or pucking a ball around with our hurleys, there was always enough space for the odd car to motor by. Eventually it was the coincidental resurfacing of the three streets that put an end to my whipping. You could not spin tops on newly laid chippings. I moved to other streets for a while but by then, having just about outgrown the top, I bowed to the inevitable and quit.

Winter sports consisted of belting hell out of one another with snowballs, rolling massive snowballs down slopes and watching them grow even bigger, making snowmen, tobogganing and sliding. The nearest thing we had to an outdoor skating rink was the enclosure on the Ferry Inch within which water was allowed to freeze. Rarely in my time was this ice sheet thick enough to withstand the weight of humans. The slide in hilly upper Botany did not require such cold conditions. Freezing point did nicely. When hard frost and snow appeared the Botany lads would lend nature a hand by sneaking out at night and pouring water on the steep section from Tommy Keating's to Tommy the Hawk's. In the morning a clear sheet of ice would

Upper New Street, Lismore, 'Botany' to us, in the late 1940's probably. The winter slide on which we skated ran down the middle of the steepest section of the street.

Skating on the level. Unidentified boys skating on a slide, probably of their own making. (Is that Michael Twomey with arms outstretched, perhaps?) Another slide is seen on the left. The place is the Ferry Inch across from Lismore Castle *(see Chapter 1)*. Probably 1940s.

cover the road from pathway to pathway, forming a slide of some thirty to forty yards. Much to the annoyance of Tommy Keating, who lived above it, because, instead of his being able to drive his ass and cart down the street as he usually did, he had to detour round by the long incline of Gallows Hill, which, though more travelled, was also fairly treacherous in those wintry conditions. As long as the frost held the lads would keep watering the slide and that, coupled with the nightly usage, ensured an increasingly slippery surface, especially on the strip down the centre of the road, which was the most testing. There would always be someone on the slope, the peak times being immediately after school and in the evening. Around eight at night was best; even the adults came out to watch. Dogs would be yapping with excitement, some having a go at the slide willingly, others being thrown onto it unwillingly. The street lights would be augmented by oil-lamps in the neighbouring windows, and the periodic opening and shutting of doors would lend the warm glow of firelight to the carnival atmosphere. The most difficult feat was to skate the full length of the slide standing up. Typically, Pedro O'Brien was best at it, with Pippa a close second. Excitement was at a peak when Pedro was having a go. His swarthy face would go taut with concentration in the run-up. Then he would launch himself onto the slide, balancing with outstretched arms all the way to the bottom. A cheer would go up at start and finish. I did not have the sense of balance for the full slide and had to be content with a standing descent on the lower half. From the top I went down sitting on my heels. Some of the older lads attempting to skate the whole way on their feet would fall over and give themselves a nasty knock. A few would retire with cuts. But all would be back again later, if not that night, then the following one.

Using his carpentry skills, Dad fashioned me a wooden sled big enough for two. A natural toboggan run was available on the long slope of the hill on the old golf course by Ballyin Gardens. At that time the course was only used for grazing sheep and cattle and the run took you straight down the hill facing the Ballyduff Road. In summer we used to lie down on the summit of the same ground with our arms stretched out over our heads and allow ourselves to roll down the longest slope till we became dizzy. We knew the snows of winter could disappear from one day to the next so we always tried to get the utmost out of the conditions, at times in desperation sledging more on the wet grass and sand than on the snow. One year, when a bright sun had all but thawed the last snow, Michael and Tom Feeney and Paddy Creane and I were down to tipping the toboggan over the rim of a small sandpit, possibly a disused bunker, on the Blackwater side of the hill and sliding down onto the stones and gravel at the bottom. We had being going over successfully and now it was Mike's turn. I had been down a couple of times and was keen to have another go. Mike was balanced on the rim under which there was an immediate three-foot drop before you hit the snow and sand. He was taking a long time getting ready, it seemed to me in my impatience, pulling on his gloves like he was settling himself behind the wheel of a racing-car. Inadvertently, or deliberately – it could have been either – I nudged the back of the toboggan with my foot and over he went unprepared, bouncing down to the bottom as if he were on a bucking bronco. He landed right side up, cursing me. I paled, expecting a wallop. But he just gave me a severe ticking off.

Gang warfare in Lismore had innocent beginnings in games of hide-and-seek, cowboys and Indians, and sword-fighting. It came about mainly over territory. The Warren and Protestant cathedral area, extending to the Mall Seat, was considered the backyard of the boys from Church Lane. The Botany boys had an extended interest beyond their street reaching from the railway station through the Fair Field and the library as far as the gully in the Villa, although their claim to the West Street end was tenuous. Main Street boys were less territorial but the Townparks lads grew nervous if the Botany boys started encroaching east of the station. Places like the Grove and the Strand, and the banks of the Blackwater and the Owenashad, were regarded as open territory so you could explore the Teampuileen caves, the underground drains of the Ferry Inch or any other niche without crossing anyone. Only in times of perceived tension would you have to watch your step. And, of course, you could roam the surrounding countryside at will. As West Street was sandwiched between Main Street and Botany, I was confused by a dual allegiance. Fortunately I never had to choose, although in my teens I spent more time in Botany than in Main Street. Warfare seldom got beyond the point of skirmishing and only then following some minor incident that had grown out of proportion. When a matter would not rest lightly older boys became involved. Then some very real hand-to-hand fighting took place. One tense autumn night I saw a Botany gang put on an impressive display of its power by parading around its patch carrying flaming torches made from 'bulrushes' (false bulrush or reedmace) dipped in tar. The bullet-headed stems, plucked from a site along the Blackwater, left an acrid aroma in their wake. In winter, snowballing fights could take a serious turn. A stone might be secreted inside the ball to give the recipient an unpleasant surprise. I heard of razor blades being placed in snowballs also but I never came across an occurrence of this. Most likely it was just a rumour. I cannot imagine that anyone I knew, or was even acquainted with, would have thought for a moment of doing so criminal a thing.

The middle class of the town tended to exaggerate such events, as they did the odd occurrence of a man giving his wife a black eye or a wife laying out her husband with the flat of a frying pan. Thus, the earliest pictures of Botany and the Lane sketched for me filled me with some trepidation. Luckily, I was well-placed to explore Botany for myself as I lived just around the corner from it. Also, and more importantly, from an early age I used to play with Barney Walsh, who lived only a hundred yards up from Ormonde's Corner. In this way, I had an earlier entrée to the street than my pals who lived up the Main Street. Similarly, those pals who lived in upper Main Street formed friendships with the boys from Church Lane. I must have been in my earliest teens before I made real contact with the Lane, by which time I knew Botany well.

The contentious area around the back of the library and the grounds of the Villa formed a playground favoured by Main Street, West Street and Botany lads. The situation changed after the Villa, unoccupied for some years was bought, or rented, by Colonel McConnell, a recently retired Palestine police commissioner, in 1948. Before that year slanging matches and mild exchanges of catapult fire would erupt between Main Street and Botany elements from time to time across the Gully, a kind of trench that marked the course of a former dirt track, now a muddy dip, that had led

Me, Gerald McConnell (back); Willie Ryan, Mickey McConnell (middle) Popsie McConnell (front). Taken at the Villa in West Street, Lismore, c. 1947.

War games at the Villa. Me sparring with Gerard McConnell (back); Mickey McConnell astride Willie Ryan (middle); Popsie holding rope. Lismore, c. 1947.

(From left on the fence) Me, Gerald McConnell, Willie Ryan and Mickey McConnell, with Popsie McConnell in front. Taken at the Villa in West Street, Lismore, c. 1947.

Pals. Mickey McConnell and Willie Ryan in front of the stand of New Zealand flax at the edge of the Villa lawn, c. 1947.

A group of us peering out through the stand of New Zealand flax that grew by *The Villa* lawn. From left to right; Willie Ryan, top of head of either Gerald or Mickey McConnell, Jim Ballantyne and Popsie McConnell with a ribbon in her hair. *c* 1947.

from the walled backyard of the house to the locked green wooden gate opposite Ormondes. Things only became serious when rivals were seen to muddy their faces and stick ferns in their hair.

The Villa was a marvellous playground. It had a variety of trees and bushes – beech, ash, sycamore, holly, laurels plain and variegated, flowering shrubs, and a splendid monkey-puzzle on the front lawn – and a thick undergrowth of briars, ground elder and hogweed which, even in the Colonel's time, was allowed to grow almost unchecked. Around these grounds we rode in posse, smacking our rumps with a hand to simulate using the whip on our horses, and whooping when cast in the role of Indians. Playing Cowboys and Indians, or hide-and-seek, we encountered incidentally many forms of life among the weeds and grasses in which we concealed ourselves, from scary slugs and scampering spiders to the mysterious, frothy exudation that we knew as cuckoo spit. Ideal territory, right on our doorstep. Barney, Hoagy and the Feeneys and I were always in there, and never without gadgets in our pockets – chipped, convex magnifying glasses from old torches with which to burn holes in paper or sting one another's skin by harnessing the heat of the sun; worthless foreign coins for swopping; magnets; penknives for carving our names or initials on trees and for cutting and trimming peashooters... In our teens we developed something of a mania for knives, in particular, throwing knives. We held the Indian and Mexican knifemen of the pictures, with their deadly accuracy from impossible angles and distances, in high esteem. The performing knife-throwers of the circuses, on the whole, disappointed us because they seemed to be no more than eight or ten feet away from the fetching lady around whom they targeted their special blades. To begin with, we made our own throwing knives out of old table knives that we sharpened to a point on the carborundum wheel in Feeney's garage. The finished product looked passable but, having little balance, seldom stuck in our tree-trunk targets. Later, through an address that I had from a comic, I sent off for what was advertised as a throwing knife. On receipt it turned out to be a kind of stiletto with no balance, useless as a throwing knife. At least, Barney and I could seldom get it to stick. The most successful throwing knife we had was a kris that Barney's brother Tom, who was in the British Army, had brought home from Malaya. It was well-balanced, possibly because the torso-shaped hilt, in the image of a goddess, and the wavy blade itself were made of the one material, a kind of aluminium alloy, it seemed to us. If you did not stand too far back from the tree you could always get it to stick. So encouraged were we by this that I was even persuaded by Barney to stand against the trunk and let him sink the knife in the wood next to me like in the circus. The knife was not used exclusively for throwing. Barney nearly took his eye out with it once when he was carving his initials on a hard beech. The blade slipped upwards and outwards and sank about a quarter of an inch into his eyebrow.

When we first heard that new people were taking over the Villa we feared that it would mean the end of our playground. They were coming from abroad, after all, and would hardly want us kids running free on their acres. When it transpired that there were two boys of our age group in the family there was hope. Hesitantly, but surprisingly quickly, we got to know one another and Gerald and Mickey were enrolled at our school. They were to attend the CBS for a year or two after which they were sent to Clongowes Wood boarding school near Dublin, a kind of Jesuit public school, I was given to understand. Mickey, home on holidays from his first term there, did not seem the slightest bit overawed by it. Willie Ryan of Townparks became a great pal of his and moved closer into what was becoming a Villa circle. Paddy Creane joined us around this time also. All part of the way children grew up in our world, discovering new allegiances and interests but also, hurtfully discarding or unhappily losing former friends in the process.

Sometimes you became acutely aware of the hurt involved. It was neither pleasant to be rejected nor to be the one who was doing the rejecting. A big, wild-looking tinker lad, a bit older than I but lacking my education, such as it was until then, used to come around the ball alley when he was in town and, because no one else seemed to be paying him much heed, I befriended him. It was okay for a while but when he began to follow me about everywhere I got annoyed. I had my other pals, my old pals, to think about, too, and was not willing to devote more time to him than to them. Eventually, I had angry words with him and told him I did not want to see him again. Puzzlement and sadness clouded his face. I felt both sorry and relieved. He was around town for a while after that. Then he was gone. I never laid eyes on him again. It was a great shame for both of us that I did not know how to handle things better.

Having made friends with the McConnells, we had assured for ourselves continued access to the Villa grounds during the Colonel's residency. The Colonel, a Corkman, had returned from Palestine after the establishment of the State of Israel with his charming wife and Mickey, Gerald and daughter Popsie. With them also lived 'Uncle Bill' who, we understood, was not so much a relative as an old friend of the family. An enigmatic figure, he was never seen near a church of any denomination and no one ever learned his surname. He always wore flecked tweed suits, a matching hat perched on the Kildare side of his head, and he carried a cane. The cane was wholly in character. He carried it jauntily when he was sober, twirling it now and again, and it held him upright when he was drunk – which, sadly, was often enough. Regularly I would glimpse him through the window of the Devonshire Arms, sitting at the bar. Every so often the Colonel would have to collect him and lend him a shoulder home. He was never loud or demonstrative when he was drunk, just quiet and sleepy, with the air of a lost child. In general, there was something lost and lonely about him and I think Mrs McConnell, who was an ex-nurse, looked after him most kindly. He seemed to be very much a guest in the McConnell household and Mickey and Gerald never seemed quite sure of how they should relate to him. I never saw him doing any work about the Villa, other than a few inadequate attempts with a billhook, aptly named, at cutting back the undergrowth in the grounds. Physically he just was not up to it. Sober, he was a most amiable, if reclusive, character and always smiled nicely at us youngsters. Dad saw in him something more sinister, the devil-may-care cut of an Auxie from the time of the Black and Tans. He would not have been at all surprised if he heard that Bill had been one. It was the jauntiness, he said; men who had been through the carnage of the First World War had lost their beliefs, their ideals, and their fear of death. Dad sighed despondently saying this for he too found Bill an amiable person.

Colonel McConnell was a bit of a puzzle to us children. He exuded an air of authority and repression and yet was always polite to us, and was gentleness itself with Popsie and Bill. With the boys he was a ferocious disciplinarian. I saw him take his heavy brown belt to them on a couple of occasions, one of which seemed to me to be totally unwarranted – Gerald had been ten minutes late for tea. I felt particularly bad about this as I was the one who had delayed my pal. But the Colonel would not heed my protests and drove Gerald off to the house with a few sound wallops on the rump. It seemed even more unfair to me as Gerald was normally very quiet and well-behaved. Mickey was more recalcitrant when he got the lash and, tough as nails, just swore under his breath. He took his phops in school in the same laconic manner. In those moments I saw the Colonel as the Charles Laughton-portrayed father in *The Barretts of Wimpole Street,* or as the same actor's Captain Bligh in *Mutiny on the Bounty.*

I was sensitive to his authoritarianism because my experience of my own father could not have been more different. Neither Dad nor Mam ever raised a hand against me, though I gave them good cause more than once. Even when Mam would happily have seen Dad give me a smack, he stayed his hand. With Colonel McConnell you felt that had it not been for his wife, who was sweet and gentle, he would have been downright unpleasant. The other aspect of him that aroused my curiosity was his Catholicism. It was strange to see someone who from his accent and manners had so obviously been a cog of the British machinery of State attending Mass with his family in our small republican town.

One of our greatest pleasures when the McConnells were in residence was building 'camps' in the dense Villa shrubbery. We would clear a space under a shady laurel, tread out a muddy floor, cut branches and entwine them into a roof and walls, make a doorway and a couple of lookout holes, and finally camouflage the whole from outside so that the casual eye would not remark it. The thick layer of laurel with which we roofed the camps made them virtually rainproof as the worst of any downpour was absorbed or deflected by the beech canopy overhead. A camp was at its most secretive on drizzly sound-quashed days when the rainwater seeping in at the underskirts infused the interior with an earthy fug. Inside, four or five of us could squat comfortably, talking and planning, planning and talking. From our secret base we would go on scouting expeditions to check whether any other camps had been erected in the area. If we found another we might wreck it, or not. Smashing another group's camp was an outright act of war. But camps fell apart from disuse, too. And sometimes we smashed one of our own if we thought it had been discovered. We tried to build camps in trees but they were very difficult to construct and anyway impossible to disguise. The whole point about camps was that they should be secret.

One of our attempts at camp-building almost cost me my life. I was fifteen feet up a sycamore near the driveway to the Villa, hacking off suitable branches with a rusty old meat cleaver that Mickey had found in an outhouse when I slipped and fell to the ground. Fortunately, the cleaver fell away from me on the other side of the tree and, even more fortunately, Popsie, who would have been standing under it if I had dropped it a few moments earlier, had moved back to another position. The cleaver bounced harmlessly off the brown earth. I hit the ground with the flat of my back and bounced, too, no doubt. I did not notice as the wallop knocked me out. I came to as Mickey and the others – Mickey was the only one I could make out – were carrying me down the narrow path toward the wicket gate opposite my home. Mam got the fright of her life when she opened the door. Barely conscious, I was carried upstairs and placed flat on my back on my parents' double bed. The blind was drawn down on the window. Then I was left alone. A short time later one of the Ormondes from Dungarvan, a nurse who happened to be visiting her relatives up the street, came in and examined me. A doctor could not be found. All she could say with certainty was that I did not seem to have broken any bones. Tom Feeney sent me an apology via Mam for not having helped to carry me.

'I was too small,' he explained, 'so I just walked behind.'

The nurse knew her stuff. I had not fractured any bones. Doc Healy examined me when he got back to town. I was badly concussed, he said, and would have to lie on my back in a darkened room for a few days. I was lucky and made a full recovery. A couple of months later I fell off a tree again but this time I was no more than six feet up. Mam learned of that May mishap from Paddy when she was attending rosary at the chapel.

He went up to her and whispered calmly, 'Jim fell off a tree again. But he's okay. Said to tell you he'd taken an aspro and gone to bed.'

She rushed home at once to see for herself and was relieved to find that it was nothing worse.

Our fondness for building camps came partly from the pictures, partly from the comics, and a lot from the lore of the local Boy Scouts – dowsing for water with a hazel twig, freshly cut in a Y-shape, was an idea gleaned from them that I fruitlessly attempted. I was sceptical about the whole thing and the dowsing-rod, held out gently in front of me by the prongs between thumbs and fingers, resolutely refused to turn it's 'nose' towards the ground of its own accord, even when I held it over open water. I quickly ascertained that if you gently forced the prongs apart the nose, or leg of the 'Y', did indeed incline downwards – or upwards depending on which way round you grasped the rod. But this was good-humoured cheating. In spite of our lack of nous and success I think we accepted that there did exist individuals who were skilled dowsers. Such divination was undoubtedly one of the Scouts' rarer notions. It only increased my desire to be one of them but Mam would not let me join. She seemed to think I was too delicate to be let off on my own with a bunch of assorted kids. On the other hand, as Seán Dennis has reminded me, people held 'views' about the Scouts, and Mam and Dad with their republican sympathies may well have shared these. For those with such reservations the Scout movement, because of its founder Lord Baden-Powell, the defender of Mafeking, was tainted by imperialist and colonialist associations.

'Barney an' Tom an' Willie are in the Scouts. So is Bags Murphy. So why can't I be?' I wailed.

But all to no avail. Every August I would watch forlornly as Kieran Fenton, the Scoutmaster, and Billy Hogan of the Main Street, the assistant Scoutmaster, made preparations at the garage to take the troop on an annual holiday to the seaside. The two bell-tents would be laid out for inspection, the canvas re-creosoted and any holes sewn up or otherwise mended. Pegs and lamps and other equipment would be counted and tested. On going-away day Kieran and Billy would be in full uniform. Two lorries would roll up, one driven by Panzer Behegan. A number of Scouts in uniform would help load the tents and other equipment. Finally, they would sling aboard their bags and cases. Then the lorries would drive off to pick up the other members of the troop. Some time later they would pass by again. I would wave to the cheering Scouts sitting on the tents as they drove off down the New Way and picture the exciting times they were going to have in Ardmore or Tramore, their usual destinations. It was a lonely moment. And it was not just that I was keen to go on annual holidays with them. They were involved in lots of other interesting activities and went on weekend camps along the Blackwater near Aglish. They had a small hall of their own, St Carthage's, a renovated church that had formerly served as a place of worship for a Protestant sect. The Scouts had done most of the renovation themselves. A hall of their own was something they had been after for a long time.

Arthur Paxman's death in 1950 brought them a different acquisition. His widow, clearing out the house, presented them with a billiard table. Until then there was only one comparable table in general use in the town, the snooker one in the green-galvanised 'Iron Room' in Fernville (or Chapel Place), which I thought was a sort of British Legion Club. Only once did I ever see the inside of this somewhat secretive place and I can neither remember who showed it to me nor what it looked like, beyond recalling that it was gloomy, and maybe that was just because the curtains were drawn. (For a brief history of the club see *The Last Forge in Lismore* by Paddy Vaughan, page 87.)

I do remember the first snooker table I ever saw. It filled the middle of a cavernous room with a huge churchy window in the old Temperance Hall in Greystone Street, Carrick-on-Suir, directly across the street from my aunts' house. Around the walls were ranged long, leather-covered seats with wooden backs that had seen better days. Everything was covered in dust, except the green baize that was an oasis of order and rectitude. It was my Uncle Mick who took me there. My uncle Jimmy, he said, was a very good snooker player. More than watching my uncles' Davin Club friends play snooker, I enjoyed listening to them talk. I had no idea why the place was called a Temperance Hall, or what 'temperance' meant (the Pioneer Total Abstinence Association had not yet surfaced in my world). Had I known I would have doubted the qualifications of my uncles and their friends for membership.

The Scouts had their counterpart in the Girl Guides. The girls had a much lower profile than the boys, suggesting that they did not have half the fun the boys had. But maybe they had, and more. How was I to know? I knew nothing at all about their activities beyond seeing them at religious ceremonies.

It was a brush with a senior Scout, Bernie Tobin, that threatened open warfare between the Villa group and a Botany gang. Bernie, known as 'Brownie', wiry, thin-lipped and a couple of years older than me, fancied himself as a bit of a Cagney though he did not look all that tough. A gang of upper Botany boys he had formed had built a camp behind the library and it had been smashed up. They knew that we had been putting up camps around the Villa over the preceding weeks and suspected us of having been the raiders. We got word that they were thinking of reprisals and held a small council of war. A quick check among ourselves confirmed that none of us had been responsible for pulling down the camp. We had no designs on what went on over the library wall but beyond the gully we had an interest. On setting out to reconnoitre the area, we ran into enemy stonefire. A catapulting exchange followed before both sides withdrew. Brownie was not present at the skirmish. On our side I could see that Mickey McConnell's face was flushed with excitement. Later on, when an embarrassed and neutral Barney Walsh was sent to us as an intermediary Mickey was in no mood for compromise. After making it clear to Barney that we had not smashed the camp, and that we did not even consider ourselves a gang as such, he added aggressively, 'But if they want a fight, we'll give them one.' It was a difficult situation for Barney. We had reached the stage where he was no longer as close to the Villa group as he had been. As against that, he was not a member of Brownie's gang either – as far as we could tell. But, being from Botany, he was inevitably inclined to view the story from Brownie's angle, which made me sad as it put our long friendship at risk. After the meeting things went quiet for a day or two then, when I was up at the Co-op on a message for Mam, I was collared at the entrance by Brownie and Barney. Brownie grabbed the lapel of my jacket, pulled me aside and demanded to know whether we were forming a gang to take on the Botany boys. I was anything but fearless under his mean gaze but was annoyed to see that my old pal had thrown in his lot with him. Not alone that, but Barney started playing Mr Soft to Bernie's Mr Hard. I did not have to lie to Brownie and eventually he seemed to accept my protestations that we had not touched his camp and did not even consider ourselves a gang. 'Okay,' he said curtly, releasing me. Barney smiled ingratiatingly. I left, feeling humiliated that I had spoken to them at all. What right had they had to jump me like that? Tension remained in the air for another week or so as Brownie continued his search for a culprit. Then the whole thing blew over. Nobody ever gave away who had smashed the camp though we all had our suspicions. Mickey, I think, was disappointed that the matter had not reached its conclusion on the battlefield. He would have relished some hand-to-hand combat.

Some time after that our Villa group was split temporarily by internal rivalry and Barney, pals with me again, backed me when I had a fierce falling-out with Willie Ryan. Who knows what we fell out about but, whatever it was, it called for satisfaction in the ring. I imagine Willie was the injured party as I had an unfortunate penchant for blurting out things I could not back up. Already in the grounds of the Villa a year or two earlier I had drawn Mike Feeney's ire down on me by insulting the quality of Feeney's BP petrol, something I knew fuckall about.

'BP' I sneered, after Mike had got up my nose about something, 'Best piss. That's what it stands for.'

'What did you say?' asked Mike, very proprietorial and very serious all of a sudden.

'Best piss,' I repeated, not very seriously as we had been half-kidding.

'Nobody says that about our petrol,' Mike snapped, 'Put up your dukes.'

'You're bigger than me,' I protested.

'Come on,' he challenged, and snaked a straight left into my eye.

'Hey!' I said and looked vainly to his brother Tom and Hoagy for support. They were even smaller than I and Tom was additionally embarrassed for had I not insulted his petrol, too?

Mike, determined to teach me a lesson, snaked out another left. I saw no way out but to have a go at him. He was too nimble for me and that left kept snapping my head back. After a while he figured he had made his point and let me off the hook. I had not managed to lay a glove on him. Hoagy seemed very annoyed with him and Tom was simply embarrassed.

On a later occasion I said something to annoy Peadar Henley, a classmate quick to take offence, at the CBS. We were upstairs in the long room with the partition and had just come back from lunch. I was in the back desk and Peadar in the one in front of me. Whatever remark I made it got Peadar's goat and without warning he turned round and unleashed a punch at me. I was in the act of sitting down and had not expected it. It caught me on the Adam's apple, causing me to choke. Tom Lineen, sitting next to me, leapt to my defence and told my attacker that he had thrown a dirty punch. Peadar had not intended to hit me there but was unrepentant. Vin O'Donoghue, our teacher came in to start the class before the matter could escalate. In a while I got my breath back and had time to consider whether I wished to take the matter further with Peadar after school. Needless to say, I did not. I saw no sense in dropping myself further in the shit. And, more than enmity toward Peadar, because I knew I had asked for it, I felt angry with myself for walking into such humiliation. But there was a bright spot. Tom had been a true friend in springing to my aid.

Still later, I muttered something to rile Seán Dennis one evening when we were playing handball. Seán, normally the quietest and most controlled of youths and, unfortunately for me, one of the strongest, lashed out with a right unexpectedly and gave me a bloody nose. Typically, he was immediately sorry for what he had done and solicitously helped me to staunch the flow of blood. 'Will I ever learn?' I asked myself.

Like Seán, Willie never went looking for trouble so the odds were on me as the culprit. Nor, as had happened with Mike Feeney, was there a way out of a scrap. But this time at least, I could consider myself fairly matched. Willie was about my build, had maybe a few pounds on me and possibly a longer reach, but nothing to suggest I did not have an equal chance against him. We decided to settle the matter in the corner of the field behind the library according to the Marqus of Queensberry rules, about which we knew nothing but the broadest concept. Jackets and pullovers defined the ring. Mickey was Willie's second and Barney was mine. 'Get in close and give it to 'im in the belly,' was Barney's advice as we waited for someone to say go. Round one consisted of me chasing my opponent like a miniature but very skinny John L. Sullivan and he pounding me on the forehead and eyebrows with classical straight lefts like an elegant Gentleman Jim. By the end of the round I had not laid a fist on him and was asking myself, 'Where did he learn to box like that?' Then I remembered he was a Scout. Round two followed the same pattern, in spite of my second's inter-round advice and shouts of support. I ended it with tears of frustration running down my face. In the third I chased my tormentor again until my angry tears were blinding me. The fight was stopped to let me wipe them clear. We started once again. And stopped once more when the tears recommenced. Willie looked worried and appealed to Mickey and Barney to stop the fight. I was not having any of that and wanted to go on. Our seconds went into a huddle and declared it a draw. Willie agreed at once. I stalled, but eventually bowed to the inevitable. I had been whipped but had salvaged some honour.

When I got home I ran into more trouble. I had delayed as long as I could in the hope that my red and swollen eyes would have returned to normal. They had not. Mam shrieked the minute she saw me and demanded to know who had been hitting me. I ran to my room and refused to tell her. She followed me upstairs and persisted, and persisted until, to add to my shame, she wore me down. I admitted it was Willie but made her swear never to say anything to him. To my surprise she seemed quite relieved that it had only been my pal who had dished out the punishment. It did not occur to me that she might have been worried that an older boy or adult had been pegging me. As far as I know, she kept her word and never took Willie to task over it.

There was one other occasion when my loose mouth nearly got me into trouble. Seán Moynihan and I had been let out of school to sort out planks from the town hall for the Christian Brothers' Corpus Christi procession altar on the coming Sunday. Having selected a number and laid them out by the Monument we decided to take a break and sat down on the steps. We were soaking up the sun when a bus-load of English tourists pulled up outside Kathleen Hogan's ice-cream parlour and poured out to stretch their legs. A few of them, including two very attractive blondes with Virginia Mayo hairstyles, one carrying a wide-brimmed hat, sauntered over to examine the inscription on the pile behind us. I pursed my lips in a kiss and made some silly remark – I have no idea what it was – to one of the blondes. A flaxen-haired good-looker who might have stepped off a film set himself, probably her bloke, minced me with a glare and stepped menacingly in my direction. But the blonde only laughed good-naturedly and pulled him away. Then Seán laughed. Then I laughed, relieved that she had not taken offence, and that the man had not taken a poke at me. Then I felt ashamed for being such an eejit. I was, after all, sixteen at the time and a long way beyond jumping on the shadows of others but, perhaps, still trying to jump over my own.

CHAPTER SIXTEEN

Law and Order

LAW AND ORDER WAS BIG in Lismore during the Second World War and postwar period. And there was a link with an earlier era in the person of Dan Lawton of Townparks who had been a sergeant in the Royal Irish Constabulary before he became town clerk. The fact that he had been a member of that unpopular force obviously did not do Dan any harm in the eyes of Lismore's citizens. He was widely liked and was genuinely mourned when he died in 1949. Dad used to say he enjoyed swapping yarns with him about the Troubles.

The *garda* station, i.e. the barracks, was the base for one superintendent, one sergeant and eight *gardaí*. Three other middle-ranking officers nosed into town regularly, Inspector John Patrick Croke (who used to write short detective fiction for the *Garda Review*) from 1942 to 1949 and Inspector Michael Teehan who succeeded him on 17 March 1949, both up from Waterford City, and the rotund and ebullient Sergeant Kelleher from Dungarvan whose generous jowls put an impossible strain on the neck of a uniform that was ever on the point of coming apart – he was the weights and measures man. I never really understood why the *gardaí* had to be responsible for weights and measures, even though my own uncle Paddy Ballantyne in Sligo was doing this job up there. I used to see Sergeant Kelleher checking scales in grocery shops from time to time but mostly I saw him around the weigh house by the salmon hatchery. The cross-hatched iron raft outside the house was used for weighing lorries and carts, loaded and unloaded, but it was also sensitive enough to weigh a child. It was fun to stand on it when it was in the weighing mode and feel it move beneath your feet. As children we never passed it without jumping on it to see if we could get it to shudder. Mostly we could not as it was locked in place. Mam had Paddy and me weighed on it often. She seldom missed an opportunity to pop us on an industrial scales. Mokie McCarthy or Paddy O'Brien would weigh us at the Wine Vaults and Dan Colbert at the railway station on brown scales with rafting three-by-three-foot bases. An arrowed weight moving along an arm recorded your poundage. At the station by the goods yard there was also a platform scales like the one at the weigh house. A third one, no longer in use, could be found in front of the old market house by the barracks.

The barracks itself was a handsome three-storey building in West Street, just across from the Monument. On the right-hand side as you entered was the large day-room where an orderly was always on duty and where I used to sit and listen to wireless commentaries of GAA games. In here too I used to poke my head to ask for Dad when I wanted to touch him for a penny or two without Mam knowing it. On the left there was another large room that served as a kind of private consultation chamber for the public. On the first floor was the superintendent's office and, next to it, the office of the superintendent's clerk. You knew there was something special about this level because the super either wore civvies or a fancy, light-blue uniform with gold braid, and the clerk, a kind of staff officer, was always in civvies. The clerk was Guard Michael Mason, a handsome man who, with his horn-rimmed spectacles, indifferent air and carefully pressed tweeds did not fit my image of a lawman at all. He rarely wore a uniform and it was not until I saw him in one for the first time that I really believed he was a guard. I used to find him cold and aloof until the day he gave me a bob out of the blue. It came about because a few days earlier I had found a full new packet of ten cigarettes in West Street and, in an uncharacteristic flush of honesty – I could, after all, have smoked them myself – handed them in at the barracks. He was chatting to Guard Moynihan (who took up duty in Lismore in February 1949) at the entrance when he called me over.

'Are you the young fella who handed in the packet of cigarettes the other day?' he asked.

'Yes,' I said, thinking nothing of it.

'You're a good lad. Here's a reward for you.' And he put a shilling in my hand.

'Jakus!' I thought, walking along in a daze after thanking him, 'a fella could make a few bob out o' finding things in the street and handing them in.'

Another uncharacteristic flush of honesty, though involving a much larger sum, brought me no recompense at all and caused me to revise this opinion. It did not happen in the street but the principle was the same. A new, young bank clerk at the Munster & Leinster Bank next door to the barracks, whom I quite liked, gave me a fiver too much in change that I was getting for Mam. I immediately noticed his error and a *frisson* of sin shot through me. I remembered the sweat and toil I had had in putting the same amount together for my Charles Atlas course. But honesty prevailed.

'You gave me five pounds too much,' I said quietly, and showed him what I had in my hand.

The young man, whose name was McMullan, gulped and glanced across at Mr O'Riordan out of the corner of his eye. 'Oh thanks.' He took back the fiver, relieved that his senior officer did not appear to have heard me, which had been the point of my speaking softly. A momentary pause before I departed with my correct change gave no hint of a reward to come so all I could savour was the glow of having done right by the commandment that exhorted us not to covet our neighbour's goods. The clerk was always very amicable with me afterwards.

On the top floor of the barracks was located Dad's office, the highest Lismore room I was ever in, other than our and Feeney's attics that only had skylights from which to look out. Here you could look vertically down and it was a long way to the ground. The office was spartan: bare floor boards – a common feature of all the rooms in the building which lent a characteristic echo to it; two grey metal cupboards, one of which was always kept locked, just on the right as you entered; and a wooden table that stood in front of the window to the back. When I was alone with him I would ask him to show me his revolvers. By this time I knew he had them because he admitted as much in a final response to a series of pestering questions that I had put to him about facing down desperadoes. He had fobbed me off for a long time. The first break came when he allowed me to handle his truncheon. I was amazed that a piece of wood could be so hard and heavy. I tapped it gingerly against the side of my head, then harder.

'You could split a man open with that!' I protested, rubbing the spot I had tapped too vigorously.

'You don't hit a man over the head with it,' he explained, 'You hit him here,' he touched the middle of my shoulder, 'on the collarbone.' He went on to clarify the disabling effect of that.

I was still not convinced that the club was anything but downright dangerous but he assured me that it was only used in extreme situations.

On the day he relented on the revolvers he closed the door of his office quietly and went over to the locked cupboard. A key from a set he had on a ring unlocked it. Then, from the highest shelf, he took down two six-guns, one a Webley .45 that was standard Army issue, the other, a smaller .38 that looked a bit rusty to me.

'Have you ammunition for 'em?' I asked.

He pointed to a couple of small, sturdy cardboard boxes, the ends of which I could just glimpse on the high shelf.

Sergeant Joseph Ballantyne, front row centre, with colleagues in the late Twenties or early Thirties. The photo was probably taken in Drangan or Fethard, Co Tipperary or in Swanlinbar, Co Cavan in all of which localities he served around that time.

Then from me came the inevitable question, delivered in a hushed voice, 'Did you ever shoot anyone?'

'No,' he said sternly, his tone indicating that he would tolerate no further questions on the subject.

He went on to stress that neither he nor any of the guards in the barracks, the super included, had the authority to use guns. They were held solely for the use of plain-clothes detectives who might be faced with an unexpected emergency in the locality. He let me handle both weapons. Even the smaller of the two I could not aim with one hand it was so heavy. But I could spin the chamber.

'You know how to shoot 'em though?' I said, knowing that he had served in the IRA during the Black and Tan war.

'Yes,' he said brusquely and took the guns from me and locked them away again.

'In America all the cops carry guns,' I pointed out. 'I bet Uncle John has one.' (Uncle John, Dad's elder brother, was a police lieutenant in the New Jersey Police Department.)

'America's a different place entirely,' he said laconically. 'They use guns for any reason there. A James McDonagh on my mother's side had been in the New York police force and after he came home to Ireland he told me that he had once come across a cat-burglar shinning up a pipe on the outside of a building. "Come down off o' there," he shouted, and when the burglar wouldn't, he just shot him off it.' Dad laughed disbelievingly. 'James was rough.' While still on the subject of the United States, Dad deflected me from guns and told me that the ill-fated President William McKinley had once shaken his father's hand. (Dad's father too had worked in the States for a time.) I was *very* impressed. Imagine having your hand shaken by the President of the Unites States of America! I would have been happy to shake de Valera's. And with that he sent me away. Going down the narrow wooden staircase I could not help wondering why so many Ballantynes had chosen to become lawmen. (A number of Sligo/Roscommon 'Ballantines' who might have been distant relatives of ours had also served in the RIC.)

In the small yard at the back of the barracks there were two barred cells like you would see in the sheriff's office in the pictures; well-swept and with low, grey, metal beds on which lay folded grey blankets. They looked business-like but not draconian. I never saw anyone in them or, more correctly, I was rightly never allowed to see anyone in them. Not that they were exactly a vital component of the police operation in Lismore. Desperadoes rarely upset the rhythm of our quiet West Waterford town where lights was the major crime.

Lights could reach epidemic proportions at times with the whole force being deployed to combat it. Curiously, or not so curiously, the perceived epidemics would often coincide with the arrival of a new super. On other occasions a committed young cop on his own was sufficient to bring the situation under control. A strange crime to target in an era of such traffic-free roads. You would rub your eyes if you saw half a dozen cars parked on the Main Street on any day other than Fair Day or Market Day. It might have been that car models, aside from Doc Healy's Studebaker and the limousines of the Devonshire and Westminster dukes, dark dragons in Henry Ford's favourite colour, were somewhat dated. Certainly, an awful lot of them needed manhandling before they shuddered off. Starting handles would almost wrench men's arms off, and might require jumping on, in generating that vital spark of ignition. The owner of a motor bicycle needed to be something of an athlete because he might have to push it a good fifty yards or more, running alongside, before he got it going and sprang onto it. Push-bikes were the least temperamental but often came down with punctures and broken axles. All modes of transport, specially the dicky ones, brought a gleam to the eye of the young *garda*; he cut his coppering teeth on lights and, in the process, was often as much a pain in the arse for colleagues as for his victims. It was not entirely his fault, though. Young guards were expected to reach a certain quota of summonses. In peaceable areas the only hope of reaching that quota, give or take the odd drunk or after hours, lay in lurking in the ditches on the edge of town and accosting unwary travellers, male and female, on their way home from the pictures or a dance. Nobody objected overmuch to the young *garda* filling his quota. It was *how* he filled it. The keen ones who wanted to establish new records in crime-busting caused mild consternation in the community, achievers like P. J. McInerney, known for the obvious reason as 'The Clareman', who was *perceived* to have chalked up more summonses than any *garda* in living memory, many more than the dour Joe Browne who replaced Jim Byrne in September 1951 or the massive and amiable Con Cahalane whose brief reigns of terror were insignificant by comparison. Con it was who earned himself a commendation when, enjoying himself at a dance in the Boathouse in Cappoquin, he happened to notice a wanted man among the dancers. He quietly alerted the local force and the desperado was taken into custody without resistance. In time, and it was in time, even P.J. mellowed and devoted his surplus energy to spare-time crooning – his big numbers, 'Because Of You' and 'A Beggar In Love'. Who did he think he was, we used to ask ourselves, Roy Rogers? A stop was usually put to the young guard's gallop when an older and wiser head was delegated to take him aside and whisper that it might be a good idea to go a little easier on the populace. The guards lived in a symbiotic relationship with the good people of Lismore and surrounding area. Why jeopardize good community relations by dragging hapless citizens before the courts for peccadilloes? All but the pig-headed got the drift. But it was not only the young guards who fished for lights. If the super, or visiting chief super, felt that the returns for arrests were down Dad and his disgruntled older colleagues were urged out to push up the figures. And not all the older *gardaí* had mellowed. One at least, the tetchy O'Sullivan, never gave up the ingrained habits of his rookie days. It was said that once toward dusk he encountered an acquaintance who displayed no evidence of having a light on his bike, engaged the man in unusually amiable and protracted conversation until it grew dark, then promptly summoned him for having no lights.

When a gang of us youngsters biked it over to Cappoquin or Tallow to the pictures we rarely had amongst us more than one lamp to every three bikes. Consequently, we walked our bikes into town and out of town. The lone light customarily switched on in town was supposed to indicate that we all had the lights required by law but had turned off the rest to save batteries, pricey and not very long-lived commodities. Needless to say, this did not cut much ice with the cops and, when they were feeling contrary, or in the mood for a laugh, they would lie in wait for us out the road, mostly after the pictures. In Cappoquin one night after the show we had just walked beyond the Boathouse without mishap, and were thinking of getting on our bikes, when a big Cornerstone *garda* launched a pre-emptive strike from the shadows.

'Where are yere lights?' he demanded gruffly.

Luckily for us it was not one of the worst nights he could have jumped us. We were four passengers on three bikes and had two and a bit out of three lamps, none of which were switched on at that moment. I was riding Dad's and had a light. Sucky and Doshin were sharing another and were also able to flash something. It was Barney we were worried about. All he had, and it was in his trousers pocket, was a little green bunny rabbit fantasy item, the battery of which was almost dead, that his brother Tom, home from England, had given him.

'Okay, okay,' the *garda* cleared Sucky and myself. 'And where's yours?' he came to Barney.

'Oh, I have it here, Guard,' said our pal, flicking the switch and keeping his fingers crossed. The light just about came on.

'What's that?' said the *garda*, illuminating it with his own powerful torch.

'Oh that's light enough in the dark, sure,' Barney maintained boldly and pointed it hesitantly at his interrogator's face. As he did so, the light flickered and died.

'Jasus, he has us now,' I thought.

To our great surprise and relief, however, the *garda* burst out laughing. 'Off with ye, out o' that, ye blackguards,' he roared, 'and be careful in the dark.' Then he hopped on his bike and rode back into town still chuckling.

"Thanks, Guard," we shouted after him. It had been our lucky night.

Another time along the same stretch of road Mike Feeney and my brother Paddy hit the wrong key in a motorcar. They had driven to a picture and on the way home ran into a trap set by two eager young guards. Mike did not have to be told why he had been stopped. When he left Lismore earlier in the evening only one of his tail lights had been working and that was wonky. He supposed they had spotted it on his way into Cappoquin and resolved to nail him on the way out.

'While I'm talking to them,' he whispered to Paddy, 'you get out and slip round the back. Give the right-hand light a kick. That'll switch it on again.'

Paddy went to the back and did as he was told. Unfortunately, he did the job too well and put his boot through glass and bulb. There was no way out of that summons.

Riotous behaviour was not so amusing for the guards. Jim Byrne had to have half an ear stitched back on after he had intervened in a tinkers' brawl. Dad said he was lucky the whole of it had not been severed. Some time afterwards, I think it was, Dad himself had a couple of ribs kicked in by Bill Buckley, a powerfully built man from beyond the top of Main Street. Bill was something of a wild man who periodically and unpredictably raced his horse and cart around town like it was a chariot and he Ben Hur. Linked to this statement of disdain for Lismore and its citizens were the severe batters he went on and it was when he ran amok on one of these, requiring several *gardaí* to bring him under control, that Dad caught his boot. I only experienced the aftermath. There was a knock on the door the next day when I was on my midday break from school having dinner. Mam went out to answer it. Then I heard her say with unaccustomed wrath, 'What do *you* want?' Her voice then dropped, to be followed by a low and intense conversation, the gist of which I was unable to catch. Intrigued, I got to my feet, went over to the living-room door and peered down the hall. On getting a glimpse of a very contrite-looking Bill I ran upstairs.

'Dad, 'tis Bill Buckley!' I said excitedly, 'He wants to see you.'

Dad pulled himself up stiffly in the bed.

Then Mam came in, her face dark as a rain-cloud. 'I don't think you should see that fella,' she said unforgivingly.

'Ah, he's okay, Mary.' Dad said with typical generosity. 'He only wants to say he's sorry. Sure he was blind drunk. He didn't know what he was doing.'

'All right,' Mam agreed dubiously, as if she feared the man was coming to stave in another couple of Dad's ribs. She grabbed my hand. 'Come on. This is no place for you.' She ushered me back down the stairs and thrust me into the living-room. 'Finish your pandy.' Then she pulled the door shut and went down the hall to let Bill in.

Still full of curiosity, I opened the door again and held it ajar. Again I glimpsed the contrite face of Dad's assailant as he entered. He looked so unhappy I forgave him there and then. Mam noticed me and snapped the latch shut once more. Bill was upstairs for about a quarter of an hour and when he came down there was a spring in his step like he had been to confession at a mission. By then Mam had accepted his reason for calling and saw him out gently. She could be fiercely protective when she perceived a slight or a threat to her man, a true Carrick woman.

I think Bill must have got off lightly. I never recall a court case about the affair. The charge of being drunk and disorderly was normally considered a minor form of riotous behaviour anyway, punishable at most by a fine of five or ten bob. Of course, if Jack O'Gorman, the flamboyant local solicitor, was defending the miscreant, he might well have been let off with a caution, much to the chagrin of the officer who pulled him in.

One could hardly argue that our community was entirely law-abiding. In addition to the above, a host of other common misdemeanours kept the *gardaí* on their toes: publicans having customers on the premises after hours; domestic squabbles – the last thing in which any guard wanted to become involved; larceny of trees; rent arrears; trespass of cows and other livestock; untaxed motor vehicles; being drunk in charge of a motor vehicle; fighting with hurleys at matches; poisoning of land by farmers; cruelty to animals (you had to be *very* cruel); school non-attendance; having an unlicensed dog or dogs (unenforceable in Botany where most mongrels were in common ownership); abusive language (that had to be something special); slinging logs of timber onto a road and damaging it; shooting and fishing out of season; failure to till by a farmer; leading an animal on the right-hand side of the road (traffic regulations stipulated that all animals should be led on the left); hackney drivers carrying more than the permitted number of passengers; minor affrays.

A memorable example of an affray became known as 'The Battle of the Spout'. The protagonists were a man named Crowley (Teddy?) and John 'Guyler' Greehy of Deerpark, two determined individuals of middle age. The cause of the shindy was debatable (as was much else about the affair) and if it ever surfaced at all, eventually sank amid a welter of accusation and counter-accusation in a subsequent court case. The problem appeared to be that no one but they had witnessed the beginning of the clash. Local hearsay had it that one of them, possibly Crowley, was drawing water from the Spout when the other, probably the Guyler, appeared on the scene with his water-cart and tried to muscle in. The first, possibly, taking exception to this, jumped onto the wide basin into which the water flowed and, with the aid of a bucket, drenched the upstart latecomer, probably, no doubt hoping that the cool spring water would take the heat out of the situation. Sadly, the opposite was the effect. The person drenched responded by throwing his chute at the other. Then they both picked up their chutes, one directing water at the other from the lip of the Spout, and one lashing out in an effort to take the legs from under the other. They were going at it like Laurel and Hardy when a pedestrian happened by to ponder the scene. By the time the guards had scrambled on their bikes in answer to an alert the combatants resembled a pair of weary crusaders who had just crawled out of the River Jordan.

Serious crime would be a house break-in or a major case of larceny. Dad had a bit of a reputation for crime detection though I never heard him expressing a desire to transfer to the Detective Division. Indeed, he never displayed any ambition to rise higher in the ranks as far as I could see, mainly I suspect because he loved Lismore and was so happy with his lot there. But he was a very capable officer, unassuming and caring of the well-being of all his colleagues. As well as standing in for the court clerk of West Waterford when the Lismore-based Mr O'Keeffe was away on summer holidays or periodically ill, he filled in for the superintendent whenever the latter was on leave or incapacitated.

His major exploit of detection, as far as I know, was to apprehend some men who had stripped all the lead from the Kiely-Ussher family vaults in the middle of scary Knocknagapall Wood. I felt sorry for the men. Anyone brave enough to go near that eerie place in the middle of the night deserved better for their endeavours. (It did not occur to me that they might have raided it by day.) When there was a robbery from a shop in Carrick-on-Suir while we were there on holidays the local *gardaí* caught the lads who had done it within two days. As Carrick was four times the size of Lismore I was impressed.

'How did they solve that so quickly?' I demanded of Dad.

'Oh they'd have a good idea which lads in the town might be up to doing a job like that and they'd round them up for questioning. They'd also keep an eye out for lads who'd be spending more money than they'd usually have in their pockets.'

The answer seemed logical enough – round up the usual suspects – but there were many more lads in Carrick than in Lismore. Two days was still good going, I reckoned. Another time he happened to comment, when reading of some criminal's activities in the newspaper, that the man would have gone to ground in the city by now and would be very difficult to find.

'Why?' I asked, surprised, 'In the city there's so many cops they'd be sure to find him. I'd hide myself in the countryside. There's hunderts o' hideouts.'

He smiled and shook his head. 'Far easier to lose yourself in city streets among the crowds. Down the country you'd be quickly spotted as a stranger.'

Four superintendents came and went during his sergeancy: Doyle, Creane, Duignan and Crummy. The first left town before I could rightly get a fix on him, the last arrived not long before we left Lismore, but I vividly remember my parents' excitement when Doyle's successor Patrick Creane arrived with his large County Dublin family in 1945. They took up residence in the Manse, a square, elegant villa behind a high wall at the top of Main Street. In front of the house there was a wide lawn with an ornamental holly tree in the middle, at the back a large fruit garden, appreciated from inside

Lismore gardaí the year of my father's retirement. The photograph appeared on the front cover of the *Garda Review*, November 1954. Back row, left to right: Guards Houlihan, Moynihan, O'Sullivan, Browne, Devanney, Murphy. Front row, left to right: Guard Mason, Superintendent Crummy, Commissioner Brennan, Sergeant Joseph Ballantyne, Guard Boyle.

through large French windows, the first that I had ever seen. Next to the Manse, and possibly once connected to it, stood a small red-brick Presbyterian church, rarely used anymore. The house was abuzz as the family moved in, adults moving furniture, children racing through the rooms on trips of discovery. Mam and other *garda* wives and the older Creane daughters were making tea and sandwiches and consoling a distraught Mrs Creane, who seemed appalled at the prospect of living in a small town like ours after having lived for many years in Skerries, near the capital, and after that in Tramore, another seaside town, from where the family transferred to us.

'I won't stay here! I won't stay here!' she kept repeating.

I looked at her uncomprehendingly. What was so bad about living in our town? Then my brother and I were hooshed out of the way to forge new friendships. In the background Dad and his new boss were manhandling a piece of furniture up the wide stairs. They were to form a firm friendship. Like Dad, Superintendent Creane was a kind and gentle man. And, like Dad, he had served in the Irish Republican Army, albeit in a different part of the country, during the War of Independence. Unlike Dad, he liked to play the horses.

Once he had settled down in the town he developed the habit of dropping into Feeney's to listen to the racing broadcasts and sometimes Mike, Panzer and Kieran would play a prank on him. They would fix it so that when the race was coming to a climax one of them would slip into the workshop and switch on a machine that they had linked to the wireless. Immediately the set began to crackle and sizzle the Super, his glasses dancing on his thin nose and the rate of his persistent sniffling increasing by the second, would launch into a string of curses against Radio Éireann, the BBC and the ESB as he desperately twiddled the knobs in an effort to get better reception. Then, having failed to make out the result, he would storm off to enquire about it elsewhere. Other times the lads would let him off the hook at the last minute and ensure that he heard who won.

Among other of his likeable eccentricities was one that was unique in my experience. Receiving a Christmas card, he would cross through the message intended for him, pen a new one to another friend and mail the card once more.

'Why are all those other names on the card?' I enquired of Dad the first time we got one.

'Ah, sure, Pat has little time for that kind of thing,' he laughed, meaning the formal business of sending cards, and he explained the Super's idiosyncrasy.

From his attitude I could see that Dad had no great enthusiasm for sending cards either. For my own part, a Christmas card was only worth receiving if it had a postal order or a banknote inside it.

Pat Creane died tragically young in June 1952, the third painful passing of a Lismore colleague for Dad. I was old enough to appreciate the hurt it caused his large family and was aware too of the fortitude with which his wife and children confronted his long and debilitating decline beforehand, especially the elder daughters Mary and Josephine who took on most of the responsibility for keeping the family together. My own sense of loss told me I was growing up. I remembered his charm, kindness and wit, and little things like the way he used to give us children a lift in his car when he came across us on the Hospital Road walking out to Scarook to pick whorts.

His successor Michael Duignan, through no fault of his own, seemed dour and colourless by comparison. But Dad found him okay. Among the guards Dad served with in Lismore he was probably closest to Paddy Martin, Jim Dennis and Christy Houlihan. The sudden deaths of the first two in mid-life had a profound effect upon him. They died within a couple of years of one another, Jim Dennis on 10 December 1948 at the early age of 49, and both left young families. The loss of a loved one who was also the breadwinner brought anxiety as well as pain to the grieving widows. A daughter again, May, with her eldest brother Seán, formed a singular support for Mrs Dennis. We youngsters, trying to understand such things, were happy to discover that our pals would be staying on in the town. Houlihan was the senior guard after Dad and part of my perception of their closeness might have had something to do with that. Mam liked him very much, too. What Paddy thought of him I have no idea but to me he came across as puritanical and oppressive. I had occasion to have my judgement tested when I had my only brush with the law.

Sucky, Boxer, Twiddles, Foxy and I had been around the Villa one afternoon after the McConnells had left town. It looked forlorn and empty. In the backyard we noticed that someone had left one of the kitchen windows slightly ajar. Natural curiosity drew us into the house. I knew the rooms on the ground floor from the times I visited the McConnells but I had never been higher than halfway up the main staircase and I had never seen the big, old-fashioned kitchen. I was keen to discover the whole house. No shutters were pulled across at the front so we could enjoy the vista over the lawn and small field beyond to Hogans' lodge. And we were aware that anyone happening by might see us too. Everywhere we trod on the bare boards the floor creaked, sending ghostly echoes through the empty house. Soon we lost our inhibitions and began to amuse ourselves sliding down the banisters and along the shiny floors. After a while we got bored with that. Then Sucky had an idea. He had noticed that bare bulbs hung from all the ceilings and, holding his catapult by the pouch, whirled it and belted the nearest one to smithereens with the tail of the fork. A wholly satisfying bang reverberated around the room, followed by the skitter of tiny fragments of glass across the polished floor.

'Ah, Jasus, Sucky!' Foxy remonstrated.

Boxer, rubbing his hands with glee, went into the next room and smashed another. Then I had a go. Then Twiddles. We were laughing our heads off by now, with the exception of Foxy, the only one capable of keeping a sense of proportion, who trailed behind us pleading, 'Ah, Jasus, lads, stop it! Ye're goin' too far.' In a sort of delirium we continued on our minor rampage until we had smashed every bulb in the house. Then we took heed of Foxy's pleas, slipped out of the house and thought no more about it.

About a week later Houlihan collared me on the corner across from the barracks as I was going down the New Way and gave me a rude shock.

'Jim,' he called me over to him confidentially.

I went across not knowing what to expect.

'You wouldn't know anything about who smashed up the Villa, I suppose?'

'Smashed up the Villa?' I said, genuinely puzzled. We had not been particularly destructive. Just the few bulbs. Had somebody else been in there after us?

'Yes.'

'What do you mean?'

'Some lads got in there and did a lot of damage.'

'Oh? Oh well, I don't know anything about it.'

'We think we know who it might be,' he said, fixing me with a stare. 'Look. You can tell me. *You* won't get into any trouble.'

'*You* won't get into any trouble,' the emphasis repeated itself in my mind. I looked at him aghast. The fucker was asking me to sell out my pals, in return for giving me a clean sheet!

'I know nothing about it,' I snapped, gave him a look of contempt and walked away. I was not feeling especially brave about brazening it out – if he had put the thumbscrews on me I might well have capitulated and told him – but I was damned if I was going to succumb to such mean *plamás*.

None of us was ever brought up over the few bulbs. I never spoke to, or even looked at, Houlihan again. Maybe I was too hard on him. Probably he was only thinking of the embarrassment for my father if I had been summoned. But, if he was, he went the wrong way about it.

Being a guard's son was restricting at times, specially knowing that Dad held the law in great respect without in any way being a disciplinarian. He was not blind about the law but saw it from the policeman's perspective. It disgruntled him that district justices occasionally let off people that he felt the guards had rightfully summoned just as he accepted that a *garda* who presented a sloppy case deserved to have it thrown out. District justices could be effective or ineffective but all of them liked to be humoured. A sergeant since March 1925, he believed profoundly in an unarmed police force. It had not been easy establishing that principle after the Civil War, he told me more than once. A number of *gardaí* had sacrificed their lives trying to apprehend armed gunmen who had hung onto their wartime habits long after they should have turned in their guns.

CHAPTER SEVENTEEN

Sickness and Health

ON THE FACE OF IT, the thousand or so inhabitants of Lismore were well looked after medically. We had three doctors in the town and a Cappoquin medic also attended patients amongst us. Dr Michael O'Farrell and Dr Dan Healy lived within a stone's throw of one another on Parks Road, where they also had time to pursue interests other than the strictly medical. The former lived at Ardagh, a fine house approached along an avenue of ornamental shrubs and trees. In a couple of fields at the back he kept some prize dairy cows. He also found time to be medical officer of health for the county. Dr Healy lived at the Lodge, a square block with a ground-floor bay entrance and a touch of southwest France about it lent by its persiennes. Along with this went a courtyard and outhouses, an orchard – the fruit of which I was able to vouch for, a walled garden that stretched across to the the top of Main Street, a field of some two acres in which he fattened a couple of heifers and, best of all, the Palladium Cinema, which stood at the north corner of the field. He counted the Ballantyne family among his patients and though he saw me often enough professionally I knew him best as 'the Doc', the man who ran the local cinema. The town perceived a certain rivalry between the two men. Dr O'Farrell, it was felt, held himself to be a cut above the Doc. *He* was the county MOH and liked to be seen at the fashionable social events held at the Castle and Fort William. To me, he was a rather grey figure. The Doc, in contrast, was a tubby, flamboyant little man who exuded a quiet showmanship, as befitted someone who ran a picture house. His showy side manifested itself graphically in the early Fifties when he flaunted a gleaming new black-and-silver-chromed Studebaker automobile, brought all the way from the United States of America. Not a scratch on it and with a boot in which you could have fitted a pair of coffins. Its owner's pride and joy. Dared you breathe on it, let alone stamp it with your greasy thumbprint, and the Doc would leap out and remove the offending smudge, real or imagined, with a dab of his perfectly ironed white handkerchief. In terms of performance the car probably never achieved its full potential under his sedate touch. On the other hand, who could tell what he got up to when he rode beyond the town? The gleam behind his spectacles when he eased himself into the driving seat suggested that he might well have put her through her paces when he got her onto an open stretch of highway. Never again after I left Lismore was I to have the pleasure of seeing my own doctor drive up to attend me in such style. Dr O'Farrell might have dismissed the Studebaker as imported fantasy of a vulgar kind but he might have found it less easy to digest the Doc's appointment as coroner for West Waterford in 1953. As with most physicians, Dr Healy saw to it that his children entered the medical profession also, his fun-loving Jack as a GP, his quiet and serious Finola as a dentist.

Dr John Dennehy was the third member of the town's medical triumvirate. A lot of people seemed to prefer his bedside manner to that of the others. Quiet and retiring, he lived out the Convent Road in yet another fine house, Headview, which was set well back from the road with a long, tree-lined avenue leading up to it. Outhouses and a parcel of land went with this as well. His extra chore was the local branch of the Red Cross which he ran until his death in 1950, after which the Doc took it over. A year or two later when civil defence was in the air I signed on for some first-aid classes at the town hall. The response was poor and after a few lessons during which the Doc taught us how to apply a tourniquet and tie bandages and splints the small group fell apart. A contributory factor may have been the Doc's inability to arrive on time for the classes. On the other hand, with so few of us, I think we were less than a half dozen, he might not have thought it worth his while.

Dr White was the man who came over from Cappoquin. It was somewhat fashionable to have him calling to see you. In his soft grey tweeds he was very much one of the old school and he did, after all, drive four miles to be at your bedside. Often ailing himself, he was chauffeured around by his dutiful daughter Winnie, who in time was to become a GP herself and take over his practice when he died.

A solitary district nurse, known as the Jubilee Nurse for a reason never explained to me, provided the essential back-up service for these four. The inimitable and dynamic Nurse Knowles fulfilled this role until, to the town's great regret, she left us in 1945. An able replacement was found in Nurse Twomey. Further back-up was supplied at the district hospital beyond the railway station by Nurses Keane, Foley and O'Keeffe. The Jubilee Nurse was paid by the town, and the Hon. Clodagh Anson of Ballyin House, who was also a director of the Lismore Estates Company, played a prominent part in raising the necessary funds to keep her in business. The district hospital, formerly an old Poor Law Union hospital dating, I think, from the decade before the Great Famine, and now known as St Carthage's, was a grim Victorian edifice with a high wall around it that reeked of workhouse and incarceration. In the late 1940s when the Department of Health, under the capable and committed direction of Dr Noël Browne, opened an onslaught on tuberculosis, the killer and disabler of thousands, it was converted into a sanitorium.

In dental terms we were less well served. Lacking a resident dentist we were reliant on a visiting one, Charlie P. O'Meara of Mallow, who had as his 'surgery' a hired room in John O'Donnell's small Commercial Hotel next door to Dennises in the South Mall. You came in contact with him early because he was responsible for school dental checks. His surgery had a gloomy, unlived-in look about it and the cold, wrought-iron chair he sat you in resembled a medieval instrument of torture, something you were well able to believe when be began poking about in your mouth. He was a man who believed in letting good teeth stay where they were until nature decided to shift them. The mouthful of crowded teeth I still have testifies to the flaw in that theory. Mam asked him to extract a couple of the smaller ones to let the others 'breathe', but she was overruled.

Two chemists, both situated in the Main Street, supplied the tonics we needed when we were down. The one I mostly patronised was J. J. Hely's, or the Medical Hall as the sign over the stepped doorway put it. It was run by the cold and austere Mr Wall assisted by his daughter Margery, a pre-Raphaelite beauty whose charming and wistful manner made you want to steal her away from the old autocrat. Round the corner from the Co-op was the other pharmacy, O'Hanrahan's, where the short-sighted and shrivelled Mr O'Hanrahan would peer at you myopically through thick-lensed glasses, cock a peaked ear of his small round head, and demand your requirements in a silky, rasping voice.

Last but not least in the medical set-up was Mr Lane, the bone-setter, who used to come over from Kanturk in the County Cork and hold his surgeries in a room in the Devonshire Arms Hotel. Harry Bolger of Nine Mile House, a friend of Mam's cousin Peg Grant (née Denn), used to provide similar services in Carrick-on-Suir. The bone-setter held a kind of witch-doctor status, and was much trusted by the public because he – in my experience it was always a man – could do things with bones through sheer manipulation that the general practitioner could not begin to emulate. Much of what he achieved was derided by the medical profession, which took refuge behind its secretive principles. Some doctors, however, were happy to recommend a visit to the bone-setter when a complaint stubbornly resisted their own efforts. I never had occasion to require the services of the bone-setter but had no reason to doubt the efficacy of his arcane art, having heard many tales of sportsmen who had gone to him to have a bone put back or righted. Anyway, did I not cure my own warts, an ailment for which neither doctor nor chemist seemed able to supply a wholly effective proprietary medicine? Weren't the spurge and pissabed juices I used also folk remedies? It is only fair to admit that the warts I had were small ones, all on the backs of my fingers. Some of the lads suffered growths the size of the rubber you saw on the end of pencils. Even a dab of sulphuric acid from the school science room would not shift those. When the tops of the warts became very hard lads would rub them with an abrasive stone in the hope of wearing them down. Sometimes the warts were impatiently clawed off, which we held was the worst thing one could do because they bled copiously, and wherever the blood of a wart touched the skin fresh warts were said to take root.

Preventive medicine was not recognised as a concept, but that is not to say that people took no steps to ward off illness. Mam used to feed Paddy and me various horrible potions from October till Christmas to build up our resistance to colds and flu. I had to be strapped down almost before she could administer me a spoon of a greasy white concoction known as Scott's Emulsion. Bizarrely, Paddy grew to like it so much he would suck it straight from the bottle. Castor oil and cod liver oil also came by the spoon and, though they too tasted unpalatable, had one big advantage over Scott's. They went down reasonably quickly and a spoon of sugar diluted the aftertaste. Scott's clung to the lining of your mouth for hours; without question the vilest stuff I ever took. Happily, there was an exception to all this disgusting Victorian fare – Virol – brown, treacly and toffee-flavoured. I was partial to it and had no doubt that it was the most effective tonic for me. Like all children, I was no subscriber to the old-fashioned idea that the lousier the taste the better was the medicine. As I saw it, if that had been the case we would still have been amputating legs without anaesthetics. My favourite medicine, used in either a preventive or pick-me-up mode, was not a proprietary product at all but my mother's home-made egg-flips. An egg, well-beaten, then stirred into a glass of hot milk with a spoon or two of sugar did you a power of good, especially psychologically as it massaged your taste buds in the right way. Mam kept a general medicine box in the house for minor upsets, a square biscuit tin containing bandage rolls, often scalded with hot water for re-use, a roll of elastoplast, aspirins and iodine. Iodine went on any scratch or cut I ever got. The sting of it I could bear but I hated its sickly smell and the way it stained your skin orange-brown. In winter Vick's Vapour Rub would be added to the box, to be rubbed on your chest at night when you had a cold. I did not like the smell of that either, nor the way it made me blink, nor the greasiness that messed up my pyjamas, or 'pyjies' as Mam used to call them.

Maintaining our personal cleanliness was a major preoccupation of Mam's. It was not easy in a house that had no running hot water. But, unlike the poorest dwellings in the town, we at least had running water. Face washing, hand washing and leg washing were easily policed. Organising a bath for all of us was something else, above all in winter. When I was little, I enjoyed winter and summer baths. Winter was cosiest, when I could bask in the glow of the living-room fire and see the water being boiled before my eyes. The tin bathtub would be placed in front of the fire and when the bathwater had been prepared Molly or Mam would place me in it and scrub me from head to toe with a block of coarse laundry soap. The soap came in hand-crafted lengths of about one foot or a foot and a half, from which manageable chunks for use were chopped. Washing your hair with it was dismal; it was hopeless for raising a lather. Jim Feeney was so disgusted with it he tried his hand at manufacturing his own once, boiling up animal fats with a strong alkali and pouring the resultant liquid soap into self-carpentered wooden moulds to harden. He did produce what looked like standard blocks but I think the product failed to meet his expectations because he did not continue the experiment for long. It was a relief for us all when Palmolive appeared after the War. (Rinso, too, appeared, or reappeared, for washing clothes.) I used to stay in the bathtub for as long as I was allowed. There was only one drawback, the way they washed my face with the corner of the towel. They rubbed so hard the soap always got in my eyes. Afterwards, I would be helped on with my pyjies and let sit close to the fire for half an hour or so before being sent off to bed.

When older, I would participate in the weekly or fortnightly family bath, a major planning exercise. The bathroom was on the first floor and in the corner by the window stood a large, white enamel bath on four curved legs. Bath and wash basin had been installed in 1938. A brief letter (dated 8 August of that year) to my father by Humphrey Eley, the then secretary of Lismore Estates, or agent of the Duke of Devonshire, states: *Dear Sir, I have been into the question of installing a bath and wash basin in your house, and I am prepared to do this work and take cold water connections to same provided you are agreeable to pay 2/- a week extra rent.* A letter from Billy King, the later manager of the company, dated 6 February 1942, gives the full cost of the operation:

Dear Sir,

With reference to your enquiry, the following statement shows the position at January 31st last:–

Installation of bathroom 1938	£14. 17. 7	By cash payments:–	
Half cost of wiring for light	£3. 10. 0	1st October 1938 to 31st January 1942	
		40 months @ 8/8	£17. 6. 8
	£18. 7. 7		£1. 0. 11

To prepare the bath, hot water had to be boiled continuously in every available pot in the house on the living-room fire and on the sawdust drum in the yard, then carried gingerly up the stairs. We required two bathfuls, one for the males and one for the females. The usual drill for the males was for Dad to have his bath first, followed by Paddy, followed by me. By the time my turn came the water would have cooled considerably and a fresh pot of hot might be added. When I had finished, I flushed the bath and rubbed it clean as best I could as the water drained away. After I had dried myself I opened the door and window to let the steam out and dashed to the cold or cool bedroom to pull on a new set of clothes. While I was doing this Mam and Molly busied themselves preparing their bath. The routine did not necessarily follow the same pattern always. Very ocasionally, if Dad was held up unexpectedly at work and if Paddy was not ready, I might get first go. Later when Molly left us, and Paddy was spending more time in Carrick-on-Suir, the routine was altered again. My parents tried to take a bath more frequently than the rest of us and sometimes if I came in and found one had been run I might ask to come in on the end of it. Might. Like most kids, I did not believe in overdoing the washing bit. Especially in winter in a damp and freezing house. Between baths as need or inclination arose you washed your body, the sweaty parts at least, standing up at the washhand basin.

Pest prevention was another preoccupation of Mam's. Blankets were regularly checked for fleas, above all in summer. *The* most regular routine was checking hair for head lice. I often had these, for which the only effective remedy seemed to be finecombing. Mam had a stock of fine-combs – flat, white, bone items about three inches long, with two rows of short, sharp teeth. I used to hate having them dragged relentlessly through my hair but could see the point of it all when Mam showed me the tiny white nits she had scraped off my scalp.

Mice were a lesser problem, in my eyes no problem at all. Regular visitors, their preferred location in the house was the living-room. Evenings, while we were reading quietly by the fire the faintest of squeaks from behind the skirting-board, followed by the light skimmer of claws over the linoleum under the dining-table by the window, alerted us to their presence. I would turn my head very slowly and watch them foraging for the crumbs that had escaped the sweeping brush. Then Mam would notice me noticing them and frighten them away. Not always, though. Sometimes she would peek at them too. It was not unusual to see three nosing over the floor until some hint of danger sent them scampering and sliding back to their hole in the skirting board. But soon they would reappear. 'The cheek of them!' Mam would laugh in wonder. But, ever practical, she would set the traps and, possibly even before you went to bed, the wicked snap of a spring would signal the end of one too daring raid on a piece of crust. By morning there might be another hapless victim. Harmless creatures. I did not like to see them die but Mam was ruthless.

She was even more ruthless with houseflies, a mainly summer irritant. The insects had easy access to the house when doors and windows were wide open. Cold food laid out for a meal would have to remain covered with tea cloths or sheets of paper until it was time to serve it. Perishables like milk, butter, meat, etc., were stored beyond access in the wire-mesh safe. Our safe was tiny compared to the walk-in one that my aunts had in the cool shade of their small stone-paved yard in Greystone Street, Carrick-on-Suir but it seemed adequate for our needs. The unfortunate flies would be swatted aside or annihilated with a rolled-up newspaper or would suffer a horrible lingering death on the fly-paper that dangled from the ceiling. I hated fly-paper. It was distressing to witness a freshly trapped creature struggling to free itself from the disagreeably smelling, sticky strip and gumming itself to exhaustion. I understood Mam's concern over 'germs' to some degree but to my mind even a fly deserved a quicker and more merciful end or, at least, an even break. The autumn glut of the leggy Daddy Longlegs (crane flies) she didn't seem to mind although she would swat them also when they became too numerous.

An epidemic of flu or mumps or other contagious disease would make Mam a bit uneasy about us borrowing reading matter from the library. She did not really credit the old yarn that one could pick up bugs from books though the story was sufficiently well-grounded among the middle class of the town for her to wonder. It was certainly not an idea that Paddy or I, both avid readers, entertained. Perhaps such concepts, of which there were a few around, helped people to accept illness as a fact of life, at least the physical side of it.

Mental illness was another matter. We had little understanding of this. Unfortunates who had suffered mental breakdown were marked for life, especially those who had had to undergo hospital treatment – they had been to the asylum, to the loony house, been 'put away'. No matter that they returned to the community with a clean bill of health. Milder symptoms indicated that someone was 'a bit queer', 'soft in the head', 'strange', 'not all there' – phrases attached also to individuals who displayed a healthy contempt for the authoritarian excesses of an often obscurantist society. Depression seemed to be regarded as the first step on the way to permanent disability instead of something that could be sympathetically treated. Doctors with their secretive ways did nothing to dispel this negative impression. Mam displayed great sympathy for anyone who suffered from depression and once when it was rumoured that a friend of hers, who had died in tragic circumstances might have killed himself, she was upset for days. My inquisitive young ears picked up the word 'suicide' and I had to approach one of my more experienced pals to discover how it was spelt and what it really meant. I encountered serious disability for the first time when Popsie McConnell came to live amongst us. Popsie was a Down's syndrome child and particularly refreshing and educative was the unabashed way her parents and brothers accepted her. She was a delightful child, shown great love and understanding by her mother. Colonel McConnell, too, so strict with his two sons, demonstrated enhanced affection in her presence. She was brought up as a full member of the family; they took her everywhere with them. Their good example, intentional or unintentional, taught us healthy children, and no doubt adults, too, to accept her on the same level. She would play with us boys in the Villa sometimes and we learned to be patient with her. What I found difficult to understand and cope with were her occasional sudden rages. I did not always know what I had done to invite her displeasure. As time passed, however, we learned better how to respond to her, and she to us.

That the common cold and influenza were regular winter complaints was hardly surprising. Many destitute children ran around in bare feet even in winter. Paradoxically they proved more resilient to colds than I. Or so it seemed to me sometimes. I was easily laid low. Their curse was the boil and the carbuncle, all called boils by us. The backs of some children's necks used to be pock-marked with the scars of these very painful inflammations. The cause, malnutrition. I was lucky. Of the few I ever had, only one grew to malignancy. I bathed it regularly with hot water for a few days to bring up the pus and, when it was deemed 'ripe', Doc Healy lanced it. Lancing and the regular bathing of the suppurating wound with hot water seemed the only cure, antibiotics being as yet unknown, or at least, unavailable in Ireland. Then for a further week or so Mam had to bathe it for me, squeezing out more pus and re-dressing the wound until all the poison had disappeared. Blood-poisoning was always something to be feared. On and off I would have an arm in a sling with a badly swollen finger that had turned septic after playing host to a thorn or a sliver of broken glass or suchlike. Often as children in short pants we would take a tumble and gash our knees. Healing a cut like that was a never-ending process because you either took another tumble or banged the sore point against a desk or something each time it was on the point of healing over. Off came the scab and you were back to square one. But a throb in the finger or a sore knee was nothing compared to the painfully stiff neck that a boil gave you. My one bad experience taught me to appreciate the dreary, gnawing torment that regular sufferers like Sucky Neville were going through when they were collared in antiseptic white.

More drastic surgery was required for the common ailments that were medically in vogue, tonsillitis and appendicitis. Among us boys it became accepted that by the time we reached the age of 12 our tonsils would very likely have had to be removed. Around that age when I was in Dungarvan Hospital awaiting an appendectomy Dan McCarthy, the surgeon, said to Mam, as if he were doing her a favour, 'I think I'll whip his tonsils out as well. They look a bit enlarged.' Mam looked at him aghast. 'Indeed an' you won't!' she exclaimed. 'Sure he's never had a day's trouble with his tonsils in his life.'

Which was true, nor have I ever had any trouble with them since, which gives some indication of the mindless mania that was prevalent among surgeons for 'whipping out' those innocuous glands. Such was the ease with which our young bodies coped with the loss of the tonsils and the appendix that we were forced to ask ourselves a number of pertinent questions. Why did we have these items in the first place if their absence seemed to make no difference? How many other redundant organs did our bodies possess? Why was it that so many of us got tonsillitis and/or appendicitis? We never arrived at a satisfactory conclusion as to why we contracted the first; a contributory factor might have been the cold and damp conditions in which most of us lived, but as children we were not particularly aware of those. As to why we got appendicitis, the least implausible among a host of implausible theories was that we were eating too many raw chestnuts. Undigested particles of these were said to find their way somehow into the one-way sac of the appendix and remain trapped there. It was only a matter of time before the sac got stuffed full of rotting nut and became inflamed. Once that happened you could kiss it goodbye.

There was an obvious flaw in the argument. How was it that people who never ate chestnuts came down with the same bellyache? My brother was a case in point. Paddy seldom if ever ate raw chestnuts yet he was struck down so unexpectedly by acute appendicitis that an emergency operation had to be performed on him at the Waterford City Infirmary in the new year of 1946. The whole family had been staying at Greystone Street in Carrick at the time, awaiting his planned admission to hospital, when the worst thing that could have happened did. The appendix burst early in the morning of January 20th. The four of us had been sleeping as usual in the back room when a scream of pain awoke my parents. I slept through it. When I eventually awoke I was told to stay in bed and be quiet. A hushed agitation was going on all around me. Now and then someone would come and stroke my head to soothe my heightening anxiety.

When the ambulance arrived I watched in fear and dread as Paddy was lifted off the bed, stiff as a board as if all his joints were locked together by the pain, and placed gently on a stretcher. Then the men carried him out shoulder high, taking great care not to trip over the step at the narrow doorway. Mam and Dad were white as sheets. An aunt held me close. Was he already dead, I wondered? They all looked so fearful. I did not know then that they had been scarred by an earlier experience. In May 1921 at the age of 12 my uncle Jack Morrissey had died of a burst appendix at the same Waterford hospital. Paddy was rushed to the theatre and operated on, on arrival.

My mother Mary Morrissey as a young girl with her younger brother Jack who was to die tragically of peritonitis in May 1921 at the early age of twelve.

During a subsequent dodgy six weeks he came as close to death as anyone could with peritonitis. It was a full two weeks before they took me down to see him. In between he had had to undergo a second operation but was recovering at last, they said. A miracle that he had come through it at all. I found him in a large ward on the second or third floor, on a bed just inside the door. He looked like a skeleton and his colourless face seemed barely able to sustain a smile. He raised himself on an arm but soon fell back. At that moment I felt closer to him than I had ever felt. I wanted to cry but did not. I was there for perhaps a quarter of an hour, then Mam took me away while Dad stayed on. It was my first visit to a hospital. The whiteness of everything, the hushed voices, and the cold brass grill of the lift that trundled us up and down intimidated me. It was a relief to be taken across the street to the elegant, if sombre, terraced house in Belle View Terrace where our cousins, the Manahans, lived. From a vantage point at the end of the terrace there were views westward over the city. In front of each house, a square of manicured lawn. It was here that Mam stayed during the worst days of Paddy's illness. We were greeted solicitously and I was parked in front of a slice of cake. It greatly eased Mam's burden that she had the kindness of Mary, Doc, Jo Denn and Biddy Denn to rely on. Dad, Molly and I returned to Lismore soon after that. Mam stayed on, now at Carrick, now at Manahans, until Paddy was well enough to be brought home again. At the first opportunity I asked him to show me his wound but when I saw the long, jagged scar I wished I had not. The flesh along the cut still looked pink and tender and was criss-crossed by the lesser scars of stitch and clip. He had to miss some months at school but, in spite of that, did not have to stay back a year.

My own appendectomy was a trivial affair by comparison. I was 11 at the time and had been having stomach pains. The Doc suggested I should see Dan McCarthy. Dan, an acquaintance of my parents, was a burly, beetle-browed man who might have played rugby. Mam and I entered his unpretentious surgery in Dungarvan and, after a bit of chat with her, he told me to lie down on a brown leather couch. I stretched out on my back. What happened next took me totally by surprise. With unerring accuracy he poked a thick index finger into my belly and I rose up with a yelp. 'That's all right,' he said, 'It will go away in a jiffy.' Then he turned to Mam who appeared a bit concerned about the way he had ambushed me. ''Tis the appendix all right. Nothing serious. We'll do that for him soon.'

He was as good as his word. Not long afterwards I was lodged in the small Dungarvan Hospital. The night before the operation I was flushed out with an enema. One of my pals had laughingly warned me to expect this, as he did the 'duck' in which I would be directed to piss. The nurse came up to my bed with a tall enamel jug and a slim length of orange-red rubber tubing on one end of which was stuck an enamel funnel. She told me to lie on my side. I looked at her apprehensively but she assured me it would not hurt. She shoved the thin end of the tube up my hole and poured into me via the funnel a lukewarm liquid that she said was composed of just soap and water. Then I had to sit on a bedpan and let it all flow back out again. It was a curious experience, not at all scary and even pleasurable, once you got over the embarrassment at having your private part inspected by a woman. The next morning I was given a heavily starched white gown to pull on – it covered me from neck to toe – and was told to walk down the corridor to the operating room. Arriving there, I was confronted with a basinful of blood from the previous patient and a number of bloody sheets lying about the floor. It seemed like an *awful* lot of blood to me. Probably it was just bloody water. It was clear I was not expected at that moment because one of the nurses let out a shriek and swept the evidence of the earlier butchery behind the door while the other smiled sweetly and told me to stretch out on the high, forbidding-looking table. Strangely enough I was not in the least put out by the sight of the blood, merely surprised that there should be so much of it. The patient must have been a very big person I reasoned as I lay on my back waiting for something to happen. I began to wonder where the ether was. I knew from my pals who had been operated on that a mask would be placed over my face and I would be told to breathe in the gas. A few masked heads began to assemble above me.

'Will I go asleep now?' I asked innocently, thinking maybe that I should be doing more myself. 'You do that darlin',' the busy nurse said, scarcely paying me attention.

I closed my eyes but nothing happened. I started to shiver. I opened my eyes again just in time to see the ether cone coming down. It fastened on my mouth and nose and I was aware of a strong hand keeping it firmly in place.

'Why is he shivering so much?' was the last thing I heard the nurse say.

Dan McCarthy's reply was only a mumble. Then I was gone.

A couple of hours later I awoke. I was back in my ward bed. My right side hurt as if my guts were strung tight like the wire of a piano, my head ached, and my mouth tasted as if I had puked in it.

Two days later one of the ward nurses let out a scream when she found me sitting on the high sill of the window above my bed, looking out at the sunny grounds below. A day ot two later Bishop Colbert arrived with his unforgettable oranges. Coincidentally, in the bed next to me there was another Lismoreman, Willie Geoghegan from the Castle Farm who was in with a hernia, probably in his upper abdomen. It was a 'man's complaint' and much more serious than what I had. He had had his operation earlier than I, and the day before my stitches were due to be taken out a nurse arrived to do the same job for him. They had strapped a four- to six-inch wide band of elastoplast across his very hairy chest and she wanted to get that off first.

She picked at it for some time amid Willie's moans and winces, then I heard her say, 'This is no good. There's only one way to get that off.'

Willlie nodded.

She took firm hold of the partly raised end of the tape with both hands. "Are you ready?"

I watched, fascinated as my fellow townsman drew breath and tensed himself.

Then before I fully realised what they had been planning the nurse, with one powerful tug, ripped the tape off Willie's chest, taking a swathe of his black hairs with it. The hapless patient uttered a loud groan and his whole body appeared to rise six inches off the mattress. I gulped. I could almost feel the pain myself. Willie sank back like a deflated balloon. The nurse did not even notice. When the same woman came to snip off my three metal clips and eight stitches the following day I was very wary of her. But I need not have worried. She did not hurt me at all.

My only other experience of hospital occurred a couple of years later when I was sent to the Bon Secours Hospital in Cork City to Dr Pat Kiely, a cousin-in-law of Mam's for observation. What my parents were worried about I am not sure; I suspect it was linked to the fall I had had from the tree in the Villa. I had an easy time there. Put in some kind of special room on my own high up under the roof and with a large round window at floor level, I had a marvellous view of the twinkling lights of the city at night, and of the pedestrians and traffic by day. I was in the place for no more than a day or two during which Pat Kiely, accompanied by a nun sister, came in and looked me over once or twice without making me any the wiser about what he was supposed to be diagnosing. After a few tests, I came away with a clean bill of health.

Mam was the third member of the family to be operated on. Doctor Healy removed sebaceous cysts from her head on two or three occasions. He gave her a local anaesthetic and with two simple incisions opened the skin and cut out the benign accumulations of fat. After he stitched the wound she was left with a scar that looked like the cross on a hot cross bun. 'The Morrissey cyst!' she would laugh, referring to the fact that the incidence of the growth seemed to come from her side of the family, and she was grateful that she would be able to comb her hair in comfort again. When I was about 16 she went away to the Bon Secours for an unspecified 'woman's operation'. I tried to elicit more information from her and Dad about the nature of her complaint but I was just told it was nothing about which to worry. I felt apprehensive as Dad and I waved her off on the Cork train. She was still waving as the train picked up speed and disappeared into the cutting beyond Ballyanchor Bridge. It worried me to see her going off on her own but I felt that if there had been anything seriously wrong Dad would have gone with her. Later that evening Dad and I went about following her instructions on how to cook something for ourselves. It was the first time we had to prepare our own meals. She returned in a week or so showing no ill-effects. Not long after though, I noticed that she needed to wear custom-made Spirella corsets which she ordered through Minnie Kiersey of the Parish Height in Carrickbeg, who was an agent for the company that made them.

Both of my parents were extremely reticent in matters of human physiology, particularly when it applied to persons of the opposite sex. It was as if I was expected to somehow pluck this knowledge from the air myself as I grew older. On one occasion when I was not so little I went to the lavatory and found blood in the bowl. I knew that Mam had been there just before me and ran up to her, worried.

'Mam, you cut yourself?' I said.

'Me? Cut myself? No,' she laughed.

'But there's blood in the bowl an' you were the last one in there?' I persisted. 'Come. Look.' I took her hand and led her into the lavatory. 'There,' I pointed at the bright red stain that was hugging one side of the bowl.

'That's not blood,' she smiled, 'Sure that's only a bit o' stain.'

''Tisn't. 'Tis red!'

'There now,' she said, hugging me, 'I haven't cut myself. Look.' She held out her hands for me to see.

'Well somebody has,' I said, perplexed, 'Maybe Dad... ?'

'Dad hasn't cut himself either. Now do your wee-wee and forget about it.' She pushed me toward the bowl and withdrew, closing the door after her.

I looked down at the discoloration again and, holding intensely to my bewilderment, dispersed it with my jet of piss. Days later, in spite of Mam's explanation, I was still trying to work it out. Eventually I gave up. It had to remain one of life's little mysteries for another while.

As a child I contracted all the usual sicknesses of my age group – whooping cough, chicken pox, measles and mumps. Mumps was the one I hated having most. My face resembled that of a bloated rabbit and I felt sick through and through. Being sick in West Street had its compensations. Once you had got over the worst you could look out and wave to your pals on their way to and from school. You could spy on the adult activities of the Fair Day and maybe sneak off a few shots with your peashooter or water-gun at unsuspecting necks. In the hustle and bustle no one ever guessed that the source of the sharp sting and the inexplicable droplets was the crack under my slightly raised window. On any working day there was a bit of life in the street, thanks to the garage on one side and the Wine Vaults on the other. I liked best being ill in early spring, which I almost unfailingly was either with flu or a heavy cold. The days would be visibly lengthening and the crows building their nests in the topmost branches of the straight-trunked beeches across in the Villa. Layer by layer the nests would thicken with the twigs beaked in by the pairs of birds that squabbled for space in the densely populated rookery. During flu epidemics, which were usually mild, the schools of the town would close for a week, or even two, as a precautionary measure. If, as happened to all of us children at one time or another, you were lucky enough to fall ill before the enforced recess or after the schools had reopened, this amounted to an unexpected holiday.

Outbreaks of more serious illnesses would hit the county, too, and one of these, scarlatina or scarlet fever, a highly contagious disease, laid me low one springtime. The only other person to get it in Lismore at the time was Thumper Lineen and it meant a long spell away from school for both of us. I was fortunate not to develop a serious strain. Just the same, my body rashed all over. The bind was that I had to remain quarantined in my room. My pals could neither come up to see me nor lend me comics or books. Anything I read had to be burned afterwards. Once I was over the worst of it I could wave from my window and hold shouted conversations. The illness was debilitating and subsequent to it I needed a long period of convalescence. I was ordered to go for walks every day, lengthening them bit by bit in order to recover my strength. It was important that I kept warm so to wear I was given a brown tweed overcoat that my brother had outgrown. Generally my walks were solitary and I liked them that way. I would go down the bridge and along the canal on the Cappoquin Road. I always went out between 2.00 and 4.00 p.m. in the afternoons so that I could avoid my schoolmates. It would have embarrassed me if they had seen me in such a weakened state. Later on, I used to meet up with Thumper and we would go off on longer walks together. Even though he was older than I – he was in Paddy's class – he used to put up with my juvenile company and tell me lots of things about the world that I had not yet experienced. His health recovered more quickly than mine and after he had returned to the CBS I resumed my unsocial outings. I switched to the other side of the Blackwater and went down by the Warren to the Rock and beyond where I enjoyed the teeming wild life of the riverbank. At the Rock I used to take off my coat and jacket and do somersaults and handstands on the moist grass to get myself fit again. I consciously delayed returning to school as long as I could because I enjoyed those excursions so much. My parents were tolerant but eventually even they would brook no further procrastination and I was sent back. I greatly missed my freedom of movement but the hours spent by the river had not been wasted. I sensed that I had enhanced my powers of observation. And perhaps I had developed some appreciation of patience too.

Diphtheria and tuberculosis were the dreaded diseases of the period, the second a particularly indiscriminate assassin. A large number of victims came through their encounter with it but many, including my delightful Auntie Bab, succumbed, she in 1947. The board of assistance for the county, in keeping with its counterparts countrywide, grew extremely worried about the seemingly inexorable spread of the disease. To combat it, a specialist regional hospital was established with central government funding at Ardkeen, near Waterford City, in the late Forties, and, at the same time, St Carthage's Hospital in Lismore became a convalescent home for those who were recovering from it. The Red Cross raised its profile by spearheading an anti-tuberculosis campaign, the Lismore branch doing its bit by organising flag-days and house-to-house collections. By the early Fifties mobile X-ray units had been established to aid a national TB survey instigated by the Department of Health. When the first such unit came to town people were very wary of it. No one wanted to be informed that they had contracted the disease. Teachers, nurses and doctors worked hard at allaying our fears and subsequent visits saw a big rise in the numbers going for X-ray (over 600 in September 1952). Mam had insisted that we all went from the start.

The unit itself, a large van parked outside the courthouse, looked harmless enough as did the reception cubicle where you filled in the small yellow application form. The forbidding bit came after you had stripped to the waist. You placed your jaw on a cold metal lip, your chest against the cold, smoked glass of the machine, then when you got the order from the radiographer, cupped your shoulders and drew in your breath. The apparatus buzzed like a Buck Rogers spaceship as it took your picture and that was all there was to it. I had forgotton about the experience when a month later a postcard arrived giving me the all-clear. After the first successful visit I did not have to be persuaded to attend regularly. Everyone had a friend or acquaintance who had been struck down by TB. I had lost an aunt and Molly came close to losing a first cousin, Aidan O'Neill from Carrick, who spent a year or more convalescing in the Lismore sanatorium. Molly had left Lismore by then but Mam and Paddy and I used to visit him in the hospital. Later on, when he grew strong enough to go on walks, he would drop in at West Street in the afternoons for a cup of tea.

An equally vigorous anti-diphtheria campaign seemed to meet with more immediate success. That this disease never assumed the epidemic proportions of TB was probably due to the programme which ensured that all children were immunised against it. Fear of both began to evaporate once the public saw that the control measures were proving effective. Besides, two even more frightening killers were also competing for the headlines, poliomyelitis and meningitis, both poignantly personalised for us by the deaths of two young people, one in Lismore, the other in a country with which we felt a strong affinity, Scotland. Simon Devereux, an 11-year-old schoolboy at the Lismore Christian Brothers' School died of meningitis in September 1952. A sunny youngster whose parents lived in London, he was staying at the time with his grandparents, the Farrells, in Ballyin. All the children in the town attended the funeral and there was an honour guard of CBS pupils. I was probably the only one who missed paying him respects because I was away on holidays in Carrick at the time.

The person whose death in 1947 instilled in us a dread of polio was Nancy Rioch, a young Scottish swimmer of great potential. She and her brother Fraser had caught the imagination of the public with their success in the pool and were a popular pair. That a highly trained athlete should be struck down in this manner seemed unthinkable. For a time after her death parents were very cautious about letting their children go near the water – there was a theory that you could catch the disease from too much bodily contact with it. However, we still went swimming and still drank freely from the Spout. In time a cure for this disease appeared to have been found in the form of a newly invented tank ventilator that looked like a miniature submarine. This became popularly known as the 'iron lung', an expression that, when I first heard it, provoked in my mind a terrifying conflation of a piece of apparatus out of Dr Frankenstein's laboratory and the grim Balaclava worn by *The Man in the Iron Mask*.

Then there was goitre which, happily for us children, seemed to be a disease of the elderly. While comparatively uncommon this uncomfortable-looking condition was not so rare that you would remark upon it after you had been told once what it was. The most mysterious and invisible of all diseases to me was lockjaw. Only very occasionally did you hear of it but what you heard was enough to send shivers down your spine. The name said it all. You could not talk and you could not eat. It was scary to think you could pick it up from something as easy as falling off a bike, a frequent enough occurrence for all of us.

An epidemic of which we were almost unaware, alcoholism, remained constantly with us. The poor openly recognised the addiction, the middle class sought to tuck it away, the rich had money enough to ignore appearances. At all levels, however, the disease brought suffering and distress. For the alcoholic himself or herself there was loneliness and decline, for his or her family, desperation and humiliation as their way of life was slowly undermined. Drunkenness in men was tolerated but attendant brutality was not excused. In women excess drinking on its own was inexcusable, something talked about in whispers and picked up in snatches by us youngsters. Men were fortunate not to have to endure this often ill-balanced, though not always ill-intentioned, form of character assassination. They merely 'liked a drop' or were 'fond of a drop', expressions that could mean anything from a man's going on an occasional batter to his being a serious alcoholic. The tolerance of our elders in this regard rubbed off on us children but we, unlike them, showed little understanding of the causes of the illness. It was only when the Pioneer Total Abstinence Association, set up to revive and continue the temperance movement established by Father Theobald Mathew in 1838, forced the issue into the open that I came to realise what the term 'gone away for a cure' really meant. The Pioneers however, for all their good intentions, pumped too much religion and not enough social concern into their message, which ultimately put me, and most other young people, off them.

My aunt Nellie Morrissey, Mam's musically talented younger sister, who died of tuberculosis at the age of 20 in November 1925.

The deadliness of disease was a concept I could accept as a child. Unexpected death was too unnerving to be explained. The shock and puzzlement of seeing my favourite aunt stretched out on her deathbed remained indelible. It had not been concealed from me how desperately ill she was. It was just that disease was too early a concept for me then. Life seemed limitless, death something that happened only to old people. But my aunt was not old, less so even her sister Nellie, who contracted TB after being ill with pleurisy and died at the age of 20 in November 1925. I was later to learn of this unbearably sad event, coming as it did four-and-a-half years

My aunt Nellie Morrissey is seated on the left with, in the background, her sister Nan Morrissey, Their younger brother Jimmy Morrissey is glimpsed lying on the grass on the left. Foreground right is their cousin Jo Denn of Castlejohn. In the background is the ruin of the old Carrick Workhouse known as 'The Union'. This is one of only a few extant photos of the Union Workhouse that was wholly or largely burnt down by Irregular forces during the Civil War in December 1922. The carpet of small flowers in the photo would appear to be either daisies or buttercups or both – spring/early summer blooms that would date the photo to this time of year, probably in 1925 as Nellie does not look at all well.

after the loss of my uncle Jack. In time it became clear to me that Mam and her sisters never really got over the deaths of their younger siblings, especially those of the twelve-year-old Jack and Nellie. On showing me old family photographs, Mam would always speak of them with great affection and sadness.

A glimpse of a child's coffin in the New Cemetery heightened my awareness of death; the child of some farming people. But then I saw another white coffin being carried out of a house in Botany. It was held delicately in the grieving father's arms like a crushable bouquet of lilies. Awareness turned to anxiety with the sudden death of Anne O'Brien, who lived just around Ormonde's Corner in Botany. A little older than I, full of life and always laughing, she played often with us in West Street. Then from one day to the next she was gone; collapsed with an anguished scream in a shop in the Main Street and died on the spot of a tumour, it was said. I had no apparatus to cope with this, and no concept of what a tumour was. It did not help much to be told that it was God's will, although I accepted that he took her because he liked little children. She was to be the only childhood pal that I would lose so tragically. As the protective shield of innocence slipped from my eyes death began to appear more and more indiscriminate. Nuala Neville of Botany died a child in March 1950. Anne and Sheila Stapleton, two sisters barely out of their teens, were taken within a year of one another in 1947–48. Paddy Ahearne, the father of our school pals Dick, Michael, Brian and Liam, dropped dead of a heart attack while out exercising a horse for the Duke of Westminster. Petey Gillen, the sacristan of St Carthage's parish church, who taught a generation of children the skills of altar-boying and put up patiently with our pranks, died also a youngish man in 1949. In the same year Barney's father, Martin Walsh the cobbler, passed away. The following year it was Mikey and Andy Coleman's turn to suffer when their father, John, died.

The year 1951 was a bad one for grocers. Dan Fleming, the round-faced, black-haired shopkeeper who specialised in bacon at his premises at the corner of South Mall and Main Street by the Mall Seat, packed in his slicer suddenly. Dan, a Mallowman, and his wife Mai (née Ross) from Killorglin, were personal friends of Mam's and she bought regularly there even though the shop was at the other end of town. 'There's a lovely bit of bacon now, Mary,' Dan would say, holding out a joint for her to inspect. 'Sure you wouldn't get the like of it anywhere else in town.' He always said the same thing, no matter what the piece looked like. The other grocer Mam lost that year, also an unexpected demise, was the quiet little Laurence Quinlan of Chapel Street. He was the one with whom I always had Mam-inspired petty arguments over brown paper wrapping. She insisted I had to have messages wrapped, even if I was only going next door to the Wine Vaults. Macs wrapped everything anyway but Larry ran a much smaller operation and probably remembered the wartime experience of Britain (and Ireland too?) where shopkeepers were not allowed to wrap up goods in order to save paper. Paper of any kind was scarce in the postwar period and you had to spend a good few bob with Larry before he reckoned you were entitled to a bag. I could see his point. I myself did not give a shit whether the messages were covered or not. Sure I only had to run a couple of hundred yards with them. But I knew that if I arrived back without the wrapping I would be scolded. Between Larry and myself we never quite managed it the way Mam would have liked so she had to resort to sending me out with a used bag in which to carry things back. Even then I was known to come home with the empty bag in one hand and the unwrapped messages in the other. There were probably two reasons for Mam's stubbornness about this: one, it was not too infrequent an occurrence for me to trip over my feet and drop the messages, bread and sausages for example, on the pavement; two, I do not think she was keen on the general public's knowing what she was buying. There was one other grocer in the town, besides McCarthy's, where you were automatically given a bag – John Moore's in the Main Street. And I had another reason for going to this shop. John's good-natured smile compensated for Larry's tetchiness. Mam was very diplomatic in her shopping habits and liked to leave a bit of business everywhere.

When men died leaving young families you felt deeply for those of your pals who were afflicted. And our elders did all they could to assist the widows whose lives had been shattered. Some adults you missed in their own right. I missed Guard Dennis and Guard Martin because they were often around our yard working timber with Dad. The adult I missed most, however, was our next-door neighbour Jim Feeney who died suddenly in February 1952. Our ties with the Feeneys were very close and we were always in and out of one another's houses. Jim himself was a stout, enormously good-humoured man from Ballysaggart, with an infectious laugh and a boyishly mischievous nature. He was as good as his sons Michael and Tom at illicitly sampling the apples of Bart Regan, his neighbour on the other side. Bart knew that the sons were at it and kept a watchful eye out for them. But he did not realise that Jim was fecking the odd one too until one day a hand snaked over the wall for a juicy red and he thumped it with his walking-stick.

'That'll teach you!' he chortled and popped his head up over the stone wall like a jack-in-the-box. He was as embarrassed as Jim when he saw who he had walloped.

Of another incident Bart remained entirely innocent. Jim was keeping a few chickens in the garden at the time and knew that a cat was worrying them at night. So he lay in wait with his shotgun. When the outline of the animal presented itself in the dark he blasted it. Instead of some expected wild raider, however, he had bagged Bart's harmless black pet. Too ashamed to admit to his neighbour that he had shot the animal, Jim spirited the body away. Bart was philosophical, though not unmoved, by his loss. Cats took off like that.

Jim delighted in the foibles of his customers too, none more than those of Mickey 'The Ram' O'Connor. Mickey was a wool dealer who kept himself afloat through thick and thin, as often the second as the first, by the sharpness of his wits. 'Just a gallon,' he would say expansively to Michael or Tom, getting out of his worse-for-wear car, 'I like to keep her topped up.' In many cases the lads would hear the petrol splashing into an almost empty tank but they acquiesced in the illusion.

Fair Day saw the Ram in his element. When the haggling with the farmers reached a critical stage he was known to tell them that he was expecting a call from Bradford on Feeney's phone *at any moment* that would give him the latest wool price from the international market, and that would settle the matter. Then, supposedly going inside the shop to check whether the call was still in, he would borrow an alarm clock from Jim and set it near the telephone to ring a couple of minutes hence.

'They're puttin' it through right now.' He would go back out to reassure his clients and engage them in small talk until the bell went on cue.

'That's it lads!' he would then cry and dash inside again to hold his one-way discussion with the imaginary Yorkshire agent.

The men gathered round the steps outside would hear snatches of an animated 'exchange' before he re-emerged, shaking his head ruefully.

'Jasus lads, 'tisn't lookin' too good. I'm afraid the price is after droppin' again.'

There were no flies on the farmers who, no doubt, were employing cunning stratagems of their own to argue up the rate but even they found it hard to keep pace with the exuberant Mickey.

CHAPTER EIGHTEEN

Family Life

OUR HOUSE WAS probably typical of many in its lack of electrical apparatus of any kind other than lighting and an electric kettle. I was coming up to my fourteenth year before we possessed a wireless. Dad purchased our first receiver, an HMV, Model 435, from Feeney's on the 7th of February 1951, paying £2-4-0 down to be followed by twelve monthly instalments of £1-11-0, a grand total of £20-16-0. At that time I had scarcely heard the word 'television'. Later that same year I was to hear more. Newspapers announced that demonstrations of the new wonder box were to be given in Ireland for the first time at the Royal Dublin Society. Our first electric cooker was also to be bought comparatively late in my young life. We never had a hair dryer or a vacuum cleaner. Ironing was done with the old reddish-coloured heating iron with the red-hot metal slugs, described in Chapter 2. Open fires supplied our heating. Dad would cut the blocks for these on the wooden horse that he had constructed himself, enlisting my assistance when I became competent enough to be trusted with the cross-cut saw. Wood was supplemented with coal that we bought from Boysie Noonan's yard at South Mall and Main Street. Good coal was hard to come by, a lot of shale being mixed in with the consignments of slack that were sent over from the British coalfields. Mam – the person with Molly who always lit the fires although she eventually taught me the knack – would angrily have to throw a sizeable quantity of it away or moisten the coal-dust into a kind of briquette that burned dully. What was left of the real coal only spluttered into flame. As the Second World War years receded the quality began to improve. Our own West Waterford-produced turf, harvested on the lower slopes of the Knockmealdowns, was poor also. A lot of it was fibrous and light-coloured rather than hard and dark, and it too burned lazily. Wood was the most effective fuel, especially oak and beech but these were dear.

The house was well roofed and, on the whole, dry. The small sitting-room on the ground floor was the exception. Sunlight never beamed directly into it and it remained cold and damp even in summer, with the wallpaper peeling away from the walls. In winter Mam would light the fire there on some Sundays to prevent it from becoming totally unliveable. It was a treat to snuggle up in one of the blue-grey armchairs with the dark blue floral motif, or on the matching deep sofa. Because fires were not lit there regularly enough, spring brought problems in the form of rooks, which tried to nest in the chimney pot. Usually we managed to put them off the idea.

Chimneys needed annual cleaning anyway and Hugo Dillon, husband to Peg Slash, would come around on his bike with his black, flat-headed brushes and expandable bamboo rods to do the job. Eugene Dennis has reminded me that Hugo, as well as being a chimney-sweep, was a pedlar, possibly the last in the Lismore area, who sold items that he carried on his bike. The sweep did not lack work in an area where open fires were universal. How long it took him to do an average house I can only guess but he certainly spent the best part of half a summer's day on our chimneys – screening off the fireplace with damp canvas bags and newspaper; sweating his guts out pumping the brush up every flue; clearing away the bags of soot and other ashy aggregate and, now and again, the twigs of an old nest. Not everybody had their chimneys cleaned annually and some had cause to regret it when the accumulation of soot in the passages caught fire. For us children, it was a real treat to watch the dark plume of a chimney fire snaking up from a spark-spitting pot while householder and neighbours ran about frantically, or at least apprehensively, with wet canvas sacks and buckets of water to quell the angry whoosh roaring up the flue. Our own living-room chimney caught fire once but, as comparatively little soot had built up in it, the blaze burnt itself out quickly. Mam got a fright all the same and made doubly sure that she kept the flues well-swept thereafter.

Such minor incidents she welcomed for a different reason; they gave her a chance to consider moving the furniture around. Not that she needed any external incentive to embark on this. She enjoyed it. One morning I would go off to school leaving the living-room as it had been for months. At lunchtime I would return to find that the bookcase that had stood against one wall now stood against another; the chairs were arranged in a different configuration; the light was somehow different. Another time it might be her bedroom. The next, the sitting-room. In time, all the rooms in the house would be revamped, and always unexpectedly – at least, nobody ever bothered to notify me of any moves in advance. I think she simply got bored with the aspect of a room after a certain length of time, or craved a bit of action perhaps? Or maybe, as with Martin Brennan's mother in Bernard MacLaverty's novel *The Anatomy School*, it was simply because we hadn't enough money to buy new furniture so she just moved the old stuff around?

Certainly, Dad had bought our old-fashioned furniture at auction sales.

For many years the flush lavatory on the ground floor had been inadequate and after a long campaign on Dad's part, with Mam applying pressure in the background, the Lismore Estates Company finally sent a team around to tear out the old one and substitute a new enlarged one. At the same time they were to repair the galvanised roof of the lean-to. The team consisted of Mick 'Cool Cock' Walsh and Mickey 'The Diddler' Flynn who, while they achieved work of a commendable standard and were the most amiable of men, were not exactly the fastest of troubleshooters. Before the term 'laid-back' was even invented they practised it. Which slightly inconvenienced us because while the repairs were underway we were having to use the 'sick' commode upstairs. The two men, Mick the stone-mason-cum-plumber and Mickey, his ever-ready assistant, were probably in their mid-fifties. Both *loved* to chat and you only had to half-draw breath within earshot of them for the one who first caught the flutter to break off what he was doing and engage you in conversation. They brewed up a lot on a Primus stove and 'The Diddler's' pipe was always going out so that had to be attended to as well. Mickey, being the one who had to keep a supporting foot on the last rung of the ladder, had more opportunity for talk than his senior partner. Mick's turn came while Mickey was mixing the cement, a task done with great deliberation. Repairing houses was only one of the many jobs delegated them. Everywhere around the town other Castle property was in need of renovation. Not a year would go by but you would see them attending to some section of the high stone walls along Gallows Hill, West Street or the New Way. And no passerby would escape an invitation to stop and exchange a word about the weather, the hurling and football matches of the previous Sunday and the next, the new curate, or the general state of the nation and the world. Failing a pedestrian, a passing car, bicycle, ass and cart, or even dog, would provide adequate cause for comment. 'Cool Cock', trowel in hand, would turn around on the ladder and peer after each object until it had moved out of range, or disappeared round a bend, or otherwise attained infinity. 'The Diddler' would shift his leg along the bottom rung, tip back the peak of his cap, and shake his head. Or then again might not, if he happened to be stuffing his pipe. Eventually the breach in the wall would be sealed, and so well that a shell from the biggest cannon in the Irish Army wouldn't have shifted it.

Organising an adequate supply of food was a major task for parents. The rationing of the Emergency lingered into the postwar years. During this lean period each member of our household held a separate ration book for which he or she was given a monthly supply of stamps. Mam kept them all and distributed our rations equally amongst us. Dad, a graceful, strikingly handsome and good-hearted man, worked tirelessly in the garden in spring, regularly planting potatoes, cabbage, carrots, parsnips, shallots, and parsley, to which he was very partial. I did not realise it at the time but he was working far too hard. There was the logging as well. Though he was tall and strong – he stood six feet and weighed thirteen stone – the extra labour he put in beyond his normal job hours appeared to have been instrumental in putting a strain on his heart. The year 1954 saw him forced into retirement through ill-health at the comparatively early age of 57. Indeed, he would have resigned a year earlier were it not that he wanted me to finish my schooling in Lismore. During that final year in town he was under doctor's orders to take as much rest as possible and every afternoon he would come home from the barracks to lie down for an hour or two. Mam was always worried at this time. The fatal heart attacks of Jim Dennis and Paddy Martin haunted her and she feared that he would suffer the same fate. I was worried, too, although I had an inadequate understanding of what was wrong with him. It was clear that I was entering a new phase of my life.

In my childhood I used to delight in watching Dad digging the furrows for the spuds and then lining them with the rich manure that Joe Kelly delivered over our end wall. The first whiff of the dung rocked you back on your heels but after a while you got used to it, and even savoured its sweet-sour tang. Next, Dad would bring up his bag of seed potatoes, slice each tuber down the middle and lay the halves or *sceallán̄s*, each with at least one eye in it and dusted with a white fertiliser, cut-side down on the manure about a foot and a half apart. After that, they were sprinkled with a further handshake of fertiliser and covered in. The eventual results were impressive. Good-sized plants – usually of the Golden Wonder or Kerr Pink variety – produced good quality tubers that were floury and tasty when cooked. Shallots, lettuce and rhubarb also thrived in the black earth of the garden. And parsley grew like a weed, happily, for we all loved the aromatic edge that it gave to Mam's delicious white sauce. Turnips and parsnips did reasonably well but Dad gave up trying to grow carrots after they had been eaten by maggots three years in a row. Half the cabbage was devoured by the yellow-greenish larvae of the white butterfly but what we salvaged was wholesome. (A less destructive larva, that of the Cinnabar moth, particularly seen on ragwort, was, I felt, wholly appropriate to Lismore on account of its bands of black and amber.) An experiment with Brussels sprouts proved disappointing. Fruit he made no attempt to grow, though we had inherited a couple of old gooseberry bushes, and tomatoes he left to Mam who often had a plant or two growing in pots. In summer fresh fruit at reasonable prices could be purchased from a number of orchards and vegetable gardens in the area. Apples came in a number of varieties: Beauty of Bath, Cox, etc, and Mam always saw to it that a supply of cookers, bought from Johnny McGrath, was laid in for the winter – she would wrap the individual fruits in newspaper and store them on the floor of the attic in a cool and gloomy corner. That way they kept for a few months.

Apple dishes were favourites in the house, from stewed apples and custard – 'apples and pink tuff' as I was said to have called it before I learned the colours – to tarts and charlotte. The last-mentioned was such a favourite with me I would assist Mam in making it. At first she would bake this in a rectangular enamel dish but, when Pyrex came in she switched to that. Not immediately, though. She took some convincing that glass, even of a reputedly specially hardened kind, could withstand the heat of an oven. It was my uncle Mick Morrissey who persuaded her to try it, showing her a sample of similar toughened aircraft glass that he had brought over from an RAF workshop. She eventually came to own two Pyrex dishes, a rectangular one that she reserved for charlotte, rice pudding and shepherd's pie, and a round one in which she cooked stews. Her tarts were less successful than her charlottes; the pastry never came out to her satisfaction. When she discovered that Hanna O'Donnell, the wife of postman Jim, had started selling the most exquisite apple and rhubarb tarts, made in a traditional bastable pot oven, she found the perfect excuse to discontinue all her efforts in that direction. Understandably, such delicacies were not cheap so it was a rare treat when one appeared in the house. There was one other rarity that I craved – the butter loaf, a special sweet white bread that Madden's bakery used to produce from time to time. As with the bastable-cooked tart, you never knew when it was going to arrive but when it did, you wolfed it. Mam had her own speciality too, and fortunately this made a more frequent appearance on the table – canary pudding, a kind of steamed sandwich mix served hot with heated jam. All these delights were served for tea and when I came in after school my nostrils would quickly detect the aroma of whichever one was on the menu. To keep me going in the interim I would be given a slice of bread and butter or a couple of plain Jacobs biscuits, or maybe goodie (bread soaked in warm milk). Occasionally I would be treated to a marshmallow-topped Mikado or a Café Noir, the coffee-flavoured one covered with brown icing. Jam was often home-made, produced annually from whatever berries that Paddy purchased at Paxman's. Johnny McGrath supplied the cookers from which, less frequently, apple jelly was made. We also bought produce from the well-tended Castle Gardens.

Breakfast was dull by comparison. Steaming porridge in winter and spring, Brown & Polson cornflakes in summer and autumn. In my teens, Nabisco Shredded Wheat from the USA hit the counters but I was not overwhelmed by that. Sometimes I might get a boiled egg. We consumed a lot of eggs, many of them bought from Ellis's. Sometimes I would ask for more than Miss Ellis had to hand in her pantry. She would then go round the chicken run picking out the extra ones from the tufts of grass where the hens had laid them. When I was visiting my cousins the Kielys' farm in Monakerka I was able to go hunting for eggs myself. Or, occasionally, closer to home, one of Jim Feeney's hens would lay one under the hedge between our gardens. Depending on my mood I might hand this over to Jim, or I might pocket it for myself. Eggs brought a little excitement too when you found a glugger (addle-egg) or, rarer still, one with a double yolk. Mam would serve eggs fried, scrambled, boiled, poached, or whipped into an omelette or flip. The only way I did not like them was poached; too vinegary.

For Paddy and me the staple lunchtime food all through our childhood and youth was 'pandy', i.e. mashed potatoes with butter or cream melted into them, and spiced with pepper and salt, and sometimes with onion. I never tired of it but was happy to see it replaced by colcannon once in a while. The cream was usually that which we could manage to skim off the top of the milk with a spoon. I used to scavenge it for my porridge as well. As a special treat Mam would buy a half pint or pint of cream direct from Jim Ormonde. There was a period, however, when we got none. A rumour had gone about that TB in cattle was the cause of TB in humans so Mam boiled all the milk we bought before letting any member of the household drink it. Whether this was an officially inspired rumour I have no recollection. There was, of course, another animal in the chain as far as farmers were concerned; they blamed TB in badgers for the TB in cows.

In my early years butter would be purchased in the form of a block of perhaps eight or ten pounds weight. From this, smaller units for use at table would be trowelled off and moulded with a pair of butter pats – wooden spatulas about five-and-a-half inches long from the base of a three-inch handle, with one side smooth and the other striated like the underbelly of a great whale. The day-to-day shape of these blocks was rectangular. In anticipation of guests small round balls would be rolled. I used to enjoy being given the chance to make a couple of these, although my shapes turned out anything but round. Pandy you could say I was addicted to. I would rush into the house at dinner time and wolf it down. In winter, I might get some stew with it, other seasons a sausage, rasher, slice of collared head, loin chop or, my favourite, minced-meatballs. Often Mam would serve meat for tea rather than for dinner. Dad always got some for his dinner, a piece of steak when Mam knew he was working extra hard. Dad also used to bolster his health with buttermilk or country butter, both too sour for me. I did not take to margarine either when that came in but, in this case, my dislike was far surpassed by that of Auntie Bab. She hated the stuff; said it wasn't a bit like butter at all, creamery or country; she could recognise it at a sniff, never mind the taste. Dad, who had a playful sense of humour, decided to put her senses to the test and, one night after she had gone to bed, took some margarine, patted it up to look like butter, and substituted it for the real thing on the breakfast table. In the morning Bab came down and happily ate the 'butter' as she always did.

'Did you enjoy the butter, Bab?' asked Dad mischievously.

'Yeh, 'twas grand,' said my aunt, little knowing what was coming.

'What would you say if I were to tell you it's margarine you're after eatin'?'

Bab's jaw dropped. At first she did not believe her ears but after inspecting the 'butter' closely her combined senses had to concur. Although she had a lively sense of humour herself this time she did not see the joke at all but swept furiously from the table and did not speak to him for the rest of the day. Only an abject apology from Dad finally persuaded her to let the matter rest. He was more taken aback than anyone at her reaction while Mam was highly amused at her sister's show of indignation.

My mother usually bought red meat from Jack Connors, the butcher across from the Co-op, but I was sent to the other Main Street butcher, McGrath's, as well. McGrath's was the bigger shop of the two and I used to be fascinated by the array of saws, knives and cleavers that hung there, and by the ease with which the burly Ned Coleman used to manhandle whole sides of beef from ceiling hook to hook. What I did not overmuch like, although I did not find it disturbing, was the sickly-sweet smell of fresh blood, masked to some extent by the aroma of the sawdust on the tiled floor.

The chickens we bought usually came straight from chicken runs and were delivered live to the house, which meant that we had to kill them ourselves. Molly was not very expert at this but would unwillingly attempt to do the job if Dad was unavailable. Mam loathed having to do it and, if the others were not around, would ask one of the lads in the garage, or one of the garage's customers like Sam McBrearty the Donegalman, who was wholly unsqueamish, to oblige her. Paddy and I, fortunately, were spared the ordeal of wringing the bird's neck or chopping its head off. Not that I was squeamish about it myself. I did watch the performance once or twice and afterwards gave a hand plucking the chicken. Our Christmas turkey was always prepared and cleaned out for us by Babe Tierney's grandmother in

Botany. Mam, paradoxically, did not mind gutting birds at all, breaking off from the task intermittently to wash the blood off her hands and dry them in her apron. (One of life's little mysteries for me as a child was how she used to tie the apron at the back when she could neither see her hands nor the strings she was tying. I would stand behind her and observe her strong fingers unerringly making the knot. Try as I might I could not manage the backward action myself.) Most chickens were kept for laying eggs so it was costly to buy one. Other than at Christmas or Eastertime Mam only purchased one when a member of the family was convalescing from an illness. Chicken broth was considered a wholesome pick-me-up.

Wartime bread and that of the immediate postwar years was greyish-white and stodgy. When Marshall Aid to Europe leavened the dampish Irish wheat with a drier American variety the loaf was transformed into something wholly white and stodgy. We survived both. Mam had always been giving out about the grey bread and was thrilled with the white at first. After the grey dough of wartime it brought a touch of glamour to her table. It was not very long, however, before she was wondering aloud whether the grey had been so bad after all. Fortunately she also made homemade bread. In her own estimation she made a reasonable wholemeal bread but she could never get her soda bread to rise properly. The acknowledged expert at making both of these was her sister Nan in Carrick-on-Suir, who never failed to produce the classic thing in height and texture in the oven of her small black range. Nan knew that we prized her bread and whenever friends or relatives were over from Tipperary, or were just passing through Lismore, a parcel would be dropped off for us. Now and again one would even arrive in the post. One of the joys of being in Carrick on holidays was the regular supply that came to table. Whatever doubts Mam had about her own bread she had none at all about her tea. Medium strong and piping hot or, when she felt the need of it, 'strong enough to trot a mouse on'. The only coffee she ever attempted to make, indeed the only one she could attempt for no other variety was available, was Irel liquid. It was not a success. Mam never regarded herself as a great cook and it was with some *searbhas* that she would say to me in perplexity now and again, "*Why* is it that chefs are always men when it is the women who do all the cooking at home?" Being already entrenched in my opinion that cooking was women's work and that no man should be seen doing it, I could furnish no adequate response except to concur in her supposition that a man's physique was perhaps more suited to the task of slaving over a hot stove for long hours of the day and night. She would then go on to balance this with the observation that the cooks in great houses were always women. The matter was to remain a puzzle for her.

On most Fridays of the year, and unfailingly in summer, a fisherman from Dungarvan or Ardmore would go around the town selling fresh herring or mackerel from the back of a small van. Usually he would have only one variety or the other, sometimes both and sometimes, but you had to be quick off the mark to catch these, a flatfish or two. On the whole, the hard-working fisherman had no easy task persuading a people to whom fish spelled penance to eat the produce of the sea. Our family, on the contrary, liked fish, particularly mackerel and, of course, the annual Lismore Estates Company's spring salmon. Mam used to bewail the fact that normally she could not get fish on any other day of the week but Friday, and was delighted with the exceptional deliveries of summer when the mackerel were shoaling and the fisherman would call on other days of the week. She herself preferred the taste of herring to mackerel but was wary of the many bones of the former. I tended to gulp down my food and was discouraged from eating herring in case I should get a bone caught in my throat. Mam did not insist on fish for the penitential day. If, in a cold winter spell, she felt we needed a hot meat stew inside us she would serve it up. And Bovril was always available. The Oxo cubes for stew had to be placed well out of my reach because I loved chewing those. My pals and I often used to buy a packet of them and pass them around like sweets. Probably they were not good for us but certainly were no worse than other things we sucked, like the hard chunks of Cleeve's and Sharp's slab toffee bought by the square that must have shifted a few teeth from their sockets; the sugar-sweet Rolos, Fruitos and Peggy's Leg that must have rotted others; the sorbet sucked from a flat paper packet with a straw – the first such suction device I had seen other than in the movies. The dog biscuit we used to buy – a flat, wheaten cake some three inches in diameter and pitted with holes – was a dietary dream by comparison.

Clothing was a major concern for parents. The maximum use had to be got out of every garment, and sometimes a bit more. Periodically Mam would try to revive fading shirts and blouses, even a frock, by dyeing them a new colour in the bath using Drummer dyes, but it was impressed upon me that this form of renewal was a tedious and imperfect art as it was extremely difficult to achieve an even colour across the whole garment. I don't think that any of her efforts turned out to her satisfaction. Dad would have a single tweed jacket and pants to go with it; a worn suit and a good one, sometimes just the good one when the worn one fell apart and he could not immediately afford to start the replacement process. He seldom possessed more than three neckties but had a heavy overcoat for winter and a light gaberdine for summer. In addition, of course, there were his *garda*

My mother, in a style that was later to be copied for the retro New Look, holding my brother Paddy in her arms, 1934–35. Photograph taken in our garden in West Street, Lismore.

clothes – two uniforms, including two pairs of shiny black leather leggings which I never saw him wear, and a weather-proof mac. Being in uniform most of the week helped him to save on civvies. Mam managed a few dresses and ran to a couple of overcoats and a light summer raincoat. A fox-fur wrap that had belonged to my grandmother hung in her wardrobe but I never saw her wear this. I used to take it down now and again and stare into the dark, malicious eyes of the stuffed head and run my fingers along the fine row of teeth. I would put it around my neck and feel the kiss of its fur on my nape. It had a hasp on a short chain to hold it in place and through the black silk that lined it you could feel the contours of the unfortunate animal's ligaments. Mam could never afford the fashion that she would have liked to wear but she managed a bit of style by having things made specially for her on occasion. She had a more practical reason for ordering the special items; with ready-made clothes she always encountered problems in getting the right fit. She was five foot six inches tall and never weighed more than nine stone, perhaps eight and a half. She was selective in her buying and would have coats or jackets sent to her 'on appro' from Newell's or Switzer's in Dublin. When the New Look came out in 1947 she was dismissive of it. 'What do they want, putting us back in long skirts again?' she snorted indignantly. 'Sure we left those behind us years ago?' She took to the new nylon stockings more readily. They did not constantly run ladders like the old ones and anything that saved her sewing, which she hated, had to be good.

Paddy, being four years older than I was, got first choice of clothes between us two and anything that he had stretched out of, and was still wearable, was retained for my later use. He liked a bit of style, too, and in his tall and handsome teens would even slip on a pair of white gloves occasionally, something that seemed inexplicably adult and posh to me. But he did not have much of a choice either. For myself, I was happy with my hand-me-downs. Lots of other boys wore second-hand clothes as well. It was easy to spot such garments. They never seemed to fit properly – 'Toulon and Toulouse', Dad would pun – or, if they did, showed all too clearly where they had been taken in. Mam took upon herself the washing and cleaning of our clothes. While Molly was helping her almost everything was washed. Afterwards, Mam made it easier for herself by sending sheets and shirts to the Metropole Laundry in Cork, which operated a regular van service in our area. She hated ironing with even more fervour than she hated sewing and knitting; the last-mentioned was rarely attempted.

But I was not always clothed second-hand. On the occasions of my First Holy Communion and Confirmation I was given a new outfit from head to toe and was even photographed in a phoney studio setting in a back room up the alley by the side of Larry Quinlan's shop in Chapel Street by Stritch of Fermoy. I was lucky to be given such an outfit. Many of my pals made their vows in the clothes in which they went to school. They might have had the addition of a new or borrowed pullover for the day but mostly just looked better scrubbed than normal and wore their hair uncommonly tidy. Shoes and sandals I nearly always got new. I liked the squeak of a new pair of Clark's but they often cost you a sore pair of heels while you were breaking them in. If they stayed tight after a couple of weeks' wear I used to take them up to Martin Walsh or his son Jackie, who was following in his father's footsteps, to be stretched on the last. I always wore leather-soled shoes. My first experience of synthetic soles came when white corrugated crepe began to appear on sandals. It was funny stuff and when it became frayed at the edges you used to pick at it the way you picked at your nose. There was no way of repairing crepe. It just wore out eventually. Shoes were resoled with leather. Heels and toes lasted longer with factory-made black rubber tips. Steel tips for heels and toes were also available. Boots were given added life when soled and heeled with strips of old car tyre, or when peppered with iron studs. I delighted in dancing out into a sunlit West Street in new shoes and for a few days was extremely wary of getting them scuffed. The sensation of wearing something brand new wore off quickly, however, and soon I would be back to booting stones and twigs and any other inanimate objects that lay across my path.

Mam, as well as doing her best to make Paddy and me look reasonably presentable, also endeavoured to instil a bit of culture into us. Among other things she came down hard on bad table manners and scolded us if we did not sit straight. She somehow scraped a few bob together to send us to Miss

McCarthy of Fernville for piano and elocution lessons. My brother was keen and profited from both. Having gained first class honours in pianoforte playing in the primary grade with the Dublin-based Leinster School of Music in 1941 he went on to become a very good piano player and used to entertain his friends with popular tunes when he wanted a change from classical pieces. In contrast, I was a miserable failure. I was able to make some fist of elocution but adjudged it superfluous as I was fluent enough in talk already. But I did learn that it was not at all as easy to pronounce the combination 'th' as I had thought before and that the word 'ballet' was pronounced 'bal-*lay*' because it was French and not English. On the keys I was hopelessly giddy. My heart was not into either subject. They were not at all the kinds of activity in which the streetwise kid to which I was beginning to aspire needed to be engaged. Had the lessons been part of my normal schooling I might have accepted them. As it was, they were crowding my fresh air. In a short time, I began to skip lessons. Mam was cross when she discovered she had been shelling out good money for classes I did not bother to attend and made me pick up again. When I skipped once more she and Miss McCarthy decided it was in all our interests to terminate the contract. With relief I returned to calling the local taxi driver 'Dinny Reagan' rather than 'Denny Regan'. However, in later life I was always to regret not having stayed with the music, and the few elocution lessons I endured planted the seeds of a future respect for language.

Dad, though a widely read, literate man, did not worry himself about conventional culture. He was even less interested in sport. Coursing he followed, all right, but that could hardly be called a sport, let alone an athletic activity. Mam had no interest in dogs or cats. It took Paddy a couple of years to persuade her to let him have a pet dog. Eventually, with Dad and I lending our voices, she consented and Dad got us a black mongrel puppy called Terry, that was, I think, the name that came with him. It was a kind of cocker–smooth terrier mix and it gave us a lot of pleasure during the short year or two we had it. When it died of distemper Mam refused to let us replace it with another, probably for the very good reason that she was the one who spent the most time looking after it.

On the whole, I think Mam was reasonably happy with Paddy and me though sometimes I used to feel that she would have liked to have a daughter as well. Happily for her, she had two surrogates among our neighbours, Margaret Feeney and Teresa Ormonde, both four years or so either side of me, the latter being the elder. Margaret would come in to have her hair braided and to dress up and practise her singing. She had a very nice voice but was terribly shy about it and would only sing when standing on the ledge behind the curtains in the living-room. She preferred to sing when Tom and I were not about because we, in our typically boyish way, used to tease her. Teresa fell madly in love with a handsome Englishman, Chris Harrington, who had bought a farm beyond Ballyanchor or Curraheen where he laboured mightily, using a new piece of equipment called a 'rotavator', to make arable the inhospitable soil there. Her staunchly Republican family took uncertainly to the idea of their daughter's going out with an Englishman, albeit a Catholic of impeccable credentials, and in anticipation of their ultimately giving in, the lovers used our house as a trysting-place. One or the other, or both, would knock on our door at all times of the evening and the house was heady with romance when they were about. Mam was thrilled to connive in their relationship, particularly when Teresa called to show off the latest dress in which she was going dancing.

Out-of town-visitors to our home were rare and were always greeted with great enthusiasm. Until her death Auntie Bab was our most regular visitor. Mam's other sisters Nan and Biddy came over from Carrick occasionally, either by train or when a drive came their way. And her brother Mick would always call when he was home from England. Old friends of Dad's always seemed to turn up unexpectedly and were usually passing through. They used to stay for a cup of tea or a glass of something – a bottle of Powers whiskey or a Sandeman sherry and a few small bottles of stout were always kept in the sideboard for such eventualities – and then resume their journey. Dad himself seldom drank and when, would just take a small bottle. Sometimes the Guinness was left untouched for so long it became flat and had to be thrown out. Now and again he would give me a sip of it but I found it too bitter and did not take to the tangy aroma. Mam used to mix herself a tonic of Guinness and milk when she felt the need of a pick-me-up and a sip of that was more to my liking. I think she may have added a spoon of sugar to it too. A drop of sherry went down well with her and she would not say no to a port on festive occasions. Like Dad though, she only drank alcohol sparingly. She found it mildly wicked to sip a glass on her own, and once or twice when I chanced upon her in the act, she grinned like a naughty child. It was rare to coax a whiskey into Dad's hand other than in the form of a hot toddy. He used to kid me, saying his appetite for alcohol had sharply diminished from the time he saw a gaggle of geese waddling around in a drunken stupor after they had lapped up dark, tantalising pools formed in the potholes and kerbs of a street after a cask of Guinness had tumbled off a dray and split open.

Among Dad's out-of-town friends who called to see him was one he appeared particularly pleased to see, Alec McCabe, a fellow-Sligoman and old comrade-in-arms of his IRA–IRB days. They would go into a huddle in the sitting-room, or go off for a pint, to reminisce about old times and friends. McCabe worked in Dublin for a 'building society' I was told, a term that raised in my mind the same kind of confusion as a 'turf accountant'. A rarer Dublin visitor was senior civil servant and Joyce scholar John Garvin, the brother of my Sligo Aunt Brighid, who called with his elegant and sophisticated wife Kathleen on their way to Cork or Kerry. Mam would look forward particularly to visits from her first cousin Biddy Morrissey, 'Nurse Biddy' as we knew her, who would fill the house with her uninhibited sense of fun. Biddy's Cork-based sister Peg Glendon and her husband George, then a captain in the Irish Army, would call in on their way to and from Kielys in Lisfennel, near Dungarvan, where they would have been visiting the third sister Mary Kiely and her husband Mattie, now farming in that townland. They were always good for a chuckle too. For a time we had a regular monthly visitor in Eddie Manahan, our Waterford City cousin, who was then a travelling salesman. He used to drop in for lunch on his way to Cork. I was always pleased to come home from school and find him there because I could pester him with questions about the two cities and all he saw on his travels.

The businesses on either side of our house were constant sources of interest and amusement. For me, the biggest attraction was the Wine Vaults' delivery cart. This was a low-slung, custom-made light-brown vehicle about five foot square with two-foot wooden sides and a removable back which was held in place by a couple of six-inch iron pins. Across its middle was fitted a foot-wide board that served as a seat; this was also removable. The cart ran on rubbered cart-wheels, was pulled by a horse, and was driven by Paddy O'Brien of Botany, in his spare time the drummer with Tommy Keating's Éire Instrumentalists *céilidhe* band. [See fine picture on page 36 of Eugene Dennis's *Images of Ireland: Lismore* (2005).] I was always after him for a spin around town on his delivery runs and frequently, particularly if Mikey or Mokie gave him the nod, he would give in. I would be sitting on one side of him and Tom Feeney on the other. With a sense of anticipation we would drive out through the archway into the street and ride off, gently at first because customarily we would be carrying a fair load. On route, as we shed our load, the pace would quicken. Paddy liked it best when he had to deliver something out the road to Paxmans, for example, or beyond. Once clear of the town he felt free to stand up like a charioteer and give the mare its head. The animal too grabbed the chance to stretch its legs. Pricking her ears, she pulled us vigorously forward with the powerful thrust of her muscular chestnut rump. Tom and I hung onto the seat with excitement, sensing something of the bravura of tinkers careering along the highway on their flat-tops.

A bitter-sweet smell of stale porter pervaded the Wine Vaults' shed because the McCarthys bottled their own Guinness. I used to watch Mokie operating the manual corking machine and would sometimes give him a small hand slapping the brown labels on the bottles. Corking was a fairly straightforward task but you had to watch what you were doing. You selected a filled bottle and placed it in the set position on the base of the wrought-iron machine. In the head above it was slotted a new cork. Quick, firm pressure on a lever drove the cork into the neck of the bottle. There were two possible hitches: one minor, you did not apply enough pressure to sink the cork first time round; one major, you overfilled the bottle, causing it to smash when the cork met the liquid. To avoid the latter the bottler had to keep a close eye on the pipe that drew off the stout from the cask. A later version of the machine used crown corks and these were easier, faster and safer to clip on. I was allowed to use this one, sometimes giving Sucky, who worked part-time there, a hand with the job. For a lark my pal used to take an occasional slug of the fresh Guinness but he did not recommend it. In that state it was practically undrinkable and could make you sick as a dog, he said. One slog was enough to convince me he was right.

Beyond the high shed there were a couple of stalls, one for the mare that pulled the delivery cart (I wish I could remember her name.) and one for her smarter stablemate which ran between the slender shafts of a trap. A high wall divided the stableyard off from the garden. To it was affixed a large wrought-iron bracket filled with hay that served customers' as well as the McCarthys' animals. Michael McCarthy had probably the finest trap in the county, and that included Lord Charles Cavendish's – an elegant, well-sprung, satinwood artefact with a brass front rail and other fittings, braided cushions on its seats, and finely-wrought wooden wheels that clipped the rays of the sun. Matching it for grace was the little dark mare that pulled it. For Mikey and his brother Danny it was the greatest of pleasures to ride out in it, an event for me too when the wooden gates of the Wine Vaults parted on a Sunday of matching splendour to send it gliding up Gallows Hill, with the shiny pates of its diminutive occupants bobbing up and down like two men in a tub. If I was lucky I might get a ride in it to the top of the hill. It was not easy for the brothers to ignore the longing looks that their neighbours' children cast over their vehicle. On my own I only coaxed the odd drive out of them. With Tom Feeney at my side I discovered I stood a better chance. Four appealing eyes were less resistible than two.

Large wooden gates led to an arch under the Feeneys' house and from there to the big galvanised repair shed at the back. It was in this archway that I discovered embarrassment. I was about six or seven years old, and had just left Tom, with whom I had been playing, to go home to tea. Short-cutting through the arch I got this sudden urge to do a pooley. Naturally, I did not waste any time and lifted up the leg of my short pants to relieve the pressure on my bladder. I was only half done when who should come around from the back but Mrs Feeney, on her way to shut the gates for the night. I muttered something apologetic about being short taken, hurriedly shut down the operation and ran off red-faced with drops of piss running down my legs. Mrs Feeney only grinned. I did not know how I was ever going to face her again.

The shed was a palace of mechanical ingenuity. At the end of it, looking out onto the garden, there was a wide, wide window under which ran a sturdy oil-impregnated workbench. To the right of the bench a door gave exit to the garden. The house end of the shed had gates that could be padlocked when the day's work was done. Outside of working hours the place was locked, more to keep us children from sneaking in and playing there than against any likelihood of things being fecked. It would have been easy for us to jag ourselves on some sharp implement, or trip into either of the two repair pits, or give ourselves an electrical shock, or scratch without meaning to the bodywork of somebody's car left in for repair; not that there were many cars going around without scratches. A fascinating array of tools littered the surface of the workbench – assorted wrenches, strange-looking hammers and drills, specialised screwdrivers and pliers, and all sorts of nuts and bolts. When Kieran Fenton or Panzer Behegan were working on a car you might see them climb out from under the oily cement pit beneath it, or pull back from under the bonnet, to go to the bench where, like a surgeon selecting a scalpel in an operating theatre, they would pick out the next tool they required. Fixed to the bench by the garden exit for many years had been a manually driven carborundum wheel on which we used to sharpen our penknives and sheathknives. Then one day a new electrically driven one was installed in its place. All you had to do to spin it was press a red button after which both your hands were free to manipulate the item you were sharpening. It was dead easy to operate, or so I thought until my hand slipped and the rapidly spinning stone tore a chunk of flesh out of the top knuckle of my left index finger and exposed the bone. The wound bled so profusely I thought I would never staunch the flow. We used the vices on the bench whenever we wanted to fix a metal band around the boss of a hurley. For amusement we would take turns balancing on the small square plate of one of the two hand-pumped jacks while being raised a couple of feet in the air; in repose these long heavy pieces of equipment resembled a pair of sleeping alligators.

For all the fascination they held for me, the cars and lorries that pulled up at Feeney's or stood under repair in the shed meant nothing unless I could get a ride in them. Trains were something else entirely. You could watch them going by time and time again and not necessarily feel the need to be travelling in them. No matter what angle you viewed them from, the massive locomotives and the snaking carriages were impressive. Even when there were no trains about I had an excuse to visit the railway station. Two of my schoolmates, Pierce and Jimmy Colbert, lived there. Dan, their father, was a gangling man who wore glasses perched on the end of a long nose. Because of this he became known to the Botany lads as 'Gandhi'. I always thought he was the spitting image of our own Dev. Dan, probably because he had a sizable family himself, was extremely tolerant of us kids playing about the station, even though we used often to hop across the double line of track from the passenger platform to the goods yard and back. He relied on our own sense of observation to tell us when the passenger trains were due but he kept a wary eye on our movements where goods trains were concerned because

Paddy out for a spin on his tricycle along the Tallow Road, Lismore c. 1936–37. Note the potholed road surface.

Auntie Bab and Paddy on the 'Tallow Bridge' on the edge of Lismore c. 1938–39. View toward the town. Note the good state of the newly surfaced road and the men in the background looking out for the next steam train to Cork.

these were not always predictable – extra ones were laid on occasionally. Seeing people getting on and off the train was an occasion of unfailing interest, often tinged with sadness when pals emigrated to look for work in England or returned to that country after spending a holiday at home. The six or seven hundred yards of straight track that took the train beyond the level crossing at Mayfield could seem very poignant when hands were waving from the carriages. On the other hand, when you knew pals were coming back it was a thrill to hear the distant whistle and see the tell-tale puff of smoke rising from the cutting before the engine charged into view.

Every summer Dad and Mam took us off to Carrick-on-Suir for a three-week holiday and in the run-up to our departure I kept a close watch on the trains. I would ask my parents to time their walks so that I could see the smoke puffing under the bridge on the Tallow Road. In the family we always referred to this bridge, situated just beyond the junction of the Tallow and Glencairn Roads, as the Tallow Bridge although the structure that really carried that name was the road bridge across the River Bride at the approach to Tallow itself. The railway bridge was humpbacked and a distinctive paling, made of old railway sleepers, ran up to its cut-stone walls from a distance of some thirty yards along either side of the road from both directions. Here, from the time when I was so little I had to be lifted up onto the parapet to the time when I was approaching my eighteenth birthday, I delighted in observing the trains go by. Sometimes I would wait for the bridge to suck the engine in, other times I would be on the opposite side to catch it spitting it out. Other times again I would wait for the first, then dash across the road to encounter the second, being careful not to collect a faceful of soot in the process. It was more dramatic to watch trains departing than arriving because those leaving the station pushed out more steam and smoke as they gained momentum. Not that our locomotives were thundering expresses. On the contrary, they moved rather sedately. All the better because you could keep them in view for longer. The bridge held another attraction for me. Below it, on the Glencairn Road, there was a wide grassy verge, much favoured as an encampment area by the tinkers of our region. Carts would be pulled in there and, every so often, a hooped green caravan or two. Asses and jennets grazed the verges of the road, the more lively ones spancelled with a length of rope. Bridges were not the only vantage point for watching the trains go by. Out walking the tracks with my pals we used to cling to the faces of the cuttings, so close to the passing locomotive you could almost reach out and shake the driver by the hand. Or we would lie on our bellies on the rims of the embankments watching the giant wheels transform our coins.

When the day came to depart on holidays Mam would get us up very early so that she and Molly would have time enough to put the house in order and complete the packing they had started the day before. At 11.00 a.m. sharp Denny Regan would call for us in his taxi. The main luggage would be put in the boot, odds and ends for the journey and ourselves on the seats inside, excluding Dad who always elected to walk up to the station. It would not have been quite right for the taxi-driver to overload his vehicle with a *garda* sergeant! And anyway, it was highly unlikely that the train would speed away without us. On the drive up Botany I might see some of my pals and wave excitedly to them. In my teens the gesture might be more wistful when I glimpsed a girl of whom I was fond. At the station I would have one eye on the track for the expected train and the other on Botany for a sight of Dad. I would have last seen him locking the front door, adjusting his brown hat, smoothing down the legs of his grey suit and folding a light gaberdine over his arm. Stepping out in civvies was a bit of an occasion for him and I think he was as excited as any of us about going on holiday.

Lismore Railway Station was a handsome limestone and wrought-iron agglomeration of buildings erected in the 1880s by the then Duke of Devonshire, whose crest could be seen on the friezes of the stone columns in the goods yard. It consisted of the station master's house, the ticket office, waiting-room, ladies' and gents' toilets, passenger and goods platforms, a signal box with an array of long steel levers that demanded muscle power, goods sheds, cattle pens, a stone-built water tower, and a manually operated turntable for turning steam engines around. Until 1939 an elegant glass roof had arched across the double line of track, covering both platforms. In that year, the structure having deteriorated so much, it had to be removed for reasons of safety, leaving me with no memory of it, alas. As an added refinement Eason's of Dublin maintained a small bookstall on the passenger platform, managed by Maurice Hartnett. When Maurice himself was in charge of the stall it ran like clockwork but whenever he was away on holiday and left matters to his brother Tom, who was unwillingly pressed into service to deputise for him, the service lived somewhat precariously. Tom was easygoing and liked a jar and the last thing he wanted to be doing was running a bookstand. But he had to oblige his brother. How disgruntled he felt could be gauged from an anecdote that Dick Power, who worked at the station, and Mam liked to relate. A well-dressed lady descended from a carriage and dashed across the platform as if she believed the train was about to depart again in half a minute, a highly unlikely occurrence.

'Have you *The Life of Christ?*' she asked Tom breathlessly.

'Madame,' Tom is reputed to have replied, 'Sure I haven't the life of a dog.'

Eleven-forty the train was scheduled to leave but usually it had not even arrived by that time. When as a child I heard the distant whistle, I used to jump up and down with excitement. A minute or two later the lanky figure of Joe Courtney, the porter, would appear and anxiously wave people back from the edge of the platform. Then the locomotive with its four or five carriages and guard's van eased into the station. That particular train was never full but we it was still a bit of a scramble along the corridor to obtain a compartment all to ourselves. Once we had achieved that we had all the time in the world to settle down. A couple of heavy, iron-wheeled, flat-topped trolleys would be waiting on the platform by the guard's van, one heaped up with parcels that were to be loaded on the train, the other empty, waiting to collect those to be unloaded, including bundles of magazines and newspapers. (In quiet moments at the station we youngsters liked to trundle these trolleys around the platform, giving ourselves rides on them. It was a practice frowned upon by the CIE staff as the long, iron tow-bar made them tricky to manoeuvre, and it was always possible that we might tip one over onto the line. Two trolleys were not always required and the one not in use normally stood unladen downtrack of the gents' toilet. On this I liked to squat and watch the trains.) Bicycles, accompanied or unaccompanied, would have to be got on and off. The driver would inspect his engine and gauge his fuel complement. Somebody would have telephoned the stationmaster with a request that he hold the train for a further minute or two as another passenger was on his or her way to the station. The train would shunt forwards and backwards, coupling and uncoupling carriages. It would appear to leave, straddle Townparks Bridge, then change tracks and back up to take on water. You learned from experience not to be fooled by these manoeuvres. The real signal for departure came when Dan Colbert emerged from his office, bristling with urgency and efficiency. After a momentary pause on the platform, a long arm pointed to the rear of the train. The guard showed his green flag. Dan strode forward to the engine and exchanged circular bands with the driver – a mysterious ritual that never failed to intrigue me. Another pause as he slung the band around his shoulder. A glance to the rear where Joe Courtney was now also signalling with a green flag. The whistle rose to his lips. A brisk blast was piercingly answered by the locomotive. The train lurched forward and wheezed its way out of the station. The buffers went clank, clank, clank. We were on our way.

To a greater or lesser extent a similar operation was mounted at each station along the route – Cappoquin, Cappagh, Dungarvan, Durrow – until we descended at Kilmacthomas. In all, a journey of some thirty miles. Cappagh was distinguished by its location near a level crossing. Queues of cars and lorries would form on the busy Dungarvan–Lismore Road until we passed, a sight familiar to me also from the road-user's perspective, from our summer outings to the sea with Denny Regan. After Dungarvan there was the excitement of riding over the waves (when the tide was in) along the causeway toward Clonea and beyond Ballyvoyle we notched up the windows to the top so as not to get a faceful of smoke as we steamed through the short tunnel before Durrow. We always got off the train at Kilmac. There awaiting us would be another ace of the highway, Paddy Drohan of Carrick-on-Suir. Paddy, I would say, drove marginally faster than Denny, even though his car, a rather boxy job with a vertical windscreen – a Morris 10 or Morris Cowley, perhaps – was not in the same class as the Lismoreman's Ford V8. But they were two of a kind and gave you the same kind of spiel about all the mad eejits they encountered on the road, some cornering at *twenty* miles an hour and some hitting *fifty* on the straight. And it was no use munching off about the slow pace. The Ballantyne family could hardly comment anyway as none of us knew how to drive. Dad was amused, and Mam and Molly loved to see Paddy because he would spend the whole drive back to Carrick bringing them up-to-date on events in their lively home town. My parents chose to get off at Kilmac as otherwise they would have had to journey on to Waterford City and wait there for a couple of hours before they could catch another train for Carrick. Even using Paddy's ambling service it was shorter to take the Comeragh route. For my own part, by day I loved to see those craggy peaks, so unlike our own smooth Knockmealdowns, and by night, the car headlights stabbing along the stonework and rusty iron gates of the high demesne walls of the vast Curraghmore Estate of Lord Waterford. At night also, I half expected the ghost of some tortured soul to pounce onto the roadway and scare me stiff with a howl, the way Paddy startled small animals here and there with a blast of his raucous horn. Kilmacthomas held another attraction for Mam. Her second cousin Katie Kent and her husband Jack owned a pub and grocery there and, time permitting, we enjoyed their hospitality.

Arriving at the hairpin bend on the hill above Carrick, I used to hold my breath. At the end of the long valley of the Suir rose the legendary rounded slopes of Sliabh na mBan. We did not have a vista like that in Lismore, not one quite so feminine. And straight across the valley, the cascading rises of South Kilkenny tumbled over one another. From the same vantage point by day Carrick town said nothing to me, but its nightscape was a garden of

My aunt Nan Morrissey, Paddy and me in our back garden in West Street, Lismore. McCarthy's shed and our lilac tree are behind Nan to the left. c. 1938/39.

lights, promising a degree of sophistication unknown in my home town – freshly-baked fairy cakes and pink iced buns from Jack and Mrs Mullins at the West Gate, a placename that imaged up an ancient walled town; *two* fish 'n chippers, Jacky O'Brien's on the Parish Height and Mrs Banks', the Welsh woman's, in the Main Street; we did not even have one in Lismore. There were delivery bikes galore – sturdy, black, low-slung two-wheelers, gripping large baskets in front brackets, and proclaiming on the triangular plates within their frames the names of butchers or grocers. I envied the young lads who rode them. There were more cars and vans than I ever saw at home. Here too I encountered a boarding school, the Mercy Convent, from which crocodiles of blazered girls would emerge to go on nun-accompanied walks up the hill. Night arrivals were dictated by family crises, or by Dad's having had to put in some unexpected hours of work that forced a postponement of our departure until later in the day. On one occasion we did not round the hairpin bend until after midnight. I think we must have taken the night express and been picked up at Dungarvan. Or maybe it was just that the 5.50 p.m. got abnormally delayed. Whatever hour of the day or night we pulled up at Greystone Street my aunts Nan and Biddy Morrissey would immediately appear at the door, wreathed in smiles, to welcome us.

My aunt Biddy Morrissey with Dad, Mam and me in the back garden of the Morrissey family home in Greystone Street, Carrick-on-Suir, c. 1949–50.

A hint of familiarity was lent my early visits to Carrick by Tom Guiry's Garage directly across the street from my aunts'. Then one year in the mid-Forties when we returned all that remained of it was a burnt-out shell. My Aunt Bab had looked out of her bedroom one night the previous autumn and seen something blazing inside. By the time people were alerted the fire had got out of hand. No attempt was made to rebuild the garage.

My aunts' house was much more imposing than our modest Lismore dwelling, although it scarcely had a garden. Its centrepiece was an elegant sitting-room with a fine ceiling of which, evidently, my grandfather was very proud as he had designed the cornice and central rosette himself and installed the whole thing. There was a tiled Victorian fireplace, above which hung a chiselled mirror in a rosewood or mahogany surround, that all too seldom warmed us with a fire. The room was furnished with a fine chaise longue made of walnut and leather upon which rested like indolent Persian cats large, dark, round silk cushions. (I never saw *round* cushions anywhere else.) There was a matching walnut dining-table and chairs, a mahogany sideboard, a plant stand and an upright piano. From the west window you looked right across to Sliabh na mBan. Underneath the room was a high cellar that used to be a bakery when my grandparents were alive and which

Original colour postcard in Milton 'Glazette' series no. 4300 of Greystone Street and the West Gate, Carrick-on-Suir; printed in Germany for the Woolstone Brothers, London. 1910. Morrissey's Bakery is on the right. The Morrissey girls are on the path outside. Mary Morrissey (my mother) is the girl in dark clothes on the edge of the pavement looking toward the shop window.

had its own heavily locked door onto the Wide Lane on the westward side of the house.

From my aunts' bedroom you could look across, over the Waterford end of the Old Bridge, to the small Friary Church perched on the side of the hill opposite. The Suir you could see at high tide or when it was in spate. It was in this chapel that the Morrissey family liked to worship and when we were on holidays in Carrick we mainly went to Mass and devotions there. My aunts were on very good terms with the friars, with one in particular, a plump middle-aged Englishman called Father Alfred, known for his mild eccentricities, who often dropped in to the house in Greystone Street for a cup of tea. It was he who stuck his head out of the confessional and called out after a man who had just left the box, 'I wouldn't worry about that, old man, if I were you.' My aunts used to fear for his safety when he was giving a sermon in his inimitable theatrical style. It was his custom to parade the whole of the altar area while he was speaking and, seemingly without regard to where he was on the 'deck', he would frequently advance to the very brink, and even teeter a moment above the top step, before withdrawing his overhanging sandaled foot. But he never toppled over and

Morrissey's Bakery in Greystone Street, Carrick-on-Suir, c. 1910. James and Anastasia Morrissey with their young family posing in front. The taller children from left are, Peg, Nan, Mary (my mother, with the white headband), and Bid. I cannot identify the younger ones.

never paused in his delivery. My aunts would breathe a sigh of relief when he retreated to place an elbow on the altar and nonchalantly lean back to conclude his peroration. It was pure theatre and, intentionally or otherwise, and I suspect in his case it may well have been otherwise, it was a good technique to keep the congregation in suspense. Whether the performance distracted from the content of the sermon is, of course, another question. An added attraction of going to the Friary was the walk down Bridge Street and across the Old Bridge on which we would pause to observe the state of, and boating activities on, the river.

Along the top of the the shop-front in Greystone Street, picked out in handsome white-and-blue faience lettering, each letter individually crafted and about nine inches high, ran the legend 'Morrissey's Bakery'. There is a colour postcard of the street and of the West Gate, shot in the year 1910 for the London-based Woolstone Brothers's Milton 'Glazette' series and printed in Germany, which clearly shows the exterior of the shop when it was in business. On the pavement outside my mother and her sisters can be seen playing. There are also many other people in the street. The bakery, sadly, no longer traded in my time but of the actual working area in the basement there was still ample evidence, the oven itself for example. This ran under the shop, to a distance of some ten feet, where it ended in a red fire-brick wall, and was roughly as wide as it was deep. It was, perhaps, a little more than two feet high and its base was lined with ceramic flooring tiles, each some ten inches square. Into this cramped space every St Stephen's Day, the one day of the year when the oven was fully cooled, my grandfather James Morrissey used to crawl to renew any damaged tiles or fire-bricks. The last batch of bread before Christmas was taken out of the oven on Christmas Eve morning. The oven was fired up again on the evening of the 27th of December when the first post-Christmas batch was prepared for sale in the shop on the morning of the 28th.

There was a double door to the oven. An exterior iron plate, level with the wall, was furnished with a 'spyhole' with a hinged lid through which the oven could be inspected. Another interior one was positioned a couple of feet inside the outside one. This was kept in place to seal in the heat while the oven was warming up. It was removed while the bread was baking, and, of course, while the oven was being loaded and unloaded. To the left of the oven door was the firing oven. This was, perhaps, five or six feet long by two feet high by two feet wide and was also furnished with a metal plate. From it, through a kind of grill, one could partially inspect the left-hand side of the baking oven. Coal was used as fuel and the sulphur fumes from this were unpleasant in the confined space of the basement. The combined effects of the heat, fumes and flour dust made bakers susceptible to drink but otherwise they seemed to avoid environmental health problems. All those my uncle knew in the town lived to a good old age. The flour was stored in the small basement room adjoining the bakery. As the storage space here was limited one-hundredweight bags were piled on top of each other from floor to ceiling. There was an advantage in this for the baker when he was engaged in the heavy work of dough making – he could more easily lift the topmost bags onto his shoulders, carry them over and empty them into the dough-making troughs ('trows' as in 'blows' the bakers pronounced it). Coal and wood were stored down a side passageway that led to the backyard, later the garden.

In place still were the four rough-hewn, fitted wooden troughs in which the dough was prepared. The dough was mixed by hand and chunks for the loaves cut out of it with a big knife and weighed as required. There was no specialist knife. The baker chose his own, his essential requirement being for a tool that was very sharp and had a strong handle grip. The troughs measured something like three feet deep by five feet long by three feet wide. Each had a removable wooden lid that could easily be stored out of the way when the bakers were working the dough. Two troughs were on the left, and two on the right-hand side as you faced the oven. Other remains were a number of rusty baking trays; iron weights; some earthenware pots; the oar-length, wooden 'float' – a kind of rod with a paddle on one end used for loading the raw dough into, and removing the baked bread from, the oven. When not in use the float lay across a pair of iron hooks in the ceiling above the bins on the left. On the wall near this there was a small wooden bracket on which a hurricane-lamp used to stand before electricity became available; a number of these lamps were used for lighting. After electrification a scales for weighing dough stood on the bracket.

Neddy Kavanagh had been the baker. My Uncle Mick also qualified as a baker, serving an apprenticeship with Neddy, with whom he worked for some six or seven years. Working hours were unsocial. From 8.00 p.m. to midnight the oven was fired and the dough prepared and covered and left to rise in the troughs. The bakers then caught a few hours' sleep. When work resumed around 5.00 a.m. the yeast-expanded dough would have pushed up the lids of the troughs. The necessary quantity of loaves, anything from 50 to 200 depending on the day, was then cut from the dough and loaded into the oven. Each loaf was individually weighed at the dough stage; one-pound or two-pound loaves being the norm. Before each baking the oven was swabbed clean using a kind of home-made mop on the end of a long pole (some dust from the fire always got into the oven). The common loaf was baked on the oven tiles. Bread baked in a tin was known as a tin loaf or a pan loaf. Between 7.00 and 8.00 a.m. the bread was removed from the oven to cool.

Our holiday accommodation was the back room beyond the sitting-room and was spartanly furnished with a double bed, two narrow single beds, a wash-stand with a large porcelain jug and basin, a dressing-table, and a wardrobe. Brown linoleum lay on the floor. Daylight filtered down from a skylight and in through a small window that overlooked the Wide Lane. Most intriguing for me was the back door of this room, which opened onto a wooden stairs that took you down to a further extension where my grandfather used to store building materials. From the extension you entered the garden, a very private place with twelve-, or maybe fifteen-foot-high walls where my Aunt Nan liked to cultivate tea roses and arum lilies. In the right-hand corner as you entered were two huge, mysterious-looking, half-globe-shaped iron vats that were cemented on top of brick furnaces. In my grandparents' time one of these had been used for cooking food for some bonhams that my grandfather used to rear – evidently he believed in a mixed economy. The weekly washing for the household, a considerable task for which two women were employed, was done in the other one. White overalls and clothes used by the bakery staff had to be boiled, starched and ironed in addition to the normal clothing of a large family. During this period James Morrissey also owned a builder's yard with outhouses and a large vegetable garden (he had a big family to feed) a hundred yards farther down the street, in or next to Salt Yard Lane. By all accounts, he was a most energetic individual.

Halfway down the garden on the left was a wooden latrine overhung with a dense growth of ivy that spilled onto it from the high brick wall that separated us from our neighbours, Mulcahys the grocers. With four or five steps leading up to the cabinet it resembled a tree house. And indeed, when as a little boy I first entered the roomy whitewashed interior and looked down through the hole of the generous wooden seat at the pile of shit that peaked below, it was a bit unnerving. I was afraid I might fall through the hole. It helped that ashes from the open fire in the house were shovelled onto the pile from time to time to dampen down the pong. Once I got used to it, I loved the place. It was so secretive and private, like no other lavatory I had ever been in. On the wall by the side of the seat cut-up squares of the *Irish Press* hanging on a string served as toilet paper. The dung was carted away every so often by a man who drove in and out of the garden through a pair of massive wooden portals that opened onto the Wide Lane. Happily for the workman it was not just human excrement he had to fork onto the cart. At the end of the garden were four kennels in which my uncle Jimmy kept greyhounds and the used straw and the muck they generated was also dumped behind the latrine.

Helping my greyhound-trainer uncle with the hounds was my favourite pastime when I was in Carrick, but only after I had learned not to be frightened of the eager animals that seemed to want to lick my head off. At least, I used to think I was helping him. Possibly I did in small ways but, probably, I was more of a hindrance than a help. I would assist in clearing out the kennels, and shaking Jeyes Fluid around the place, and sharpening his knife on the worn patch of the doorstep outside the kitchen where all knives were sharpened. But not in the preparation of food for the dogs. The sorcery of that he kept to himself. In the late afternoon of every day he would arrive with a few sheep's heads and a few loaves of bread under his arm. The heads, cloven in half, were boiled in two large pots on an open-air sawdust stove, like the one we had in Lismore, in the small shed beyond the kitchen. While they were cooking an appetising aroma tantalised our nostrils. When they were done Jimmy would cut all the meat off them and mix it with chunks of bread into a thick porridge with his bare hands.

Sometimes he used to take tablets or powders from a chest of small drawers in the shed and mix these through the food before giving it to a particular dog. Each animal was given a large bowlful of the prepared food and Jimmy would run an experienced eye over them as they fed. So generous was he in answering my many questions that my aunts had to drag me away from him at times to allow him to concentrate fully on his work. In time I learned when to talk and when to be silent. He had to concentrate especially hard when he was combing an animal, or rubbing it down with the special pads that carried leather bands into which fitted his hands. In those moments you would only hear the swish of the grooming tool on the smooth sinews of the dog, Jimmy's hard breathing, and the scrape of his boots on the blue flagstones. The dog, held firmly between my uncle's thighs, seemed to like the treatment.

A full-grown greyhound is a powerful animal and I learned to respect its strength. I was well into my teens before Jimmy would trust me to walk such a hound on the open road. You had to keep it gently but firmly reined in at all times because if it spotted a cat or a rabbit it might suddenly sprint away from you. Jimmy exercised his dogs in a number of long fields around the town. One year he favoured a stretch out the Clonmel Road just past the Cottage Boreen. The first time he ran a dog at me there I had not yet learned how to walk one. It was a somewhat unnerving experience, even though he had explained in advance what he was going to do. He left me standing at one end of the field while he took the two dogs to the other end. I watched intently as he prepared to slip one of them. He shouted a renewed warning that I should stand stock-still. Then he slipped the animal. The dog raced toward me, its yard-long strides devouring the ground, its long snout skimming the grass. It seemed to be making a beeline straight at me. Apprehensively, I watched it bearing down on me. At all costs I had to hold my ground, I told myself. I trusted my uncle when he had said that if I moved at the last minute the hound might not have time to change direction and might crash into me, injuring itself or me. The moment of doubt passed and the dog shot harmlessly past.

The recreational side of the Carrick vacation was going for walks. We followed the Suir downstream to the bend behind the Ormonde Castle to watch Shanahans the basket-makers harvesting sallies, or we took our favourite route up Grubbs' Hill, so named after a Quaker family who had been wealthy landowners and millers in the town. From its northern slopes one secured marvellous views of the Suir Valley and from its southern ones of the Comeragh Mountains. A short distance up the hill on the right was Dick Sinnott's fine market garden to which we often called for produce on

A 1778 engraving showing the Ormonde Castle on the right and, upriver, the then ruined parish church of Carrickbeg and the medieval Old Bridge.

the way back from our walk. Mam would buy apples and soft fruits in season and a bunch or two of her favourite flowers – roses, sweet pea or sweet william, usually. Sometimes too, Dick, an old family friend, would give my aunts cuttings from roses and other shrubs to plant in their garden. Like our own Johnny McGrath in Lismore he was a fully professional horticulturalist. Halfway up this hill an iron pipe set in a cement block drained off spring water as clear and sweet as that which flowed from the Spout in Lismore. And around the bend farther up there was a mossy rock shaped like a great chair upon the seat of which I would ask to be perched when I was little so that I could indulge my fantasy about Fionn MacCumhail's having carved it with a chop of his hand. At the top of the hill on the right you could glimpse through the pines the Grubbs' grand old wooden house, now inhabited by Captain Downey, no ordinary captain but a seaman who came home to rest between voyages on the seven seas. Away to the left the waves of a gentle, undulating landscape broke on the craggy slopes of Knockanaffrin, one of the highest peaks of the Comeraghs. We walked also on the eastern extension of Grubbs', called Seskin Hill, from which we would descend by a plateau known as Gees' Hill, where there was

Period postcard of the River Suir at full tide, looking in the direction of Clonmel. County Waterford is on the left, County Tipperary on the right. On the right is the river bank walk, a favourite of my parents and indeed, of most people in the town of Carrick-on-Suir. A fisherman's cot peers out from the undergrowth by the bank. Cots were always moored, and still are, at this point. Amid the trees at the end of the path Dr Murphy's cottage can be seen.

a pitch and putt course, to the New Cemetery where respects would be paid to the Morrissey dead. Strolling was done along the river-bank in the direction of Clonmel. Mostly we just went as far as the Cottage Boreen, a mile or so from the town. On occasion, however, Dad used to take Paddy and me on a longer walk up to Arrigans' Boreen, and beyond to Dovehill Castle, the grey-green ruin of an old Norman keep, the battlements of which it was possible to mount via the substantial remains of a stone staircase, and view the sweep of the river valley and imagine the French invaders who had usurped our lands.

In the town itself I was fascinated by the network of narrow lanes between the Main Street and the quays, and by the long weir, over which the Suir tumbled copiously when the tide was out, that angled across the full width of the river-bed just above the Old Bridge. The medieval bridge, a pleasing multi-arched stone structure, had housed, I was told, a nailer's workshop in the western rectangular recess halfway across its span within the memory of my mother's generation. As intriguing as the image of a building on the bridge was the idea of someone making nails by hand. Along the quays there were cement steps leading down to the water and

Paddy Ballantyne up the bank by the Suir in Carrick-on-Suir, c. 1946/47.

My father Joseph Ballantyne relaxing in civvies. Carrick-on-Suir, Mid to late Forties.

weathered flagstone slips up which flat-bottomed fishermen's cots could be drawn. The slips extended upstream as far as the Cottage Boreen and in mid-Suir across from the one below the Cottage, in which Dr Murphy lived, there was a boulder known as the Friar's Rock from which the bigger lads of the town used to dive when swimming. The Friar's Rock was nothing like the Rock we had in Lismore. It lay permanently submerged – aside from periods of drought when its tip might just be glimpsed, I was told.

Swimming was what I missed most in Carrick. The Suir around the town with its sharp-smelling tannery effluent did not look at all as appealing to me as the crystal-clear Owenashad or the sombre Blackwater. Upstream of the tannery outlet, across on the Carrickbeg bank of the river, there were shallows where the smaller kids used to bathe but, as the river was tidal well beyond this point, effluent would disperse itself in that direction too. But it was not really the state of the water that prevented me from swimming. I was not greatly worried about that. It was more that I was shy of making friends and those few I had in Carrick did not go swimming themselves. But I did have occasion to bathe in the Suir at Deerpark when my parents were visiting the farm of Ma-Jo Arrigan, an old friend of the Morrissey family. My eldest first cousin Tony O'Mara has informed me that Ma-Jo, Mrs Ellen Davin of Deerpark, Mrs Fleming of the Cloth House [?], Main Street,

Carrick, and our grandmother Statia Morrissey formed a close-knit group of friends. (Ellen Davin was the wife of Pat Davin, youngest after Tom of the three renowned athlete brothers. The eldest, of course, was Maurice, the upright and inspirational first president of the GAA.) Dad would take me to a spot near Arrigans' Boreen where the water curled and pooled and sparkled over stony shallows in which you could roll and tumble and skim stones across to Coolnamuck.

The Suir from Carrick to Waterford then, unlike the Blackwater around Lismore, was still very much a working waterway. (Up to the very early years of my childhood coastal topsail schooners like the *de Wadden* and the *Lizzie May*, later *Kathleen and May* – now restored with a home port in Bideford in North Devon – carried coal, pit-props and other cargo to and from Killahaly Quay on the wide Blackwater opposite Dromana House and, in earlier times, barges used to ply the Lismore Canal.) On the Suir two riverboats, the *Knocknagow I* and the *Knocknagow II*, operated commercially, one piloted by Captain Jimmy Jacques (the surname was pronounced 'Jakes' locally) who was to become the last captain on the river. It was educating to sit on a bollard and observe the boats being loaded and unloaded at Dowley's Stores. Heavy overhead cranes travelling on gantries would roll in and out of two warehouses slinging sacks of grain. One of these warehouses, a fine massive granite building with red stone edging, was built by my grandfather James Morrissey who also erected the large granite pillars either side of the entrance to the town hall. The *Knocks* came and went with the tide. Watching them dock, or weigh anchor, was another unfailing pastime. The clanking activity of the day gave way at night to a stealthier, but no less commercial form of endeavour. Working in pairs of cots, with a snap-net stretched from one boat to another, the salmon fishermen would signal their presence with muffled voices, muffled paddles, and the glow of lighted cigarettes. Often a white terrier, standing at a prow, could be made out.

It took some time to get adjusted to Carrick. There was a smoky dankness to it at times and from it emanated different sounds to those of our small West Waterford town. A working town clock a few doors away at the West Gate chimed the hours long before that of Lismore was back in operation. And it gave you information other than the time. 'Look at the salmon, and tell me which way the wind is blowing,' my Aunt Nan would say, pointing up at the fish-shaped weather-vane that surmounted it. The cement surface of Greystone Street, stretched like a membrane between the stone walls of the houses, lent a constant echo to the activity of the town. Two sounds in particular still reverberate in my mind – the short-lived flurry of feet, overlain with animated voices, of the cinema patrons making their way home to Treacy Park and Mill Street around 10.30 p.m. after the evening show, and the nocturnal barking of dogs. Many dogs were strays but there were also the persistent, lonely cries of greyhound pups housed for the first time on their own, which would echo distantly from Lough Street, Treacy Park, or maybe from across the river in Carrickbeg. In the morning people were up and about much earlier than in Lismore, especially the tannery workers, the beginning of whose main shift was raucously signalled at eight o'clock by a hooter.

Silence in Carrick was never the absolute stillness that I was used to in Lismore. The town's stone and slate centre and river valley setting heightened the various echoes. This was most apparent on the hill above the town to where a variety of sounds, from the voices of children pucking a ball around on some green or other to the clanking of tools, the hoot of a car horn, a chapel bell, the chugging of a *Knock*, or the calls and yelps of animals, clearly floated up. For anyone who paused on the height under the clear blue sky of a winter's morning to look out over the valley from which a shroud of fog had not yet lifted, the intermittent harmony and discord were the only pointers to the town that lay beneath.

Visual stimuli could also be confusing. In Lismore when a small group of boys coalesced threateningly on a street corner and looked me over coldly I could cope with it because I knew the score. In the larger town, gangs

My cousin 'Nurse Biddy' Morrissey and my uncle Mick Morrissey do a Bonnie and Clyde in Greystone Street, Carrick-on-Suir in the early 1930s. *(Ballantyne family photo)*

seemed to hover more menacingly and issue more uncertain signals. Sound and vision came together in the sophisticated centralized cash collection system operated by Paddy Bourke's drapery in the Main Street. This curious mechanism, an overhead rapid wire system engineered by a firm called the Lamson Store Service Co. Ltd. (later the Lamson Engineering Co. Ltd.), and acquired through the Lamson-Paragon Supply Company of Cheapside in the City of London, was catapult rather than pneumatically driven, which made it somewhat unusual, although both firing systems operated on the same propulsion principle. All I knew was that when Hugh Ryan, the shop manager, book collector, and local historian, or one of the Drohan brothers Pat or Billy, took my elders' money, it and the bill were slipped into a metal carrier, or cartridge, which one twisted to open and shut. The carrier was then clipped onto a mechanism just above head height. A pull on a cord, a swoosh, and the capsule was sucked away to the cashier's office behind a window on the mezzanine floor above. Seconds later the machine would splutter again and a bell would tinkle. The shop assistant would reach up, deftly unclip the carrier and deposit change and receipted bill on the counter all in one move. A miracle of modern technology but mean in conception, expressing as it did to me at any rate a distrust of shop assistants.

Shyness limited my circle of acquaintances in Carrick. I played only with my first cousins the O'Maras of Mill Street, none of whom was the same age as I, and Mick and Jim O'Keeffe, who lived across the road from my aunts. My uncle Jimmy's kids were mostly girls and were too young for me. The O'Keeffe home had two attractions for me, a fine walled garden with a lawn on which we used to tumble and an eerie, empty shop with many, many shelves and compartments that was a bit spooky to walk through. A former pawnshop, still known as 'The Pawn', it had been owned by the boys' late father, Jack 'Busty' O'Keeffe, who had been a lifelong friend of my mother's and her sisters and brothers.

Of the O'Maras, Noel was the one who was around most often. When I was small he used to take me for walks along the river and once narrowly avoided slipping me downstream in a boat on my own. He had sat me in one of the many cots moored near Bóthairín na gCapall and was gently rocking me in and out like I was in a pram when the iron ring to which the mooring chain was attached came away from the wall. I gazed at him in fright and hung onto the seat as the current began to take me out. But he reacted swiftly and, jumping into the water, drenching his long trousers to midthigh in the process, managed to grab the end of the cot and haul me back in again. When his mother asked him later why his trousers were all wet he

'Molly and me' edging into the Forties. Taken in the back garden of Morrissey's Bakery, Greystone Street, Carrick-on-Suir. c. 1941.

My aunt Bríghid Ballantyne (née Garvin) on the left, with my mother and brother Paddy on the threshold of the Ballantyne family home in Carrowreagh, Keash, Co. Sligo. Late 1930s.

just muttered that it was because he had had to 'save a life'. I was most impressed that he had risked the depths of the Suir to rescue me.

Left to my own devices, I liked to muck around the open spaces of the Wide Lane. Piles of rubble lay about where all but one or two of the derelict old cottages that had formerly huddled there had been pulled down. But there was space enough for a small boy to puck a ball around and I could also hide amidst the debris. And there was the forge on the corner where I could watch Paddy Dwyer, the tall angular blacksmith, knocking sparks off glowing horseshoes, the way the Vaughans did in Lismore. I saw much less of Molly when we were in Carrick because she would stay at her mother Annie's place, first in Salt Yard Lane and later in Treacy Park. But she would often drop into Greystone Street to give me a cuddle. At the end of the Forties she did not return to Lismore with us because she was needed in her own home. The break was tearful.

My brother, who had been born in Carrick, seemed to have more of an affinity with that town than I did. He developed a wide circle of friends and went on holidays there whenever he had a chance, even at Christmas when

The Ballantyne family farmhouse in Carrowreagh, Keash, Co. Sligo. My brother Paddy is standing on the window sill. In front of him are Aunt Bríghid (known in her locality as Bridget Maggie), Dad (or possibly Uncle Larry) and Mam. Late 1930s.

he was older. He was also allowed to go to Sligo to visit our relatives in that region. Which made me envious, of course, but being substantially younger than he, I knew that I could not expect such freedom of movement yet. After he passed his School Leaving Certificate with honours in 1950 he went to live in Carrick for long stretches of the year. There he studied further, following a course in business methods at the technical school in the Main Street. Some two years later, in January 1953, he started his first job, a clerkship with Bórd na Móna in the tiny village of Rathangan in County Kildare, home of the writer Maura Laverty. It was hardly the posting of his dreams but jobs were hard to come by and it was a start. Soon he gave it up and went to stay with our uncle Mick Morrissey in Birmingham where he spent a summer lounging by the swimming pool at Cadbury's chocolate factory in Bournville – because the weather was too hot for the job he had been assigned, painting squiggles on chocolate sweets – and gestating plans to emigrate to Canada. I never saw him in Lismore again and I last glimpsed him in Carrick in September 1955, almost a year after I myself had said goodbye to my home town. He called to see us at Greystone Street before he took the boat to North America. My parents, particularly Dad, were very lonely seeing him go. Canada was a twelve- to fourteen-hour flight away in a Lockheed Constellation. How much further it must have seemed to them by ship? Paddy was dead cool about his departure and emotionally I showed little response – I was used to his being away. Inwardly though, I was excited and was looking forward to the letters that would arrive from him in due course. I already had vague impressions of the far-away land from postage stamps and the odd Mountie or Mohawk I had seen in the movies. But I was a bit puzzled that he had chosen North America in which to start a new life. His interests appeared to lie so much in the great European events of preceding centuries. In reality, I had no idea at all of what he was thinking. He never confided in me, nor I in him. Four years was just too wide a childhood gulf for us to bridge. And our interests were totally dissimilar. He was to sail from Southampton on the *Franconia* but, when this ship developed engine trouble, found himself crossing the Atlantic tourist class on the *Queen Mary* instead, which was an unexpected thrill for him. It was to be seventeen long years before we met again, in London in 1972, where he stayed with my first wife Ulrike Arp and me for three weeks. He returned to live in Ireland in June 1977.

I was always pleased to return to Lismore, or mostly I was. The prospect of returning to school would depress me sometimes. There were two years when I had a bit of a let-off. Dad had been unable to take his holidays as early as planned and we found ourselves in Carrick until the end of the first week of term. When I appeared for classes on the following Monday P. D. Lee, the superior, made it clear to me that he was not in the least impressed by my excuse, even though I had brought him a written note from Dad. The train ride back was a more subdued affair for my parents, the end of their holiday. Usually we caught the midday train at Kilmac that got us to Lismore a couple of hours later. Otherwise it meant a wait for the six o'clock and an arrival home in the late evening.

Until we purchased our first wireless in 1951 our only form of home entertainment was the gramophone unless you counted Mam's musical box in the shape of Our Lady's Grotto at Lourdes which tinkled out a hymn; fun to wind up occasionally but hardly inspiring. It was much more amusing to screw in a Songster or HMV steel needle and wind up the gramophone – one full wind per 78 waxed record. This instrument belonged to Mam but she did not own many records, a swing number or two like 'Black Bottom', a few romantic ballads such as 'It Happened in Monterey' and 'For You', jaunty pieces like 'Roll Out the Barrel', Gigli singing *Core 'ngrato* and a couple of John McCormacks. Gigli and McCormack were her favourite tenors. She also possessed a few Delia Murphys amongst which were 'If I Were a Blackbird' and 'Three Lovely Lassies from Bannion'. I bought a record from Feeneys myself, the Irish tenor Josef Locke belting out a couple of rousing numbers from *The White Horse Inn* one of which went, *And so I go to fight the foreign foe although, I know that I'll be sometimes missed by the girls I've kissed...* You had to start somewhere.

One item we had, 'The White Cliffs of Dover', was the cause of my throwing tantrums when I was little. I had not minded it until Dad jocularly said that the line, *And Jimmy will go to sleep in his own little room again*, referred to me personally. I took him seriously and vehemently denied that the words were about me. For some reason, known only to myself at the time, I angrily rejected the notion that I might be called Jimmy. Jim was my name, not Jimmy! I had nothing against the Jimmys of the world. Wasn't one of my favourite uncles called Jimmy? I just saw myself as Jim. I felt like a Jim. That was the name I had grown up with. And that was that. Dad and Mam used to tease me at first but then laid off when they saw how incensed I used to become.

The wireless brought us complete home entertainment. Dad really got it for Mam, who quickly grew to love it. For him it served merely as a vehicle for news. For her it was a new window on the world. I was most excited by it also. Paddy was almost as selective as Dad in his tastes, and was soon into the BBC Third Programme. Details of Radio Éireann programmes were given in the daily press and we started to take the *Radio Times* so that we could plan our BBC listening. The first thing that struck me about the set was its dial. Obscure placenames like Hilversum, Sundsvall and Sottens, and even Athlone, were accorded equal status to some of the grandest capitals on earth. So I learned about transmitters. Another path of discovery was switching channels, especially late at night when all the languages of the planet seemed to be vying for airspace. I would seek to understand a word here, a word there, usually a place-name, or come across a familiar piece of music in a different setting. One station, AFN, the American Forces Network, caused me no difficulty and I quickly became an addict of the Groucho Marx and Dennis Day radio shows. Of prime interest to me on the home station were the hurling and Gaelic football broadcasts, of course, and I also enjoyed programmes in the Irish language.

Mam would choose piano recitals by Eileen Joyce, and song recitals by her favourite singers, Delia Murphy, Cavan O'Connor, Gigli, Owen Brannigan, Edmund Hockridge, Michael O'Duffy, Anne Ziegler and Webster Booth, Kathleen Ferrier and Gracie Fields. She was very fond of Paul Robeson, too, and never failed, after listening to him, to comment on his great dignity and on how unjustly he had been hounded by his own country, the United States of America. In a different vein she would listen to Sydney Thompson and his Olde Tyme Orchestra, Bill McGuffie or Charlie Kunz on piano, and Sandy MacPherson or Reginald Dixon on the BBC theatre organ. She liked her singers to be melodious and had no time at all for the popular American singer Nellie Lutcher who, to her ears, merely growled her way raucously through her numbers. 'Sure that's not singing at all,' she would laugh as I was struggling to find a frame of reference myself. As against that, she thoroughly enjoyed the baby voice of the American Rose Murphy. I shared her taste in Rose and Delia, as I did in O'Connor, the 'Vagabond of Song', but I was able to resist Owen Brannigan singing 'On the Road to Mandalay' for the hundredth time.

A mania that swept the country, *Question Time*, on Radio Éireann, I soon grew bored with. Joe Linnane, and later Niall Boden, compered it to a national disease and soon every society and club in every townland, village and town were organising quizzes of their own. The radio version even toured by the Happydrome with Linnane after the War. *Farmer's Forum*, presented by Michael Dillon, though outside my field of interest, seemed eminently worthy by comparison.

The big thrill the wireless offered me was the chance to cliff-hang regularly with *Dick Barton* and his pals Snowy and Jock in my own home. Until we had our own set I had only been able to pick up the odd episode at Feeney's. Nothing in that sound recordist's delight was too much for me. I winced with every thud, recoiled from every trapdoor that sprang open, hissed with every hiss, and gritted my teeth when abyss and snake-pit beckoned. Radio Éireann, to my delight, came up with an unexpected and very effective series in some ten or twelve parts called *Michael O'Sullivan, Detective*. This home-grown product, about the pursuit of a master spy or master criminal, contrived to be more menacing than anything in Barton. Sadly, an anticipated sequel never materialised. Perhaps I was alone in expecting one?

Mam and I discovered a shared taste in BBC humour – *Educating Archie, Take It from Here, Ray's a Laugh, Life with the Lyons, Bedtime with Braden, Charlie Chester*, and *Hancock's Half Hour*. The zany antics of the *Goon Show*, my favourite, baffled her a bit. Sunday dinner-times we liked to take in the *Billy Cotton Band Show* before eating. Vic Oliver, and Wilfrid Pickles' *Have a Go*, were also favourites of hers but these were a bit too grown-up for me. Another penchant of hers I did not share was switching on to hear the Angelus every evening. She would say a short prayer, sure, but I think she also trusted the radio version more than the real thing that pealed across from the Catholic church – Petey Gillen did not always manage to ring on the stroke of six.

Whenever I became ill my listening pattern altered appreciably. Once strong enough to sit up in the living-room after a heavy cold or flu – the wireless was a mains one and the aerial led only to that room – I would start at 10.30 a.m. with the half-hour instrumental *Music While You Work*, which featured on good days the best dance bands in Britain and on bad ones, gasworks and colliery brass bands. Among the conventional bands, it was possible to discern different styles. Syd Dean and His Band and Sid Phillips and His Band played a kind of ragtime dixieland and were almost as indistinguishable in their rhythms as they were in name. Another grouping would be Troise and His Banjoliers or Troise and His Mandoliers, as the mood struck him, and Primo Scala and His Accordion Band. There was the Latin-American of which Edmundo Ros was king, with a whole phalanx of lesser bands competing to come up with the most colourful and original name: the Hermanos Deniz Cuban Rhythm Band, Roberto Inglés and His Rumba Band, Bernard Moonshin and His Rio Tango Band – a touch of old moonshine about that one. All of those with their piping clarinets, rattling strings and pounding drums gave you a lift when you were suffering from post-flu depression. Good value also were the big bands, with flashy numbers orchestrated by such leaders as Joe Loss, Lou Praeger, Victor Sylvester, Geraldo, Cyril Stapleton, Eric Winstone and, yet another Sid, Sidney Lipton. Top end of this galaxy was probably the posh-sounding and posh-playing Anton and His Orchestra.

Come 3.45 p.m. I got a second half-hour of the same and in between I might listen to *Workers' Playtime*. The emphasis on work and worker puzzled me. Did the English workforce down tools specially to listen to these programmes? The most startling departure from my normal habits was *Mrs Dale's Diary*. Hard to imagine anything less relevant to a small-town Irish schoolboy. Yet, whenever I heard its rippling signature tune I homed in on the latest events in the life of the decent Dr Jim and his family. But I would no sooner be current with it than I had to go back to school again and would be out playing thereafter when it was on. The beauty of it was that by the time I became ill again in a few months, or a year, nothing much would have transpired in between and I was easily able to pick up the threads once more. With *The Archers* it was analogous although I had more chance of catching that programme as it was transmitted at a later time of day. *The Archers*, as one might expect from an everyday story of country folk, struck more of a chord in me than the genteel goings-on of the Dales. The high point of its earthiness for me was a long and squelchy kiss between a reluctantly charmed Chris Archer and the bounder Nelson Gabriel in the latter's car. I was listening to it with Mam and felt too embarrassed to enjoy it fully.

Extracts from the sound tracks of moving pictures – usually romantic dialogues that appeared to have been recorded inside the torpedo chamber of a submarine – were instantly recognisable on the wireless. Even the odd action sequence sounded artificial, which, of course, it was. The cinema programme I tuned into now and again was *Current Release*, a BBC production that went out in the late evening. Leslie Mitchell, the *British Movietone News* newsreel commentator, also had a BBC lunchtime film slot on Thursdays and Fridays but I only ever caught this during bouts of illness. Wondermen cropped up on the BBC in the personalities of Leslie Welch, the Memory Man, whose recall of sporting data was so total you felt there had to be a catch in it, and Ronnie Ronalde, a one-off whistler who could do the music *and* the birds of 'In a Monastery Garden', and who could yodel as well as any cowboy on the silver screen. *Book At Bedtime* at 11.00 p.m. on the Light Programme was something I tried not to miss, especially when a novel I liked was scheduled. Roger Delgado was the best of the storytellers. I fancy I heard him reading *The Hound of the Baskervilles* more than once.

With the wireless came the pop stars of the early Fifties, mature men and women rather than the teenage idols who were to emerge in the later years of the decade. The focus was the United States of America where performers like Guy Mitchell, Rosemary Clooney, Eddie Fisher, Doris Day, Jo Stafford, Mario Lanza, Dinah Shore and Tennessee Ernie Ford were cutting their first million-selling discs. All of them featured songs I liked, especially Mitchell, but it was other singers and groups who were developing styles that were wholly their own that really caught my imagination – Nat King Cole, Les Paul and Mary Ford, Frankie Lane, Johnny Ray, the Weavers, the Four Aces. Cole with hits like 'Too Young' and 'Unforgettable' was my favourite but the group that most broke the mould of earlier pop traditions, paradoxically because its members rooted themselves in traditional song, was the Weavers with numbers like 'Good Night Irene', 'Tzena, Tzena, Tzena', and 'On Top of Old Smokey'. I was not quite sure what to make of Johnny Ray but any man who could get away with such outrageously sentimental and tearful singles as 'Cry' and 'The Little White Cloud That Cried' had to have something going for him. Other singers grabbed my attention with just one hit, e.g. Teresa Brewer with 'Music, Music, Music', Kay Starr with 'Wheel Of Fortune', Kitty Kallen with 'Little Things Mean a Lot' – a number I liked a lot, and Hank Williams with 'Your Cheatin' Heart'.

By comparison, British music had little to offer: Dickie Valentine, a romantic vocalist; Steve Conway another ('I'd Give My Life and All My Love for You'), The Stargazers vocal group; Winifred Atwell on honky-tonk piano; Mantovani and His Strings with 'Charmaine'. Looming into earshot was the sound that was going to totally change our perceptions of pop – rock 'n roll, already with us in the rhythms of Fats Domino though we did not recognise it. It would not be too long before I would read about a dynamic young male performer from the Southern United States whose most ardent female fans were taking to carving his initials on their forearms with penknives.

One could have predicted that I would become a fairly regular listener of Raymond Glendenning's soccer commentaries on winter Saturdays, though I always compared him unfavourably with our own Mícheál O'Hehir because he never gave me the impression that he kept up with the play the way the latter did. Indeed, of the Irish commentator it was sometimes hinted that he was ahead of the play! When in doubt about either of the two, the cheers and shouts of the crowd were the giveaway. Less predictably, as I knew little about motor cars, I became hooked on the annual Monte Carlo rally that was held in January–February. Raymond Baxter's late night reports on its progress filled my mind with images of glistening vehicles with flashing lights powering over snowy mountain passes in all manner of road and weather conditions. Cricket I never got into on radio. It was all talk intermingled with brief flurries of action. But it was less comical than the breakneck surrealism of tennis commentaries. Its saving factor was the calm and unmistakeable Hampshire accent of John Arlott. The BBC Light Programme and Radio Éireann were the stations I listened to most. On the Home Service I might be attracted by a play, or repeats of something I had missed on the Light. The Third Programme was all Virgil and madrigals. Irish music that had for so long seemed but fiddles and repetitions to me was beginning to make sense through the fresh and enthusiastic approach of a new Radio Éireann presenter, Ciarán MacMathúna. From February 1951 to December 1954 I listened more intensely to the wireless than at any other period of my life. But it never kept me indoors on summer evenings.

CHAPTER NINETEEN

School

SCHOOL WAS A FUNNY BUSINESS. I do not think I ever realised quite what it was supposed to do for me. Certainly I was happier out of the place than in it and greatly envied those of my pals who were allowed to leave at the age of 14, the official school-leaving age. Would I have felt more positive about it if, like Bill Dineen, a sturdily built secondary-school classmate, I had had to cycle from beyond Ballynoe in County Cork in all weathers to attend? Bill, a farmer's son, *never* missed school. Not even on a day when it rained so heavily and stormed so hard I was sent to class unwillingly by a strangely unrelenting Mam who discounted my protests that none of the lads from outside the town would be able to attend in such weather. Indeed, I was dubious that all the lads from the town would show up. Of the dozen or so boys in my class only Tom Lineen, Des Frawley and Chris 'Scanner' Scanlan, all townies, had arrived by the time I got in. Other classes were equally sparse in numbers. Among the four of us we agreed that of all of the boys from the surrounding villages and countryside only one was likely to put in an appearance. And sure enough, it was not long before we spotted an army cape cycling around Dunne's corner, flapping furiously in the high wind and driving rain, and under it Bill Dineen. Admirable it was but sure he needn't have bothered. We were all sent home an hour later and he had to head off again in the opposite direction. Such desire for learning set me thinking – for a while. The Cappoquin lads stayed at home in bed, a not very impressive performance when they only had four miles on the flat to bike, and put into perspective when one considered that Bill had travelled all of eleven miles, if not more. Those further east, from Modeligo, or from the south-east, Affane, Aglish and Villierstown, had more reason not to attempt the journey, specially the lads from the last-named villages who used to shortcut via the ferry across one of the Blackwater's widest stretches at Camphire rather than go the roundabout route through Cappoquin. The ferry would not have been operating on such a day.

I was first sent to a place of learning at the age of 4 1/2, being taught initially in the long room that overlooked the front gardens of the Presentation Convent nursery school. Officially one started at 5 but the nuns were willing to take children a few months earlier if parents wanted to accustom them to being with other kids before starting school properly. It was here I had my first brush with romance in the celestial image of Sister de Lourdes. I was left in the coeducational care of the nuns for the best part of three years, during which I fell in love with the same number of female classmates: Joan Boyle, Sadie Glasse and Janey Dunne. They all had lovely long tresses and it was most conflicting sorting out which one I loved best. I suspect I was in love with all three at once, or with whomever would smile the most sweetly at me at any one time. Probably it was Joan I was really smitten with. She had the waviest hair and exuded a kind of wise gravity that made her smiles all the rarer and more alluring. Playing tag in the small leafy playground, you could actually touch the object of your desire. And when the class stood up to say prayers in the room on the left as you entered the yard – that in which we spent our final coeducational year – it was a pleasure to watch the sunlight dancing on the admired locks of hair. It was all too good to last and, having been guided through the responsible age of seven and having earned my few bob making my First Communion, I was separated from the girls whose company I enjoyed and delivered into the hands of the Christian Brothers who were to complete the job and make a man of me. The best years of my schooling had come to an abrupt end.

The all-male environment was strange at first. I did not understand why at the time, but with hindsight I think I may have had some glimmer of a realisation that an important dimension of human experience had been curtailed for me. I did not have a lonely feeling as such – my male classmates had transferred with me – but there was a sense of loss. And probably anxiety. At the purely arbitrary age of seven I was to start acquiring the traits of adulthood. How the girls felt about this hiving off of the boys I have no idea. They probably took it in their stride. After all, they were staying on at a familiar institution.

Three classrooms, all on the ground floor, formed the primary school of the CBS. In fact, there were only two rooms but the larger was split in half by a sliding, wooden partition that had a door in it, to make the third. In the primary we were the charges of the Brothers only, the senior one being Brother Murphy, who was a fixture in the place. It was hard to like Murphy and, to give him his due, he did not seem to care overmuch whether anyone liked him. Generations of Lismore lads went through his hands, enduring his phops, wiggings and snide remarks. Parents argued that his strictness did us no harm – he made us learn in spite of ourselves – but this apologia

My CBS classmates and I from Lismore and surrounding area. School photo taken when we were eleven or twelve, c. 1948-49. Back row, left to right: Michael 'Murph' Murphy, Seán Dennis, Michael Scanlon, Frank Frawley, Richard Broderick, Joe Tobin, Andy Coleman. Middle row, left to right: Ned Doherty, Tom O'Connor, Michael Doocey, Bertie Nugent, Tommy Maloney, Terry Forde, Alfie Whelan. Front row, left to right: Des Frawley, Tommy Cahill, Patsy Bray, Patsy Hickey, Willie Walsh, Jim Ballantyne.

cut no ice with his pupils. He was a thin, peevish Corkman with a repressed air who could raise no more than a snigger when he attempted a laugh. What I disliked about him most was the way he picked on some youngsters and sneered at the duller ones amongst us. Compounding that was the manner in which he favoured others, among whom, I am glad to say, I was never counted. He was well thought of by the middle class because he kept us in our place, it appeared to them. In Botany and Church Lane he was more sharply appraised.

Happily, you were not thrown straight to him when you arrived at the school. Younger Brothers eased the transition from the convent school. But you got a glimpse of what he could be like when your own teacher happened to fall ill. The partition would be rolled back and he would give us written exercises to keep us quiet while he concentrated on teaching the Primary Certificate class. All the time we were within range of his fierce glare, and anyone who did anything to upset the rhythm of his instruction was called

School photo. Paddy Ballantyne and his CBS classmates from Lismore and surrounding area. Second Year, 1946. Back row, left to right: John Murphy, Seán O'Connell, John Joe O'Donnell, Noel Doocey, Billy O'Brien, Michael Twomey, Michael Madden. Centre row, left to right: Michael Feeney, Jim Lineen, Robert McCarthy, Tom Ryan, Paddy Walsh, Paddy Ballantyne, Michael O'Farrell, John Arrigan, Joe Daly, Front row, left to right: Brian MacSweeney, Walter Creane, Michael Coleman, Pat O'Donoghue, Maurice Hickey, Paddy Browne, Billy Stack, Michael Troy, Michael 'Coz' Madden, Bernard Lonergan.

up before both classes and phopped. A second transgression earned a couple of extra phops. And if, in his eyes, you were being particularly difficult he would grab your hair above the ear with his thumb and index finger and force you up on your toes – his infamous wigging – and maybe knuckle the side of your head as well. After that he might stand you outside the classroom door where the Brother Superior could make negative assumptions when he passed. I think I would not be exaggerating if I said that at worst I hated his guts and at best I was very suspicious of him when he came on friendly.

I had Brother Kelly to begin with and he was okay. By the time I reached him he had had some of the corners knocked off him. One occasion, in particular, was said to have opened his eyes. He made the mistake of giving Fisser Neville a couple of phops above the odds. What he did not realise was that Fisser's mother Kit, while a disciplinarian in ensuring that her kids attended school, was adamant that if any flaking was to be done to any of her family she would be the one handing out the clouts. She stormed up to the school and banged on the door of the long narrow classroom that overlooked the playground. When Kelly came out he got an earful. One more incident like that, she warned, and she would lay into him with a stick. It was a highly embarrassed and deservedly chastened brother who withdrew back into the classroom to face the sniggers of his pupils. Afterwards though, Kit and he got on fine and when she delivered another son, Michael, known as 'Lochrann', sometimes abbreviated 'Loch', to the door of the same classroom after she caught him mitching, Kelly immediately despatched the truant to his desk and listened sympathetically as she explained at length about all the trouble the kids were giving her. While they were talking Lochrann, who detested school, hopped out through the back window and ran off again to resume his mitch.

Kelly was famously accurate at lobbing a piece of chalk and used this skill to revive the flagging interest of inattentive pupils. You would be daydreaming out the window when you felt a sting on the side of your cheek. Or your head would be dropping onto your exercise book when a piece of chalk would land on the page in front of you and make you start. Or, as happened to Toddy Uniacke, who used to yawn slothfully and uninhibitedly in the back row, you might be unlucky enough to have a missile lobbed into your gaping gob. The rest of us laughed as Toddy coughed and spluttered to get rid of the unwelcome object. Schoolchildren like nothing better than to see one of their number discomfited. But even our rueful pal had to admire Kelly's aim. The teacher left us in the summer of 1946 and was replaced by Brother Beare in the autumn. Beare was the one who was to launch us on the boards of the entertainment halls of West Waterford.

The lads who got an unfair deal in primary school were those from the poorest sections of the town whose parents had no hope of keeping them on in secondary school. But there were those who were even more disadvantaged: poor kids from out the country for whom a primary school was not always within easy reach and, most of all, tinkers' children who were lucky if they encountered any formal education at all. Primary school education was completed at the age of 12. School leaving age was 14. So in theory the children of the poor were destined to form a sort of supernumerary Primary Certificate class until such time as it was legally in order for them to leave. In practice, many youngsters left before this legal limit was attained. For those who did not, the authorities took a lenient view of truancy. People had to live. People had to earn their bread.

The Brothers, to their credit, did their utmost with meagre resources to assist disadvantaged pupils and students who showed a commitment to learning. The real problem remained outside their control. How could a boy, or girl, develop a taste for learning in a small cottage crammed with brothers and sisters who all had to fight for space? It was hard enough finding a crust just to stay healthy. Only an exceptionally determined child could make space for himself to read and study in such conditions, even with parental encouragement. The Brothers demanded no fees from impoverished parents whose bright kids wanted to continue through secondary school. Which was commendable, but it did not except these children from having to fetch wood, draw water, and seek paid work in their spare time. The teachers might have done more to encourage slower boys, and the quick-witted ones who manifestly possessed the capabilities for, but who showed no interest in, pursuing their education. Perhaps they did discreetly? It was hard enough for them to persuade me, with the comparative advantages I had.

A Manual Room in the school was well equipped with stout workbenches and an array of saws, chisels and planes, etc. Here basic training in carpentry was given to all of us by our vocational instructor, Seán Baston. Poorer boys staying on in primary could at least develop some useful skills by using this facility. More often than not, sadly, they were used as cheap labour by the school. In my ignorance, I used to envy pals who were in this predicament when I saw them called out to pick fruit or do other odd jobs in the Brothers' garden, or to lift the potato crop in the small field adjoining the Manual Room but, at the same time questions niggled uneasily at the back of my mind. Why was it only my poorer classmates who were asked to volunteer for this unskilled work? Why did they have to do it during class time when the rest of us were being taught? Were they getting paid for it? Why couldn't I go out and help as well? Why was I in a privileged position? *Was* it a privilege to be kept inside while my pals were out in the open air? Girls found themselves in a similar situation when it came to vocational education. We had carpentry and allied skills from Baston. Miss Veale taught them domestic economy, a subject that basically prepared them for the task of cooking, washing up and keeping house for the eventual man of their dreams. We boys, for our part, expected to be waited upon by the eventual woman of our dreams.

Physical training classes provided the bizarre shock in the move from convent school to CBS. This was the real business of becoming a man. Every Wednesday morning our drill instructor Sidney Fraser would drive up in his little Morris 8 and take all grades in turn, finishing with the Leaving Certificate lads at lunchtime. It was odd seeing a strongly built man, all of six foot plus, unravelling himself out of such a small vehicle and I never got over that initial impression. Coincidentally, his brother Jack was a PT instructor also, but the two were said to be professionally at odds with one another and to hate one another's guts. The brother, who also operated in West Waterford, and over into east County Cork, never came to our School but we used to see him passing through town regularly in a flashier-looking Morris 8 than our instructor had, a kind of two-tone black-and-maroon job. I myself only came across second-hand evidence of the supposed animosity between the two men when, during my higher schooling, Sidney turned up for work one sunny day wearing a lovely black eye. Having had advance notice of it on the grapevine and having been impatiently awaiting a gander at it, we grinned like Cheshire cats. He scowled and gave us a hard time. 'Up down, up down, in out, in out, faster, boy!' Fortunately, halfway through the session Brother P.D. Lee ambled over, as he sometimes did, to see how things were doing.

'At ease, boys!' Sidney barked and turned to the Superior.

P.D. raised his eyebrows when he caught the violaceous sheen of the shiner.

'Oof!' he exclaimed with a sharp intake of breath and recoiled as if he had just taken a wallop himself. 'That's a bad one.' He peered solicitously at it. 'How did you get that at all?'

'Ah sure, wasn't it my own fault,' said Fraser and launched into an elaborate explanation of how he came to collect the shiner. Delivered in a kind of improved English for the Superior's ear, it ran something like this: 'One of those days. I'd had trouble with the car and got home late. Made myself a cup of tea. Relaxed over the paper. Maybe that wasn't the best thing with the state the country's in.' He forced a laugh.

P.D. nodded attentively.

We grinned from ear to ear.

'Then I went out and got the things from the car and ran a bath. You get very sweaty in my line of business.'

'Yes,' agreed P.D.

'While the tap was running I threw off my shoes and went back to the kitchen. The kitchen is off the bathroom, you see. How it is, the kitchen is over here,' he blocked off a chunk of air with his muscular hands. 'And the bathroom is over there,' he cut out another chunk. 'And the door to the bathroom opens like this,' he waved a hand. 'And when it's open it normally stands at an angle like this,' he made an angle of thirty degrees with the palms of his hands.

P.D. nodded intently, no hurry on him at all. I began to wonder from where the hot water for the bath was coming. Maybe tough gym instructors just used cold?

'I had one ear to the bath while I washed a few dishes. They pile up, you know,' he laughed.

P.D. smiled.

We maintained our collective happy grin.

Fraser angled us a quick flash of malice, disguised for P.D.'s consumption as no more than a cursory glance to check that we were maintaining ranks. 'When it was ready, the bath that is, I got myself a towel and strolled over to the door but, if I did,' he flapped his arms, 'didn't the feet suddenly go from under me. I fell forward and cracked my face against the edge of the door.'

Our steady grin broadened.

'Uuh! That must have hurt,' P.D. commiserated.

'Took my breath away, I can tell you. Tripped over my shoes. I'd forgotten all about them. That was how it happened. As simple as that.' He paused to see how the Superior was taking the yarn then went on to milk a little more sympathy. 'I had been stretching the towel, you see, softening it like,' he demonstrated with a twist of his hands, 'And because I fell so quickly, I couldn't free my hands in time to break the fall.'

'Can easily happen,' said Lee and shook his head.

Fraser looked relieved that his story had been credited.

'But it's on the mend now, isn't it?' P.D. turned on his heel and walked away, allowing us a glimpse of more than the ghost of a smile.

We felt Sidney's glare on us and stifled our grin. It was obvious that P.D. had heard the same story that we had, and had given our drill instructor a bit of rope to see to what heights of invention he would go in explaining away the shiner. The real story, if accounts were to be believed, was that the two brothers had had a one-to-one punch-up at a dance in the Glebe Hall in Aglish the Sunday night before and Sidney had come off the worst. A couple of senior students from beyond Cappoquin who had been hanging around outside the hall had seen the action. Hence, our awareness of the matter. From whom P.D. got wind of it, who could say?

'Push-ups!' Fraser bellowed in the sergeant-major manner he affected. "Up down, up down, up down... .'

We collapsed onto our bellies, the grin wiped from our faces.

The instructor liked to keep us in our place, what you might expect from someone who had been in the Army. 'Chin up, boy!' he would bark, tipping up your chin with the tips of his fingers, then suddenly dropping the same hand and rapping you in the belly with the back of it so that you gasped and doubled up. You walked into it the first time but after that you were ready for him, well, nearly always. He could still catch you unawares if you were in a dozy mood. He was also fond of marching us around the school yard, normal pace and at the double. On the face of it this was a cinch. What was it only walking fast? But when you had a collective go at it, it proved to be not as easy as you had expected. We were a rumpled lot to begin with, some straight, some slouching, some skipping, some loping, all of us falling over our feet or someone else's in our efforts to keep time. Just when you thought you were in step the fella in front of you would do a skip and put you out again. A few of the lads genuinely had problems in following Fraser's instructions and, instead of swinging the right arm in time with the left leg they would swing it in time with the right, even though normally they achieved the correct gait without thinking. The result was comical and used to infuriate Fraser while throwing the rest of us into confusion as well. Sometimes when he had managed to get us marching in style Fraser's attention would wander. Noting this, one of us might wilfully change step, or swing the wrong arm, taking the formation apart again just for a laugh. I liked Fraser, though. I think most of us did. And even though I laughed about his black eye I was disappointed that his brother appeared to have bested him, in that particular scrap anyway. His only fault in our eyes was that he was a bit full of himself. He was a good gymnast as well as being a good instructor. In a good mood he would display his prowess for us on the parallel bars or on the vaulting-horse. I used to ask myself why such a physically fine man showed no interest whatsoever in field games, but never dared ask him for a reason.

Wednesday afternoon was devoted to sport, i.e. Gaelic games, so all in all Wednesday was not a bad day to attend school. Lads who had no interest in hurling and Gaelic football just went home, unofficially because theoretically the afternoon session counted as class time. On occasion they would be made to hang around the school building for an hour or so before they were let go, or they might have to go up to the playing field and watch from the sidelines. I skived off now and again myself when the mood for organised play was not on me. Mostly, I was glad to participate. The standard of play was fairly high because the town contingent was augmented by some very handy players from outside – the catchment area of the school covered a radius of some ten to twelve miles. In my class alone Charlie Bolger, John Herr and Michael MacSweeney from Cappoquin, Peadar Henley from Tallow and Bill Dineen from Conna were good enough for any team in Waterford. The Hurling Field would usually host two games simultaneously, the Fifth and Sixth classes taking over the two-thirds of the pitch at the town end for a hurling match refereed by Vincent O'Donoghue (Mícheál U. Ó Donnchadha), our Irish teacher known to us as Vin, the juveniles being allocated the other third for a game of Gaelic football controlled by Brother Barrett, the Latin teacher. That was the usual pattern but sometimes the games would be reversed and Vin would take charge of the juveniles for a hurling session.

Barrett was known to us as 'Fishy' for two very good reasons: one, his wan, round visage and the black yank of hair plastered sideways across his bald pate gave him the appearance of a sly old cod, and two, he used to sneak on us to the Superior. A silky-spoken individual, he was a good teacher of Latin and English but it taxed his somewhat frail health to control an unruly class. We did not always give him an easy time and took unfair advantage of his reasonable efforts to keep us in check by compelling him to resort unwillingly to the phop now and again. On the other hand, he brought it on himself to some degree with an ingratiating sense of humour that got under our skin. He might not have had a taste for phopping but when he laid a few across you, you remembered it. Rising on the balls of his feet to give himself extra leverage he would balance delicately for a moment before cracking the leather down on your outstretched palm with an acute sense of timing. It stung. When he saw that phopping was no solution to a problem of indiscipline he simply sneaked on us. Drawing the Superior's attention to a particularly disruptive display of behaviour by a student would have been acceptable, even to the perpetrator. It was his habit of retailing peccadilloes that lost him our respect and goodwill, mine at any rate. As well as his immaculate ability with a phopper Fishy had, on the plus side, one other rare skill; he was an ace at taking football penalties. He was only a slim wraith of a man but when his polished pigskin shoe – he never turned out in sports gear – connected with the ball there was not one of us, from senior to juvenile, who could save his shot. There was always rivalry to see which of us would be the first to make a save but none of us ever did, or if one did, it was due to Fishy's miskicking the ball, in which case a retake left the goalie floundering as usual. In spite of misgivings, I got on okay with him – until he sneaked one story too many about me to P.D. I was 13 years of age in First Year, when a crude sketch I had pencilled of my crude impression of a naked woman, her vagina arrowed with the word 'slit', was picked up by him as it circulated from giggling hand to giggling hand among the desks. I had improvised it following some classroom banter about girls. Fishy's white face went whiter when he laid eyes on it. His thin lips pursed in pious distaste.

'Who did this?' he asked quietly, shielding the cartoon from those who had not yet been circulated with it.

I held up my hand and tensed myself for a barrage of phops. My classmates' reactions varied from apprehension to amusement at my embarrassment. Those whom the offending item had not yet reached showed a mixture of curiosity and disappointment. But Fishy just stuck the slip of paper into his pocket, told me to sit down, and resumed the lesson. I knew that was not the end of it and, sure enough, at the break P.D. called me into the empty Manual Room on my own. It was like being sent to the torture room. I braced myself for the hiding of a lifetime. Fishy's sense of propriety was small beer compared to that of the Superior's. Also, while I was sure I could outlast the former's capacity for dishing our physical punishment, I was very uncertain about how much I could take from P.D. If he chose to lay into me he could bounce me around the room till dinner time without raising a sweat.

'What's this?' said the Superior quietly in his soft Cork accent and pointed with distaste at the scarcely detailed line drawing that he had placed beside him on the heavy workbench on which he was half-perched.

I just shrugged my shoulders and remained silent. What could I say? My debauchery spoke for itself.

'This is not the kind of thing I'd expect from you,' he said next and launched into a quiet sermon about the sins of the flesh.

He quickly succeeded in making me feel very ashamed and I found myself wishing he would just shut up and get on with handing out the pasting I knew was my due. Waiting for punishment was often worse than the actual thing when it arrived because your imagination tended to sketch in the worst possible scenario.

P.D. exhausted his homily and, exasperated I suppose by my hangdog look, looked around for a long ruler to phop me. 'If I had a... ', he gritted his teeth. Failing to spy a ruler within reach, his eyes fell on the wooden block of a blackboard duster that lay on the bench.

'Jasus!' I thought in a sudden panic, 'Is he goin' to lay into me with that?'

Just then the virginal chimes of the school bell signalled the end of recess. The old boxing cliché didn't enter my head until later. The Superior glared at me as if trying to figure out whether his words had had any effect at all, then roared, 'Get out of my sight!'

The last of my classmates was disappearing up the wide wrought-iron staircase to the secondary classrooms when I came out into the yard. I walked slowly across the open space, drawing in mouthfuls of air with relief, but cursing myself for my stupidity and for the humiliation I had brought upon myself. Lee, whether he guessed it or not, had handled it right and I bore him no malice. Even if he had beaten me I would have accepted it. About Fishy, however, I was unforgiving. My sketch, misguided prank that it was, had been wholly innocent. It was based on a coy, full-frontal nude that Mickey McConnell had shown me in a copy of the English magazine *Coronet* that had somehow fallen into his hands.

'Look at that!' Mickey had exclaimed, opening the pages to reveal the nude.

It was one of those pseudo art photographs with the head turned sideways and locks of long black hair falling down over the face, informative about basic physique but hardly very provocative.

'You can see *everything!*' Mickey enthused. 'Look! Jesus!'

It was the first nude picture of a woman I had ever seen but it left me cold. 'So that's all there is to it?' I thought.

'You can have it,' Mickey pressed the magazine upon me as if he were presenting me with the most valuable item in his possession. 'Here.'

I declined, not knowing what further use I could have for it.

'You don't want it!?' Mickey exclaimed. 'You can *keep* it. I'm not just lending it to you.' He looked at me expectantly.

Shyly I declined again. I did not wish to hurt his feelings when he clearly thought he was giving me something of great value but I just could not see what I could do with the illustration. It held no erotic attraction for me. I could hardly stick it up on the wall of my bedroom – my parents would have blown their top. I would not have wanted to stick it up anyway. I had no pictures of any kind on my walls. Furthermore, the rest of the magazine looked even more uninteresting. Shaking his head, my pal pocketed the small magazine and went off through the wicket gate of the Villa.

Neither of us recognised that a repercussive seed had been sown.

My classmates looked at me apprehensively when I re-entered the room. Vin O'Donoghue studiously ignored me and went on writing on the blackboard. I wondered whether he knew as well. Did the whole school know?

'How many did you get?" Murph, a connoisseur of phopping, whispered as I sidled in alongside him on the bench.

'None.'

He looked at me incredulously.

'But he gave me an awful talking to.'

I did not elaborate, nor tell anyone that Brother Lee's tongue-lashing had wounded me more than a hundred phops. You did not dwell on humiliation. I was certain of one thing though. I wanted nothing more to do with Fishy. Unfortunately, I had no option but to remain in his classes for another two years during which my disdain for him showed in plummeting marks in Latin and, eventually, English. He had not been taking me for the second subject at the time of the incident. My English teacher then was Tommy Keane, a Kerryman.

Keane was the most remarkable teacher I ever had, the only one who ever generated real enthusiasm in me for a subject. He was a young teacher when he came to Lismore CBS. Possibly it was his first job after graduating. When I upgraded to secondary in September 1949 he had been in town for about a year. Aside from any consideration of his worth as an educationist he was also a good enough Gaelic footballer to have had played junior for his footballing county. That only did him good in our eyes. He was quickly snapped up for the black and amber in the hope that he might shed some of the illustrious Kerry tradition on the Lismore juniors. Sadly, the Kingdom magic failed to rub off on the local players and Lismore football remained in a trough. In spite of these extra and welcome credentials that Tommy bore, our immediate concern as schoolboys was with his skills and habits as a teacher.

The first thing he stuck under the collective nose of our class was *The Wind In The Willows,* which I had never heard of before. It was this story by the English writer Kenneth Grahame, of whom I was also ignorant, and the manner in which Tommy taught us to appreciate it, that made me alive to language. He was so enthusiastic about the book himself he made it live for us, too. It was a joy to listen to him reading it. His longish nose would tilt, he would cock his head slightly, then his musical accent would carry you off into the world of Mole and Ratty. I had never seen a mole in my life but I could identify with water-rats, which were plentiful along the Blackwater. Tommy encouraged us to read aloud too, with feeling. He spoke of language and how it was, and should be, used. The essays he set made sense to me. Above all, he was straight. When he was in a good mood he let you know it. Equally, if he was hung-over after an all-night dance he made no attempt to disguise this. He could be bitchy now and again, but in a forgivable way. Possessing the ability to maintain discipline on the strength of his personality, he had little need of a phopper. I don't think I ever once got phopped by him. If that is so, he would be the only teacher never to have crossed my palm with leather. Which is not the same as saying I never got up his nose, just that I did not get far enough up it.

One incident certainly earned me his displeasure. I had allowed Beaver Doherty to cog a drawing using tracing paper. Keane happened to look at Beaver's work first and congratulated him on it. 'Very good, Ned,' he said, 'I never thought you were so good at drawing.' Then he picked up my sheet. 'Cog!' he snapped and clipped me over the ear. Then he gave my pal a clout as well. Our obvious attempt at cheating wasn't worth a phop. You had to be really bad, be a smart arse, or be afflicted with an excess of goodness, to grate on Tommy.

Unfortunately, he was to remain with our class for barely a year or so. A posh school up in Dublin, Blackrock I think, made him an offer that our underfunded Collegiate School could not match and he moved away. I was bitterly disappointed as, at last, I seemed to have had a reason for going to school. I think I felt offended too that he should have quit us to take a job in a school which probably already had more than its share of good teachers and where pupils and students most likely did not need to cover their books in brown paper the way we did so that we could maintain them in reasonable condition for re-sale to the class coming after us. Under his influence, I had even taken to studying my other subjects assiduously and some evenings would go up to Tom Lineen's house in the Main Street so that my pal and I could jointly work out the answers to the more difficult mathematical problems. I liked going to Tom's house. Like ours, it had a shop window, but unlike ours, it still had a counter and shelves as well because Tom's father had had a licensed premises there at an earlier stage. My pal's Dad, also called Tom, was very friendly and his mother, a gentle, beautiful woman, would smile benignly on our diligent efforts.

After the Kerry lay teacher left there was a period of uncertainty when we were subjected to inexperienced young teachers who were given short-term contracts to hone their skills on us. We also had one or two student teachers on placement. One of these was an ex-Lismore CBS student from Cappoquin who was faced with the additional hazard of coping with faces that were already familiar to him. For whatever reason, and it may have been connected with this unstable situation, although it could just as easily be down to my own negativity, my interest in learning waned and I began to rely on cogging to keep me afloat. I did not like copying. It seemed unfair to profit from another's hard work. But I did it. We all did it to some degree or other. Peer pressure saw to it that a cog was seldom refused. Only the inveterate practitioner might suffer rejection when his demands became excessive.

P. D. Lee was the third Brother Superior to work in Lismore during my time at the CBS. I never learned the names behind the initials. His precedessors, Brother McGovern and Brother O'Connor, were only vague figures of authority to me as I was attending primary school during their terms of office and scarcely came in contact with them. Brother McGovern left town in 1946, the same year as Brother Kelly, to be replaced by O'Connor, who only stayed a couple of years. Neither of these appeared to have been particularly authoritarian. The real bogey in this respect in the secondary school was a senior called Brother Brady, who mercifully moved on in 1947. The secondary school boys above us spoke of him in hushed voices because of the ferocity with which he laid about him with the lash.

Their stories may have been exaggerated to scare us smaller ones but I saw no reason to doubt them when I came across him strolling down West Street, stately and unsmiling, and alone, a big walking stick in his hand and a glint that suggested he would use it if he encountered any students engaged in behaviour of which he did not approve outside the school.

My only experience of him revealed him to be anything but an ogre. It was during his final year at the CBS. He called to offer his condolences to Mam on the death of her sister Bab. Standing at the living-room door, I saw her take this forbidding-looking figure by the hand and, with tears welling in her eyes, lead him into the sitting-room where they had a private chat. In the few moments I saw him he spoke very softly and very feelingly to her. My brother Paddy must have escaped any serious phopping as he never complained of him. Also on the positive side, Brady was very fond of Lismore and did not wish to leave it when transferred. Before he left he gave Dad some notes on local place-names in his own handwriting and a number of cuttings from books that he had accumulated about the area, which I also read with interest, especially one about the *Rian Bó Phádraig*. (I still have these notes and cuttings.) All of which suggested he may have been something of a Jekyll and Hyde. In spite of these personal impressions, I breathed a sigh of relief when I heard he was going for good. Almost certainly I would have come out on the wrong side of him myself at some stage and I had no desire to see him laying into my pals either.

Brother Beare, a good-looking, studious man who wore glasses, was the one who taught us showbiz. (He stayed until 1953 to be replaced by Brother Blake.) Before his arrival my only brushes with the theatre had been a nativity play that the Creanes and a few of us had put on one Christmas in a small meeting room known as the School Room that adjoined the Manse, and a kind of sketch that Kate O'Connell had had some of us kids do at a variety concert at the Happydrome. The nativity play we wrote, designed, lit, directed, and produced ourselves. On top of that we handled our own publicity and it was on this that we failed miserably. At 3.00 p.m. on the Saturday afternoon in mid-December when the curtain was due to rise on our biblical extravaganza only one theatre-goer had paid her penny entrance money, the redoubtable Annie Campion. While she waited obdurately for the lights to go down we scanned the Main Street up and down for the missing punters. We double-checked what we had written on the poster outside. Where *was* our audience? There was no counter-attraction that we knew of. We kept apologising to Annie for the delay in starting, hinting that perhaps she might not wish to stay if nobody else turned up. She remained adamant that as she had bought her ticket she expected to see a show. Finally, and totally oblivious to the fact that we were upholding a great tradition of the theatre, we were forced to draw back the curtain for our solitary customer. Well, perhaps we did not quite live up to the highest tradition. We performed a hurried and abbreviated version only, then called it a day. Our audience was very disgruntled as she left. She had, understandably, recognised a certain discontinuity in the production and took us to task for our free interpretation of the Christmas story. 'What d'you expect for a feckin' penny?' someone muttered as she swept off, saying that she would not be hurrying to our next production. At least she did not ask for her penny back. She need not have worried. That was the one and only effort of our company. There had to be better ways of making a buck. The act Kate put on at the Happydrome was more successful. At least we had a proper audience. It was given the title 'McNamara's Band' and consisted of a bunch of us schoolboys singing a few songs and doing a couple of numbers with combs and paper under the stern gaze of our taskmistress.

Beare demanded a higher level of professionalism but had one unfortunate tendency with which I was wholly out of sympathy; he always seemed to pick on me when he needed a woman in the cast. He first subjected me to this assault on my manhood in 1947 when I was 10. Brother O'Connor and he organised a St Patrick's Day concert in which the whole school was involved. Michael Feeney and I were delegated to sing the duet 'Mollie Bawn'. No need to ask who played Mollie. Being shoved into female attire was no light thing for a growing boy, but I managed to cope with the cracks of my pals. Happily, that was only one item on a full card. Fraser had us doing tableaux, flag drill, and a further variation called wand drill; he himself layed on a bit of magic with the Indian clubs and parallel bars. He liked the limelight, Sidney, and I have to admit we were a little proud of him. The centrepiece of the show was an act entitled 'The Singing Sailors'. About thirty of us primary kids were dressed up in 'jolly tar' costumes and given a half-hour medley of sea shanties, well, most of them were shanties, to sing. The drapers of the town made a few bob out of all the material that went into the making of the costumes. The sewing and stitching was undertaken by mothers and sisters. I cannot remember who sewed mine but I know it was not Mam. Beare was the one who coached us and, needless to say, Kate O'Connell was our accompanist on the piano. Why our teachers went for the sailor idea when we lived so many miles inland was anybody's guess but we enjoyed the occasion. We began and ended with, of all numbers, 'All the Nice Girls Love a Sailor' and in between tackled such classics as 'The Larboard Watch', 'Haul Away Joe' and 'What Shall We Do with the

Drunken Sailor?' Because of all the effort and the expense incurred, we gave two concerts, matinee and evening. The involvement of the CBS in the traditional St Patrick's Day concert was nothing new. My brother Paddy and my co-duettist Michael Feeney had been soloists at earlier events as had other of their classmates, e.g. Finbarr Kearney on the violin and Jack Healy, the Doc's son, reciting 'The Green Eye of the Little Yellow God' or 'Pearse's Farewell'. It was the scale of the 1947 production that attracted attention.

Encouraged by their first success, Beare and O'Connor moved on to more extravagant ventures in 1948. We started in early January with a rag day in aid of the parochial building fund. The whole town took part in this and we were led by the Lismore Brass Band on foot and by an 'Irish rebel' clad in 1798 green, mounted on a white steed. Barney Walsh and I were mounted too, albeit not so elegantly as our leader. We travelled on Jocklin's ass, lent specially to us for the afternoon. Barney did the jockeying and I rode pillion on the hard bone of the rump, which left me with a bloody sore arse and walking like a bandy-legged cowpoke at the end of the pageant.

The blockbuster of the year, however, took place a month later, a total entertainment presented by the pupils and students of the CBS, which we had been rehearsing since the autumn of the previous year. It consisted of a short play in Irish, *Seán ar an Aonach*, a physical culture session organised by, and with the participation of, Sidney Fraser and, the icing on the cake, a comic opera in four acts entitled *Columbus in a Merry Key*, all of which ran for some three hours. The short play was put on by my brother's class. Paddy himself was in it with such pals as Michael O'Farrell, Pat O'Donoghue and Jim Fives. It was a farce about a farmer called Seán who sells his only cow to a succession of buyers to pay the rent and, in spite of its being in Irish, which many in the audience had difficulty in understanding, went down well as an opener. Fraser pulled out all the stops for his section which followed, adding bolas and Indian club swinging to our usual routines. Then came *Columbus*.

Brother Beare had auditioned us for the various parts and it was probably late September or early October when he lined up the various classes after school to announce who was to play who. It had appeared to me that the plum part of Columbus was between Pierce Colbert and myself but that he had an edge over me. Maybe it was a sense of foreboding that Beare was going to stick me in the woman's role again. When Pierce was duly confirmed as Columbus I promptly lost interest in the proceedings. On being offered the part of Queen Isabella I protested angrily that I could not, and would not, play a woman again. Beare, whom I liked as a teacher, used cajolery and a little emotional blackmail from the other leading players who had been chosen to wear me down, and in the end I grudgingly accepted the part. It was Thumper Lineen, chosen to play the blacked-up Caribee King, who really swung me round. He took me aside and pointed out that Michael Feeney would also be playing a woman, Mademoiselle Sago Palm, so I would not be the only female in the cast. If Mike did not care about appearing in a frock why should I? Notwithstanding my acceptance, I went home in a sour mood, in no way looking forward to the day when I would step up to sing 'Madame, Will You Walk?' with the rival who had trumped me for the male lead. The advance publicity for the entertainment had been so effective we were billed to tour the show over to St Michael's Hall in Ballyduff a week after the Lismore première. We packed them in there as well, hardly surprising as that venue was much smaller than the Happydrome. By that time I was so content in my role I might have been playing Hopalong Cassidy. The part had its advantages. Certain details of the female anatomy were confirmed to me, for example. As I was waiting in the wings in Ballyduff Mary Willoughby from the Lismore Dramatic Society, who was helping us out, came up to me with a couple of balls of newspaper in her hand.

'We can't have you looking that flat,' she chuckled and stuck the balls under my bodice to give me more chest. At the same time Mike Feeney was bolstering himself with the same material.

The Brothers must have made a few bob out of the concert because they threw a party for all participants in St Carthage's Hall some time later. Lots of cake and lemonade.

There was a bit of a lull in my dramatic career after that. I watched enviously as the Colbert brothers, Pierce and the younger Jimmy, hit the spotlight, the former with his impersonation of Micheál O'Hehir, the Radio Éireann sports commentator, the latter with his two-fingered whistling and bird-calls. Jimmy was an accomplished whistler and, with his versions of 'Sorrento', 'Tritsch Tratsch Polka' and 'Birdsong at Eventide' was soon being billed as Lismore's Ronnie Ronalde at concerts all around Munster. Another member of that talented family, the boys' sister Claude, accompanied him on the piano. The two brothers, and Thumper and I were thrown together in January 1952 in a one-act comedy, *The Old Bucket*, directed by Brother Lee, who had decided to revive his predecessor's tradition. Mercifully, I was not cast as a woman in this one. It was Jimmy's turn and he had accepted the part of Miss Julia Hayes without any of the tantrums that I had displayed. Again, the piece formed only one facet of a whole spectrum of entertainment. This time the adults were in on the act. Yet another Colbert, Dan, the station master himself, in Dublin drag sang

Biddy Mulligan. Chrissy O'Brien and P. J. McInerney, the singing *garda*, shared romantic hits. Billy Hogan and Pete Gillen, Jr. shimmied 'Walking My Baby Back Home' and effortlessly followed it with a series of accordion and saxophone solos. Jack Fogarty, the singing bank clerk, did his usual comic number, 'To Be a Farmer's Boy'. Willie Sargent, the Cappoquin tenor, sang 'Catarri'. A schoolmate of Jimmy's, Noel O'Connor, who specialised in holy numbers, rendered, as they used to say, 'Ave Maria'. For the first time the Presentation Convent participated – with a choir. There was even a visiting company, the Dungarvan CBS, who put on a serious one-acter entitled *Campbell of Kilmore*. And, of course, there was Fraser. He did his parallel bars bit at the shorter matinee programme but, with everyone trying to get in on the act in the evening, suffered the indignity of being deleted from the second performance by P.D. who felt that the variety section was running over. A decision which did not make Sidney very amiable for the remainder of the night.

The Old Bucket went down a bomb at both shows and, wholly accidentally, I got the laugh of the day at the second performance. P.D., when he was coaching us, had bowdlerised the script, instructing us to substitute the word 'blooming' for 'bloody' whenever this occurred, which was frequently. It did not seem right to him that the boys in his charge should be heard using such strong language in the legitimate theatre, even though he knew full well that we used 'bloody' and worse terms regularly in our vernacular. I was taken aback and was worried whether I could adhere to this decision. 'Blooming' was a word I had never used in my life, though I had come across it in the English comics where it tended to be employed by public school prefects and the like. 'Bloody' rolled freely off my tongue every day. There was also an artistic consideration. None of the characters in *The Old Bucket* would have included in their vocabulary such a mild expletive. But, P.D. had decreed and we were stuck with it. After a lot of rehearsal the four of us got it right. 'Bloody', however, was always hovering on the tip of my tongue, waiting to catch me unawares.

The matinee performance went without a hitch, except that it threw up another problem in Lee's estimation. It did not seem a problem to me. There was a moment in the play when I, playing James Malloy, had to hurl the old bucket of the title offstage, and this I had performed with gusto. The bucket had been heard rolling along the boards and clattering down the steps that led up to the stage for an unconscionably long moment, a thoroughly satisfying *coup de théatre* as far as I was concerned. Unfortunately, it nearly took the shins off someone on the way. P.D. decided he could not allow me to repeat the action, brilliantly realistic as it was, at the evening performance because of possible danger to life and limb, and came up with an alternative scenario. I should not jettison the galvanised vessel so graphically but should swing it into the wings and hand it to P.D., who would be acting as prompter there. He would then rattle it vigorously to simulate its being slung out. This prosaic production change did not appeal to me at all but I had to accept it. In the evening, coming up to the big moment, which happened to coincide with the moment when I was to utter my most exasperated 'blooming', I was still brooding on the matter. I swung the bucket as directed and shouted, 'I don't give a damn about Pakie and his bloody... ', my mouth fell open as I came face to face with P.D. '...ah, *blooming* old bucket,' I rectified, and handed him the vessel to shake. The audience twigged at once and fell off their seats laughing. Pierce and Jimmy were struggling to keep a straight face and, to my great relief, P.D. started laughing too.

I may have had a few clashes with Brother Lee but I greatly respected him. Like Tommy Keane, he had the knack of bringing out the best in me. That I did not perform better as a scholar under him was due to my own intransigence rather than to any shortcomings on his part. He was a fine teacher and was deeply concerned about the welfare of all his students. Mathematics and science were his own subjects. Once, through sheer chance, I had the pleasure of solving a problem in algebra that he had posed to a joint class composed of mine and the one above. We were in the science room staring blankly at the array of symbols on the big, sliding double blackboard while he stood by impatiently. This room was the only classroom that had a board of this type and P.D.'s algebra used to regularly spill off the outer section onto the inner one. All the other rooms were equipped with either free-standing wooden easel boards or with the usual wall boards. After what seemed like five minutes' silence I raised my hand. P.D. held out a piece of chalk and asked me to write my solution, which I did. To my surprise it was wholly correct.

'Good lad, Ballantyne,' Lee said, 'You're the only one who knows anything about mathematics.' And he cleared the double board with typically energetic sweeps of the duster and went on to the next problem.

I returned to my seat pleased with my unexpected coup but not showing it as I did not want Seán Dennis and his pals in the senior class, who were looking at me in some wonder, to think I was showing off. It was an unusual position in which to find myself. 'Did P.D. *really* mean what he said?' I wondered, and recalled another occasion when he showed some belief in my scholastic ability. I had returned to school content with the Pass I had gained in my Intermediate Certificate earlier in the summer. He was welcoming new students at the top of the wrought-iron staircase.

'Why didn't you get Honours then?' he snapped. 'I'll see to it that you work from now on.'

I was sorry to disappoint him but saw no reason to change my ways. Probably my parents too shared his hopes of an improvement, but I regarded myself in a more modest light, as some kind of child of nature, I suppose, who would somehow work out his own way in the world. At the same time, I sensed the long shadow of my brother's school record weighing on me. Paddy, it was said, had 'brains to burn' or 'too many brains' and had done well at his studies.

Brother Lee introduced educational trips to the Lismore CBS when, in one of my senior years, he took a busload of us on a double visit to Rineanna Airport and the Ardnacrusha hydroelectric scheme in County Clare. The airport, strangely enough, made little impact on me but I was thrilled with the power station. Its setting on a wide arm of the River Shannon, the carefully landscaped grounds, the almost monastically clean interior with the mighty generators and turbines, all left a lasting impression on me. Our small school had very limited resources for science teaching that, for me at any rate, made it difficult to take the subject seriously. After the visit to Ardnacrusha, however, I was instilled with a new respect for science and technology.

The Superior arranged one other visit for us, this time in the arts field in October 1953, and one to which we had to travel under our own steam. We were in Fifth Year, about to embark on the study of Shakespeare's *Julius Caesar* for our Leaving Certificate the following academic year. Anew McMaster, the Shakespearean actor-manager, who shrewdly kept an eye on the schools' curriculum, was bringing his 'Full International Company' to the Friary Hall in Dungarvan in October to perform just that play. It was too good a chance to miss. The real thing on stage. Not just a flowery text on the printed page. The school had few funds and, if we wanted to see it, P.D. explained, we would have to pay for our own tickets and cycle down to Dungarvan. We would get the day off from normal classes, of course. I needed no further enticement. A holiday from school was always a cause for celebration. We did not get that many of them aside from Christmas, Easter, St Patrick's Day, Point-to-Point, Ascension Thursday and other holy days of obligation, and a few days when there was a lot of influenza about, so we accepted P.D.'s offer with alacrity. I did have some doubts though, and cycling fifteen miles there and fifteen back on Dad's big bike was one of them.

Lee arranged for a group of us to attend the Thursday matinee at 3.00 p.m., so around mid-morning on that day a number of us set off from

Lismore. It was dull and cloudy and we expected some rain. At Cappoquin Charlie Bolger, John Herr and Michael MacSweeney joined us. They, used to cycling to the CBS every weekday, were pedalling effortlessly. For the Lismore contingent it was more of a slog. Being in a group, laughing and telling yarns, shortened our journey and we broke off en route to eat our packed lunches before arriving at our destination. Immediately we could see that we were about to participate in something of an event. Bikes were stood around in bunches, looked after by the minders who customarily performed this task at hurling and football matches. Students were also arriving by car and on foot. Was the whole of West Waterford studying *Julius Caesar?* Inside, boys and girls filled every available space – seats, window-sills, even the rafters. Our group had been allotted seats on the ground floor near the back. Everyone was on the top of their voice, boys and girls flirting, rival groups slagging each other off. A few studious types were actually head down in the text of the play. Someone started banging with a hammer. Nobody took any notice. The hammering was repeated. Still no notice was taken of it. One more time and we started to get the drift. The lights began to dim and the curtains began to slide open. Noise and chatter went on unheedingly. Bang, bang, bang, went the mallet for the last time and silence finally descended. Onto the stage strode a funny looking Roman in a white sheet.

On the whole, the performance seemed to go well, although it was difficult to be enthralled as the action was punctuated frequently by titters from the audience. Anew himself stomped upstage and glared at us more than once, not for a moment stepping out of his Brutus. On the way home afterwards we stopped off at the Halfway House before Cappagh for refreshments. John Herr downed a couple of small bottles of Guinness but the rest of us were more abstemious. Then we set off again. At the level crossing we had to wait for a train to pass. A creamery lorry pulled up alongside us. Charlie Bolger, seeing the possibility of a tow to Cappoquin, wheeled himself into position at the tail of it. The rest of us laughed at his antics. The truck would not be taking it easy along the straight four miles of good highway to his home town. Then we watched the train go by. I glanced back at my schoolmate. He was calmly testing his grip on the corner post of the lorry. 'Is he *really* thinking of hanging on all the way?' I asked myself. The answer came quickly. The gates opened. The truck accelerated away, taking Charlie with it. Soon they were lost in the dusk. Next day he told us he had held on for the whole four miles and we believed him. He was not one to bullshit. I admired his nerve. Grabbing a tow in town, going up a hill, or dawdling on the flat was standard practice – I had done it myself – but maintaining your grip on the flat on a fast stretch of road, that was daring. Having caught hold, Charlie had committed himself until the lorry slowed down again. Had he let go at speed, he would almost certainly have thrown a wobbly and come off in a heap, possibly suffering serious injury. As the rest of us resumed our pedalling I envied his free-wheeling decision. Those of us from Lismore still had half our return journey to complete and my arse was already sore from a combination of the saddle and the hard bench in the Friary Hall. I rode the last four miles standing. But it had been worth it, something of an adventure, and the Bard had come off the page for the first time.

Of the two Brother Superiors with whom I had personal contact, P. D. was easily the most committed. Or so it appeared to me. My opinion may be coloured by the fact that he was the one in charge throughout all my secondary years. I think we all respected him, and many of us liked him. He never phopped without good reason but when he did, you felt it. Though deep into Mariology he seemed shy and awkward when chatting even briefly to our mothers. A feeling I had, possibly gathered from our mutually embarrassing exchange in the manual room, that he was intolerant of our schoolboy humour with regard to women was confirmed by a minor skirmish in the Fifth Year instigated by the irreverent John Herr. Our science teacher Vin O'Donoghue was late back from lunch and while we were awaiting his return John held up a narrow-necked laboratory flask and chuckled, 'Our next experiment will be how to get a woman to piss into a pint bottle without splashing.' We all burst out laughing, even belatedly Seán Dennis, who could take umbrage at such quips. A second later P. D. irrupted into the room from the neighbouring class and, fixing us with a fearsome stare, shouted, 'Who said that? I heard it.' None of us gave way. He continued eyeing us for a minute or so, during which I with my record felt particularly uncomfortable, then snorting and muttering in disgust, went back to his class, leaving the door open. When Vin came in a little later he was scowling too, or almost. He could not quite conceal from us a flicker of amusement as he closed the door. But he was most likely annoyed as well. Had it not been for our disruption he could have entered the room via the door leading to the Intermediate Certificate class and the Superior might never have realised he was late.

Wholly modest, Lee only ever displayed one trace of vanity, the pride he took in his ability to draw perfect circles freehand on the blackboard. We had never known anyone else with this accomplishment. Every time, swish, and it was there, compass perfect. P.D. knew we admired this rare geometric skill of his and whenever he drew an exceptionally perfect example – how perfect is perfect! – his pleasure at our gawks of admiration would reveal itself in a brief, self-conscious smile. In his absence we used to try to emulate his artistry but even our best efforts failed to match his worst.

Not quite so flawless was the Superior's conspiracy theory of the history of Christianity upon which he would digress on occasion. He exhorted us always to employ the full word 'Christmas' rather than 'Xmas' when referring to, or writing about, this festival. 'Xmas' was an excrescence urged upon us by the forces of evil to shut Christ out of the season. 'X' equalled 'Mr X', the anonymous cliché of police thrillers. Hence, the reduction of the Lord's name to anonymity. He saw the machinations of the Antichrist in the destruction of Hiroshima and Nagasaki, the second the most Catholic city in Japan, and in the levelling of Monte Cassino by the Allied Military Forces. In the case of the Italian monastery, why were the Germans not simply starved out? There was no other way to explain the barbarity of such events. As to the Dark Ages, this era was so-called by Protestants and anti-Catholic individuals who were jealous of a period that was, in fact, a golden age of early Christianity. Here, as later scholarship was to testify, he was on surer ground.

In a wholly innocent manner he gave me the impression he had little idea of how to communicate with those who were not of his own faith. When Paul Rice, the Protestant son of the new owner of the Devonshire Arms Hotel, surprisingly joined our class for a period Lee had difficulty in coping with him. Not that Paul was in any way disruptive. On the contrary, he was a model pupil. It was as if the Superior resented the English boy's presence. Paul, it was obvious, did not know what was required of him, either. And who could blame him? Coming into our class, as he did, in the middle of the school year it was hard enough for him to acclimatise to our free-wheeling ways, let alone to the peculiarities of our teachers. There was for him the added embarrassment of having to sit on his own at the back of the class reading a book while the rest of us were given Catholic religious instruction. He would sit out this period with his hands over his head, looking down at the page, and sometimes out of boredom used to peer at Lee through the slits of his fingers, which greatly irritated the teacher for some reason. The unhappy relationship did not last long. Paul soon, and wisely, left the school.

Brother Lee himself left Lismore to take up a post in faraway County Monaghan in the August of 1954 after I had done my Leaving Certificate in which, sadly, I was again to fall short of his expectations. He was replaced by Brother Doody. That I managed to pull up so much in English and Latin was due to Brother Cullen, who had replaced Barrett in 1952. It was no fault of Lee's that I was weak in maths; I had decided that I had no real interest in this subject. Had it not been for him and Cullen I would probably not even have gained the Pass I did. But one other factor had concentrated my mind. I knew that Dad was ailing and was only hanging on in his job until such time as I had completed my secondary education. For the first time, possibly, I had been forced to think seriously about my responsibility to my parents.

For me the most welcome aspect of my success in passing my exam was coming so close to Honours in Latin and English. I had lost all interest in these under Fishy, and Cullen's arrival did little to improve things at first. Fifth Year was a cushy number because you had no exams at the end of it so I had seen little of him during that period. It was when our class started its last year that he took us over fully. A number of traits made Cullen memorable. He was a tall lean man with a stoop. Thin-rimmed glasses and a long, inquisitive nose lent him an icy air and he could burn you with caustic wit. Around town he sported a hat that had a wider brim than the usual Brothers' headgear. In church he gave the impression he was not over-concerned with the religious demands of his calling. Years later I was to find a ringer for him in 'Bec-de-Gaz' of Jean Vigo's revolutionary French film *Zéro de Conduite*. In sport he had no interest whatsoever but one day, idly tapping on his snuff-box, he let out a remark about the time he had 'topped Mount Brandon', one of the highest peaks in the country. There was a stunned silence in the science room where we were sitting. Seán Dennis, who had gained an Honours Leaving Certificate the previous year and was doing some extra study before going on to teacher training, broke it with a loud guffaw. Wide grins suffused the mugs of the rest of us.

'What's so odd about me climbing a mountain?' Cullen snapped and zapped us with a long dictation.

Long dictations were a real sweat and he dished them out fast, so fast your wrist would be hanging off at the end of them.

'Aisy!' Charlie Bolger used to exclaim, head down.

'Whoa!' John Herr would add.

Cullen's eyes would smoke like an open freezer. He might pause, or he might turn up the heat.

For Seán, dictations were a cinch. He was ambidextrous. You went green with envy when you saw him calmly switching his pen from one hand to the other while your own wrist was going numb. A better implement would have helped. The pencil-slim wooden holder tired your wrist quickly and it was difficult to avoid making blobs with the splayed and scratchy nib. Such items as fountain pens and propelling pencils were prized possessions. Not lightly used on dictation exercises. Cullen always availed of the quiet of the dictation session to stuff some snuff up his nozzle. Knowing this was going on, our heads would invariably angle upwards, as if controlled by a single mechanism, to catch the wonder of it. For our teacher, it was an irritation so intense he would pay us back twice over – double the speed and double the length of paragraph.

A battle of wills developed between Cullen and me during the first six months of our acquaintance. I distrusted him as he was Fishy's successor and he, with his cold sarcastic manner, made no concessions to me, nor indeed to any of us. Slowly, however, and very much in the teeth of opposition from me, he revived my interest in Latin and English so that I began to study these subjects willingly again. I even found myself enjoying some of the poems in our pale blue anthology, *Senior Poetry – Matriculation and Leaving Certificate Poetry*, edited by Patrick J. Kennedy, especially Coleridge's *Rime of the Ancient Mariner*. One of our earlier clashes centred on an essay he had asked us to write, taking as a theme a favourite landscape in our region. The last evening before I was to hand in my effort I still had not written anything and was casting around in desperation for something to inspire me. By chance I came across in our bookcase an old orange-coloured *County Waterford Official Guide* that was very descriptive of the Knockmealdowns and there I found the spur I needed, a passage about Baylough that I could easily doctor. In a phrase I had lifted wholly, 'a small tarn overshadowed by the mountains', Cullen's long nose quickly detected the stench of plagiarism and he confronted me about it when he was returning the marked essays. There was a genuinely humorous side to him and when he was in the mood, which was rare enough, he could grin in an engaging way.

'Did you really write that yourself?' he asked with a lift of his eyebrows.

He had put me on the spot in front of the class but I had no intention of giving in to him. Besides, the rewritten paragraph from the pamphlet only constituted one section of the essay. There was some of my own stuff in there as well.

'Yes,' I brazened.

'Hmm,' he grunted reflectively and stroked his chin. 'And how did you come up with the word "tarn"?' His eyes scanned the two and a half pages of foolscap again.

'I found it in the dictionary we have at home,' I put on a hurt expression.

'Hmm, he hummed again, "and you really wrote it all yourself?'

'I did.'

'Fine.' He handed me back the pages. There was a gleam of admiration in his eye, I thought, which could have been interpreted either as a compliment to my writing or to my bare-faced chancing.

Either way I was happy, although I was less pleased at being forced to lie in public. Shortly after that incident the teacher and I seemed to acquire a greater tolerance of each other, with the benefit for me of knuckling down belatedly to studying for my Leaving. Subsequently, the only thing I held against him, hardly his fault as it was on the curriculum, was the turgidity of Chesterton and Belloc, writers so excruciatingly dull I was forced to believe that only one reason kept them on our reading list, their trumpeting Catholicism. A further chore was the poetry of the Armagh essayist George William Russell, who fancied himself as a pair of initials. Fortunately, we only touched on the trio, who gave me the distinct impression that they had never known a childhood.

Getting phopped was an occupational hazard of school attendance. Every teacher could find a reason to lay into you, even if that reason was generated by his own excess, i.e. a momentary surge of contrariness or a simple hangover. In such moments you could get picked on as easily for being good as for being bad. On the whole, we accepted a system that was connived at by parents and teachers, even when a particularly painful barrage brought tears to our eyes, the tears as much the fruits of public humiliation as of pain. Not that we always took our phops without protest. 'Whoa!' a hardened student might grin as he took his medicine, causing the exasperated teacher to throw in an extra phop in answer to such insolence. As we grew older corporal punishment tended to decrease. Possibly it was we ourselves who were in the process of maturing but, just as likely, our teachers recognised that there could be hazards for them in confronting with the strap hulking lads who were fast approaching manhood. Michael Doocey of Ballyea, one such lad then in Fifth or Sixth year, left one teacher in no doubt that if an attempt was made to use the leather on him any more the teacher would meet with physical resistance. The Brother saw the logic of the challenge and backed off. It was a comforting encounter for the class.

The Christian Brother favoured a custom-made black leather strap, slotted into a specially tailored, thigh-high pocket in his long flowing gown. Some leathers were said to have had pennies, or even strips of lead, sewn into them for added weight in the strike, a rumour I was never able to substantiate from any of the instruments that I peered at, or handled surreptitiously. Lay teachers who used the strap might slip it self-consciously into the inside pocket of their jacket like it was a .38 automatic – Tommy Keane, who mostly kept his holstered, did this – or keep it in the drawer of the teachers' desk where it was vulnerable to our thieving fingers.

Vin O'Donoghue actively disliked the instrument, which is not to say that he did not phop us as well. His preference was for a well-seasoned ash or hazel plant that he liked to lay across the very tips of our fingers, a tingling refinement for the recipient compared to the crude phop on the flat of the hand. Three feet long, the plant just fitted into the drawer of the high desk in the Intermediate Room. Fortunately for us, this desk often remained unlocked so it was common for his canes to disappear. Vin, an easy-going man, did not relish phopping but there were periods when, for one reason or another, he decided he had to make a point of showing us who was boss. When I was in Second Year or Inter he was making free with a very nice piece of hazel to which he had become particularly attached. Chatting one lunchtime to Mikey Coleman, who was in a more senior class, I discovered that we had both smarted under it that morning.

'Time we did something about this,' Mikey said. 'Where is it now?'

'In the desk in our room,' I answered, 'but he might have locked it.'

'He might not too. Let's go and have a look.'

We strolled up the wrought-iron staircase and entered the first classroom on our right. Mikey went straight to the desk and tugged at the heavy drawer. It opened immediately and there, invitingly lying across a few books and a duster, was the cane.

'Bit long to take outside,' I observed.

'Not a problem,' said the cool senior. He snapped the cane once, then twice, over his knee and went over to the corner by the window. There he lifted a loose floorboard and shoved the broken pieces down as far as he could. Then he replaced the board and stood up.

'He'll phop no more with that,' he said with satisfaction.

We rejoined the lads in the yard and passed the word along. Later in the afternoon Vin went round the back of the desk to get out the stick and phop one of us, Murph probably, who had provoked him just to see his reaction when he discovered the cane was missing. He opened the drawer with a flourish. Our expectant eyes noted his lips forming a curse but he sought no explanation of us. He snapped the drawer shut, stalked into the First Year room, borrowed a leather from the Brother there and dished the willing recipient who had had nothing to do with the fecking of the cane an extra couple of phops for good measure. 'Pissing agin the wind,' I could sense him thinking. He had had to put up with a lot from us too.

My own first contact with the Irish lay teacher had not been very promising.

'Ballantyne? What kind of a name is that?' he said in Irish with some disparagement, on my joining his class. 'What's the Irish for it?'

'O'Bailintín,' I said hesitantly, thinking he had to know because he had been teaching my brother for four years by that time, and because it was the version I had been given in the primary school.

'I shall call you '<u>de</u> Bailintín',' he decided authoritatively, following Norman practice although my surname was Scottish.

I was annoyed that he saw fit to make a bit of a fuss about it. Was he implying that because I had a strange name there was something foreign about me? There was also something snobbish about the 'de'. Minor as it was, the episode caused me to search out the Irish names in my family – McDonagh, Morrissey, Cullinane, Magrath, Duffy, Phelan. I was especially proud of the first-mentioned when Dad told me that his mother was descended from the Sligo McDonaghs who had gone off with the Wild Geese to distinguish themselves in the Irish Brigades of France in the eighteenth century.

After that contretemps I got on well with Vin, give or take a few phops here and there. I liked him because he was straight. And we had an affectionate nickname for him, 'Finooka' (associated with 'Pooka', I suppose). He was an excellent Irish teacher; the language being his *raison d'etre*. And he was good at geography, another subject for which I had a taste. For a time I was heavily into the geology component of this subject, especially drumlins and eskers, and I became obsessed with the age of the Earth, struggling to imagine how *anything* could be as old as the pre-Cambrian and Jurassic rocks of our islands. Newfoundland, combining our teacher's interests, came over the horizon as *Talamh an Éisc,* the land to which earlier hardy generations of fishermen from the estuarine basin of the Three Rivers spilling into Waterford Harbour, and the wider catchment area along the coast, set hazardous sail to catch the teeming cod on the Grand Banks.

I was able to graft on archaeological and anthropological questions too. There was good reason to wonder what ancient remains were under my feet when I stood on the summit of the Round Hill. At home I drew myself a map of North America on to which I used to record, as I came to learn of them from my private reading and from the movies, the names of the Indian nations of that huge continent and the regions that they traditionally inhabited. Vin also taught us general science, but this was not a subject in which he was especially accomplished at imparting knowledge. We learned a smattering of biology, chemistry and physics from notes that he had put together years previously. Of the three components I think I only managed biology with any success. His methodology, probably a product of its time, was scarcely geared to rivet you, e.g. in teaching biology he would come in with a box full of coloured chalk and proceed to copy meticulously onto the blackboard from his notes, or from an advanced textbook, multicoloured illustrations of cross-sections of plants and trees. We would laboriously copy these into our jotters with the aim of memorising the facts illustrated. Chemistry was more practical. We used to gather in groups around Bunsen burners or balances and attempt a variety of experiments – rekindling flames on wax tapers with oxygen, boiling water in glass beakers and adding sawdust to show up the circulation patterns, pHing acids and alkalis with litmus paper, measuring the meniscus on liquid surfaces, titrating with pipettes and burettes, weighing salts before and after burning, messing about with mercury and sodium. The balances, each in a separate glass case, were ranged around the perimeter of the Science Room. Behind the desks in the middle of the room stood a large black-topped bench on which a number of Bunsens rested. Mishaps occurred from time to time when somebody mixed the wrong chemicals. When I was in First Year some of the seniors burst out of the Science Room, followed by clouds of black smoke. Nothing special. The smoke quickly dissipated once the windows were opened. A dark stain remained on the white ceiling for some months afterwards, testimony to the backfired experiment. P.D. took us for science in the first years, Vin in Fifth and Sixth years. In my final year, however, the Superior appeared to be initiating a change when he took over the teaching of this subject to the Sixth Year.

Some of the boys were keen enough to try a few experiments of their own, like silvering copper pennies with mercury to make passable half-crowns. Now and again a few of these 'forgeries' would turn up in shopkeepers' tills and complaints would be made to the school. The Brothers had to treat such discontent seriously and the mercury would be locked away until the heat was off. We youngsters had little sympathy for the complainant. If a man was eejit enough to let someone slip a bad lookalike across him – the silvered penny was smaller in circumference and lighter in weight than the silver half-dollar – he could hardly complain afterwards. Better forgeries were made of lead. These were detectable because they were heavier and less silvered than the real thing. But you might not necessarily spot one in a handful of change. The leaden coins, it was commonly supposed, were made from moulds by some of the more accomplished metal workers among the tinkers, who were known for their expertise in repairing pots and pans. No doubt there were other adventurous metallurgists in the settled community who tried their hand too. I do not recall hearing of any local tinkers being hauled before the courts for forgery. But these coins did circulate. I was allowed to handle one furtively on a couple of occasions and Dad showed me one in the barracks. Such experiments illustrated the everyday possibilities of science, at least.

Tweeds were favoured by lay teachers, male and female. Vin's own choice was a heavy grey suit, flecked with brown and green, which he wore winter and summer. Miss Eva Wright, his sartorial counterpart at the Presentation Convent, liked to appear in tweeds also. The drawback of tweed was that it made an irresistible target for sticky-backs when the teacher was writing on the blackboard. Miss Wright's slim shoulders may not have had to endure them but Vin's broad back was wide open to attack. One day he appeared in the Science Room hosting about ten burrs, which provoked a wave of giggling around the class. John Herr happened to be sitting in the front row and gave us reason for further merriment when he leaned forward and picked a couple off the back of the teacher, who was busy chalking up a diagram, and lobbed them back on the suit again. Vin looked around and shook his head.

'What's the matter with ye?' he asked, perplexed, and surveyed our juvenile faces for a clue to the skittishness. 'Ye're like a bunch of little children.'

Paul Rice was also in the front row and we had failed to appreciate that he did not find the situation at all as funny as the rest of us did. 'It's those things on your back, sir,' he said, putting himself in our black books as a tell-tale.

'What things?" Vin looked over his shoulder.

"These, sir,' Paul picked off a burr and showed it to him.

'Thank you, Paul,' said Vin courteously and took off his jacket and peeled off the rest of the offending objects. 'Babies ye are,' he glowered witheringly at the rest of us and sermonized us to grow up.

The irony of the situation was that we were taking the rap for one of the seniors, Michael O'Farrell, who was in my brother's class doing his Leaving. In that same class was Vin's son Pat and it must have been a bit of a trial for him to see a classmate taking the piss out of his father. Or maybe not? Perhaps he enjoyed it as much as anybody? Being a teacher's son, you had to live with these things. O'Farrell it was, we learned later, who had popped the burrs, one by one, onto Vin's back. Michael came from a landed family and lived in a fine dwelling, Ballyanchor House, situated a mile and a half out the Ballyanchor Road beyond the school. An uncle, Seán O'Farrell, a gregarious man with a sense of style, lived in equally fine accommodation at Ashbourne House, about a mile out the Hospital Road in Townparks East. His nephew, with his round face and full lips, resembled a cherub, or a youthful Charles Laughton. Everything he did was fastidious. He carried himself fastidiously, dressed fastidiously in the best tweeds, ate fastidiously, rode a bicycle fastidiously, drawled fastidiously in both Irish and English. During his senior years at the school he went through an intense Gaelic phase after he discovered that he was a distant descendant of the Tipperary writer, Charles Kickham. Thenceforth, designating himself 'Michael Charles Kickham O'Farrell', he would bombard the local newspapers with letters and poems on matters of local and national interest. At the Wine Vaults he used to try Mary McCarthy's patience by insisting on being served in Irish, a practice in which he was joined for a time by Dervla Murphy who refused to hand over the money for her groceries until she too was given the amount in our native tongue. He developed a habit of going to auctions, at times taking my brother along with him. 'You never know where you might pick up an Old Master,' he confided to Mam, who viewed his airs and graces with amusement. His making fun of Vin was in line with his general reputation as a prankster. He had been known to fill balloons with water in the Science Room and drop them on the heads of unsuspecting students and teachers in the yard below. When Tommy Keane incurred his wrath through some injudicious remark Michael, in true patrician fashion, armed himself with a gun, albeit a pellet gun, and sought satisfaction by sniping the teacher in the back of the ear from an upstairs window of the school when the Kerryman was parking his bike, a stunt that almost got him expelled.

Our Irish teacher represented more than just education to us. We read about him regularly in the national newspapers because of his senior administrative role in the running of the affairs of the GAA. He achieved the highest office in that body when he was elected president in April 1952. On his return to our classroom John Herr, so often the bane of his life, rose to his feet as our spokesman to offer congratulations. John spoke haltingly but effectively in Irish after which we all applauded, moving Vin to respond quietly and fluently in Irish and English, 'Of all the congratulations I have received this is the nicest. Thank you, boys.' We all liked Vin though we may not have taken his concepts of nationality and honour as seriously as he did, particularly when he argued in a GAA address that these had 'little chance of existence in the sensual atmosphere of the dance hall and the cinema'. You had to feel warm toward a man who would turn his back in disgust on an unruly class, as he once did with us, and hiss, 'Piss down my back and tell me I'm sweating.'

Because I liked Irish I had less reason to be troublesome in his class than in others. In fact, I was so keen to progress in the language I used to pester my parents to allow me to study for a month at the summer school in the nearby Gaeltacht of Ring. Children came from all over the country to attend the school, run by a man known simply as 'An Fear Mór', a pretentious soubriquet, the authoritarian overtones of which were lost on us youngsters. As with my efforts to be permitted to join the Lismore Boy Scouts, these pleas also fell on deaf ears. It did not occur to me that there might be financial considerations in this case. I was particularly disappointed with Mam because her mother Anastasia Cullinane, who came from Ballyneale in the Parish of Mothel, was a native speaker; hardly surprising as Irish was widely spoken in County Waterford up to the late nineteenth century. Dad, who had taught himself the language using a Linguaphone course in order to be accepted for training as a *garda*, had forgotten most of it and could only help me with my lessons when I was little. When I scolded them for their lack of encouragement it was firmly emphasised to me that neither of them had had the benefit of the schooling I was getting.

My grandfather James Morrissey, in contrast to his wife, was also ignorant of Irish. Mam and her brothers and sisters only heard their mother speaking the language when she and her mother, Mary Magrath, were discussing something that was not intended for young ears or when relatives and friends of the Cullinanes from the Comeragh district came to visit. What smattering the children picked up was through attendance at Gaelic League classes where the girls also learned step dancing. What seemed to me on my grandmother's part a shameful lack of interest in furthering the re-establishment of Irish was explained by my Aunt Nan as a simple matter of economics. Her mother had more than enough on her hands in trying to rear a family of nine. Within the family she never expressed a preference for Irish over English, or English over Irish, but my aunt felt that it was unlikely that she would have wanted her children to follow the precedent of the day and learn English only.

For all my love of the language I never got round to entering for the gold *Fáinne*, although I did gain the silver one (long lost) early on. Outside school hours there were other possibilities of furthering one's knowledge. Diarmuid Ó Drisceoil, a feverish enthusiast, used to teach both the Irish language and Irish dancing at evening classes organised by the *Conradh na Gaeilge* and the *Cumann Culthúrtha na h-Aiséirighe* in the town. Billy 'Irons' O'Brien of Lower Botany, one of my brother's classmates, played a leading part in these activities and used to compere *céilidhes* every Friday at the town hall. In addition to Irish, only two other adult education classes were offered. Over the winter months in the evenings Seán Baston taught woodwork in the manual room at the CBS and Miss Veale domestic economy at the Presentation Convent.

Overall, I would say again that what I enjoyed most about school was being away from it. Which is not to say that I did not enjoy learning. I had good times at school and was happy to be given new perspectives on the world. But something always seemed to come between me and the subjects on which I was keen. At times it was the understandable limitations of our small school. The Brothers could cope with six or seven subjects for Inter Cert (with history and geography counting as one) but could only manage five, maybe six, for Leaving. In large towns and in the cities students could attempt as many as eight subjects in both examinations. Not a range I would have wanted to undertake myself! But I would have welcomed more choice. I was very fond of drawing when I was in junior secondary, which is not the same thing as saying I was any good at it, and would have liked very much to take the subject beyond Inter Cert but this was not possible. There just were not facilities for teaching it after the middle year. History I dropped also, though this may have been my choice. Other times a personality clash between a teacher and me arrested my progress. My problem was that the learning I enjoyed above all was that which I acquired through an everyday awareness of my surroundings and of the people amongst whom I lived. It was a lazy man's approach to education, I suppose, but in the idyllic setting of Lismore I was in no hurry to grow up. I became expert at screwing an extra day or two of convalescence after I was ill, playing my solicitous mother off against my sceptical father. When classes came to an end at lunchtime I would be in the first charge of juniors through the school gate on the Ballyanchor Road. We exited on foot, on roller-skates and on bikes and continued our career down Gallows Hill, occasionally with mishap.

John O'Riordan narrowly avoided cracking his skull when he accepted a lift on the bike from his classmate Michael Dennis. They were blazing down the hill shouting their heads off when the screws fixing the carrier to the frame beneath the saddle suddenly gave way. I saw the carrier slip back over the wheel and hit the ground with John still sitting on it. The axle screws held and as he was towed along, showering sparks in his wake, he somehow managed to maintain his balance. After a momentary fright he started laughing and hung on like he was tobogganing in the snow until Michael ground to a halt. When he rose to his feet he did not have a scratch on him. Which was more than could be said for the road.

Natural curiosity and incidental learning left you with lifelong nuggets of useless information. For many years it confounded and annoyed me that I could not hold a pencil behind my ears like most of my pals could. This small mystery dogged me in spasms until one day I read in a film magazine a piece of gossip about Clark Gable which implied that the star had had a cosmetic operation to have his big floppy ears pinned back to the sides of his head because it was reckoned they stood out too much. 'Jasus!' I thought, 'that's it!' I picked up a pencil and ran to the bathroom to have a peek at my closely shorn head in a mirror. Sure enough, I had jug ears. No wonder I could never lodge a pencil behind them. I tried again. The pencil just fell off. It was a disappointment to me that I would have to go through life without this accomplishment but the situation was hardly drastic enough to merit surgery.

Birthmarks also intrigued us. Pete Neville had the most famous one, a white patch on the side of his otherwise black head of hair. Seán O'Connell had a sizable brown one on one of his thighs. Nobody else had anything as dramatic as those although there were many smaller and less conspicuous examples for us to wonder at. Curiosity about people's names would remind me that I had read in Ripley's *Believe It or Not* that the man who claimed to have the shortest name in the world was one citizen of the United States of America (where else?) called Ed Ek. Ripley obviously drew solely from Western sources. A Burmese politician called U Nu was soon to appear on the world scene.

In spite of indifferent students like me the Lismore Christian Brothers' School regularly produced good results in State examinations. Students also won county council scholarships for entry to higher education courses – Seán Dennis and Joe Martin were two who succeeded in 1949. There was a catch about these, however. The amount won was only large enough to cover fees and books. Unless your parents could afford to pay your board and lodging, or unless close relatives in a university city could put you up for little or nothing, you had no option but to refuse your prize for excellence. The cash value of the award could only be claimed if you went on to higher education. Students from disadvantaged families, consequently, suffered the disillusionment of knowing they had the ability to take a degree but not the means of achieving it. My classmate, Chris 'Scanner' Scanlan, and Kip Tobin from the class under me, both Botany lads, won county council scholarships and had to turn them down. There was no doubt that, given the chance, they would have graduated successfully. Kip, for example, was very good at mathematics. Army cadetships were much sought after. Two of my brother's classmates, Jim Fives of Tourin and Michael Browne of Cappoquin, gained these in the one year, 1949. Successful Leaving Certificate students who gained a job in a bank were considered a success as well, which mystified me, as any such environment that I had ever had occasion to visit was stultifyingly dull and unimaginative.

In their quiet way, it was the girls of the Presentation Convent who were achieving the most success. But they worked for it. In the run-up to examinations the nuns would have them back at school from 6.00 p.m. to 8.00 p.m. for extra study, something unheard of at the Brothers'. And it paid off. The girls won numerous county council and Earl of Cork scholarships. The Earl of Cork, won on Intermediate results, was of particular assistance to the poor student because it enabled her to stay on and do her Leaving. An economically deprived family would have found it difficult, if not impossible, to support the student otherwise. When it came to academic excellence the best of the girls produced results at which the best of the boys could only wonder. Guard Murphy's daughter Rosie won prizes at everything she attempted. Margaret McCarthy of the Wine Vaults came first in Ireland in the Civil Service Examinations in November 1947. And Carmel Byrne, an ex-student of the Presentation sent away to a posh school in Limerick by her bank-clerk father to better pursue music at which she was especially accomplished, showed just what the girls were capable of in averaging a staggering 90% in eight subjects for her Leaving! A feat beyond my comprehension.

For the disadvantaged boys and girls of the town London, Coventry and Birmingham – the English cities to which most Lismore people emigrated – held the future. But across the water a possible pitfall lay in wait for the boys. National Service was mandatory and after two years working in Britain young Irishmen, like their British counterparts, became eligible for call-up into Her Majesty's Armed Forces. A few of the lads did their stint but most managed to stay ahead of the British authorities by moving around from city to city. There was one unfailing method of buying time – personation. If you had a brother, relative or close friend whose circumstances were such that it was highly unlikely he would be emigrating to England (he might already have emigrated to Australia or the United States even), you could come home, close the book on your own identity and return to a different city in Britain a short time later in the person of the co-operative relative or friend. That allowed you to work for another two years. Sometimes the person co-operating might charge for this service. Other times permission might not be sought at all. Emigrants who had been personated without their knowledge turned up in England to find call-up papers slapped on them with undue haste. School did nothing to prepare you for this eventuality.

CHAPTER TWENTY

Sexuality and Sin

IT HAD TO BE SAID that school did not help very much in matters of sexuality either. We were in the Leaving Certificate class before P.D. tried his well-meaning best to put us straight on procreation. Too late on bald facts. From street conversations with my pals, the study of dictionaries and encyclopaedias and other literature of a less academic nature, from the observation of my own body and those of others, male and female, and from the rutting of dogs and farm animals, I had already sussed out that babies were not found under cabbages. But his unusual sensitivity effectively re-pictured the somewhat crude images that I had created until then.

My first real sexual encounter, aside form a few potty fantasies about my favourite Auntie Bab, was wholly accidental. I was about 11 years of age, recovering in bed from a bout of flu, when out of sheer boredom I discovered that I could give myself some nice sensations by idly stroking my prick. I do not think there was an erotic thought in my mind. I was merely enjoying the feeling. Vague misgivings suggested that anything so pleasurable had to be sinful somewhere along the line but I preferred not to heed those. At most, I figured, the transgression could only be venial, certainly nothing about which to make me want to rush off and make hasty enquiries. The sensations grew stronger, as if my prick was trying to tell me something. I eased off. After a short time, however, I resumed my new-found pleasurable pursuit, rather in the manner in which I was later to play with the gob of spittle above Annie Campion's nose. Then, as with the gob, I overplayed my hand. Waves of voluptuous feeling swept over me and my hand grew sticky beneath the bed-clothes. It could not be piss I knew because piss was 'dry' like water. I was in no hurry to seek an explanation for this new phenomenon. It was enough that it felt so good. I just lay there with a happy grin on my face.

Suddenly Mam shouted from downstairs, 'Jim, Paddy Creane is coming up to see you.'

'Feck!' I cursed. I dried my hand hurriedly on the leg of my pyjamas and tried to compose myself against the bolster.

Paddy bounded into the room on his long legs with a couple of comics for me.

'What are you looking so happy about?' he said. 'I was expectin' to find you sick as a dog.'

'Oh, I, I was just thinkin' of somethin' I read in a comic,' I slurred, twinges of delight still suffusing my body. 'I am really sick, honest. But I'm gettin' better.'

'Here's a couple o' comics for you,' Paddy held them out for me to take.

I drew my left hand out from under the clothes and accepted them. I did not dare uncover my right. For all I knew it could be blood that was all over it.

'Don't come too near me,' I warned, in case he might catch the strange smell that reached my nostrils as I uncovered my hand. 'You might get the flu.'

'I'm after havin' it, sure,' he said unconcernedly and, thankfully, sat on the end of the bed and looked across to the Villa.

'Oh yeh, I forgot. Are you goin' over playin'?'

'Yeh. Mickey and the lads are over at the camp. You can see 'em from here,' he invited.

'I don't think I'd better get up yet,' I drew my left hand back under the covers.

We conversed in that vein until Paddy decided that I was not, perhaps, as well as I looked. He excused himself and left. I waited until I heard him leave the house. Then I sat up and peered out as he crossed the road and climbed in over the Villa wall opposite Feeney's where we had created well-worn toe-holds. Assured that he was gone, I examined my wet pyjamas. No blood. Just something like the paste Dad used for hanging wallpaper. I dashed to the bathroom, washed my genital region with freezing-cold water as best I could, and bounded back into bed again. As I lay there re-warming myself I sensed that I had conjured up one of life's major mysteries. 'What was it at all that could make you feel so good?'

I was to work this unexpected seam of physical delight for the best part of a year before, influenced by my puritanical schooling, I decided that such gratification had to have a darker side to it. That was my mistake. From the moment I confessed in church I moved for the first time from simple, if slightly dubious, venial innocence to the arena of mortal sin. Thereafter every bit of pleasure had to be snatched secure in the knowledge that God was somewhere up there waiting to pull the plug on me – *Ye know not the hour nor the place*. In my agonies of indecision I convinced myself that the mortal bit was in going over the top. Stroking my hard-on was merely a peccadillo, though it did not escape me that prolonging the moment of ejaculation only served to heighten the ecstasy. Happily, like my pals probably – none of us would ever admit to masturbation and, oddly enough, it never occurred to me that girls might have been confronting a similar predicament – I was prepared to take my chances when my need was too great.

As it was one day a year or two later when I found myself down Ballyrafter Flats by the Current, upstream of Bullsod Island. It was warm and sunny and as I lay alone on the grassy bank above the sallies the sensuous rush of the fast-flowing water and the buzzing of the insects combined to make me feel like doing myself a favour. I raised my head and peered across the field behind me to the Canal Bridge. Not a soul in sight. I scrutinised the slopes of the fields on the other side of the river, up to the wooded Warren on the right of them, for a human face or the telltale glint of binoculars. No man, woman, boy or girl to be seen. It was between God and me now. I looked up at the sky. It was hazy, lazy and blue. Even *He* was unlikely to rouse Himself enough on such a gorgeous day to want to launch a sudden thunderbolt at the speck of existence that I represented. I felt a little bad about my guardian angel who, I knew, was right there next to me doing his utmost to redirect my thoughts to higher things but, when the cards are down, it's hard not to ignore the invisible. I reached down inside my trousers. Afterwards, I took out some insurance in the form of a quick act of contrition, washed my hand in the Blackwater, and lay back to dream.

By this time it was clear to me that my sexual activity was inextricably associated with contemplation of the opposite sex. In the early days I just jerked off because it was nice. It made you feel good, so why not? Later I became more adventurous, which forced me to start washing my own socks. I often wondered to what cause Mam attributed this turn of domesticity. Did she believe I was beginning to assume a little responsibility for the clothes I wore? Or did she just think, 'Ah, he's at that stage now'. She never volunteered an observation and I maintained a poker face. The most embarrassing thing about the whole business was coming face-to-face with your priests in the confessional. Oh it was dark and dingy in there and though you kept your head down and the priest only showed you his profile you knew that he had figured out who you were. The trick was to do the rounds of them all so that you would not be confronting any one of them with the mortal too regularly. And in between, when you were good, you would come up with the venials like, 'I cursed ten times' or 'I told lies' (unspecified) or 'I had immoral thoughts' (specified on request). When you did have a mortal to confess you always started with a few inconsequential items to soften up the priest. He kept saying 'Yes, yes' as you reeled these off, like he knew a big one was coming. After you hit him with it, the next question was, 'How many times?' which always knocked me back a bit. Upon your reply to that depended your penance. I usually came out with anything from a couple of decades of the rosary to the full string. Most priests took it in their stride but one man, a tall, severe friar in Carrickbeg (I was active in Carrick-on-Suir too), quizzed me at length before throwing in a novel slice of scaremongering.

'You could become impotent from doing that. Did you know that?' he said, turning to me full face.

'Yes, Father,' I said, just wanting to get the hell out of there.

'Do you know what "impotent" means?'

'Yes, Father,' I bluffed. 'It means you can't stop doing it.'

He smiled in a superior sort of way. 'Well, yes, you could say that.' Then he put me straight and gave up on me.

Funnily enough, not one priest asked me if I enjoyed myself while I was doing it. But I was offered the consolation of one day legitimising my sexual needs in the eyes of God by getting married. That seemed an awfully long-term solution to someone who was still a schoolboy but I decided that if that was how it would have to be eventually I ought to cast an eye over the marriage business. So I sneaked into the back of the chapel one day to have a peek at a ceremony. Near me, indulging a more romantic curiosity perhaps, sat a few other spectators, mainly women in varying degrees of adulthood, clearly knowledgeable about what was going on. The wedding guests, perhaps twenty persons, were standing in the front pew of the centre aisle while the priest and the man and woman who were tying the knot sustained a mumbled dialogue. It was all over before I realised it. Immediately, the newly married couple, as I supposed they now were, disappeared into the sacristy. Everybody else sat down and chatted animatedly. Before long the couple re-emerged and marched down the aisle in my direction. I did not hang about for the sequel. I had seen enough to inform me that the adult ritual I had heard so much about was surprisingly ordinary.

Busy with my own voyage of discovery, I had for a long time no conception of what girls were going through. I did not even stop to ask myself whether they got any more sex education from the nuns than we got from the Brothers. I suspect we were kept mutually ignorant. Ordering the two sexes in your mind was a painstaking and time-consuming endeavour. When you were very little it was, for example, a thorny problem to address grown-ups. 'Hey, Mrs Woman, can you tell us the time?' you might ask, pluralising yourself as we often did. Tom Feeney was faced with this question when he got onto the wall separating our house from the garage by clambering over the back of a lorry. It had been a simple matter to get that far but now he was faced with a five-foot drop into our yard. The only person in the yard at that moment was Dad who was sitting in an armchair reading a newspaper. Clearly the thing for Tom to do was call Dad and ask him to lift him down off the wall, but how was he to formulate his request? He had never been faced with the problem of addressing Dad directly before. To complicate matters further, Dad happened to be in uniform. Eventually my little pal overcame his bewilderment and spoke to Dad in a way that he felt would uniquely identify him. 'Jim Ballantyne's father, take me down off the wall,' he called out. Which Dad, greatly amused, did. A child from Tallow might have found the situation less problematical and employed the familiar 'You sir' of his locality.

After the early experience of being in school with girls I lost the facility of making conversation with them. Having no sister myself, I was possibly more disadvantaged than my pals but I think most of us boys were awkward in the company of girls. When I was maybe 13 or 14 my gaucherie left me confused and embarrassed before a girl of my own age from Dundalk who had wavy red hair, a vivid personality, and a lilting accent that I had heard her employ in a shop. (Frank Mason has informed me that my description fits Bernadette Smyth who used to holiday with her aunt Maisie O'Gorman in Chapel Street.) She came speeding down from the Monument on a bike toward Hogans' gate where Hoagy, Mickey McConnell, Willie Ryan and I were lounging about. I immediately expressed to my pals my admiration for her.

Coincidentally, we had been practising a bit of two-fingered whistling, not the easiest of boyhood arts in which to achieve efficiency. Whistling, in general, was not something that just came to you. You had to work at it. We employed three methods: one, you put your lips together and blew, as Lauren Bacall put it to Humphrey Bogart in *To Have and to Have Not*; two, you drew your lips back tightly against your teeth and blew; and three, you stuck two fingers in your mouth – long and index fingers or thumb and index finger – and blew. If you were Jimmy Colbert, of course, you stuck a variety of fingers in your mouth and vamped with the other hand like you were playing the harmonica. Style one was the basic method and you spent many hours acquiring the technique. Learners always pursed their lips too much and blew too hard to begin with so that they only managed a wheezy exhalation. You had to learn to take it gently. 'Watch me,' a pal who already had the knack would invite and you would focus intently on his mouth as he made it look so easy. Then you would bite your lip in annoyance when you failed to replicate the sound yourself. You would go home, stand in front of a mirror, and try again. Eventually, almost by accident, it clicked. You had picked up an important lifetime skill. Thumper Lineen, after he had perfected the basics, taught himself to whistle breathing in and breathing out so that he was able to produce a seamless tune. His first cousin, Jim 'Plug', adding to his spitting achievement, was a master of the second style, as were Beaver and Cal. This was the style that the Lone Ranger employed to call his horse Silver, especially handy when the baddies had left him tied to a tree. I never managed to become proficient in this technique. I did okay on style three though. Even managed a bit of a tune after some tuition from Jimmy Colbert.

'Bet you wouldn't whistle after her,' Mickey challenged.

'I would,' I said defiantly.

'Go on, then. Now's your chance.'

Instinctively I felt it was not the right thing to do but, having been snared into a dare, I saw no option. As the girl passed, I put my fingers in my mouth and whistled as loudly as I could. To my horror I saw the object of my approbation snap on her brakes and spunkily wheel about. I fled into the bushes at the bottom of the nearby *Reilig* and cowered behind them as she coolly rode up to my pals and stopped.

'Well?' she demanded with an imperious toss of her red head. 'What do ye want?'

Her singsong accent cut into me because I had so much wanted to meet her, but not in this way.

'We don't want anything,' said Hoagy curtly.

'Ye whistled, didn't ye?'

'No, it wasn't us at all,' said Mickey defensively.

'You bollocks!' I thought. 'After puttin' me on the spot.'

'Course it was. Do ye think I'm an eejit?'

'No, it wasn't us,' Willie assured her.

'Then who was it? The whistle came from here.'

I sank behind the dense foliage.

'It was that fella in there in the bushes,' said Mickey.

'You fuckin' bollocks!' I swore to myself.

'What bushes?' She waved an arm around in a half circle.

'Beyond,' said Hoagy, nodding in my direction and he and Mickey, real pals, laughed as I probably would have, had I been in their place.

'Hey, you in there, what do you want?' the girl, still standing astride her bicycle, called out from the gate.

'Jasus Christ, will she never go away!' I asked myself but remained silent.
'I think ye're coddin' me,' she said to the others. 'There's no one in there.'
'Oh he's in there all right,' Mickey assured her.
'You in the bushes,' she shouted again, now to my despair, icy and impatient as well as persistent, 'what do you want?'

A long silence ensued during which I crouched like a frog, cursing myself as much as my pals, and tried to compose the humiliating apology I would have to offer my princess when she took the inevitable next step and came in to unmask me.

Fortunately, she decided otherwise. 'Aren't ye *silly*,' she said in a raised voice, very grown-up and obviously including me, then as abruptly as she had descended from her saddle, she remounted and rode off again.

I waited for a while in case she might suddenly return. Then I emerged shamefacedly to endure the jibes of my friends. Mickey was fuming over her parting shot. That a girl should have addressed him in that way! But what could he say? He was the one who had put me up to it. It was only water off a duck's back to the rest of my pals. For myself, it had been a well-deserved comeuppance. My first encounter with a sophisticated girl had left me floundering ignominiously. I had a long way to go to acquire the skills of addressing the opposite sex effectively.

My wolf-whistle had backfired so totally there was scant hope that I would achieve any greater success with a wink, that other weapon in the male armoury of communication. You could not avoid noticing that whistling and winking were male accomplishments. In a girl, or even a woman, they were remarked upon. And adults seemed to favour the wink over the whistle, hardly surprising in a nation where a nod and a wink is as much a greeting as anything else. As a means of non-verbal communication the wink had its limitations but, that said, it was possible to convey a certain range of meaning with it. There was the greeting wink accompanied by a suitable inclination of the head, the bold wink of the young fella who fancied a young one, the nudge-nudge wink of the three-card-trick man, the tortuous wink of the man who wanted to be certain sure you had got the message, the Robert Mitchum droop – more a sore eye than a wink.

As with whistling, winking was not a skill that just grew on you. You worked at it from an early age. By the time I had moved up from primary school I had acquired it myself. My first attempts were complete and utter failures. Both eyes kept snapping shut instead of one. I used to screw my face up with concentration then tell myself, 'Now!'. But again and again both eyes would close. I sought hints from the lads who already knew how to do it, some of whom were proficient with either eye. Then, as with whistling, I took to practising in front of a mirror. Finally, the day came when I succeeded in uncoupling the movement of one eye from the other. From there I progressed relatively quickly to a mastery of winking with either peeper. The aim after that stage was to be able to wink like James Cagney, mean and meaningful; when and where I would hope to employ this eventual enhancement of my skill was unclear to me. I would be guided by experience. Of one thing I was already sure. I would be wary of using any form of wink to transmit feelings of admiration to females.

Early enough I formed an impression of the shape of women – rounder than men and softer. What was something of a mystery, however, was the kind of underwear they wore. The word 'knickers' sounded odd, if not funny. 'Corset', on the other hand, had a forbidding ring to it. Later on, through reading American film magazines like *Screen* or *Modern Screen,* that my brother used to take, I learned that there were newer sleeker garments to be had nylons, panties, girdles… 'Lingerie' first impacted on me when I read a gushing interview with the American film starlet (as she was then) Shelley Winters about her unlikely – in the context of the Hollywood scene – marriage to the Italian Romeo, Vittorio Gassman, in which she casually let it be known that she had bought 'some sexy lingerie for Vittorio's gaze'. Nearer home, Foxy Flynn was adding another dimension to my understanding in describing what had happened when he took a new girlfriend, home from England, to the one-and-three-pennies at the Palladium.

'I asked her,' he said to me quietly afterwards, 'what do you wear down there?' She just reached down, pulled on the elastic of the knickers and let it slap against her thigh."

'Go on!' I said.

'Aye,' he nodded with such conviction I could almost hear the fleshy twang.

The memory of it was to exercise my imagination for a long time.

Foxy was always ahead of me when it came to an understanding of sexual connotations and techniques. Another time, when we were about 15, he nodded me aside and, peering furtively over his shoulder, opened a Friendly matchbox. In it lay a flesh-coloured piece of rubber that I took to be a balloon.

'Do you know what that is?' he asked. Knowing Foxy as I did, it was a cinch it wasn't a balloon so I decided to play safe and shook my head.

He picked up the item carefully by the tip and dangled it between his index finger and thumb so I could better inspect it. Then he looked at me quizzically again. It still looked like a balloon. Again I shook my head.

'*That*,' said my pal, 'is a French letter.'

'A *French letter!*' I gasped, open-eyed. I had heard about this oddly named number but until that moment had struggled to form an impression of what one looked like – 'French' I could nudge at but why 'letter'? I peered at it closely. 'Can I touch it?'

'Sure.'

I rubbed it gently between my fingers. It was evident how it was supposed to fit on. 'Where did you get it from?'

'One o' the lads home from England,' he said cagily.

'Has it been used?'

'Yeh.'

'How many times can you use it?'

'As many as you like till it wears out,' he said knowledgeably, 'You have to wash it after each time.'

'Have you used it already?'

'I got it off one o' the lads,' he deflected my question, knowing that if he said 'yes' I would then want to know with whom. After that he tucked the item away and shut the matchbox. 'I'll wash it,' he said calmly and added cryptically, 'Then I'll use it.'

While I was impressed with Foxy's know-how, I was not convinced that he kept the piece of rubber with the intention of using it, with a partner at any rate. But I was grateful to him for showing it to me. I knew it would be a long time before I would be experienced in the use of a condom but, at least, I could now say that I had seen one.

The intimate darkness of the cinema was, of course, a conveniently safe ambience in which boys and girls could educate themselves in matters of human physiology. And not always in terms of what went on on the screen. At a matinee in the fourpennies one summer I encountered more than I expected. Twelve, perhaps 13 years of age, I was sitting next to a girl whom I had met for the first time a week earlier. She was from outside the town and had been to England, from where she picked up a veneer of sophistication that made her bolder and more adventurous than me. As the film progressed she inched her warm buttock nearer to mine. It was pleasant and I had no objection. Until suddenly in a prolonged blackout between two scenes her hand slid across and grabbed my penis through my trousers. I sat forward with a start, not knowing how to react, but made no move to push her hand away. As the action resumed on the screen she smiled at me very warmly.

'Do you mind if I leave my hand there?' she whispered.

'No,' I gulped unsurely, not wishing to offend her, and stared intently at the screen, maintaining my awkward posture.

She did not take her hand away until just before the film ended, by which time I was so utterly confused I had lost track of what was going on.

Thereafter, she assumed such proportions in my mind as an occasion of sin I thought it wiser to steer clear of her. It was a great mistake as she could undoubtedly have taught me much more than Foxy Flynn.

One's knowledge of female anatomy was painstakingly acquired. At an early age you spotted the basic difference between boys and girls; we had a mickey and they didn't. Later, they were to gain protuberances that we lacked. Girls, for their part, appeared to be inquisitive about us boys, too, so the obvious solution to both of our quests for understanding was for some of us to get together with some of them. The bushes around the library became our hedge-school. It was indeed, though we were not cognisant of this, a fitting place in which to pool our knowledge. The girls had been taught two basic rules by their mothers: never go off with a fella on your own, and always keep your legs together. We boys had been told nothing by either parent. After some exploratory chats, Barney, Foxy and I embarked on a series of rendezvous with three of our female contacts who, depending on their mood on the night, might or might not decide to turn up. If they did, and often enough they kept their word, class could begin. We operated systematically, each taking an initial partner who was swopped around after a while, then swopped again after another while, so that each boy and each girl had a turn with every member of the opposite sex who was present. Complications would arise when either group brought along a spare face without notice. When it came to choice of partner we all had our preferences but, at the exploratory age of 13 or so, we boys not long out of short pants, the passion of first love was still some way off. Having sorted out the matter of initial partnerships, each pair retired to a different, but proximate, niche of the shrubbery. The girls always kept within earshot of each other so that anything too adventurous could be stamped on quickly. Within this generally agreed framework we chatted softly to our partners, kissed tentatively with tightly closed mouths or more daringly touched one another, again very tentatively, down below. The 'feel' was not something lightly accorded by the girls. And we boys were even slower to allow them to touch us up. Some trait of our upbringing, perhaps, that suggested it was okay for us to give them a feel but not for them to reciprocate. When I did get my first feel of a girl through layers of clothing I was amazed and moved by the softness and firmness of the hidden flesh. I was aware of the warm arms around my neck and the scented smell of my partner. Most of all, I was conscious of my own clumsiness.

Swopping time could be contentious when you and your partner of the moment were enjoying a mutual attraction. You would both delay the moment of change-over as long as possible before surrendering to the demands of the agreed system. Of course, there were occasions too when you or your current partner could not wait to swop. She was bored with your lack of experience or your mind was on another. Nearly always there was one amongst us who wanted to defer the switch.

'Aw, come on lads, 'tis time to change round,' Foxy might moan.

'In a minute,' Barney might respond. 'Sure we're only at it five minutes yet.'

'Five minutes! 'Tis ten at least,' would counter our aggrieved pal, 'Isn't it, Baler?'

'I don't know,' I could usually answer truthfully because I invariably lost track of the time on such occasions.

Sometimes you had barely begun to converse with your partner when one of the girls, piqued for some reason by the fella she was with, would call a swop. The girls would then go into a huddle while we boys idled sheepishly about. After a while they might allow us to resume or, if they were so inclined, might just buzz off and leave us flat. When they followed the second course we would then bawl out the one amongst us who was at fault. The reason for the girl's dissatisfaction could centre on anything from petty jealousy to incompetence. In my case, it was usually the latter, certainly on my first encounters. I was so slow in learning the ropes that on one occasion Barney was forced to take over my experienced, in relative terms, partner who was voicing displeasure at my lack of technique and was threatening a walkout.

'Look!' he said exasperatedly, 'This is how 'tis done,' and in the light of the street lamp that glistened on the evergreen laurel and escallonia I watched his hand snake down my erstwhile partner's thigh.

I could understand my pal's concern and knew it was in his interest to sort out the situation. If I did not measure up, the girls might not agree to meet our particular group again. As it happened, I did not find his particular technique all that illuminating but every little helped.

In time we got to the stage where we became daring enough to ask the girls to show us what they had got down there – in the glint of the lamplight only. By then we knew what they had above, 'dugs'. Or, as one of the lads jocularly christened them, 'creameries'. 'A nice pair of creameries', one of us might remark among ourselves when a well-built woman passed by. Neither term turned me on exactly. The girls had a ready response to our demands that greatly disconcerted us.

'Show us yere's first,' they chorused, 'then we'll show ye ours.'

We came up with unconvincing arguments like, 'Aw 'tis easier for ye to show us than for us to show ye,' or, 'If we show ye first, then ye won't show us,' which were smartly thrown back at us. The mutual distrust saw to it that none of us saw anything of the opposite partner's privates.

But I was also resorting to Dad's *New Gresham Dictionary of the English Language* by Charles Annandale for enlightenment. A knowledge of one or two medical terms was enough to get you started on this and then you were away, at least, in terms of the bald geography of the human reproductive system. Learning that my balls were testicles, my prick a penis, or a woman's cunt a vagina, contributed nothing to my knowledge of human sexuality.

At the age of 12 going on 13 I still was not sure how babies came into the world, and was in no hurry to get to the bottom of the matter. I'd had leads from earlier experiences but had not yet fitted things together. When I was eight my first cousin Michael O'Mara was born in Carrick-on-Suir. I was brought up to my Aunt Peg's bedroom in Mill Street to be shown the new arrival. It was the first baby I had ever seen at close quarters and I wondered why my aunt needed to be in bed to present him to us. It seemed such a tiny thing. I was told that I had been just as tiny when I was 'found'. Three years later, again in Carrick, my Aunt Mary and Uncle Jimmy Morrissey showed me another new baby in their small, galvanised-roofed, Park View home that resembled an upper Botany cottage. The interior was dark and dank and my aunt sat in an old armchair with my tiny cousin Jim resplendent in a froth of white lace. Again I sensed a mystery but again nothing was explained to me. By the second occasion, however, I had made some advance. I was no longer grappling with the yarn that babies were found under cabbages. That, like Santa Claus, had long since been discarded.

It was our observations of the animal world that really started us putting two and two together. What was that dog doing on the other one's back? Why was he thrusting in and out so vigorously, and so obliviously to us? And why was his thing three times its normal length? Why was that stallion's, ass's or jennet's tool hanging down like that? Were the animals in pain? Why were bullocks always jumping up on one another? Why was the cock jumping on the hens? Why were the tiny kittens with their eyes yet unopened sucking at the mother cat's belly? Nor did our innocence stop at that. Feeney's next door had an affectionate old Irish setter called 'Cruiser' and we used to tuck his front paws around our waists and delight in the way he would squeeze us from behind. One day Mrs Feeney came across us playing like that and, with a mingled look of humour and disgust, forbade us ever again to allow the dog to come near us in this way. We were greatly puzzled. Cruiser was the most lovable and harmless of animals.

Glimpses of the private parts of adults were other pieces of the jigsaw you were constructing. Mam used to ask me to scrub the middle of her narrow back sometimes when she was washing herself standing up in the kitchen because she could never quite reach the centre point. She used to cover her breasts decorously with a towel but from behind I could usually see the swell of her flesh when I purposely leant to the side. The first full view of an adult male's penis was accorded me in my aunts' garden in Carrick when my Uncle Jimmy, whom I had been 'helping' in my fumbling 7 or 8-year-old way to clean the greyhound stalls, stood up to relieve himself against the garden wall. I decided I ought to have a piss as well and, positioning myself beside him, pulled up the leg of my short pants. Before I could get my flow underway I was startled by a noisy gush of water that hit the wall next to me. I had never seen a man pissing close-up before and was intrigued by the forceful delivery. My fascination turned to astonishment when I glanced across and saw what Jimmy was holding in his hand, something reddish-brown and thick that looked like a rod of hazelwood.

'Jakus!' I gasped involuntarily.

'What's wrong with you?' Jimmy grinned.

'I never saw a one like that before,' I replied in a hushed voice.

'Sure you'll have one like it yourself when you grow up,' he said calmly and, finishing his business, tucked his thing away and went back to work.

I eyed my tiny prick dubiously.

'Will I?' I asked, finishing a minute later.

'Will you what?'

'Will I really have one as big as yours one day?'

'Sure you will,' Jimmy chuckled.

The next time I laid eyes on a full-grown tool was some seven or eight years later down at the Rock in Lismore. Brooky Lynch from Townparks, home from a spell of working in England, and Mick Coleman from Church Lane were stretched out unselfconsciously on the grass after a nude swim, soaking up the sun and chatting away as coolly as if they were lounging around the Mall Seat fully dressed. Lads home from London always brought with them the saucy flavour of that free-living city, a veneer of cockney perhaps, a slick haircut, a jazzy shirt or tie and, sometimes too, handwritten versions of torrid and explicit sexual encounters that had been copied down from the kind of costly sex books that we understood could be obtained 'over'. Lads would produce these sexy, dog-eared samizdats at the Rock and it was difficult to read them in company without a blush, or maybe a telltale bulge in your swimming togs. By this time, of course, I had learned exactly where babies came from. Beaver Doherty it was who rocked me back on my heels with the truth of it all when the two of us happened to be sitting alone at the Mall Seat.

'That's how it is,' he summed up. 'The man puts his into the woman and they make the baby.'

'Ah, that can't be,' I murmured incredulously. "I don't believe it."

Beaver eyed me a little uncertainly. He appeared apprehensive that he had had to be the one to shatter my illusions, whatever illusions I'd had. It wasn't that we had approached the subject in any deliberate way. It had just surfaced and he, surprised that I, at the age of 13 or maybe even 14, still did not know that there was another use for my tool aside from pissing (and masturbating, but we didn't talk about that), laid the facts on the line.

''Tis true, Jim,' he said apologetically. 'Honest.'

'Ah that can't be,' I repeated, shaking my head.

''Tis,' he assured me quietly.

'I don't know,' I said and, still shaking my head, walked off in a daze and left him.

Why I reacted with such disbelief is difficult to say. I had often seen dogs and other animals coupling and I knew the result of this. Perhaps the idea of humans doing it seemed faintly ridiculous, or maybe I felt that copulation constituted an unworthy method of reproducing the human species?

Other than the handwritten literature that was passed around, access to steamy text and illustration was rare. Easily the sexiest female figure I came across was the *maja* of the painter Goya's *La Maja Desnuda* and *La Maja Vestida* that appeared in a copy of the weekly magazine *Everybody's*, although I was unsure whether it was the look in her eyes rather than her divine body that turned me on. The magazine was my brother's but as he was working in Birmingham by this time I gave myself licence to go up to the attic and remove her from the trunk where he had lodged his journals to take a peek at her.

My first read of a pornographic paperback happened fortuitously when I was 16. Paddy was home from Birmingham on holidays and in the inside pocket of the raincoat he left hanging on the door of the sitting-room I discovered a work by one Hank Janson. I was afraid to ask him if I could borrow it so I used to slip into the room when he was out and snatch a read of it. It did not take long to finish. The explicit sections, on which naturally I concentrated, were exciting to my questing mind but left little to the imagination. In a Zane Grey western, of all things, I had earlier come across just one phrase that conjured up a set of images far more vivid and lasting. The taciturn hero had trekked his new bride across miles and miles of unknown territory, accompanied by a cow, a bull and a wagon, until he reached his dream site by a river. Here, he declared, he was going to build their ranch house. As they set about staking their claim to the surrounding hectares he made it plain that he was thinking of starting a family too.

'Can I come to you tonight?' he asked the heroine simply.

'Of course,' she whispered, after which they continued winning their bit of the Old West.

I filled that scene under the prairie stars with the perfume of wild grass and sage, and the sound of rushing water.

The Janson disappeared from Paddy's pocket a few days before he returned. Presumably he had passed it on to one of his pals.

It took me some time to absorb the full implications of Beaver's revelations. But he had not explained everything. Such things as conception and contraception still had to be cleared up. And here Jim 'Thumper' Lineen came to my assistance when we were on one of our post-scarlatina walks along the Blackwater. As we crossed over the tongue of water by the head of the Current to join Ballyrafter Flats it was explained to me for the first time that a woman was subject to periods. In imparting this information, Jim inadvertantly solved the long-standing mystery of the blood I found in the toilet bowl at home to which no one had ever owned up. 'So that's what it was,' I thought. 'Mam having her period, and she was too embarrassed to tell me.'

'When a woman has her period,' Thumper said authoritatively, 'you can stay on all day and there's no danger of making a baby.' He laughed. 'If you can keep it up and don't mind being covered in blood.'

I was very impressed with Jim's mastery of the facts and wondered how he came to possess them. My own brother, who must have known as much as Jim, never passed on such wisdom to me. Maybe he just figured I knew these things already? Once he nearly caught me with a girl when a few of us younger ones were courting in our exploratory way in the triangle of tree and shrub that tapered down to the Spout between the New Way and Ferry Lane. This triangle, Eugene Dennis has reminded me, was known as the Small Wood to differentiate it from the Plantation Wood farther up in which St Carthage's Well was located. In the gloom of a late October evening he and his classmates Coz and Michael Madden came upon us by accident on the lane side. They had heard us in the bushes and came over to the wall.

'What's goin' on in there?' one of them shouted in mock horror. 'Why aren't ye at the Rosary?'

'Have ye young ones in there?' said another.

And so on.

'Shit!' I panicked when I recognised Paddy's voice. ''Tis my brother,' I whispered to my partner who was enjoying the situation and dived under a bush when the older lads threatened to come in over the wall to see who we were.

But they only leant over the low wall and beat the bushes with their hands. Paddy came within a few feet of me. Then they laughed and continued on their walk down toward the bridge. At the age of 13, as I then was, I would have been very embarrassed if Paddy had caught me out.

At the top of the Grove by the Green Road there was another shrubbery where Barney, Foxy and I liked to meet the girls. It was here I encountered smoky kisses for the first time. The girl I was with liked to alternate the offering of her tightly closed lips with puffs from a Woodbine.

But the back of the library remained our favourite venue. It was our territory and we did not take kindly to others using it, or any part of the area around the buildings. We became incensed when we caught Michael Broderick from the Main Street, who was much older than us, courting in the grassy corner on the other side of the library from where we conducted our activities. To add insult to injury we discovered he was *gláming* one of 'our' girls who had quit us in search of wider experience.

'Come on out,' we chanted jealously. 'We can see ye.'

They sank farther into the dark. When we saw they were not going to come out we rooted up sods of grass with the heels of our shoes and hurled them at the pair. Still they would not emerge. Mercilessly we let fly another barrage. This time we were rewarded with angry cursing. We chanced one last sod before taking to our heels. We knew that Michael had a short temper and if he had chosen to catch one of us the unlucky one would have earned a right flaking. But he never budged, nor did he try to take it out on us afterwards even though he well knew who we were. Probably he was too embarrassed by the whole thing.

I knew nothing of my brother's activities in this respect, except that he liked the company of Ann Quinlan, Anne Madden and Dervla Murphy and other girls in the tennis set. I imagined that he and Dervla were always talking about art, classical music and history, subjects distant from my own interests. I liked Dervla. She was always friendly, would greet you in Irish like her father sometimes, and had an independent attitude to life that was impressive, even to a schoolboy. It was good to encounter someone who did not give a shit about convention, an attitude that earned my respect, although her tough and robust physique represented a challenge to my ideas of femininity.

But, being with girls did not mean you had to be courting them all the time. It was also fun to be in their company. A mixed gang of us often went for walks together when we would talk about the pictures, dancing, hurling and Gaelic football matches, clothes ... The last-mentioned item became more important to us as we advanced into our teens. Without going overboard about the whole thing we used to indicate our likes and dislikes for certain garments or colours. The sexual element, however, was always there. One summer's evening one of the girls and I ran up to the top of the grassy slope at the end of the Warren and waited for the others to catch up. As we lay down to take a breather I asked her what colour knickers she was wearing. She jumped up, pirouetted above me so that I could see for myself, then threw herself down upon me, gave me a quick hug, sprang to her feet once more and ran off down the hill to join the others. I sat up as if in a dream, enchanted by the tantalising glimpse of her bronzed thighs. I hardly noticed her knickers.

The sadness of teenage relationships, male and female, was evident in the manner in which you began to grow away from pals with whom you had spent years in school to form new friendships with others whose interests were developing in line with your own. It was a wholly organic process, a natural part of growing up, but you felt somewhat bewildered when you discovered that old friends did not necessarily share your newly acquired tastes. Sometimes you were the one who was left behind, clinging to old rather than exploring new pathways. Fortunately, some friendships remained durable and promised to have a lifetime of running in them.

A far bigger threat to comradeship was emigration – very high in the early Fifties - which especially affected young and unskilled working-class men and women. British cities offered the main hope of employment to emigrants who left of necessity rather than choice. Those of us who remained in the town could look forward to the pleasure of seeing them return for two-week summer holidays, and possibly a week at Christmas. At such seasons the picturesque railway station would be thronged with people awaiting the arrival of the morning boat-train. The smiles of welcome, the hugs, the kisses and the handshakes were a celebration of family emotion in particular. But the joy of those welcoming family back was tinged with regret for those who would be seeing family off later in the day. An old friend, just arrived from Coventry, would grab the opportunity of seeing an old friend working in London who was due out the same evening. Intense hours of conversation would conclude with the latter accompanying the former to the Station to wave goodbye for another year. It was unlikely they would meet in England in between. Sometimes brothers and sisters endured such transient moments. It was not always easy to get away on holidays at the time of one's choosing. But it was good to cherish your loved ones again. Even for a short two weeks, even for a short few hours. Those seeing relatives off on the Rosslare train in the evening were already anticipating the return of the following summer, if not Christmas. As the train pulled away unsteadily from the platform, last-second hugs, snatched under the worried but understanding eye of the station master, despairingly willed it back. Passengers who had joined it farther up the line looked on in sympathy, having already put their own goodbyes behind them.

The break was most intense for the young man or woman, furnished perhaps with a sympathetically worded medical certificate, who had stayed on an extra week, or two or three, beyond the official annual leave in the vain hope that a permanent job might come up at home. Sometimes it took two or three visits, with as many postponements, to convince the emigrant that there was no hope of work, other than seasonal, in the locality. But not all of those leaving were sad. A few were going to England for a holiday, accompanied by family who were established there. And the eyes of the first-time emigrant could be filled as much with hope and curiosity as with the sadness of parting from loved ones. Most emigrants, in spite of educational shortcomings, managed admirably the transition from country to city life, some in time returning with an English boy- or girl-friend whose accent had us pricking up our ears to understand. All, when mired in mean city streets where poor accommodation had to be won against ingrained English prejudice, learned to appreciate more than they had ever done, the physical beauty of their native landscape. When as teenagers word reached us that one of our pals was due back in town we would be at the station too, hanging around in the background until the family welcome had been observed. Then we would acknowledge each other and arrange to meet later that day or the next, when he might regale us with tales of the Hammersmith Palais or the lovers who touched so brazenly on the grass in London's Hyde Park. While waiting, we availed of the chance to appraise the urban attire of the returned travellers.

At 16–17, we boys were beginning to ease ourselves into the Blue Gillette and Brylcreem phase. By now we had learned that a girl looked at you with more interest if you could flaunt a little style. Or, rightly or wrongly, that was what we thought. After all, if the girls took great pains to get their rouge and lipstick right why should we not grease our hair up and maintain a crease in our pants? Humble efforts that would never achieve the same effect on their senses as the intoxication of their sticky lips on ours. Style for me meant no more than a loose-fitting tweedy jacket, baggy blue or grey trousers with turn-ups, a white shirt, the collar of which I wore over the collar of the jacket, and a pair of sturdy black or brown shoes. In the lapel of the jacket I would have the Pioneer shield of total abstinence, total abstinence from alcoholic drink, that is. There was a limit to this abstinence business and even that from alcohol was never total for me. But I tried.

Also in my lapel, inserted vertically in the stitching along the top edge, glistened the heads of a few plain pins. Just a few. I was comparatively restrained in this habit. Some of the lads used to keep a whole row on each lapel. Acquired in a haphazard fashion, the pins served a practical rather than decorative purpose. We often cut or scratched ourselves in minor ways, or got thorns lodged in our hands. Pins were useful tools for extracting slivers of wood or glass, or for deflating pus-filled pimples. On medical grounds Mam was always warning me not to prick my skin in this way – the pins were never sterilised and were sometimes a little rusty even – but I ignored her well-meaning advice as there was no evidence to show that I or my pals had suffered from the practice. Well, not in any major way. I could see that pimples pricked with a pin did not really heal any quicker than those left to scab off naturally. In fact, the healing process could be prolonged by the meddling. The pins were not employed solely for medical purposes. For fun we might prick one another in the arse with them. And, very occasionally, they served as paper-clips, non-existent items of stationery in Lismore. Safety pins could also be used for this purpose. These were less common and when acquired were affixed to the back of the lapel. They were most handy when you lost a button on the fly of your trousers, or along the waist where your braces were attached.

It was my custom to wear either a belt or braces. Some of the lads, and a lot of working men, wore both at the same time. I had something of a passion for belts although I never possessed more than one or two. The belt of my dreams was owned by an Irish–American kid who came to holiday in the town not long after the end of the Second World War. His mother, a sister of Father Teddy O'Brien of lower Botany who worked in California and who was a good friend of my parents, had married a well-to-do American painter. Demonstrably an Ivy League type in his expensive tweed jackets, and with his pipe, moustache and glasses, he did a lot of sketching around Lismore. I used to play with their boy, who was about the same age as me, on the steps of the Devonshire Arms Hotel where they were staying and coveted a beautiful cowboy belt with a fancy buckle that he wore. In an effort to work a swop I showed him everything I owned but there was no deal. My meagre possessions held little attraction for him.

Two events greatly contributed to the social life of the town for us teenagers in 1953. Mr Boam, the latest owner of the Devonshire Arms,

Two Corkmen, Jim [surname ?] and Dick Long at the entrance of the Devonshire Arms Hotel where they worked. Early Fifties.

opened a small café toward the back of the building, with a separate entrance that faced down the New Way, and Kathleen Crowley, by then Mrs Billy Hogan, opened an ice-cream parlour in the old market house situated between the barracks and the courthouse. At last boys and girls had a couple of places where we could mix in public. Previously we boys on our own had not lacked for a site at which to congregate: the Mall Seat and the Red House Corner being our favourites among a number of corners. Girls did not hang around these male centres of gossip and yarning; they usually met at one another's houses. Boam had drafted in two young Corkmen to help him liven up the staid image of the old hotel, Dick Long and his mate Jim, whose surname escapes me. Dick was small and slim with jet-black hair combed straight back off his handsome forehead. He was the junior of the pair and held the main responsibility with Boam's daughter Dorothy for running the café. Jim was a Dennis Price look-alike and had the same sauvity of manner, if not of accent, as the British screen actor. There was a whiff of urban danger about him, something of the croupier whom we encountered in the movies, that seemed to attract women. His long wavy hair was parted in the middle, something you did not see often in our part of the world. The senior in responsibility as well as age to Dick, he was a sort of major-domo who, among other things, ran the bar with great authority – a good man to mix a cocktail, it was said. Unlike Dick who was solid and down to earth, he fancied himself as a bit of a man about town and, like his look-alike in *Kind Hearts and Coronets,* could scarcely conceal his *ennui* when forced to spend too much time in the company of us uncultured *villageois*. Both lads had brought with them cross-channel experience. Dick had spent a year working as a conductor on the London buses and had done other jobs in South Wales. Jim, presumably, had acquired his skills in the hotel and catering trade. Dick became a pal and would spend time with us on his days off. He was indulgent of his countyman's foibles and loyally defended him whenever we became *searbhasach* with our comments. The attractions of Boam's café were table football, the first such game we had seen, and Dorothy. Boam himself may have been a somewhat humourless Groucho Marx but Dorothy was pure steamy Jane Russell. I did not know what the word complexion meant until she blossomed in my eye. Much as I enjoyed Dick's company, I was more inclined to while away the time in the café when Dorothy was in charge. It was a hopeless cause, however. She was already going to dances at a time when I was only allowed to peer through the door at the town hall céilidhes.

The big attraction at Hogan's ice-cream parlour was Kathleen herself, the loveliest woman for miles around. Looks, personality, warmth, good humour, she had all in abundance but was pedastalled irretrievably beyond our dreams, being older than us and with a husband who knew better than anyone how to croon her a tune and serenade her on any one of a dozen different musical instruments. We all fell in love with her at one stage or another of our development. I sometimes bought a cone just for the pleasure of being bathed in her sunny smile. The soft vanilla with the red cordial on top seemed doubly sweet on such occasions. For the girls there was also a thrill. Kathleen's cousin Michael was the handsomest man for miles around.

But there were girls of my own age of which to dream, too. One came from Dublin to holiday with relatives on Parks Road and unknowingly dazzled me with her long fair hair bound in strands. I never exchanged more than a smile with her although I strove mightily to put myself across her path. Did her relatives wonder why I used to pass along that stretch of road between the Palladium and Fernville with unaccustomed frequency on those bright summer evenings with my brylcreemed head shining in the sun and my best white shirt ironed to a 'T'? All to no avail. One evening on the Blackwater Bridge she passed me with her parents. As I gazed wistfully after her, words from a popular song of the time, *Tell Me Why,* rose unconsciously to my lips.

'*I know I haven't a chance,*' I sang lightly. But not lightly enough.

'You're dead right, you haven't,' guffawed Thumper Lineen who, approaching with his pals from behind, had overheard me.

I blushed and smiled ruefully. But I could have kicked him in the teeth because he had hit the nail on the head. I had a tendency to put girls on a pedestal. Many of us did, I imagine. Except for Beaver Doherty, who seemed to keep a sense of proportion.

'Pity she shits,' he would murmur when any of us got too ecstatic about a female and it was difficult to muster an answer to that.

Sucky Neville liked to undermine your illusions on occasions, too, by referring to the act of making love as 'having a scrape', a phrase which conjured up no pleasureable sensation whatsoever. Or he might deflate us with a crudity more to our liking like:

BRIDE: *(on her wedding might, taking the groom's hand and placing it on her knickers) Shot silk, 1920.*

GROOM: *(taking her hand and placing it where his private parts should be) Shot off, 1916.*

prompting someone else to counter it with an image equally crude but less alarming,

A storm blew down the power lines one night leaving the nuns in the convent in the dark so the Reverend Mother sent a telegram to the ESB saying, 'Please send men with tools. Nuns are using candles.'

This vulgarity, like our coarseness of language, came to us naturally but it was more an expression of defence, perhaps even of fear, than aggression. Behind it lay an ignorance of women and a conflict over sexuality that made each of us youths a possible calamity for any girl who became involved with us. Fortunately, the girls had more sense than we had and knew where to draw the line. Or at least, most did. A rare whisper would go the rounds about someone who had 'got into trouble'. The cruelly unlucky girl, conspicuous by her absence, had probably gone to England, the deliverer of all such Irish woes, to be relieved of her pregnancy under the cold eyes of nuns. Her rumoured lover, unless he was uncharacteristically courageous and chivalrous, would connive in the obfuscation and continue to live at home, diminished but not cast out like the woman. As to the unwanted child, the holy sisters could be counted on to place it somewhere where it would no longer embarrass the two families. But not all such children were born into the darkness of anonymity. Amongst us lived the fruits of passionate encounters, usually working class, who were no different to us. In time you learned the real meaning of the word 'bastard', a noun we hurled at one another so freely and so flippantly, and you thought twice before you used it again. Later still you came across the adult expression 'illegitimate'. Very rarely – I only recall one instance in our locality – a whisper reached you of a newly born infant that had been found dead and abandoned in some field or farm outhouse.

Youths and young men might get into trouble of a different kind. To be caught 'interfering with young girls' stigmatised an unfortunate for life. A 16-year-old I knew, who had been 'put away' for a time, told me on his return that while he was inside he had been made to take a 'white powder' to stop him getting an 'erection'.

'An erection?' I, a couple of years his junior, queried.

'A horn,' he said with a grin of infinite sadness.

'Oh,' I nodded and filed away another adult word.

Then he changed the subject and looked across from the lip of Jackie White's cave where we were sitting on our haunches sheltering from a shower at a man drawing water from the Spout.

CHAPTER TWENTY-ONE

Politics

ELECTIONS BROUGHT A periodic swirl of excitement to the centre of town after Mass on Sundays or during the early evenings of the six-day working week. And tangible local successes like the installation of the town clock in July 1950, for which Jack Campion had long pushed, or the building of the new council houses opposite the Palladium cinema in 1951–52 for which the lanky Main Street electrician Jimmy Glasse installed the electric light, were firm evidence of the political process. However, recognising the existence of politics was one thing, understanding it another. It wasn't history for sure because that was about heroes and battles. And there was a dirty side to it. After the Second World War whispers reached even my young ears, in fact I think it was said aloud in chapel, that Tom Kyne, the Labour Party politician from Dungarvan, who was outspoken on workers' rights, was a communist. A communist? What in the world was that? All I could glean from my parents, who were no way vociferous about it, was that it was a godless creed against the Church. But neither of them believed for a moment that Kyne was secretly a member of this party. The smear cost the politician votes in the short term but, to the credit and good sense of the people of County Waterford, he won a seat in Dáil Éireann in the General Election of 1948.

What was startling about that particular election was that Eamon de Valera and his Fianna Fáil Party lost power for the first time in my young lifetime. Dev, like him or not, was a part of everybody's life, a hero of 1916. And had he not put Churchill to shame with a dignified riposte at the end of the Second World War? It seemed ungrateful to turn him out. During that hard-fought election, en route from a big meeting in Cork, he paused briefly and unexpectedly in Lismore to give a short address and rally the party workers. The word spread quickly. 'Dev's in town! He's up at Kate O'Connell's.' Kate, as well as being the chapel organist, ran a small guest-house in Chapel Street and she and her brother Niall Darragh were staunch Fianna Fáil supporters. Dad, coming in to grab an overdue bite of supper after keeping en eye on the crowd at a local Fianna Fáil meeting earlier, broke the news at home. This was something big in our little town and, even though it must have been after ten o'clock, I asked excitedly if I might be allowed to go and see the great man. Dad said okay but warned me that I would be lucky to catch a glimpse of him as a crowd had gathered outside O'Connell's. Mam had a couple of autograph books in the house that many of her friends had signed – this Victorian hobby was still a fad in her teens – so I asked her if I could borrow one to get Dev's signature. She hummed and hawed and eventually gave me neither. But she did fish out a third one that was tattered and torn and had only one or two signatures in it so, armed with this in one hand and a fountain pen in the other, I ran off down West Street to accost Dev. When I got to Kate's there were supporters milling about all over the place. Being little, I managed to crawl through to the front where Niall Darragh was telling everyone that the Taoiseach was exhausted after a long day and needed to grab some refreshments. I waved my notebook and pen and pleaded to be let through. At first I got a dusty answer but, finally, someone let me up the steps and into the hall. How to get into the back room where Dev was holding a brief parley presented a further obstacle. People were fighting for space at the door. I could gauge from the direction in which everyone was looking where he was in the room so I got down on my knees and bored through to the front. I emerged where he was sitting by a table and spread an open page in front of him. Without halting the flow of his conversation he reached down, took the pen and signed the book. Then I was yanked away and bundled out into the street again. A short time later Dev himself was bundled out, shoved into the back of a big black car to cheers of 'Up Dev!' and driven off down the New Way. The autograph shed its novelty quickly and not long afterwards I mislaid it or passed it on.

Tom Kyne was a more permanent figure and, after his first election success, was regularly returned as a TD for the county. As well as being in the national parliament, he was also an urban district councillor for Dungarvan. A reflective man, with a fine head and profile, he pressed, among other things, for a better deal for libraries and librarians and spoke out against oil deposits on beaches. He was interested in reafforestation and advocated the scaling down of the Irish Army in the wake of the Emergency while all other politicians seemed to be still squabbling emotionally over the issues of the 1922-23 Civil War. In Lismore we had a Labour stalwart in Jack Campion, the man who had hung out the Union Jack on VE-Day. Once he put that behind him, and he never felt the need to apologise for it, Jack steadily built up support for himself and his party as a town commissioner, going on to win a seat on the Waterford County Council as well where he was solid in putting forward Lismore's claim to a greater slice of the county cake. Always his own man, he brooked no bullshit. He never went out without his cloth cap, resplendent with salmon flies, and under his wide trousers flapping at half mast he wore no socks. He talked in a sharp, barking manner, even when handing us kids a slice of bread pudding – Chester cake we called it, as Josie Drislane (née Flynn) has reminded me – baked professionally by himself, or a piece of slab toffee, or a Woodbine or two, over the counter of the small shop that he and his sisters ran in lower Botany. But, skilled as he was as a baker, it was as a rod fisherman for salmon that he excelled. Naturally, this caused him to focus on the question of fishing rights along the Blackwater. Around Lismore the best stretches of the river were preserved for net fishing by the Lismore Estates Company and for rod fishing by the Duke of Devonshire and his friends and bailiffs. The ordinary licence holder was relegated to the less bountiful waters, a galling situation in particular for the few really good rod men like Jack and the Keyes brothers who had the skill and ability to land the biggest and best fish.

''Tis a well known fact that British landowners hold all the rights on the Blackwater from Fermoy to Youghal,' he once said at a council meeting, or words to that effect, proving that while he might wave the Union Jack on a great international issue he was not going to roll himself in it on a local matter.

His political philosphy was simple and undogmatic; he supported the rights of the working man. In this he put his weight behind Tom Kyne, whose meetings in Lismore he always chaired. He was, as far as I could understand it, the only politician in our town to buck the prevailing orthodoxy.

Fine Gael (the 'Fine' was frequently pronounced as in 'fine day.', possibly a deliberately malicious mispronunciation put about by the Fianna Fáil side, but more likely a confusion of Irish and English) was led in the county by Mrs Willie Redmond. Its main claim to a philosophy lay in an Inquisition-like approach to law and order. Other than that and the still festering Civil War argument, there was little else to distinguish it from Fianna Fáil. Mrs Redmond, as she was known, was the widow of Major Willie Redmond, the son of the old nationalist leader in the Irish Parliament who had made an absurd appeal to his fellow-countrymen on the outbreak of the First World War to sacrifice themselves on the fields of northern France for the British Empire, a singularly fatuous and insensitive call while the ravages of the Great Famine were still well within living memory. So it seemed to me. The aura of Redmondism was still potent enough to assure Mrs Redmond of a permanent seat in the Dáil and lent her, perhaps, an air of authority that was inherited rather than won on merit. A puritanical-looking woman, she dressed in black and spoke in a very high-pitched, school-marmish voice as if she were handing down a definitive text. It needled her once when a heckler, presumably from the Fianna Fáil side, was ill-mannered enough to bawl out, 'What about the 77?' (This was a regular taunt hurled at Fine Gael speakers.) But she ignored the intervention and ploughed on with her prepared speech. The significance of the question was lost on me then but, a year or two later when it was hurled vehemently and persistently at her senior party colleague Richard Mulcahy and he scowled angrily by way of response, I turned to Dad for enlightenment. Shaking his head in sorrow, he put me straight.

Hecklers brought to the surface the best entertainment of the election campaign. To stir things up a bit more we youngsters used to cheer and jeer and repeat the sallies that got through to the speaker. But not for long. The committee members of the party holding the meeting would infiltrate the crowd and pick us off. Grown men and women who became too obstructionist would be bustled away protesting by the guards. More usually the heckler was male rather than female, but the latter could be thornier and more vociferous when she got her dander up. The politicians were accustomed to seeing off their tormentors – they had to be if they wanted to remain in politics – but some were more accomplished at it than others. One man who had no need of protection by his handlers was the Fine Gael deputy who represented Monaghan, James Dillon, easily the best orator I heard on a Lismore platform. An impressively bulky man in a black, wide-brimmed hat, black flowing coat and black-rimmed spectacles, he filled the air around the Monument with a booming voice in a manner in which I had not heard from anyone else. As far as I could judge, he made mincemeat of hecklers, although what he said in substance in the course of his speech was beyond my interest and understanding. I only recall him visiting the town once. It must have been an important occasion that brought him the length of the country to address the electorate of Lismore. Local Fine Gael support was led by George Heskin, a farmer, and David 'Boysie' Noonan, the ironmonger and auctioneer from the Main Street. The party's meetings were usually chaired by one or other of the pair. George's brother Denis, however, went his own way and added to his county councillorship a seat in the Dáil as an Independent Farmer.

The big Fianna Fáil guns in the county were little: P.J. who was Little in surname, a soft-spoken, bespectacled man who was TD for a number of years, and our own Seán Uí Guilídhe, i.e. Seán Goulding, who was little in physical stature and even more quietly spoken than his colleague. Seán had been a TD also but in my time had been elevated to senator. His dapper presence in the town was a constant reminder to the citizens to vote for Dev, to whom, it was said, he was close. Redmondism died with the black widow in 1952 and let in a third Fianna Fáil deputy who was going to be around for a while – William Kenneally from Waterford City, who pledged himself with a straight face, in the classical tradition of his party, to 'straight dealing and honest government'. And still later, Jacky Ormonde, a national teacher in Dungarvan and brother of our neighbour Jim, filled another Fianna Fáil seat. Jim himself, with Horace Dowd, both town commissioners at one time or another, were active in organising and chairing the party's meetings.

It was the 1948 General Election that really brought the politicians out in force. Seán MacBride and his new fast-growing party *Clann na Poblachta*, was upsetting the cosy Civil War duopoly, stealing their republican clothes and draining off support from each. Meetings formerly announced in advance by Jim Slog, the town crier, were now increasingly being publicised over loudspeakers installed in the private cars of party supporters. They were held every other day, on Sundays a succession of them from last Mass to mid-afternoon. For me it meant excitement in our otherwise sleepy streets and the pleasure of seeing adults slagging one another off in public. For Dad and his colleagues it meant extra hours of work and the odd minor fracas to be sorted out. Not all hecklers were amateur. Far from it. Often they were campaigners for other parties. Jack O'Gorman, the wily local solicitor and bane of the *gardaí* because he frequently won cases against them, was always good value at meetings. A Fine Gael man until he turned Clann na Poblachta in 1948 to chair that party's meetings, there was nothing he liked better than to stand on the fringe of the Fianna Fáil crowds and heckle his opponents, especially those like him, who happened to be ex-IRA.

Mam was the politician in our family as Dad, being a *garda* and thus, servant of the State, had no vote. Her view of politicians was without illusion. 'Promises, promises, they promise you the earth before they get in, and when they're in, forget about you until they want your vote next time round,' she would laugh.

But in spite of that, she voted regularly. She enjoyed being wheedled for her vote and listened to the arguments of *both* sides – for her it could only be either Fianna Fáil or Fine Gael. As far as I know, however, she always put her 'X' by Fianna Fáil names. With one exception, probably. She and Dad knew Denis Heskin very well and greatly respected him. It would not surprise me if she crossed over to give him her first preference vote when he was seeking office. On one occasion, certainly, after he called to canvass her, the independent politician departed with a particularly big smile.

For our town commissioners, politics was all too real. Responsibility for the failure to attract an industry other than the seasonal ones of tourism and river fishing to Lismore could hardly be placed at their door. Members of all parties were united in this endeavour and could not be faulted for want of trying. In more humble ways they did succeed in bringing us improvements. Better, and long overdue, fire-fighting equipment was secured for our voluntary fire brigade. Mick Ward was the fire chief and he and Bert O'Donnell and the others now had Grecian helmets and proper oilskins and, more importantly, a splendid new hessian-enshrouded hose that required the muscle of two men to control. They would train with it at the Point, arching an exhilarating jet of sparkling Owenashad high over the Blackwater under the blue of an early evening sky. Behind these aesthetically pleasing exercises lay a more sinister purpose. The period of postwar rearmament carried the threat of nuclear extinction. In a new civil defence organisation set up by the State, which citizens were exhorted to join, fire brigades had an obvious role to play. The town water supply was another headache for the commissioners. In long dry spells townspeople grew accustomed to having their water cut off two, three, or even four times a day on a rota system. Usually you received advance notice of this. Mam would fill a few saucepans, and maybe half a bath if she was intending to do some washing that day, to tide her over until the supply resumed.

We were lucky to have running water piped directly to our home. In Botany people had to queue on the corner of the Boreen at the public tap, a chunky cast-iron piece with a mushroom-shaped head, striated sides and a fat round handle, set in a niche in the wall on a cement dais with steps leading up to it – a familiar sight in many Irish towns. At Devonshire Cottages near the Presentation Convent there was another one. Church Lane was furnished with a standpipe that was situated outside the Dohertys' cottage, near the ball alley. The town was fortunate to have the never-ending flow of the Spout as back-up. After a successful experiment to divert water from this into the distribution system a pump was maintained by the Spout and the good-natured Paddens Ryan, the father of my pal Willie and one of Lismore's best senior hurlers of the Twenties, was put in charge of it. In time he gained the stature of a mythic Keeper of the Source on whom the village depended for life. As youngsters we never passed the place without dipping our mouths in the basin and enjoying a chat with Paddens, however brief.

Cappoquin was also linked to the Lismore system and when it came to rationing the requirements of both towns had to be taken into account. Nor was it only dry spells that had to be considered. Cold winters burst pipes, which also interrupted distribution. Whichever time of the year a problem arose it was quickly apparent at the point of delivery from the muddy-coloured water that flowed from the taps. Shortly after, the supply would be cut off.

All politics, national and local, were imbued with the poisonous legacy of the Civil War, an event that we knew had traumatised our country but about which our leaders and our elders were noticeably shy to comment, as if they were ashamed that such a thing had been allowed to happen. It wasn't that the subject was taboo as such. More it was that no one wanted to be the first to mention it. School history stopped at 1916. What came after was some kind of hiatus.

Family photograph of Joseph Ballantyne in the uniform of an Irish Volunteer. Most probably taken in Keash, Co. Sligo c. 1917–1919.

Which left us youths and girls to access an understanding of this event through our own devices, much in the manner in which we acquired a knowledge of sex. At least, in contradistinction to sex, I could count on my parents for some enlightenment on this matter. At school we were neither taught about the War of Independence nor the Civil War. We learned something of the great men of the period but not why or how Michael Collins had been killed in an ambush or why or how Liam Lynch came to die of gunshot wounds received on the lonely slopes of our nearby Knockmealdowns where a modest monument now stood to his memory. It eventually became clear to me that Dad regarded the Civil War as the greatest deception of his life. He had been in both the Irish Republican Brotherhood and the Irish Republican Army, initially joining these organisations in Sligo and subsequently serving in Belfast ('A' Company), when Joseph McKelvey was the Company Captain there, and actively with responsibility for Special Services (copies of two 1923 letters I hold from the Office of Director of Intelligence, GHQ, Dublin, suggest Intelligence) in Liverpool (Liverpool Company) where he rose from Section Leader via First Lieutenant to become Vice-Commandant, under Commandant Denis Fleming, of the Battalion. He served in the Irish (National) Volunteers/IRA from the autumn of 1916 until Easter 1922. (A brief supplementary appeal he compiled for the Military Service Pensions

Board when applying for a military service pension in October 1940 outlines his active service in Liverpool. That and other relevant documents of the same period, including references from comrades supporting his application as well as letters from other Liverpool comrades – IRA and Cumann na mBan – requesting references from him for their pension application, are now with his campaign medals on deposit with the Sligo County Library Museum Archives in Sligo. There are papers in the Military Archives in Cathal Brugha Barracks in Dublin also.) These papers Mam showed me for the first time after his death on the 29th of March 1974. During his lifetime Dad himself *never* discussed with me his own role in any of the organisations. Even when I pressed him for such information he would not be drawn. Occasionally though, he would volunteer something about a comrade with whom he had served or about a well-known veteran of the War of Independence who was in the news. It might have been prompted by a death notice, for example, that of Ernie O'Malley (in March 1957, just over two years after we moved from Lismore to live in Carrick-on-Suir) or Barney Mellows (the 1942 *Irish Press* obituaries of which I found among his papers), or by a commemorative notice that he had seen in the daily paper. (The Mellows obituary notices may be an indication that Dad had also encountered Barney's brother Liam, a fellow IRB member, on one of Liam's trips to Liverpool as IRA Director of Purchases.) My father spoke briefly but feelingly of Joseph McKelvey, always referring to him as Joe, whenever the name of this Commanding Officer surfaced. Clearly he thought highly of the man and greatly deplored his and Rory O'Connor's reprisal execution, with Liam Mellows' and Richard Barrett's, at the hands of the William Cosgrave/Kevin O'Higgins/Richard Mulcahy dominated Dáil in 1922. Dad admired O'Connor as well. (I was to discover later that he had shared briefings with him and worked under his personal direction for a time.) But he also found him 'distant', which suggested to me that he regarded McKelvey in a warmer light and had been closer to him. Mam immediately sensed the sadness that enveloped him on these occasions and would quietly draw me away from his presence.

'There's nothing as bitter as civil war,' she would say, 'It's brother against brother, sister against sister, family against family.'

One thing I did overhear him confide to my uncle Liam O'Mara of Carrick-on-Suir who had also served as a senior IRA officer in South Tipperary and had escaped from Kilkenny Gaol in a mass tunnel escape - prior to that, after he was arrested, the Tans or Auxies, as was sometimes their wont with captured soldiers, had lashed him to their open Crossley tender to deter ambush as they patrolled the streets and roads and also to taunt their enemies. During the Truce of 1921, in preparation for future

My father Joseph Ballantyne in the centre with two unidentified men (IRA/IRB comrades, probably) during the War of Independence era. Place: Sligo Station? Or Belfast or Liverpool?

Studio portrait of my father Joseph Ballantyne in man-about-town pose. Photo taken during War of Independence era, probably in England.

hostilities should there be a breakdown in the peace talks, Dad and his comrades were engaged in procuring arms and smuggling them to Ireland by passenger boat.

'A risky business,' he remarked matter-of-factly, 'Because if we were caught breaching the terms of the Truce our own side would have had to disown us.'

He did not take sides in the Civil War although friends in both political factions had approached him for support. 'I did not take up arms against the British to turn my gun on my own comrades,' Mam said he told them. One of the sides, probably out of fear that he would go back on his word and join their opponents, held him prisoner for a short time in an effort to make him change his mind but he did not budge from his position. Eventually they let him go. He never involved himself in politics again other than voting Fianna Fáil after he left the *gardaí*. He never expressed any virulent feelings about Fine Gael although, perhaps instinctively, he shied away from the repressive philosophy of the party that had ruthlessly and illegally shot

Photograph taken most likely in Cammell Laird's shipyard, Birkenhead, Merseyside, (possibly on behalf of Bootle Technical School) c. 1920-21. Joseph Ballantyne is seated front row on the right. The man with the shiny shoes seated front row centre has the air of a foreman or instructor. Were any of these men IRA or IRB comrades? Dad learned his carpentry skills there.

A receipt, found among Dad's papers, from the County Borough of Bootle Technical School, dated 18th November 1920. It states that 'J. Ballantyne' enrolled for a course in building for the session 1920–21 and paid a fee of £0-13-00.

his former comrades and dabbled in the trappings of fascist ideology in the Thirties. His brother Paddy, who had served with the IRA in Sligo and been interned in Ballykinlar Camp where he made the acquaintance of Peadar Kearney and Seán Lemass among others, demonstrated a similar reserve with regard to postwar politics.

It is possible that my brother, either through Mam or Dad, knew more about our father's IRA career than I did. Perhaps he was more probing than I in his questioning or benefited from the trust accorded to a first son. I recall that he once told me he had suggested to Dad that he should write his memoirs but that Dad had laughed and shrugged off the idea. He would have read Edward M. Brady's book *Ireland's Secret Service in England* (Dublin: Talbot Press, 1928) and, whether he agreed with this version of events or not, may have felt that Brady had said enough about the Liverpool Company. Dad's first-hand account of the Company's activities, certainly with regard to the role of Special Services, would have been illuminating, given the dearth of written records about this undercover war. Like many a steadfast soldier of the War of Independence, he was not a man to blow his own trumpet and I feel sure that he would have been an honest chronicler of the period, to a point – he would not have found it easy to say a bad word about any of his comrades, volunteers all.

In the post-1916 vacuum floated the feeling that the final chapter, the reunification of Northern Ireland with the South, was all that remained to be written. The history that was taught us in school, and such articles as we read in newspapers and magazines, ill-prepared us for understanding the complexities of the political scene in the 'Six Counties'. England was the source of all our disasters. The word 'British' was incomprehensible to us. Most mystifying of all was the manner in which our Protestant fellow-Irishmen and -women in the North proclaimed that they were British above all else, a stance from which even the English seemed to recoil. Was there something about the possession of a black bowler hat that drove men to extremes? Whenever Mam saw a picture of Orangemen in their sombre attire (sombre yet with bizarre frills and accoutrements) she would shake her head and say with *searbhas,* 'Sure they're not like our Protestants (meaning those of *Éire*) at all. Nobody could live with them.' Dad would just laugh sadly and comment, 'They'll never give up.' I heard both their opinions with respect because Dad had worked for a time as a carpenter in the shipyards in Belfast (he later worked at Cammell Laird's in Birkenhead) and, after he became a civic guard, served in Swanlinbar in County Cavan where Mam joined him. 'Swad', as they referred to it, was situated just across the Border from Enniskillen, which they used to visit regularly on shopping expeditions to buy certain goods, including stockings for Mam, that were dearer in the South. Of the two, Mam was the more republican in utterance, quick to pour scorn on the reactionary speeches of Lord Brookborough. The feisty English Labour politician Manny Shinwell endeared himself to her for life when she heard him say on the wireless, 'The North of Ireland gives me the horrors.' He meant the government of the day, of course, not the people or place. Dad was more circumspect. Respect for the Law, and the impartiality he felt he had to maintain as a *garda*, combined to limit anything he wished to say about politics. But he never left me in any doubt of his contempt for the attitude of the Great Powers toward small nations. Of his time in Belfast I learned little though he did mention once how two Catholics he had known had had to fight their way out of a shipyard, back to back swinging shovels, during a Unionist-fomented pogrom. And on another occasion he referred to a street he had known in a Republican area where the inhabitants had cut holes though the connecting walls of a terrace of houses and masked them with dressers and cupboards so that wanted men could slip from house to house when evading the RIC.

Of the Black and Tans and Auxiliaries you heard plenty, none of it good. Dad gave the battle-hardened Auxies credit for one thing. 'They feared neither God nor man,' he said with a mixture of perplexity and admiration. His comment impressed me because I knew that he was respectful of courage but did not make a song and dance about it. Neither did he admire people lightly. One man he held in high regard was Abd el-Krim, the Berber chieftain of the Rif region who, until his eventual surrender in 1926, led a successful guerilla campaign against the Spanish and French troops in Morocco from 1921 to 1925. It was an unlikely name to drop from his lips and I eagerly pressed him for further information about the exploits of this warrior of whom I had previously known nothing. Abd el-Krim! I imagined him on a prancing Arab stallion sweeping down in ambush on the French Foreign Legion. Dad was less enthusiastic when I questioned him about Napoleon. Had not the French under that self-styled emperor trampled on the rights of small nations? In spite of his reservations, he deplored the treatment meted out to the former ruler by the British on the island of St Helena and the name Hudson Lowe came to signify for me a pettifogging gaoler. As to the Black and Tans, what were they but criminals let loose on the populace? Mam's cousin-in-law, Jack Kent of Kilmacthomas, had been beaten to within an inch of his life by them, his health and hearing impaired for the rest of his life. Superintendent Creane's brother had been beaten to death in Leinster. The City of Cork and other towns had been torched.

Of the Flying Columns who fought the guerilla war of independence against the Tans you heard plenty, none of it bad. The military feats of Tom Barry, Florrie O'Donoghue, Dan Breen of the 'sulky bulldog appearance' of the British wanted posters, and Seán Treacy were known far and wide. We were able to read Barry's own first-hand account of his famous exploits in his book *Guerilla Days in Ireland* when it was published in May 1948. It appeared in instalments in the *Irish Press,* also. But we could take some pride in the less spectacular achievements of our own tough countyman, Pax Whelan of Dungarvan, as well.

These events, and those of the Great War, though lived through first-hand by our elders, seemed as distant to us children and youths as the Great Famine. I was not in the least surprised that Britain was still meddling in our affairs, however. From the arrival of Strongbow and his adventurers, brought over by the traitor Dermot MacMurrough, had not England treated us perfidiously? But had we not brought disaster on ourselves too by our internal divisions? The Irish nobles' practice of hiring foreign mercenaries to fight their wars was incomprehensible to me, as was the manner in which Irish informers betrayed us at critical junctures of our history. Did not the beautifully proportioned shape of our island, perfectly balanced on the edge of Europe, demand of its warring clans an end to divisions and the reunification of our country under one flag? I reserved my greatest contempt for mercenaries and informers, not difficult as I had no idea of the complex factors that led men to hire themselves out as cannon-fodder or of the economic or psychological pressures, or tortures, or sheer greed that could force or tempt a man or a woman to betray a cause. History as I encountered it failed me on this. Which left other questions hanging in the air. If mercenaries and traitors were men without honour what was I to make of a man like James II, or of allies like the Spanish at the Battle of Kinsale? Often even the fates seemed to have conspired against us. Where bad tactics could not account for our defeats, as at the Battle of Kinsale, bad luck took a hand, as in the untimely death of Owen Roe O'Neill, the only leader who might have saved us from the massacres of, and enslavement by, the arch-scourge of the Irish, the tyrant Oliver Cromwell. Loyalty to Crown and Empire was the oddest concept of all. How Irishmen, no matter what their religious persuasion, could consider fighting England's wars was beyond me. Yet I could find ready evidence of men who had been willing to do this on the walls of the Protestant cathedral of Lismore. White and grey marble plaques informed me of the Villiers-Stuarts who had died in the Boer and Great wars, and of the splendidly named Major George Sheaffe-Montizambert who was 'killed in action before Moolton (Multan?) in the East Indies in 1848' while the Famine raged at home. What the Major was doing in such an obscure (to me) place thousands and thousands of miles from home I could only conjecture. And why was he fighting in someone else's country anyway? I could find in my heart neither understanding of, nor sympathy with, his motives.

Against the inspiring and tragic backdrop of history the politics that prevailed in the Ireland of the 1940s and '50s appeared very small and shifty, and equally puzzling. At one minute past midnight on Easter Monday 1949 the Free State left the British Commonwealth to become the Republic of Ireland. Both Ireland and England made a bit of a fuss about it but what it signified in practical terms I had no idea. Lismore looked the same the morning after as it did the night before and we did not even get a day off from school because the event took place over the holiday. Still, anything that got up England's nose could not be bad. What gave me more cause for thought a couple of years later was the manner in which the Catholic bishops were allowed to abort the obviously fair Mother and Child Scheme of the Health Minister, Dr Noël Browne. I inadequately understood the issue but the basic principle of providing better health care for the public, and especially the poor, was beyond dispute. I spoke to Mam heatedly about it and, although she seemed to accept the decision of the Government, she was somewhat embarrassed in her defence of it, saying that if Browne, who was a 'difficult' man, had been prepared to compromise on the plan it might have been acceptable to the clergy. However, the callous indifference of the Church scarred me, perhaps much more deeply than I realised at the time, and flushed out other questions that were latent in my uneasy mind. By what right, for example, did the Church demand that all children of a so-called 'mixed' marriage, itself frowned upon, be brought up as Catholics? I could never understand how any self-respecting Protestant could a), acquiesce in this arrangement and b), live with the clear slur on his or her own long-held beliefs, and remain a Protestant. If both faiths, and they were confusingly two of a kind, agreed to be bound by the toss of a coin in the matter, fine, but for one to claim absolute right seemed wholly unfair.

Inextricably bound up with our identity as Irishmen was the Irish language. In school it was the medium through which we were taught all subjects, except English and Latin. I liked it and did not find it difficult. I was lucky. For some of my pals it was very hard. We were taught the language in an old-fashioned way but it was not so much this as the ambivalent attitude of respective governments to it that fostered in us a cynicism and a doubt about its future. Many educated people scoffed at it as a dying language, or pronounced it dead already. The disadvantaged had more pressing reasons for doubting it. They were the ones who bore the brunt of the emigration to the English-speaking countries of the world.

'What's the bloody use of teaching them Irish?' Kit Neville, who was not lacking in patriotism, used to say to me, referring not just to her own sons and daughters. ''Tisn't here they'll be working after they finish school.'

While cursing the Irish government for its shortcomings, she could say with fire in the same breath, 'I hate the English!' The statement was more personal than nationalist. The first of her large family were already working in Coventry and she was only too aware that England would siphon off the rest, one by one, as they grew to school-leaving age, and place temptations in their paths that might undermine not only their Irishness but their Catholic religion.

On *Conradh na Gaeilge* and the *Cumann Gaedhealach* rested the main hopes of reviving the language. Vin O'Donoghue, Fergus Murphy and Diarmuid Ó Drisceoil as educationists took leading roles in these organisations and enlisted keen support from Willie 'Teller' Walsh, Pad Tierney and Billy 'Irons' O'Brien from Botany, Michael Nolan from Main Street and Liam Leddy from Araglin. An early success of this group was the re-establishment of the Lismore Feis in May 1948. It was held in the Hurling Field where there were sporting competitions like the *poc fada* and the longest kick in Gaelic football, as well as Irish dancing, ballad singing and melodeon and fiddle playing. I entered one of the singing grades, the one and only time I tried to sing through a mike in the open air. I think I came second or third. In any case, I did not win a medal for my efforts.

Teller Walsh wore a different hat entirely in another field of endeavour. He was the Lismore gossip columnist for the *Dungarvan Leader* in the early Fifties. Under the byline 'Pot-Pourri' in the 'Lismore Notes', which he also wrote, he did his best to embarrass courting couples, and would-be courting couples with teasing lines and thinly veiled clues to identity like:

So some of the old reliables were missing at the céilidhe. Tough luck M-y!!!!!

We heard some remarks passed about a chap with lovely waves and smashin' eyes!!!!

F-xy seemed to have taken a liking to his namesake but she seemed to prefer a certain farmer's young son from D-k!!!!

We hope P-y and E-ie enjoyed dancing in the hall by the sea.

The old bridge below the town has more than scenic attraction for N-l and J-my!!

Who was the gent that escorted the lady home as she was afraid of black dogs?!!!

We heard that two gentlemen travelling to Cappoquin had to abandon their automobile outside the Weaver's!!! Maybe the petrol shortage was the cause of it - or was it?!!!

Is it true that a certain person is going to buy a book all about "dates"?!!!

Who is the gent that does the nightly beat in Cappoquin?!!!

Is it true that T-s is very upset about last week's Pot-Pourri?!!!

We heard that Jimmin is setting up a detective agency!!!

M-k got no dance from C-k - . Boy! Was he mad!!! We heard that he blamed the dust. Is that true?

A word of advice K-n. Don't change the old love for the new!!!

Mostly, Teller was merely mischievous in his comments but occasionally, when a little peevish, he could dip his pen in acid and sharpen the embarrassment for his target. Like all gossip columnists, however, he had to tread a fine line. A wrong perception on his part and an aggrieved party could be provoked beyond endurance. Which could have led to a black eye or at least, a firm warning, as happened. But his sharp tongue was more than a match for most and when his eyes glistened coldly behind his rimless spectacles lovers thought twice before crossing him. The *Leader* and the other Dungarvan paper, the *Observer,* both featured regional sections like 'Portlaw Pickings', 'Ballyduff Broadcast', 'Coast to Comeragh Chips' or 'Mid-Deise Mems', even 'East Cork Jottings', but only the 'Lismore Notes' seemed to harbour a regular gossip columnist.

The *Leader* and the *Irish Press,* the papers my parents took, had precious little Irish language material in them. But they had no such inhibitions about party politics, especially the *Press,* the organ of Fianna Fáil, which unceasingly plugged that party's policies and politicians, never more clearly than when Seán T. O'Kelly ran for president of the country in 1945. No one seemed to have been particularly aware of the harmless little candidate with the big brawny wife before, but suddenly he was being hailed as a great Irish patriot, his likeness plastered over numerous pages of the *Press* and every available billboard. A Sunday paper did not cross our threshold until the *Sunday Press* appeared in 1949. Over in England a Lismoreman, Thomas J. Hickey, became news in September 1943 when he was appointed editor of *The Statist,* a London weekly of the period. He also co-founded the Irish Club in Eaton Square, London. Guard Martin's wife was his sister. I never saw a copy of his paper in our town.

Politics would show in the local papers in reports of town council and county council meetings and, less directly, in the few readers' letters that appeared. The letter writers frequently cloaked themselves in the anonymity of a pseudonym, e.g. 'Incognito' (you couldn't argue with him), 'A Gael' (unchallengeable), or 'The Man Without A Name' (far in advance of Clint Eastwood). Correspondents who were respected pillars of society – priest, librarian, or teacher – were sure enough of themselves to append their own names. Poems that appeared in the locals also tended to carry a pseudonymous byline, e.g. 'Ballyduff Bard' or 'The Wandering Bard'. These were often long rhyming ballads dedicated to winning hurling and football teams and made reference to many persons and place-names. *We'll sing ye too of hurlers true/ with skill and daring grand* would be typical lines. Local newspapers were noteworthy for their obsequiousness toward the affairs of the gentry. 'Fashionable' weddings and balls were vividly described, with the presence of those perceived to be leading figures noted. Obituaries were fulsome. One might read that 'Major So-and-So', who died last Thursday had had a brilliant career in the Jockstrap Highlanders, i.e. he did a bit of fancy soldiering on a horse for a time, or that 'Colonel Hobnob' who succumbed after a long illness, was one of the most popular sportsmen in Munster, i.e. he liked to go to the races and probably drank himself to death. Young male emigrants at the other end of the social register in age and possessions (or lack of possessions) drew more unintentionally poignant comment. Always, it was noted, they left to take up a 'lucrative position' in England. The positions young women emigrated to fill were seldom accorded a comment.

CHAPTER TWENTY-TWO

The World Outside

THE SUREST INDICATORS of a world outside our own were the swallows, swifts, house martins and sand martins that migrated to nest amongst us under the eaves of our buildings (we had a pair of swallows at the back of our own house in West Street for a few seasons) and in the sand-pit and along the river banks. They never failed to delight with their scimitar skims through the air and over the surface of our waters and inches; even when occasionally I slung a missile in their direction with my catapult I knew that I hadn't a hope in hell of bringing one down and would have had mixed feelings if I did anyway. In April, sometimes March, we welcomed the swallows especially as harbingers of summer and in the autumn, over days, observed them congregating silently in lengthening rows along the telegraph wires, as if tuning up for their hazardous journey back to the heat of southern Africa, confirming that our long and delightful daylight hours were drawing in. At some innate signal they would take off as one and almost instantly whirl out of sight. On the one occasion when I witnessed this departure, in the late afternoon above the Castle Farm fields bordering the Tallow Road, it engendered in me an acute sense of loneliness. But there was anticipation too of the return the following spring.

The telegraph wires themselves hummed with news of other places. Down at the post office the tapping of Morse code was regularly heard, telegraphs incoming or outgoing. Now and again one would be delivered at home. Mam was always apprehensive when it came and steeled herself to open it. They were uncommon enough to warrant worries about serious illness and death in the family or among close friends, an unease fulfilled on at least one occasion. But, more often than not, they merely signalled arrival times for someone coming to visit, unexpected congratulations of one kind or another, or last-minute Christmas greetings. Mam would sigh with relief when the news was good.

The world outside West Waterford began close to home, at the railway station from which the single ribbon of track ran eastward towards

Lismore Railway Station in 1964. The railway was closed to all traffic three years later.

Paddington. Which of our pals who had emigrated would be next to arrive with news of the latest fads and fashions from the English capital? At the castle the hoisting of the flag bearing the Devonshire coat of arms would announce that the Duke and Duchess had arrived via Dublin in their black limousine. Was it to be Fred Astaire, or Bing Crosby, who was guesting with them this time? The dancer stayed with the Cavendishes at least once in my lifetime and was mobbed for autographs at the station by the film fans of the town in May 1937 while awaiting the night express to London, an event through which it can safely be assumed I slept blissfully in my mother's arms. She was not out looking for an autograph. Whether any of Crosby's rumoured sojourns was translated into reality is doubtful.

It was through our returning pals that the outside world really came alive. They would bring with them the glamour of the Hammersmith Palais, the movie premières of Leicester Square, the lights of Piccadilly, but also the poisonous smog and the sordid job and accommodation advertisements in newspapers and in newsagents' shop windows that stipulated 'No Irish need apply', or 'Dogs and Irish not allowed', and the like, clichés now but revelations to us. First-hand accounts of the emigrant's life in the United States of America were rare. From our part of the country only nuns and priests seemed to take the Atlantic route to betterment and, cosseted as they were in presbyteries and convents, their experience hardly mirrored the daily grind of the ordinary Irishman and Irishwoman who went to America to earn a living. When someone did go to the States or Canada it was anticipated that it would be years before they would be seen at home again, if ever. The voyage across the Atlantic from Cobh took a week to ten days and the one-way ticket was not cheap. The cost of the alternative mode of travel, an air trip in a lumbering Constellation from Rineanna, was prohibitive for the emigrant, unless he or she had the good fortune to be funded by relatives who had succeeded in establishing themselves in the host country.

Returning emigrants, no matter what country they had settled in, brought mixed messages from the lands of opportunity. Only the more thoughtful and realistic of them gave you the negative as well as the positive aspects of their new home towns. Some would argue vehemently in favour of the personal freedoms they encountered. A few would blind you with the gloss of city-centre entertainment. Others would relate frankly how they had had the corners knocked off them in adapting to big city life. From all rang the conviction that if a man made a bit of money he worked his guts out for it. Luck played a painfully small part. Dissatisfaction with both home and abroad was often revealed by an emigrant during his or her two-week holiday but it was not always easy to ascertain the truth of his or her feelings.

Holiday funds came in hard cash and Botany lads who spent injudiciously in the euphoria of the early days found themselves broke by the end of the first week, leaving them with three options. They could return to England ahead of time, borrow from friends or, as they most frequently did, live out the remainder of the vacation on the charity of their hard-pressed families. Those who were more careful with their money would enjoy their stay if the weather was good, but if it turned out poor, would complain about the lack of amusement facilities in the area. In particular, young men and women would bemoan the paucity of dances, though efforts were made to put on extra hops during the summer influx of visitors. It was at dances that they could best show off their sophistication, with city style and the latest steps. But many loved the *céilidhe*s too and would take in as many as they could during their brief stay.

What I wanted to know most from the lads who had been 'over' or abroad was what the life and people of other places were like. London alone seemed to be populated by Frenchmen, Poles, Chinese, Indians; Americans, North and South; Italians, Spaniards, and every other nationality you could think of, as well as the English, and not to mention the Irish. Millions of them! How they all fitted into one city, however great, was beyond my comprehension. If they had not had something bizarre called a Tube they would not have been able to move around at all. The idea of travelling underground I found difficult to grasp, even though I had seen examples of such transport systems at the pictures. How the thing operated and how you found your way around it was often described to me in words but I still did not take to the idea of being down in a hole, squashed face to face with thousands of people. It was too incredible. Fortunately there were buses as well. Dick Long used to talk about the year he spent working on them as a conductor with West Indians – he liked and got on well with his fellow-immigrants from the other side of the Atlantic. He had also spent a year or two working in South Wales in a town called Mountain Ash, a name so captivating I at first refused to believe it was anything other than a place of rowans, a favourite tree that dotted the Mountain Road to Carrignagour. However, he assured me that it was a town and, moreover, one to which generations of Corkmen and Corkwomen had gone to make a living. Further corroboration that Britain did not consist of wall-to-wall cities arrived when I was 16. Three very interesting young English lads from the West Country rode into town on a tandem and a bicycle and camped out in the area for a week. Tom Feeney and I befriended them and they told us a lot about life in the English countryside that, to our surprise, did not seem very different from life in Lismore. Another aspect of life over, about which our returning pals spoke, was the new welfare system that provided free medical treatment. My brother, on his first trip home, mentioned an Englishman he had met on the boat who had *six* pairs of spectacles on his person, all obtained gratis on the National Health Service. Which appeared a bit excessive. Or, at least, Paddy thought so. But by then he was used to the oddities of the English. Had he not also roomed for a while with a bloke who knitted his own socks!

Older, well-established emigrants, like my Uncle Mick Morrissey and his Oughterard-born wife Ann, would refer now and again to the Blitz. Mam could scarcely believe that people could survive such a rain of bombs and I, in spite of a diet of British and American war pictures, could not comprehend the event either. By the time I left Lismore in 1954 a full realisation of the cataclysmic effects of World War Two was only beginning to seep into my mind. That the Germans and Japanese had behaved evilly was beyond question but such were the brutal caricatures of them that I encountered in the pictures and in the English comics and adventure stories I read, that I was forced to ask myself how much was truth and how much was British propaganda. It was the American film *Escape,* with Robert Taylor and Norma Shearer, that first filled me with a dread of Nazi Germany. The film was made in 1940 but I could not have seen it until a number of years later, I imagine. It is about an American of German descent who goes to Germany to rescue his mother who is under sentence of death in a concentration camp. He smuggles her out of the camp in a coffin then, after a tense train journey by night, out of the country by plane. It was probably the first film that alerted me to the reality of the Nazi persecution of the Jews. Images from it remain with me to this day although I have never seen the film since. Curiously enough, it was in another Robert Taylor film of the Forties, *Bataan*, that I encountered grim images of the Japanese Imperial Army, a force, I think, that filled me with even more apprehension than the Nazi hordes.

References to wartime slipped easily into my parents' conversations. Mam would call any man who affected a posh accent or manners 'Lord Haw Haw'. Kit Neville had another phrase for the same type of individual, a 'Mickey the Lady'. When I queried Mam's expression she explained to me that the original Lord Haw Haw had been a Mayoman (in fact, he was born in Brooklyn of Galway parentage) who spoke posher than the British aristocracy and who broadcast propaganda for the Nazis during the War. After the War when the British captured him they executed him for treason.

'We heard him a few times. Sure he was only an eejit,' said Mam. 'They were silly to take him so seriously.'

Dad thought that hanging was an excessive punishment for him. The man was more a fantast than anything else. 'But, that's the British way,' he shrugged.

Mam was more appreciative of J. B. Priestley, one or two of whose early wartime radio *Postcripts* she had picked up on somebody's wireless. A copy of his novel *The Good Companions* rested in our bookcase and she may have read others of his works as well.

Another time Dad would talk disparagingly of David Gray, the United States ambassador to Ireland at the outbreak of the War. He felt the American had over-stepped the bounds of his diplomatic role in attempting to bounce the neutral Irish government into entering the War on Britain's side. And there was the postwar incident when Dev had gone to the German Embassy in Dublin to offer his condolences on the death of Hitler.

'A mistake,' Dad shook his head, 'Dev was a stickler for diplomatic niceties and felt it was his duty as prime minister to offer his regrets to the German nation on the death of its constitutionally elected leader. But it was very naïve of him.'

My Uncle Mick Morrissey's Royal Air Force duties saw him based in Stafford during the War and, when home on leave afterwards, he left me a few wartime mementos – an English gas mask, an enemy aircraft identification manual, and a Nazi swastika. The mask came in a black tin canister. I would stick it on my head from time to time and try to breathe through the perforated green cup that hung below my chin. It was a suffocating experience, not helped by the strong smell of the black rubber of the mask. How someone was expected to breathe through it for more than a few minutes in an emergency I could not imagine. Mick told me that all homes in the cities of England had them during the Blitz, in case of gas attacks by the Luftwaffe. The swastika was a small aluminium pin that he had picked up in the postwar period when he was stationed at Gütersloh transit camp in Germany. I added it to a few Irish and British military badges that I already had, the small collection eventually to be swapped for something more desirable.

In spite of my reservations about his serving in the British forces, Mick remained my favourite uncle. There was a touch of the big wide world about him and, perhaps, a bit of the glamour of the RAF, although his higher ambitions in this force had been thwarted. On the ground staff, he had applied to become a gunner on the bombers but was turned down on account of poor eyesight. Lismoremen, too, had fought, and were fighting, for the British Crown, one, an Alexander of Mayfield, soon to die in Korea. Nor did the Irish Army fail to attract local recruits. Some years after the end of the European conflict Botanyman Pad Tierney confided in me that he had spent the Emergency years guarding German internees at the Curragh. The prisoners, some of them spies, were for the most part delighted to remain incarcerated and guarding them was a cushy number, he chuckled. At Christmas he would share a bottle of whiskey with them.

An echo of an Irishman's role in a much earlier war of Empire reached me when I went on holidays from Lismore to my aunts' house in Carrick-on-Suir. A Mayoman from Swineford called Mick Hurst had come to live out his retirement years in Mill Street with his Clonmel-born wife Mary (Gleeson?), who used to work as a laundress for my grandmother. They had no children. When his wife died my grandfather, who appeared to have become a close friend of his, offered him a room in Greystone Street – the room beyond the back bedroom where we were accustomed to sleeping when staying in Carrick. There he lived almost until his death 'not long after the outbreak of the First World War', according to my Aunt Nan Morrissey, at the Carrick hospital and former Workhouse, known as 'The Union'. An ex-British soldier, Hurst had seen action in the Crimean War (1853–56). There were military barracks in Clonmel and Carrick and the likelihood is that he maintained some connection with one or both of these after he retired on pension. My aunts, who always spoke of him in respectful tones, remembered him as a tall, spare slightly stooped grey-haired man with a grey moustache and a small goatee, who kept himself very neat and clean, 'as most ex-Army men did', and always carried a walking-stick. War wounds contributed to a poor state of health in his declining years. His gold watch-chain passed to my father and eventually to me with a silver South African half-crown, to which a pin may have been soldered. Dated 1897 it bears the bearded likeness of Paul Kruger. Thus, by this indirect path, I also heard of the Boer Wars (1st, 1880–81; 2nd, 1899–1902). My uncle Mick Morrissey in Birmingham held his campaign medal until 21 November 2002 when he most kindly gave it to me to act as its future custodian. According to my Aunt Nan again, Mick Hurst is buried in the Friary churchyard in Carrickbeg, presumably with his wife, in a single unnamed grave marked today by a rusty iron cross with a circle on it, standing on a small cement plinth. It may be found to the right of the church about ten yards from the corner at the top of the outside steps, near the hedge and between a stunted block on the left bearing the name John O'Neill and a large grave with fancy iron railings behind a Galvin grave. [*See Appendix for further information on Hurst.*]

After World War Two the red on the map of our planet began to shrink inexorably, beginning with the establishment of the State of Israel in 1948, an event which imprinted itself on my memory soon afterwards when Colonel McConnell, having served as a commissioner in the Palestine Police in Haifa, came to live in the Villa. Among souvenirs of the East that he had brought back with him were two curved Arabian daggers, one a silver-hilted, silver-pommelled weapon from the silver scabbard of which a deadly blade unsheathed itself with a hiss, filling my imagination with the heroics of distant frontiers. The Colonel also kept photographs that his son Gerald showed me of the rioting which preceded the setting up of the State. They captured graphically the sunlit streets littered with the paraphenalia of riot – stones, sticks, and bottles. Frozen in them were policemen on foot with round shields on their left arms and long batons in their right hands, mounted policemen keeping a tight rein on their horses, rioters in a variety of costumes in the act of throwing missiles while they scattered in all directions, and on every flat roof in sight spectators looking down on the excitement. Later in the same year extremist Jewish gunmen created a more negative image by assassinating a Swedish diplomat with the odd-for-a-Swede name, I thought, of Count Bernadotte.

'They shouldn't have done that,' I overheard Mam mutter among the adults, 'He was a man of peace.'

Once Israel had opened the floodgates other countries began to shed their red, first India, clearing a vast swathe but sacrificing her revered leader Gandhi at the moment of independence. Then in 1951 Premier Mohammed Mossadegh of Persia, whom the newsreels liked to portray in pyjamas, and sometimes seemingly weeping, further undermined the stained reputation of Empire by nationalising the Anglo-Iranian Oil Company, a move fully justified in my republican eyes. Not long after, Egypt was pushed into the headlines when a group of army officers led by General Neguib threw out the fast-living King Farouk, a not unreasonable coup as the playboy monarch was more into studding belly dancers' navels with diamonds than relieving the appalling poverty of his people – more than a match for Lady Docker when it came to flaunting wealth. In the midst of the crisis the ubiquitous Ali Sabry strove to keep the country going. Further south on the same continent a chilling, to white planters, new phrase, 'Mau Mau' was entering the English language.

As the British Empire was crumbling the new Soviet Empire of Joseph Stalin was rising out of the ashes of a broken Europe, a process not viewed with any enthusiasm by my parents. In 1948 they spoke in shocked tones of the death of Jan Masaryk, the Czech statesman. It was rumoured that he had committed suicide by throwing himself out of a high window, but they harboured suspicions that the defenestration might not have been of his own volition. Mam said prayers for him, as she was to say later for Cardinal József Mendszenty, the Hungarian churchman after he was imprisoned by the Communists. I too joined the crusade of prayers and Masses for the Cardinal. The reason was simple. The man was suffering for our faith. Or so it was presented. I had no understanding of the real issues. A-bombs and H-bombs were being tested by the Americans the Russians and the British in their respective wastes of Nevada, Siberia and Australia, lending a frightening perspective to the drift into war in the Far East. It was Hannah Drohan, calling to see Mam one afternoon when I was alone with her, who announced that war had broken out in Korea between the United Nations and the 'Reds' – the *Irish Press* always referred to the communists of the globe, and some non-communists of the Left, as 'Reds'. Mam sat down on the nearest chair in a state of shock and blessed herself. Then she and Hannah began to converse in hushed voices. When I asked what it all meant, this war on the other side of the planet, I was told to go out and play with my pals. But I had understanding enough by then to realise that the world was becoming a smaller and more dangerous place. The Korean War was in full spate when the death of Eva Perón in Argentina swung attention for a brief time to convulsions in another hemisphere. I mourned her out of respect for her rapport with the ordinary Argentinian people.

But all was not gloom in those years. A coup against the very heart of Englishdom brightened our Christmas in 1950. The talismanic Stone of Destiny was nicked from under the coronation chair in Westminster Abbey by a commando of Scottish Nationalists. Up to that time I had never heard of this mythic block of granite nor, it appeared, had most other people in these islands, although it had been languishing under the chair for half a millenium. We learned that it was also known as the Stone of Scone, Scone being a parish in Scotland. And there was a further intriguing revelation. There was a very good chance that the stone did not really belong to the Scots either but was our own Lia Fáil that they had snatched from us a further five hundred years back. The English did not see any humour in the situation at all and diligently set about dragging the Thames and the Serpentine in Hyde Park in a fruitless trawl for the sacred relic. A few months later the robbers relented and turned it in. It had been a wizard prang while it lasted, with the newsreels getting more than a bit of mileage out of it.

Mam had an enduring interest in a very different kind of story, one that had begun before I came into the world. I cannot recall at what stage I first heard of the Dionne Quintuplets, who had been born to French–Canadian farmers in 1934, but apparently they were creatures of great fascination across the continents. Twins people were used to, triplets were not that rare, but quins! And all of them lived! Mam saw something miraculous in their birth and though she liked to hear news of them she could not stomach the intrusive reporting of the newpapers and newsreels, which portrayed them as freaks. When they were already out of their teens she was still bemoaning the fact that they were not allowed to escape commercialisation. For my own part, I could not muster any interest in such an accident of birth.

Human interest stories began for me with the serialisation by the *Irish Press* of the Aga Müller adventure in 1950. Müller was a young German woman who had set out from Hamburg in a small dinghy with her father Paul in an effort to escape the poverty and hunger of postwar Germany and start a new life elsewhere. After a 'dangerous and stormy' voyage her father died off the coast of Liberia. Some time later she came to live in Ireland. In the two-year gap between this serialisation and Thor Heyerdahl's account of the *Kon-Tiki* voyage, which the *Press* also carried, there blew up off the coast of Cork a classic confrontation between man and the sea – the lingering death of *The Flying Enterprise*, which commanded the headlines of press and newsreel over Christmas 1951 and into the new year. On board the ship during those days, his crew having already been winched to safety, remained the Danish–American Captain, Kurt Carlsen, determined to save his vessel or, in the best tradition of the sea, go down with her. Standing by in the storm was the British tug *Turmoil*, and on board her the first mate, Kenneth Dancy, desperately trying to get a towline onto the stricken *Enterprise*. Somehow he managed to get aboard the ship himself and talk some sense into the Captain. The two men returned safely to the *Turmoil*, leaving *The Flying Enterprise* to drift helplessly to destruction. We lived through it all, with regular reports in the press and on the wireless, aerial photos in the papers and, though it reached us late, live action in the newsreels, right through to the final flip under the waves. All that was missing was Sonja Henie in the role of the distressed then joyous wife, poised on her flashing skates for the moment of her Scandinavian hero's return.

Kenneth Dancy proved that while Britain might be losing an empire she could still produce selfless and courageous men of action. A more telling metaphor of her postwar state, however, was provided by a carrier of a different kind, the giant Bristol Brabazon airliner. You saw it on the newsreels from time to time, a magnificent bird taxiing around the runway. The question was, would it ever get off the ground? It did, in managing a test flight. It did not, in being overtaken by the jet age.

CHAPTER TWENTY-THREE

The Cinema

MY CINEMA-GOING HABITS were formed almost exclusively at the Palladium, Dr Daniel Healy's house of dreams on Parks Road. Supplementary excursions to the Desmond in Cappoquin and the Regal in Tallow were not as frequent as I would have liked. Transport to these had to be by bicycle and Dad, with good reason and not a little foresight, would not lend me his big Raleigh until he was sure I had mastered the technique of riding it. Tucked away at the westernmost end of the county in a thinly populated area, our small halls lacked the frills and bright lights of their counterparts in the larger towns and cities of our east and west but, once the screen flickered into life, size and sophistication mattered not in the slightest.

The Regal with 300 seats was the smallest cinema in the region but it had a big-town element that the Palladium and the Desmond lacked – a small balcony with four or five rows of soft seats. The Doc's was a 350-seater while the Desmond, although serving a population roughly equivalent to that of Lismore, about 1,000 inhabitants, had a capacity of 500. It was a sobering thought that had there been a disastrous fire during a performance more than one third of our townspeople could have perished in the Palladium and half those of Cappoquin in their movie house. The palaces started at Dungarvan, with its 960-seater Ormonde serving a population of some 5,000. By the River Suir, the 4,700 residents of Carrick Mór in Tipperary and Carrickbeg in County Waterford could attend the 800-seater Castle Cinema or the smaller, barrel-vaulted Park View, a 400-seater barn of a place like our own Palladium. The plushest picture house of all was the Savoy, situated in the busy Barronstrand Street of Waterford, one of a number in that city. Seating 1,200 patrons, it even had a restaurant on the first floor. With its big screen and soft red seats it was a magnet not just for the 28,000 inhabitants of Waterford but for the whole county and for the neighbouring regions of South Kilkenny, South Tipperary and East Wexford as well. And the man in charge of all this luxury was Mam's cousin-in-law, another doc, Doc Manahan. Confusingly, unlike our Lismore

The Palladium Cinema, Lismore, sadly up for sale in summer 1990.
The Lodge, Doctor Healy's former home, is on the right. The cinema has
been demolished since then.

Doc, the small, natty man was not a member of the medical profession. I only discovered this when, extrapolating from the two examples within my narrow experience, I innocently asked Mam why doctors seemed to have their well-manicured fingers in the entertainment pie.

'Ah sure, Doc isn't a medical man at all,' she said.

'Then why is he called "Doc"?'

'I have no idea. We never called him anything else,' she answered and that was that.

He treated Mam, Paddy and me to a slap-up tea and a picture whenever we were down in Waterford from Carrick during our holidays. Dad would not be with us because he hated shopping and had no interest whatsoever in the pictures. Not only did he never take me to the pictures, he never even knew what was playing. Yet by his own account, on the couple of occasions that he had been to the cinema – he was a youth or young man then – he had enjoyed some Charlie Chaplin shorts enormously. I found his lack of enthusiasm for what for me was becoming an absorbing form of entertainment puzzling. Someone who always had his head in a book should have fancied a movie now and again?

Coincidentally, the Palladium arrived in Lismore the same year as me, 1937. It had been preceded in the town by another picture house called the

Mall Cinema (or Carron's Cinema?) that was situated in the South Mall. The big attraction of the new 'cosy and well-appointed' Palladium was that it was a 'talkie' cinema, the first in the area. But not for long. Cappoquin, ever anxious to keep up with our pace-setting innovation, installed its talkie equipment later the same year. The Palladium stood right next to the Doc's residence, the Lodge. Between the Lodge and the actual cinema there was a wide yard onto which led two side exits from the auditorium, one from the one-and-threes and one from the fourpennies. Further access to the road was through a tall wide gate or an adjoining wicket set in heavy granite walls. On the other side of the building was the entrance to the cinema. From the side, the cinema resembled a large shed with a sloping, galvanised roof. From the front when it was closed, you saw a plain, white or pastel-coloured facade with a flat, brown, wooden double gate set in it on the left. From wall height a series of 'steps' led up from left and right to the pediment and beneath the pediment, stood out in tall, unserifed letters the word PALLADIUM.

Queuing for a show, we would wait at the gate, peering impatiently through the keyhole as the screening time neared, until we heard or glimpsed the Doc himself, or his master of ceremonies, Kevie Noonan, coming up the short gangway from the box-office, jingling a set of keys. The wings of the gate would scarcely have parted before we wriggled through and, clutching our four pennies, charged down the ten yards or so to the tiny box-office window facing us. Inside would be Mrs Healy with a roll of tickets. You gave her your coins and she peeled off your passport to dreamland, entered via heavy brown curtains immediately on your right. Kevie or the Doc, or both, would check you in. The back row of the fourpennies ran straight across from the curtains to the yard exit on the opposite side. For evening shows the fourpennies were really not the fourpennies but the bobs. As we understood it, the Doc charged us fourpence, not out of the goodness of his heart, but to save himself the hassle of filling in a lot of tax forms, or some such complication, which he would apparently have had to do if he had charged us the higher rate. The way we heard it, if he charged us a bob the government took away eightpence, leaving him with fourpence. If he charged us fourpence they demanded nothing. So why charge a bob, the Doc sensibly is supposed to have figured. Logical. Evidence for this theory was to come when, after some of us had behaved somewhat riotously during a film that displeased us, the Doc arbitrarily put the price up to the full amount.

The fourpennies consisted of about six rows of hard wooden benches on the flat. (Dubliners called theirs the 'woodners'.) Some eight to ten feet from the front row there was a shallow stage that remained curtained off with heavy brown drapes until the film started. The curtains were opened by Kevie, the top of whose head reached just above the floor of the stage. From the back of the fourpennies up a slight rake sloped the bobs proper, some ten rows of padded seats with wooden arms. The padding was not very soft and the seats were a bit tight for those with long legs. Between them, the fourpennies and the bobs took up about half the auditorium, leaving the other half to the one-and-threes of soft red velveteen and extended leg room. The prices I quote were the matinee ones. For the evening performance the bobs went up to one-and-three and the one-and-threes to one-and-six. Doc willing, the fourpennies remained the fourpennies. Prices went up again for particularly popular films that the Doc obtained earlier than usual after the first run in Dublin, *Gone with the Wind* or *The Quiet Man*, for example. Half a crown was probably the limit the market would bear. There were aisles running along both sides of the hall. At the back of the left one, as you faced the screen, the Doc had installed the plushest seating of all, three double seats, one behind the other, cordoned off by red ropes with brass hooks and reserved for family and friends. When all six places were occupied the people in them looked like they were sitting in a roller coaster car. Mrs Healy was an avid cinemagoer and if no other member of the family appeared through the curtained side exit just in front of these seats you could be fairly certain that she would. But all the family took their turn, even the Doc.

At the very back of the other aisle there was another bastion of privilege, one acquired by dint of squatters' rights, in the manner in which some churchgoers liked to lay claim to particular pews. The door of the projection box led on to this and, on the right as you came out, there was a high stool on which the projectionist Michael Lineen used to sit to keep his eye on the sound and image quality when the film was running. The three or four seats on the back row to his left were the contentious ones, squatted with regularity by the members of the O'Brien family of upper Main Street, who were undoubtedly the Doc's most faithful and lucrative adult customers. The senior member of the family was Old George, the often grumpy builder and carpenter who had an Aladdin's cave of a workshop full of different lengths of wood, strange tools and the aroma of glue. He liked a movie now and again but his sons and daughters, especially Chrissy, who sang in the choir and at local concerts, and John, who was a teacher in Dublin and very active in the Irish Film Society as Seán, were addicted. Family members would get quite, even very, huffy when they came along and found someone else sitting in their favourite places. The two outer seats were particularly prized because they offered an unimpeded view of the screen. Anything up to three or four O'Briens at a time might be huddled in that corner, sometimes twice that complement when Seán was down with friends from the capital. Listening to them, you could tell that what they didn't know about the pictures wasn't worth knowing. Liking those outer seats as well, I braved their displeasure on a number of occasions myself in my last years in the town. After all, there was nothing they could do about it if you had occupied a place first. I also slipped into the Doc's private section now and then when the Healys were away, not always without incident as the Doc could unexpectedly materialise in the middle of a performance. He *could* shift you. On the other hand, often when he had a full house he would allow customers to occupy the family seats.

Sneaking back into the better seating, especially from the fourpennies to the bobs, was normal practice once the lights were dimmed. Those in the bobs took their chances to slip into the one-and-threes too. It was not that easy to slip back because the Doc used to position himself by the bobs with a torch while Kevie was opening the curtains and he would flash it around at the slightest sound. But he had to check latecomers' tickets at the same time and it was while he was occupied with them that you made your play. Sometimes so many of us youngsters would have traded places he would stop the projection, bring the lights up again and herd us back to the fourpennies, checking maybe too the tickets of some suspected adults in the one-and-threes. Jeers from friend and foe accompanied those of us who had been caught out as we were shepherded back to the right pen. Not much escaped the Doc's eagle eye.

When the Doc was away it was left to Kevie, assisted by Jack Healy when he was home on vacation from university, to keep order. We youngsters liked Kevie but, in spite of our liking him, gave him a hard time when he was on his own. Because he was small and slight and shy, and had a harelip which impeded his speech, it was difficult for him to keep us under control. When he employed his sense of humour he was most successful with us. When he was peevish we took it out on him, sadly, cruelly mimicking his impediment at times. The devil-may-care son, so obviously bored with his cinema duties, if anything wielded even less authority than Kevie so, between the two of them, they scarcely constituted a deterrent to our frequently mischievous behaviour. Fortunately for them they had an ally to rely on, Michael Lineen, the projectionist, who would come out of his box to dampen things down. But all was not a bed of nails for Kevie. It was for him that we regularly reserved the biggest cheer of the programme, and sometimes received an answering grin and wave, when he walked to the stage and reached for the wooden pegs around which were fastened the ends of the ropes that operated the screen curtains. We would settle down with anticipation as he unwound first one rope, then the other, and watch eagerly as the curtains slowly parted to reveal the screen.

This ceremonial act of Kevie's was the overture to a couple of hours' entertainment that did not always turn out as expected. Invariably the only consistent feature of the show was the poor quality of many of the prints the film rentners used to send to the Palladium. Not that we particularly minded, or even noticed the scratches on the image. It was more that the films often came apart and often right in the middle of an exciting action sequence. Wild Bill Elliott, say, would be throwing a punch but before it could land on the ugly mug of the baddie, the film would snap and the screen would explode with light, then quickly go black. Moans of disappointment and outright derision would fill the hall. Out would come Kevie and the Doc's torches. The beams would criss-cross like searchlights as they sought out the faces of those amongst us who were sounding off the most. A bad tear and the house lights would come on. When the film came on again the baddie would be stretched out unconscious on the floor, giving us further cause for dissent as the essence of the action had passed us by. Sometimes the print used to rip apart not once or twice but five or six times during a screening, giving Michael Lineen a real headache. Other times a tear might take five, or even ten minutes to repair, leaving the houseful of patrons sitting around wondering if the show was finished for the night. When that happened, the film not only jumped a few frames but a whole scene or two, giving our imagination plenty of rein for filling in the missing action.

It was not unknown for a print to simply fall apart, in which case the Doc had no option but to give the patrons their money back. He had good cause to be disgruntled when he was saddled with such a lamentable product. There were times when the show was cut short by an agent other than the film rentner. The weather, for which the Doc was not unprepared, played a part too. In an outhouse in the yard he kept a small electricity generator for the not infrequent occasion when the town lights would suddenly fail. The machine appeared adequate to drive the projector for a quarter of an hour to thirty minutes but it could not generate enough power to run a whole feature. If the lines supplying the town were blown down the Doc would again refund his customers. On one such night I was at the Palladium with my brother Paddy and Mike Feeney. A storm had been blowing up as we entered the cinema and the Doc was already looking subdued as it was clear that many punters had decided to remain at home in deference to the weather forecast. Not long into the programme the lights suddenly went out. The Doc did not waste time. He came on with his flashlight and announced that the lights had gone off all over town. A violent gale would hit us before long. It was advisable for everyone to go home. One by one the small attendance filed out past the box-office where the Doc, his round face glistening in the light of an auxiliary oil lamp, refunded us our money.

As Mike, Paddy and I walked down Main Street we could see candles flickering in the pubs. Outside, the darkened street was eerie with menace. High winds swirled and gusted through it, lifting slates off the roofs and shattering them on the flagstones of the pavements. We kept close together and held onto the crown of the road. Local experience held, rightly or wrongly, that that was the safest place when slates were falling, advice similar to that that warned you never to seek shelter from lightning under a tree. Instinct suggested you did the opposite but you tried to respect the empiricism of your elders in such things. Leaden clouds, racing low, lent a ghostly sheen to the blackness. We eyed the tops of the houses warily but maintained a normal walking pace. Now and then we would peer around apprehensively in case a rogue slate might be planing down on us. Not more than a half dozen fell during our passage. It was difficult to pinpoint where they hit. After you heard them grating off the roof there was a moment of suspense before they fragmented on the ground with a smack. We arrived home without injury to be greeted by our anxious mothers. In bed after a cup of hot cocoa, I lay supine listening for new impacts, now near, now farther up the street, before drifting off to sleep. When I awoke in the morning the storm had subsided. The streets were dotted with broken slates.

Another hazard for the Doc and Kevie was the peashooter, when in season. We liked to turn round in those moments when the screen went dark for a night scene and loft a mouthful of haws, or a fistful, high over the heads of the bobs into the one-and-threes. It was always satisfying to hear the resultant squawks of annoyance from the patrons who got rained on. We hoped we had the good sense to shoot high so that no one would catch a haw in the eye. A lone missile might nick Kevie on the neck when he went to work on the ropes. Nor would the Doc escape. When one was feeling daring one picked him off as he exited through the yard door near the fourpennies, having got the programme underway. Balled-up sweet papers; chestnuts, edible and horse; apple hearts (i.e. cores); and other bits and scraps were tossed about in similar fashion. A refinement of this procedure involved one of us slipping back into the bobs and showering a section of the fourpennies, provoking retaliatory action. The skirmish that followed would cause such an uproar among the patrons caught in the crossfire that the projection would be halted and the house lights flung on. A flinty lecture from the Doc, coupled maybe with an ejection or two, restored order. During the peashooter season the Doc took steps to prevent such behaviour by standing at the entrance and eyeing us up and down as we went in. He never went as far as frisking us but he did confiscate the odd shooter sticking too boldly out of a pocket. We took steps to counter him, concealing derringer versions of our normally long shooters down our crotch, or down our socks if already we wore long pants. He would have done better to hang out a sign that said LEAVE YOUR PEASHOOTERS ON THE WAY IN.

When we finally provoked the Doc to our disadvantage it was not with our haws but with his own choice Bramley apples (or they might have been Ross's). Choice the fruit undoubtedly was but, as we were to discover, it was too sour to eat uncooked. It was a scorching summer's afternoon. The town on four wheels, including the Doc and his family, was away in Clonea, Ardmore or wherever. That on two wheels was off at matches of one kind or another. The Scouts were away on their annual camp. Boxer and Euge Dennis, Doshin Keating, Paddy Creane and I seemed to be the only kids left in town and we were bored out of our skulls, so bored we decided to go to the pictures, even though the main feature, *Jennie* (the original American title was *Portrait of Jennie*), looked anything but promising to us. First, as we knew the Healys had taken part in the general exodus, we thought we would stock up with some nice apples from the Doc's orchard. It was a cinch to get in over the wall from the field at the back of the cinema. The yellowing Bramleys were so big and juicy two or three were enough to stuff our pockets. Then we went and took our places in the fourpennies. Only a scattering of patrons was in the auditorium, we in the fourpennies, a few in the bobs, the O'Brien's in the one-and-threes. The first third of the show was passable, an uninspiring selection of travelogues and cartoons. During this period we sampled our apples and found them unbelievably sour, which added to a growing feeling that this was not going to be one of our better days. The main feature came up, a story about an artist and a beautiful ghost, with Joseph Cotten looking all dreamy and helpless and Jennifer Jones of *The Song of Bernadette* looking edgily rapturous. What was a bunch of youngsters in a small town in the back of rural County Waterford on a hot summer's day to make of this? The answer was not much. We sat out the first ten minutes in expectation. Ghosts were always good for a tingle. We tasted all our apples and still found them unbelievably sour. We gave the film another five minutes. It did not seem to be going anywhere. We muttered to one another in discontent. After another five minutes it still had not picked up. Doshin yawned out loud. Kevie, antennaed to the burgeoning situation, bounced up with his torch. We retreated into sullen silence. Up in the one-and-threes an enrapt silence reigned. A cough or two was starting to emanate from the bobs. Euge coughed once, then twice, then the whole fourpennies coughed, a sure indicator that our boredom threshold had been reached. Kevie came at us again with the flashlight. The ensuing five minutes confirmed us in our opinion of the film. It was going nowhere. A word from someone went along the bench. Up went our arms and bang, bang, bang went the big Bramleys against the wooden partition beneath the screen. I was sorely tempted to shy one at Cotten but, fearing that I might do untold damage to the magic screen, lashed out at the boards also. The salvo of discontent unleashed, we raced to the side door, pulled aside the heavy curtains, flung open the door, ran out into the sunny yard, then out through the wicket gate into Parks Road and off down the Main Street, avoiding the melting pools of tar, and laughing and shouting our heads off. The apples had been lousy, the film had been lousy, but we had salvaged some bit of enjoyment from the experience.

The following Wednesday evening we got our comeuppance. We turned up for a western with our fourpences in our hand as usual. Unusually, the Doc was standing *outside* the box-office looking very businesslike. Mrs Healy surveyed us coldly from inside. A few of our other pals who were hanging around regarded us sullenly.

'Fourpenny please,' said Doshin, cool as ever.

'There are no fourpennies anymore,' snapped the Doc, 'on account o' the ruckus ye created on Sunday.' He eyed us vengefully. ''Tis a shilling from now on.'

'What ruckus?' I was going to bluster but, like the others, I knew Kevie would have had to fill him in on the incident, so I prudently withdrew.

'What's goin' on?' Doshin, with sweet reasonableness, asked the other lads who were waiting at the outer gate, hoping the Doc would change his mind.

'Ye ought to know,' said one of them accusingly. 'He's goin' to charge us a bob from now on. Officially he should be doin' that anyway an' payin' tax. Because of Sunday he's puttin' it up to the full whack.'

The Doc had turned the tables on us all right, hitting our pockets and laying the blame for the rise clearly where it belonged. But he was hitting his own pocket, too, and maybe complicating his tax return, so a couple of weeks later he brought the price back down to its original level. The fourpennies, after all, were his bread and butter.

A few years later Doshin, Boxer, Sucky and I were to be provoked into one other public display of consumer dissatisfaction but, this time more restrainedly, and at the Desmond Cinema in Cappoquin. We had cycled over to the neighbouring town to enjoy what we expected to be a tense double bill of murder and gangsterism – the titles of both, sadly, are beyond my recall. The first feature had lived up to our expectations but the second turned out to be a dead loss. After a quarter of an hour or so, during which we ran through our customary coughing procedure, we decided to call it a night. We rose from our front bench seats with as much clatter and bang and scrape as we could muster. Doshin turned and faced the audience.

'This film is no bloody good,' he announced calmly and deliberately, 'We are going home. To Lismore. I advise ye to do the same.'

Then, to laughter that suggested we had the sympathy of most of the gathering, we marched out of the cinema.

I attended the Desmond fairly regularly once I had mastered Dad's Raleigh. A real gate of a thing with 28-inch wheels, it had neither a three-speed gear nor a dynamo. In the dark I used one of those black clip-on lamps with a double battery. Learning how to ride it was not easy. To a young teenager it was a massive, unwieldy contraption. It was the only bike in the house and as we could not afford another I had no option, if I wanted to learn to ride, but to practise on that. The cost was many skinned ankles and abrasions on my legs. I first got to grips with it by inserting my body precariously under the crossbar and balancing it at an angle. Already at 13 or 14 my legs were long enough for me to cycle in the normal position with the saddle screwed down to its lowest height, but not long enough for me to throw my leg over the saddle.

I was in this middle phase when I suffered my first crash, coming down upper Botany at speed when the brakes failed. Realising this to my horror, I managed to drag my right leg over the saddle with difficulty and tried to slow the bike down by grinding the sole of my shoe along the ground. But I had reacted too late. The right-angle corner with lower Botany was coming up fast and in the position in which I was riding I could only manoeuvre to the left. I shot across the lower Botany road – luckily neither man, woman, dog nor vehicle, was coming against me – onto the opposite path and up the slope of a pile of earth and gravel that happened to be heaped up against the four-and-a-half-foot-high wall to within six inches of the top. The front wheel hit the six inches with a shudder, throwing me back on the ground and the bike up in the air. A second later the bike came down on top of me. After I had gathered my senses I reached a finger into my bleeding mouth and discovered I had chipped a piece off a front tooth and loosened a side one. My nose did not come out of it so well, either. As for the bike, the front wheel was buckled beyond redemption and I was forced to roll it home on the back one under the amused gaze of some women who were drawing water from the nearby public tap.

Within a year or so I was to crash spectacularly again, this time bringing down half a dozen other riders as well as myself. A gang of us had been to a Cagney picture at the Desmond in Cappoquin and, in the still bright summer night, came over the summit of the Kennel Heights in a phalanx, cramming the narrow road from ditch to ditch with an array of bikes of all shapes and sizes. Boxer was leading the downhill charge, the rest of us close behind. I was near the front on the right and, seeing Pete Neville pressing me on the left, moved over toward the ditch to let him overtake. Unfortunately, at the same moment, Pete decided to change course and go for the gap between me and the ditch. His front wheel locked with my back one and over we keeled, bringing down all the riders to our rear. Boxer, and the others who were ahead, pulled up when they heard the crash and cruised back, roaring with laughter at the tangle of frames and aimlessly spinning wheels. We were laughing-moaning as we checked our cuts and bruises. Then I saw my front wheel neatly bent at a right angle, forming two half circles.

'Oh Jasus!' I exclaimed, the grin wiped off my face in a flash, 'Dad won't be half mad about this. ''Tisn't long since I smashed the other one.'

My pals commiserated, but the problem now was to get the unridable object home. We had some three miles to go and it was unpushable. The other bicycles had come through unscathed so Barney and most of the lads remounted and rode off, there being nothing constructive they could do about mine. Boxer, Sucky and Pete stayed behind. We were planning to walk back together with the wreckage straddled across the others' bikes when an angel of mercy in the form of Sonny Dawson of Ballyanchor happened along in his Austin 7 car.

'What's up lads?' he asked, shoving his head out of the window.

'Ah sure, we had a crash and we're wonderin' how to get my father's bike home,' I said.

'You did a right job on it, sure enough,' he grinned genially. 'I'll take it home to your door for you.'

''Tis a big bike, Mr Dawson,' I said, eyeing his little car dubiously.

'No trouble.' Sonny got out and inspected the damage. 'I'll get that on the back easily.'

'That's real nice of you, but we have no straps or anythin' to tie it on with.'

The little man looked at me calmly. 'I have binder twine in the car.'

'Oh great!' I said. 'How would you like us to tie on the bike?'

'Don't worry lads. I'll do that. Ye go ahead. I'll catch up with ye. Sergeant Ballantyne's house in West Street, right?'

'Yeh,' I said gratefully.

Pete gave me a lift home on the crossbar of his bike, which had only suffered a bent front mudguard. As we came around by the Co-op I could see ahead of me the light of our open door throwing a beam across West Street. Dad, I was to discover, had just come in late and Mam was telling him that Barney Walsh had called to say that I had crashed the bike. I was explaining to them what had happened when Sonny, not noted for his velocity on the highway, finally caught up with us. Dad did not take it badly and Mam let me off with a scolding.

When bicycle crashes occurred en route to and from the cinema the main cause was lack of lights. We knew every curve, dip and rise of the main and back roads to Cappoquin and had no difficulty negotiating our way in the dark. Usually. At times it could be pitch black. One such night at Ballygallane, Fisser Neville, who was ahead of a group of older lads, crashed straight into a cow that was standing in the middle of the road. The lads coming up behind heard a thump, then a startled 'moo!', then Fisser's bike hitting the tarmacadam, then the cow's hooves cantering off and finally, Fisser fuckin' and blindin'. Their pal was okay but the bike had to be walked home. It was presumed that the animal, which had disappeared into the night, was only dented.

Simple punctures caused most breakdowns. Our bicycle tubes were covered with patches because it was easy to pick up thorns or glass, or even nails, along the way. In daylight if we had a repair kit amongst us, we would fix the puncture. At night we would not even try. I became fairly expert at patching tubes at home, stripping off the tyre with the aid of a spoon handle, immersing the pumped-up tube in a basinful of water to pinpoint the tiny prick, sand-papering clean the area around the puncture, applying the adhesive, sticking on the patch, and dusting the finished job with kaolin scraped off a sweet-sized block. The slim yellow kit box made of tin was carried in a black leather pouch hung at the back of the saddle. Like pumps they were feckable. Consequently, we mostly went out without them.

Trips to the Regal in Tallow were less frequent for me. Aside from the pictures, Tallow offered a thrill of its own, the mile-long hairpin Sweep down to Tallowbridge. It was a killer to bike your way back up it, impossible if you had someone on the bar. In the Regal I discovered a projection problem different to anything I had encountered elsewhere. The attraction we went to see was the new 3-D film *House of Wax*, with Vincent Price. Not a version for which you needed the special 3-D green-and-red glasses – such sophistication was beyond the dream houses of West Waterford – but vivid just the same. Foxy, Barney and I had given Kay Tobin, Breda Behegan and Mada Cahill a bar over to see it. We did not realise that we were going to be in for a protracted show. One of the two projectors broke down which meant that each reel of the film had to be rewound after projection before the next could be laced up and rolled. During these switchover periods of some ten minutes each the house lights were turned on, dispelling totally the hoped-for illusion of horror. At least we were sitting in the comfort of the balcony seats. Some patrons went home when they realised what was happening. We, having made the journey over the hard way, were not so easily put off. It was Kay rather than anything scary in the picture who made the audience jump at the end of the second reel. Just before the lights came on she screamed, 'Jim, take your hand off my knee!' leaving me blushing with innocence. She caught me out again at the end of the third and after that we took to uttering mock screams when Price and his henchman, played by the young Charles Bronson, shadowed into close-up. It was well after eleven when the picture finished, past midnight when we reached the top of the Sweep.

The only other cinema I frequented with any regularity, and that was during holidays, was the Castle cinema in Carrick-on-Suir. The second Carrick picture house, the Park View cinema, was in its declining years, giving me but one opportunity to patronise it. Molly took me there to see a Joe E. Brown comedy one sunny Sunday afternoon. The atmosphere was febrile and a cliff-hanging sequence had the audience in a spin. It was a small-town house like our own. In contrast, the Castle, with its castellated frontage and wide concrete awning, was the kind of place you would expect to find in a bigger town. It had a foyer with a real box-office, a sweet shop, girls serving icecream during the intervals, a central staircase leading to a wide balcony, gold-coloured screen curtains that opened *automatically* to reveal a large screen, music before and after the performance and during the intervals. Certain songs I always associate with it – 'The Folks Who Live on the Hill', 'There's a Small Hotel', 'Harbour Lights', 'Could I Forget You', 'In a Cream Caravan There's a Lady They Call the Gypsy'. And it issued pocket-sized programmes for every month. For all that, however, the pictures were not that different from those I saw at the Palladium. The advantage was that you saw them earlier. But not that much earlier either. Nothing like as early as the movies shown in the first-run cinemas in Dublin. In West Waterford it sometimes seemed to us that we saw in the Forties what

Typical monthly programme of the Castle Cinema, Carrick-on-Suir. This one, for the month of August 1955, offers a varied and most entertaining programme, including three all-time favourites of mine – *Body and Soul*, *Narrow Margin* and *Ramrod*. *(The Castle Cinema no longer exists.)*

the Americans and the rest of the sophisticated world saw in the Thirties, and in the Fifties what they saw in the Forties. With some exceptions, *Gone with the Wind* and *The Song of Bernadette* maybe, *The Quiet Man* certainly. John Ford's picture was given a blanket release throughout Ireland in 1952–53 to the huge enjoyment of many and the chagrin of many others.

'Sure we're not like that at all!' expostulated Mrs Feeney to Mam as the two of them were sitting through it in a packed Palladium.

'Ah sure, 'tis only a picture, Mary,' whispered Mam, wiping the tears of laughter from her eyes.

'I don't find it that funny,' Mrs Feeney said and stared stonily at the hair of the person sitting in front of her.

The picture had generated enormous publicity from the moment when the famous Irish–American purveyor of sentiment and shamrock descended on Galway with his retinue of stars and technicians to shoot it. Its reception on release did not do it any harm either. Curiosity more than anything else brought Mam and Mrs Feeney to see it. Neither woman I regarded as a cinemagoer. Mam rarely went to the cinema and Mrs Feeney appeared there with only marginally more frequency than Dad, who did not express the slightest interest in viewing the object of so much ballyhoo. I was not complaining, as Mam had treated me to a seat in the one-and-threes alongside them.

On the way home afterwards Mrs Feeney continued her attack on the movie. 'Stage Irishry, that's all it is,' she commented icily, with some reason. 'We're not like that at all.'

''Tis a bit exaggerated I admit, but sure don't we often fight among ourselves and, God knows, the trains are *never* on time,' replied Mam.

'They're never *that* late,' Mrs Feeney snapped. 'And what about the way he dragged her around by the hair? That doesn't happen.'

'Sure didn't she deserve it? With her greedy little mind.'

'I'm surprised at Maureen O'Hara. Acting in a picture like that.'

'The bit I had to laugh at was where May Craig handed John Wayne a stick and said, "Here's a stick to beat her with, mister."'

'Draggin' her around by the hair like that!' Mrs Feeney looked at her reproachfully, 'You ought to be ashamed of yourself for enjoyin' it.'

'Sure Mary, 'tis only a film,' was all Mam could plead in her defence again.

They were still arguing the toss when they got to their front doors in West Street. I stayed out of the argument but I had my own thoughts. I thoroughly enjoyed the film but had to agree with our neighbour that the hair-pulling sequence was a bit over the top. Not that I was in any doubt that the like of it was occurring somewhere in our own county. In Tallow or Ballyduff maybe, but not in Lismore. Never in our civilized town.

The May Craig sequence was to join two others, both from a Deanna Durbin picture, I think, that Mam found irresistibly funny. Unfamiliar and unfunny to me, one had Durbin struggling to eat peas off the back of a fork at a stuffy dinner party, and the other an obsequious waiter in a posh restaurant enquiring of an obese woman, 'May I press you to a little jelly, Madam?'

Other whiffs of film-making in Ireland came our way in the early Fifties with the production of *Knights of the Round Table* and *Moby Dick*. The first, with Robert Taylor, was shot in part in 1953 at Luttrellstown Castle in County Dublin, hardly a stone's throw from County Waterford. The Lismore connection was one Major Robert Porter who had bought and restored an old cottage out the Mayfield Road where he lived with his exotic Filipino wife. Well over six foot tall, rangy and rakishly good-looking, he stunted in the jousting scenes, not too successfully, apparently. He returned from Luttrellstown with one leg in a plaster cast. With a wife the twin of Dorothy Lamour to look after him, I felt little desire to be sympathetic when I saw him hobbling in and out of the Wine Vaults on a pair of crutches. A year later John Huston was setting up the opening scenes of *Moby Dick* in Youghal, County Cork, a seaside resort regularly visited by Lismore people as it lay only eighteen miles distant from our town. I was a rare day-tripper there. The fascias of many of the shops and bars along the old seafront were repainted and given names to coincide with those of Melville's novel. People came from miles around to experience the buzz. The filming was over and the film crew long departed by the time I got there from Carrick-on-Suir to which place I had moved by then.

My understanding of the physical artefact that produced the images on the screen was more modestly acquired. I would scavenge the small rubbish dump at the back of the Palladium projection box for pieces of film that Michael or Jim Lineen – Thumper assisted his first cousin for a time – had discarded after repairing a print. Most of these were nondescript so I used to greatly value the few stills of Hopalong or Alan Ladd, and others of my heroes that turned up. The treasured items would be put away in a cardboard box with a rubber band around each one, to be unscrolled and viewed under an electric light bulb when I so desired. The frames I did not cherish were either swopped for other things or set alight for the thrill of seeing the strip of film burn.

These snippets of the real thing meant much more to me than the movie magazines I used to come across. I occasionally bought *Picture Show* or

Picturegoer but I was never fan enough to want to subscribe to them regularly, or to want to start a film scrapbook. The two English periodicals looked dull - they were printed in an uncertain sepia tinged with red - and, of necessity, were dull in content as they predominantly covered British cinema. My brother used to borrow a glossy American fanzine entitled *Modern Screen* or something like that, from some friends of his. Strong on bathing beauties, provocative by the standards of the time in Ireland, and on gossip about the stars, this periodical contained little information about the actual movies. For a serious discussion of cinema I turned to a general English magazine to which Paddy himself subscribed, the sepia-coloured *Everybody's*. He took it mainly for the articles on kings and emperors and palaces, for music, art and short stories. These were the features in which it specialised, it seemed to me. But it was worth combing for other subjects too. As well as cinema, it covered the infant television and, surprisingly, sport – its reports of the two Turpin–Robinson world championship fights were particularly good.

In Lismore, films were screened on Monday, Wednesday and Thursday evenings and on Sunday afternoon. The Thursday programme was usually a repeat of the Wednesday one. On all other days of the week, including Sunday evening, you could choose to go to Tallow or Cappoquin. The Regal in Tallow had two shows on Sunday and, during the week, Monday–Tuesday and Thursday–Friday programmes. Cappoquin's Desmond favoured an evening slot on Sunday, a single show on Tuesday, a repeat programme on Thursday–Friday and, occasionally, a Saturday performance. Larger cinemas like the Castle in Carrick-on-Suir or the Ormonde in Dungarvan would feature four or five different programmes a week. In West Waterford extended runs, maximum a week, were rare and were only accorded to films for which an unusual demand was perceived. An obvious candidate, dealing as it did with miracles and Mariology, subjects dear to the Irish Catholic heart, was *The Song of Bernadette,* shown at the Palladium in 1945. *The Quiet Man* stayed for a week as well.

Like Hollywood, the Doc recognised the potential of religion. On free days the Palladium would be hired out to religious orders who would screen independent productions made to promote religious fervour and attract acolytes to the orders. Feature-length titles that we were released from school to attend included *The Life of St John Bosco, Our Lady of Fatima* and *Monsieur Vincent,* which just might have been the first French film I ever saw. Neither as education nor entertainment did these pictures inspire me. The less said about the even more turgid religious shorts we were shown about the Holy Land and the missions, the better.

A full programme at a West Waterford cinema was offered from the following menu: a short, a James A. Fitzpatrick travelogue (How *many* did the guy make?), a cartoon, a serial, a newsreel, and the feature film. Within this broad classification there were many variations, the most welcome of which was the substitution of the James A. by a second cartoon, or anything, and the most unwelcome of which was the substitution of the cartoon or anything by a James A. B-features, i.e. supporting features or co-features, offered two possibilities: a double bill with an abbreviated shorts list or a single B with an expanded shorts programme. Shorts came in many guises and in varying lengths. There was comedy, for example, from the Three Stooges, the Bowery Boys, Joe McDoakes, Laurel and Hardy, Pete Smith (Specialities), and Ma and Pa Kettle; cowboy adventures with Hopalong Cassidy, Roy Rogers, Whip Wilson, Bill Elliott, etc.; serials like *Flash Gordon, Zorro,* and *The Clutching Hand;* crime series such as *Crime Does Not Pay* and *Scotland Yard.*

The newsreel we saw in West Waterford would probably have been either *British Movietone News* or *Pathé Gazette/Pathé News,* tailored with an eye to the Irish censorship. It was, in effect, a local version of the British national reel with stories of Irish interest replacing British regional news items. But it did not stop there. The producers would edit in for our consumption any story from anywhere in the world about the Catholic religion on the assumption that it had to be of interest to us. Or they just filled in with non-controversial and boring topics like fashion shows and 'strange' sports from around the world. Stories of direct Irish interest included GAA Finals, home countries rugby internationals, Irish ceremonials and political events, international sports events in which there was Irish participation, horse-racing, anything to do with religion in Ireland. *Universal News* was also shown in Ireland, exclusive to Rank Cinemas. (A wholly Irish newsreel did not appear until 1956. This was Gael Linn's excellent Irish-language weekly reel, *Amharc Éireann,* which ran over 256 issues until 1964.)

Most youngsters of my age came to the newsreels unaware that the British companies that produced them had suspended their circulation in the Free State from mid-1943 to sometime in late 1946, or early 1947, owing to wartime shortage of film stock. At least, that was the reason the companies offered. Another possibility was that Allied wartime trading sanctions against our country might have been in operation. The reels were primarily of interest to us when the sports stories came on, in particular the Hurling and Gaelic Football Provincial and All-Ireland Finals. Less absorbing were the much more frequent soccer matches and rugby games.

Major horse races, especially the Aintree Grand National, also held our attention. The National, spectacular in the awesome heights of its jumps and in the length of the course, was always of interest. Irish horses were consistently good competitors in it, from the magnificent Prince Regent to the gallant little Lough Conn, the surest each-way bet of all, and we had winners in Lovely Cottage in 1946 and Sheila's Cottage in 1948. Success on the flat was more elusive for the Irish-trained animals until Vincent O'Brien's Tulyar swept across our screens in 1952. Championship boxing contests were a major attraction, with any fight with the Brown Bomber a sell-out. Even if the rest of the programme were rubbish in our eyes we would crowd in to see Louis deliver his latest kayo. Unfortunately, I myself missed a number of his fights in the Forties because my parents did not yet allow me to stay out late enough to see a programme through to the end. Our strategy when we had to miss programmes in which we were interested, for reasons of age or lack of money, was to put our ears to the auditorium door, or skulk behind the projection box, and soak up with bated breath what we could hear of the soundtrack.

The Doc and Kevie were sympathetic to disadvantaged children and often, when they found them listening outside, would let them into the show for nothing if there was room in the fourpennies. I could have been let in free on a couple of occasions also, only I was under curfew. Ruefully, I watched Doshin and a couple of others take up the offer. The biggest yawn in the newsreel was the society wedding, of which there was far too much. Vying with this was the Channel swim. While there was much to admire in the endurance of the redoubtable Florence Chadwick and her adult and teenage peers, the images of them smearing their bodies with thick grease before starting out on the swim, battling through the choppy waters of the English Channel guided by a small accompanying boat, and emerging exhausted at either Calais or Dover (those like Miss Chadwick who were successful) were singularly uninspiring. Visually exciting events like the drama of *The Flying Enterprise* were rare, although the reels were keen on disasters. Often news items were mere headlines, so that a really interesting story like the shooting of the Sicilian Robin Hood, Salvatore Giuliano, in 1950 could have been missed if you blinked.

My short comedy favourites were undoubtedly Laurel and Hardy and their regular antagonist, the Scot James Finlayson. The Three Stooges mayhem was less to my liking, but the lads from Botany and Church Lane enjoyed it. Between these two contrasting styles we found mutual pleasure in other comedians. Leo Gorcey and the Bowery Boys (occasionally in their earlier guise, the Dead End Kids) went down well with us. Joe McDoakes never quite lived up to his engaging credits sequence which saw him emerge from behind a large eight-ball, the significance of which was lost on us, tip his pork pie hat back over his forehead, roll his eyes and ripple his fingers. A standard title phrase, *So You...,* was his other trademark, e.g. *So You Think You're a Nervous Wreck, So You Want to Hold Your Wife,* etc. Leon Errol was more to my liking in supporting roles than in his own series, Edgar Kennedy a laugh in spots only. Chaplin's tramp was a rarity at the Palladium – I do not recall ever seeing him anywhere on a West Waterford screen – although the character was instantly recognisable to us from magazine and newspaper articles. His great contemporaries, Buster Keaton and Harry Langdon, did appear on our screen; I remember seeing a number of their shorts. The other silent entertainers, the Mack Sennett comics and the Keystone Kops careered regularly across our screen, the custard pie slapstick and inspired acrobatics of Chester Conklin and his pals always arousing us to a frenzy. Larry Semon I found less appealing but I laughed willingly with him, too, at times. The *Ma and Pa Kettle* series, with Marjorie Main and Percy Kilbride, of the early Fifties took us beyond the slapstick we enjoyed so much. Main's rough-spoken Ma and Kilbride's shrewdly mild-mannered Pa were perfect foils. The lasting image of Pa for me comes from *Ma and Pa Kettle Go to Town;* intrigued by an automatic door he elegantly skips through it again and again.

Of humorous supporting films, the cartoon seldom failed. When the Looney Tunes and Merrie Melodies logos hit the screen a spontaneous cheer rose from the fourpennies and we all sat up in anticipation. The cheer would double in volume when it became clear that we were about to see Tom and Jerry, Bugs Bunny, or Sylvester and Tweetie Pie even when, as often occurred, we had already seen the film not once but twice or three times before. The range of cartoons I myself saw was limited. Popeye, Donald Duck and Mickey Mouse were only known to me through the comics that my cousin Catherine used to send me from New Jersey. Only one feature cartoon came my way, *Snow White and the Seven Dwarfs.* I enjoyed the dwarfs.

Feature-length comedy reached us with less frequency. Danny Kaye was a comic with whom I could go only so far down the line. He could be very funny and lovable, but also, and frequently, very silly. Zaniness was something else, the Marx Brothers – our favourite main feature comics by a street. Even their corny musical interludes we could accept. They had their indelible heroine too in Margaret Dumont, who suffered indignity after indignity with equanimity. I did not know her name then, nor that of the brothers' other admirable and indispensible foil, Sig Ruman. Fast-talking too were Abbott and Costello whose wise-cracking routines creased us. Feature-length comedy was in a state of transition in the postwar period but from my point of view, the older the comedy, the riper it was, right back to the Keystone Kops. In between I enjoyed Jimmy 'Schnozzle' Durante, Joe E. Brown and Jerry Colonna, the bizarre lanky guy with the Mexican moustache, high-pitched voice and bulging eyes. Bob Hope I preferred in anything without Bing Crosby. The crooner was a pill, as was Dean Martin, the other half of a new comedy duo styled on the *Road* pairing. Martin could not act for toffee and his sleepy singing pulled my eyelids right down. Jerry Lewis, at least, had his moments, even if he was not the funniest act around. One thing I could compliment the pair on: they introduced Elaine Stewart to the screen in *Sailor Beware*. The oddest comedian to come my way was Francis, the Talking Mule, his voice immediately recognisable as that of Chill Wills whom we knew from many cowboy pictures. While he and his buddy Donald O'Connor did not knock us out, they gave us a share of laughs. Francis, after all, was a damn sight funnier than Tarzan's tiresome chimp.

When it came to other genres, our young tastes centred on westerns ('cowboy films' we called them), swashbucklers, horror films, gangster films and jungle thrillers. I could never accept the big-name stars in cowboy films. Errol Flynn and Tyrone Power, acceptable in sword-fighting roles, came across as dudes in their fancy western regalia. But they were only two of a number of glamorous stars that looked unconvincing in cowboy outfits. Even Cagney looked out of place in them. Mel Ferrer was another, a real dude in *Rancho Notorious,* when he came up against the gritty Arthur Kennedy. Nor was it just their outfits that made us wince. In action sequences they seemed to be riding hobby-horses rather than the real thing, bobbing up and down in the ridiculous Anglo-Irish fashion instead of riding low and tight like the real cowboy and Indian. But they brought one slice of reality to the western; they stopped to load their guns. One star, Randolph Scott, was an exception. He was to become my archetypal western hero, outdoing even Wild Bill Elliott. His face, lined and full of character, had a lot to do with it. I took to faces. Some I liked instantly – Ladd, Bendix, Lancaster, Conte, Raft, Duryea. Others, like Cagney, Edward G., Garfield and Bogart I had to work on. Veronica Lake was instantly divine, Gloria Grahame instantly and indelibly bitchy. Stanwyck I could not make up my mind about; was she a goodie or a baddie? Joan Crawford's accusing eyeballs were too much for me, but I liked her voice. However ambiguous I felt about them, it was the stars who drew me to the feature films. I never missed the Marx Brothers, George Raft, Dan Duryea, Errol Flynn, Karloff,

Abbott and Costello, and Weissmuller, for example. I tried hard to catch Joel McCrea, Rod Cameron, Jon Hall. With luck a favourite male actor would be teamed up with a favourite actress – Lake, Virginia Mayo, Ruth Roman, Ava Gardner, Bacall,... .

The dreams the cinema peddled were real enough even though we instinctively knew that an awful lot of the imagery we were soaking up was crap, for example, the heroine who battled through mud and rain and always came through with hairdo and make-up intact, the villains whose hats never fell off during a punch-up, the hero who talked aloud in the silence of the night when a whisper was called for, the cowboys who never had to load their six-guns – sometimes we used to count the shots for fun; I cannot recall the highest total we came up with. We spotted tell-tale traces of invention in the darkness that was never really dark and in the stagecoach wheels that revolved with a backward motion. We recognised that there was a limit to the money spent on a production when we regularly hooted a sequence that showed the same posse coming around the same outcrop of rocks and the same copse of trees in different cowboy films. Indeed, we noted costumed baddies cornering the same sweep in swashbucklers. And we sensed how music was used to play on our emotions – the taut, discordant strings that underwrote the credit sequences of gangster films, the weepy violins of love scenes, and so on. In saying 'we' I do not mean to imply that all the youngsters in the town were as attracted to the cinema as I was. Tom Lineen was one who could confidently ignore this aspect of American and British culture. He rarely if ever went to the pictures.

Imagination, being a free spirit, could cause you to lose your way in a dream, as happened to Paddy Creane when he was little. Molly had taken him and me to see George Formby in *Let George Do It*. In it there is a scene in which the comedian falls into a vat of dough or a bin of flour and stands up looking like a ghost. Which was exactly what Paddy's fertile mind took it to be. He started crying hysterically and Molly had to usher the two of us out of the cinema. It took her a long time to calm him down during which I, who was a year or two older, unsympathetically sulked at having to miss the rest of the film. I was to be unsettled myself, though not so dramatically, in a later year when I was confronted by a tarring and feathering scene in a film about the southern United States. My mind seized on the appalling incident and for a long time it appeared to me in a succession of dreams so vivid that I began to think I had witnessed it for real in Lismore.

The screen worked negatively in other ways. As we had no scale in our own lives against which to judge otherwise we took racial stereotypes at face value. 'Chinamen' were funny and easily scared, with the exception of

Charlie Chan who, of course, was played by a white man. Blacks (usually Willie Best) rolled their big white eyeballs fearfully in the dark. New York's finest were lovable, slow-in-the-head Paddies. German officers liked to address their prisoners as *Schweinhund*, a term that the comics used to translate bizarrely as 'pigdog', a linguistic abomination that never failed to make me grin. Frenchmen could not speak English properly. Neither could 'greasy Mexes', and they, with the exception of Gilbert Roland, were irredeemably lazy and low on guts to boot. Even at best, Red Indians were untrustworthy. And so on. To such extremes were the stereotypes carried, however, that eventually you were forced to question them. For a start the best boxers in the world – Joe Louis, Sugar Ray Robinson, Archie Moore, to name but the greatest, were black and brave and regularly seen on the newsreels thrashing white men. Then there were the Red Indians, so obviously underdogs who were having their lands stolen from them. Why was it so necessary for the whites to insult them, break agreed treaties again and again and slaughter them over and over with superior firepower? Soon enough you reached the stage where you were hoping the cavalry would *not* arrive in time, a wish fulfilled when *They Died with Their Boots On*, the big one to which the cavalry came too early, unfolded on our screen. It cheered me no end to see Errol Flynn cashing in his chips in a western.

For us kids it was the cowboy short, of which Bill Elliott was king, that provided the real thrills. Hopalong Cassidy, too, earned a high approval rating from us although some of his B-features had their longueurs. Johnny Mack Brown was a third who gave value for money. The Doc kept us reasonably well supplied with these westerns although it was always a matter of curiosity to us why he chose some sagebrush heroes rather than others. Hoppy, Wild Bill and Johnny Mack rode regularly at the Palladium. We did not get too much of Rogers and, mercifully, nothing of Gene Autry, the other singing cowboy. The Desmond in Cappoquin was his hunting ground. If you wanted to catch Charles Starrett or Tex Ritter you went to the Regal in Tallow. I suspect the vagaries of the film renting business accounted for these anomalies.

Weary of the diet of cowboy and gangster movies that monopolised the Lismore screen, Mam would periodically say to the Doc, '*Why* don't you get good pictures? If you did, I'd go more often.'

'I put in for them, Mrs Ballantyne,' he would say, shaking his head wearily, 'But they don't let me have what I ask for. Except now and again.'

The cowboy yarns might have counted as rubbish in Mam's eyes but they were seat-gripping stuff to me, the pabulum of a lifetime. Excepting Roy Rogers, of course. The only thing you could admire about him was his smart horse Trigger, and he was no smarter than Hoppy's Topper. In one of his pictures there were even motor cars! No, it was too much to ask us to take seriously someone whose first Rider's Rule was 'Be neat and clean'. I would have been very surprised, and not a little disappointed, to discover that the Roy Rogers Riders Club had succeeded in recruiting even *one* member in the town of Lismore, let alone in West Waterford. Rogers' biggest failing in our eyes was that he looked about as tough as the insipid Englishman, Leslie Howard; or the super-quiffed Austrian, Paul Henreid; or the oddly-named American, Franchot Tone; all carriers of a disease known as milky patriotism. To the Palladium also came the curious Whip Wilson, about whom I could never make up my mind. 'Better than nothing, i.e. Rogers and Autry' was, I think, my final analysis. As his name suggested, he was supposed to be more at home with a bullwhip than a six-shooter. And he did have a few snappy routines with this instrument. What puzzled me, however, and made me distrust the reality of his whipwork was how, after he had looped his lash around the branch of a tree or the balcony rail of a saloon and swung his pudgy frame aloft, he could then free it so easily again. He did not look very tough, either. Every time he raised his arm to crack the whip you could sense him creak and his ample belly used to ride up over his belt. His saving grace was that he had Andy Clyde, on loan from Hoppy, as a side-kick. Clyde was always good for a laugh. The whip man I would really have liked to see was Lash Larue, a leaner, meaner-looking exponent of this skill, whom I knew from the comics. But I am not sure if he ever rode out on a West Waterford screen. A number of other range-riders never made it off the pages of the comics either, Monte Hale and the Lone Ranger and Tonto, for example. Still others, like Allan Rocky Lane (I would have liked to see more of him), Ken Maynard and the Cisco Kid appeared out of the blue for an odd screening, as if the rentner had sent the Doc the wrong reel of film by mistake or, unable to supply Hoppy, sent a filler instead. Hoppy was the smartest cowboy of them all, thoughtful, cool, and with a sense of humour – *Ha, ha, ha!* We used to take off his laugh. Hoppy did not go in for frills, except maybe for a fancy gunbelt. He was a dead shot. He wore a plain black shirt and trousers and a distinctive high-domed, black sombrero; and when subterfuge demanded, a grey tweed suit and a white sombrero. The actor William Boyd's hair used to puzzle us. Was it really white as it appeared in monochrome or was it just very fair? We never solved that one. Hoppy's partners were okay as well – Gabby Hayes and later Andy Clyde for laughs and Russell Hayden for punch-ups and a *little* romance. (We were not impervious to romance; as long as it did not get too mushy it was acceptable.) Robert Mitchum, sneering and leering, was often a worthy opponent. If Hoppy had a failing it was that he was too much of a gent.

For a brawl you went to Wild Bill Elliott. When he tangled with roughnecks whole saloons fell apart. He did not mind going in with the boot either, which made him seem a bit more human. He rode, and looked, like a real cowboy, i.e. our idealised cowboy, went for the crossdraw, and did not wave his Colt .45 around as if it was something he buttered bread with. Above all, he looked tough; strong jaw, tight lips, and with a mean glint for the meanest killer in the West, Bob Steele. Steele, small, cold-eyed and menacingly voiced was fated to be the second-fastest gunslinger in countless westerns. No one could take a slug in the guts and writhe in his death throes better. Andy Devine, the big, fat, dewlapped, timorous comedian also rode with Elliott. For action and thrills only one cowboy outrode Wild Bill Elliott – Randolph Scott, a man in the same mould. The rugged Richard Dix, a couple of whose features I managed to view, was the only other western star that I was willing to bracket in their company. Scott may not have been tougher or more rugged than Elliott but he had the advantage of B-feature scripts, bigger co-stars, and better direction. Mostly. He starred in some poor westerns, too, but even in those he was watchable. A hole he could not shoot himself out of, he would talk himself out of. He could deliver a bizarrely humorous line with relish. His square-jawed good looks and weather-beaten face lent him credibility as a man who lived the outdoor life and he brought an unquenchable honesty and dignity and a kind of tenderness to his roles. We believed he always did his own stunts. Barney Walsh had it on authority that Scott's big fight scene with John Wayne at the end of *The Spoilers,* a full-length feature in which our hero was cast as a kind of good-hearted baddie, was the real thing because the two actors had lost their rag with one another.

Of two Canadian Indian 'canoe' pictures it was Scott's *The Last of the Mohicans* (1936) rather than Spencer Tracy's *Northwest Passage* that left a lasting impression on me, even though he had a rather subdued role, playing a British officer. Uncas the Mohican was the real hero of *The Last of the Mohicans,* throwing himself and his sworn Huron enemy Magua to death off a precipice. In the Fifties Randolph Scott was already coming to the end of a long career, one that had begun, like that of many other big names, John Wayne, Bogart, Bela Lugosi, etc, in the multiple episode serials.

The Doc, for some reason, did not appear to take serials so you had to go to either Tallow or Cappoquin if you got hooked on them. I mostly heard of them second-hand from my Botany pals who had more freedom of movement and fewer restrictions placed on their cinema-going than I had.

I only ever managed to pick up an odd, out of context, episode of this or that. *Buck Rogers* and *Flash Gordon* were favourites but the serial that most seemed to grab my pals' imagination was a Craig Kennedy thriller called *The Clutching Hand*. Whether *The Hand* was on at the Regal or the Desmond or, as I suspect, both, I cannot recall but as Sucky and Doshin did not miss one of the fifteen parts that had gripping individual titles like 'The Phantom Car', 'The Evil Eyes' and 'The Steps of Doom', I suspect the Doc might have screened it in the evenings too. I would hear of hooded villains, secret chambers, treacherous trapdoors and, above all, the perilous endings that kept them in suspense until the next episode. Not even one episode of this cliff-hanger did I manage to view. The nice twist about the serials was that the villain, his masked identity cloaked under pseudonyms like 'The Scorpion', 'The Gargoyle' or 'The Rattler', was a much more exciting and entertaining character than the hero.

The lads from Botany and Church Lane identified wholly with the characters played by Cagney, Ladd, Raft, Richard Conte, Mickey Rooney and John Garfield and, to a lesser extent, with Edward G. Robinson, possibly because the characters often came from poor and disadvantaged backgrounds like themselves, and possibly because these particular stars, like many of the Botany and Lane boys, were physically short. They would also have been proud of Cagney's Irish descent. Rooney we reckoned as Irish too and it would have greatly disappointed us had we learnt that his real name was Joe Yule. On the other hand it was a long time before we realised quite how short some of these larger-than-life screen figures were. The studios saw to it that they were shot from carefully studied angles and teamed up with petite female stars, Ladd with Lake, for example. I was sharply disillusioned when I discovered that he stood only five foot six inches in his socks. On screen he had appeared so tall and muscular. William Bendix, his sidekick in many pictures, was not much taller, although he was beefier and just as tough. Bit of a slob with it. Who else could have uttered such words as, 'Heart, Jim, heart. The world's cryin' for a bit o' heart,' and made you believe he believed them? Any of the actors Bendix sidekicked, for example, Ladd in *The Blue Dahlia* and *Two Years Before the Mast*, Raft in *The Glass Key*, Mitchum in *Macao*, Kirk Douglas (the most heavily muscled shorty of them all) in *Detective Story*, would have been value on their own. Bendix was the icing on the cake.

Leading players like Bendix – Claude Rains, Brian Donleavy, our own Barry Fitzgerald, Sidney Greenstreet, Peter Lorre, Victor McLaglen etc. – were as attractive to us as the big names. And along with them came a host of great Hollywood supporting players, many émigrés from the troubled continent of Europe, who never failed to lift a picture with their cameo roles. Over time they became instantly recognisable to us as they were constantly turning up in different genres. However, as we tended to chat impatiently through the credits, we could seldom put a name to the faces. Which did not worry us in the slightest. It was enough that we could identify them physically, e.g. 'the big fella with the beret and the funny accent' (Dan Seymour), 'the fussy little clerk with the moustache' (Franklin Pangborn), 'the big guy, full of himself' (Sig Ruman), 'the mangy-lookin' fella' (Charles Halton), and so on. Once settled into a definite characterisation the supporting performer seemed to be stuck with it. I did my own loose categorisation, bracketing those 'unnamed' actors and actresses into those I loved to love and those I loved to hate. Among the former were Mike Mazurki (favourite heavy), Nat Pendleton and Donald McBride (favourite dumb cops), William Demarest (fast-talking heart of gold), Allan Hale (cheerful, dependable big man), Ward Bond (dependable but a little dumb), Guinn 'Big Boy' Williams (beefy, slow-thinking grinner), Gloria Grahame (sultry), Thomas Mitchell (dry Irishman), Gilbert Roland (Mexican charmer), Claire Trevor (wise-cracking heart of gold), S. Z. Sakall (favourite funny foreigner), and Margaret Dumont (serene amidst the chaos of the Marx Brothers). In the second slot I fitted among others Raymond Burr (enormous, sweaty and cowardly baddie), Marie Windsor (bug-eyed, treacherous, but also damn sexy), Bruce Cabot (dry-gulcher), Victor Jory (ditto), Barton Maclane (brutal), Ray Teal (big, mealy-mouthed), and Henry Daniell (a rat).

It was the American cinema that held all the attractions for us. The only other industry within our experience was the English one in which all the music scores were directed by one man, Muir Mathieson. Two factors combined to make the British pictures, with a few exceptions, interminably dull to a youthful cinemagoer. One, the only thing that moved fast enough in them to generate any excitement was the black police car that went ring, ring, ring, down city streets and country lanes in the *Scotland Yard* series of shorts presented by the smug, rotund little Edgar Lustgarten from behind his massive, ego-boosting desk. And two, most of the great British screen stars – Colman, Laughton, Rains, Sanders, Rathbone, Greenstreet, Karloff, Lanchester, Lupino, and no less unforgettable supporting talents such as Wallace Ford and Eric Blore – had taken their distinctive and imperishable talents to Hollywood. That said, however, I think we did appreciate as we grew older the downbeat realism of the British pictures, especially the documentaries. On the whole, there seemed to be no spurious glamour about them of the kind that we readily saw through in the Hollywood output. The few exceptional features were well worth waiting for: Sabu in *The Thief of Baghdad*, James Mason in *Odd Man Out*, Robert Newton again in *Odd Man Out* and *Treasure Island*, Trevor Howard in *The Golden Salamander, I See a Dark Stranger* and *An Outcast of the Islands*, were among my personal favourites. Less enjoyable, but interesting because of their Irish themes, were *Captain Boycott* with Stewart Granger and *Hungry Hill* with Dennis Price. British comedians were exceptions also, especially Will Hay and Alistair Sim. From pictures that dealt with the British Empire, for example, the British-produced *The Drum* and *The Four Feathers* and the American-produced *Gunga Din* and *The Charge of the Light Brigade* (Errol Flynn dying with his boots on again), we emerged with divided loyalties. It was okay to see the bad guys getting beaten, although we were not wholly convinced always that they really *were* bad guys. What was not so much to our liking was that they should be defeated by the bugle-blowing British, even if now and again a token Paddy, usually played by Victor McLaglen, was thrown in on the Imperial side. (The historical reality was that a very high percentage of the British army of occupation in India at the height of Empire was Irish.) There was something corrupt going on that we could only sniff at, a parallel with the bugle-blowing US Cavalry, amongst whom often rode too a token Irishman, who slaughtered the Sioux and the Apache. I never saw the British film that generated the most publicity, *The Third Man*. It was probably screened in Lismore but I do not recall it coming to the Palladium. I may have been away on holidays at the time. Everyone talked about it but I had to be content with hearing on radio the haunting theme music on the zither that became an unlikely hit in 1950.

Not all war films we saw dealt with the British Empire. Most were about the Second World War, the subjects of which included, for example, escape from Nazi Germany *(Desperate Journey* with Errol Flynn); resistance to Nazi occupation *(North Star* with Dana Andrews and Anne Baxter); the war against the Japanese *(Home of the Brave* with Frank Lovejoy and Lloyd Bridges and *Objective Burma* in which Errol Flynn destroyed the enemy to the real-life chagrin of the British who had done all the fighting there); spy stories *(13 Rue Madeleine* with James Cagney, *Odette* with Anna Neagle); the Spanish Civil War *(For Whom The Bell Tolls* with Gary Cooper and Ingrid Bergman); and so on. Overall the war pictures, of which there were many, were popular with us. Of the genre, I myself tended to prefer the spy stories.

There were curious absences from the screens I patronised. I cannot be certain about this as I did not see or hear of every film that passed through Lismore itself. It would require an inspection of the Doc's booking records, if these are extant, or of those of the film rentner who supplied him with prints, to establish a comprehensive exhibition list. The Doc's publicity matter may also have survived. During my childhood I was only allowed to go to matinees (exceptionally I was taken to an evening programme), but even then I usually saw the notices listing what was on, or had information through my pals who regularly went to evening shows. W. C. Fields and Mae West were unknown to me – they may have been too hot for our repressive state censorship. Don Ameche and Rita Hayworth were merely names. After her steamy role in *Gilda* in 1946 and her highly publicised marriage to the fabulously rich Prince Aly Khan in 1949 she too may have proved too hot to handle for the censorship. But Don Ameche – who was this name I came across periodically that could turn the collective head of the Daughters of the American Revolution? And Clark Gable? If he came to town, other than in *Gone with the Wind*, I missed him too. And did the Doc really not take serials? As I explained above, these could have been screened in the evenings at a time in my young life when I was not allowed to stay out late. Betty Grable's legs I did see sometime, but only just, in one of those films in which Hollywood liked to be seen supporting the war effort. Many pictures came to the Palladium that I as a child, and later as a youth, had no interest in seeing. Mam would be on the lookout for stars like Bette Davis or Greer Garson, Ronald Colman or Cary Grant. She loved Norma Shearer's Elizabeth Barrett Browning in *The Barretts of Wimpole Street* as much as she despised the tyrant father portrayed by Charles Laughton – 'Sure you couldn't live with the likes of him?' she commented. Anything with Jeanette MacDonald or Deanna Durbin in it also drew her. I was dragged along unwillingly with her to a packed Palladium to see the big-jawed co-star of Nelson Eddy in *Maytime* and *Rose Marie*, probably because she did not trust me to be on my own at home, or possibly because she felt I could do with a little shock treatment to wean me off my diet of B-westerns. I escaped seeing Deanna Durbin, even in *Can't Help Singing*, a favourite of Mam's, I seem to recall. Mam was more successful with *Wuthering Heights*. The passionate romanticism of Laurence Olivier and Merle Oberon captivated me as much as Mam. On the whole, I had little time for musicals although I was not averse to the odd song, for example, 'Balalaika' from the film of the same title with Eddy and Ilona Massey and Allan Jones's 'Donkey Serenade' from *The Firefly*. My weak spot was the one that came up with an Irish accent, *My Wild Irish Rose*, with the wavy-haired Dennis Morgan (real name Stanley Morner) who passed for an acceptable Celt. Another 'Irish' musical, *Little Nellie Kelly* with Judy Garland, packed them in but I was too small when this hit town. It was often talked about. As for dancing pictures, in spite of the Astaires' connection with our town, the only hoofer I wanted to see was George Raft. Nobody could tango like George Raft. Except maybe our own 'Mick the Bird'.

Romance I sought in the exotic, and there was not much that was more exotic than the swordfighting film, a genre ranging from *The Mark of Zorro* in Mexico through *The Three Musketeers* of France to *The Prince Who Was a Thief* of Bagdad. Interestingly, in these pictures our tastes as boys coincided with those of our girlfriends. Tyrone Power, for instance, a great favourite with the girls, won us all over in *The Mark of Zorro* and *The Black Swan*. I was totally indifferent to his charms in other films. Louis Hayward, more to my liking, gave us a *frisson* when we heard that head grille snap shut in *The Man in the Iron Mask* and the elegant and beautifully spoken Robert Donat was unforgettably romantic and steely in *The Count of Monte Cristo*. Only those three came near to challenging the hegemony of the arch-swashbucklers, Errol Flynn (*The Sea Hawk, Captain Blood,* etc.) and Douglas Fairbanks Jr. (*The Corsican Brothers, Sinbad the Sailor,* etc.). Impressive too the smooth-talking, sword-wielding villains, George Sanders, Basil Rathbone and Robert Douglas. The last-named carried his suave expertise over to a new generation of costume heroes, appearing opposite Burt Lancaster in *The Flame and the Arrow*. Lancaster was somewhat upstaged in his second attempt at a swashbuckling role in the hugely successful (to us anyway) romp, *The Crimson Pirate,* by a diminutive supporting acrobat called Nick Cravat. Another new star, Tony Curtis, grabbed his chance in *The Prince Who Was a Thief.* The two last-mentioned were the last movies of the genre that I was to see in Lismore.

Exoticism did not end with the swashbuckler. It only began there. Never too far away from the corny, it found expression as freely in Biblical extravangaza – de Mille's *Samson and Delilah* with Victor Mature's magnificent tits – as in Marlene Dietrich's gipsy piercing the ear of Ray Milland's British intelligence officer in the Nazi Germany of *Golden Earrings*; or in Anton Walbrook's blinding by a red-hot sabre in the Russian tale of *Michael Strogoff,* or in the war canoes of Jon Hall's *South of Pago Pago,* or in the lost valleys of Tarzan or, indeed, in the Mexican jungles of *The Treasure of Sierra Madre,* the picture that shattered my prejudice against stars in westerns. Bogart convincingly managed the transition from the gangster movie and Tim Holt, known previously to me only in the guise of an above-average sagebrush hero, brought an unexpected depth to his role. They needed to be convincing with Walter Huston, a new actor to me, memorable as the third lead. Around this time also, Jeff Chandler, a new male Hollywood actor being groomed for stardom, was beginning to appear on our screen. With prematurely grey hair, and one of those faces it took a while to get used to, he could be solid or awful – solid in the *Iron Man,* in which he plays the heavyweight boxing champion of the world until Rock Hudson's Speed O'Keefe runs rings around him, or as Cochise in *Broken Arrow,* awful as some kind of sheikh in *Flame of Araby.* 'Come with me to the black tents of my people,' he keeps entreating Maureen O'Hara. The lines entered our library of catch-phrases alongside ones such as, 'Shut mouth, dust no get in' (our variation of the Indian cook's 'Keep mouth shut, dust not get in' to Walter Brennan in *Red River)* or the immortal 'White man speaks with forked tongue,' or (from the Tyrone Power version of *The Mark of Zorro),* 'The Capitán's blade is not so firm. Firm enough to run you through!'(as our pal John 'Cal' Callaghan loved to act out). And probably every boy in the English-speaking world stuck out his chest at some time or other and shouted hopefully, 'Me Tarzan!'

Our catch-phrases never issued from the mouths of child actors, probably because nothing they ever said struck us as worthy of our mimicry. All in all, we did not go overboard for kids of our own age on the screen. With the exception of the Dead End Kids/Bowery Boys (whose Huntz Hall was one of fourteen children of an Irish immigrant father, but we did not know this), Sabu, and Mickey Rooney, who won our applause in *Boys' Town,* those in our own age bracket were either insufferably cute or insufferably well-spoken. Freddie Bartholemew, however, did overcome both of those disadvantages in *Captains Courageous.* Only two other child stars made any impression on me, Dean Stockwell in *Kim* and Claude Jarman in *The Yearling.* What the girls of Lismore made of Shirley Temple I have no idea but I do know the boys were unimpressed. The only girl that won my heart on the screen was the plucky Elizabeth Taylor of *National Velvet.* Never since has she been as beautiful.

Before you grew into your teens female stars were just something that interfered with the action. As you stretched into youthfulness you began to see them in a different light. Who did not dream a little when Veronica Lake or Lizabeth Scott raised a lid from under their long blond tresses? Who did not feel a shiver when Gloria Grahame came on, all pouting lips and swinging hips, and who did not feel a pang when she got a raw deal one more time? Only one other woman with a heart, Barbara Stanwyck, got a rawer deal and she usually deserved it. When Stanwyck was bad (as in evil) she was really mean, and on the rarer occasions when she was good (as in kind), e.g. as the fiery Irish postmistress in *Union Pacific* (co-star Joel McCrea), she sparkled like a firecracker. In facial terms she was only equalled in full-jowled menace by the heavily padded Raymond Burr, then peddling a dark vein of sado-masochism. Her voice was so unmistakeable you picked it up at once when you heard it on the wireless. Stars on the radio convinced you that the cinema could offer delights that sound alone could never pass on. Over the airwaves you couldn't hear Ava Gardner's shoulders raise a shrug, nor experience Ruth Roman's impressive bosom straining to contain a passion that was threatening to run away with her, nor be unsettled by Dorothy Malone's smoky eyes and the wanton lift of her chin. How could you appreciate Carmen Miranda if you only heard her on the wireless? Two women who exploded onto our screens in the early Fifties were not products of the American cinema at all, Kerima, the Algerian actress, passionate and unforgettable in *An Outcast of the Islands*, and Silvana Mangano, daring and voluptuous in the Italian *Bitter Rice,* the first film to really make me aware that there was a cinema outside the English-speaking world of the USA and Britain. But Hollywood, latching onto a new postwar sensibility, already had a star to equal and surpass them, a blonde who was supposed to have posed *in the nude* for a calendar. I was to leave Lismore before she reached its screen. In the meantime, I had Elaine Stewart with her long dark hair, Veronica Lake-style, to think about – when I was not dreaming about Virginia Mayo. Mayo was a technicolor lady all the way down to her delicious ankles and I could not have cared less whether she could act or not. That sincere, solicitous look of hers melted me. I could hardly miss her pictures anyway. Like William Bendix, she was the icing on the big male star cake – with Lancaster in *The Flame and the Arrow,* Cagney in *White Heat,* Kirk Douglas in *Along the Great Divide,* Danny Kaye in *The Secret Life of Walter Mitty...*

Horror and sport were other themes that drew us, as boys and youths, into the cinema. Tarzan pictures were full of athletic endeavour, much of their attraction due to the swimming talents of ex-Olympic champion Johnny Weissmuller, who looked less sure of himself on land than in the water. Like Charlton Heston who surged to our attention in *The Greatest Show on Earth,* he always looked as if his somewhat shaky legs were about to buckle under the weight of his large torso. The more muscular Heston sloped around as if he was knee-deep in quicksand. He was very good in *The Greatest Show on Earth* but it was Cornel Wilde who won attention for athleticism. A sports film I really liked was *Jim Thorpe, All-American,* in which Burt Lancaster plays the Indian who is robbed of his Olympic gold medals on a technicality. It was boxing, however, which came tops with us. John Garfield, with his New York East Side background and rugged good looks, had us slugging with him all the way in *Body and Soul.* I was less pleased to see a dancing Errol Flynn whip the great John L. in *Gentleman*

Jim. Champion and *Iron Man* were the other boxing features that really made me sit up.

Horror films came in two categories, pure horror and creepy. To the latter belonged chillers like *The Lodger* (something of a legend amongst us for creepiness) with Laird Cregar, *The Beast with Five Fingers* with Peter Lorre and the elegant *Picture of Dorian Gray* with Hurd Hatfield and George Sanders. The last-mentioned I found quite disturbing; I was not yet ready to be confronted with the thought of bartering one's soul to the devil. In the creepy range I also included Sydney Greenstreet's sinister Japanese collaborator in *Across the Pacific*, Edward G. Robinson's obsessed farmer in *The Red House* and the same actor's obsessed sea captain in *The Sea Wolf*. In terms of sheer sadism, the performance I recoiled from most was Hume Cronyn's senior prison guard/warden in *Brute Force*, neither a horror nor a creepy film but a powerful prison drama. Genuine horror was the province of three men exclusively, Boris Karloff, Bela Lugosi and Lon Chaney Jr., and two gorillas exclusively, *King Kong* and *Mighty Joe Young*. *Mighty Joe Young* was used as a vehicle for pint-sized starlet Terry Moore who, with Piper Laurie of *The Prince Who Was a Thief*, was being hailed as an exciting new Hollywood property. Of the three men I liked Lugosi in anything, Karloff in most things, Chaney now and again. Chaney, I felt, was the favourite among the Botany boys, unusually as he was such a huge man compared to the small tough guys they revered. But that was just a feeling I had. They made sure they did not miss Karloff or Lugosi either. The horror and creepy movies remained resolutely monochrome, which suited their subject matter well. In general, I preferred black-and-white to colour pictures. Except for westerns. Colour celebrated the magnificent landscapes of these.

We talked a lot about the pictures we saw. ''Member the time he fell through the roof?' ''Member the way he (the stunt man Yakima Canutt probably) went under the horse's belly?' ''Member how Harpo took away his hand and the building fell down?' Any such comment was sufficient to set us off on an animated discussion. Favourite sequences would be rerun in words. Sometimes we would run through a whole film, one of us always finding a moment that struck him as peculiarly funny or significant. Action scenes we discussed most – those that made us first tingle, then hold our breath, and finally cheer when the hero or heroes came out on top. These were scenes like Errol Flynn's swordfight with Basil Rathbone at the end of *The Adventures of Robin Hood*, Joel McCrea's knife duel with Yellow Hand in the wide Missouri of *Buffalo Bill*, and Burt Lancaster's duel in the dark with Robert Douglas in *The Flame and the Arrow*. We gained a quieter satisfaction from moments such as Bogart and Lorre's escape from Devil's Island in *Passage to Marseilles*. On the humorous side there were Groucho Marx's and Lou Costello's wisecracks to be retailed, S. Z. Sakall's routines to be aped, Laurel and Hardy's mayhem to be described… . In the wake of a good swashbuckler the Villa would ring with the clash of our hazelwood rapiers. After a cowboy-and-Indian movie, arrows and whoops would fill the air. We grew out of these juvenile activities to pursue our cinematic dialogues in the cosy and intimate snugs of Joe O'Donnell's pub in Ferry Lane and Coghlan's in the Main Street where a discreet level of underage drinking was tolerated. Joe's was our preferred establishment until he threw us out one night after one of our number, who shall be nameless, could not hold his liquor and pissed on the floor of the snug.

'Ye committed yereselves,' said Joe disgustedly and barred us forever.

CHAPTER TWENTY-FOUR

Show Business

ONE MAN WAS INDISPENSIBLE TO the theatrical companies, variety shows and circuses that came to Lismore: Jim 'Slog' Ahearne, the town crier. We youngsters knew him simply and appropriately, and affectionately, as Jim Slog. The middle class tended to refer to him as Slog Ahearne, which I found odd. There were other Ahearnes in the town but only one Jim Slog. Visiting repertory companies clearly viewed him as a cost-effective and efficient advertising medium. Every evening after six during their visit, Jim would come down our street, slogging his large brass bell, announcing the evening's programme.

'Tonight at the town hall at 8.00 p.m. Carrickford Productions present *East Lynne,* a drama of...' .

Or he might be contracted to announce a company's arrival in advance.

'Next week at the town hall Mr Ernie Clegg's Play Company returns with a season of new plays and old favourites.' Then he would read from his list. 'On Monday *The Colleen Bawn*...'.

They also used him to signal changes to the programme or cast. Jim was small, stocky and weather-beaten, and when he loped around town making his announcements people came to their doors to listen. In my time he was limited largely to news of the entertainment world but now and then he would be contracted by the town commissioners, or the ESB or water utility, to proclaim the cutting off or curtailment of the electricity or water supply. Whatever his message he seldom walked alone. To us children he was something of a Pied Piper. Invariably there would be a scattering of boys and girls scampering at his heels, aping his walk and repeating his announcements. And mongrel terriers would trot along for company. When the kids of one part of town left off those of another would pick him up. As long as his announcements could be heard Jim patiently endured the unwanted company. Understandably, there were times when we became too much for him and he would hunt us all away. I was proud that we had a town crier. No other town of my acquaintance had one. It seemed to be an isolated tradition, possibly resulting from the English settlement in Lismore. If so, he did not preface his proclamations with 'Oyez!', at least as far as I could tell. By the time I left Lismore Jim had already adapted to change, defeated by the car loudspeaker, the flexibility of which the theatre companies, circuses and funfairs, political parties and sports organisations quickly came to appreciate. If I recall correctly, when the loudspeaker first came in he was called upon to make some announcements over this medium. But, probably, a voice accustomed to trumpeting information without the benefit of amplification (I don't think he had ever even used a megaphone) was ill-suited to the low-key delivery required by the new instrument. Jim took to playing the triangle with the Éire Instrumentalists Band and local marching groups, and appeared content that he could continue in this alternative public role. But he was a different man. Gone was the raucous West Waterford cry and the purposeful stride. Succeeding them, we saw a dignified cog of a music machine, daintily picking at his instrument.

I remember my incredulity when he first put his new persona on display. Then I thought, ''Tisn't that different from ringing a bell. More power to you, Jim.' But I felt a pang that his old role was in decline.

Not all of Slog's town commissions came via the town hall. Challenging Doc Healy's hegemony as the town's leading impresario was the canny, sharp-featured Jackie Scanlan who had set up his centre of entertainment, the Happydrome, on the wrong side of the tracks. He too employed the crier to advertise the funfairs, variety shows and other spectacles that he brought to this venue. Live entertainment was his speciality but he must have given the Doc some anxious financial moments with his counter-attractions. He was in competition with the town hall more directly. The latter was the longstanding venue for concerts, theatre, dances – especially short hops and *céilidhe*s – as well as providing floor space in the courthouse for badminton and table tennis, and, of course, it held the advantage of a central location. But Jackie had an edge as well – a much larger hall and a half-acre of land at the front where he accommodated the funfairs. Smaller events like whist drives, forty-five drives, and Kate O'Connell's annual party for the members of the Catholic choir (a stirring event in the annual calendar), kept to St Carthage's Hall. In the summer months a further place of entertainment came into play, the Stage at Ballygallane, situated in a glen a few hundred yards off the main Cappoquin Road about a mile and a half from the town on the left. Here on warm, and not so warm, Sunday evenings scores of young, and not so young, men and women would gather to dance on a small wooden platform about the size of a small disco floor. Refreshments were available from crates.

The stage at Kilclooney Bridge, Coolnahorna in the townland of Clonea (known as Clonea Power) in the parish of Mothel, my Cullinane grandmother's part of the County Waterford in the foothills of the Comeragh Mountains. This vivid photograph (taken in the late Forties or early Fifties?) was given to me by Michael Coady of Carrick-on-Suir. He in turn received it from Seamus McGrath who was given it by Paddens Nolan. A print of the same used to hang in Kenny's pub in Clonea. The man playing the melodeon is Tom Neill. For the names of those dancing the Lancer see '*In the Shade of the Comeraghs: A profile of Rathgormack/Clonea*', Rathgormack Press, 2000, which credits the late Maurice Quinn of Carrick-on-Suir and West Derby, Liverpool as the photographer. I include it here as a rare record of a County Waterford stage dance. In a Lismore Ballygallane stage setting the boy looking over the hedge could have been one of my pals or me.

Further beyond the confines of the town there were other West Waterford venues that attracted Lismore audiences, including two other stages at Monalour and Camphire. The Boathouse in Cappoquin was a favourite for ballroom dances. Dances, concerts, and socials run by a variety of organisations, many with religious affiliations, were held in the Arch Ballroom in Tallow, the Glebe Hall in Aglish, St Michael's Hall in Ballyduff and Bennett's Hall in Ballysaggart. And those who had four wheels under them made it to the Red Barn in Youghal. Of those halls, St Michael's was the only one I ever attended, and that was just for the school entertainment we put on there. After the Palladium, it was Jackie Scanlan's hall that attracted me – to the funfairs and the variety shows.

Dances were off-limits to me because my parents decided I should not attend these until after I was eighteen. I was unhappy about this. My pals, male and female, from Botany and Church Lane had been going to dances since they were sixteen, or even younger. Not all did. The point, however, was that those like Sucky, who was not particularly interested in dancing, could have gone if they so wished. I had no such option. But I respected Dad's and Mam's wishes, to a point. They could not prevent me from hanging around outside the halls when dances were taking place, at least for the earlier part of the evening. At the station side of the Happydrome, a big, barn-like shed with a black, galvanised gable roof and a black, galvanised front, it was possible to cling to a large window and peer in over the top of the shutters at the dancers inside – provided Jackie's stewards were not about. Sneaking a view of the town hall scene was more difficult. The town hall, synonymous with the courthouse, was an attractive, granite-grey building surmounted by the town clock and fronted by a semi-circle of tall, wrought-iron railings painted green. Heavy wrought-iron gates were set in the middle of the semi-circle. Through these one approached the entrance up a wide flight of steps and across an exterior landing. Dances took place in the main hall on the ground floor, accessed over a tiled foyer and through tall, elegant doors, or in the smaller upstairs room. The only way you could get a glimpse of the dancers on the ground floor was by standing at the box-office, or by the small table near the door that often served as one, particularly for hops, and angling your head around each time a patron entered. How revealing a view you managed to get depended on the mood of the person who had the role of doorkeeper. 'Irons' O'Brien was the most accommodating. 'Teller' Walsh was so-so. Michael Nolan took a perverse delight in blocking off your view.

One flight up was a smaller hall, the courtroom itself, again entered through elegant doors. Along the left-hand side as you entered ran an impressive mahogany balustrade. On the raised floor behind this stood seats and compartments of the same wood, reserved for legal proceedings and, beyond these, on a still higher elevation, the circuit judge's canopied bench, to which a side door gave access via Chapel Street, from which he dispensed justice from an upholstered chair on which I often sat for the fun of it. Other entertainments took place in the long, rectangular space outside the balustrade. At the opposite end of this from the entrance theatrical companies would perform on a specially erected proscenium stage. The badminton and table tennis clubs would set up their nets and tables in this space too. Looking down on all the activites from both sides of the room were high, vaulted windows.

Dance forms in West Waterford fell into three categories, *céilidhe*, old tyme and modern. I was proficient in none. Hardly surprising, as the only dances I ever attended were a couple of *céilidhes* in the town hall that 'Irons' had let me into free so that I could educate myself in the customs of this adult world. 'Irons' organised the *céilidhes* on behalf of the Gaelic League, acting as MC as well. His talents in the last-mentioned direction were also in demand by the Boy Scouts, another body to which he adhered, for their whist drives. I earned my free entrance by helping him prepare the dance floor. He would hand me a slim round carton of paraffin wax and instruct me to scatter the white crystals on the surface and slide them flat. This I did with enormous pleasure. The stuff really worked and in no time the shiny wooden boards would take on the lubricity of a skating rink, which added to my general bafflement as to how dancers, especially women in high heels, managed to stay upright when they were performing those intricate, twirling movements. *Céilidhes* and modern hops were short. They began at eight and ended at eleven with the playing of the National Anthem. All dances, and indeed all concerts and similar entertainments, wound up with the National Anthem. Often the whole of it would be played, the patrons singing to the music with the words in Irish. Alternatively, a few bars were swiftly dashed off. My own feeling was that it should be reserved for state occasions and not devalued at every little event up and down the country. As that seemed highly unlikely, I preferred to stand through the complete version rather than the truncated one, believing that a National Anthem should be played *in toto* or not at all. Many people ignored it whichever version was played.

It cost two shillings and sixpence to attend the weekly *céilidhe*, four or five shillings to attend those held on special occasions – at Christmas-time or on St Patrick's Day. The special events went on until 2.00 a.m. Almost exclusively the music was provided by Lismore's own Éire Instrumentalists Céilidhe Band, known in its formative years as the Tom Keating Céilidhe Band. Regular musicians who played with the band were Tom himself, a fine box player; Jack Healy, also on box; and Paddy O'Brien on drums. Another Healy, Tommy, was a well-known Irish dancer who would often entertain with reels and hornpipes at the *céilidhes*. In time, Tom Keating did well enough to be able to style his musicians in grey-green jackets with black lapels. But the Instrumentalists remained essentially a working-class band for a working-class audience. *Céilidhes* were not totally devoted to Irish music. Old tyme waltzes were allowed as well. An old tyme dance was something else. A touch of old Ruritania. Mazurkas, veletas, palais glides, and Lambeth walks, into the small hours. All for five bob. The dance people paid most to attend, and stayed latest at, was the modern ballroom dance. As I understood it, this cost five shillings to twelve shillings and sixpence, depending on whether things ended at 2.00, 3.00 or 4.00 a.m., the last, the so-called 'all-night dance'. There was an even longer one, the Hunt Ball, which went on until 6.00 a.m and cost £1 (incl. supper). The ball, run by the West Waterford Hunt, was the exclusive event of the dance calendar. Favoured also by the better-off were dances organised by the tennis club, the point-to-point committee, the Lismore Agricultural Society, and the badminton club. Wider and less stuffy audiences were attracted by the dances of the coursing club, the Knockmeal Co-operative Society, the table tennis club, the Lismore Dramatic Society, the Waterford Farmers Union and the Cow Testing Association. The Pioneer Total Abstinence Association ran 'socials' and if you wanted an alcoholic drink at those dances you had to slip a noggin of something into your back pocket before you entered. The dry occasion was one for which Billy Baldwin provided a mineral bar.

The Hunt Ball, at Lismore Castle, naturally booked the best bands in the land, e.g. those of Mick Delahunty or Peggy Dell. Mick Del was much favoured by tennis clubs also. Peggy Dell was the most successful of a number of female bandleaders, emulated at Youghal by Miss Nancy Crowley and Miss Sheila Hitchen. Outside of one or two top bands in Dublin, the Clonmel-born and Clonmel-based Delahunty was reckoned to have the best outfit in Ireland but in the early Fifties another Tipperaryman, the young Seán Healy from Carrick-on-Suir with his nine-piece band was rapidly building up a reputation to match him. Indeed, Healy was a much livelier performer on stage than Del. Carrick, with many fine young musicians graduating through the Carrick Brass Band, was notable for providing musicians for both of these dance bands, and for the more specialised circus bands. In nearby Tallow the Brideside Serenaders Band was formed, among its best musicians Lismoremen Billy Hogan and Pete Gillen, and in Lismore itself there was the Marino Band. Both played at the Sunday night hops in the town hall and at other short ballroom dances in the area for which the entrance fee was probably of the order of two shillings and sixpence to four shillings. Dance organisers had to be very careful in selecting their dates. An unforeseen clash with a counter-attraction could risk not only some loss of revenue but a total flop, something a club, whose main purpose in holding the event was to raise cash, could ill afford. Cancellations or postponements resulted when an oversight was spotted in advance. Atrocious weather was the other cause of disruption.

In any one winter two or three variety concerts would be held in the town, the Happydrome being the major venue for these. Whenever well-known

Munster, or even national, figures appeared, the 'variety concert' became a 'celebrity concert'. A celebrity was someone like Frank Ryan from Tallow, 'Ireland's Leading Tenor' or 'The New McCormack' as he was usually billed. The Forties and Fifties were the great years of the 'Irish tenor'. Father Sydney McEwan was another one who did the rounds of West Waterford. Most regular of tenor visitors were Cappoquinman Willie Sargent (until his tragic death in 1953) and Paul Twomey, who was also much in demand as a compère. Of comedians, Danny Hobbs of Cork was the most frequently seen on our stage. Frank Donovan of Radio Éireann brought his revue artistes to town once or twice. And the first lady of Irish song, Delia Murphy, visited once, I believe. Two sopranos, Eily Murphy and Enda Whelan, were popular throughout Munster. They would sing numbers that drove me under the seat – 'Oh, the Days of the Kerry Dances' and 'The End of a Perfect Day' – and numbers that I would not admit to myself that I liked – 'When We Were Young One Day' and 'The Old Rustic Bridge by the Mill'. And they engaged in Victorian duets with tenors – 'Life's Dream Is O'er' or 'My Hero'. The only duettists I appreciated were Pete Gillen and Billy Hogan, whose theme song was 'Walking My Baby Back Home'. Pete would be on sax ('Ramona' a favourite piece) and would also sing items from the Hit Parade like 'Too Young' or 'Because of You'. Billy was the more versatile musican. In duets he favoured the accordion but also played sax and piano and just about any other instrument to which he cared to turn his hand. Earthiness was provided by Kathleen Neville, Sucky's sister, who belted out 'Galway Bay', 'Tonight Is Our Last Night Together' and two songs written by William Campion of Botany, 'The Scenes around Lismore' and 'The Shamrock from Lismore'. (Two other songs about our town, 'The Mall of Lismore' and 'The Lismore Turkeys' I was not to come across until many years after I had left there.)

The tenors, sopranos and baritones (something or a rarity) would stand erect on the stage, clasping in their hands at waist level in front of them a rolled-up slip of paper with the words of the song or songs in their repertoire in case they should suffer a sudden lapse of memory – as happened now and again. On the whole, I found tenors heavy going. I could enjoy numbers that had a bit of bounce to them, 'Valencia' or 'Take a Pair of Sparkling Eyes' or Moore's 'The Minstrel-boy', but I fell asleep over 'The Holy City', 'The Dear Little Shamrock', 'Don't Be Cross Dear', 'Darling I Am Growing Old (Silver threads among the gold)', 'Mary of Argyll' (I have heard the mavis singing...) and 'I'll Walk beside You'. After the tenor the most popular male singer was the crooner but it was not easy to get him on stage, even for a celebrity concert – the problem was, he was constantly on the road with the dance bands.

We were fortunate to be able to count on Pete Gillen and Billy Hogan, who were semi-professional. Otherwise available crooners were amateur, e.g. Guard P. J. McInerney, the female equivalent of whom was the vocalist Chrissy O'Brien, whose favourite number for a time was 'Love's Roundabout', the English-language version of the theme song from Max Ophuls' 1950 French film *La Ronde*. The pair sometimes sang romantic duets together. In time Chrissy became semi-professional, too.

Of all vocal performers there was only one type that evoked a *nul* response in me, the recitationist. The fault was not necessarily his (it usually was a he). It was just that I had no sympathy with his material, which was either mushily sanctimonious, 'The Green Eye of the Little Yellow God', or mushily patriotic, 'The Rebel' or 'The Old Fenian Gun' (Diarmuid Ó Drisceoil's favourite). There was one other style of vocalist, the specialist in comic songs, but I bracketed him (it was always a he) with the comedians. Here we had all the talent we needed locally. Dan Colbert, the stationmaster, who was also a good fiddle player, used to have us falling off our seats when he came on in drag doing his 'Biddy Mulligan'. Jack Fogarty, the bank-clerk, used to sing and act out 'I'm Ninety-Four Today' and 'The Farmer's Boy'. Across from Cappoquin would come a big national teacher, revelling in the cinematic name of F. X. O'Leary, to sing 'My Grandfather's Moke'. Of the three, Jack was perhaps the one who missed his true vocation in life. Appropriately enough, he died backstage in November 1952 after delivering 'The Farmer's Boy' for the last time. A lot of fun went out of concerts after that.

Fun informed many of the performances of the Lismore Dramatic Society as well. The long established LDS knew its West Waterford audiences and served them up such popular successes as George Shiels's *The New Gossoon* and *Paul Twyning* and Edward McNulty's *The Lord Mayor*. *The New Gossoon* was probably its most frequent production. Melodramas like Charles Kickham's *Knocknagow,* J. Bernard MacCarthy's *The Down Express* or Louis D'Alton's *Lovers' Meeting* drew in the crowds too. The three-act plays were often supported by humorous one-acters which carried titles such as *High Finance, Outwitted* or *The Rainy Day* in which younger and newer members of the society like Janey Dunne or Seán O'Connell cut their dramatic teeth. The established players included Jack Singleton, Mary Willoughby, Jim Campion, Monica Noonan and Kieran Fenton. Aside from plays put on by the Christian Brothers' School the only other local competition came from the Gaelic League, who would occasionally produce a play in Irish, Domhnall Ó Corcora's *Aiséirighe,* for example. The highlight of Lismore theatrical life in my time in the town was provided neither by the LDS nor the Gaelic League but by Boysie Noonan's daughter Eeelagh who had gone off to Dublin to study elocution and drama. In 1951 she was picked from among hundreds of young hopefuls to appear with Micheál MacLiammóir in Donagh MacDonagh's new play *God's Gentry* at the Gate Theatre in Dublin. You could hardly make a more auspicious start as a professional than that.

For a diet of Irish theatre then, we could count on home talent. It was left to the touring professionals to bring us dramatised versions of the classics of Victorian, tear-jerking melodrama, *Wuthering Heights* or Mrs Henry Wood's *East Lynne* for example, or stage adaptations of Hollywood successes like *Gone With the Wind* (!), *Little Nellie Kelly* or *Dracula*. Carrickford Productions was probably the most frequent touring company to visit Lismore and always played at the Courthouse. Others were Equity Productions, Mr Ernie Clegg's Play Company, Dennis Murray and His Players, and the Shannon Players. Carrickford would stay for seven days and feature, between evening and matinee performances, almost as many productions. Time was allowed too for a repeat of the play that drew in the largest crowd in the earlier part of the week. It was serious stuff. Regrettably, I never managed to see their highlights from *Gone With the Wind*. It must have been some experience on the small Courthouse stage. Mam did take me along to see them in *East Lynne* and in an Irish melodrama, Boucicault's *The Colleen Bawn* (or possibly it was another play, *The Bride of Carrickbawn)*, performances enlivened by dramatic gestures, flapping cloaks and much toing and froing through the wings. It was all very adult and above me at the time. Indeed, judging by the reactions of the small number of other children at the half-full evening show, it was above all of us. I had to be tugged a few times and warned to shut up because I was inclined to shuffle my hard chair around on the wooden floor when the sad and romantic sequences dragged on. I was cheering at the end, though, when the villains got their just deserts.

Commercially the touring companies did okay as long as they presented comedy and melodrama. When they tried to break the pattern and put on serious works such as Paul Vincent Carroll's *Shadow and Substance* (a favourite play of Mam's) they had to surrender a few meals. The touring actor's life was at best precarious. Moving from cheap boarding-house to cheap boarding-house, battling continuously against the counter-attractions of the cinema and other entertainments, they could ill-afford to be self-indulgent about their choice of material. Compared to the life of circus and funfair people who moved about with the freedom of tinkers almost, theirs seemed a more conventional existence. Between the poles of theatre and circus–funfair I counted a third group, the variety companies.

Whether you lived in Lismore or London how could you resist an attraction billed as 'Miss Vic Loving and Her Flash Parade Review'? Less captivating, but no less entertaining, were the Daniels Variety Company, Mack's Variety Entertainers, Edwill Productions, and Mr C. Bailey. All of these performed exclusively at the Happydrome. A large element of their glamour and excitement was due to the high-kicking chorus girls. Once, a few rows only back from the stage at a matinee, I sat spellbound by the array of flashing brown legs and sky-blue knickers (probably Miss Loving's Flash Parade) cavorting above me. A glimpse of anything female above the knee was rare for a West Waterford boy, and evenly bronzed legs were even rarer. It was odd that they managed to maintain the tan over the winter. The companies also brought their own bands with them, or at least the nucleus of a band that could be supplemented by local musicians. Other acts they offered that were beyond the scope of the local and celebrity concerts were the ventriloquist and the magician. I delighted in the magician with his sleight of hand and repertoire of colourful illusions but felt slightly uneasy about the ventriloquist, or more properly about his dummy that, although funny, even very funny, gave me a somewhat eerie sensation. There was only one drag act for me – I am not sure if there ever were any others – the sophisticated Billy Quinn. All blonde and bouffant, shimmering in sequinned black down to his high heels, and wearing arm-length black gloves, he did a whale of an impersonation of Marlene Dietrich and was like nothing I had ever seen before. Whether we took him as he intended to be taken is a moot point but, judging from his flashing smile, he seemed happy enough with the encores we lavished on him. My brother and some of his classmates got to know him quite well and he used to fascinate them with his tales of being on the road.

Funfairs came to town in the autumn after they had closed down their summer operations by the sea. Perks Amusements and MacDonalds Amusements, both Youghal-based, were the regular visitors. A third, Tower Amusements, put in an infrequent appearance. October and November were the preferred months, the Happydrome again the preferred venue. In the grounds in front of it the bumpers (contrasting wittily with the English usage, 'dodgems'), swinging-boats (as we called them), chairoplanes, and other roundabouts would be set up. A particular fairground ride gave us a lot of fun one year; it ran on an undulating track, like a waltzer except that its seats did not swivel round. Inside the hall standards were: the shooting range, bagatelle, darts, pongo (bingo), wheel of fortune, and that knacky meshed round table where you rolled your penny down a little chute to try to land it inside a winning box (e.g. alight within a '5' and you got five pennies back;

the odds weren't in your favour). One year McDonalds brought along a Wall of Death as well but I was considered too young and impressionable to be allowed to attend this. When some years later a Globe of Death mushroomed by the entrance to the hall you could not keep me away from it. How the metal latticework shook as the leathered rider swirled and swooped inside it, sometimes with his woman partner riding pillion, other times cutting around her erect figure posed on the base! At sixpence a time, I quickly squandered my pennies on that. I never had much to spend but it was surprising how far a bob or two would go when, during the course of an evening, you spent a penny on this, twopence on that, and won some extra coin on the wheel of fortune or at pongo occasionally. And sometimes you found the odd piece of change that had slipped out of somebody's pocket. Generally, I was satisfied if I had enough cash in my pocket to enjoy a spin or two on the bumpers, a couple of pulls in the swinging-boats and a few rounds at the shooting gallery, my favourite indoor attraction.

Many of us youngsters had access to pellet guns and the gallery gave us a chance both to engage in target shooting and to gain experience with the larger calibre .22 lead pellets. Something like a tanner entitled you to four shots so you had to be sparing in your challenges. The man in charge of the range counted out your ammunition, directed you to an 'alley', pulled the target holder to him along the wires, inserted a new card and set the target at the requisite distance. You licked your lips as you lined up your first shot. How you did with that one was crucial because it gave you an indication of the way your particular weapon was sighting. On your performance with that one pellet you based the rest of your shots. The accuracy of the guns was variable and usually you managed to convince yourself that one was sighting better than the others. It was intensely satisfying to get your card back and discover that you had scored a few bulls.

Money wasn't essential to the enjoyment of the fairground. When broke, I was content to hang around and soak up the buzz – the tunes that crackled over the loud-speaker system, 'You Can't Be True Dear', 'Let the Rest of the World Go By', 'I'll Be Your Sweetheart', 'Among My Souvenirs', 'Cruising Down the River' and so on; the hum of the oily generator, the coloured bulbs, the rumble and clack of the merry-go-rounds, the flashing sparks and distinctive nitro mix given off by the bumpers. And the fairground represented more than just a place of lights and entertainment. It licensed us boys to stay out later and rendezvous in the surrounding shadows with the equally licensed girls whose thighs had flashed on the swinging-boats and chairoplanes.

As with the funfair, there was something liberating, yet still more captivating, about the circus. Like the funfair scene, two names dominated the world of sawdust and tinsel, Duffy and Fossett. John Duffy advertised himself with some flair, and not a little hubris, as 'The Irish Barnum', and his company more accurately as 'An Irish Circus for the Irish People'. The national element was provided by a troupe of Irish dancers. In time John Duffy was to go into partnership with his brother James. Fossett's, never quite in the same class, was less ambitious in the scale and range of its presentations although these did improve over time. In Lismore the dominance of the two was only challenged once in my time, in August 1951 when the 'Great Jeserich Circus' came to the Fair Field, the traditional venue for circuses.

Circuses arrived in the middle of the night, transported in multicoloured wagons and caravans drawn perhaps by some thirty to sixty horses, many piebald, and ponies. Motor-driven vehicles were not common in my childhood but as I grew up the number of these being acquired by the circuses increased. To reach the Fair Field the cavalcade usually rumbled up West Street from the direction of Cappoquin. The only other direction they came from was down Gallows Hill from Tallow. We always knew when to expect the circus. We would have had notice weeks ahead. Then, some days before it appeared in town a small advance party, including a clown, would arrive to put up colourful posters and, with the consent of the nuns and Brothers, come round to the schools to whet the appetite of the pupils and students with brief displays of juggling, acrobatics or other easily portable stunts. The night the circus was expected I tingled with excitement but still managed to sleep through the first arrivals in town. At some point in the small hours I would become aware of the trek of horses' hooves and the creak of heavily laden wheels. Wrapping a blanket around me, I would position myself at the bedroom window and quickly focus my eyes on the dim shapes of horses and ponies. Lighted cigarette ends would betray the drivers on the caravan seats and the handlers who ghosted among those animals that were being herded along. They came strung out, sometimes a half-dozen caravans together, sometimes only one, all straining to reach their destination and grab a short few hours' sleep before the back-breaking work of erecting the big top began all over again. Beyond the dawn there would always be a straggler, a van that had broken down en route perhaps. I might catch it if I had re-awoken from my disturbed sleep. Whether I got up earlier or later than I planned, I would be sure to allow myself enough time to dawdle in the Fair Field on the way to a half-day's schooling to watch the circus hands laying out the awesome canvas of the circus tent and the planks that were to form the seating. The men worked furiously, dragging at the ends of the tent and driving long wooden pegs and iron bars into the ground with weighty sledgehammers. By the time I returned at lunchtime the sheer manual strength would have erected the big top. Its tiers of seating would be almost installed; its side canvas almost secured, shutting in the familiar clammy spice of trampled grass. More hands were needed for all this work than the circus brought with it. Among the local lads drafted in as supplementary labour would unfailingly be Tommy Parker of Church Lane. Tommy loved the ambience of the sawdust ring and, whenever it came to town, was sure to wander off with it as a seasonally employed hand. For months at a time he used to be away, sleeping rough under the caravans. Come two o'clock there would be a switch in activity, the permanent hands disappearing among the wagons to grab an hour's sleep as the artistes began to loosen up for the first show of the day. The acrobats would stretch, the knife-thrower would get his eye in, the high-wire artiste would check her equipment. A small troupe – the strongman, a bareback rider, a few clowns – might form up behind the band and an elephant to parade the length of the Main Street. I would regard them with wonder and marvel at the exciting lives they had to be leading. Like all travelling people, they represented a different set of values to those in which I was being raised, a freer, more open society. They spoke foreign languages, wore differently cut clothes and appeared in the ring in glamorous and daring costumes. And there was a healthy sexuality about them. Sucky told me, much more matter-of-factly than I in his place could have done, how he had seen one of the women in a team of four Hungarian trapeze artistes at practice, raise her pullover with a giggle and expose her bare breasts for one of her male partners to fondle.

'Which one was it?' I asked breathlessly as the foursome performed above us at the evening show.

'The blonde,' he said and pointed.

I watched with enhanced admiration as her lithe, sequinned figure somersaulted from one swinging trapeze into the safe hands of her stocky, powerfully built male partner, suspended from his knees on another. The Four Passos the group called themselves, I think, and they were easily the best trapeze act I ever saw in Lismore. A black-and-white publicity postcard I purchased posed them in their acrobatic tights. It was a memento I held onto for many years until it went the way of most boyhood treasures. At the circus I usually sat on the highest tier at the back of the tent. There was a good view of the ring from this level and it also had the advantage of distancing me from the clowns, amongst whom performed always one or two of the shambling short-statured little men known universally as 'midgets', who were accustomed to dragooning the boys and girls occupying the lower seating at the front into active participation in their anarchic routines.

Duffy's high-wire man was known as Blonden (as distinct from the famous Charles Blondin of Niagara Falls), his strongman as 'The Young

Atlas', his long-term clown, simply as Johnny Quinn, a favourite of ours as Paddy Vaughan has reminded me in *The Last Forge in Lismore* (page 84). Atlas was tightly muscled and his feats of strength were sufficiently convincing to my young eyes. A tall and rather flabby looking Samson put up by the competition at one stage singularly failed to impress; his big act saw him standing between two shire- or Clydesdale horses with his arms linked around a harness trailed by each, his fingers interlocked across his belly, holding the animals back as they strained in opposite directions. Or that was what he was supposed to have achieved. When I saw him at the matinee he had no sooner shouted 'Go!' as a signal to the handlers that they should release the horses they were reining in than one of the harnesses snapped. After time-consuming preparations! No effort was made to supply a replacement piece of equipment so that he could try again. We felt cheated and booed. It seemed to me that this was his normal routine. Or, like Samson, he had had a haircut the night before. Our show of disapproval did not put him out in the slightest. He then proceeded to lift a few weights that our own Ned Coleman or Bill Landers or Harry Vaughan could have tossed around with ease. The strongest man of all who came to town preferred his own earthy Irish name to any fancy classical pseudonym. Butty Sugrue, the Kerryman, raised awesome-looking blocks and barbells.

The most sensational act to hit Lismore in my eyes was neither acrobat nor strongman nor lion-tamer but the female fakir, Koringa, who came just once with the Great Jeserich Circus in 1949 or 1950. Dark-eyed and dark-skinned, she wore her hair long and wavy over a leopardskin, like a character out of a Tarzan picture. Her assistants buried her alive under sand in an airtight coffin. For five long minutes we bit our nails in silence until they let her out again. We cheered as she emerged a little dazed but smiling. More fearsome still was another number in her repertoire, ascending and descending barefoot a stepladder of shining scimitar blades. I winced as each pretty foot in turn pressed gently down on the razor-sharp edges of the ten or so weapons that a minute earlier had shredded slips of paper. The tent was stunned to even greater silence. A goddess of the jungle, she came through the ordeal without a scratch, provoking a collective sigh of relief as her foot came off the last blade and touched down safely on the sawdust. That won her possibly the biggest ovation that I ever heard in a Lismore ring. The next morning I saw her in close-up. Every inch the star she was wrapped in a fur coat, telephoning urgently from Feeney's. It was monsooning down outside, the circus delayed by the atrocious weather. She spoke with an accent but I was too mesmerised to judge whether she was speaking English or a foreign language. She sounded very brisk. When she finished her call she paid Mrs Feeney, then got into a long black car with the lucky man who was accompanying her and drove off up Gallows Hill. She did not even notice me. Later in the day when the rain had eased off I went up to the Fair Field to retrieve the memory of her magic. The grass was deeply rutted and here and there my nostrils recoiled from the foul-smelling dung of the wild animals fed on meat. Of the illusions of the day before only a soaked circle of sawdust gave evidence. A couple of Botany lads were nosing around for lost coins. Koringa stayed in my thoughts for a long time. She never returned to our town. *(See black and white pictures and colour posters of her on the* Web on Google Images*)*

Another circus to do the rounds of Munster in earlier years was the Heckenberg Super Circus (Berlin Tower 1937). Whether it came to Lismore this early in my life I cannot say but *The Nationalist* newspaper of Clonmel carried a sizable ad on page 5 of its 15 May 1937 edition for forthcoming visits to nearby Cahir and Clonmel, among other places. Among the swirl of attractions promised were such acts as the Great Pekin Troupe of horizontal bar performers, the 'famous Shaun O'Connor' as 'Mrs Casey', the Headless Girl, Johnnie the Boxing Deer, the Namrehs (name alone – no indication of their stunts needed?), Zozi & Zizi the musical clowns, the Indian Wonders Abdal Asita Troupe (exotic stunts with swords and snakes); Dessie Ray (pun?); lightning tap dancer (flamenco?) 'escaped from Madrid' (political point here); and the Rudinoff Troupe – dancing aces of the air. I would have jumped at the opportunity to see these spectacular promises fulfilled.

In April 1953 the arts came under the spotlight. The first Tóstal was taking place all over the country and Lismore was accorded a modest crumb of the nationwide artistic cake. In the room in the town hall where the *céilidhes* were held I wandered among the painted landscapes, copies for all I knew, of Paul Henry and other Irish artists. My first visit to an art exhibition. I liked the graded blues of Henry's mountains but not much else. A replica of the Book of Kells defeated me with its complexity of Celtic forms. Aware as I was that I was in the presence of a facsimile of a work of art held to be our greatest treasure, I could not muster the reverence expected of me. Indeed, I was distinctly under- rather than overwhelmed by the book. The home crafts that completed the exhibition seemed to be aimed at women. On the whole, I was satisfied to encounter things outside my normal experience and took in the exhibition a second time at least.

Art was not the only focus of the Tóstal. The word *tóstal* or *tóicheastal*, a complex Irish word conveying, among other things, the sense of 'pageant', 'display', 'parade' and 'pride', lent itself ideally to a festival of Irishness. The driving forces behind this display of Gaelic culture were the *Conradh na*

Gaeilge and the GAA, so on the Lismore organising committee sat representatives of those bodies, e.g. Pad Tierney, 'Teller' Walsh, 'Irons' O'Brien, and Harry McGrath. The GAA laid on a full programme of hurling, football and handball tournaments. My pals and I were involved in these and they brought crowds to the town on the lengthening evenings. There was a monster fancy dress parade for which many people made a real effort to come up with an original costume, our neighbour Margaret Feeney winning a prize for her 'Gay Nineties' dress. By special permission the Castle Gardens were opened to the public every day of the week-long event. Beyond our borders, the members of the Lismore Fire Brigade proved the worth of their new, efficiency-enhancing equipment by winning a tournament of fire brigades in Dungarvan. The Tóstal was celebrated again in 1954 but the second festival lacked the fizz and enthusiasm of the first. However in May 1954, as part of that year's celebrations, we had the pleasure in Lismore of seeing the brilliant Mount Sion beat Blackrock from Cork in an exciting game for medals by the score of 4-4 to 3-5. Both Tóstals flopped in terms of pulling in the Irish-Americans to glory in the culture of their forefathers and spend millions of dollars in the process, but I was not complaining. I enjoyed myself.

Up to the end of the Forties excursions, mainly to GAA matches, and pilgrimages, mainly to Knock in County Mayo, were run exclusively by train. In 1951 a privateer, the Dungarvan Bus Company, started running a special service from Lismore to Youghal via Tallow every Tuesday of the summer months, enabling people who did not possess a car to access the pleasures of nightlife by the sea into the small hours. The bus excursion had arrived. A three-bob fare took the dancers to the Showboat Ballroom and back. I never felt attracted to Youghal. I did not like the way its long sandy beach was disfigured at regular intervals by wooden groynes. And I was too young to be allowed to go dancing there anyway. Once the idea of the excursion took off the day-tripper became a familiar sight, arriving in and venturing out from our town. Among the first to organise annual outings from Lismore to Ballycotton, Glengarriff, and on to Kerry, was the Pioneer Total Abstinence Association. Pilgrims were taken farther afield, to Knock and Lough Derg, places as foreign to me as Timbucktu. Mam had been to Lough Derg once, long before I was born, and that one experience had scarred her for life. Neither she nor Dad ever expressed any interest in participating in such junkets. Nor did either of them ever suggest to Paddy or me that it might do us some spiritual good to go on one. It seemed to me that pilgrimages were well-named. They were a pill, they were grim, and they put years on you.

CHAPTER TWENTY-FIVE

Departure

EARLY IN THE NEW YEAR of 1954 it dawned on me that I was spending my last winter in my home town. My parents had already forewarned me that it was their intention to go to live in Carrick-on-Suir after I had finished my secondary schooling. Now, however, I could glimpse the writing on the wall. There would be no more St Stephen's Days like the one I had recently spent with Boxer, Sucky, Foxy, Doshin and Val Foley in the snug of Coghlan's bar in the Main Street.

We had talked cinema, the state of the world, told yarns about those people we liked and those we disliked, and were now engaged in a game of poker. Boxer and I, still adhering to out teetotaller commitments, although in my case precariously so, were drinking Club Orange. Val was on Coca-Cola and the other three on bottled Guinness. Foxy was having a run of luck and decided to switch up to rum and Coke, a recently introduced concoction – to me at any rate; it was the first time I had heard of it. He downed two in quick succession then the danger signals began to appear.

'Ye'll have another one, lads,' he invited, smacking his lips.

'Take it aisy, Foxy,' Doshin tried to calm him down. 'Sure we have all night.'

But Foxy would not be put off. 'Same again, right?' He got to his feet and rapped on the flat of the snug window with the edge of a coin.

'Okay,' we all nodded.

'Jasus, he'll be on his ear if we don't slow 'im down him,' murmured Boxer.

'What can we do?' said Val unconcernedly.

'Leave 'im at it,' Sucky grinned.

'We can't stop him if he wants to drink?' sighed Doshin wickedly.

'Ah, he's half-tore already,' I protested. 'We don't want to be carryin' him home.'

'All right, all right,' Doshin sighed again. 'Leave it to me.'

Foxy turned and placed half the round on the table, his own rum and

Probably the last photograph of my brother Paddy in Lismore.
Taken in our back yard in West Street in summer 1953. Mam's expansive
castor-oil plant is running wild behind him.

Coke ostentatiously first. When his back was towards us again Doshin effected a thimblerigger move. Quickly he poured Foxy's drink into one of the empty glasses on our table and placed it in front of himself. Into Foxy's emptied glass went an appropriate measure of Val's Coca-Cola. Then down Doshin's gullet washed the rum and Coke. I had my own problem in the form of three bottles of orange that were still sitting in front of me waiting to be drunk. 'Jasus, I don't want another one o' them,' I was thinking when Foxy planked one more on the table.

'Drink up, Baler,' he said, lifting his glass and downing a slog of his supposed short. He drew in his breath and licked his lips. 'A real drink, that,' he purred with satisfaction.

Doshin, on whom alcohol seemed to have no effect, took care of the 'rum and Cokes' for the rest of the evening, Foxy, blissfully unaware that every time he bought himself one we distracted his attention while the drink was switched and, when our own rounds came, simply bought him a Coke and poured out the appropriate amount. As for my problem, the sight and taste of all that sickly sweet orange proved too much for me. I set aside my half-hearted pledge and drank my first small bottle of Guinness. Foxy made it home on his own legs, surprised by, and impressed at, his ability to hold his liquor.

Beyond the end of 1954 I was totally unable to project. For the first time I sensed some parental pressure upon me to achieve something at school. It was imperative that I should at least pass my Leaving Certificate. Dad was staying on that extra year, at a possible cost to his health, to allow me to complete my basic education at the school at which I had always studied, among the schoolmates with whom I had grown up. I gave no thought at all to the after-time – how I was going to seek out and hold down a job. I vaguely imagined I would be following my brother across the water to some kind of job in England but I scarcely gave the matter much thought. Instinctively, I decided that if this was to be my last year in Lismore I was going to make the most of it.

I managed to get through my Leaving, surprised that I had done reasonably well, a little disappointed that I had missed getting Honours by a comparatively small margin, in contrast to my brother who had strolled through his exams. Paddy by now had quit a clerkship he held with Bord na Móna in Rathangan, County Kildare and had emigrated to Birmingham so I was the only one at home. By this time Dad was unable to cope with a full day's work. Under doctor's orders, he had to lie down for a few hours every afternoon. Mam worried about him. All she knew of his medical condition, as far as I could see, was that he had a weak heart. Whatever it was, he certainly did not look the tall, straight figure of a couple of years earlier, having acquired a slight stoop and lost some weight. And he was prone to listlessness. I now began to fret about him, about Mam, and about my impending departure from Lismore. I had asked why we could not stay on and Dad had patiently explained to me that it was better we went to live in Carrick because if anything happened to him Mam would have family there amongst whom to live. I would be going my own way in due course. I had to accept this. Many of my own friends and acquaintances had already emigrated, or were preparing to take up jobs or go to university in other parts of Ireland.

On the 28th of September Mother Brendan, the mother superior of the Presentation Convent, a native Irish speaker, a Cullinane from the Kilmacthomas area and a cousin of Mam's, died after a long illness at the age of 84, presaging the cutting of all family links with the town. She had been at the Convent for over forty years, most of that period as Reverend Mother. Bishop Cohalan came up from Waterford to preside over the funeral ceremonies. The interment took place in the nuns' own burial ground in the convent. Mam was deeply saddened by her passing but I shrugged it off with the indifference of youth. I used to like Mother Brendan but nuns were always something of a mystery to me. Concerning me more was the thought that my own life in Lismore was ebbing away. It would not be long now before I would have to say farewell to the friends and places that had formed me. I took to going on solitary walks around the haunts I loved best, down the Grove, along the Warren, along the canal, along the Blackwater, up the Strand and the Mountain Road, out Mayfield, out the railway line to the Round Hill... . I biked it further afield. It was my way of endeavouring to let go. Instead of that, however, the opposite happened. It became inconceivable to me that I should ever leave the town I knew so intimately and loved so much, ultimately a self-defeating thought.

The last days neared. We acquired empty tea chests and large cardboard boxes from McCarthy's next door and started packing china, glasses, and other breakables. Dr Healy arrived to present us with a table lamp for our new home, although as yet we had no home to which to go. First we were to reside with my aunts, Nan and Biddy Morrissey of Greystone Street, until such time as we would be in a position to purchase a lease on a home of our own. The days were speeding up horribly. I called to see all my friends in turn, my sense of loneliness augmenting in the wake of each visit. At six o'clock in the evening of the 13th of December Mossie Pollard, confirmed as town clerk in succession to Dan Lawton after Jack O'Gorman had filled in as acting town clerk for a time, arrived on our doorstep and asked for

Dad. Two other town commissioners were in the shadows behind him, Jack O'Donoghue and Thomas Crotty. I scarcely noticed them in my distraction. When Dad came out I returned to the living-room to help with the last bit of packing. After a while I heard the door close and he returned with a wallet of notes in his hand. The commissioners had taken up a collection in recognition of his services to the town. He was greatly moved. Mam embraced him gently.

After supper I went up Botany for the last time to say goodbye to Kitty Keyes and her daughter Kay Tobin. Kay, whom I was very fond of, and I went for a walk around by the railway station. The air was clear, the sky as full of stars as I had ever seen it. We chatted. Hugged. I presented her with a small blue-labelled bottle of eau-de-Cologne that I had bought at the Medical Hall. It was not much but it was all I could afford. We knew we were saying goodbye. Who could say if and when we would ever meet again? We returned to Kitty's and took leave of one another. I walked away with tears in my eyes and did not look back. I went past my home and on down the New Way to the two bridges. I wanted the last smell of the rivers, the last earful of their rushing waters. And I wanted my eyes to cool down before I got home. I returned via the ball alley, the Palladium, Fernville and Chapel Street. I did not sleep much that night.

Early the next morning a lorry sent by Nat Ross, the Cork furniture remover, pulled up outside our front door. The driver and his helper spent the morning piling our belongings onto it – they did not amount to much when skilfully loaded. The sky was grey, the street quiet and empty even though it was only eleven days to Christmas. Immediately after some tea and sandwiches my parents left the town in Denny Regan's taxi, Mam and Mrs Feeney having bid one another a tearful farewell. I had already said my goodbyes to Tom and Margaret, who were at school, and to Michael, who was elsewhere. I was to travel in the front seat of the lorry in order to direct the driver to the address in Carrick-on-Suir. I spotted Pete Neville and 'Cox' Doherty sitting below at the Monument and went down to chat to them for the last time. Cox hated goodbyes and there were tears lurking in his eyes as well as mine. Pete made a joke in an effort to brighten me up. Then I went back and got into the lorry alongside the driver's helper. I could barely hold myself together. I waved goodbye to Mrs Feeney. As we turned into the New Way Snobby Barry waved from the seat across from the barracks. We were well out the Cappoquin Road when the helper, seeing my distress, gently asked me, 'Did you live there for a long time?' I could find no words and nodded through the tears I was no longer holding back.

Appendix

*A Mayo man in Carrick-on-Suir: the Search for
Mick Hurst, a Veteran of the Crimean War*

An echo of an Irishman's role in a much earlier war of Empire reached me when I went on holidays from Lismore to my aunts' house in Carrick-on-Suir. A Mayoman from Swineford called Mick Hurst had come to live out his retirement years in Mill Street with his Clonmel-born wife Mary (Gleeson?), who used to work as a laundress for my grandmother. They had no children. When his wife died my grandfather, who appeared to have become a close friend of his, offered him a room in Greystone Street – the room beyond the back bedroom where we were accustomed to sleeping when staying in Carrick. There he lived almost until his death 'not long after the outbreak of the First World War', according to my Aunt Nan Morrissey, at the Carrick hospital and former Workhouse, known as 'The Union'. An ex-British soldier, Hurst had seen action in the Crimean War (1853–56). There were military barracks in Clonmel and Carrick and the likelihood is that he maintained some connection with one or both of these after he retired on pension. My aunts, who always spoke of him in respectful tones, remembered him as a tall, spare slightly stooped grey-haired man with a grey moustache and a small goatee, who kept himself very neat and clean, 'as most ex-Army men did', and always carried a walking-stick. War wounds contributed to a poor state of health in his declining years. His gold watch-chain passed to my father and eventually to me with a silver South African half-crown, to which a pin may have been soldered. Dated 1897 it bears the bearded likeness of Paul Kruger. Thus, by this indirect path, I also heard of the Boer Wars (1st, 1880–81; 2nd, 1899–1902). My uncle Mick Morrissey in Birmingham held his campaign medal until 21 November 2002 when he most kindly gave it to me to act as its future custodian. According to my Aunt Nan again, Mick Hurst is buried in the Friary churchyard in Carrickbeg, presumably with his wife, in a single unnamed grave marked today by a rusty iron cross with a circle on it, standing on a small cement plinth. It may be found to the right of the church about ten yards from the corner at the top of the outside steps, near the hedge and between a stunt-

ed block on the left bearing the name John O'Neill and a large grave with fancy iron railings behind a Galvin grave. (From Chapter 22, p. 495–6)

Over the years 1999 to 2001 curiosity led me to search for a written record of the Mayoman who had settled in our Tipperary town, taking into account that his surname might have been spelt Hirst, Herst, Hearst, or even Horst. The surname Hurst is anchored in the counties of Berkshire, Kent, Northumberland and West Yorkshire (in this county also in the form 'Hirst') and this seemed to me the most likely spelling. Mick Hurst's burial plot is unrecorded in the Friary records (as are others). The date of his marriage and death would certainly be in the Irish records, his date of birth less likely as I surmised he was probably in his nineties, but I had no precise dates on which to start searching. A first exploratory search for a record of his death at the General Register Office in Dublin covering the three-year period from January 1914 to December 1916 inclusive proved fruitless. A further search of the years 1917 to 1919 by the diligent staff of the office unearthed the record of his death. He died a widower aged 86 at the Workhouse (i.e. Union) in Carrick-on-Suir on 27 November 1918 at a time when the great flu epidemic that had claimed at least a dozen lives in the town was finally abating. The next step was more challenging. Tracing the military record (discharge papers, pension details, etc.) of non-commissioned men without knowing the regiment in which they served is notoriously difficult and time-consuming. Hurst I guessed was most likely a private, corporal or sergeant in an infantry battalion and, as a Mayoman, might have been with the Connaught Rangers but this was by no means certain. He might even have joined an English regiment in Ireland or England. Not knowing his regiment was a major drawback. Initially I researched fruitlessly in the military records held in the Public Record Office (PRO) at Kew, London. I also drew a blank at the British Library Newspaper Library in Colindale where I failed to find a death notice for the old soldier for the years 1914–1919 in the pages of the main local twice-weekly Irish newspaper of the period, *The Nationalist* (Clonmel).

That the men who had fought in the Crimean War were dying off at this time is evidenced by the following two items from the Clonmel paper:

Death of Crimean veteran
The death occurred on yesterday, at O'Neill Street, Clonmel of Mr William Hurley. He was a native of Clonmel and had reached an advanced age. He joined the 13th Light Infantry in his early days, was a clarionet player in the regimental band, and served through the Crimean War. In later years he was a gate keeper at Clonmel Asylum, and retired on pension. The interment takes place tomorrow at St Patrick's

cemetery at 3 o'clock. (*The Nationalist*, 19 October 1915, page 3, bottom of column 5.)

Military funeral
An officer and twelve men came from Clonmel barracks to Carrick-on-Suir on Wednesday for the funeral of the late Mr Jas. Flynn, a Crimean War veteran, who died on Monday, aged 90 years. The members of the local comrades of the Great War and D&D.S.S.F. and a large number of the general public accompanied the remains to their last resting place. The coffin was covered with a Union Jack. (*The Nationalist*, 15 November 1919, page 8, under 'Carrick News'.)

My not locating a similar record in the press for Hurst might have been due to a number of factors. Only deaths of local worthies or newsworthy persons were mentioned in *The Nationalist* at this time. Clearly, some Crimean veterans counted as newsworthy, as did the Young Irelanders of 1848 and the old Fenians who had taken part in the insurrection of 1867 in Tipperary, who were also disappearing. I might not have been looking in the right place or in the right time-frame. I might have missed the item. Not being a local man, Hurst might not have counted as local news. He might have wanted to go without a fuss, passing away quietly as old soldiers often do. On the other hand I now had confirmation on his death certificate that, sadly, he had become senile three months before his death. This could account for his dying at the workhouse rather than at my grandparents' home in Greystone Street to which address the certificate also attests. With the onslaught of senility he was probably more than the busy James and Statia Morrissey and their large and young family could handle round the clock.

Only with the acquisition of this official document did it dawn on me to ask my Uncle Mick to examine Hurst's campaign medal. Belatedly, this proved a revelation. For a start, I now knew with certainty that his surname was spelt 'Hurst' and that his first name was indeed 'Michael'. He had served with the 9th Regiment at the siege of Sebastopol. The date on the medal was 1854, the second year of the Crimean conflict, when he had reached 22 years of age (or 20 as I would have cause to believe later?). Armed with this information I returned to the Public Record Office. The 9th Regiment, I discovered, was known officially as The Royal Norfolk Regiment (The 9th Regiment of Foot), and was founded in 1685. It was also known familiarly as the Royal Regiment, its men as the Royals. The *Army List* of 1854 records the 9th Regiment of Foot (The East Norfolk) as having headquarters at Fermoy in County Cork. Perhaps it was there that Hurst joined up? Document file WO 100/26 *(Campaign Medals 1793–1912)* at the PRO carries on page 303 under 9th Regiment of Foot a 'Nominal List of Officers, Non Commissioned Officers and Soldiers entitled to receive a Medal for Service in the Crimea.' The alphabetical list running over a number of pages is handwritten and dated 26 March 1855. Page 307 of the list names Michael Hurst and gives his medal number (306) and regimental number (3230). The medal is recorded as having being awarded with clasps for the Alma (dated 20 September 1854) and Inkerman (dated 5 November 1854) although these battles had been fought by the time the 9th landed near Balaclava on 27th November 1854. The medal that my uncle held was not accompanied by these, which suggests that the 9th did not, in fact, receive them.

Also at the PRO I found a further brief reference to 'Michl' Hurst in file WO 25/3342, a handsome brown leather (very foxed) volume with, on the front cover, an ornate title panel in red leather with gold lettering which read *1st. 9th Foot* (i.e. 1st Battalion, 9th Regiment of Foot). This is the 'Index to Casualty Returns ca 1850–1910' confirming that Hurst had, as my Aunt Nan said, suffered war wounds. The one-line entry under the alphabetical heading 'Hu' gives Hurst's rank as Private and confirms his regimental number – 3230. What follows is cryptic. I make it to read 'To Dep:B2.Limerick.PL 12/61 To a H.l. 31.12.62 DH12' and squiggle. 'Dep' is most likely 'Depot', 'B2' – Barrack 2, 'PL' probably 'Pay List' and 'Hl' hospital?

Finally, I unearthed in file WO14/39, one of two 'Muster Books and Paylists for the Crimean War Scutari Depot, 3rd Division, 9th Regiment', a third reference to the soldier. This is a slim blue volume, foolscap size, labelled on front '9th Regiment, 3rd Division', in the florid bookkeeping style of the time. At the top of unnumbered page 10 there is the heading 'Muster for the Month, ended the 30th of April 1855', and on the very bottom line this entry for Hurst – (regimental number) '3230, pte, "Michl" Hurst' (from period) '22 to 15', (and in the remarks, column, i.e. 'REMARKS, explanatory of the Reasons and Durations of Absence, and Causes of broken Periods...)' 'joined 22' (the hospital, it seems), confirmation again that he had been wounded. The 9th Regiment left the Crimea on 1 May 1856 having lost more men to rampant disease than as a result of enemy action. The names of Crimean War killed and wounded (in varying degrees) contained in the hand-written despatches from the field were published at the time in the *London Gazette*. In 1976 all these details were brought together in the following work published by J.B. Hayward & Son of London: *Casualty Roll for the Crimea. The Casualty Rolls for the*

Siege of Sebastopol and other Major Actions during the Crimean War 1854-1855, compiled by Frank & Andrea Cook. Edited and arranged by John B. Hayward with a foreword by Vivian Stuart. However, there is no mention of Michael Hurst among the list of casualties listed for the 9th Regiment of Foot on pages 147 and 148. The circumstances of his wounding are thus unremarked.

Armed with the exact date off his death, I revisited the British Library Newspaper Library at Colindale for a further search. This time I had more success. I found the death notice that follows duplicated in the two Clonmel papers of the period, i.e. in *The Nationalist* of Wednesday, 4 December 1918 (page 4, column 1) and *The Clonmel Chronicle* of Wednesday, 4 December 1918 (page 2, column 6). *The Nationalist* entry I had missed the first time round as it was the 7th short item tucked in against the spine of the large bound volume under the heading 'Local & General News'. *The Chronicle* I had not checked before. Here the entry came under a florid bold heading, 'Obituary Notices'. The immediate notice read:

Death of a Crimean Veteran
The death has occurred in Carrick-on-Suir in his 86th year of Mr Michael Hurst, who fought in the Crimean War. The late Mr Hurst, after leaving the army, was a warder in an English convict prison and was in charge of the late Michael Davitt when that gentleman was in the prison hospital.

The reference had to be to Michael Davitt, the Land League Founder, whose son at that time in 1918 was canvassing in the County Waterford elections for Dr Vincent White of Sinn Féin who was opposing the Redmondites. This was an unexpected twist and posed the question of whether I could find a document that would testify to the simultaneous presence of Hurst and Davitt in a particular place or institution. There are records at the Public Record Office in Kew giving the names of convicts and prisoners held in gaols but I did not come across any records suggesting the names of the staff who were responsible for guarding them. There are letters dealing with the working conditions and remuneration, etc. of prison staff but these only carry the names of senior officials, chaplains, etc. I did find the record for London's Millbank Prison that marks the beginning of what was to become seven-and-a-half purgatorial years of incarceration for Davitt. File number HO 24/11 'Millbank (male) 1869–1874', volume 11, is a huge bound volume in the series 'Home Office: Prison Registers and Returns'. There is an alphabetical list of names at the beginning of the volume where each prisoner's name and register number can be found. Each brief entry is then arranged horizontally in an unnumbered section under register number across two A3-sized (approx.) pages. Michael Davitt's reads:

Register number	Name	Age	Married or single	Read or write	Trade
6721	Michael Davitt	25	Single	Imp [Imperfect? This could be read as either an ironic or irksome comment.]	Printer

CONVICTED

When	Where	Crime*	Sentence
11 July 1870	C.C. Court	Compassing to de *(sic)* from the Queen & any (?) War agt [against?] her.	Fifteen PS [Penal Servitude, presumably]

RESERVED

When	From what gaol
1870 29 July	Newgate

Substance of gaoler's report of character
(Blank)

REMOVED

When	Whither
25 Mar 1871	Dartmoor prs.

*This I could not decipher properly.

The grim Millbank Prison, where Davitt was held for ten months from 29 July 1870, seemed an unlikely place to start. That left Dartmoor Prison, where the nationalist was held from mid-1871 to 19 December 1877 in extreme conditions which lastingly undermined his health; Portsmouth Prison, where he spent a month in the infirmary from 16 July 1872 before being returned to Dartmoor again; and Portland Prison, where he was detained from 5 February 1881 to 6 May 1882 under a more benevolent regime with a far more humane governor than he had experienced at Dartmoor. The indomitable Fenian also had experience of penitentiaries as diverse as Clerkenwell and Newgate prisons in London, and the Richmond Bridewell and Sligo Gaol, but I felt that he was not imprisoned long enough in any of these to have required, or merited in the eyes of his gaolers, hospital care.

So the next step was to try to locate Michael Hurst at, or in the vicinity of, either Dartmoor, Portsmouth or Portland prisons during the years of Davitt's imprisonment, using the *Census of Population* records housed at the Family Records Centre, Myddleton Street, London EC1R 1UW. Census returns for England and Wales for the years 1871, 1881 and 1891 are held there. Hurst may not have been living in or near those localities when these censuses were taken and, if this were so, I had no idea in which other town, village or hamlet in England he might have been resident. Princetown is the small town adjacent to Dartmoor Prison in which prison officers were accustomed to living so this was a likely place to start.

The census of 2 April 1871 does not reveal a record of Hurst and his wife in or near Dartmoor Prison. This census, unlike that of 1881, has no 'General Surnames Index', nor is one immediately envisaged, so for this period there is no quick route to locating individuals. I opted to search files RG10/2142, RG10/2144 and RG10/2148 that cover the Parish of Lydford (also Lidford) and Princetown, as well as part of Tavistock. These did bring up the names of perhaps a dozen other Irishmen resident in Princetown (one a Michael Walsh which initially raised my hopes) who worked at the prison. A cursory check of the list of convicts in file RG10/2144 did not reveal Michael Davitt's name. I may have missed it, or it is possible that the Fenian was still in transit to Dartmoor when the census was taken. The Millbank Prison entry records that he was removed to Dartmoor on 25 March 1871. The census was taken on April 2nd. His presence could have been recorded at some other location. For Hurst, I also checked the 1871 file RG10/1127 that covers Portsea and the part of Portsmouth that I thought offered a similar possibility for Portsmouth Prison. No luck there either, although I did find a number of occupations classed as 'warder, convict prison'.

I then turned to the records of the census of 3 April 1881. Here in the 'General Surnames Index' appears a reference to Michael Davitt. This led me to the 'Enumeration Book for Her Majesty's Convict Prison' – Portland, Dorset, England, File RG 2108, folio 31, page 7, on microfilm. Among the warders, guards and prison officers listed there are six Irish-born personnel but no Michael Hurst. Among the long list of convicts that follows there is this bald entry for Davitt:

Name	[Status]	Conditions as to marriage	Age	Rank, Profession or Occupation	Where born
Michael Davitt	Convict	Unm.	35	Printer	Ireland

In the *General Surnames Index* for 1881 I then found a reference among a number of Michael Hursts to the Swineford man, identified by age and occupation as an infirmary nurse, in this entry:

Surname	Forename	Age	Sex	Relationship to Head	MARITAL CONDITION	Census Co.	Parish
Hurst	Michael	47	M	Head	M	Dev	Lidford (sic)

Occupation	Name of Head	WHERE BORN	
		Co	Parish
Infirmary Nur+	Self	Ireland	—

REFERENCES

Public Record Office			*G.S.U. Film*
Piece	Folio No	Page No	Number
RG11 2218	117	36	1341534

This in turn led me to his census entry in File RG11/2218, folio 117, page 36 that confirmed the above as follows:

Civil Parish	Village	Rural District of	Ecclesiastical Parish of
Lydford*	Princetown	Tavistock	St Peter's [?]

No of Schedule	Road, Street, etc.	HOUSES		Name and Surname of each person	Relation to Head of Family	Condition as to marriage	Age		Rank, Profession or Occupation	Where born
		In-habited	Unin-habited				Male	Female		
143	Barracks	1		Michael Hurst	Head	M	47		Infirmary Nurse	Ireland
				Mary Hurst	Wife	Mar		31	Wife	Ireland

*[Note: Lydford is situated 7 miles north of Tavistock and the parish takes in a large part of Dartmoor.]

This entry confirms that Hurst's wife's name was indeed Mary. Her maiden name is not given, unfortunately, so there is still a query over that. A discrepancy is revealed between the age given for Michael Hurst in this record and that given on his death certificate. According to the latter, he died in 1918 at age 86. This would mean that he was born in 1832. But add 47 to 1832 and you get 1879. This would indicate that the man was aged 84 rather than 86 when he died and so was born in 1834. (Or that he *was* born in 1832 and his age should have been recorded as 49 years in the census of 1881.)

The 1881 entries for Davitt and Hurst make it clear that in April 1881 the two men were resident in different places. However, the entry for Hurst places him in the immediate vicinity of Dartmoor Prison where Davitt had been held up to December 1877. It also confirms that he was an infirmary nurse and not a warder as such. This strongly suggests that it was at Dartmoor in the mid-1870s, rather than at Portsmouth in 1872 or Portland in 1881–82, that Hurst was in charge of Davitt when the latter was hospitalised. From the Census of 1871 one gains an indication of the staffing of Dartmoor Prison infirmary. Four infirmary nurses are listed, two of whom were born in Ireland (a third had an Irish wife). Two lived with their wives in the barracks (like the Hursts later) and two in Princetown itself. The two living in the barracks were aged 45 and 46, the others aged 46 and 33. Hurst's age was given as 47 when the 1881 census was taken. Assuming a general retirement age of 50 for prison personnel (which is no more than a guess on my part), one could speculate that Hurst in the mid-1870s might have replaced one of the two who lived in the barracks. The Irish connection may have encouraged him to take up the job that testifies to an early Irish involvement in British nursing, albeit of a specialist kind.

There remain a number of questions about Hurst that may yet find an answer. Aside from the scant reference to Davitt, I can only speculate on the events in the soldier's life between the time of his return from the Crimea in 1856, his transfer to the hospital in Limerick on 31 December 1862, and the census record of 1881. The probability is that he met his future wife Mary (Gleeson?) in Carrick-on-Suir or Clonmel, or even Cahir, when he was stationed in this region and, most likely, they married locally. Possibly it was his experience of hospital, coupled with events in the Crimea, that gave him the incentive to become an infirmary nurse. But where did he acquire the skills for this career? When and where did he receive his discharge papers from the British Army, and was he still in the 9th Regiment of Foot at that time? My first cousin Tony O'Mara has informed me that his mother, my Aunt Peg (Morrissey), told him that Hurst was with the South Irish Horse in Carrick-on-Suir. This regiment was raised on the 7th of March 1900 for the South African War (i.e. the 2nd Boer War), which may explain how the 1897 South African half-crown with the likeness of Kruger, which I mentioned above, came into his possession. He himself, then in his late sixties, could not have served actively but the coin could have been a present or memento from a fellow-soldier who did go to war. Reorganised a number of times in its short lifetime, the South Irish Horse was renamed the 7th Battalion, Royal Irish Regiment on 1st September 1917, then reformed as the South Irish Horse in June 1918 before finally being disbanded on 31 July 1922. I also do not know when Hurst re-emigrated with his wife to join the prison service in England and when they came back to live in Ireland again. My grandfather James Morrissey was already living at Greystone Street, Carrick, when he married Anastasia Cullinane on 27 June 1896 so it would have been some time after this that Mary Hurst, now turning fifty, came to work for them. Did the Hursts stay on in England for a time after Mick's work at the prison finished or did they go straight back to Tipperary? If, as my aunt maintained, he was with the South Irish Horse, this would imply that he had re-joined the British Army on return. (His brief obituary notice in the two Clonmel papers of 1918 notes that he was a warder in an English convict prison *after leaving the army.*) Files RG12/1750 and RG12/1751 of the census of 1891 show no record of the pair still living in Lydford Parish in the village of Princetown, which would suggest that, at least, they had left that immediate locality by then.

The Devon Record Office at Exeter may hold documents recording Hurst's years in the West Country that would shed some light on this blank period. The General Register Office in Dublin should hold a record of his marriage as well as his wife's death certificate. But all this research requires a wider trawl than I am able to contemplate. There is still the possibility that I overlooked an entry for the Swineford man and his wife in the 1871 census as the eye-straining and time-consuming process of checking the heavily used records at the Family History Centre has to be performed on microfilm, in which format at times the handwritten text is barely legible, or is even illegible. A lingering doubt persists that his attestation/discharge papers lie somewhere in the PRO at Kew but have eluded me. I believe I was quite thorough in the searches I undertook but I cannot claim to have been exhaustive.

One wonders what the two Mayomen, near neighbours (Straide where Davitt was born is no more than 10 miles from Swineford), probably of similar backgrounds, sharing a common first name, and cast on opposing sides, had to say to one another. *If* they were allowed an exchange of words beyond the immediate matter of Davitt's health. Contact between warders and prisoners in that era of draconian sentencing and harsh confinement was highly restrictive. For example, we have it on Davitt's own authority that during his ten months of almost total isolation at Millbank Prison, 'his entire conversation with other prisoners, as well as with chaplains and warders... hardly amounted to twenty minutes in all.' (see *Michael Davitt: Revolutionary, Agitator and Labour Leader,* by F. Sheehy-Skeffington. London, Macgibbon & Kee, 1967, page 45).

Hurst would have seen at first hand the scars, physical and mental, left by the tyrannical, petty and vindictive regime to which Davitt, without any concession to his one-armed disability, was subjected in Dartmoor. Was he sympathetic to his great countyman? Did he admire the man's ability to maintain his dignity while surviving humiliating treatment, arctic winters, nauseating food and stinking cells? Or did his role as a servant of the Crown make him impervious or indifferent, or even antipathetic, to the prisoner's plight? I ask myself if he ever spoke to my grandfather about these prison encounters, or indeed, about any of the events of his soldiering and warding years? Soldiers, for their own good reasons, are often reticent about their military and associated experiences.

I have laid out the rather haphazard procedure I followed so that anyone who might wish to extend my research may build on this foundation. I am sure that a seasoned researcher would have taken much less time to come up with the same result and might well have located other data that escaped my attention. I am glad, however, that my digression has retrieved some interesting fragments of the life of that faraway stranger from County Mayo who unknowingly left an imprint on my boyhood years. As in the example of my father's War of Independence years (*see* Chapter 21), it underlines how little we often know about the adventurous past of people who live within the circle of our own family.

Coincidence drew my eye to an entry for another Michael Hurst in the 'General Surnames Index' of the census of 1881 and in file RG 11/3540, folio number 131, page 25, at the Family Records Centre. This person, aged 26, lived with his mother Dina, aged 56, at a place called Monks Coppenhall in the district of Crewe in Cheshire and worked as a 'general labourer'. What is of interest is that both were born in 'Mayo, Ireland'. Might this Michael Hurst have been a relative, or even a nephew, of the Crimean veteran? And what of Dina (Dinah), a singular first name for an Irishwoman of the period?

There were two other coincidental footnotes to my researches. I discovered an earlier connection between the 9th Regiment of Foot and West Waterford. General William Steuart (*sic*) (1652–1726) of the Villiers-Stuart family of Dromana, Cappoquin, was given the command of the Regiment by William of Orange in 1689 just before the Battle of the Boyne. (See *The History of the Norfolk Regiment 1685–1918,* by F. Loraine Petre, OBE. 2 volumes. Published at Norwich by Jarrold & Sons, The Empire Press, – no date, but early twentieth century.) And there was a further echo of my schooldays. The 9th had fought at the Battle of Coruña under the command of Sir John Moore of whose fame we learnt in the Irish poet Charles Wolfe's popular poem, 'The Burial of Sir John Moore' ('Not a drum was heard, not a funeral note...').

Index

Index entries are for: **personal names** of family, friends, local people, Irish performers, writers, politicians, sportsmen and women, and some national and international public figures; **place-names** in Ireland; **titles** (in *italics*) of newspapers, magazines, plays, Irish radio programmes, cinema newsreels and books of local interest; and subject **terms** for topics covered in the book.

Not included in the index are: **titles** of popular songs and films; and **names** of internationally popular singers and films stars.

Bold number page references refer to illustrations

AAU, *see* Amateur Athletics Union
abstinence movement, 92, 104, 331, 366, 468, 539, 549
Affane, 414
Aglish, 132, 134, 414, 421, 536
agriculture, *see* farming
Ahearn, Andy, 153
Ahearne, Brian, 368
Ahearne, Dick, 368
Ahearne, Jim ('Slog'), 35, 477, 534–5
Ahearne, Liam, 368
Ahearne, Michael, 368
Ahearne, Father Michael, 89–90, 103, 108
Ahearne, Paddy, 368
Ahearne, Tony, 121
Ahern, James, 50
Aiséirighe, (stage play), 541
alcoholism, 365–6
Alexander, Captain, 49
Alexander of Tunis, Earl, 49
Alfred, Father, 394
All-Ireland Football Finals, 138, 139, 140, 183, 198, 517
All-Ireland Handball series, 158
All-Ireland Hurling Finals, 125, 126, 132, 198, 517

Allison, Bobby, 299
Amateur Athletics Union (AAU), 159
American films, 507–8, 511–12, 514–15, 518–21, 522–6
Amharc Éireann, 517
angling, *see* fishing
Anglo-Irish War, *see* Irish War of Independence
animated films, *see* cartoon films
Anson, Hon. Clodagh, 350
anvil lifting, 119
appendicitis, 357–60
Araglin, 147
Arch Ballroom, Tallow, 536
Ardmore, 1, 180, 185, 187, 228, 379
aristocracy, 15–16, 47–56, 221, 491
armed forces, British, Irishmen serving in, 8, 326, 449, 494–5, 495–6
Army, Irish, 8, 96, 346, 495
barracks, 8, 13, 32
hurling team, 13
manoeuvres, 11–13
Arp, Ulrike 408
Arrigan, John, **417**

Arrigan, Ma-Jo, 402
Arrigan, Mick, 171, 183
Arrigan, Paddy, 171
Astaire, Adèle, 52, 169
Astaire, Fred, 49, 52, 491
athletics, 158–60
Athlone, 5
Atomic bomb testing, 497
aurora borealis, 238
Auxiliaries, 484
Avonmore Bridge, 232

BBC, *see* British Broadcasting Corporation
badgers, 260
badminton, 121, 192, 537
Bailey, C., 543
bakeries, 13–14, 375, 394, 395–7
Baksi, Joe, **197**, 197–8
Baldwin, Billy, 94, 259, 279, 539
Baldwin, Johnny, 71, 303
ballad sheets, **209**
Ballantyne, Bridget (née MacDonagh) (JB's Paternal Grandmother), 2
Ballantyne, Brighid (née Garvin) (JB's Aunt), 309, 384, **406**, **407**

INDEX

Ballantyne, Catherine (JB's Cousin), 80, 519
Ballantyne, James Joseph Patrick ('Jim'), 11, 15, 30, 76, 324, 325, 392, 393, 406, 416
birth, 1,
childhood, 8–23, 24
  bathtimes, 353–4
  birthdays, 312
  Christmas celebrations, 98, 300, 308–9
  family walks, 17–18, 399–401
  games, 83, 295, 315–16, 317–18
  holidays, 1, 388–406
  love of books and comics, 77–85
  love of railways, 387–90
  making toys, 299
  mealtimes, 24–5, 375–9
  mimickry, 33, 55
  nativity play, 428–9
  obtains Eamon de Valera's autograph, 474
  Pancake Day, 308
  pet dog, 382
  piano and elocution lessons, 382
  picnics, 165, 185–7
  rescues birds, 237
  sees flooding, 234–5
  trips to the seaside, 179–87
  understanding of sickness and death, 366–8
  understanding of war, 8, 10, 11–14
  watching stars at night, 238
  wolf whistling, 454–6
family relations, 1, 2–7
  brother, 5, 7, 19, 180, 249, 312, 407–8, 464
  father, 14–15, 144–5, 185, 204–5, 297–8, 322, 328, 336, 337, 374, 407–8, 552–3
  mother, 9, 26–7, 130, 195, 207, 227, 302, 328, 334, 382, 434
health, sickness and accidents, 14–15, 19, 21, 29, 57, 58, 81, 329, 349–50, 352, 355–64, 411, 450
  accidents, 15, 19, 81, 224–5, 329, 357, 509
  appendectomy, 101, 357, 359–61
  fear of polio, 365
  injuries from fights, 333
  scarlet fever, 29, 363–4
  X–ray tests for TB, 363
home, 9, 10–11, 24–32, 58, 236, 237, 371
  garden, 374
  heating and keeping warm, 10–11, 59–61, 371–2
  new bathroom, 353
  new lavatory, 373
recreations, games and hobbies, 295–334
  bird's egg collecting, 262–8
  bird's nesting, 268–72
  card games, 303
  catapulting, 270, 272–5
  Charles Atlas body-building course, 176, 201–7, 337
  fishing, 218–30
  gramophone records, 408–9
  hare coursing, 217
  helps construct a racing car, 194–5
  hunting, 254–9
  in gangs, 323–34
  making a fishing rod, 218–20
  Monopoly, 302
  peashooting, 295, 316–17, 506–7
  pitch-and-toss, 303–4
  playing street games, 25, 316–20
  robbing orchards, 93–5
  rolling hoops, 318–20
  shooting, 217–18
  stamp collecting, 307
  swimming, 1, 162, 164–73, 174–6, 179, 183–7
  tobogganing, 320, 322
  watching horse races, 208–10, 211–12, 213–14
religious beliefs and experiences, 87–118 *passim*
  altar boy, 98–101
  awareness of mortal sin, 451
  chorister, 113–17
  Christmas, 98
  church going, 68
  confessions, 89, 91–2, 451, 452–3
  Corpus Christi procession, 93, 96–7, 334
  First Communion and Confirmation, 111–12, 195, 381, 415
  missions, 88–92
  observance of Lent, 113
  opinions of priests, 98–9, 101–2, 103–5, 107
  pledge of abstinence, 104, 111
  retreats, 87–8, 92
  rosaries for world peace, 104–6
schools, 8–9, 33, 36, 93, 290–1, 408, 414–49, 552
  concert and stage performances, 428–33
  English classes, 425–7, 438–40
  infants, 8–9
  Irish studies, 445–6
  Leaving Certificate, 552
  nursery, 414–15
  primary, 415–23, 427
  religious instruction, 87, 437
  secondary, 423–49
  visits, 434, 440–1
sports, 68, 119–61, 162–87, 188–207
  athletics, 159, 160
  boxing, 82, 196–201
  cricket, 68, 188–92
  equipment, 7, 141–2
  Gaelic football, 68, 123–35
  handball, 123, 148–51, 153–4, 156
  hurling, 68, 126–7, 134–5, 136–7, 140–2, 144–6
  softball, 149
  table tennis, 192
teenage years,
  cinema going, 306, 317, 500–33
  circuses, 545–8
  clothes, 64, 143, 381, 467–8
  cycling, 157, 280–1, 340–1, 434, 500, 509
  dances, 537, 549,
  fighting, 333–4
  fun-fairs, 543–5
  hunting rabbits, 254–9
  leaves Lismore, 550–4
  listening to the wireless, 130, 139–40, 198–9, 336, 371, 408, 409–13
  sexual experiences, 450–2, 458–61, 464–6
  shotgun, 217
  smoking, 306
  theatre, 541–3
  understanding of World affairs, 490–9

Ballantyne, John (JB's Uncle), 80, 338
Ballantyne, Joseph Albert, (JB's Father), 2, 7, 23, 30, 31, 216, 233, 338, 345, 393, 402, 407, 479, 481, 482
  birth, 3
  character and appearance, 54, 122, 183, 185, 186, 344, 348, 374, 382, 383
    clothes, 183, 185, 379–80
    contempt for the Great Powers, 484
    contributes to cost of published history, 118
    deplores exile of Napoleon Bonaparte on St Helena, 484
    opinion of the Irish Civil War, 479–82
    political views, 330, 477, 481, 483–4
    sense of humour, 85–6, 377
    teaches himself Irish, 446
    voracious reader, 75–6, 85–6, 382
  family relations,
    mother, 5
    sons, 144–5, 185, 297–8, 328
    wife, 186, 342, 374, 352–3
  health and sickness,
    death, 480
    ill health, 294, 322, 374, 377, 438, 552–3
    injuries, 342
  home, 10, 27–8, 371–4
    carpentry skills, 28, 322, 371
    grows vegetables in back garden, 374
    saws and splits firewood, 10, 294
  recreations and sports,
    fishing at Ardmore, 228
    hare coursing, 216, 217, 382
    keeps greyhounds, 216
    swimming in the sea, 183–7
  religious beliefs and experiences, 104, 108
  work,
    as Sergeant in the Lismore Garda Síochána, 2, 3, 67, 122, 336–9, 342, 343–8
    at Carrick-on-Suir Garda Barracks, 3, 216
    at Drangan Garda Barracks, 3, 216, 338

at Fethard (Tipperary) Garda Barracks, 3, 338
at Swanlinbar Garda Barracks, 216, 338, 483
attitude to guns, 357–9
deputizes at Dungarvan Court, 179–83, 228, 344
in the Irish War of Independence, 335, 338, 479–80, 485
in shipyards at Belfast, 483, 484
Irish Volunteers, 479
office at Lismore Garda Barracks, 32, 336, 337
retirement from the Lismore Garda, 54, 374, 554
Ballantyne, Larry (JB's Uncle), 309
Ballantyne, Mary Frances (née Morrissey), (JB's Mother), 1, 3, 6, 7, 15, 30, 31, 51, 358, 380, 393, 394, 395, 407
  birth, 3
  character and appearance, 383
  attitude to women's sports, 159
    clothes, 379, 380
    helps poor families, 62, 63
    political views, 330, 477, 484
    taste in reading, 85, 86
  childhood, 3
  family relations, 1, 3, 5–6, 9, 10, 17–18, 371–413 passim
    husband, 186, 342, 374, 552–3
    sons, 9, 26–7, 72, 130, 195, 207, 227, 249, 302, 328, 334, 351, 382, 434
  health and sickness, 6, 9, 131, 179–80, 361–2
  home, 10–11, 24–32, 59, 371–413 passim
    Christmas celebrations, 308
    moving furniture, 372–3
    pest prevention, 354–5
    cooking, 10–11, 24–5, 27, 59, 63, 223, 246, 289, 309–10, 373–9
  recreations,
    autograph collection, 473–4, 491
    favourite film stars, 528
    holidays 389

horse races, betting on, 209, 211
listening to the gramophone, 408–13
listening to the wireless, 198
love of wild flowers, 289
picnics, 165, 183–7
playing cards, 303
religious beliefs and experiences, 86, 88, 96, 97, 103, 104–5
Ballantyne, Joseph Patrick Conor (JB's Son), 7
Ballantyne, Paddy (JB's Uncle), 335, 483
Ballantyne, Patrick (Paddy) Anthony (JB's Brother), ii, 11, 15, 19, 30, 31, 39, 51, 100, 216, 380, 387, 392, 402, 407, 417, 551
  birth, 5–6
  character and appearance, 7, 72, 408
    clothes, 380–1
  childhood, 6–7
    holidays, 187, 401, 406
    parlour games, 297
    pet dog, 382
    piano and elocution lessons, 7, 382
    rescues birds, 237
    picnics by the sea, 179–87
  family relations,
    brother, 5, 7, 19, 180, 249, 312, 407–8, 464
    father, 297, 483
    mother, 72, 382
  health and sickness, 349, 352
    appendicitis/peritonitis, 358–9
    death, 6
  home, 24–32
  recreations and sports,
    badminton, 192
    lawn tennis, 193
    greyhounds, 216
    watching the stars at night, 238
  school, 407, 428, 430, 434
    in Carrick-on-Suir, 407
    teenage years, 341, 465
    cinema going, 505–6
  work, 407
    at Bórd na Móna, Rathangan, 407, 552
    in Birmingham, 407, 463, 493, 552
    leaves for Canada, 407–8

INDEX

Ballantyne, Patrick, (JB's Paternal Grandfather), 2, 3, 5
Ballinamult and Dungarvan Co-Operative Creameries, 242
Ballinvella, 111
Ballinwillin, 45
ballroom dancing, 539
Ballyanchor House, 46
Ballycotton, 549
Ballyduff, 18, 41–2, 89, 431, 536
Ballyduff Castle, 44
Ballyduff hurling team, 119, 121, 130, 131, 132
Ballyea, 43, 167, 259
Ballygallane, 535
Ballygallane Bridge, 265
Ballygallane House, 43
Ballygally House, 44
Ballyin, 18, 20, 36, 42, 234, 313, 365
Ballyin Gardens, 42, 49, 53, 71, 322
Ballyin House, 163, 258, 350
Ballyin Wood, 261, 262
Ballykinlar Camp, 483
Ballyneale, 3, 143
Ballynelligan Cottage, 35
Ballynelligan Glebe, 167
Ballyrafter, 36
Ballyrafter House, 42, 276
Ballyrafter Wood, 43, 136, **168**, 291
Ballysaggart, 46, 111, 123, 535
Ballysaggartbeg Glebe, 45
Ballysaggartmore House, 42
bands,
    brass, 539
    ceilidhes, 155, 384, 535, 538
    dance, 411, 539
banks, 70–1, 177, 203, 336
Banks, Mrs, 392
Bannister, Roger, 159, 198
banshees, 288
Baptist, Sister, 9
barley growing, 247
Barna, Victor, 192
Barracks, Garda, Lismore, 8, 13, 32, 335–7
Barranamanoge Wood, 42
Barrett, Brother ('Fishy'), 423, 437
Barrett, Richard, 480
Barry, John Joe, 159
Barry, Mick, 151
Barry, Ned, 311
Barry, Paddy (Cork hurler), 129
Barry, Paddy ('Snobby'), 36, 554
Barry, Tom, 485

Baston, Seán, 419, 446
Baylough, 178, 280–1, 439
The Beano, 77–8
Beare, Brother, 135, 418, 428
bee keeping, 247, 278
Beecher, Mick, 131
beet thinning, **285**, 285–8
Behegan, Breda, 105, 512
Behegan, John ('Panzer'), 142, 194, 215, 319, 330, 346, 386
Behegan, Mick, 121, 146
Belfast, Northern Ireland, 479, 484
Belfast 'A' Company, IRA, 479
Bell, Isaac, 47–9, 258
Bell, Mrs, 53–5, 258
Bennett's Hall, Ballysaggart, 536
Bernadotte, Count, 496
birds, 262–72
birds nesting, 263, 268–72
birds eggs collecting, 263–8
Bishops Fishery, 37, 41, 225, 228, 231–2, 266
Bishopstown Wood, 46
Black and Tans, 338, 484
Blackrock hurling team, Cork, 549
blacksmiths, 119, 406
Blackwater Bridge, 161, **220**, 220
Blackwater Ramblers, 5, 121–3, 133
Blackwater River, 18, 20, 36, 37, 40, 41, 42, 43, **43**, 44, 162–7,**163**, **168**, 174–6, 178, 218, 220, 231–4, 266, 322, 475, 553
Blankers–Koen, Fanny, 159
Blitz bombing of English cities, 493
blizzards, 236
bluebells, 289, 290
Blueshirts, 483
Boam, Dorothy, 104, 469–70
Boam, Mr, 302, 468
Boathouse, Cappoquin, 340, 341, 535
Boden, Niall, 410
Boer War, 555
Bolger, Charlie, 134, 145, 422, 435–6, 438
Bolger, Harry, 351
The Book of Kells, 548
bookmakers (bookies), 212–13
Bórd na Móna, Rathangan, 407, 552
Bóthar na Naomh, 45
Boucicault, Dion, 542
Bourke, Paddy, 409

bowling, 151
boxing, 82, 196–201
Boxing News, 200
Boy Scouts, 96, 97–8, 312, 329–31, 538
Boyle, Guard M., 17, 150, 304, **345**
Boyle, Jerry, 17
Boyle, Joan, 415
Boyle, Richard, 117
Boyle, Robert, 117
Brackett, Ned, 119
Brady, Brother, 427–8
Brady, Edward M., 483
Bransfield, Sonny (Declan), 125, **125**, 132
brass bands, 539
Bray, Patsy, 94, 276, **416**
bread, 378
    home made, 378
    making, 13–14, 375, 395–7
    staple diet, 58, 63
Breen, Dan, 485
Brendan, Mother, 9, 93, 553
Brennan, Commissioner, **345**
Brickey Rangers, 133
Brickey River, 133
Bride, River, 44, 46
Bride of Carrickbawn, 542
Brideside Serenaders Band, 539
bridges,
    Avonmore Bridge, 232
    Ballygallane Bridge, 265
    Blackwater Bridge, 161, 220, **220**
    Lady Louisa's Bridge, 163, 293
    Lismore Bridge, 18, 37, 41, 162, 235, 263, 302
    Lismore Canal Bridge, 261
    Owbeg Bridge, 45
    Owenashad Bridge, 260, **261**
    Strand Bridge, 11, 42, 165, 232, 234, 235–6, 292
    Tallow Bridge, 44, 388, 511
    Townparks Bridge, 242
    Youghal Bridge, 45
British Broadcasting Corporation (BBC), radio programmes, 346, 409–13
British Movietone News, 412, 517
Broderick, Michael, 120, 121, 465
Broderick, Richard ('Ritchie' or 'Bawgie'), 120, 153, 156, 175, **416**
Broghill Tower, 169
Brohan, Jimmy, 146

INDEX

Brooke, Sir Basil, Viscount Brookeborough, 484
Browne, Guard Joe, 340, **345**
Browne, Michael, 448
Browne, Dr Noël, 351, 486
Browne, Paddy, **417**
Buckley, Bill, 342
Budd, J. J., 279, 282, 291
bulls, 243–4
Bullsod Island, Blackwater River, 37, 167, **168**, 175, 219, 232, 266
Burgess Anchor, 46
butter, 34, 242, 376–7
Byrne, Carmel, 449
Byrne, Guard Jim, 133, 340, 342

Cahalane, Guard Con, 340
Cahill, Dodo, 105, 147
Cahill, Mada, 105, 512
Cahill, Tommy, 147, **416**
Caldwell, Johnny, 200
calendar customs, 308–12
Callaghan, Dr. Pat, 143
Cammell Laird Shipyard, Birkenhead, **482**, 483
camogie (womens' hurling), 128
Campbell of Kilmore, (school play), 432
Camphire, 536
Camphire House, 44, 45, 414
Campion, Annie, 114–17, 428
Campion, Jack, 13–14, 72, 231, 473, 474–5
Campion, Jim, 541
Canal, Lismore, 11, 43, 226, 261–2, 269
Canning, Jim, 243
Cantillon, Mr, 55, 56
Canty, Janey, 22
Cappagh, 180, 391
Cappoquin, 41, 43, 71, 123, 132, 134, 160, 193, 217, 232, 285, 340, 391, 414, 478, 500, 508, 510, 516, 522, 524–5, 535
Cappoquin Rowing Club, 193
card playing, 68, 71–2, 303
Carew, Eddie, 127
Carey, Johnny, 196
Carlos, Bill, 138
Carlsen, Captain Kurt, 498–9
Carnegie, Andrew, 73
Carnegie Public Library, Lismore, 73–7, **74**
Carrick Brass Band, 539
Carrick-on-Suir, 1, 8, 57–8, 63–4, 74, 102, 142–4, 240, 278, 330, 344, 351, 391–408, **394**, 500, 512, 513, 516, 555
Carrickford Productions, 534, 542
Carroll, Paul Vincent, 542
Carrowreagh, 2, 3, 406
Carter, Raich, 196
Carthage, St, 117
cartoon films, 519
Casey, Jim ('Bladder' or 'Blather'), 189
Casey, Steve, 207
Cassidy, Paddy, 18
Castle Cinema, Carrick-on-Suir, 500, 512, **513**, 516
Castle Farm, Lismore, 15, 18, 208, 211, 216, 243–4, 314, 490
catapulting, 259, 262, 270, 272–5, 323, 331
cattle markets, 240, 243
Cavan hurling team, 140
Cavendish, Andrew Robert Buxton, 11th Duke of Devonshire (1920–2004), 475
Cavendish, Charles, Lord, 15–16, 50, 52, 385
Cavendish, Deborah Vivien (nèe Freeman-Mitford), 11th Duchess of Devonshire, 47, 49–50, 51–2
Cavendish, Edward Spencer, 10th Duke of Devonshire (1895–1950), 221, 491
Cavendish, Mary Alice (nèe Gascoyne-Cecil), 10th Duchess of Devonshire, 491
Cavendish, William, Marquess of Hartington, 52
Cavendish, William George Spencer, 6th Duke of Devonshire (1790–1858), 117
céilidhes, 128, 156, 446, 492, 535, 538
celebrity concerts, 540
censorship, 112, 517
Chadwick, Florence, 518
charcoal burning, 55–6
Charles, Ezzard, 198
Charles I, King, 73
Chavasse, Colonel, 214
Chavasse, Mrs, 253
chesnuts, 291
Chester cake, 475
chickens, 377–8
children,
 barefooted, 57
 poorly clothed, 59
Children of Mary, 92, 96
chimney sweeps, 372
Christian Brothers' School, *see* Collegiate School of Christian Brothers
Christmas celebrations, 98, 300, 308–9
Churchill, Winston, 86, 473
cinema-going, 500–33
cinemas,
 Castle, Carrick-on-Suir, 500, 512, **513**, 516
 Desmond, Cappoquin, 500, 508, 510, 516, 522, 524–5
 Ormonde, Dungarvan, 500, 516
 Palladium, Lismore, 500, **501**, 501–8, 516
 Park View, Carrick, 500, 512
 Regal, Tallow, 500, 511, 516, 522, 524–5
 Savoy, Waterford, 500
circuses, 544–8
Cistercian Order, religious houses, 44, 111
Civil War, *see* Irish Civil War
Clann na Poblachta, 477
class structure, 67
Clegg, Ernie, 534, 542
Clements, Willie, 190
clergy, *see under* individual names
Clifford, Tom, 194
Clonea Bay and Strand, 1, 179, 183–6, **184**
Clongowes Wood College, 326
Clonmel, 553, 556–7
The Clonmel Chronicle, 559
clothes,
 black shawls, 63–4
 shortage, 57
coal, 371
coarse fishing, 220
Cohalan, Bishop Daniel, 111, 553
Colbert, Bishop, 100–3, 360
Colbert, Claudette ('Claude'), 192, 431
Colbert, Dan, 36, 102–3, 105, 335, 387, 390, 431–2, 541
Colbert, Jimmy, 192, 387, 431, 433, 454–5
Colbert, Pierce, 72, 101, 135, 137, 387, 430, 431, 433
Coleman, Andy, 368, **416**
Coleman, John, 368,
Coleman, Michael ('Mikey'), 93–6, 99, 147, 276, 368, **417**, 441,

Coleman, Mick, 63, 149, 158, 196, 257, 314, 462
Coleman, Ned, 119, 377, 547
Coleman, Tom, 175
The Colleen Bawn, 534, 542
Collegiate School of Christian Brothers, 33, 34, 36, 93, 97, 134, 148, 278, 302, 326, 365, 415–48
Collins, Michael, 479
Columbus in a Merry Key, (school performance), 430–1
comedy films, 517, 518–20, 521, 533
Comeragh Mountains, 3
comics (children's magazines), American, 80–1
English, 77–80, 82
Irish, 82–3
concerts, 535, 538, 539–41
Conn, Billy, 140, 198
Connell, Kate, *see* O'Connell, Kate
Connors, Jack, 293, 377
Connors, Willie, 211
Connors, Mrs Willie, 216
Conradh na Gaeilge, 446, 487, 548–9
Conway, Billy, 133
Cooney, Agnes, 63
Cooney, Burke ('Mikey'), 62–3, 120
Cooney, Mary, 63
Cooney, Michael, 150
Cooney, Mrs, 62
Coppi, Fausto, 160–1
Cork, City of, 41, 129, 161, 484
Cork Athletic Football Club, 196
corn farming, 249–50
Coronation stone, theft from Westminster Abbey, 498
Corpus Christi Procession, Lismore, 93, 96–7, 334
Cosgrave, William, 480
Courtney, Joe, 390
Cow Testing Association, 539
cowboy films, 517, 520, 522–4, 532–3
creameries, 242
Creane, Josephine, 346
Creane, Mary, 346
Creane, Paddy, 202, 206, 263–5, 302, 322, 326, 428, 450, 507–8, 521
Creane, Superintendent Patrick, 167, 344–6, 484

Creane, Walter, 137, 167, 302, **417**, 428
cricket, 68, 121, 125, 188
crime, 343–4
Crimean War, 495–6, 555–65
Croke, Inspector John Patrick, 335
Cromwell, Oliver, 73, 485
Crosby, Bing, 52, 491
Crotty, John, 20, 192, 193
Crotty, Peter, 197
Crotty, Thomas, 554
Crotty, Tommy, 17
Crowley, Jim, 136
Crowley, Kathleen, 469, 470
Crowley, Michael ('Harry'), 110
Crowley, Michael ('Lala'), 110, 120, 470
Crowley, Nancy, 539
Crowley, Teddy, 343
Crummy, Superintendent, 344, **345**
Cuchulain's London Irish hurling team, 124
Cullen, Brother, 437–9
Cullinane, Anastasia, *see* Morrissey, Anastasia,
Cullinane, Geoffrey, 3
Cullinane, Mary (née McGrath) (JBs Maternal Great-Grandmother), 3, **4**, 446
Cullinane, Michael (JB's Maternal Great Grandfather), 3,
Cullinane, Philip, 3
Cullinane, Walter ('Wattie'), 33
Cully, Jim, 197, **197**
Cumann Culthúrtha na h-Aiséirighe, 446, 487
Curley, Con, 132
Curley, Mick, 132
Curley, Sonny, 132
Curragh, 495
Curraghmore Estate, 391
Curraghmore House, 49
Currey, Francis Edmund, 235
Currey, Frances Wilmot, 235
cycle racing, 160–1
cycling, 157, 160–1, 280–1, 340–1, 434, 500, 509
The Cygnets (GAA team), Carrick-on-Suir, 142–4

Dáil Éireann, 473, 475, 480
D'Alton, Louis, 541
Daly, Charlie, 132
Daly, Dorothy, 192
Daly, Joe, **417**
Daly, Ned, 126, 127

Daly, Redmond ('Rem'), 303, 304
Daly, Sheila, 128
dances, 213, 253, 340, 492, 535, 536, 537–9, 549
  ballroom, 539
  céilidhes, 128, 156, 446, 492, 535, 538
  old tyme, 538–9
  stage, 535–6
Dancy, Kenneth, 499
The Dandy, 78
Daniels, George, 543
Daniels, Mick, 127
Daniels Variety Company, 543
Darragh, Niall, 114, 473–4
Dartmoor Prison, England, 560–3
Davin, Ellen, 402–3
Davin, Maurice, 403
Davin, Pat, 403
The Davins (GAA club), Carrick-on-Suir, 142–4
Davitt, Michael, 559–64
Dawson, Sonny, 510
de Lourdes, Sister, 8–9, 415
de Porres, Blessed Martin, 88
de Valera, Eamon, 473–4, 494
Deerpark Woods, 278–9, 292, 402
Delahunty, Mick, 539
Dell, Peggy, 539
Denn, Biddy, 359
Denn, Eddie or Ned, 250–1, **251**
Denn, Jo, 359, **367**
Dennehy, Dr John, 350
Dennis, Peter ('Boxer'), 100, 108–10, 114, 135, 136–7, 155, **172**, 209, 221–3, 230, 253, 257, 270, 273–4, 280, 291, 294, 507–8, 510, 550
Dennis, Eugene, 18, 97, 151, 181, 230, 235, 240, 280, 285, 313, 372, 384, 464, 507–8
Dennis, Guard James ('Jim'), 10, 139, 347, 369, 374
Dennis, Mrs James, 347
Dennis, May, 347
Dennis, Michael, 155, **172**, 278, 280–1, 285, 447
Dennis, Seán, 61, 145, 153, 175, 176, 277, 330, 333, 347, **416**, 433, 438, 448
dentists, 351
Derrynane, 3
Desmond Cinema, Cappoquin, 500, 508, 510, 516, 522, 524–5

Devanney, Guard, **345**
Devereaux, Simon, 365
Devonshire, Dukes of, *see* Cavendish
Dillon, Hugo, 372
Dillon, James, 476
Dillon, Michael, 410
Dineen, Bill, 414, 422
Dionne Quintuplets, Canada, 498
diptheria, 364,
doctors, 349–51
dogs, hunting, 215, 216, 257, 260, 398–9
Doherty, Edward (known as Ned) ('Beaver'), 60–1, 131, 150, 151, 153, 154, 156–8, 171, 175, 176, 303, 304–5, 313, **416**, 426, 455, 462–3, 471
Doherty, 'Parrot', 97
Doherty, Peter ('Cox'), 61, 150, 153, 156–8, 303, 554
Donkey Protection Society, 54
donkeys, 53–4
Donohue, Peter, 140
Donovan, Frank, 540
Doocey, Michael, **416**, 440
Doocey, Noel, **417**
Dooley, Joe, 14
Dooley, Paddy, 14, 61, 231, 291
Dowd, Horace, 477
Dowd, Peter, 167, 302
Dowling, Liam, 129
The Down Express, 541
Downey, Captain, 400
dowsing, 329–30
Doyle, Eddie, 143
Doyle, Jack, 197
Doyle, John, 129
Doyle, Superintendent, 344
Doyle, Tommy, 129
Dracula, (stage adaptation), 542
drinking, 365–6
  after licensed hours, 122
Drislane, Josie, (née Flynn), 475
Drohan, Andrew ('Andy'), 75, 218–20, 225–8, 230
Drohan, Billy, 405
Drohan, Denis, 43,
Drohan, Hannah, 72, 497
Drohan, Paddy, 391
Drohan, Pat, 405
Dromana House (Castle), **43**, 44
drovers, 62–3, 240
Drumroe House, 45
Ducey, Dick, 133
Ducey, Tom, 133
Duff, Frank, 104

Duffy, John, 545
Duffy's Circus, 545, 546
Duggan, Joe, 124–5
Duignan, Superintendent Michael, 344, 346
Dungannon, 89
Dungarvan, 73, 74, 105, 142, 157, 179, 197, 217, 236, 285, 379, 391, 434, 474, 500
Dungarvan Bus Company, 549
Dungarvan Hospital, 359–61
Dungarvan Leader, 49, 71, 202, 487–8
Dungarvan Observer, 13, 49, 71, 156, 231, 232, 245, 478
Dunne, Cyril, 301–2
Dunne, Jack, 149
Dunne, Janey, 53, 415, 541
Dunne, Mary, 23,
Dunne, Molly, 149
Dunne, Pa, 149, 154, 156, 172
Durrow, 391
Dwyer, Paddy 406

ESB, *see* Electricity Supply Board
The Eagle, 81–2
East Lynne, 534, 542
education, 414–49 *passim*
  nursery, 8–9, 414–15
  primary, 415–23
  secondary, 423–49
Edwill Productions, 543
Éire Instrumentalists Céilidhe Band, 155, 384, 535, 538
el-Krim, Abd, 84
elections, 473, 477
Electricity Supply Board (ESB), 236, 274
electrification, rural, 236, 241
Eley, Humphrey, 353
Ellis, Alec, 34, 243, 248, 253, 276
Ellis, Miss, 34, 248, 253, 376
emigration, 466–7, 491–2
  to Britain, 8, 158, 449, 466, 487, 489, 491, 553
  to North America, 3, 407, 491–2
employment, 50–1, 285
Endersen, Kitty, 114, 275
Endersen, Trevor, 275
English, Paddy, 132
English Channel swim, 518
English films, 516, 521, 526–7
Equity Productions, 542
Erin's Own hurling team, 124
Everybody's, 86, 463, 516

FCA, *see* Fórsa Cosanta Áitiúil
fairgrounds, 209, 240
fairs and markets, 209, 240
  cattle, 240
  fun-fairs, 543–5
  pigs, 240
  potatoes, 240
farm labourers' wages, 51
farmers, 211, 240–2
Farmers' Forum (Radio Éireann), 410
farming, 55, 234, 240–52
  arable, 383,
  cereal, 55, 245–6, 247
  cattle, 34, 240
  milk, 242
  potatoes, 245, 247
  sheep, 231–2
farms,
  machinery, 244
  use of chemicals, 242
Farouk, King, 497
fascism, 483
Feeney, Jack, 190
Feeney, Jim, 93, 140, 228–9, 247, 301, 353, 369–70
Feeney, Margaret, 105, 165, 228–9, 296, 320, 325, 376, 382–3, 549, 554
Feeney, Mary, 140, 215, 228–9, 386, 461, 514, 554
Feeney, Michael, 11, 19, 20–1, 194, 217, 238, 271, 320, 322, 325, 332–3, 341, 346, 369, **417**, 429, 431, 505–6, 554
Feeney, Pad, 188, 189–90, 243, 314
Feeney, Tom, 11, 21, 93, 104–5, 136, 165, 169, 172, 189, 194, 228–9, 271, 273, 302, 314, 317, 319, 320, 322, 325, 329, 330, 332, 333, 365, 369, 383, 384–5, 454, 493
Feeney's Garage, Lismore, 139–40
Fenton, Kieran, 98, 142, 194, 215, 319, 330, 346, 386, 541, 554
Fermoy Gaelic football team, 138
ferreting, 255, 256–7
Ferry Inch, 20, 44
Fianna Fáil Party, 83, 154, 181, 473–4, 476, 477, 481, 488
field athletics, 158–60
film magazines, 515–16
film stars, 503, 507, 512, 514–33 *passim*

INDEX

American, 507, 512, 515–17, 518, 521, 522–6, 527–33
English, 521, 526–7
Irish, 514, 525–7, 530, 542
film-making in Ireland, 514–15
films, 507–8, 511–2, 513–33 *passim*
films (genres)
   cartoons, 519
   comedies, 517, 518–20, 521, 533
   cowboy, 517, 520, 522–4, 532–3
   gangster, 525–6
   historical, 527
   horror, 512, 532
   musicals, 528–9
   religious, 516
   serials, 517, 524–5
   sports, 531–2
   swashbuckling, 529–30
   war, 527
   westerns, 520, 522–4, 532–3
films (nationality)
   American, 507–8, 511–12, 514–15, 518–21, 522–6
   English, 516, 521, 526–7
   Irish, 517
Fine Gael Party, 83, 475–6, 481–3
firewood collecting, 60–2
fishing, 217, 218–19, 379, 442
   eels, 58, 164, 218–23
   illegal, 231
   licensed, 475
   mackerel and herring, 187, 228–30
   salmon, 20, 42, 51–2, 172, 230, 231
   trout, 58, 218, 221, 225–8, 230, 243
Fitzgerald, Bertie, 141–2, 292
Fitzgerald, John, 244–5
Fitzpatrick, James A., 305, 517
Fives, Jimmy, 133, 430, 448
Fives, Mossie, 133
Fives, Tom, 253
flax growing, 55
Fleming, Dan, 368
Fleming, Denis, 479
Fleming, Mrs, 402
flooding, 233–6
flowers, wild, 289–90
fly-fishing, 221, 225
The Flying Enterprise, 498–9
Flynn, James, 557
Flynn, Michael ('Foxy'), 94, 105–6, 173–4, 257, 259, 267, 276, 314–15, 347, 457–8, 459–60, 465, 412, 550–2

Flynn, Mickey ('The Diddler'), 373
Flynn, Paddy, 115, **120**
Fogarty, Jack, 71, 432, 541
Foley, Bill, 69
Foley, Bing, 257
Foley, Jimmy, 160
Foley, Nell, 69
Foley, Nurse, 350
Foley, Val, 257, 550–6
food,
   rationing, 10, 22, 58–9, 373–4
   shortage, 58, 373–4
Forde, Terry, **416**
An Fórsa Cosanta Áitiúil (Local Defence Force), 12–13, **13**
Fortwilliam House, 44, 47, 51, 53
Fossett's Circus, 545
Fourmilewater hurling team, 133
Fox, John, 155
foxes, 215, 260
   hunting, 214–15
foxgloves, 290
Fraser, Jack, 419–20
Fraser, Sidney, 206, 419–22, 429, 430, 432
Frawley, Des, 71, 414, **416**
Frawley, Frank, 71, **416**
Frawley, Jack, 71
frogs, 261–2
fruit,
   farm, 282
   picking, 276, 278–82
   stealing, 93–5
fun-fairs, 543–5
funerals, 189
Furey, Seamus, 172

GAA, *see* Gaelic Athletic Association,
Gael Linn, 517
Gaelic Athletic Association (GAA), 68, 121, 125–6, 130, 139, 146, 157, 158, 191, 193, 445, 549
Gaelic football, 5, 121, 123, 137, 409, 422, 487, 549
Gaelic language, *see* Irish language
Gaelic League, 446, 538, 541
Gaelic sports, 119–61
Gaeltacht of Ring, 445–6
Gallagher, Jessie, 151
Galway University hurling team, 121
games, 295–322 *passim*
Gandhi, Mahatma, 497

gangs, 322–34
gangster films, 521, 525–6
Garda Review, 335
Garda Síochána, 335–6
Garvin, John, 384
Garvin, Kathleen, 384
Gate Theatre, Dublin, 542
Gavilan, Kid, 200
Geary, Joe, 122
General Election, 1948, 473, 477
Geoghegan, Willie, 360–1
Geraldines hurling team, Aglish, 132, 134
German internees, 495
Gigli, Beniamino, 408
Gillen, Peter ('Petey') (Sacristan), 96, 411
Gillen, Peter (musician), 411, 432, 539, 540–1
Girl Guides, 96, 321
Glasse, Jimmy, 72, 473
Glasse, Sadie, 415
Glebe Hall, Aglish, 536
Glen Rovers, 147
Glen View, 43, 235
Glenaraha, 34
Glenbeg House, 44
Glencairn, 44, 51, 146
Glencairn Abbey (Cistercian), 44
Glendon, George, 384
Glendon, Mary, 187
Glendon, Peg, 384
Glengarriff, 549
Glenmore House, 42, 44
Glenmore Wood, 42
God's Gentry, 542
Godfrey, Lady, 33–4, 276
Gone With The Wind, (stage adaptation), 542
Gorman, Father T., 103
Gough, Matt, 75, 86, 190–1, 192
Goulding, Seán (Seán Uasal Uí Guilídhe), 154, 476
Grand National, Aintree, 211, 518
Grangemockler Creamery, 242–3
Grant, Peg (née Denn), 242–3, 351
Grant, Phyllis, 243 **251**
Gray, David, (US Ambassador to Ireland), 494
The Great Jeserich Circus, 545, 547
Great Potato Famine, 3, 475
Greehy, John ('Guyler'), 343
greyhounds, 11, 216, 258, 398–9

Grimes, Philly, 127
Grosvenor, Hugh Richard Arthur, 2nd Duke of Westminster (1879–1953), 47, 53
Guinness (drink), 385
Guiry, Tom, 393
guns, use of, 217–18, 357–9

Hallowe'en celebrations, 311
Hammersmith Palais, London, 467, 491
handball, 148–58
Hanlon, Jimmy, 155
Hannigan, Mary ('Petticoat Loose'), 178
hardball (handball), 155
hare coursing, 216–17
Harraher, Paddy, 143
Harrington, Chris, 383
Harris, Reg, 160
Hartington, Marquess of, *see* Cavendish, Lord William,
Hartnett, Maurice, 389
Hartnett, Tommy, 83, 120, 266–8, 389
harvesting, 249–51
Haw Haw, Lord, (William Joyce), 494
haymaking, 247, 248
Healy, Aggie, 72, 299
Healy, Dr Daniel ('Doc'), 53, 276, 277, 329, 339, 349–50, 359, 500, 502–8, 518, 522, 553
Healy, Jack, 350, 430, 504, 538
Healy, Seán, 539
Healy, Tim, 117
Healy, Tommy, 538
'The Heap', Lismore, 61, 148, 154, 155
Heckenberg Super Circus, 548
Hehir, Brendan, 283–4
Hely, J. J., 351
Henley, Peadar, 132, 134, 211, 332, 422
Hennebry, Father, 103
Henry, Paul, 548
herbal remedies, 290, 352
Herr, John, 134, 422, 435, 438, 444, 445
herrings, 379
Heskin, Denis, 476, 477
Heskin, George, 211, 476
Hick, Sam, 227
Hickey, Maurice, **417**
Hickey, Mick, 127, 131–2
Hickey, Papa, 313
Hickey, Patsy, 57, **416**

Hickey, Peadar, 122
Hickey, Thomas, 488
Higgins, Mick, 12, 131, 140
High Finance, (short stage play), 541
Hill's Lending Library and Reading Room, Dungarvan, 73
Hillary, Edmund, 198
historical films, 527
Historical Sketch of Lismore Parish, 117
Hitchen, Sheila, 539
Hobbs, Danny, 540
Hobson, Mr (Vet), 178
hockey, 125
Hogan, Billy, (musician), 120, 469, 470, 539, 540–1
Hogan, Billy ('Hoagy'), 5, 168–70, 175, 198–9, 221–3, 273, 278, 291, 302, 314–15, 317, 325, 330, 432, 454–6
Hogan, Garrett, 5, 121–2
Hogan, Jim, 110, 121, 122
Hogan, Kathleen, 32, 470
holy wells, 94, 97–8
hoop rolling, 318–19, 320
Horan, Mick, 217
horror films, 512–532
Horse Fair, Tallow, 213
horse-racing, 17, 208
horses,
  fairs, 213
  jumping, 252
  racing, 211
  shires, 247
hospitals, 45–6, 350, 351, 359–61, 364
The Hotspur, 78, 80
Houlihan, Guard Christy, 72, 345, 347–8
Howard, Dan, 241
Howard, Jimmy, 34, 251
hunting,
  foxes, 214–15
  rabbits, 254–9
Hurley, William, 556–7
hurling, 13, 43, 120–1, 123–5, 191, 409, 422, 549
Hurst, Mary, 495, 555, 563, 564
Hurst, Michael, 495–6, 555–65
Hynes, C. P., 17
IRA, *see* Irish Republican Army
IRB, *see* Irish Republican Brotherhood
ice houses, 18, 20, 42, 117
ice skating, 20
Industrial Development Authority, 285

Ireland, Republic of,
  establishment of, 486
  map, **xvi**
  National Anthem, 538
  neutrality during World War Two, 494
Images of Ireland: Lismore, 235, 384
Ireland: Photographs 1840–1930, 235
Ireland's Secret Service in England, 483
Irish Civil War, 474, 479–81
Irish Defence Forces, 11–13
Irish Film Society, 503
Irish Independent, 83
Irish language, 409, 445–6, 486–8, 541
Irish literature, 85, 541–2
Irish Press, 83, 102, 198, 485, 488, 497, 498
Irish Republican Army, 346, 479
Irish Republican Brotherhood, 479
Irish Times, 83
Irish Volunteers 479
Irish War of Independence, 346, 473, 479–81
'Iron Room', Lismore, 108, 330
Israel, establishment of the State of, 327, 496

Jacob, Miss, 136
Jacques, Captain Jimmy, 403
Jameson, Captain, 49
Japan,
  Imperial Army, 494
Jews, persecution of, 494
Jocklin, John, *see* O'Donnell, John
Julius Caesar, 434–5

Kavanagh, Neddy, 397
Keane, John, 127
Keane, Nurse, 350
Keane, Tommy, 137, 425–7, 440, 445
Kearney, Peadar, 483
Keash, 2, 3, 309, 406
Keating, Donie ('Doshin'), 35, 58, 107, 108–10, 130, 252, 257, 259, 270, 341, 507–8, 525, 550–2
Keating, Johnny, 107
Keating, Minnie, 107
Keating, Tom ('Tommy'), 107, 293, 321, 384, 538
Kelleher, Sergeant, 335
Kelly, Brother, 417–18
Kelly, Joe, 374

Kelly-Lynch, Peter, *see* O'Kelly-Lynch, Peter
Kenneally, William, 477
Kennedy, Jimmy, 146
Kennedy, Kathleen, 52
Kennedy, 'Moses', 35
Kennedy, Paddy, 138
Kennedy, Rose, 52
Kennel Heights, 43
Kenny, Paddy, 129
Kent, Jack, 391, 484
Kent, Katie, 391
Kerry, 549
Keyes, Gordon, 120, 225
Keyes, Jacko, 123
Keyes, Kitty, 123, 554
Keyes, Mickey, 225, 230
Khyber Pass Wood, 44
Kickham, Charles, 445
Kiely, John, 127, 157, 211
Kiely, Mary, 187, 384
Kiely, Mattie, 187, 384
Kiely, Paddy, 211
Kiely, Dr Pat, 361
Kiely, Tom, 143
Kiely-Ussher Vaults, 42
Kiernan, Peter, 36
Kiersey, Minnie, 36
Kilclooney Bridge, Coolnahorna, stage dance, 536, **536**
Kilgobnet, 157
Kilkenny, 128
Kilkenny Gaol, 480
Killahala Wood, 45
Kilmacthomas, 391
Kilrossanty, 121, 131, 138
King, Billy, 51, 52, 353
Kingston, Gus, 190
Kirwan, Billy, 138
'Kitty the Hare', 82
knife sharpening, 65
Knockanaffrin, 400
Knockmeal Co-Operative Society, 285, 539
Knockmealdown Mountains, 17, 34, 162, 236, 292, 371, 479
Knocknagapall Wood, 42
Knocknagow, (stage adaptation), 541
Knockroe, 4
'The Knocks', (*Knocknagow I/II* river boats), 403
Knowles, Nurse, 21–2, 350
Korean War, 497
Koringa (circus performer), 547–8
Kyle, Jackie, 195
Kyne, Tom, 473, 474, 475

LDF, *see* Local Defence Force
Labour Party, 13, 473, 475
Lacey, Mick, 133
Lady Louisa's Bridge, 163, 293
Landers, Bill, 119, 149, 547
Landers, Dick, 149, 153
Landers, Mick, 149, 154, 156–8
landowners, 47–9, 53
Landy, John, 159
Lane, Mick, 195
Lane, Mr (bonesetter), 351
Langford, Michael, 291
Langton, Jimmy, 129
The Last Forge in Lismore, 36, 164, 180, 211, 331, 547
Laverty, Maura, 407
law and order, 335–48 *passim*
Lawn, Father, 111–12
lawn tennis, 121, 125, 192–3
Lawton, Dan, 335, 553
Leahy, Terry, 129
Leddy, Liam, 487
Lee, Brother P. D., 91, 98, 116, 241, 408, 417, 420–1, 423–4, 427, 431–4, 436–7, 443, 450
Legion of Mary, 104
Lemass, Seán, 483
Leslie, Shane, 52
libraries, 73–7
lilacs, 32, 290
Linnane, Joe, 410
Lineen, Babe, 181
Lineen, Bill, **120**
Lineen, Jim ('Plug'), 455
Lineen, Jim ('Thumper'), 11, 36, 72, 120, 234, 305, 363, **417**, 431, 455, 464, 471, 515
Lineen, Kitty, 126
Lineen, Michael, 72, 503, 515
Lineen, Pad, 119, 130, 232, 234
Lineen, Tom, 36, 46, 63, 127, 130, 134–5, 136, 195, 198–9, 234, 292–3, 296, 414, 427
Lineen, Willie Bob, 127, 172
Lismore, xvii (map), 1, 119, 553
bridges,
 Lismore Bridge, 18, 37, 41, 162, 235, 263, 302
 'Tallow Road' Bridge, 44, 388, 511
 Townparks (Railway) Bridge, 242
churches,
 Presbyterian Church, 345
 St Carthage's (Catholic) Cathedral, 38–9, 68, 83, 88
 St Carthage's (Protestant) Cathedral, 16, 37, 38, 39, 53, 117
commercial and public buildings,
 Courthouse/Town Hall, 32, 40, **41**, 253, 537
 Garda Barracks, 8, 13, 32, 335–7
 Gas Works, 234
 Happydrome, 39, 70, 104, 128, 197, 253, 292, 410, 429, 535, 537, 539, 543
 'Iron House', 108, 330
 The Monument, 1, 32, 40–1, **41**, 96
 Palladium Cinema, 53, 199, 349, 500, 501–8, **501**
 Post Office, 38
 Public Library, 73–7, **74**
 Railway Station, 39, 240–1, 387–8, 389–90, 490–1, **491**
 St Carthage's Hall, 535
 St Carthage's Hospital, 45–6, 350, 351, 364
 St Carthage's Well, 94, 97–8
 Town Clock, 473
events,
 Annual Seed Potato Market, 32, 240
 Corpus Christi Procession, 93, 96–7, 334
 Fair Day, 26, 66, 240, 370
 Gymkhana, 68, 213
 Hunt Ball, 68, 539
 Pig Market, 32, 240
 Point-to-Point Races, 68, 208–13
 St Carthage's Day, 97–8
 St Patrick's Day, 429, 430, 538
officials,
 Town Clerk, 553
 Town Commissioners, 73, 231, 285, 477, 478, 553
 Town Crier, 35, 477, 534–5
parks, gardens and open spaces, 17–18
 Ball Alley, 148, **148**, 153
 Canal, 11, 43, 226, 261–2, 269
 Castle Gardens, 36, 93–5, 162, 168, 276, 549
 Fair Field, 24, 29, 39, 135–6, 213, 240, 252, 315, 322, 545

576 INDEX

Lismore, (*cont.*)
  Ferry Inch, 20, 44
  Gaelic (Football) Field, 123–4, 144
  The Grove, 40, 313
  'The Heap', 61, 148, 154, 155
  Hurling Field, 12, 123, 134, 159, 422, 487
  Lady Louisa's Walk, 17, 37
  The Warren, 17, 37, 40, 313, 322, 553
  Warren Gardens, 38, 235, 303
  private houses,
    Ardagh, 141, 349
    Ashbourne House, 46
    Bushfield, 33
    Castle View, 38
    Deanery, 38, 40, 277
    Devonshire Cottages, 8, 153
    Headview, 350
    Hill Cottage, 33
    The Lodge, 53, 168, 349, 502
    Mall House, 38
    The Manse, 40, 202, 344
    Roseville, 124, 276
    The Villa, 21, 31, 33, 40, 97, 202, 276, 323–9, **324**, **325**, 331–2, 347–8
    Woodview, 34, 243, 248
  public houses, bars and hotels,
    Coghlan's Bar, 279, 533, 550
    Commercial Hotel, 351
    Devonshire Arms Hotel, 21, 40, **41**, 68, 104, 213, 302, 351, 468–9, **469**
    Geary's Public House, 122
    Madden's Public House, 22, 157
    O'Donnell's Public House, 122, 533
    Red House, 40, **41**
    The Wine Vaults, 15–16, 24, 33, 49–50, 56, 68, 213, 317, 335, 384–5
  schools,
    Collegiate School of Christian Brothers, 33, 34, 36, 93, 97, 134, 148, 278, 302, 326, 365, 415–48 *passim*
    Presentation Convent School, 8–9, 36, 93, 117, 148, 276, 278, 415, 449, 553
  shops and services,
    bakery, 13–14, 375
    banks, 32, 33, 70–1, 177, 203, 356
    bookmakers, 212–13
    butchers, 377
    café, 32, 469–70
    chemists, 351
    co-op, 40, 97, 234
    dairy, 33
    dentists, 351
    doctors, 349–51
    drapery, 32, 35, 72
    fire-brigade, 478
    garage, 21, 24, 32, 139–40, 234
    grocery, **13**, 33, 70, 368
    ice-cream parlour, 32, 469–70
    library, 73–7
    newsagents, 32, 79
    post office, 38
    shoes, 22
    sweets, 22–3
    toys, 98, 164, 300, 301, 318
  streets,
    Ballyanchor Road, 18, 34, 45, 46, 97, 242, 282
    Ballyduff Road, 18, 20, 46
    The Boreen, 13, 83, 239
    Botany, 13–14, 33, 34, 36, 39, 40, 59, 60, 93, 97, 100, 123, 135, 146, 254, 257, 289, 314, 320, **321**, 322
    Chapel Street, 34, 40, 83, 96, 123
    Church Avenue, 53
    Church Lane, 36, 38, 40, 60, 63, 100, 147, 153–4
    Convent Road, 350
    Deerpark Road, 8, 45
    Fernville, 38
    Ferry Lane, 122
    Gallows Hill, 1, 33, 73, 97, 321
    Glencairn Road, 44
    Green Road, 17
    Green Walk, 17, 18
    The Grove, 291, 322, 553
    Main Street, **13**, 40, **41**, 96, 97, 124, 135, 240, 322, 351
    Mayfield Road, 45, 292, 553
    Mountain Road, 46, 98, 167, 234, 235, 289, 291, 351
    New Street, *see* Botany
  New Way, 18
  North Mall, 38, 96
  Parks Road, 349
  South Mall, 38, 40, 96, 351
  Station Road, 239
  Tallow Road, 18–19, 34, 60, 97, 248, 276
  Townparks Road, 45, 135
  Upper Chapel Street, 38
  Upper Main Street, 38
  Upper New Street, **321**
   see also Botany
  West Street, 1, 31, 32, 97, 322
Lismore Agricultural Society/Show, 251, 252, 253, 539
Lismore Board of Fishery Conservators, 231–2
Lismore Brass Band, 430
Lismore Bridge, 18, 37, 162, 235, 263, 302
Lismore Camogie Team, 128
Lismore Canal, 11, 43, 226, 261–2, 269
Lismore Castle, 15, 36, 44, **48**, 73, 117, **163**, 220, 539
Lismore Crozier, 117
Lismore Coursing Club, 216
Lismore Dramatic Society, 431, 539, 541–2
Lismore Estates Company, 2, 10, 16, 20, 41, 50–1, 55, 231–2, 240–1, 253, 350, 353, 373, 379, 475
Lismore Feis, 487
Lismore Fire Brigade, 478
Lismore Handball Club, 148–9, 150, 153–8
Lismore Hurling & Football Club, 121, 133, 137
Lismore Junior Hurling Team, 120, 121
Lismore Library, 73–7, **74**
Lismore Point-to-Point Races, 17, 68, 208–13
Lismore Railway Station, 39, 240–1, 387–8, 389–90, 490–1, **491**
Lismore Ramblers, 121
Lismore Sinn Féin Club, 43
Lismore Table Tennis Club, 192
Little, P. J., 476
Little Nellie Kelly, 528, 542
Liverpool Company, IRA, 479–80, 483
Local Defence Force (LDF), **13**, 12–13, 96
Locke, Josef, 409
London,

INDEX 577

Blitz, 493, 495
Irish emigrants in, 466, 477, 488, 491–3
Lonergan, Bernard, **417**
Lonergan, Cheasty, 138
Long, Dick, **125**, 469–70, **469**, 493
The Lord Mayor, (stage play), 541
Lotty, Allan, 129
Lough Derg, 549
Louis, Joe, 81, 140, 198, 522
Lovers' Meeting, 541
Loving, Miss Vic, and Flash Parade Review, 543
lumberjacks, 292–3
Lynch, Brooky, 154, 173, 314, 462
Lynch, John, 172–3, 231
Lynch, Liam, 479
Lynch, Pakes, 149

MacBrearty, Sam, 215–16, 377
MacBride, Seán, 477
McCabe, Alec, 383–4
McCarthy, Dan, 359–60
McCarthy, Danny, 16, 33, 118, 385
McCarthy, Florence ('Mokie'), 49, 192–3, 196, 335, 384–5
McCarthy, Franco, 134
MacCarthy, J. Bernard, 541
McCarthy, Margaret, 449
McCarthy, Mary, 50, 192, 193, 445
McCarthy, Michael ('Mikey'), 16, 49, 56, 118, 385
McCarthy, Miss, 381–2
McCarthy, Robert, **417**
McCarthy Cup (hurling), 127
McConnell, Colonel, 306, 323, 327–8, 356, 496
McConnell, Gerald, 291, 302, 307, 314, **324**, 326, 327, 496
McConnell, Mickey, 64, 65, 221, 291, 302, 306, 314, **324**, 326, 327–9, 331, 424–5, 454, 455–6
McConnell, Popsie, 312, **324**, 327, 356
McCormack, Count John, 85, 408
McDermotts hurling team, 13
McDonagh, Bridget (JB's Paternal Grandmother), 3, 5
MacDonagh, Donagh, 542
McDonagh, James, 338–9

McDonalds Amusements, 70, 197, 543–4
McEwan, Father Sydney, 540
McGovern, Brother, 427
McGrath, Father Denis, 68, 72, 98, 103–5, 106, 107
McGrath, Canon Frank, 107
McGrath, George ('Haudles'), 133
McGrath, Harry, **120**, 123, 549
McGrath, Joanna ('Annie'), 64, 406
McGrath, Father John, 89, 103, 107–8
McGrath, Johnny, 18, 55, 253, 375, 377, 400
McGrath, Liam, 193
McGrath, Mary, *see* Magrath, Mary
McGrath, Molly, 1, 9, 17–18, 30–1, 64, 67, 86, 97, 164, 165, 179–80, 184–7, 234, 293, 309, 377, 406, **406**
McGrath, Myler, 117
McGrath, Paddy, 193
McHugh, Father, 89, 91
McInerney, P. J. ('The Clareman'), 340, 432, 541
McKelvey, Joseph, 479, 480
Macken, Walter, 75, 76
McKeon, Mick, 200
McKibben, Harry, 195
McKinley, President William, 335
MacLiammóir, Mícheál, 542
McMaster, Anew, 434–5
MacMurrough, Dermot, 485
McNulty, Edward, 541
MacSweeney, Brian, **417**
MacSweeney, Michael, 422, 435
mackerel fishing, 187, 228–30
Macks Variety Entertainment, 343
Macra na Feirme, 241, 247
Madden, Anne, 193, 465
Madden, Michael ('Coz'), **417**
Madden, Michael ('Mick'), 121, 162, 195–6, **417**, 464
Madden, Willie, **172**
Madden's Bakery, Lismore, 375
Magrath, Mary, *see* Cullinane, Mary
Maher, Sonny, 129
Malachy, St, 117
Malachys, 152
malnutrition, 58, 356
Maloney, Tommy, **416**
Manahan, Doc, 359, 500–1

Manahan, Eddie, 384
Manahan, Mary, 359
maps,
 Ireland, Republic of, **xvi**
 Lismore, **xvii**
 Waterford, County of, **xxvi**
marble playing, 295, 317–18
margarine, 377
Marino Band, 539
markets, 209
 cattle, 240
 pigs, 240
 potatoes, 240
Martin, Joe, 448
Martin, Guard Paddy, 10, 347, 369, 374
Masaryk, Jan, 497
Mason, Frank, 235, 303, 454
Mason, Guard Michael, 10, 336, **345**, 488
Mason, Mickey, 123
Master McGrath Monument, 180–1
Mathew, Father Theobald, 366
Matthews, Stanley, 211
Maxwell, Major, 49, 253
Mayfield Lodge, 45
Meade, Jimmy ('The Gurkha'), 35
Meade, Teasy, 98, 164, 300, 301, 318
Meagher, Canon William, 213
medical services, 349–52
medicines, 352–3
Mellows, Barney, 480
Mellows, Liam, 480
melodeon player, **536**
Mendszenty, Cardinal, 497
meningitis, 365
mental illness, 356
Mercy Convent, Carrick, 392
The Messenger, 86
Metropole Laundry, Cork, 381
Michael O'Sullivan, Detective, (Radio Éireann), 410
middle classes, 67–72 *passim*, 100
milk production and supply, 242
Mill Hill Fathers, 92
Mill Vale Creamery, 242
Millbank Prison, London, 559–60
Mills, Albert, 276–7
Mills, Frankie, 276
Mills, Freddie, 82
Mills, Herbert, 124, 276–7
Mills, Laura, 276–7
Mochuda, St, 117

578   INDEX

Modern Screen, 516
Mollerans (GAA club), Carrick-on-Suir, 142
Monahan, Rinty, 197
Monakerka, 376
Monalour, 34, 536
Monavullagh Mountains, 121, 181
Monopoly, 302
Moore, Archie, 198
Moore, Bill, 307
Moore, Mrs Bridget, 306
Moore, John, 369
Morrissey, Anastasia (née Cullinane) (JB's Maternal Grandmother), 3, 4, 6, **395**, 403, 446, 557, 563
Morrissey, Anastasia ('Bab') (JB's Aunt), 9, 23, **23**, 364, 377, 383, **387**, 393–5
Morrissey, Bridget ('Biddy') (JB's Aunt), 3, 309, 383, **393**, 392–5, **395**, 553
Morrissey, Jack (JB's Uncle), 4, **358**, 358, 368
Morrissey, James (JB's Maternal Grandfather), **4**, 4–5, **395**, 396, 398, 403, 446, 557, 563
Morrissey, James ('Jimmy') (JB's Uncle), **6**, 11, 143, 216, **216**, 217, 331, **367**, 461–2
Morrissey, John, 5
Morrissey, Mary Frances (JB's mother), *see* Ballantyne, Mary Frances
Morrissey, Mick (JB's Uncle), **6**, 39, 291, 309, 331, 375, 383, 397, 398, **404**, 407, 493, 555
Morrissey, Nellie (JB's Aunt), 366–8, **366**, **367**
Morrissey, Norah ('Nan') (JB's Aunt), 3, 6, 309, **367**, 378, 383, **392**, 392–7, **395**, 403, 495, 553, 555, 558
Morrissey, 'Nurse Biddy', **51**, 384, **404**
Morrissey, Peg (JB's Aunt), *see* O'Mara, Peg
Morrissey's Bakery, Carrick-on-Suir, **394**, **395**, 395–7
Mosley, Lady Diana, 52
Mosley, Sir Oswald, 52–3

Mossadegh, Mohammed, 497
motor cycling, 194
Mount Melleray (Cistercian Abbey), 111
Mount Sion (GAA club), 128, 131, 133, 549
Mountayne, Miss, 72
movies, *see* films
Moylan, Christy, 127
Moynihan, Guard, 137, 139, 336, **345**
Moynihan, Seán, 123, 135, 136, 137, 334
Mulcahy, Richard, 476, 480
Mullen, Karl, 195
Mullins, Jack, 392
Mullins, Mrs, 392
Munster & Leinster Bank, Lismore, 32, 70–1, 177, 203, 336
The Munster Express, 5
Munster (Hurling) Finals, 127, 129, 132
Murphy, Brother, 112, 248, 278, 415–16
Murphy, Delia, 540
Murphy, Dervla, 178–9, 193, 445, 465
Murphy, Eddie, 299
Murphy, Eily, 540
Murphy, Fergus, 74–7, 86, 178, 487
Murphy, Guard P., 139, **345**, 449
Murphy, John, **417**
Murphy, John ('Spud'), 36, 105–6, 314
Murphy, Michael ('Murph'), 135, 136, **416**, 425, 441
Murphy, Father Michael, 103
Murphy, Pat ('Bags'), 135, **172**, 330
Murphy, Rena, 296
Murphy, Rosie, 449
Murphy, Tom, 107
Murray, Dennis, and His Players, 542
mushroom picking, 289
music, 408–9, 538–41
musical films, 528–9
musicians, 66, 155, 384, 535, 538–9
myxomatosis, 58–9, 218, 254–5, 260

NACA, *see* National Athletic and Cycling Association
National Anthem, Irish, 538
National Athletic and Cycling Association (NACA), 158–9, 160, 161

National Bank, Lismore, 33, 70–1
National Health Service, British, 493
National Service, British, 449
The Nationalist, 5, 556–7, 559
nativity play, 428
Nazi Germany, 493–4
Neill, Tom, **536**
Nemo Rangers, 146
Neville, Billy, ('Fisser', later 'Guiney'), 35, 173–4, 305, 417–18, 511
Neville, Kathleen, 59, 280, 540
Neville, Kit, 58, 246, 417–18, 487, 494
Neville, Michael ('Lochrann' or 'Loch'), 418
Neville, Nuala, 368
Neville, Peter, 60–1, 150–1, 153, 154, 156, **255**, 298, 303, 313, 448, 510–11, 554
Neville, Philip ('Sucky' or 'Blackie'), 35, 58, 59, 105–6, 108–10, 130, 133, 134, 136–7, 140, 244, 246, **255**, 255, 257, 262, 270, 292, 305, 314–15, 316, 341, 347, 357, 471, 510, 525, 550
The New Gossoon, 541
New Year's Eve, 311
Newfoundland, 442
newspapers, 83, 102, 198, 485, 488, 497
newsreels (cinema), 412, 517
Newtown School, Waterford, 189, 191
nicknames, 35
Nolan, Bob, 282–4
Nolan, Michael, 104, 487, 537
Nolan, Violet, 128
Noonan, John, 162, 178
Noonan, David ('Boysie'), 371, 476
Noonan, Eeelagh, 541–2
Noonan, Kevie, 55, 502, 504–5, 508, 518
Noonan, Monica, 128, 192, 193, 541
Northern Ireland, 483
Northern Lights, 238
Norton, George, 195
Nugent, Bertie, **416**
Nugent, Eddie, 22
nuns, *see* individual names
nursery rhymes, 297–8

O'Brien, Anne, 368
O'Brien, Billy ('Irons'), 72, 104,

417, 446, 487, 537–8, 549
O'Brien, Chrissy, 114, 432, 503, 541
O'Brien, Colonel, 49
O'Brien, Dorothy, 38
O'Brien, Georgie, 120, 152, 264, 503
O'Brien, Jacky, 392
O'Brien, Jimmy ('Jimmy the Hawk'), 130, 254, 288
O'Brien, John, 503
O'Brien, Mick ('The Bird'), 36, 255–6, **255**, 529
O'Brien, Ned, 53–4
O'Brien, Paddy, 335, 384, 538
O'Brien, Pedro, 120, 146, 196, 257, 265, 321
O'Brien, Pippa, 254, 257, 291, 302, 321
O'Brien, Father Teddy, 468
O'Brien, Tommy ('Tommy the Hawk'), 35, 120
O'Callaghan, Jackie, 13, 149
O'Callaghan, John ('Cal'), 58, 120, 149, 150, 152–3, 156–8, 172, 174, 178, 455, 530
O'Callaghan, Dr Pat, 143
O'Carroll, Father, 89, 90–2
Ó Colmáin, Gerry, 200
O'Donnell, John Joe, **417**
O'Connell, Kate, 113–14, 117, 428–9, 473–4, 535
O'Connell, Mr (National Bank), 155
O'Connell, Seán, 156, 178, **417**, 448, 541
O'Connor, Brother, 147, 427, 429
O'Connor, Johnny, 127, 216
O'Connor, Mickey (Cappoquin hurler), 127, 133
O'Connor, Mickey (wool dealer), 370
O'Connor, Noel, 432
O'Connor, Pat, 110
O'Connor, Rory, 480
O'Connor, Thomas, 235
O'Connor, Tom, 241, **416**
Ó Corcora, Domhnall, 541
O'Donnell, Dodo, 282
O'Donnell, Frank, 19, 289
O'Donnell, Hanna, 375
O'Donnell, Jim, 113, 308
O'Donnell, Joe, 122, 533
O'Donnell, John (John 'Jocklin'), 293
O'Donnell, John F., 120, 124, 133, 351

O'Donnell, Mrs, 285–6, 287
O'Donnell, Ronnie, 120, 121, 127, 137
O'Donnell, Seamus, **172**
O'Donnell, Tommy, 302
O'Donoghue, Florrie, 485
O'Donoghue, Frank, 134, 135
O'Donoghue, Jack, 554
O'Donoghue, Pat, 120–1, **417**, 430, 444
O'Donoghue, Tommy, 122–3
O'Donoghue, Vincent (Vin) (Mícheál U. Ó Donnchadha), 135, 147, 158, 191–2, 247–8, 333, 422, 425, 436, 441–2, 444–5, 487
Ó Drisceoil, Diarmuid, 446, 487, 541
O'Dwyer, William, 139
O'Farrell, Michael ('Mickey'), 22
O'Farrell, Michael (Charles Kickham), 317, **417**, 430, 444–5
O'Farrell, Dr Michael, 22, 141, 215, 349–50
O'Farrell, Seán, 444
O'Gorman, Crony, 175–6
O'Gorman, Jack, 216, 342, 343, 477, 553
O'Gorman, Maisie, 454
O'Grady, John, 113
O'Hanrahan, Mr, 351
O'Hehir, Mícheál, 139, 413, 431
O'Higgins, Kevin, 480
O'Hugain, Seán, 133
O'Keeffe, Jack ('Busty'), 405
O'Keeffe, Jim, 405
O'Keeffe, Mick, 405
O'Keeffe, Nurse, 350
O'Kelly, Nicholas G., 181
O'Kelly, Seán T. (President of Ireland), 111, 488
O'Kelly–Lynch, Peter, 71, 145–6
O'Leary, F. X., 541
O'Malley, Ernie, 480
O'Mara, Brendan, 144, 278
O'Mara, Liam, 6, 480
O'Mara, Michael, 461
O'Mara, Noel, 405–6
O'Mara, Peg (née Morrissey), 6, **395**, 461, 563
O'Mara, Tony, 402, 563
O'Meara, Charlie P., 351
O'Neill, Aidan, 364
O'Neill, Bill, 123
O'Neill, Con, 40, 104
O'Riordan, Berry, 177
O'Riordan, Billy, **172**, 175

O'Riordan, John, 110, **172**, 447
O'Riordan, Mr (Munster Bank), 167, 177, 203, 205
O'Sullivan, Guard, 340, **345**
O'Sullivan, Pat, 43
oats growing, 247
The Old Bucket, (school performance), 432–3
old tyme dancing, 538–9
Olympic Games, 1948, London, 159
Olympic Games, 1952, Helsinki, 159, 197
open-air platform dances, *see* stage dances
Ormonde, Cora, 19, **19**
Ormonde, Jacky, 477
Ormonde, Jim, 12, **13**, 75, 242, 279, 376, 477
Ormonde, John, 19
Ormonde, Patty, 19–20
Ormonde, Teresa, 19, **19**, 382, 383
Ormonde Castle, 399, **400**
Ormonde Cinema, Dungarvan, 500, 516
Osborne, John, 134
otters, 260–1
Our Boys, 82–3
Outwitted, (short stage play), 541
Owbeg Bridge, 45
Owbeg Stream, 45
Owenashad Bridge, 260, **261**
Owenashad River, 20, 34, 37, 162–3, **163**, 165–7, 170, 218, 230, 234, 260, **261**, 262

Palladium Cinema, Lismore, 500, **501**, 501–8, 516
'pandy', *see* potatoes, mashed
Park View Cinema, Carrick-on-Suir, 500, 512
Parker, Tommy, 61, 153, 546
parlour games, 296, 301
Pathé News, 517
Patterson, Jackie, 197
Paul Twyning, (stage play), 541
Paxman, Arthur, 42, 276, 330
Paxman's Butter Factory, 42
Paxton, Joseph, 117
Pearse, Patrick, 26
Pearse, Willie, 26
peashooting, 295, 316–17, 506–7
Pender, Kate, 38, 203
Pericho, Miss, 22

Perks Amusements, 70, 197, 543
'Petticoat Loose' (Mary Hannigan), 178
Peyton, Father Patrick, 105–6
Phelan, Margaret, 5
Picture Show, 515
Picturegoer, 516
'the pictures', *see* films
pig market, 240
Pinkert, Jim, 133–4
Pioneer Total Abstinence Association of the Sacred Heart, 92, 104, 331, 366, 468, 539, 549
Pirie, Gordon, 159
pitch-and-toss, 303–4
Place Names of Decies, 40, 118
plays, 430, 534, 541–2
  see also titles of individual plays
poaching, 37
The Point (convergence of the Blackwater and Owenashad Rivers) 163, 164–5
Point-to-Point Races, Lismore, 17, 68, 208–13
police, *see* Garda Síochána
poliomyelitis, 365
politics, 473–89
Pollard, Mossie, 120, 133, 553
popular songs and singers, 409–10, 412–13, 539–41, 544
Porter, Major Robert, 515
potatoes,
  blight, 245
  growing, 245, 274
  market, 240
  mashed, 376
poverty, 57–65 *passim*, 356, 418–19, 449
Power, Dick, 51, 389
Power, Jimmy, 57
Power, Canon Patrick, 40, 117, 118
Power, R., (bookmakers), 213
Power, Seamus, 127
Presentation Convent School, 8–9, 36, 93, 117, 148, 276, 278, 415, 449, 553
Priestley, J. B., 494
Prileaux, Mr, 53
prisoners of war,
  Japanese, 14
Proclamation of the Dogma of the Assumption, 92
Queen's Gap and Weir, Blackwater River, 40, 178, 233–4, 266, 271

Question Time (Radio Éireann), 410
Quinlan, Ann, 465
Quinlan, Laurence ('Larry'), 368–9
Quinlan, Peg, 70
Quinlan, Philip, 3
Quinn, Billy, 543
Quirke, Mikey, 131

rabbits,
  dazzling, 254
  hunting, 58, 217–18, 254–9
  myxomatosis, 58–9, 218, 254–5, 260
  snaring, 255
racism,
  in comics, 80
  in films, 521–2
  in nursery rhymes, 297
Radio Éireann,
  programmes, 112, 346, 409–13, 540
radio listening, 139, 408, 409–13, 540
Rafferty, Pat, 132
railways, 180, 388–91, 490–1
The Rainy Day, (short stage play), 541
Raleigh, Sir Walter, 117
Rás Tailteann (Tour of Ireland cycle race), 161
Rath, 136
Rath House, 136
Rathangan, 407, 552
rationing, 10, 22, 58–9, 373–4
recitations, 541
Red Barn, Youghal, 535
Red Cross, 22, 350, 364
Reddan, Tony, 129
Redmond, Major William (Willie), 475
Redmond, Mrs William (Willie), 67, 475–6, 477
refugees,
  German refugees in Ireland, 495
Regal Cinema, Tallow, 500, 511, 516, 522, 524–5
Regan, Bart, 29, 369–70
Regan, Denny, 179, 184, 228, 382, 389, 391, 554
Regan, Mick, 125
religion, 87–118 *passim*
  mission, 88–92
  processions, 93, 96–7, 344
  retreats, 87, 92, 542–3
religious orders,
  Cistercian, 44, 111
religious retreats, 87, 92, 542–3

repertory theatrical companies, 534, 541–2
Rian-Bó-Phádraig, 45, 225, 428
Rice, Paul, 302–3, 437, 444
Richards, Gordon, 211
Rineanna Airport, 434, 492
The Ring, 82, 200, 201
Ring, Christy, 126, 129, 132, 133
Rioch, Fraser, 365
Rioch, Nancy, 365
Riordan, ('Stylo'), 132
rivers,
  Blackwater, 18, 20, 36, 37, 40, 41, 42, 43, **43**, 44, 162–7, 174–6, 178, 218, 220, 231–4, 266, 322, 475, 553
  Brickey, 133
  Bride, 44, 46
  Lismore Canal, 11, 43, 226, 261–2, 269
  Owbeg, 45
  Owenashad, 20, 34, 37, 162–3, **163**, 165–7, 170, 218, 230, 234, 260, **261**, 262
  Suir, 164, 399, **400**, 402–3
roads, 239
  maintenance, 239–40
Robeson, Paul, 409–10
Robinson, Sugar Ray, 198, 199, 516, 522
The Rock, Blackwater River, 167, **168**, 171, 174–5
roller skating, 301–2
rolling hoops, 318–19, 295
'Rosary Priest', *see* Peyton, Father Patrick
Roscommon, County,
  Gaelic football team, 138, 140
Ross, 3
Ross, Nat, 554
Round Hill, 44, 45, 117, 225
The Rover, 78–9, 80
rowing, 193–4
Royal Air Force, 494
Royal Irish Constabulary, 89, 335, 339, 484
  see also Auxiliaries; Black and Tans
Royal Norfolk Regiment, 557–8
rugby, 125, 195
rural electrification, 236, 241
Rustchitzko, Paddy, 128
Ryan, Frank, 540
Ryan, Hugh, 3, 405
Ryan, John, *172*
Ryan, Michael, 57
Ryan, Paddens, 478

INDEX

Ryan, Tom, **417**
Ryan, Willie, 160, 170–1, 175, 179, 192, 221–5, 314, 324, 326, 330, 332–4, 454–6

St Carthage's (Catholic) Cathedral, 38–9, 68, 83, 88
St Carthage's (Protestant) Cathedral, 16, 37, 38, 39, 53, 117
St Carthage's Hall, Lismore, 535
St Carthage's Hospital, Lismore, 45–6
St Malachy's hurling team, 134, 145, 152
St Michael's Hall, Ballyduff, 536
St Stephen's hurling team, 124
saints, local, 117
salmon fishing, 20, 42, 51–2, 172, 172, 230, 231
salmon hatchery, 163, 165–6, 232–4
Sargent, Bud, 11, 43, 194, 234
Sargent, Michael, 193–4
Sargent, Willie, 193–4, 432, 540
Savoy Cinema, Waterford, 500
sawmills, 292
Scanlan, Jackie, 39, 70, 79, 197, 292, 535
Scanlon, Chris ('Scanner'), 230, 414, 448
Scanlon, 'Gandóg', 35, 244
Scanlon, Mike ('Gander'), 35, 244
Scanlon, Kathleen, 170–1
Scanlon, Michael, **416**
Scanlon, Patrick 'Bishop', 16, 56, 292
Scanlon, Patsy ('Young Bishop'), 108, 135, 257, 268
scarlet fever, 29, 363–4
Scarook Wood, 29, 45, 278
The Schoolfriend, 82
schools, 8–9, 33, 34, 36, 93, 97, 117, 134, 148, 276, 278, 302, 326, 365, 415–48, 449, 553
Scone, Stone of, theft from Westminster Abbey, 498
Scott-Allan, John, 231
Scott-Allan, Mrs John, 72, 231
Seán ar an Aonach, (school performance), 430
Seemochuda, 34

Selzner, Horst, 22
serial films, 517, 524–5
Sexton, Sean, 235
Shadow and Substance, 542
Shakespeare, William, 434
shamrocks, 147, 290
Shanavoola, 34
Shannon Players, 542
Shaw, George Bernard, 86
shawls, 63–4
Sheaffe-Montizambert, Major George, 485–6
sheep farming, 251–2
Shelta (tinker's language), 65
Shiels, George, 541
Shinwell, Emmanuel ('Manny'), 484
shipyards, **482**
Shrough, 46
sickness and health, 349–70 *passim*
Silcox, Major, 56
singers, popular, 409–10, 412–13, 539–41, 544
Singleton, Jack, 541
Sinn Féin, 43, 559
Sinnott, Dick, 399–400
Sinnott, Mr and Mrs, 306
Slash, Peg, 372
Slattery, Dick, 155
Sligo, 2, 3 480, 484
Smyth, Bernadette, 545
snaring rabbits, 255–6
snow, 236–7, 295, 300
soap, wartime quality, 353
soccer, 125, 195–6
society, religious differences, 67, 167
softball (handball), 149, 154
soldiers, 11–13
sopranos, 540
South Irish Horse Regiment, 563
spinning tops, 295, 319–20
sports films, 531–2
The Spout, Lismore, 37–8, 343, 478
squirrels, red, 261
Sruh, 136
Stack, Billy, **417**
stage dances, 535, **536**
standpipes, street, 478
The Standard, 86
Stanley, Dean Charles, 16, 167, 188, 189, 276, 278, 302
Stapleton, Anne, 368
Stapleton, Pa, 35
Stapleton, 'Phopper', 35, 119, 292

Stapleton, Sheila, 368
Stapleton, 'Storc', 35, 119, 292
The Stars (GAA club), 143–4
The Statist, 488
stonemasons, 107
storms, 60, 236, 238, 505–6
Stradbally, 1, 121, 123, 185, 187
Strancally Castle, 44, 45
Strand Bridge, 11, 42, 165, 232, 234, 235–6, 260, 292
Strathdee, Ernie, 195
street games, 25, 83, 316–20
Suir River, 164, 399, **400**, 402–3
Sunday Press, 488
Sutton, Muriel, 87
swallows, 490
Swanlinbar, County Cavan, 3, 6, 7, 140
The Swans (GAA club), Carrick-on-Suir, 142–4
swashbuckling films, 529–30
Sweeney, Johnny, 243
swimming, 121, 162–87
  in rivers, 162–79
  in the sea, 179

TB, *see* tuberculosis
table tennis, 121, 192, 537
Talamh anÉisc, 442
Talbot, Matt, 82
Tallow, 41, 119, 130, 132, 147, 213, 500
'Tallow Road' Bridge (railway bridge), 44
Teampuileen Caves, 56, 322
Teehan, Inspector Michael, 335
teetotal movement, 92, 104, 331, 366, 468, 549
television, 516
temperance movement, 92, 104, 331, 366, 468, 549
tennis, 71, 121, 125, 192–3, 537
tenors, 409, 540–1
Tenzing, Sherpa, 198
theatrical companies, touring, 534, 541–2
theatrical performances
  local dramatic society, 431, 539, 541–2
  school productions, 428–33, 541
  visiting repertory companies, 534, 541–2
Thornton, Martin, 197
Tierney, Frankie, 190, 192
Tierney, Pad, 487, 495, 549
timber, 292–4
tin-smithing, 66
tinkers, 65–6, 209, 240, 418

Tipperary, County, 3, 128, 142–3
Tobin, Bernie ('Brownie'), 331–2
Tobin, Joe, **416**
Tobin, Kay, 512, 554
Tobin, Kip, 121, 141, 282, 284, 448
Tobin, Nuala, 105
Tooraneena, 153, 154
Toortane, 68
Tóstal (Irish Arts Festival), 40, 135, 138, 157, 160, 548–9
Tour of Ireland (cycle race), 161
Tourin, 45, 132
Tourin Castle, 43
Tower Amusements, 543
Tower Glen, 42
The Towers, Barranamanogue Woods, 42
Town Crier, Lismore, 35, 477, 534–5
toys, 299, 300, 301
trains, *see* railways
travelling people, *see* tinkers
Treacy Park, 63
Treacy, Seán, 485
Treacys, Seán, (GAA team), 143, 485
Troubles, *see* Irish War of Independence
trout fishing, 58, 218, 221, 225–8, 230, 243
Troy, John, 243
Troy, Michael, **417**
tuberculosis,
  in animals, 260, 376
  in humans, 23, 364–5, 366, 376
Tullahought, 5, 57
Turpin, Randolph, 198–9, 516
Twomey, Michael, **417**
Twomey, Nurse, 350
Twomey, Paul, 540
Tyers, Paddy, 192

Uniacke, Toddy, 418
Union Workhouse, Carrick, 367, 555, 556
United States of America,
  emigration to, 8, 338–9
  Gaelic football, 139
Universal News, 517
The Universe, 86

VE Day, 13–14
variety concerts, 543
variety shows, 539–41
Vaughan, Ann, 77
Vaughan, Harry, 119, 547
Vaughan, Johnny, 120, 129, 133
Vaughan, Paddy, 36, 164, 180, 211, 303, 331, 547
Veale, Miss, 419, 446
vegetable growing, 374
Villierstown, 414

wages, 50–1
Walcott, Jersey Joe, 198
Wall, Margery, 351
Wall, Mr (chemist), 351
Walsh, Bernard ('Barney'), 112, 120, 201, 221–4, 252, 266–7, 270, 293, 318, 323, 325, 330, 331–2, 333–4, 341, 430, 459–60, 464, 510–11, 512
Walsh, Billy, 151, 155
Walsh, Jack, 151, 155
Walsh, Jackie, 87, 381
Walsh, Lucy, 22–3
Walsh, Martin, 368, 381
Walsh, Canon Michael, 89, 98–9, 107, 108
Walsh, Mick ('Cool Cock'), 373
Walsh, Paddy, **417**
Walsh, Tom, 326, 341
Walsh, Willie ('Teller'), 310, **416**, 487, 537, 549
war films, 527
War of Independence, Irish, 346, 473, 479–81
Ward, Mick, 260, 478
Ware, John, 127
Warren Gardens, 38, 235, 303
wasps, 248
water supply, 478
Waterford, City of, 41, 128, 129, 285, 358
  Infirmary, 358
Waterford, County, **xxvi** (map), 1
  Library Service, 74
Waterford, Lord, 49, 56, 391
Waterford Farmers Association, 539
Waterford hurling team, 121, 126
Waterford United Football Club, 196
weather,
  cold, 59
  flooding, 233–6
  snow, 236–7, 295, 300
  storms, 60
weight lifting, 119
Weir, and Queen's Gap, Blackwater River, 40, 178, 233–4, 266, 271
Weissmuller, Johnny, 172, 175, 202, 531
Went, Dr A. E. J., 231
West Waterford Hunt, 56, 208, 214, 539
western films, 517, 520, 522–4, 532–3
Westminster, Duke of, *see* Grosvenor
wheat growing, 245, 247
Whelan, Alfie, **416**
Whelan, Enda, 540
Whelan, Michael ('Mickey'), 120, 247
Whelan, Nabbsy, 20, 217, 225, 230
Whelan, Paddy, 160
Whelan, Pax, 485
Whelan, Tommy ('Bomber'), 160, **172**
whippets, 258
whist drives, 71–2
White, Dr (Cappoquin), 350
White, Dr Vincent, 559
White, Jackie, 37
whorts (bilberries) picking, 278–82
wild flowers, 289–90
Willoughby, James (Jim), 49
Willoughby, Mary, 431, 541
Willoughby, Nora, 7, 98, 301
Windgap, 5
winter sports, 320–2
wireless, *see* radio listening
The Wizard, 78, 80
women's sports, 128, 192–3
wood, collecting for fires, 59–62
Wood, Mrs Henry, 542
Woodroofe, and Kiely–Ussher vaults, 42
World War One, 162, 475, 485
World War Two, 8, 10–14, 335, 371, 378, 493
  bombing of English cities, 493, 495
  emergency preparations in Lismore, 8, 11–13
wrestling, 207
Wright, Eva, 444
Wuthering Heights (stage adaptation), 542

X-ray units, mobile, 364

Youghal, 45, 535
Youghal Bridge, 45
Young, Jim, 129

Zatopek, Emil, 159